Frederick Carder's Steuben Glass

Guide to Shapes, Numbers, Colors, Finishes, and Values

Marshall Ketchum

Revised and Expanded 2nd Edition

Schiffer Publishing Ltd

4880 Lower Valley Road, Atglen, PA 19310 USA

Dedication

This book is dedicated to the three people who have been most
influential in my studying and collecting Carder Steuben:
**Thomas P. Dimitroff,
Robert F. (Bobby)Rockwell III
and Robert F. Rockwell Jr.**

Designed by John P. Cheek
Cover design by Bruce Waters
Type set in ZapfCalligraphyBT/Korinna BT

ISBN: 0-7643-2411-X
Printed in China

Published by Schiffer Publishing Ltd.
4880 Lower Valley Road
Atglen, PA 19310
Phone: (610) 593-1777; Fax: (610) 593-2002
E-mail: Info@schifferbooks.com

For the largest selection of fine reference books on
this and related subjects, please visit our web site at
www.schifferbooks.com
We are always looking for people to write books on
new and related subjects. If you have an idea for a
book please contact us at the above address.

This book may be purchased from the publisher.
Include $3.95 for shipping.
Please try your bookstore first.
You may write for a free catalog.

In Europe, Schiffer books are distributed by
Bushwood Books
6 Marksbury Ave.
Kew Gardens
Surrey TW9 4JF England
Phone: 44 (0) 20 8392-8585; Fax: 44 (0) 20 8392-
9876
E-mail: info@bushwoodbooks.co.uk
Website: www.bushwoodbooks.co.uk
Free postage in the U.K., Europe; air mail at cost.

Contents

Acknowledgments

Many people have been helpful in making this work possible. Robert F. Rockwell Jr. was one of the first to see a preliminary version and offered helpful hints that improved the accuracy. He offered corrections to the location of shapes within the line drawings where I was not aware there were errors. Mr. Rockwell also allowed me to photograph Carder Steuben that was for sale in his shop. Many of the new photos in the second edition are also from this source. Ms. Robyn Peterson, the former Curator of Collections at the Rockwell Museum, offered suggestions and support. Bob Dander and Neil McPhee offered the use of their extensive library of auction catalogs. I am profoundly thankful for the help that Tom Dimitroff gave me on this project. It was he who suggested that the work would be more valuable if auction results were included and encouraged me to continue with that effort. He spent many hours helping me error check the many technical aspects that occur in this kind of book. It should be noted that any errors that remain are mine alone. He was also gracious enough to offer to contribute the Foreword, which gives a broad background for Carder Steuben. Finally, I must thank my wife, Carol, who encouraged me all along the way and who didn't seem to mind the time I spent on the computer accumulating auction results from eBay.

Foreword

The 100th anniversary of Steuben Glass occurred in 2003. It all began over a century ago when Thomas G. Hawkes and Frederick C. Carder combined talents and resources to convert the old Payne Foundry on Erie Avenue in Corning, New York, into a new glass factory, the Steuben Glass Works. The story of Steuben glass was an exciting adventure then and it continues to be so to this day. Corning is nestled in a typical east-west valley on the great Allegheny Plateau in western New York State. By the early 1900s, Corning had become a bustling community proud of its status (1890) as a city. Although still very much a railroad town, it had industry, the most important being the Corning Glass Works, which had its beginnings in the community in 1868 as the Corning Flint Glass Works.

By the early 1900s, both the city and the Corning Glass Works prospered. The Corning Glass Works made a variety of glass products, especially railroad lenses and light bulbs. Also prospering were Corning's dozen or so glass cutting shops led by the largest, T. G. Hawkes & Co. Thomas G. Hawkes, its owner, noticed that Corning Glass Works was losing its commercial interest in producing blanks for the cut glass industry as other of its products became more profitable. This prompted him to seek out Frederick Carder, who was a successful English glass designer and chemist, and bring him to Corning to start a new firm, the Steuben Glass Works.

Since its founding over one hundred years ago, the Steuben Glass Works has undergone many important changes including, among others, its acquisition by Corning Glass Works in 1918. Perhaps Steuben's greatest change occurred in 1931-32, when Frederick Carder was removed from active leadership of the company and replaced by Arthur A. Houghton, Jr. Arthur Houghton revolutionized Steuben first by phasing out the use of Carder's colors and types of glasses and then by replacing them with Corning's new, very clear, optical glass. Further, he began to seek out a variety of designers to work with this wonderful new material. These changes in the leadership and direction of Steuben define the end of Steuben's Carder or Colored Steuben Era and the beginning of the Houghton or Modern Steuben Era. Most importantly, however, regardless of these changes, Steuben today continues its 100-year uninterrupted tradition of American excellence in art glass production based upon commitment to craftsmanship, quality, and the wonder and inherent beauty of glass.

This Guide and prices realized compilation addresses the Carder Era of Steuben glass history. In addition to guide material and auction prices realized, it presents photos of Carder pieces seldom illustrated in other publications. As such, it is a valuable tool for collectors, scholars, and anyone interested in learning more about Frederick Carder's Steuben glass, its identification and values.

Collectors of Carder era Steuben are presented with an array of glass exhibiting tremendous varieties in color, types of glasses, decorative techniques, and styles. Carder was, indeed, a most prolific designer. This fact combined with his longevity resulted in the production of significant numbers and combinations of styles, colors of objects, and new techniques both at Steuben and after, stretching from 1903 to his final retirement in 1959. All of this offers glass lovers challenges and potentials in collecting his glass by color or type of glass, by shape number or type of object, or by any one of numerous other possible groupings. This richness of variety, opportunity, and choice also presents collectors with problems, especially in the identification of Carder Steuben glass.

The single most important factor in identifying Carder Steuben pieces is shape. This is because throughout the company's history, Steuben has kept fairly complete records including accurate line drawings of their objects. These line drawings are readily available to collectors particularly through two publications: *The Glass of Frederick Carder* by Paul V. Gardner and *Frederick Carder and Steuben Glass: American Classics* by Thomas Dimitroff. This Guide is an especially valuable tool in using shape to help identify Carder Steuben pieces, as it provides easy reference for collectors and others via illustrations of pieces in various shapes from several reference books. Care must be taken by users to understand that shape alone cannot usually guarantee a positive identification of an object. Such identification of Carder Steuben objects is a process that should involve several of many factors in addition to shape alone, including colors, types of glasses, decorative techniques, and signatures.

Determining the value of a given piece of Carder Steuben at a given time is also a dynamic and complex process. The addition to this Guide of auction prices realized for Steuben pieces at both traditional and electronic auctions is a valuable aid. Individual auctions can be prone to unpredictability and the whims and emotions of human individuality. Therefore, the use of several prices realized at different auctions at different times is most helpful. By doing this, the given prices can indicate a trend rather than a "one time price." This, in many cases, avoids the danger of suggesting an item's value based upon a single "unusual" example of either an inordinately high or low price realized at a particular auction. Using prices from different auction houses also tends to modulate the affects of differing markets in different parts of the country. It is hard to argue that a given piece isn't worth a value established by the sale of several comparable pieces at auctions in different parts of the country.

Even several different price examples from sales in different auctions may not adequately factor in things affecting value such as condition, color intensity, and over-all quality of a given piece. Care must be taken to consider all relevant factors when deciding upon the value of Carder Steuben objects.

The joy of collecting is enriched through familiarity with and knowledge about the items being collected. This Guide and value guide is a valuable resource in helping all who seek to better know and understand the wonderful world of Carder Steuben glass.

Thomas P. Dimitroff
January, 2005

Preface to the Second Edition

This edition is a continuation and expansion of the first edition published in 2002. It corrects a few mistakes such as the shape number for Figure 32 and places the auction information for goblet shape 7160 where it belongs with shape 5154. It has expanded the auction results from about 2000 to over 8500 and includes additional auction houses that were not included in the first edition. In addition, it includes some new glass shapes that were found in the archives of the Rakow Research Library at the Corning Museum of Glass in Corning, New York. For reasons that are not understood, they were left out of the line drawings that Paul Gardner included in his book, *The Glass of Frederick Carder*. This edition also expands the number of photographs and adds a new chapter on Steuben candlesticks. The new photos are of glass in the author's collection and also glass from other collections.

Introduction

This Guide sorts the line drawings found on pages 137 through 310 of *The Glass of Frederick Carder* by Paul V. Gardner in numerical order. The first five columns from the left refer to the line drawings in Gardner. The left column lists the shape numbers. The next column to the right gives Gardner's description as found in the book. The third column from the left lists the page on which the line drawing is found. The next two columns list the column, from left to right, on that page and the row, from top to bottom, of that column where the shape is to be found.

The next three columns are used to list recent auction results for many of the shape numbers and the final section on the right provides comments and many references to photographs for pictures of Carder Steuben that are found in several books.

There are four appendices that provide additional information. Appendix 1 decodes the color abbreviations that were used in the Auction Result section. Appendix 2 provides information about the auction companies that were used. Appendix 3 is a discussion of a number of anomalous features that have turned up in *The Glass of Frederick Carder*. Some of these may be well known but

many beginning collectors may not be aware of them. Appendix 4 is a cross reference of Steuben colors and finishing techniques to the same list of nine reference books that were used to cross reference line drawing numbers in the Photographic References section of the Guide. Using this cross reference, a photograph of most of the colors and finishing techniques for Carder Steuben can be found.

There will be cases where the phrase "shade vase" is used. This applies to shapes 913, 929, 938, 2230, and 2533. For most of the life of these shapes they were lamp shades and are shown in the "Shades" section of the line drawings. In about 1932, these five shapes were redesigned, inverted, and used as vases. The Guide lists both types. Shape 938 was available in three configurations as a lamp shade, as a shade vase, and as footed vase. The footed vase seems to be the most common. Further research has revealed that shade 2390 was also made into a vase in 1929. The archival information does not state if the vase had a separate foot or not but it is almost conclusive, based on the available evidence, that the vase shown as Ill. 103 on page 69 of the Gardner book is a 2390 shade vase.

Auction Results

Three columns in the Guide to Shape Numbers are used to provide recent auction results of Carder Steuben. The results cover approximately the last ten to fifteen year history of auction sales from several well known auction companies. The first column lists the price realized at auction and includes any applicable buyer's premium. The second column lists the type of glass that was auctioned. This list is highly abbreviated and in many cases cannot be complete for lack of space. A list of the abbreviations used can be found in Appendix 1. The third column lists an abbreviation of the auction company that conducted the auction and the month and year of the auction. A list of the auction companies is given in Appendix 2.

The space available will not usually be sufficient to describe the colors of the piece that was auctioned but a couple of standards were used. When the glass is two colors and is designated as Topaz/Celeste Blue, for example, the first color mentioned, in this case Topaz, is the major color of the piece. The second color, in this case Celeste Blue, will be the more minor color. The more minor color may be the color of the foot, the rim or some other decoration. If the listing is for an acid cut back (ACB) and the color is listed as, for example, Green Jade/Alabaster ACB then the color can be read "Green Jade over Alabaster" with etched decoration. If the etched pattern is known it may be listed in the Comments section.

The prices realized are for single items and are rounded to the nearest five dollars. If a lot contained multiple items of different shape numbers it was omitted from this listing. If multiple items of the same shape number and size were auctioned, for example a pair of candlesticks, the price listed here was the total for the lot divided by the number of items in the lot. It should be recognized that this is not an ideal situation. Often when multiple items are in a lot, for example a dozen goblets, the price realized on a per item basis may be lower than if a single item had been auctioned. The opposite may be true where a pair of candlesticks could bring a premium compared to twice the price realized for a single candlestick. If the lot description mentioned any significant damage it was omitted from this listing. The only damage that was acceptable was minor chipping to the fitter rim of lamp shades and possibly very small losses to threading. Wear on the bottom of a foot or on the base is inevitable and was not considered although it might be a factor in the purchase of a plate.

It should be noted that these auction results are examples of what a particular piece of Carder Steuben sold for at a particular point in time. They should not be used as appraisals or an estimate of what a similar piece might be worth because the value of a particular piece of glass depends upon its condition and many other variables that cannot be covered in this condensed list.

Color Photographs

The color photographs have been included to show a wide variety of Carder Steuben. Pieces were chosen for inclusion here because they have not been published elsewhere. A mix of both common colors and color combinations as well as colors that are not often seen has been included. The values placed on the pieces are intended to be an estimate of the retail price one might expect to pay for essentially a perfect piece. The only wear or damage should be normal wear that occurs on the bottom of the base. The actual wording or signature that is inscribed on each piece is shown between the curved brackets {}.

Figure 1
Topaz and Celeste Blue goblet
Shape 3140
Not signed
Height 5.8 inches
Value $80-$125

Figure 2
Colorless Toothbrush holder with Mirror Black threading
Shape 6767
Fleur-de-lis acid-stamped factory signature on bottom
Height 4.75 inches
Value $100-$150

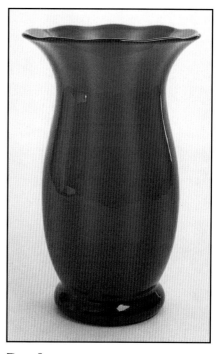

Figure 3
Dark Blue Jade vase
Shape 2230
Fleur-de-lis acid-stamped factory signature on bottom
Height 6.7 inches
Value $1500-$1800

Figure 4
Calcite vase with Gold Aurene decoration
Shape 649
{Aurene 649} factory engraved signature on bottom
Height 2 inches
Value $1200-$1500

9

Figure 5
Tyrian vase
Shape 2408
Not signed
Height 8.25 inches
Value $12,500-$14,500

Figure 6
Citron Yellow goblet
Shape 3140
Not signed
Height 5.75 inches
Value $110-$150

Figure 7
Sea Green Bowl
Shape 7307
{Steuben} script acid-stamped factory signature on bottom
Height 6.4 inches
Value $200-$275

Figure 8
Special Green champagne
Shape 7385
Not signed
Height 4.25 inches
Value $200-$275

Figure 9
French Blue cigarette holder
Shape 7529
Not signed
Height 3 inches
Value $80-$125

Figure 10
Flemish Blue goblet
Shape 5088
{Steuben} block letter acid-stamped factory
signature on bottom
Height 6.5 inches
Value $100-$175

Figure 11
Antique Green goblet
Shape 3140
Not signed
Height 6 inches
Value $100-$175

Figure 13
Verre de Soie perfume with Gold Ruby threading
Shape 6619
Not signed
Height 3.5 inches
Value $350-$450

Verre de Soie puff box with Gold Ruby threading
Shape 6600
Not signed
Height 3.5 inches
Value $350-$450

Figure 14
Selenium Red and
Colorless goblet
Shape 6522
Fleur-de-lis acid-
stamped factory
signature on bottom
Height 8 inches
Value $150-$200

Figure 12
Wisteria vase
Shape 7433
Fleur-de-lis acid-stamped factory signature on bottom
Height 6 inches
Value $275-$350

Figure 17
Amethyst cased colorless bowl
Shape 7049, engraved in "Crescent #2" pattern
Fleur-de-lis acid-stamped factory signature on bottom
Diameter 14 inches
Value $500-$600

Figure 15
Selenium Red compote
Shape 6043
Fleur-de-lis acid-stamped factory signature on bottom
Height 7.75 inches
Value $350-$450

Figure 18
Celeste Blue covered box
Shape 6786
Fleur-de-lis acid-stamped factory signature on bottom
Height 5.5 inches
Value $275-$375

Figure 16
Topaz and Pomona Green champagne
Shape 6303
{Steuben} block letter acid-stamped factory signature on bottom
Height 6 inches
Value $175-$250

Figure 19
Alabaster bowl with Rosaline lining
Shape 6415
Not signed
Height 4.5 inches
Value $275-$350

Figure 20
Bristol Yellow goblet
Shape 6242
{Steuben} block letter acid-stamped factory signature on
bottom
Height 5.6 inches
Value $100-$150

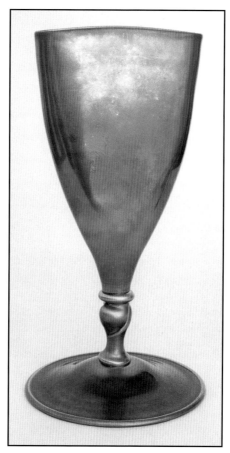

Figure 21
Blue Aurene vase
Shape 6679
{Steuben Aurene 6679} factory engraved
signature on bottom
Height 10 inches
Value $1750-$2250

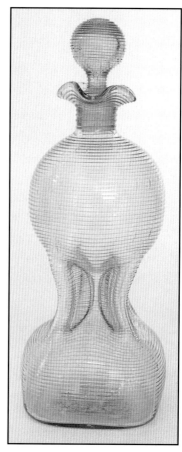

Figure 22
Orchid decanter
Shape 6343
Fleur-de-lis acid-stamped factory
signature on bottom
Height 10 inches
Value $250-$350

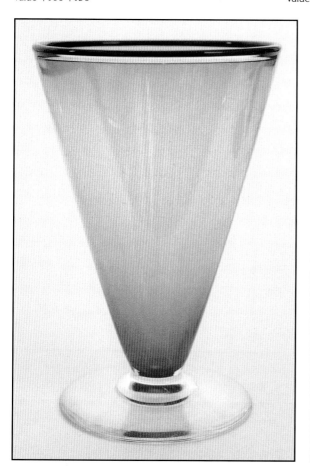

Far left:
Figure 23
Grenadine goblet with black
rim
Shape 5130
Not signed
Height 5.25 inches
Value $100-$175

Left:
Figure 24
Wisteria goblet
Shape 7182
Fleur-de-lis acid-stamped
factory signature on bottom
Height 9 inches
Value $500-$800

Figure 25
Gold Ruby puff box
Shape 6237
Fleur-de-lis acid-stamped factory signature on bottom
Height 4.5 inches
Value $300-$400

Figure 28
Marina Blue candlestick
Shape 6626
{Steuben} block letter acid-stamped factory
signature on bottom
Height 7 inches
Value $600-$800

Figure 26
French Blue compote
Shape 6355
Fleur-de-lis acid-
stamped factory
signature on bottom
Height 8.25 inches
Value $275-375

Figure 29
Alabaster Vase with Mirror Black Decoration
Shape 7459
Not signed
Height 6 inches
Value $275-$325

Figure 27
Yellow Jade compote
Shape 2760
Not signed
Diameter 10 inches
Value $800-$1000

Figure 30
Colorless compote with matte Wisteria engraved stem
Shape 7183
Fleur-de-lis acid-stamped factory signature on bottom
Height 6.75 inches
Value $275-$350

Figure 31
Flemish Blue and colorless bowl
Shape 7520
{Steuben} script acid-stamped factory signature on bottom
Diameter 11 inches
Value $275-$350

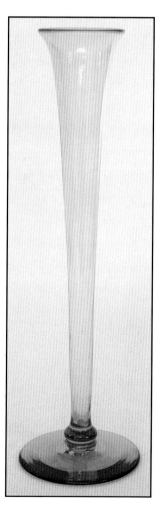

Figure 32
Celeste Blue goblet
Shape 5067
Not signed
Height 5.25 inches
Value $80-$125

Figure 33
Amethyst and Colorless compote
Shape 6110
{Steuben} block letter acid-stamped factory signature on bottom
Height 7.25 inches
Value $300-$400

Figure 34
Russian Amber vase
Shape 7671
Not signed
Height 10 inches
Value $175-$250

Figure 35
Gold Aurene candlestick
Shape 6384
{Steuben Aurene 6384} factory
engraved signature on bottom
Height 3.6 inches
Value $350-$400

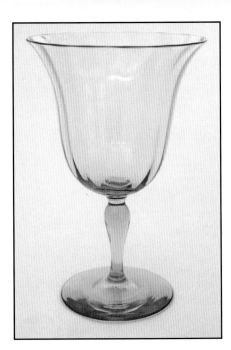

Figure 38
Olive Green goblet
Shape 1692
Not signed
Height 6 inches
Value $80-$125

Figure 36
Calcite bowl with Blue Aurene rim
Shape 2851
Not signed
Diameter 10 inches
Value $700-$850

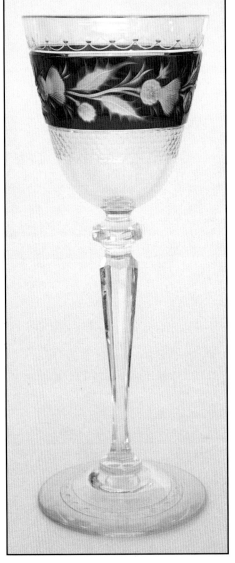

Figure 37
Verre de Soie compote with Coral decoration
Shape 5155
Not signed
Height 6.25 inches
Value $350-$450

Figure 39
Flemish Blue and colorless goblet
Shape 6861
Not signed
Height 10 inches
Value $600-$800

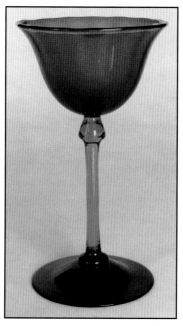

Figure 40
Colorless compote with Gold Ruby decoration
Shape 3332
Fleur-de-lis acid-stamped factory signature on bottom
Height 8 inches
Value $300-$375

Figure 41
Amethyst and Celeste Blue goblet
Shape 6062
Not signed
Height 5.8 inches
Value $150-$250

Figure 42
Unconfirmed color, possibly Nile Green champagne
Shape 6692
Fleur-de-lis acid-stamped factory signature on bottom
Height 5 inches
Value $100-$150

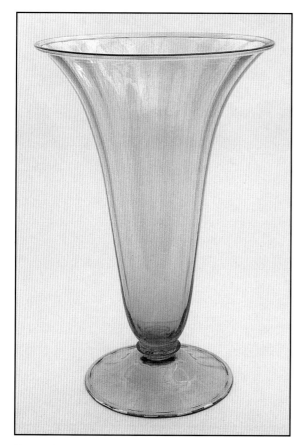

Figure 43
Pomona Green vase
Shape 2909
{Steuben} block letter acid-stamped factory signature on bottom
Height 8 inches
Value $150-$200

Figure 44
Amethyst cased and colorless champagne
Shape 6505, engraved "Harvard" pattern
{Steuben} block letter acid-stamped factory signature on bottom
Height 6.1 inches
Value $250-$300

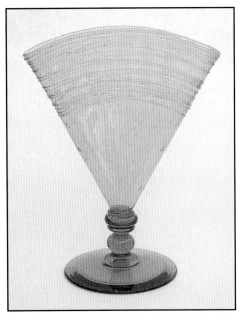

Figure 45
Spanish Green fan vase
Shape 6287
Fleur-de-lis acid-stamped factory signature on bottom
Height 8.25 inches
Value $350-$450

Figure 46
Colorless and Gold Ruby sherbet and underplate
Shape 6596, engraved "Cordova" pattern
{Steuben} block letter acid-stamped factory signature on bottom
Plate 8.5 inches in diameter
Value $400-$500

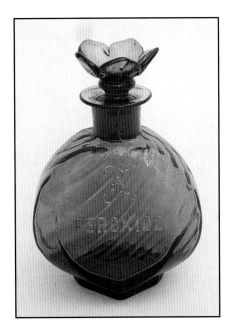

Figure 47
Amethyst cologne
Shape 7325
Fleur-de-lis acid-stamped factory signature on bottom
Height 5 inches
Value $350-$450
Note: The "K" and "Peroxide" may not be original.

Figure 48
Green cased and colorless engraved goblet
Shape 3321, engraved "Etruscan" pattern
{Steuben} block letter acid-stamped factory signature on bottom
Height 8.2 inches
Value $350-$450

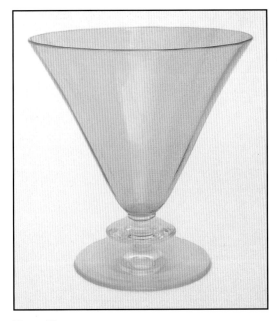

Figure 49
Bristol Yellow and colorless vase
Shape 6419
Not signed
Height 7.3 inches
Value $250-$350

Figure 50
Ivory vase
Shape 6030
Not signed
Height 7 inches
Value $300-$400

Figure 51
Cinnamon Florentia candlestick
Shape 6593
Fleur-de-lis acid-stamp factory signature on bottom
Height 4.5 inches
Value $550-$650

Figure 52
Mirror Black sherbet
Shape 2680
Not signed
Height 3.75 inches
Value $200-$300

Figure 53
Amber and Celeste Blue sherbet and underplate
Shape 2680
Fleur-de-lis acid-stamped factory signature on bottom
Height of sherbet 3.75 inches
Value $150-$200

Figure 54
Gold Ruby bowl
Shape 6106
Fleur-de-lis acid-stamped factory signature on bottom
Diameter 11.5 inches
Value $150-$200

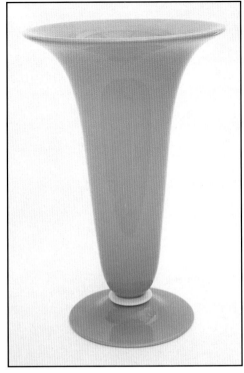

Figure 55
Light Blue Jade and Flint White vase
Shape 2909
Not signed
Height 8.3 inches
Value $600-$800

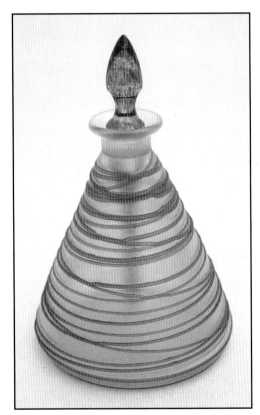

Figure 56
Gold Ruby threaded Verre de
Soie perfume
Shape 6600
Not signed
Height 4 inches
Value $300-$400

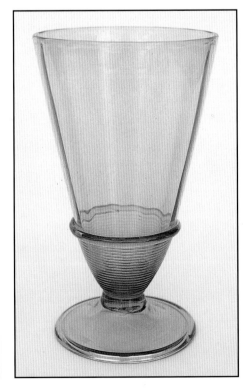

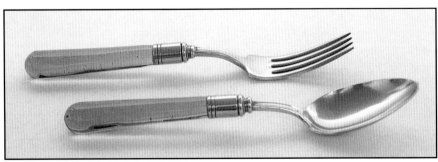

Figure 57
Fork and spoon with Spanish Green handles
Shape 7478
Not signed
Fork 7.7 inches long, spoon 7.6 inches long
Value $150-$200 each

Figure 58
Blue-gray and Amber Goblet
Shape 6026
Not signed
Height 6 inches
Value $100-$175

Figure 60
Yellow Florentia lamp
Shape 6731
Glass is not signed, metal is signed "Crest"
Height of glass 11.75 inches
Value $4000-$5000

Figure 59
Antique Green goblet with colorless mica flecked stem
Shape 3140
Not signed
Height 5.8 inches
Value $175-$250

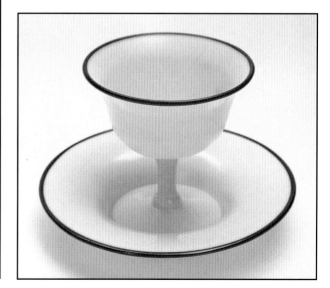

Figure 61
Opal candlestick with Amethyst Cintra trim
Shape 2933
Not signed
Height 9 inches
Value $500-$600

Figure 62
Opal vase with Amethyst Cintra trim
Shape 2987
Not signed
Height 12 inches
Value $600-$800

Figure 63
Calcite sherbet and underplate with Mirror Black trim
Shape 2680
Not signed
Height of sherbet 3.75 inches
Value $400-$500

21

Figure 64
Rosaline and Alabaster compote
Shape 5194
Not signed
Height 7 inches
Value $250-$350

Figure 65
Gold Ruby threaded colorless compote
Shape 6357
Not signed
Height 7 inches
Value $275-$375

Figure 66
Selection of stems
Shape 3551, two on right are engraved "Van Dyke" pattern
Height 8.25-8.50 inches
Value $150-$350 each

Figure 67
Cluthra bowl
Shape 6906
Fleur-de-lis acid-stamped factory signature on bottom
Height 5 inches
Value $600-$800

Figure 68
Colorless fingerbowl and underplate
Shape 6936, cut "Warwick" pattern
{Steuben} script acid-stamped factory signature on bottom
Bowl is 4.25 inches diameter
Value $200-$300

Figure 69
Blue Aurene sherbet
Shape 2680
{Aurene 2680} engraved factory signature on bottom
Height 3.8 inches
Value $300-$400

Figure 70
Gold Calcite demitasse
Shape 2723
Glass not signed, metal signed "J.E. Caldwell & Co."
Glass is 2.24 inches high
Value $125-$300

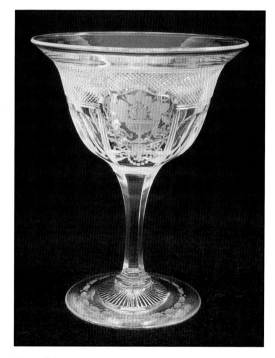

Figure 71
Colorless engraved champagne
Shape 1530, Engraved in Sinclaire's "Adams" pattern
{Steuben} block letter acid-stamped signature on bottom
Height 4.5 inches
Value $150-$250

Figure 72
Verre de Soie engraved sherbet and underplate
Shape 2680
Not signed
Height 3.75 inches
Value $150-$250

Figure 73
Orchid goblet
Unknown shape
{Steuben} block letter acid-stamped signature on bottom
Height 8.25 inches
Value $250-$350

Figure 74
Colorless cut goblet
Shape 6959, cut in "Lambeau" pattern
{Steuben} block letter acid-stamped signature on bottom
Height 6 inches
Value $100-$150

Figure 75
Colorless cut goblet
Shape 6936, cut in "Leaves" pattern
Fleur-de-lis acid-stamped signature on bottom
Height 5.3 inches
Value $100-$150

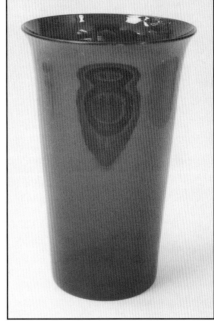

Figure 76
Selenium Red tumbler
Shape 2361
Not signed
Height 5.6 inches
Value $125-$175

Figure 77
Etched Green Jade vase
Shape 6287, etched "Sculptured" pattern
Not signed
Height 9 inches
Value $400-$600

Figure 78
Pomona Green vase
Shape 8368
Fleur-de-lis acid-stamped factory signature on bottom
Height 8.5 inches
Value $300-$375

Figure 79
Selection of vases
Shape 6119
Left; colorless with Flemish Blue foot
Center; Amber with Pomona Green foot
Right; colorless with Topaz foot
Value $200-$400 each

Figure 80
Topaz vase
Shape 6425
Not signed
Height 7 inches
Value $250-$350

Figure 81
Cluthra bowl
Shape 6804
Not signed
Height 4.7 inches
Value $500-$600

Figure 82
Celeste Blue puff box
Shape 6786
Not signed
Diameter 5.7 inches
Value $350-$450

Figure 83
Green threaded colorless puff box
Shape 6786
Not signed
Diameter 5.8 inches
Value $200-$300

Figure 86
Verre de Soie compote with Green Jade trim
Shape 2760
Not signed
Diameter 7.5 inches
Value $350-$450

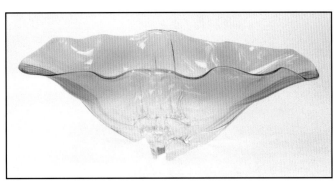

Figure 84
Green shaded to colorless Grotesque bowl
Shape 7537
Not signed
Width 12.5 inches
Value $500-$600

Figure 87
Verre de Soie perfume
with Celeste Blue stopper
Shape 2833
Not signed
Height 3 inches
Value $300-$450

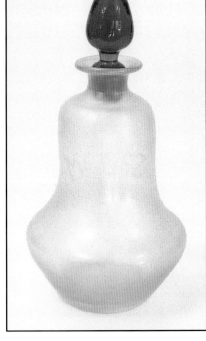

Figure 85
Celeste Blue compote
Shape 5194
Fleur-de-lis acid-stamped factory
signature on bottom
Height 8.5 inches
Value $400-$600

Figure 88
Pair of ash trays
Shape 7026
Left; Celeste Blue
Right; Amethyst
Diameter 3.5 inches
Value $300-$400 each

Figure 89
Pomona Green Silverina Airtrap vase
Shape 2390
Not signed
Height 7 inches
Value $600-$750

Figure 91
Verre de Soie pump perfume
Unknown shape
Not signed
Glass height 3.3 inches, overall height 4.75 inches

Figure 90
Etched Green Jade flower pot
Shape 6676, etched "Mansard" pattern
Not signed
Height 6.5 inches
Value $1000-$1200

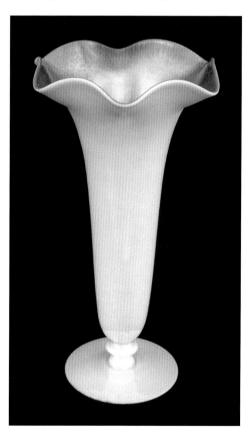

Figure 92
Blue Calcite vase
Shape 312
Not signed
Height 10.5 inches
Value $2500-$3000

Figure 93
Gazelle
Shape 7399
{Steuben} diamond point factory signature on bottom
Height 7 inches
Note: This is a rather rare version where only the gazelle itself has a matte finish. The more common forms have either the entire piece matte or the entire piece polished.

Figure 94
Blue-gray and Amber sherbet and underplate
Shape 5154
Not signed
Sherbet height 2.75 inches
Value $75-$150

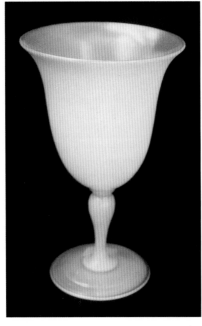

Figure 95
Gold Calcite goblet
Shape 1044
Not signed
Height 6 inches
Value $300-$400

Figure 96
Blue Aurene master salt
Shape 3067
{Aurene 3067} engraved factory signature on bottom
Diameter 6 inches
Value $600-$800

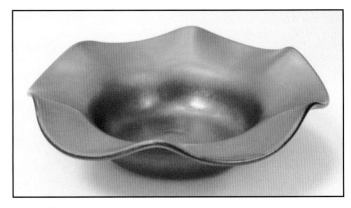

Figure 97
Blue Aurene bonbon
Shape 138
{Aurene} engraved factory signature on bottom
Diameter 6 inches
Value $400-$600

Figure 98
Gold Aurene nappie
Shape 2670
{Aurene 2670} engraved factory signature on bottom
Length 4.5 inches
Value $700-$900

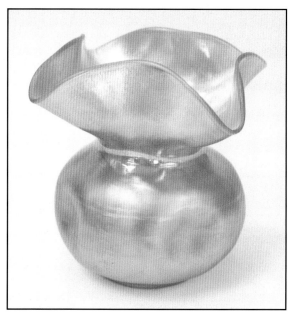

Figure 99
Gold Aurene vase
Shape 151
{Aurene 151} engraved factory signature on bottom
Height 3.7 inches
Value $500-$700

Figure 101
Gold Aurene vase
Unknown shape
Haviland paint stamped factory signature on bottom
Height 5.2 inches
Value $400-$600

Figure 102
Gold Aurene salt
Shape 269
{Aurene 269} engraved
factory signature on
bottom
Diameter 2.5 inches
Value $300 to $500

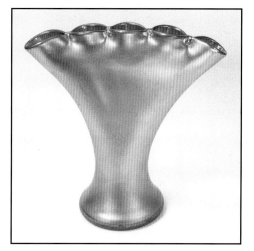

Figure 100
Gold Aurene vase
Shape 208
{Aurene 208} engraved factory signature on bottom
Height 5.2
Value $800-$1000

Figure 103
Gold Aurene vase
Shape 2762
{Aurene} engraved factory signature on bottom
Height 6 inches
Value $800-$1000
Note: Probable variation of shape 2762, which has
four openings rather than five.

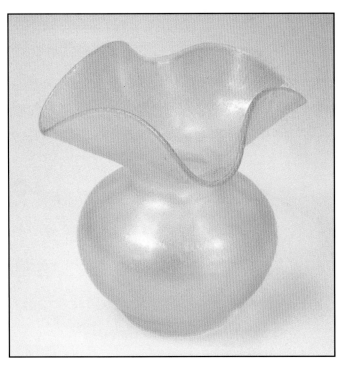

Figure 104
Verre de Soie vase
Shape 369½
Not signed
Height 3.5 inches
Value $150-$250

Figure 106
Blue Aurene vase
Shape 2776
{Aurene 2776} engraved factory signature on
bottom
Height 6.4 inches
Value $1000-$1200

Figure 105
Gold Aurene vase
Shape 162
{Aurene 162} engraved factory signature on bottom
Height 3.4 inches
Value $300-$500

Figure 107
Blue Aurene vase
Shape 2408
{Aurene 2408} engraved factory signature on bottom
Height 5.3 inches
Value $1000-$1200

Figure 108
Blue Calcite compote
Shape 1983
Not signed
Height 4 inches
Value $600-$800

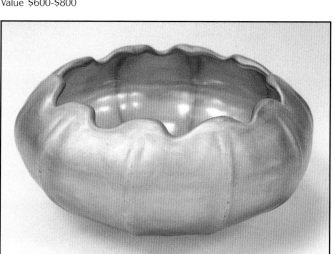

Figure 109
Gold Aurene bonbon
Shape 565
{Aurene 565} engraved factory signature on bottom
Diameter 6 inches
Value $600-$800

Figure 110
Bristol Yellow threaded Persian
Blue compote
Shape 6886
Not signed
Height 7 inches
Value $400-$600

Figure 111
Blue-gray vase
Shape 2908
Not signed
Height 9.7 inches
Value $400-$600

Figure 112
Cyprian goblet
Shape 6134
Not signed
Height 5 inches
Value $150-$250

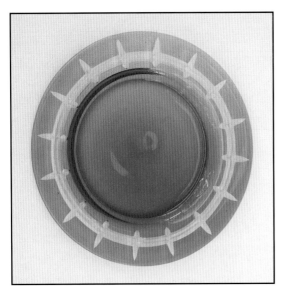

Figure 113
Flemish Blue and colorless plate
Shape 2028
Not signed
Diameter 8.2 inches
Value $75-$150

Figure 114
Flemish Blue champagne
Shape 7057
Not signed
Height 5.6 inches
Value $100-$200

Figure 115
Three French Blue stems
Shape 6603
{Steuben} block letter acid-stamped factory signature on bottom
Center stem 8.4 inches high
Value $100-$200 each

Figure 116
Colorless sherbet and tumbler with red and blue decoration
Shape 7472
{Steuben} script acid-stamped factory signature on bottom
Tumbler 4 inches high
Value $75-$150 ea

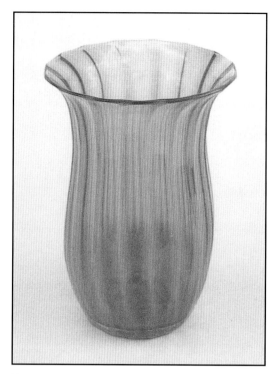

Figure 117
Oriental Poppy toothbrush holder
Shape 6767
Fleur-de-lis acid-stamped factory signature on bottom
Height 4.7 inches
Value $600-$800

Figure 119
Amethyst and colorless vase
Shape 7730
{Steuben} diamond point engraved factory signature on bottom
Height 7.2 inches
Value $150-$250
Note: This was probably made during the transition from colored to colorless glass after 1932. This shape is almost always seen colorless.

Figure 118
Flemish decanter and cup
Shape 2685
Not signed
Height 9.7 inches
Value of decanter $400-$600
Value of cup $100-$200

Figure 120
Blue-gray and Amber sherbet and underplate
Shape 2680
Not signed
Height of sherbet 3.7 inches
Value $125-$175

Figure 121
Flemish vase
Shape 2614
Not signed
Height 8.1 inches
Value $250-$350

Figure 122
Yellow Verre de Soie vase
Shape 938
Not signed
Height 5 inches
Value $400-$500
Note: This may be the same color that the
factory records call iridized Topaz.

Figure 123
Engraved Amethyst over colorless candlesticks
Shape 6863, engraved in "Crescent #2" pattern
Fleur-de-lis acid-stamped factory signature on bottom
Height 6.2 inches
Value $400-$600 each
Note: See Figure 17.

Figure 124
Cut and engraved Mirror Black over colorless champagne
Shape 7234
Not signed
Height 6.3 inches
Value $300-$400

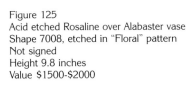

Figure 125
Acid etched Rosaline over Alabaster vase
Shape 7008, etched in "Floral" pattern
Not signed
Height 9.8 inches
Value $1500-$2000

Figure 126
Amethyst and colorless bowl
Shape 2896
Not signed
Diameter of top 8 inches
Value $300-$400

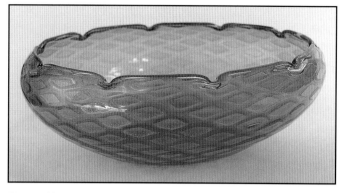

Figure 128
Amethyst Silverina Airtrap bowl
Shape 6997
Fleur-de-lis acid-stamped factory signature on bottom
Diameter of opening 10.5 inches
Value $1000-$1200

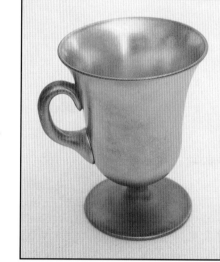

Figure 129
Gold Aurene punch cup
Shape 2367
{Aurene 2367}
engraved factory
signature on bottom
Height 3.5 inches
Value $350-$450

Figure 127
Ivory vase
Shape 6968
Not signed
Height 10.1 inches
Value $1000-$1200

Figure 130
Amber over colorless cut sherbet
Shape 7161
Fleur-de-lis acid-stamped factory signature on bottom
Diameter 4.6 inches
Value $350-$450

Figure 131
Colorless acid etched bowl
Shape 6415, etched in "Moderne" pattern
Fleur-de-lis acid etched in pattern on the side
Height 4.4 inches
Value $450-$550

Figure 132
Acid Etched Mirror Black over Amethyst Cintra lamp
Shape 3273, etched in "Adams" pattern
Not signed
Glass height 14 inches
Value $1500-$2000

Figure 134
Cut colorless goblet
Shape 7270, cut in
"Georgian" pattern
Not signed
Height 5.3 inches
Value $250-$350

Figure 133
Flemish tumble-up
Shape 3064
Not signed
Height 6 inches
Value $350-$450

Figure 135
Cut colorless dessert bowl and underplate
Shape 7270, cut in "Georgian" pattern
{Steuben} block letter acid-stamped factory signature on bottom
Bowl height 2.5 inches
Value $150-$250

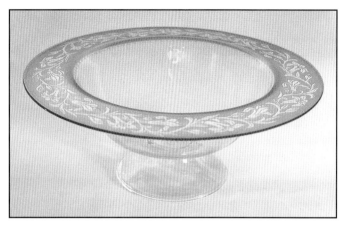

Figure 137
Colorless bowl with Gold Ruby acid etched cased rim
Shape 5194
Not signed
Diameter 9.7 inches
Value $250-$350

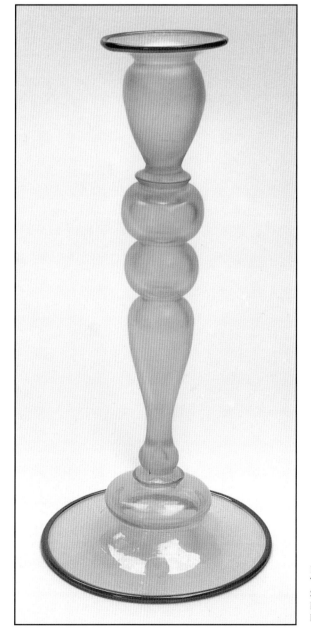

Figure 138
Colorless vase with engraved and fumed pattern
Shape 7406, Teague T-132 pattern
Not signed
Height 9.7 inches
Value $400-$500

Figure 136
Yellow Verre de Soie candlestick with Amethyst trim
Shape 2956
Not signed
Height 10 inches

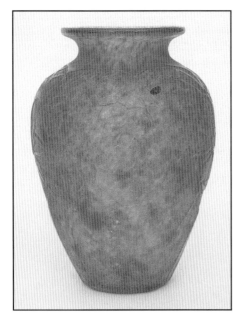

Figure 139
Rose Quartz vase
Shape 6501
Fleur-de-lis acid etched in pattern on the side
Height 6 inches
Value $600-$800

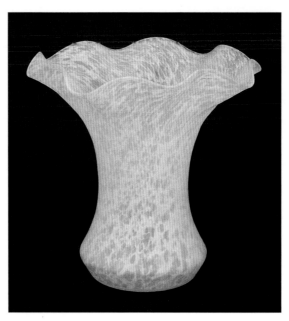

Figure 140
Blue Cintra vase
Shape 6813
Fleur-de-lis acid-stamped factory signature on bottom
Height 12 inches
Value $2000-$2500

Figure 141
Aqua Marine covered vase
Shape 2945
Not signed
Height 12 inches
Value $700-$900

Figure 142
Topaz goblet
Shape 5088
Fleur-de-lis acid-stamped factory
signature on bottom
Height 6.5 inches
Value $80-$125

Figure 144
Blue Aurene vase
Shape 2649
{Aurene 2649} engraved factory
signature on bottom
Height 2.5 inches
Value $400-$600

Figure 143
Engraved Gold Ruby over colorless stem
Shape 6114, Engraved "Thistle" pattern
Not signed
Height 4.2 inches
Value $100-$150

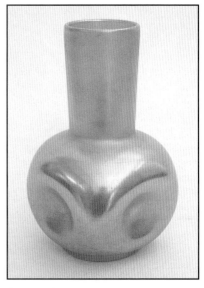

Figure 145
Gold Aurene vase
Shape 158
{Aurene 158} engraved factory signature
on bottom
Height 5.5 inches
Value $600-$800

38

Figure 146
Selection of bottles
Shape 6590
Left: Gold Ruby; Center: Bristol Yellow; Right: Amethyst
Height 5.2 inches
Value $125-$200 each

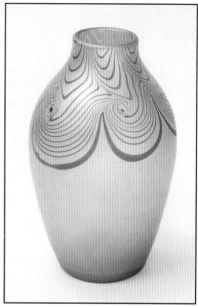

Figure 147
Gold Aurene decorated vase
Shape 645
{Aurene 645} engraved factory signature
on bottom
Height 5 inches
Value $1500-$2000

Figure 148
Blue Aurene vase
Shape 6512
{Aurene 6512} engraved factory signature on bottom
Height 5.5 inches
Value $1000-$1500

Figure 149
Flemish Blue champagne
Shape 6969
Fleur-de-lis acid-stamped factory
signature on bottom
Height 4.5 inches
Value $150-$200

Figure 150
Blue and colorless compote
No shape number
Not signed
Height 7 inches
Value $250-$350
Note: This is a Corning Inc. product
produced in the 1960s for internal sale.

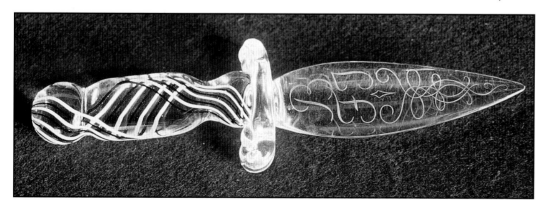

Figure 151
Colorless letter opener with
blue and white stripes
Whimsy, no shape number
Not signed
Length 8.2 inches
Value $400-$600
Note: This was made by Neil
Hardenberg, engraved by Max
Erlacher, and presented to Mr.
Franklin Blake, a resident of
Corning, New York.
Provenance: Mrs. Franklin
(Amy) Blake

Figure 152
Green vase
Whimsy, no shape number
Not signed
Diameter 4.2 inches
Value $100-$200
Provenance: Mr. Robert F. Rockwell Jr.

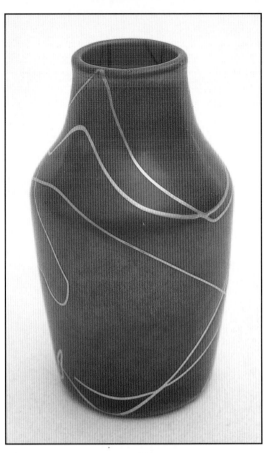

Figure 153
Experimental Gold Aurene decorated
Selenium Red vase
No shape number
Not signed
Height 3.2 inches
Value $3500-$4500
Provenance: Mr. Thomas P. Dimitroff
and Dr. and Mrs. L. G. Wagner

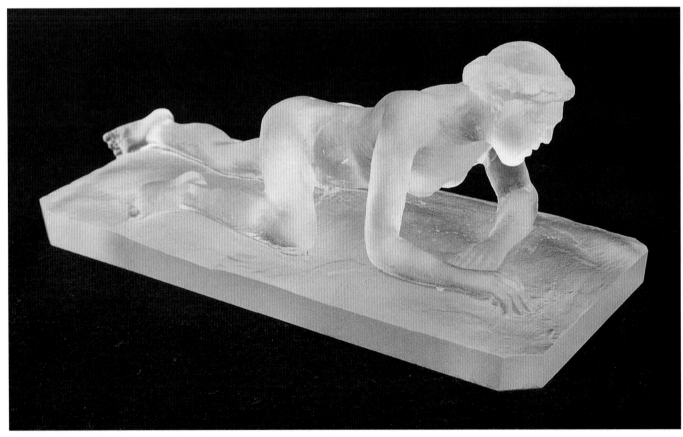

Figure 154
Colorless Cire Perdue figure of a woman
Frederick Carder, maker
No shape number
Signed {FC 44} in the casting, {F. Carder 1951} engraved on the bottom
Length 8.5 inches
Value $10,000-$12,000

New Drawings

The following drawings were found in the Carder Steuben archives of the Rakow Research Library at the Corning Museum of Glass in Corning, New York. For reasons that are not clear, they were not included in Paul Gardner's book *The Glass of Frederick Carder*. Some of the drawings, such as the 686 Compote and the three 6602 shapes, were found on pages in much the same format as the rest of the drawings in the archives. A few of the drawings were found penciled onto more formal drawings and at least two were found drawn in ink on blueprints. The drawings included here were electronically scanned from photocopies of the originals or blueprints, and in all cases were processed to remove extraneous material that was clearly not part of the original drawings. Many of the drawings showed water damage and it was this type of extraneous staining that has been removed. In the case of the drawings that were found as "black on black," where they had been inked onto blueprints, considerable effort was required to obtain the drawing free from background clutter. While every effort has been made to make these drawings follow the originals as closely as possible, they are not "photographic" copies and slight variations may be found if compared with the originals. There is **no scale** between the several drawings shown here.

Included with these drawings is much of the textual material that was found with the original drawings. This type of material, while not included in Gardner's book, provides an insight into the sizes and colors in which the various pieces can be found. Most of the text is undated. Where dates were found, they have been included. An effort has been made to present the text in the same order and with essentially the same abbreviations and punctuation as was used in the original text. It should be stressed that **this information is not complete** in the sense that all of the sizes and colors that a particular shape might have been made in were not necessarily included in the original material now available. This textual material must be looked at as only a **"snapshot in time."** The material was probably accurate at the time it was written but a particular shape could have be made in other sizes or colors previous to the original being generated and certainly other sizes and colors could have been made at some later date. There is evidence that many textual records were updated as changes were made but it cannot be depended upon to have happened with any consistency. Where comments have been made that were not on the original materials they have been added in *italics*. The cost numbers on the original generally did not include the dollar sign ($). The dollar sign has been added here for clarity.

The format of original records changed somewhat over time and there is evidence that some shapes were redrawn at least three times. The first records had the drawing and text on the same sheet of paper. It must have become clear fairly early that this would be inadequate because as the text was updated the information became confusing as parts of the text were crossed out and replaced with updated material. Most of the records are found with the drawing on one sheet, on the left as bound in a notebook, and the text on a second sheet on the right. As the text was updated, additional sheets could be added to accommodate it without the labor-intensive job of redrawing. Since three to five different shapes were normally found on each sheet, redrawing one meant redrawing them all.

All of the drawings fall within the same series as the drawings found in Gardner with the exception of the automobile dome lights that are found with numbers 6000 through 6005. These appear to be another number series, as tableware already exists with these same numbers.

When the Rakow archive drawings are compared with the drawings found in the Gardner book it is evident that the Rakow does not now have all of the drawings that he used. The Gardner book has about 500 to 600 shapes that are not found in the Rakow collection. In particular, the Rakow collection has very few of the 8000 special order series. Most of the "missing" drawings can be found in the collection of the Paul Vickers Gardner Glass Center at Alfred University in Alfred, New York.

And now a note about colors. Carder Steuben was made in a wide array of colors. By some counts, there are 140 or so listed in the records. Many of the colors that are attached to these names are unknown at this time. The original records also list some colors somewhat differently from how we know them today. The common colors that may cause confusion are:

- Blue Aurene is found as Cobalt Blue. The term Blue Aurene is not found until probably about 1925. The term Aurene in the factory records specifically meant Gold Aurene

- Gold Aurene over Calcite (Gold Calcite) is found as "Calcite G/L," which is interpreted to be Calcite (with a) gold layer or liner.

- Blue Aurene over Calcite (Blue Calcite) is found as "Calcite B/L," which is interpreted to be Calcite (with a) blue layer or liner.

- Today, most collectors generally name the Jade colors by having the color precede the "Jade" term, e.g. Green Jade. In the records, the Jade term generally precedes the color and we find it called Jade Green.

• The factory records indicate that Royal Purple must have been a popular color as it was offered in many shapes over most of the time Steuben was produced. Collectors today do not recognize Royal Purple as a separate color. It is almost certain that the dark Amethyst that collectors just call "Amethyst" is, in fact, Steuben's Royal Purple. Carder used the term "Mousselene" in conjunction with some of his transparent glasses. The definition of the term is somewhat obscure but, from context, Carder seems to have used it to define a glass with optic ribs and possibility as a term synonymous with transparent glass. Many of the references to Royal Purple are entered as "R. P. M." and Royal Purple, i.e. Steuben's dark Amethyst, is commonly found with optic ribs.

• The factory records indicate that a great deal of a glass called "Flemish" was made. Much of this glass was made in various shapes numbers concentrated in the 2000 range. The description of shape 2701 seems to define the word "Flemish." For this shape, prices are entered in the a column where the heading says, "Amber with Flemish Blue line" and then directly underneath "Flemish." From this, one can assume that the glass that is Amber with Flemish Blue decoration is, in fact, what Carder called "Flemish." Care must be used, however, as Amber glass decorated with Celeste Blue is not uncommon.

• Although the color Flint White exists and was often used with Light Blue Jade, the term "Flint" used in these records seems to mean lead glass and not the separate color.

The two vases shown to the right are found on a page in the factory records that immediately precedes the page that has cruet number 97. Number 97 is the earliest shape that can be found in the records with a factory number. At some point in time, someone made a notation beside each of these two vases speculating that they may be number 95 and number 96. They are included here for completeness.

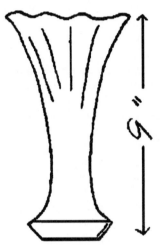

259½ Vase $2.50

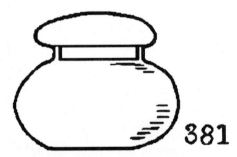

381 Puff Box and Cover $5.00doz

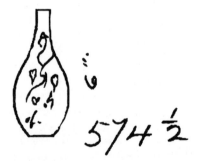

574½ Vase $4.50

686

686 Compote
7x7	Trans. Plain	$2.50ea
7x7	Trans. Rd	$3.00ea
7x7	Trans. Silverine	$3.00ea

5x5 Comp. same price as 6" per Mr. C. 5/12/?5

	Trans.	Cyprian	Cal. G/L	Aurene	Cer. Ruby	
5x5	$24.00doz					
6x6	$24.00doz	$30.00doz	$4.00ea	$4.50ea		
7x7	$27.00doz	$33.00doz	$4.75ea	$6.25ea	$42.00doz	11/11/24
8x8	$30.00doz	$36.00doz	$5.50ea	$8.00ea		
8x10	$37.50doz					

1926 Prices
	Trans.	Cyprian	Cal. G/L	Aurene	Cer. Ruby
6x6	$27.00doz			$5.00ea	
7x7	$30.00doz		$5.25ea	$7.00ea	
8x8			$6.25ea	$9.00ea	

8x8 Comp. Pom. Green Eng. #10008	$3.50ea
6" Diam x 8" high Amber Comp.	$2.50ea (1923)
7x7 Comp. Smoked Cry. Eng. Grape	$6.00ea (3/12/31)

Additional Set of 686 Compote price data that was undated.
7x7 Compote:
Verre de Soie	$30.00doz
Pomona Green	$30.00doz
Celeste Blue	$30.00doz
Amber	$30.00doz
Black	$33.00doz
Cyprian	$33.00doz
Jade Green	$63.00doz
Rosaline	$63.00doz
Aurene	$84.00doz
Cobalt Blue	

8x8 Compote:
Grenadine
Violet
Verte d'eau

794

794 Vase. No further data.

1038

1038 Cruet	$12.00doz
Cutting	$16.00doz

1039

1039 Cruet	P./B.	$15.00doz
	S./B.	$16.00doz

24 pt star *on base*

1044 Goblet
All regular colors see special memorandum

	Pomona Green Celeste Blue Amber, VDS Amethyst	Flint	Calcite G/L Cerise R.
Goblet	$13.25($12.00)Doz.	$10.00($9.00)Doz.	$21.50($19.50)
Saucer Champ.	$12.25($11.00)	$9.75($8.75)	$20.75($18.75)
Claret	$10.50($9.50)	$8.25($7.50)	$18.50($16.75)
Cocktail	$9.75($8.75)	$7.75($7.00)	$17.75($16.00)
Wine	$9.75($48.75)	$7.75($7.00)	$17.75($16.00)
Sherry	$9.75($8.75)	$7.75($7.00)	$17.75($16.00)
Cordial	$9.75($8.75)	$7.75($7.00)	$17.50($15.75)
Highball Tumbler & Ice Tea	$13.75($12.50)	$11.00($10.00)	$26.50($24.00)
Brandy & Soda Tumbler	$15.25($13.75)	$12.25($11.00)	$29.75($27.00)
Half Pint Tumbler	$9.50($8.50)	$7.50($6.75)	$14.50($13.00)
Finger Bowl	$10.50($9.50)	$8.25($7.50)	$20.00($18.00)
Finger Bowl Plate	$10.50($9.50)	$8.25($7.50)	$20.00($18.00)
Whiskey Tumbler	$8.25($7.50)	$6.75($6.00)	$13.25($12.00)
Handled Iced Tea Glass	$15.50($14.00)	$12.50($11.25)	$26.50($24.00)
Apollinaris Tumbler	$9.00($8.00)		
Champagne Tumbler	$8.25($7.50)		
Finger Bowl Engraved 10011	$20.25($18.25)		

The prices in parenthesis are updated prices that were added at a later date.

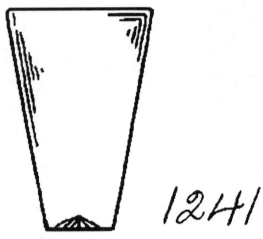

1241

1241 Cocktail Mixer
3.5oz $6.00
Alvin #040

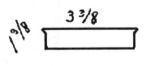

1566

1566 Pin Tray $2.00

1704

1704 Bonbon
8" $25.00/lb.   Light for Eng.   8" 3 feet $12.00
9"   no feet $9.00

2155 Cruet
Silversmith Co.

a. $9.00
b.   "
c.   "

a. $3.50
b.   "
c.   "

2155

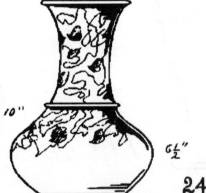

2437

2437 Vase
10" $10.00
8" $7.50

Information from a later date
Aurene   8" $13.00ea
          10" $17.50ea

44

2438

2438 Vase $15.00

Information from a later date.
Aurene $26.00ea

1397 s/s
3024

3024 Marmalade Jar $21.00
It appears that the 3024 is the same as the small size of the 1397 with an engraved pattern. In the original records s/s means "small size."

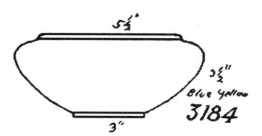

3184

3184 Bowl
10" Black green trim $4.50ea
10" Aurene $7.75ea
Plain Cintra $6.50ea Trim $7.50ea

10" $10.00
7" $7.00

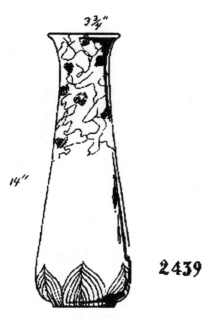

2439

2439 Vase $18.00

Information from a later date
Aurene $31.50

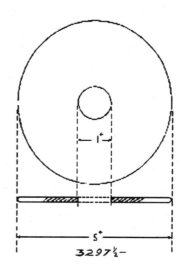

3297½

3297½ Bobeche
Amber Blue Edge $16.00
Trans. Colors $13.50doz
Flint $12.00
Cerise Ruby $18.00doz

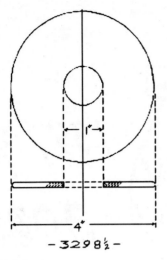

$-3298\tfrac{1}{2}-$

3298½ Bobeche
Trans. Colors	$12.00doz	Col. Edge
$15.00doz		
Flint	$10.50doz	
Grenadine plain	$18.00doz	
6/4/27		

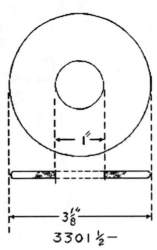

$3301\tfrac{1}{2}-$

3301½ Bobeche
Trans. Colors $10.50doz

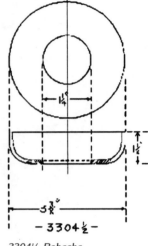

$-3304\tfrac{1}{2}-$

3304½ Bobeche
Trans. Colors $10.50doz

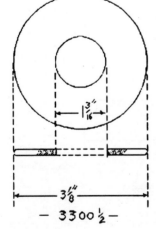

$3299\tfrac{1}{2}-$

3299½ Bobeche
Trans. Colors $12.00doz

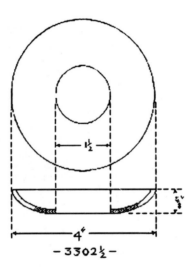

$-3302\tfrac{1}{2}-$

3302½ Bobeche
Trans. Colors $12.00doz

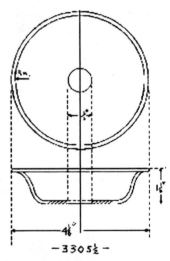

$-3305\tfrac{1}{2}-$

3305½ Bobeche
Trans. Colors	$12.00doz
Mirror Black	$15.00doz

$- 3300\tfrac{1}{2}-$

3300½ Bobeche
Trans. Colors $10.50doz
changed to $11.75doz, 1926

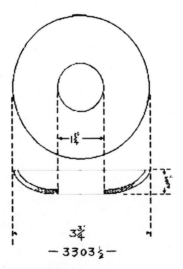

$-3303\tfrac{1}{2}-$

3303½ Bobeche
Trans. Colors $12.00doz

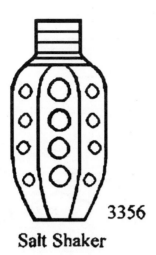

3356

Salt Shaker

3356
No further information

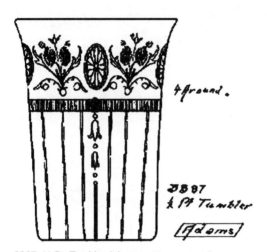

3387 ½ Pt. Tumbler Adams *pattern engraving*

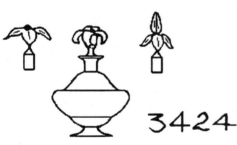

3424

3424 Cologne. No further information.

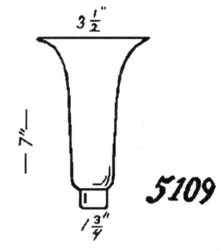

5106

5106 Vase
Rouge Flambé $2.50ea
Later price $4.50ea

5109

5109
Amber $6.00doz
Later price $12.00doz

5114 Comp.
7x7 Comp. Black on Crystal stem white edge on bowl only $6.00ea

	Jade	Pale Topaz &Crystal	Colors
7x7	$10.50ea	$3.00ea	$5.50ea
8x8		$4.00ea	$7.00ea

	Cyprian	Trans.	Black & Color
7x8	$5.35ea	$5.25ea	$6.00ea

7x8   Cyprian, Amber & Celeste Blue, Antique Green, Black & Green,
       Black & Turquoise, Black & Cinnamon Black & Crystal, Amethyst
       & Crystal, Pomona Green

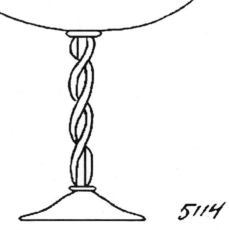

5114

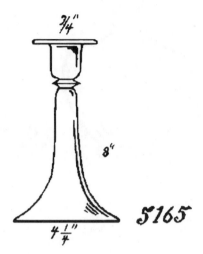

5165 Candlestick

	R.P.M	Flemish
8 inch	$27.00doz	$31.50doz
10 inch	$31.50doz	$36.00doz

5212 Same as shape 5067 only less work
Jug $4.00ea
Glasses $12.00doz. M.F.
Presumably M.F. stands for Marshall Field & Co. in Chicago.

Oval **6000**
2" x 3"

6000 Auto Dome Light. No further information.

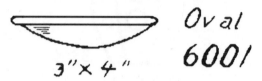

Oval **6001**
3" x 4"

6001 Auto Dome Light. No further information.

Round **6002**
$3\frac{3}{4}$ Diam

6002 Auto Dome Light. No further information.

Round **6003**
$4\frac{3}{4}$ Diam.

6003 Auto Dome Light. No further information.

Round **6004**
4" Diam.

6004 Auto Dome Light. No further information.

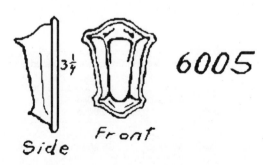

6005
Side   Front

6005 Auto Dome Light. No further information.

6099 12½" Vase
Black over Cinn.
With Cinn. Line or dots $2.50 ea

Art Light Fix Co. Black Rosa dots $2.50each
To Fit Mtg. #30

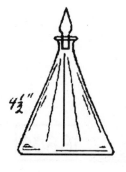

6600 Long Stpr. Cologne
V.D.S. with Jade Green or
Celeste Blue L/S $1.25 ea.

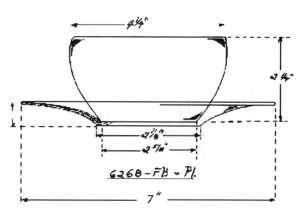

6268 Finger Bowl and Plate
This information taken from 6268 stemware data.

Bristol Yellow – Plain

6269
Goblets	*$18.00doz*
Champagnes	*$16.00doz*
High Ball	*$18.00doz*
7½" Plate	*$18.00doz*

Alexandrite crystal stem and foot cut Old English   #1 $78.00doz
                                        #2 $75.00doz

Crystal Cut "Queen Anne"   *$6.50ea goblet*
8" Plate Cut "Queen Anne"   *$9.50ea (1926)*

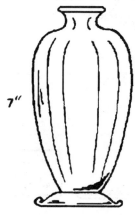

6601 Vase   7"
Crystal & Black
Moonlight
Bristol Yellow plain $1.75 ea

Reeded & bubbly $2.50 ea

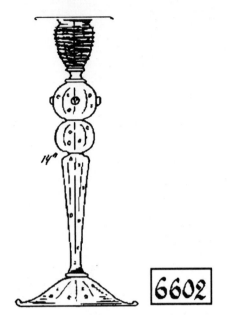

6602 Candlestick 14"
Moonlight reeded and bubbly $7.75ea

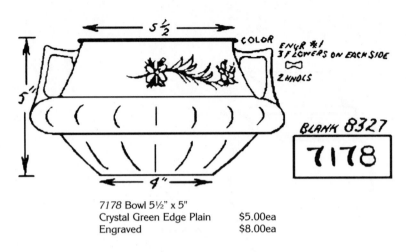

7178 Bowl 5½" x 5"
Crystal Green Edge Plain $5.00ea
Engraved $8.00ea

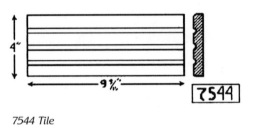

7544 Tile

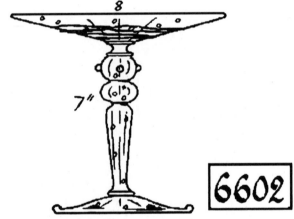

6602 Comport 7 x 8
Moonlight reeded and bubbly $7.75

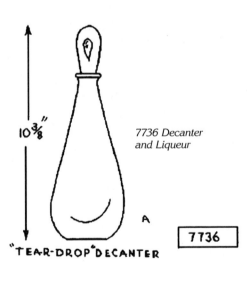

7736 Decanter
and Liqueur

"TEAR-DROP" DECANTER

"TEAR-DROP" LIQUEUR

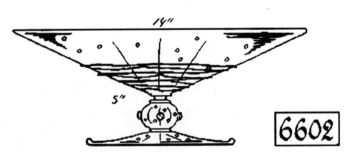

6602 Bowl 14"
Moonlight reeded & bubbly $12.25ea

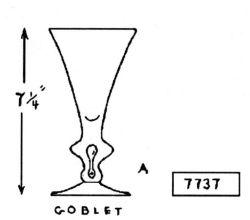

GOBLET

7737

7737 Goblet. No further information.

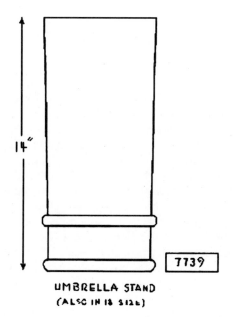

UMBRELLA STAND
(ALSO IN 18 SIZE)

7739

7739 Umbrella Stand

BEER·GLASS

7738

7738 Beer Glass

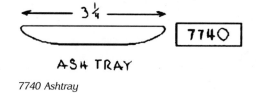

ASH TRAY

7740

7740 Ashtray

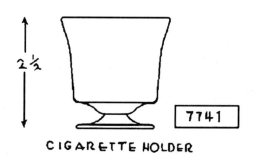

CIGARETTE HOLDER

7741

7741 Cigarette Holder
Drawings 7738, 7739, 7740, and 7741 were on a sheet dated 10/17/35

Steuben Candlesticks

Steuben made a wide range and number of shapes of candlesticks. There are over 280 different designs shown in *The Glass of Frederick Carder*. Many of these candlesticks were made in a number of sizes. For example, design 686 was made in 6", 8", 10", 12", and 14" sizes and the popular 2956 was made in 8", 9", 10", 12", 14", 15", and 18" sizes. All of the sizes on any one design look alike. By just looking at one of the sticks it is difficult to tell what size it is without an external reference. What may not be generally recognized is that Steuben redesigned several of its taller designs into a shorter version called a "Low candlestick" in the factory records. There are no drawings in the records to show us what these designs looked like. Several have turned up, however, so we can get an idea of what Steuben was trying to do. Basically Steuben took a tall candlestick with a long, rather straight stem and removed the stem. This produced a stick about 6" high that has the basic look of the original but is considerably shorter. The factory records list a number of candlesticks that were made in the "low" version. These are 3399, 6355, 6444, 6453, 6506, 6507, and 6734. In addition, there are at least two others that have turned up that were not listed as being available in a "low" version in the records. These are the 6110 and the 6602. Be-

cause several of these have turned up on the collector market, the drawing for the tall version can be modified to show what this low version looks like. This has been done here for shapes 6110, 6506, and 6602.

In each of these drawings, the tall candlestick has been scanned from the factory records. The drawing for the short candlestick was then formed by modifying the drawing of the tall stick to match the appearance of the photograph or actual glass of the short version.

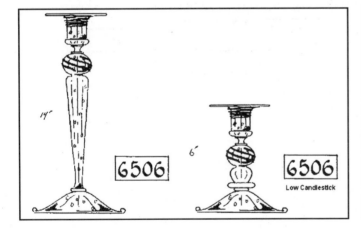

Collecting Steuben

Collecting Steuben can be very enjoyable. With over 7000 shapes and 140 colors, the combinations that can be found are almost limitless. But how does one begin? The first thing to do is to acquire, read, and study as many of the books listed in this volume as you can. It is also important to attend as many shows as possible, so that you can begin to see the actual pieces of glass. Museums that specialize in glass can be helpful, and probably the best in the world is the Corning Museum of Glass in Corning, New York. It houses the Carder Steuben collection of the Rockwell Museum that has over 2000 pieces on display.

The identification of Carder Steuben is always somewhat of a problem. As Tom Dimitroff says, and he is absolutely correct, the identification of Steuben is a process that one must go through. One cannot depend upon signatures alone, for example. One must use the shape, the color, the surface finish, some aspects of the way the piece was made, and finally the signature if it has one. Unfortunately, where there is money to be made there will be people who will go outside the realm of civilized decency and forge signatures on glass. All of the Steuben signatures have been forged and a Steuben signature on a piece of glass is therefore worthless, by itself, for authentication. Several years ago, Bob Rockwell, who owns a shop in Corning where he buys and sells Steuben, bought some 6303 stems from a seller. When he received them, he found that many of them had forged signatures alongside genuine signatures. It is beyond imagination why someone would do something like that.

Forged Steuben signatures have been around for a long time. Most of the early ones—from, say, twenty-five years ago—were fairly easy to spot because when held in reflecting light only the outline of the signature's features could be seen. There was no frosting on any of the features as there should have been. In more recent years, the forgers have improved. In a booth at a show a few years ago I picked up a piece of glass and noticed a Steuben signature that I would not have thought about twice except that I found it on a piece that wasn't Steuben. Great care must be used to make sure that signatures do not play too large a role in identification. Chapter 10 of the Dimitroff book has photos of most of the genuine and a number of the forged signatures. It would be well to study this section carefully.

One good way of getting started is to find a seller you feel you can trust that has a lot of experience with Carder Steuben. Buying primarily from one individual until you feel more confident may be a bit more expensive in the short run but in the long run, if there should ever be a question about a piece, a reputable seller will take it back. Another avenue is to find an advanced collector whom you can use as a mentor. Such a person should have collected for fifteen or twenty years or more. Such a mentor will warn you that he or she can make mistakes and that what he or she will give you is an opinion. An opinion from such a person is much more valuable than no opinion at all, however. Still another method is to join a group who all enjoy collecting Carder Steuben. One such group is the Carder Steuben Club, which is headquartered in Corning, New York. This group gener-

ally meets for a symposium each September on the weekend closest to September 18, which is Frederick Carder's birthday. The group's website at http://brokenshards.homestead.com/ CARDERSTEUBENCLUB.html has much useful information.

Be very careful of some of the online auction sites, even the big ones. While there is a lot of Steuben auctioned on these sites many of the sellers are not very knowledgeable or worse, they are just what I call "fast buck artists." A number of sellers take items on consignment and know very little about anything they are selling. They just use descriptions supplied by their consignors and it seems to matter little if the description is right, wrong, or indifferent.

Collecting Steuben as an Investment

Many collectors who must spend from about $50 into the thousands of dollar for items for their collections would like to believe that they are also making an investment that may, sometime in the future, be worth more than they paid initially. This can often be shown true for "high end" items. As an example, a red decorated Aurene vase shape 547 sold at auction in the fall of 2004 for $27,500, including the buyer's premium. The same identical piece was sold by the same auction house in the fall of 1993 for $13,750. This results in an equivalent compound interest rate of slightly less than 7% over the eleven year period.

It was hoped that some of the auction data that is presented in this book would show value trends over the ten to fifteen years for which the data was collected. This does not seem to be the case for the fairly common shapes and colors. For example, the data for Gold Aurene 2683 vases shows a lot of scatter and no discernible trend. There may be a couple of reasons for this. The data itself may be incomplete. There has been no attempt, for example, to include an item's size in the database. A 2683 Gold Aurene vase was made in a number of sizes and the smaller sizes may be more popular with collectors because they are easier to display. On the other hand, the larger sizes may be more popular with some because they are more ostentatious. Another factor may be condition. While damaged pieces were not included in the database, the factory clearly produced pieces where one might have had a better color or finish even on pieces of nominally the same size and color. There have been several instances where multiple pieces of the same shape and color have been in the same auction. The piece with the better color and finish always brings a premium. There was no way of accounting for these differences in the current database. It is also possible that the time span for this data is just too short for the relatively common items to show any trends.

So, what can we conclude? It would seem we should collect because we like what we collect. We should try to keep track of the current market values for what we collect so that we pay reasonable amounts to add pieces to our collections. We should keep in the back of our minds that what we collect may be a long term investment, but that reason alone should not be the major reason why we collect.

Photographic References

The following is a listing of the nine reference books where photographs of Carder Steuben have been cross-referenced into this Guide. The photos in this book are now included. The **FORMAT** describes the manner in which the photographs have been listed in the Guide. Because of limited space in this section, the listings are coded. In all cases, the listing is preceded by the initials of the book's author, e.g., JSS) for Jane Shadel Spillman. For Paul Gardner's two books, the headings start PG1) or PG2).

1) Gardner, Paul V., *The Glass of Frederick Carder.* New York, New York: Crown Publishers, Inc., 1971, and Atglen, Pennsylvania: Schiffer Publishing, Ltd., 2001.

FORMAT: PG1) PAGE NUMBER, ILLUSTRATION NUMBER, A where A is an alphabetic character that shows the position of the piece in the photograph from left to right. "A" would be the leftmost piece in the photo, "B" would be the next piece to the right, etc. In at least one case, TL is used for "top left" and TR is used for "top right." etc.

Example: PG1) 108, 171, B is bowl number 6081 found on page 108 in illustration 171 and is the second item from the left in the photograph.

For articles that are shown on the color plates, the format is:

FORMAT: PG1) PLATE NUMBER A, B where A is the photo designation on the plate number page and B shows the position of the piece in that photograph as described above.

When the reference is to the photographs found on pages 347 through 355, the format is:

FORMAT: PG1) PAGE NUMBER, X where X refers to the photograph designations that are captioned on pages 344 through 346.

When a reference is made to drawings in the Appendix of the 1932 Steuben Catalog on pages 312 through 322, the format is:

FORMAT: PG1) PAGE NUMBER

---

2) Gardner, Paul V. *Frederick Carder: Portrait of a Glassmaker.* Corning, New York: The Corning Museum of Glass, 1985.

FORMAT: PG2) PAGE NUMBER, A where A is an alphabetic character that shows the position of the piece in the photograph from left to right. Where two pieces are shown directly in front of one another, an "f" will designate the piece in front and "r" the one in the rear.

---

3) Rockwell Jr., Robert F. *Frederick Carder and his Steuben Glass 1903 – 1933.* West Nyack, New York: Dexter Press Inc., 1968. This is now available on a CD ROM.

FORMAT: RFR) PAGE NUMBER, SHELF NUMBER, A where the shelf number is listed from top to bottom, 1, 2, 3 etc., and A is an alphabetic character that shows the position of the piece from left to right.

---

4) Grover, Ray and Lee. *Art Glass Nouveau.* Rutland, Vermont: Charles E. Tuttle Company, 1967.

FORMAT: RLG) PAGE NUMBER, ILLUSTRATION NUMBER, A where A is an alphabetic character that positions the piece from left to right where it is required.

---

5) Revi, Albert Christian. *American Art Nouveau Glass.* Exton, Pennsylvania: Schiffer Publishing Ltd., 1968.

FORMAT: ACR) PAGE NUMBER, FIGURE NUMBER

For color plates that are shown between pages 142 and 143 the format is:

FORMAT: ACR) COLOR 1..4, T or B, A where COLOR 1..4 refers to color plates 1 through 4. There are four color plates that show Steuben. Color 1 is the first plate and faces page 142. T or B refers to the location of the photograph on the page (top or bottom) and A is a character that positions the piece from left to right.

---

6) Shuman III, John A. *The Collector's Encyclopedia of American Art Glass.* Paducah, Kentucky: Collector Books, 1988.

FORMAT: JAS) PAGE NUMBER, POSITION OF PHOTO ON PAGE, A where the position of the photo is similar to that used in the photo captions, i.e. TL is top left, BR is bottom right etc., and A is an alphabetic character that positions the piece from left to right.

---

7) Spillman, Jane Shadel. *The American Cut Glass Industry, T. G. Hawkes and His Competitors.* Woodbridge, Suffolk England: Antique Collectors Club Ltd., 1996.

FORMAT: JSS) PHOTOGRAPH NUMBER, POSITION OF OBJECT IN PHOTO where the photograph number is as in the photo captions and the position of the object in the photo is designated as L, C, or R for left, center or right as required.

---

8) Dimitroff, Thomas P. *Frederick Carder and Steuben Glass: American Classics.* Atglen, Pennsylvania: Schiffer Publishing Ltd., 1998.

FORMAT: TPD) FIGURE NUMBER where the figure number is that listed for each figure.

---

9) Ketchum, Marshall. *Frederick Carder's Steuben Glass.* Atglen, Pennsylvania: Schiffer Publishing Ltd., 2005.

FORMAT: MDK) FIGURE NUMBER where the figure number is that listed for each figure.

In many cases, there are two or more photographs referenced from the same book for the same drawing number. Where this occurs, the references are separated by a colon. For example:

TPD) 7.11: 7.13

These are two references for shape number 1284 shown in Figures 7.11 and 7.13 in the book by Thomas P. Dimitroff.

Guide to Shape Numbers

SHAPE NO.	ITEM	PAGE	COL	ROW	PRICE REALIZED	GLASS TYPE	AUCTION HOUSE	COMMENTS & PHOTO REFERENCES
0044	Tray	158	2	16				This number is an error, see #0411.
0097	Cruet	178	1	1				
0098	Cruet	178	1	2				
0099	Cruet	178	1	3				
0100	Cruet	178	1	4				
0101	Cruet	178	1	5				
0102	Cruet	178	1	6				
0103	Cruet	178	1	7				
0104	Sugar & Creamer	234	1	1,2				
0105	Sugar & Creamer	234	1	3,4				
0106	Nappie	233	1	6				
0107	Compote	171	1	1				
0108	Goblet	190	1	1				
0109	Goblet	190	1	2				
0110	Bowl	141	1	1				
0111	Bowl	141	1	2				
0112	Bowl	141	1	3	$1035	Blue Aurene	EAC-11/03	
0113	Decanter	180	1	1				
0114	Decanter	180	1	2				
0115	Pitcher	212	1	1				
0116	Tumbler	198	4	4				
0117	Spooner	233	1	1				
0118	Spooner	233	1	2				
0119	Spooner	233	1	3				
0120	Spooner	233	1	4				
0121	Nappie	233	1	7				
0122	Cruet	178	1	8				
0123	Vase	246	1	1				
0124	Pitcher	212	1	2				
0125	Cruet	178	1	9				
0126	Nappie	233	1	8				
0127	Nappie	233	1	9				
0130	Vase	246	1	2	$2475	Gold Aurene	Cott-08/01	PG1)351,A; TPD)5.1
0130					$805	Gold Aurene	FtnA-02/03	
0130					$4310	Gold Aurene	EAC-11/03	
0130					$1880	Gold Aurene	Sknr-12/03	
0130					$1800	Gold Aurene	Dalla-10/04	
0130					$1255	Gold Aurene	ebay-11/04	
0130					$1150	Gold Aurene	EAC-04/05	
0130					$1275	Gold Aurene	ebay-05/05	
0130a								PG1)V C,A:352,V; TPD)5.1 (optic)
0131	Vase	246	1	3	$1265	Decorated Gold Aurene	Sknr-10/96	PG1)351,E
0131					$545	Gold Aurene	Sknr-10/96	
0131					$325	Gold Aurene	ebay-10/00	
0131					$1750	Gold Aurene	JDJ-05/03	
0131					$590	Gold Aurene	ebay-08/03	
0131a								Threaded
0131b					$2010	Gold Aurene	JDJ-05/03	Threaded pulled up in festoons
0132	Vase	246	1	4	$375	Gold Aurene	ebay-11/04	PG1)351,I
0132					$345	Gold Aurene	EAC-04/05	
0132					$440	Gold Aurene	ebay-06/05	
0133	Compote	171	1	2				
0134	Vase	246	1	5	$725	Gold Aurene	ebay-02/03	PG1)351,G; TPD)4.19:4.22
0135	Vase	246	1	6	$1155	Gold Aurene	JDJ-05/94	PG1)32,55:351,K
0136	Vase	246	1	7	$920	Gold Aurene	Sknr-10/97	TPD)8.55
0136					$3080	Gold Aurene	EAC-08/00	
0137	Vase	246	2	1	$485	Gold Aurene	Sknr-02/01	PG1)351,K
0138	Bonbon	233	2	14	$190	Gold Aurene	EAC-10/91	PG1)VI,C,C:353,EE; RFR)9,3,B;
0138					$150	Gold Aurene	JDJ-10/94	TPD)10.123; MDK)97
0138					$300	Gold Calcite	EAC-07/96	
0138					$1045	Blue Calcite	EAC-10/96	
0138					$545	Blue Aurene	Sknr-10/96	
0138					$275	Gold Calcite	EAC-07/97	

SHAPE NO.	ITEM	PAGE	COL	ROW	PRICE REALIZED	GLASS TYPE	AUCTION HOUSE	COMMENTS & PHOTO REFERENCES
0138					$220	Gold Calcite	EAC-10/97	
0138					$195	Gold Aurene	EAC-10/97	
0138					$255	Gold Aurene	JDJ-06/98	
0138					$230	Gold Aurene	JDJ-05/99	
0138					$475	Gold Calcite	Ogal-02/00	
0138					$195	Gold Calcite	ebay-03/00	
0138					$300	Gold Calcite	EAC-05/00	
0138					$460	Blue Aurene	Sknr-06/00	
0138					$385	Gold Aurene	EAC-08/00	
0138					$180	Gold Aurene	ebay-10/00	
0138					$325	Gold Calcite	Ogal-10/00	
0138					$225	Gold Aurene	ebay-11/00	
0138					$90	VDS	ebay-02/01	
0138					$170	Gold Aurene	EAC-04/01	Haviland signature
0138					$75	Gold Calcite	ebay-06/01	
0138					$200	Gold Calcite	ebay-06/01	
0138					$165	Gold Aurene	ebay-07/01	
0138					$690	Blue Aurene	Cott-08/01	
0138					$145	Gold Aurene	Jack-09/01	
0138					$195	Gold Aurene	EAC-11/01	
0138					$260	Gold Aurene	EAC-11/01	
0138					$280	Blue Calcite	ebay-11/01	
0138					$485	Blue Aurene	Jack-12/01	
0138					$130	Gold Calcite	ebay-02/02	
0138					$170	Gold Aurene	EAC-04/02	Haviland signature
0138					$225	Gold Aurene	EAC-04/02	Haviland signature
0138					$145	Gold Calcite	ebay-04/02	
0138					$400	Blue Aurene	ebay-07/02	
0138					$335	Blue Aurene	EAC-09/02	
0138					$135	VDS	ebay-10/02	
0138					$225	Gold Aurene	ebay-10/02	
0138					$775	Blue Aurene	Jack-11/02	
0138					$95	VDS	ebay-03/03	
0138					$315	Gold Aurene	EAC-06/03	
0138					$105	Gold Calcite	ebay-08/03	
0138					$150	Gold Calcite	ebay-09/03	
0138					$135	Gold Calcite	ebay-10/03	
0138					$225	Gold Calcite	ebay-11/03	
0138					$125	Gold Calcite	ebay-11/03	
0138					$150	Gold Aurene	ebay-12/03	
0138					$190	Gold Calcite	ebay-03/04	
0138					$405	Gold Aurene	ebay-03/04	
0138					$225	Gold Calcite	ebay-04/04	
0138					$400	Gold Calcite	EAC-04/04	
0138					$50	Gold Calcite	ebay-05/04	
0138					$250	Gold Aurene	ebay-05/04	
0138					$230	Gold Aurene	JDJ-05/04	
0138					$180	Gold Calcite	Cinc-06/04	
0138					$130	Gold Calcite	ebay-06/04	
0138					$175	Gold Calcite	ebay-07/04	
0138					$110	Gold Calcite	ebay-07/04	
0138					$180	Gold Calcite	ebay-07/04	
0138					$135	Gold Calcite	ebay-09/04	
0138					$135	Gold Calcite	ebay-11/04	
0138					$150	Gold Aurene	ebay-11/04	Haviland signature
0138					$110	Gold Aurene	ebay-12/04	Haviland signature
0138					$135	Gold Aurene	ebay-12/04	Haviland signature
0138					$175	Gold Aurene	ebay-12/04	Haviland signature
0138					$350	Blue Aurene	ebay-12/04	
0138					$250	Gold Aurene	Ogal-01/05	
0138					$140	Gold Calcite	ebay-03/05	
0138					$160	Gold Calcite	ebay-03/05	
0138					$80	Pomona Green	ebay-04/05	
0138					$135	Gold Calcite	ebay-05/05	
0139	Bonbon	233	2	15	$575	Gold Aurene	EAC-07/93	PG1)353,EE
0139					$255	Gold Aurene	EAC-04/94	
0139					$190	Gold Aurene	EAC-10/97	
0139					$350	Gold Aurene	ebay-05/02	Haviland signature
0139					$465	Gold Aurene	ebay-08/04	
0139					$390	Gold Aurene	ebay-08/04	
0139					$305	Gold Aurene	ebay-10/04	
0139					$455	Gold Aurene	ebay-06/05	Haviland signature
0139					$575	Blue Aurene	EAC-07/05	
0139	Salt				$300	Gold Aurene	EAC-04/99	

SHAPE NO.	ITEM	PAGE	COL	ROW	PRICE REALIZED	GLASS TYPE	AUCTION HOUSE	COMMENTS & PHOTO REFERENCES
0139					$525	Blue Aurene	ebay-06/01	
0139					$140	Gold Aurene	Dalla-05/03	
0139					$400	Gold Aurene	ebay-01/04	
0139					$475	Gold Aurene	ebay-02/05	Haviland signature
0139					$560	Gold Aurene	ebay-07/05	
0140	Vase	246	2	2	$575	Gold Aurene	ebay-01/00	PG1)351,H
0141	Vase	246	2	3	$385	Gold Aurene	JDJ-05/94	PG1)351,C
0141					$215	Gold Aurene	ebay-09/02	
0142	Vase	246	2	4	$750	Gold Aurene	ebay-10/03	
0143	Vase	246	2	5	$510	Gold Aurene	ebay-02/05	PG1)351,B
0144	Vase	246	2	6	$2680	Gold Aurene	JDJ-11/02	PG1)351,I
0145	Vase	246	2	7				
0146	Compote	171	1	3				
0147	Compote	171	1	4				
0148	Vase	246	3	1				
0149	Vase	246	3	2				
0150	Vase	246	3	3	$675	Gold Aurene	ebay-03/00	PG1)353,FF
0150					$1100	Gold Aurene	ebay-11/03	
0151	Vase	246	3	4	$470	Gold Aurene	EAC-10/95	PG1)353,FF; MDK)99
0151					$425	Gold Aurene	ebay-04/00	
0152	Vase	246	3	5	$1615	Gold Aurene	ebay-02/03	PG1)351,B
0153	Vase	246	3	6				PG1)351,J; TPD)10.84
0154	Vase	246	3	7	$2775	Engraved Aurene	ebay-11/99	PG1)351,G; TPD)5.38
0154					$730	Gold Aurene	ebay-03/02	
0154					$1225	Decorated Gold Aurene	ebay-08/04	
0154					$805	Decorated Gold Aurene	EAC-04/05	
0155	Vase	246	3	8				PG1)351,I
0156	Compote	171	1	5				
0157	Compote	171	1	6				
0158	Vase	246	4	1	$575	Gold Aurene	Sknr-05/94	PG1)351,C:353,FF; MDK)145
0158					$430	Gold Aurene	ebay-03/02	
0158					$410	Gold Aurene	ebay-06/03	
0158					$340	Gold Aurene	ebay-11/04	
0159	Vase	246	4	2				PG1)351,E
0160	Vase	246	4	3				
0161	Vase	246	4	4				PG1)351,J
0162	Vase	246	4	5	$805	Gold Aurene	Sknr-10/95	PG1)32,56,B:351,E; MDK)105
0163	Vase	246	4	6				PG1)352,X; TPD)5.38
0164	Vase	246	4	7	$720	Gold Aurene	JDJ-11/02	PG1)352,O; TPD)4.67
0165	Vase	246	4	8	$690	Gold Aurene	ebay-12/99	PG1)351,B
0165					$485	Gold Aurene	ebay-08/02	
0165					$1035	Gold Aurene	JDJ-05/04	
0166	Candlestick	160	1	1				
0167	Vase	246	4	9	$400	Gold Aurene	Jack-06/02	PG1)351,A
0167					$450	Gold Aurene	ebay-07/02	
0167					$350	Gold Aurene	ebay-09/02	
0167					$1435	Blue Aurene	FtnA-08/03	
0168	Vase	246	4	10	$880	Gold Aurene	Cott-08/01	
0168					$750	Gold Aurene	EAC-04/04	
0169	Candlestick	160	1	2	$380	Gold Aurene	ebay-10/01	PG1)351,L
0169					$1120	Gold Aurene	EAC-04/02	
0170	Vase	246	5	1	$880	Gold Aurene	EAC-10/99	PG1)III B,A:352,O
0171	Finger Bowl	189	1	1	$300	Gold Aurene	EAC-10/91	PG1)353,EE
0171					$1540	Gold Aurene	EAC-10/93	
0171					$250	Gold Aurene	ebay-04/00	
0171					$250	Gold Aurene	ebay-10/03	Signed "Haviland"
0171					$225	Gold Aurene	ebay-11/03	Underplate only
0171					$170	Gold Aurene	JDJ-11/03	
0171					$300	Gold Aurene	ebay-01/04	Finger Bowl only
0171					$510	Gold Aurene	Cinc-06/05	
0172	Compote	171	1	7	$520	Gold Aurene	EAC-10/91	PG1)352,O
0172					$1725	Gold Aurene	EAC-06/03	
0174	Vase	246	5	2	$2930	Gold Aurene	ebay-06/05	PG1)351,L
0175	Vase	246	5	3	$975	Gold Aurene	ebay-03/03	PG1)351,F; TPD)4.50
0175					$1500	Gold Aurene	ebay-08/03	
0176	Vase	246	5	4				PG1)352,N
0177	Vase	246	5	5				PG1)352,N; ACR)144,270
0178	Vase	246	5	6				PG1)352,N
0179	Vase	246	5	7				PG1)351,D
0180	Vase	247	1	1				PG1)352,M
0181	Vase	247	1	2				PG1)352,M
0182	Vase	247	1	3	$735	VDS	Tway-09/04	PG1)XV B,C:352,M
0183	Vase	247	1	4				PG1)351,F
0184	Vase	247	1	5				PG1)351,F

SHAPE NO.	ITEM	PAGE	COL	ROW	PRICE REALIZED	GLASS TYPE	AUCTION HOUSE	COMMENTS & PHOTO REFERENCES
0185	Vase	247	1	6	$2990	Gold Aurene	EAC-07/05	PG1)352,R; TPD)8.55
0186	Vase	247	1	7	$6600	Gold Aurene	Cott-08/01	PG1)351,H Compote in factory records.
0187	Cologne	240	1	1	$640	Gold Aurene	ebay-01/00	PG1)352,W
0188	Cologne	240	1	2				PG1)352,W
0189	Cologne	240	1	3				PG1)351,H
0190	Cologne	240	1	4				PG1)352,W
0191	Nappie	233	1	10	$575	Gold Aurene	EAC-07/98	PG1)353,EE
0191					$330	Gold Aurene	ebay-04/04	
0192	Bonbon	233	2	16	$605	Gold Aurene	EAC-04/90	PG1)353,CC
0193	Vase	247	2	1				PG1)351,G
0194	Vase	247	2	2				PG1)351,L
0195	Vase	247	2	3	$1430	Decorated Gold Aurene	EAC-04/92	PG1)351,D; RFR)11,4,A; ACR)133,241
0195					$4675	Gold Aurene "B"	Cott-08/01	
0196	Candlestick	160	1	3				PG1)351,D;
0197	Bowl	141	1	4				PG1)353,Y
0198	Bowl	141	1	5				PG1)353,Y
0199	Bowl	141	1	6				PG1)353,Y
0200	Vase	247	2	4				
0201	Vase	247	2	5	$1380	Decorated Gold Aurene	Sknr-05/96	PG1)351,J
0202	Vase	247	2	6				
0203	Vase	247	2	7				PG1)351,A
0204	Finger Bowl	189	1	2	$150	VDS	ebay-07/04	PG1)353,CC
0205	Nappie	233	1	11				PG1)353,EE
0206	Cruet (Decanter)	178	2	1				PG1)353,Z
0206	Wineglass							PG1)353,Z
0207	Vase	247	2	8				PG1)351,K
0208	Vase	247	2	9	$350	Gold Aurene	ebay-02/03	PG1)352,S; MDK)100
0208					$840	Gold Aurene	JDJ-05/04	
0209	Vase	247	2	10	$1035	Decorated Gold Aurene	Sknr-03/99	
0209b	Vase							PG1)352,S
0210	Vase	247	3	1				PG1)353,CC,FF
0211	Vase	247	3	2	$525	Gold Aurene	ebay-02/01	
0211b	Vase							PG1)352,S
0212	Vase	247	3	3				PG1)353,FF
0213	Vase	247	3	4				PG1)353,FF
0214	Vase	247	3	5				
0215	Vase	247	3	6				TPD)5.22
0216	Vase	247	3	7	$385	Gold Aurene	EAC-10/91	
0216b	Vase							PG1)352,Q
0217	Vase	247	3	8	$985	Gold Aurene	ebay-09/02	PG1)352,Q; TPD)10.93
0218	Vase	247	3	9				
0218b	Vase							PG1)352,V
0219	Vase	247	3	10				RFR)10,4,D; TPD)10.93
0219b	Vase				$2000	Decorated Gold Aurene	Cinc-06/03	PG1)352,V
0219b					$2000	Decorated Gold Aurene	EAC-04/05	
0219b					$1495	Decorated Gold Aurene	EAC-07/05	
0220	Vase	247	4	1				PG1)352,R
0221	Vase	247	4	2				PG1)353,AA
0222	Vase	247	4	3				PG1)353,AA; RFR)7,1,C
0223	Vase	247	4	4	$1105	Blue Aurene	ebay-12/01	PG1)353,AA
0224	Vase	247	4	5				PG1)352,X
0225	Vase	247	4	6				PG1)352,P
0226	Vase	247	4	7				PG1)352,P
0227	Vase	247	4	8	$475	Gold Aurene	ebay-05/01	PG1)352,R
0227					$520	Gold Aurene	JDJ-05/01	
0227					$500	Gold Aurene	Tway-05/04	
0228	Bonbon	233	2	17				
0229	Vase	247	4	9				
0230	Vase	247	5	1				PG1)62,95,TL
0231	Nut Dish	211	1	1	$165	Gold Aurene	ebay-04/00	
0231					$230	Gold Aurene	ebay-01/02	
0232	Nut Dish	211	1	2				
0233	Vase	247	5	2				
0234	Vase	247	5	3				
0235	Vase	247	5	4				PG1)353,BB
0236	Vase	247	5	5				PG1)353,BB
0237	Vase	247	5	6	$330	Gold Aurene	JDJ-10/94	
0238	Vase	247	5	7	$325	Gold Aurene	ebay-11/02	PG1)352,Q
0238					$375	Gold Aurene	ebay-12/03	
0238					$295	Gold Aurene	ebay-06/05	
0239	Vase	247	5	8				PG1)353,DD
0240	Vase	247	5	9	$1100	Gold Aurene	EAC-07/99	PG1)353,DD
0241	Vase	247	5	10	$530	Gold Aurene	ebay-09/03	
0242	Vase	248	1	1	$330	Blue Aurene	JDJ-10/94	PG1)353,DD; TPD)4.56

SHAPE NO.	ITEM	PAGE	COL	ROW	PRICE REALIZED	GLASS TYPE	AUCTION HOUSE	COMMENTS & PHOTO REFERENCES
0243	Vase	248	1	2				TPD)10.155
0244	Vase	248	1	3	$4950	Decorated Green Aurene	EAC-04/93	
0244					$4600	Decorated Gold Aurene	JDJ-06/97	
0245	Vase	248	1	4	$990	Gold Aurene	EAC-07/97	PG1)352,X
0245					$1205	Blue Aurene	ebay-03/00	
0246	Vase	248	1	5				PG1)352,P
0247	Vase	248	1	6				
0248	Vase	248	1	7				
0249	Vase	248	1	8				
0250	Vase	248	1	9				
0251	Cruet	178	2	2				
0252	Sugar & Creamer	234	1	5,6	$440	Gold Aurene	EAC-07/91	Creamer only
0252					$300	Gold Aurene	Cinc-12/99	Sugar bowl only
0252					$340	Gold Aurene	ebay-03/02	Creamer only
0252					$325	Gold Aurene	Cinc-11/02	Sugar bowl only
0252					$700	Gold Aurene	ebay-04/04	Set
0253	Vase	248	2	1				PG1)352,U
0254	Vase	248	2	2				PG1)352,U
0255	Vase	248	2	3	$3300	Decorated Gold Aurene	EAC-04/95	PG1)352,U
0255					$7840	Decorated Gold Aurene	EAC-09/02	
0255					$2465	Decorated Gold Aurene	EAC-01/03	
0256	Vase	248	2	4	$4600	Decorated Green Aurene	EAC-06/03	PG1)62,95,BOT
0257	Vase	248	2	5	$7776	Decorated Green Aurene	ebay-09/02	PG1)62,95,TR
0258	Vase	248	2	6				PG1)352,T
0259	Vase	248	2	7				PG1)352,T; JAS)160,C; TPD)8.5
0259½	Vase							9" high, See New Drawings section
0260	Vase	248	3	1	$860	Decorated Gold Aurene	Sknr-10/96	PG1)352,T; RFR)12,2,B; TPD)5.50
0261	Vase	248	3	2	$4310	Decorated Gold Aurene	Sknr-10/98	PG1)353,BB; RFR)12,3,A
0262	Vase	248	3	3	$475	Gold Aurene	ebay-10/01	JAS)161,TL,B
0262					$1400	Decorated Gold Aurene	ebay-03/03	
0262					$4200	Millefiori on Gold Aurene	JDJ-06/05	
0263	Vase	248	3	4				
0264	Nut Dish	211	1	3				
0265	Vase	248	3	5				
0266	Vase	248	3	6				
0267	Vase	248	3	7				RFR)10,4,B
0268	Salt	217	1	1	$880	Blue Aurene	EAC-07/96	
0268					$335	Gold Aurene	ebay-10/01	
0268					$230	Gold Aurene	ebay-10/03	
0269	Salt	217	1	2				MDK)102
0270	Vase	248	3	8	$4400	Decorated Red Aurene	EAC-10/94	TPD)5.10:5.21
0270					$13000	Decorated Red Aurene	Cinc-11/02	
0270					$13800	Decorated Red Aurene	Jack-06/03	
0271	Vase	248	4	1				
0272	Vase	248	4	2				
0273	Vase	248	4	3	$4600	Decorated Gold Aurene	Sknr-10/96	
0274	Shade	218	1	1				
0275	Vase	248	4	4	$8400	Decorated Green Aurene	EAC-04/02	RFR)12,4,A
0276	Vase	248	4	5	$3300	Decorated Green Aurene	EAC-10/90	RFR)10,2,A; RLG)138,267; TPD)5.5
0277	Vase	248	4	6				
0278	Vase	248	4	7				
0279	Vase	248	5	1	$515	Blue Aurene	Jack-11/02	PG1)VII B; RFR)10,3,A:11,2,B:11,3,B;
0279					$810	Gold Aurene	ebay-10/04	RFR)31,1,A; ACR)140,259
0280	Vase	248	5	2				
0281	Vase	248	5	3				
0282	Vase	248	5	4				
0283	Vase	248	5	5				
0284	Vase	248	5	6				
0285	Vase	248	5	7				
0286	Vase	248	5	8				RLG)137,264; RFR)10,1,A
0287	Nappie	233	1	12	$400	Gold Aurene	Wint-12/01	
0287					$500	Gold Aurene	ebay-07/03	
0287					$495	Gold Aurene	ebay-10/03	
0288	Vase	249	1	1				
0289	Vase	249	1	2				
0290	Vase	249	1	3				
0292	Vase	249	1	4				
0293	Vase	249	1	5				TPD)5.20
0294	Vase	249	1	6				
0295	Vase	249	1	7				
0296	Vase	249	1	8				PG1)IV A,B
0297	Vase	249	1	9				TPD)5.15
0298	Vase	249	2	1				PG1)VII A,F:VII C; RFR)12,4,C;
0298								RLG)137,263; TPD)10.125

SHAPE NO.	ITEM	PAGE	COL	ROW	PRICE REALIZED	GLASS TYPE	AUCTION HOUSE	COMMENTS & PHOTO REFERENCES
0299	Vase	249	2	2				
0300	Cologne	240	1	5				
0301	Cologne	240	1	6				
0302	Cologne	240	1	7				
0303	Cologne	240	1	8				
0304	Cologne	240	1	9				
0305	Cologne	240	1	10				
0306	Cologne	240	2	1				
0307	Cologne	240	2	2				
0308	Cologne	240	2	3				
0309	Vase	249	2	3	$250	VDS	ebay-02/01	PG1)353,II
0309					$850	VDS	ebay-07/05	
0310	Sherbet	216	4	1				
0311	Vase	249	2	4				PG1)XV B,B
0312	Vase	249	2	5	$935	Gold Aurene	EAC-07/93	PG1)353,GG; MDK)92
0312					$950	Gold Calcite	EAC-04/01	
0312					$645	Gold Calcite	EAC-09/01	
0312					$750	Blue Aurene	ebay-11/01	
0312					$925	Gold Calcite	ebay-11/01	
0312					$1440	Gold Aurene	JDJ-11/02	
0312					$1840	Gold Aurene	Jack-06/03	
0312					$1410	Blue Aurene	EAC-11/03	
0312					$1840	Gold Aurene	EAC-11/03	
0312					$1150	Gold Aurene	EAC-04/04	
0312					$410	Amber/Amethyst stripe	ebay-05/04	
0312					$360	VDS	Crft-05/04	
0312					$305	Gold Calcite	ebay-06/04	
0312					$200	VDS	Crft-09/04	
0312					$1000	Blue Aurene	ebay-03/05	
0312					$380	Gold Calcite	ebay-04/05	
0313	Vase	249	2	6				PG1)XV B,A
0314	Vase	249	2	7	$805	Gold Aurene	JDJ-11/01	PG1)353,GG
0315	Basket	139	1	1				
0316	Basket	139	1	2				
0317	Bonbon	233	3	1				
0318	Bonbon	233	3	2				
0319	Bonbon	233	3	3				
0320	Bonbon	233	3	4				
0321	Bonbon	233	3	5				
0322	Bonbon	233	3	6				
0322	Cologne	241	1	2				This number is an error, see #3222.
0323	Bonbon	233	3	7				
0324	Bonbon	233	3	8				
0325	Bonbon	233	3	9				
0326	Bonbon	233	3	10				
0327	Bonbon	233	3	11				TPD)10.2
0328	Bonbon	233	3	12				
0329	Bonbon	233	3	13				
0330	Bonbon	233	3	14				
0331	Vase	249	3	1				
0332	Vase	249	3	2				
0333	Vase	249	3	3				Same as #332 but with crimped top.
0333					$550	VDS (E)	EAC-04/05	
0334	Vase	249	3	4	$1610	Orange Cintra	Sknr-10/95	
0334					$430	VDS	Sknr-10/96	
0335	Vase	249	3	5	$230	VDS	ebay-09/01	Same as #334 but with crimped top.
0336	Sugar & Creamer	234	1	7,8				
0337	Goblet	197	2	1				
0338	Punch Cup	216	1	1				
0339	Vase	249	3	6				
0340	Vase	249	3	7				
0341	Cologne	240	2	4				
0341	Vase	249	3	6				This number is an error, see #0344.
0342	Vase	249	4	1				
0344	Vase	249	3	6				This shape is shown as #341 in Gardner.
0343	Knife Rest	237	3	6				
0345	Vase	249	4	2				PG1)353,HH
0346	Vase	249	4	3	$770	Gold Calcite	EAC-04/91	PG1)VI C,D; PG2)54,Br&C; RFR)14,3,C
0346					$935	Blue Aurene	EAC-10/91	
0346					$660	Blue Aurene	EAC-07/93	
0346					$575	Gold Calcite	Sknr-05/98	
0346					$660	Gold Aurene	EAC-07/98	
0346					$495	Gold Calcite	EAC-07/99	
0346					$880	Gold Aurene	EAC-07/99	

SHAPE NO.	ITEM	PAGE	COL	ROW	PRICE REALIZED	GLASS TYPE	AUCTION HOUSE	COMMENTS & PHOTO REFERENCES
0346					$300	Gold Calcite	Tway-03/00	
0346					$900	Gold Aurene	ebay-04/00	
0346					$610	Gold Calcite	ebay-06/00	
0346					$475	Gold Aurene	Ogal-06/00	
0346					$290	Gold Calcite	JDJ-11/00	
0346					$665	Blue Aurene	ebay-01/01	
0346					$590	Gold Aurene	ebay-02/01	
0346					$895	Rosaline/Alabaster	EAC-04/01	
0346					$700	Gold Aurene	ebay-05/01	
0346					$620	Gold Aurene	ebay-07/01	
0346					$1540	Blue Calcite	Cott-08/01	
0346					$430	Rosaline/Alabaster	JDJ-11/01	
0346					$840	Gold Aurene	EAC-11/01	
0346					$260	Green Jade/Alabaster	ebay-12/01	
0346					$400	Gold Calcite	JDJ-05/02	
0346					$500	Gold Calcite	ebay-06/02	
0346					$460	Gold Calcite	ebay-07/02	
0346					$815	Gold Aurene	ebay-08/02	
0346					$1200	Gold Aurene	JDJ-11/02	
0346					$995	Gold Aurene	ebay-11/02	
0346					$330	Gold Calcite	ebay-11/02	
0346					$225	VDS	Cinc-11/02	
0346					$425	Gold Calcite	Cinc-11/02	
0346					$230	Gold Calcite	ebay-12/02	
0346					$280	Gold Calcite	ebay-02/03	
0346					$385	Gold Calcite	ebay-02/03	
0346					$1200	Blue Aurene	ebay-03/03	
0346					$1005	Gold Aurene	ebay-03/03	
0346					$410	Gold Calcite	ebay-06/03	
0346					$860	Gold Aurene	EAC-06/03	
0346					$3065	Blue Calcite	EAC-06/03	
0346					$325	Gold Calcite	ebay-09/03	
0346					$175	Gold Calcite	ebay-09/03	
0346					$95	VDS	ebay-09/03	
0346					$460	Celeste Blue	EAC-11/03	
0346					$750	Gold Calcite	EAC-11/03	
0346					$355	Gold Calcite	ebay-03/04	
0346					$405	Gold Calcite	ebay-03/04	
0346					$450	Gold Calcite	Tway-05/04	
0346					$730	Gold Calcite	Ogal-05/04	
0346					$785	Gold Aurene	ebay-07/04	
0346					$225	Gold Calcite	ebay-07/04	
0346					$260	Gold Calcite	ebay-10/04	
0346					$440	Gold Calcite	EAC-10/04	
0346					$1680	Blue Aurene	ebay-11/04	
0346					$1440	Blue Calcite	JDJ-11/04	
0346					$1440	Gold Aurene	Crft-01/05	
0346					$1680	Gold Aurene	Crft-01/05	
0346					$405	Gold Calcite	ebay-02/05	
0346					$1140	Gold Calcite	Tway-03/05	
0346					$300	Gold Calcite	ebay-03/05	
0346					$720	Gold Aurene	JDJ-06/05	
0346					$2100	Blue Aurene	JDJ-06/05	
0347	Vase	249	4	4	$150	Ivrene	ebay-02/02	
0347					$990	Blue Aurene	EAC-10/04	
0348	Vase	249	4	5				
0349	Candlestick	160	1	4				
0350	Sugar & Creamer	234	1	9,10				
0351	Sugar & Creamer	234	1	11,12				
0352	Puff Box	244	1	1				
0353	Cracker Jar	309	3	2	$825	Gold Calcite	EAC-04/93	
0354	Vase	249	4	6	$550	Gold Aurene	EAC-07/97	PG1)353,HH; TPD)4.82
0354					$250	Ivory	ebay-11/99	
0354					$210	Ivrene	ebay-11/99	
0354					$385	Ivrene	ebay-07/01	
0354					$145	Ivrene	EAC-06/03	
0355	Vase	249	4	7	$965	Gold Aurene	ebay-12/99	PG1)353,JJ
0355					$690	Gold Aurene	Sknr-02/01	
0355					$430	Gold Aurene	ebay-04/01	
0355					$950	Gold Aurene	EAC-01/03	
0355					$510	Gold Aurene	ebay-03/03	
0355					$500	Gold Aurene	ebay-03/03	
0355					$800	Gold Aurene	ebay-06/03	
0355					$1000	Gold Aurene	ebay-12/03	

SHAPE NO.	ITEM	PAGE	COL	ROW	PRICE REALIZED	GLASS TYPE	AUCTION HOUSE	COMMENTS & PHOTO REFERENCES
0355					$425	Gold Aurene	ebay-05/05	
0355A	Vase							PG1)353,HH
0356	Vase	249	5	1	$5960	Decorated Gold Aurene	ebay-02/01	PG1)353,JJ; TPD)5.19
0357	Vase	249	5	2				PG1)353,JJ
0358	Vase	249	5	3				PG1)353,JJ
0359	Vase	249	5	4	$230	VDS	ebay-12/01	PG1)353,JJ
0360	Vase	249	5	5				PG1)353,HH
0361	Vase	249	5	6				PG1)353,HH
0362	Bowl	141	1	7				PG1)353,HH
0363	Vase	249	5	7				PG1)353,GG
0364	Vase	250	1	1				PG1)353,GG
0365	Vase	250	1	2				PG1)353,GG
0366	Vase	250	1	3				PG1)353,II
0367	Compote	171	1	8	$575	Gold Calcite	EAC-07/93	PG1)353,JJ; PG2)57,A; RFR)7,2,B;
0367					$880	Gold Aurene	EAC-04/96	ACR)135,245; JAS)150,TR,A
0367					$550	Gold Aurene	EAC-07/96	
0367					$1265	Blue Aurene	Sknr-10/97	
0367					$660	Gold Aurene	EAC-04/98	
0367					$140	Colorless	ebay-02/00	
0367					$300	VDS	Tway-10/00	
0367					$2035	Blue Aurene	Cott-08/01	
0367					$385	VDS	Cott-08/01	
0367					$360	Mirror Black	ebay-01/02	
0367					$1990	Blue Aurene	ebay-06/02	
0367					$1400	VDS	JDJ-11/02	
0367					$1490	Gold Aurene	ebay-11/02	
0367					$1400	VDS	ebay-11/02	
0367					$1025	Blue Aurene	ebay-11/03	
0367					$100	Colorless	ebay-12/03	
0367					$850	VDS	ebay-02/04	
0367					$350	VDS	ebay-08/04	
0367					$450	VDS	ebay-09/04	
0367					$1280	Blue Aurene	ebay-11/04	
0368	Vase	250	1	4				
0369	Vase	250	1	6	$350	Gold Aurene	ebay-07/01	
0369½	Vase	250	1	5				MDK)104
0370	Vase	250	1	7				
0371	Basket	139	1	3				
0372	Basket	139	1	4				
0373	Goblet	190	1	3				
0374	Goblet	190	1	4				
0375	Nut Dish	211	1	4				
0376	Candlestick	160	1	5				
0377	Compote	171	1	9				
0378	Compote	171	2	1				
0379	Candlestick	160	1	6	$305	Aqua Marine	ebay-02/00	PG1)44,79,A,C
0380	Mayonnaise Bowl	210	4	5				
0381	Puff Box and Cover							See New Drawings section
0382	Punch Cup	216	1	2	$210	Gold Aurene	JDJ-06/05	
0383	Tea Cup	216	2	5				
0384	Mushroom Dish	210	1	1				
0385	Caviar Dish	210	1	2				
0386	Pitcher	212	1	3				
0387	Sugar & Creamer	234	1	13,14				
0388	Sugar & Creamer	234	2	1				
0389	Puff Box	244	1	2				
0390	Bonbon	233	3	15				
0391	Vase	250	1	8				
0392	Vase	250	2	1				
0393	Bonbon	233	2	13				
0394	Compote	171	2	2				
0395	Salt	217	1	3				
0396	Salt	217	1	4				
0397	Salt	217	1	5				
0398	Salt	217	1	6				
0399	Salt	217	1	7				
0400	Salt	217	1	8	$400	Blue Aurene	ebay-06/01	
0401	Compote	171	2	3				
0402	Compote	171	2	4				
0403	Bonbon	233	3	16				
0404	Bonbon	233	3	17				
0405	Bonbon	233	4	1				
0406	Bonbon	233	4	2				
0407	Bonbon	233	4	3				

SHAPE NO.	ITEM	PAGE	COL	ROW	PRICE REALIZED	GLASS TYPE	AUCTION HOUSE	COMMENTS & PHOTO REFERENCES
0408	Bonbon	233	4	4				
0409	Bonbon	233	4	5				
0410	Basket	139	1	5				
0411	Tray	158	2	16				This shape is shown as #44 in Gardner.
0412	Compote	171	2	5				
0413	Sugar & Creamer	234	2	2,3				
0414	Bonbon	233	4	6				
0415	Nut Dish	211	1	5				
0416	Salt	217	1	9				
0417	Basket	139	1	6				
0419	Goblet	190	1	5				
0420	Vase	250	2	2				
0421	Vase	250	2	3				TPD)10.46
0422	Vase	250	2	4				
0423	Vase	250	2	5				
0424	Decanter	180	1	3				
0425	Decanter	180	1	4				
0426	Decanter	180	1	5				
0427	Vase	250	2	6				
0428	Vase	250	2	7				
0429	Vase	250	2	8	$760	Decorated Calcite	ebay-04/05	
0430	Vase	250	3	1				
0431	Vase	250	3	2				
0432	Vase	250	3	3				
0433	Vase	250	3	4				
0434	Vase	250	3	5				
0435	Vase	250	3	6				
0436	Vase	250	3	7				
0437	Vase	250	3	8				
0438	Vase	250	4	1				
0439	Vase	250	4	2				
0440	Bowl	141	1	8				
0441	Bowl	141	1	9				
0442	Decanter	180	1	6				
0443	Decanter	180	2	1				
0444	Decanter	180	2	2				
0445	Cruet	178	2	3				
0446	Cruet	178	2	4				
0447	Cologne	240	2	5				
0448	Cologne	240	2	6				
0449	Decanter	180	2	3				
0450	Cologne	240	2	7				
0451	Vase	250	4	3	$990	Blue Aurene	EAC-07/92	TPD)10.46
0451					$650	VDS	EAC-10/00	
0451					$1020	Blue Aurene	JDJ-05/04	
0452	Basket	139	1	7	$365	VDS	ebay-12/04	
0453	Basket	139	1	8	$1100	Gold Aurene	EAC-10/92	RFR)9,1,D:14,2,C:21,3,A;
0453					$2750	Blue Calcite	EAC-04/95	ACR)132,237; TPD)9.35:10.39:10.143
0453					$1840	Blue Aurene	Sknr-10/95	
0453					$865	Gold Aurene	JDJ-10/96	
0453					$2070	Gold Aurene	JDJ-06/97	
0453					$1495	Gold Calcite	JDJ-06/97	
0453					$2070	Gold Calcite	JDJ-10/97	
0453					$1485	Gold Calcite	EAC-07/98	
0453					$660	Gold Aurene	Cinc-12/99	
0453					$1525	Gold Aurene	ebay-01/00	
0453					$3410	Blue Aurene	EAC-05/00	
0453					$1870	Gold Aurene	EAC-05/00	
0453					$1300	Gold Aurene	Tway-10/00	
0453					$1680	Gold Aurene	EAC-04/01	
0453					$795	Gold Aurene	ebay-08/01	
0453					$175	VDS	ebay-08/02	
0453					$35	VDS	ebay-10/02	
0453					$1100	Gold Aurene	ebay-11/02	
0453					$595	VDS	ebay-01/03	
0453					$1100	Gold Aurene	Cinc-06/03	
0453					$480	VDS	ebay-06/04	Rose flowers & green leaves for prunts
0453					$760	Gold Calcite	ebay-10/04	
0453					$805	Green Jade/Alabaster	EAC-07/05	Alabaster handle
0454	Basket	139	2	1				
0455	Basket	139	2	2	$2585	Blue Aurene	EAC-10/93	TPD)10.143
0455					$1150	Gold Aurene	Sknr-10/94	
0455					$1045	Gold Aurene	EAC-10/96	
0455					$6035	Blue Aurene	JDJ-06/97	

SHAPE NO.	ITEM	PAGE	COL	ROW	PRICE REALIZED	GLASS TYPE	AUCTION HOUSE	COMMENTS & PHOTO REFERENCES
0455					$4025	Blue Calcite	JDJ-06/97	
0455					$3450	Blue Aurene	JDJ-10/97	
0455					$2645	Gold Aurene	JDJ-10/97	
0455					$1035	Blue Aurene	ebay-02/01	
0455					$1395	Gold Calcite	ebay-06/01	
0455					$495	VDS	Cott-08/01	
0455					$2910	Blue Aurene	EAC-04/02	
0455					$1675	Gold Aurene	ebay-07/02	
0455					$300	Colorless (E)	ebay-09/02	
0455					$2550	Gold Aurene	ebay-03/03	
0455					$3000	Blue Aurene	ebay-03/03	
0455					$3000	Blue Aurene	ebay-04/03	
0455					$1900	Blue Aurene	Cinc-06/03	
0455					$2300	Gold Aurene	Jack-06/03	
0455					$1600	Gold Aurene	J&W-09/03	
0455					$2000	Gold Aurene	ebay-02/04	
0455					$2000	Gold Aurene	ebay-03/04	
0456	Basket	139	2	3				
0457	Sugar & Creamer	234	2	4,5				
0458	Sugar & Creamer	234	2	6,7				
0459	Decanter	180	2	4				
0460	Decanter	180	2	5				
0461	Decanter	180	2	6				
0462	Decanter	180	2	7				
0463	Decanter	180	3	1				
0464	Decanter	180	3	2				
0465	Sugar & Creamer	234	2	8,9				
0466	Nappie	233	1	13				
0467	Cologne	240	2	8				
0468	Cologne	240	2	9				
0469	Basket	139	2	4				
0470	Jar	209	1	1				TPD)4.54
0471	Jar	209	1	2				
0472	Salt	217	1	10				
0473	Sugar & Creamer	234	2	10,11				
0474	Sugar & Creamer	234	2	12				
0476	Goblet	190	1	6				
0477	Goblet	190	1	7				
0478	Goblet	190	1	8				
0479	Goblet	190	2	1				
0480	Vase	250	4	4				
0481	Vase	250	4	5				
0482	Vase	250	4	6				
0483	Vase	250	4	7				
0484	Vase	250	4	8	$450	VDS	ebay-11/99	
0485	Goblet	190	2	2				
0486	Vase	250	4	9				
0487	Vase	250	5	1				
0488	Vase	250	5	2				
0489	Vase	250	5	3				
0490	Vase	250	5	4				
0491	Vase	250	5	5				
0492	Vase	250	5	6				
0493	Basket	139	2	5				
0494	Puff Box	244	1	3				
0495	Puff Box	244	1	4				
0496	Puff Box	244	1	5				
0497	Puff Box	244	1	6				
0498	Basket	139	2	6				
0499	Basket	139	2	7				
0500	Vase	250	5	7	$7700	Decorated Gold Aurene	EAC-07/97	TPD)10.98
0500A	Cologne	240	3	1				
0501	Vase	251	1	1				
0501A	Jar	209	1	3				
0502	Vase	251	1	2				RFR)11,2,C
0503	Vase	251	1	3				RFR)10,2,C
0503A	Tray	158	2	17				
0504	Vase	251	1	4				PG1)VIII A,D:VIII B,B; RFR)12,4,B
0504A	Candlestick	160	1	7				
0505	Vase	251	1	5				
0506	Vase	251	1	6	$8250	Gold Aurene/Yellow Jade	EAC-04/93	TPD)10.128
0506					$5175	Decorated Gold. Aurene	Sknr-01/98	
0507	Vase	251	2	1				TPD)5.24
0508	Vase	251	2	2	$3850	Decorated Green Aurene	EAC-04/95	ACR)140,261

SHAPE NO.	ITEM	PAGE	COL	ROW	PRICE REALIZED	GLASS TYPE	AUCTION HOUSE	COMMENTS & PHOTO REFERENCES
0508		233	4	7	$7840	Decorated Green Aurene	EAC-09/02	
0509	Bonbon	233	1	14				
0510	Nappie	233	1	14	$500	Gold Aurene	ebay-01/01	
0511	Vase	251	2	3	$360	Gold Aurene	EAC-10/99	
0511					$325	Gold Aurene	ebay-12/01	
0511					$200	Gold Aurene	Wint-12/01	
0511					$355	Gold Aurene	ebay-08/03	
0511					$150	Gold Aurene	ebay-04/05	
0512	Vase	251	2	4	$400	Gold Aurene	ebay-12/01	
0512					$300	Gold Aurene	ebay-02/02	
0513	Vase	251	2	5	$320	Gold Aurene	ebay-04/05	
0514	Vase	251	2	6				
0515	Vase	251	2	7				
0516	Vase	251	2	8	$280	Gold Aurene	ebay-07/04	
0517	Vase	251	2	9				RFR)12,1,C; TPD)5.7
0518	Vase	251	2	10				
0519	Vase	251	3	1				
0520	Vase	251	3	2				
0521	Vase	251	3	3	$4175	Decorated Green Aurene	ebay-12/03	RFR)14,2,A
0522	Vase	251	3	4				RFR)11,4,D; TPD)5.23:10.28
0523	Vase	251	3	5				
0524	Vase	251	3	5	$2000	Gold Aurene	EAC-04/05	Same as 0523
0525	Vase	251	3	6				
0526	Vase	251	4	1				PG2)50,B; JAS)162,T,B
0527	Vase	251	4	2				
0528	Vase	251	4	3				
0529	Bonbon	233	4	8				
0530	Bonbon	233	4	9				
0531	Bonbon	233	4	10	$200	Gold Aurene	ebay-12/99	
0531					$250	Gold Aurene	ebay-12/99	
0532	Bonbon	233	4	11	$215	Gold Aurene	ebay-07/01	
0532					$290	Gold Aurene	ebay-04/02	
0533	Vase	251	4	4	$5600	Decorated Green Aurene	ebay-12/01	PG2)50,C; RFR)10,4,A&E; JAS)162,T,C;
0533								ACR)COLOR 3,B,B; TPD)5.10
0533					$2100	Opal/Green Cintra ACB	JDJ-05/04	
0534	Vase	251	4	5				PG1)VIII C
0535	Vase	251	4	6	$3910	Decorated Green Aurene	Sknr-01/98	RFR)12,4,B
0535					$16605	Decorated Green Aurene	ebay-04/05	
0536	Vase	252	1	1				RFR)11,4,C; TPD)5.14
0537	Vase	252	1	2				
0538	Vase	252	1	3				TPD)5.15
0539	Vase	252	1	4				PG2)50,A; JAS)162,T,A
0540	Vase	252	1	5				
0541	Vase	252	1	6	$12650	Decorated Red Aurene	EAC-10/90	PG1)IX C,B; RFR)11,4,B;
0541					$1850	Blue Aurene	ebay-11/99	TPD)10.101; ACR)138,254
0541					$1725	Blue Aurene	ebay-02/00	
0541					$1325	Gold Aurene	ebay-02/02	
0541					$1000	Blue Aurene	ebay-11/03	
0542	Vase	252	2	1				
0543	Vase	252	2	2				ACR)140,260
0544	Vase	252	2	3				
0545	Vase	252	2	4				
0546	Vase	252	2	5				TPD)5.15
0547	Vase	252	2	6	$13750	Decorated Red Aurene	EAC-10/93	RFR)8,2,A:12,1,A; TPD)5.62:8.39
0547					$455	Gold Calcite	ebay-03/01	
0547					$27500	Decorated Red Aurene	EAC-10/04	Same piece as EAC-10/93
0548	Vase	252	2	7	$3300	Decorated Green Aurene	EAC-07/93	RFR)10,1,B:31,2,A; ACR)COLOR 3,B,A
0548					$195	Ivory	ebay-10/03	
0549	Vase	252	2	8	$3450	Decorated Aurene	Sknr-05/96	PG2)51,B; ACR)COLOR 3,B,D; TPD)5.10
0550	Vase	252	3	1	$2475	Decorated Green Aurene	EAC-10/90	TPD)5.5
0550					$4885	Decorated Gold Aurene	Sknr-01/98	
0550					$3390	Decorated Green Aurene	EAC-06/03	
0551	Vase	252	3	2				
0552	Vase	252	3	3				TPD)5.10
0553	Vase	252	3	4	$1980	Decorated Green Aurene	EAC-10/90	
0553					$3360	Millefiori	JDJ-11/04	
0554	Vase	252	3	5				
0555	Vase	252	3	6				
0556	Vase	252	3	7	$1000	Gold Aurene	ebay-03/00	
0557	Vase	252	3	8				
0558	Salt	217	1	11				
0559	Vase	252	4	1				
0560	Vase	252	4	2	$465	Gold Aurene	EAC-10/94	
0561	Vase	252	4	3	$950	Gold Aurene	Tway-10/00	

SHAPE NO.	ITEM	PAGE	COL	ROW	PRICE REALIZED	GLASS TYPE	AUCTION HOUSE	COMMENTS & PHOTO REFERENCES
0561					$1320	Blue Aurene	Cott-08/01	
0561					$900	Gold Aurene	ebay-03/03	
0562	Vase	252	4	4				
0563	Vase	252	4	5	$430	Gold Aurene	ebay-12/02	
0564	Bonbon	233	4	12	$385	Blue Aurene	EAC-04/94	
0564					$275	Gold Aurene	EAC-10/96	
0564					$325	Gold Aurene	ebay-11/99	
0564					$200	Gold Aurene	ebay-04/01	
0564					$520	Blue Aurene	Cott-08/01	
0564					$300	Blue Aurene	ebay-10/01	
0564					$420	Blue Aurene	EAC-11/01	
0564					$300	Gold Aurene	JDJ-06/05	
0565	Bonbon	233	4	13	$375	Gold Aurene	Sknr-10/97	MDK)109
0565					$460	Blue Aurene	FtnA-08/03	
0565					$360	Gold Aurene	ebay-12/04	
0566	Vase	252	4	6				
0567	Vase	252	4	7				
0568	Vase	252	4	8				
0569	Vase	252	4	9	$789	Gold Aurene	ebay-11/02	
0569					$745	Gold Aurene	Hrtg-03/05	
0570	Salt & Pepper	217	3	6				
0571	Vase	252	4	10				PG1)IV A,A; JAS)161,TR,A
0572	Vase	252	4	11				
0573	Vase	253	1	1	$1980	Decorated Gold Aurene	EAC-10/90	JAS)161,TR,B; TPD)10.93
0573					$2760	Decorated Gold Aurene	Sknr-05/98	
0573					$4510	Millefiori Decorated Aurene	EAC-08/00	
0573					$3810	Decorated Gold Aurene	EAC-04/01	
0573					$3300	Decorated Gold Aurene	ebay-06/01	
0573					$7840	Decorated Gold Aurene	EAC-11/01	
0573					$2520	Millefiori Decorated Aurene	EAC-09/02	
0573					$2900	Millefiori Decorated Aurene	Cinc-06/03	
0574	Vase	253	1	2				
0574½								Six inch vase. See new drawing section
0575	Vase	253	1	3				
0576	Vase	253	1	4				RFR)12,1,B; JAS)160,A; ACR)139,257;
0576								TPD)10.93
0577	Vase	253	1	5				JAS)160,B; TPD)9.33
0578	Vase	253	1	6	$5900	Decorated Gold Aurene	ebay-02/03	
0579	Vase	253	2	1				
0580	Vase	253	2	2	$3025	Decorated Gold Aurene	EAC-04/95	
0580					$3920	Decorated Gold Aurene	EAC-09/02	
0581	Vase	253	2	3	$8550	Decorated Gold Aurene	ebay-02/00	RFR)12,4,D
0582	Vase	253	2	4	$6900	Decorated Gold Aurene	JDJ-05/04	
0583	Vase	253	2	5				
0584	Lamp	200	1	1	$3575	Decorated Green Aurene	EAC-10/92	Lamp base only TPD)4.96:9.36
0584					$3520	Decorated Green Aurene	EAC-04/91	Lamp base only
0584					$1540	Decorated Green Aurene	JDJ-06/96	
0584					$4500	Decorated Green Aurene	JDJ-11/02	Lamp base only
0584					$2050	Decorated Green Aurene	ebay-07/03	Shade only
0585	Vase	253	2	6	$3575	Decorated Gold Aurene	EAC-10/94	
0585					$4600	Decorated Gold Aurene	JDJ-05/01	
0586	Vase	253	2	7	$6720	Tyrian	JDJ-05/01	
0587	Vase	253	2	8				
0588	Vase	253	3	1				
0589	Vase	253	3	2				
0590	Vase	253	3	3				
0591	Vase	253	3	4				ACR)139,255; TPD)10.93
0592	Vase	253	3	5				RFR)11,2,A; ACR)139,256;
0592								TPD)4.56:5.25:5.56
0593	Vase	253	3	6				
0594	Vase	253	3	7				
0595	Vase	253	3	8	$2420	Decorated Gold Aurene	EAC-10/90	RFR)11,3,A
0595					$3910	Leaves and Vines	Jack-06/03	
0596	Vase	253	3	9				PG1)68,101
0597	Vase	253	4	1	$11200	Decorated Green Aurene	EAC-09/01	
0598	Vase	253	4	2				
0599	Vase	253	4	3	$2530	Decorated Gold Aurene	JDJ-06/97	RLG)166,301; ACR)139,258; TPD)5.16
0599					$4200	Decorated Gold Aurene	EAC-07/04	
0599					$4105	Decorated Gold Aurene	ebay-01/05	
0600	Vase	253	4	4				PG1)IX B,A
0601	Vase	253	4	5				
0602	Vase	253	4	6				
0603	Vase	253	4	7				
0604	Vase	254	1	1	$6325	Decorated Green Aurene	EAC-11/03	PG2)51,A; RFR)10,3,C

SHAPE NO.	ITEM	PAGE	COL	ROW	PRICE REALIZED	GLASS TYPE	AUCTION HOUSE	COMMENTS & PHOTO REFERENCES
0605	Vase	254	1	2				
0606	Vase	254	1	3				TPD)5.16
0607	Vase	254	1	4				
0608	Vase	254	1	5	$1100	Decorated Green Aurene	Sknr-10/93	TPD)5.16
0609	Vase	254	1	6				
0610	Tea Cup	216	2	6	$275	Gold Aurene	J&W-09/03	
0611	Punch Cup	216	1	3				
0612	Punch Cup	216	1	4				
0613	Finger Bowl	189	1	3				
0614	Sugar & Creamer	234	2	13,14	$260	Gold Aurene	ebay-12/04	Creamer only
0615	Tea Cup	216	3	7				
0616	Tea Cup	216	2	7				
0617	Bowl	141	1	10	$710	Gold Aurene	ebay-01/00	PG1)32,56,A
0617					$60	VDS	JDJ-05/00	
0617					$500	Gold Aurene	ebay-02/03	
0617					$850	Blue Aurene	Dalla-05/03	
0617					$150	Gold Calcite	Hrtg-03/05	
0618	Vase	254	1	7				
0619	Vase	254	1	8				
0620	Finger Bowl	189	1	4	$550	Gold Aurene	EAC-04/97	
0620					$170	VDS	ebay-05/02	
0620					$250	Gold Aurene	ebay-10/03	Signed "Haviland"
0620					$1840	Millefiori dec. Gold Aur.	EAC-11/03	Signed "Haviland"
0621	Vase	254	2	1				
0622	Vase	254	2	2				
0623	Vase	254	2	3				
0624	Vase	254	2	4				
0625	Vase	254	2	5				
0626	Vase	254	2	6				
0627	Vase	254	2	7				
0628	Vase	254	2	8				
0629	Vase	254	2	9				
0630	Vase	254	2	10				
0631	Vase	254	2	11				
0632	Sugar & Creamer	234	3	1,2				
0633	Goblet	197	2	2				
0634	Vase	254	3	1				
0635	Vase	254	3	2				
0636	Vase	254	3	3				
0637	Vase	254	3	4				
0638	Vase	254	3	5				
0639	Vase	254	3	6				
0640	Vase	254	3	7				
0641	Vase	254	3	8				
0642	Vase	254	3	9				
0643	Vase	254	3	10				
0644	Basket	139	2	8	$690	Colorless	Sknr-01/97	TPD)4.58
0644					$900	Pomona Green	ebay-12/99	
0644					$625	Colorless	ebay-05/00	
0644					$285	Pomona Green	Sknr-02/01	
0644					$230	Colorless	ebay-09/01	
0644					$380	Colorless	ebay-12/01	
0644					$180	Colorless	ebay-03/02	
0644					$130	Colorless	ebay-12/02	
0644					$340	Colorless	ebay-10/03	
0645	Vase	254	3	11	$795	Decorated Gold Aurene	EAC-10/94	TPD)10.127; MDK)147
0645					$1200	Decorated Gold Aurene	ebay-10/03	
0646	Vase	254	4	1				PG1)VIII,A,C:IX B,B; RLG)138,265;
0647	Bowl	141	1	11				TPD)10.14:10.1
0647								
0648	Vase	254	4	2	$6290	Decorated Turquoise	ebay-11/03	TPD)10.127
0648					$2000	Decorated Calcite	ebay-11/04	
0648					$840	Decorated Calcite	JDJ-06/05	
0649	Vase	254	4	3	$920	Gold Aurene/Calcite	Sknr-01/98	MDK)4
0649					$2175	Decorated Gold Aurene	ebay-01/00	
0649					$1570	Gold Aurene/Calcite	EAC-01/03	
0650	Vase	254	4	4				
0651	Vase	254	4	5				JAS)161,TL,A
0652	Vase	254	4	6	$1100	Decorated Gold Aurene	ebay-08/04	
0653	Bowl	141	1	12				RFR)10,2,B
0654	Salt	217	1	12	$500	Blue Aurene	ebay-06/03	
0655	Vase	254	4	7	$19040	Decorated Turquoise	EAC-07/04	
0656	Vase	254	4	8				TPD)4.38
0657	Vase	254	4	9				

SHAPE NO.	ITEM	PAGE	COL	ROW	PRICE REALIZED	GLASS TYPE	AUCTION HOUSE	COMMENTS & PHOTO REFERENCES
0658	Nut Dish	211	1	6				
0659	Nut Dish	211	1	7				
0660	Vase	254	4	10				
0661	Vase	254	4	11	$2575	Decorated Gold Aurene	ebay-03/02	RFR)11,1,C
0662	Vase	254	4	12				RFR)11,1,A
0663	Vase	254	4	13	$1495	Decorated Gold Aurene	EAC-04/04	
0664	Basket	139	3	1				TPD)10.143
0665	Basket	139	3	2				
0666	Basket	139	3	3				
0667	Vase	255	1	1				
0668	Vase	255	1	2				PG1)114,181
0668					$17,640	Black/Amethyst Cintra ACB	EAC-09/02	
0669	Vase	255	1	3				
0670	Vase	255	1	4				
0671	Shade	227	1	1	7625	Decorated Blue Aurene	ebay-02/05	Handel floor fixture
0672	Shade	218	1	2				
0673	Vase	255	1	5				
0674	Vase	255	2	1	$1100	Aurene	EAC-10/95	
0675	Vase	255	2	2				
0676	Vase	255	2	3				
0677	Bowl	141	1	13	$1680	Decorated Gold Aurene	ebay-04/04	
0677					$3050	Decorated Gold Aurene	ebay-05/04	
0678	Vase	255	2	4				
0679	Bowl	141	1	14				
0680	Vase	255	2	5				
0681	Vase	255	2	6				
0682	Vase	255	2	7				
0683	Vase	255	3	1				
0684	Vase	255	3	2				
0685	Candlestick	160	1	8				
0686	Compote				$880	Blue Aurene	EAC-10/91	See New Drawings section
0686					$465	Gold Aurene	ebay-12/03	
0686					$1210	Blue Aurene	EAC-10/04	
0686	Candlestick	160	2	1	$605	Gold Aurene	EAC-10/90	RFR)7,2,A&C; TPD)9.31
0686					$660	Blue Aurene	EAC-10/90	
0686					$455	Gold Aurene	EAC-02/92	
0686					$770	Gold Aurene	EAC-10/95	
0686					$330	Gold Aurene	JDJ-06/96	
0686					$290	Blue Aurene	Sknr-10/96	
0686					$920	Blue Aurene	Sknr-10/97	
0686					$1045	Blue Aurene	EAC-04/98	
0686					$635	Blue Aurene	Sknr-01/98	
0686					$545	Gold Aurene	Sknr-06/99	
0686					$715	Gold Aurene	EAC-07/99	
0686					$265	Pomona Green	ebay-12/99	
0686					$2775	Blue Aurene	ebay-12/99	
0686					$385	Amethyst	Cinc-12/99	
0686					$2000	Blue Aurene	ebay-01/00	
0686					$1925	Blue Aurene	ebay-02/00	
0686					$810	Gold Aurene	ebay-03/00	
0686					$655	Rosaline/Alabaster	ebay-03/00	
0686					$245	Pomona Green	EAC-10/00	
0686					$950	Blue Aurene	ebay-02/01	
0686					$115	Pomona Green	Sknr-02/01	
0686					$1325	Blue Aurene	ebay-03/01	
0686					$860	Blue Aurene	ebay-04/01	
0686					$660	Gold Aurene	ebay-04/01	
0686					$2015	Gold Aurene	EAC-04/01	
0686					$305	Amethyst	ebay-05/01	
0686					$525	Gold Aurene	ebay-07/01	
0686					$765	Gold Aurene	ebay-07/01	
0686					$990	Gold Aurene	Cott-08/01	
0686					$1280	Blue Aurene	ebay-11/01	
0686					$310	Amethyst/Colorless	EAC-11/01	
0686					$1320	Blue Aurene	JDJ-11/01	
0686					$745	Blue Aurene	JDJ-11/01	
0686					$890	Gold Aurene	JDJ-11/01	
0686					$805	Gold Aurene (FC)	JDJ-11/01	
0686					$840	Gold Aurene	EAC-11/01	
0686					$700	Blue Aurene	Tway-03/02	
0686					$460	Rosaline/Alabaster	ebay-06/02	
0686					$425	VDS	ebay-07/02	
0686					$905	Blue Aurene	ebay-07/02	
0686					$1405	Blue Aurene	ebay-09/02	

SHAPE NO.	ITEM	PAGE	COL	ROW	PRICE REALIZED	GLASS TYPE	AUCTION HOUSE	COMMENTS & PHOTO REFERENCES
0686					$765	Gold Aurene	ebay-09/02	
0686					$985	Gold Aurene	ebay-09/02	
0686					$1345	Blue Aurene	EAC-09/02	
0686					$650	Blue Aurene	ebay-10/02	
0686					$760	Gold Aurene	ebay-10/02	
0686					$1020	Blue Aurene	JDJ-11/02	
0686					$900	Blue Aurene	JDJ-11/02	
0686					$535	Gold Aurene	ebay-11/02	
0686					$750	Gold Aurene	ebay-12/02	
0686					$955	Blue Aurene	ebay-12/02	
0686					$910	Gold Aurene	Sknr-12/02	
0686					$890	Blue Aurene	ebay-01/03	
0686					$335	Pomona Green	ebay-01/03	
0686					$535	Gold Aurene	ebay-01/03	
0686					$685	Gold Aurene	ebay-01/03	
0686					$1340	Blue Aurene	ebay-02/03	
0686					$875	Gold Aurene	ebay-02/03	
0686					$750	Gold Aurene	ebay-02/03	
0686					$500	Gold Aurene	ebay-04/03	
0686					$600	Gold Aurene	ebay-05/03	
0686					$775	Rosaline/Alabaster stem	EAC-06/03	
0686					$250	Bristol Yellow	ebay-07/03	
0686					$610	Blue Aurene	ebay-09/03	
0686					$225	VDS	ebay-09/03	
0686					$1035	Blue Aurene	EAC-11/03	
0686					$190	Pomona Green/Colorless	ebay-12/03	Colorless stem
0686					$620	Amethyst	ebay-01/04	
0686					$200	Rosa	ebay-01/04	
0686					$1900	Blue Aurene	FtnA-06/04	
0686					$1145	Blue Aurene	ebay-06/04	
0686					$500	Gold Aurene	ebay-08/04	
0686					$300	Pomona Green	ebay-08/04	
0686					$185	Amethyst	ebay-09/04	
0686					$470	Green Jade/Alabaster	ebay-10/04	Alabaster stem and foot
0686					$660	Gold Aurene	Wesr-12/04	
0686					$290	Rosa	ebay-01/05	
0686					$945	Green Jade/Alabaster stem	ebay-01/05	
0686					$605	Gold Aurene	ebay-01/05	
0686					$1260	Blue Aurene	Crft-01/05	
0686					$265	VDS	ebay-01/05	
0686					$200	VDS	ebay-01/05	
0686					$1050	Blue Aurene	ebay-02/05	
0686					$1800	Gold Aurene	ebay-03/05	
0686					$505	Gold Aurene	ebay-04/05	
0686					$960	Blue Aurene	Cinc-06/05	
0686					$195	VDS	ebay-06/05	
0686					$215	Topaz	ebay-07/05	
0686					$690	Gold Aurene	Cott-06/05	
0686					$575	Colorless/Amethyst shaded	EAC-07/05	Amethyst shaded bowl and foot
0687	Nut Dish	211	1	8				
0688	Vase	255	3	3	$1490	Gold Aurene	ebay-10/99	
0689	Vase	255	3	4				
0690	Vase	255	3	5	$1265	Decorated Gold Aurene	JDJ-10/94	
0690					$1265	Decorated Gold Aurene	Sknr-10/95	
0691	Vase	255	3	6				
0692	Candlestick	160	2	2				
0693	Candlestick	160	2	3				
0694	Vase	255	3	7				
0695	Vase	255	3	8				
0696	Puff Box	244	1	7	$250	Gold Aurene	ebay-12/00	
0697	Bowl	141	2	1				
0698	Vase	255	4	1				
0699	Nut Dish	211	1	9				
0700	Vase	255	4	2				
0701	Vase	255	4	3				
0702	Vase	255	4	4				
0703	Lamp	200	1	2				
0704	Basket	139	3	4	$1290	Gold Aurene	ebay-04/05	
0705	Goblet	190	2	3				
0706	Nut Dish	211	1	10	$400	Gold Aurene	ebay-07/01	
0707	Nut Dish	211	1	11	$210	Gold Aurene	ebay-05/04	
0708	Nut Dish	211	1	12				
0709	Bonbon	233	4	14				
0710	Vase	255	4	5				

SHAPE NO.	ITEM	PAGE	COL	ROW	PRICE REALIZED	GLASS TYPE	AUCTION HOUSE	COMMENTS & PHOTO REFERENCES
0711	Bowl	141	2	2				
0712	Basket	139	3	5				
0713	Basket	139	3	6				
0714	Basket	139	3	7				
0715	Basket	139	4	1				
0716	Basket	139	4	2				
0718	Vase	255	4	6				PG1)32,56,C
0719	Vase	255	4	7				
0720	Vase	255	4	8	$3335	Decorated Calcite	Sknr-05/94	TPD)4.31
0721	Vase	255	4	9				
0722	Vase	255	5	1				
0723	Vase	255	5	2	$825	Blue Aurene	EAC-07/90	TPD)4.56
0723					$490	Gold Aurene	Sknr-05/95	
0723					$550	Blue Aurene	JDJ-10/95	
0723					$195	Gold Calcite	EAC-07/96	
0723					$920	Gold Aurene	JDJ-06/97	
0723					$825	Gold Aurene	EAC-04/98	
0723					$745	Gold Aurene	Sknr-05/98	
0723					$690	Gold Aurene	JDJ-05/99	
0723					$315	Gold Aurene	Sknr-10/99	
0723					$550	Gold Aurene	ebay-12/99	
0723					$605	Gold Aurene	Cinc-12/99	
0723					$1485	Blue Aurene	ebay-02/00	
0723					$810	Blue Aurene	ebay-04/00	
0723					$1210	Gold Aurene	EAC-05/00	
0723					$425	Gold Aurene	Ogal-05/00	
0723					$1250	Blue Aurene	ebay-06/00	
0723					$660	Blue Aurene	EAC-08/00	
0723					$350	Blue Aurene	Ogal-09/00	
0723					$230	Gold Aurene	ebay-10/00	
0723					$750	Gold Aurene	Sknr-10/00	
0723					$285	Gold Aurene	ebay-11/00	
0723					$1035	Gold Aurene	Sknr-02/01	
0723					$380	Gold Aurene	ebay-03/01	Haviland paper label
0723					$840	Gold Aurene	EAC-04/01	
0723					$650	Gold Aurene	Ogal-09/01	
0723					$500	Gold Aurene	ebay-01/02	
0723					$535	Blue Aurene	ebay-05/02	
0723					$2300	Blue Aurene	ebay-10/02	
0723					$615	Gold Aurene	ebay-10/02	
0723					$255	VDS	ebay-10/02	
0723					$690	Gold Aurene	JDJ-11/02	
0723					$890	Blue Aurene	ebay-12/02	
0723					$975	Blue Aurene	ebay-12/02	
0723					$585	Gold Aurene	ebay-02/03	
0723					$600	Blue Aurene	ebay-03/03	
0723					$865	Blue Aurene	ebay-03/03	
0723					$800	Blue Aurene	JDJ-05/03	
0723					$1290	Blue Aurene	Sknr-05/03	
0723					$860	Gold Aurene	EAC-06/03	
0723					$670	Gold Aurene	ebay-10/03	
0723					$550	Gold Aurene	ebay-11/03	
0723					$1380	Blue Aurene	ebay-01/04	
0723					$665	Blue Aurene	ebay-05/04	
0723					$850	Gold Aurene	Tway-05/04	
0723					$1010	Blue Aurene	EAC-07/04	
0723					$1100	Gold Aurene	ebay-08/04	
0723					$895	Gold Aurene	ebay-09/04	
0723					$900	Blue Aurene	ebay-11/04	
0723					$615	Blue Aurene	ebay-01/05	
0723					$515	Gold Aurene	ebay-02/05	
0723					$695	Gold Aurene	ebay-02/05	
0723					$760	Blue Aurene	ebay-02/05	
0723					$1320	Gold Aurene	Tway-03/05	
0723					$1000	Blue Aurene	ebay-04/05	
0723					$1090	Gold Aurene	EAC-04/05	
0723					$1035	Blue Aurene	EAC-04/05	
0723					$765	Blue Aurene	ebay-05/05	
0723					$630	Gold Aurene	JDJ-06/05	
0723					$545	Gold Aurene	Cott-06/05	
0723					$720	Gold Aurene	Dalla-06/05	
0723					$1680	Blue Aurene	Dalla-06/05	
0724	Vase	255	5	3				
0725	Vase	255	5	4				

SHAPE NO.	ITEM	PAGE	COL	ROW	PRICE REALIZED	GLASS TYPE	AUCTION HOUSE	COMMENTS & PHOTO REFERENCES
0726	Vase	255	5	5				RFR)10,4,C
0727	Vase	255	5	6				
0728	Vase	255	5	7				
0729	Vase	255	5	8				TPD)5.57
0730	Vase	255	5	9				
0731	Vase	256	1	1				
0732	Vase	256	1	2				
0733	Vase	256	1	3				
0734	Vase	256	1	4	$1960	Decorated Blue Aurene	EAC-09/02	TPD)5.64
0735	Vase	256	1	5	$1320	Decorated Blue Aurene	JDJ-05/94	
0736	Vase	256	1	6				
0737	Bowl	141	2	3				
0738	Bonbon	233	4	15	$795	Green lines/Gold interior	ebay-11/04	
0739	Bonbon	233	4	16				
0740	Bonbon	233	4	17				
0741	Vase	256	1	7				
0742	Vase	256	1	8				
0743	Vase	256	1	9	$635	Gold Aurene	Sknr-05/96	
0743					$825	Gold Aurene	EAC-07/96	
0743					$710	Gold Calcite	ebay-11/00	
0744	Vase	256	2	1				
0745	Vase	256	2	2	$385	Gold Calcite	EAC-10/94	
0746	Vase	256	2	3				
0747	Vase	256	2	4				
0748	Vase	256	2	5				
0749	Vase	256	2	6				
0750	Vase	256	2	7				
0751	Vase	256	2	8	$2805	Decorated Gold Aurene	JDJ-06/96	TPD)5.17
0751					$6325	Gold Aurene	EAC-11/03	Signed "Haviland"
0752	Vase	256	3	1				
0753	Vase	256	3	2	$825	Decorated Green Aurene	EAC-04/98	
0754	Basket	139	4	3	$805	VDS	JDJ-10/97	ACR)143,269
0755	Vase	256	3	3				
0756	Sugar & Creamer	234	3	3,4	$45	VDS	ebay-11/03	Sugar bowl only
0757	Compote	171	2	6	$440	Gold Calcite	EAC-04/98	
0758	Vase	256	3	4	$2500	Gold Aurene	ebay-10/01	
0759	Vase	256	3	5				
0760	Vase	256	3	6				RFR)10,3,B
0761	Vase	256	3	7				TPD)10.148
0762	Vase	256	3	8				
0763	Vase	256	3	9				
0764	Vase	256	4	1				
0765	Vase	256	4	2				
0766	Vase	256	4	3				
0767	Vase	256	4	4				
0768	Vase	256	4	5				
0769	Vase	256	4	6				
0770	Vase	256	4	7				PG1)32,53
0771	Vase	256	4	8				
0772	Vase	256	4	9				
0773	Vase	256	5	1				
0774	Vase	256	5	2				
0775	Vase	256	5	3	$225	Selenium Red	ebay-04/04	
0775					$325	Rosaline/Alabaster foot	ebay-08/04	
0775					$340	Green Jade/Alabaster	ebay-11/04	Alabaster foot
0775					$575	Rosaline/Alabaster	Hrtg-03/05	Alabaster foot
0776	Vase	256	5	4				
0777	Vase	256	5	5				
0778	Vase	256	5	6				
0779	Vase	256	5	7				
0780	Vase	256	5	8				
0781	Vase	256	5	9	$2415	Blue Aurene	EAC-11/03	
0782	Vase	256	5	10				
0784	Vase	257	1	1	$250	VDS	ebay-05/05	
0785	Jar	210	1	3				
0785½	Goblet	197	2	3				
0786	Vase	257	1	2	$5300	New Intarsia	ebay-05/05	PG1)76,119,A
0787	Vase	257	1	3				PG1)76,119,C
0788	Vase	257	1	4				PG1)76,119,B; TPD)10.90
0789	Vase	257	1	5	$3520	Green Jade/Alabaster ACB	Cott-08/01	PG1)75,118,C; TPD)10.90
0790	Vase	257	1	6				
0791	Vase	257	1	7				PG1)75,118,A
0792	Vase	257	1	8				PG1)75,118,B
0793	Vase	257	1	9				TPD)10.90

SHAPE NO.	ITEM	PAGE	COL	ROW	PRICE REALIZED	GLASS TYPE	AUCTION HOUSE	COMMENTS & PHOTO REFERENCES
0794	Vase							See New Drawings section
0795	Shade	218	1	3	$225	Gold Aurene dec. Calcite	ebay-03/03	
0795					$250	Gold Aurene dec. Calcite	ebay-05/03	
0795					$275	Gold Aurene dec. Calcite	ebay-12/03	
0795					$150	Gold Aurene	ebay-03/04	
0796	Shade	218	1	4				
0797	Shade	218	1	5				
0798	Shade	218	1	6				
0799	Shade	218	1	7	$160	Pulled Feather	ebay-05/01	TPD)10.9
0799					$250	Pulled Feather	ebay-06/01	
0799					$210	Pulled Feather	ebay-06/01	
0799					$340	Pulled Feather	ebay-06/01	
0799					$150	Pulled Feather	ebay-07/01	
0799					$225	Pulled Feather	ebay-03/02	
0799					$155	Pulled Feather	ebay-09/02	
0799					$300	Pulled Feather	ebay-10/02	
0799					$150	Pulled Feather	ebay-01/03	
0799					$125	Pulled Feather	ebay-06/03	
0799					$175	Green Pulled Feather	ebay-11/04	
0799					$200	Green Pulled Feather	ebay-12/04	
0799					$150	Green Pulled Feather	ebay-03/05	
0799					$50	Green Pulled Feather	ebay-03/05	
0800	Nut Dish	211	1	13				
0801	Vase	257	2	1				
0802	Vase	257	2	2	$1380	Blue Aurene	ebay-11/99	
0803	Vase	257	2	3				
0804	Vase	257	2	4				
0805	Compote	171	2	7				
0806	Vase	257	2	5				
0807	Nappie	233	1	15				
0808	Vase	257	2	6				
0809	Shade	218	1	8				
0810	Shade	218	1	9				
0811	Sugar & Creamer	234	3	5,6				
0812	Bowl	141	2	4				
0813	Sherbet	216	4	2				
0814	Goblet	190	2	4	$95	Celeste Blue/Colorless	ebay-08/03	Colorless stem
0815	Sugar & Creamer	234	3	7,8				
0816	Candlestick	160	2	4				TPD)10.121
0817	Jar	209	1	4				
0818	Finger Bowl	189	1	5	$220	Gold Aurene	EAC-04/94	
0818					$90	Gold Aurene	JDJ-06/96	
0818					$245	Gold Aurene	EAC-04/97	
0818					$700	Gold Aurene	Ogal-01/01	
0818					$265	Gold Aurene	ebay-06/01	
0818					$650	Gold Aurene	Ogal-07/01	
0818					$315	Gold Aurene	ebay-01/02	No underplate
0818					$50	VDS	ebay-02/02	
0818					$345	Gold Aurene	ebay-08/02	
0818					$375	Gold Aurene	Ogal-10/02	
0818					$90	VDS	ebay-12/02	
0818					$460	Gold Aurene	EAC-04/04	
0818					$60	Flemish Blue	ebay-05/04	
0818					$55	VDS	ebay-02/05	
0819	Shade	218	1	10	$170	Pulled Feather	ebay-03/02	
0819					$230	Pulled Feather	ebay-03/02	
0819					$810	Red Pulled Feather	ebay-08/02	
0819					$1050	Red Pulled Feather	ebay-09/02	
0819					$300	Pulled Feather	ebay-10/02	
0819					$200	Pulled Feather	ebay-12/02	
0819					$490	Pulled Feather	ebay-04/03	
0819					$250	Pulled Feather	ebay-05/03	
0819					$110	Pulled Feather	ebay-11/03	
0819					$245	Green Pulled Feather	ebay-07/04	
0819					$250	Green Pulled Feather	EAC-07/04	
0819					$195	Green Pulled Feather	EAC-07/04	
0819					$480	Green Pulled Feather	ebay-08/04	
0820	Shade	218	1	11	$300	Pulled Feather	ebay-01/02	
0820					$180	Pulled Feather	ebay-05/03	
0820					$245	Red Pulled Feather	ebay-09/03	
0820					$300	Pulled Feather	ebay-10/03	
0821	Shade	218	2	1	$230	Pulled Feather	ebay-10/01	TPD)10.10
0822	Shade	227	1	2	$7850	Decorated Red Aurene	ebay-02/01	
0822½	Shade	218	2	2	$120	Gold Aurene	ebay-12/00	

SHAPE NO.	ITEM	PAGE	COL	ROW	PRICE REALIZED	GLASS TYPE	AUCTION HOUSE	COMMENTS & PHOTO REFERENCES
0822½					$290	Gold Aurene	ebay-02/01	
0822½					$315	Gold Aurene	ebay-05/02	
0822½					$200	Gold Aurene	Sknr-12/02	
0822½					$200	Gold Aurene	ebay-07/03	
0822½					$225	Green Pulled Feather	ebay-02/04	
0822½					$230	Gold Aurene	JDJ-05/04	
0822½					$15	VDS	ebay-10/01	
0822½					$135	Gold Aurene	ebay-12/04	
0823	Shade	218	2	3	$100	Gold Aurene	ebay-03/02	
0823					$125	Gold Aurene	ebay-04/02	
0823					$160	Gold Aurene	ebay-12/02	
0823					$145	Gold Aurene	EAC-07/04	
0823½	Shade	218	2	4	$120	Gold Aurene	ebay-04/01	
0823½					$175	Gold Aurene	ebay-05/01	
0823½					$65	Gold Aurene	ebay-04/02	
0823½					$130	Gold Aurene	Jack-06/02	
0823½					$60	Gold Aurene	ebay-07/02	
0823½					$245	Gold Aurene	ebay-09/02	Diamond Quilted
0823½					$140	Gold Aurene	EAC-09/02	
0823½					$135	Gold Aurene	Cinc-06/03	
0823½					$75	Gold Aurene	ebay-07/03	
0823½					$120	Gold Aurene	ebay-02/04	
0823½					$100	Gold Aurene	ebay-03/04	
0823½					$185	Gold Aurene	EAC-04/04	
0823½					$180	Gold Aurene	JDJ-05/04	
0823½					$190	Gold Aurene	ebay-06/04	
0823½					$120	Gold Aurene	ebay-07/04	
0823½					$195	VDS (E)	EAC-07/04	
0823½					$125	Gold Aurene	EAC-07/04	
0823½					$75	Gold Aurene	ebay-07/04	
0823½					$100	Gold Aurene	ebay-09/04	
0823½					$125	Gold Aurene	ebay-11/04	
0823½					$1095	Gold Aurene	EAC-04/05	
0823½					$200	Gold Aurene	ebay-05/05	
0824	Shade	218	2	5				
0825	Shade	218	2	6	$200	Brown Pulled Feather	Jack-06/02	Calcite base; TPD)5.49
0825					$250	Brown Pulled Feather	ebay-02/05	
0826	Shade	218	2	7				
0827	Shade	218	2	8				
0827½	Shade	218	2	9	$945	Green Pulled Feather	ebay-05/05	
0828	Shade	218	2	10				
0829	Shade	218	2	11				
0830	Shade	218	2	12				
0831	Bowl	141	2	5				
0832	Shade	218	2	13	$170	Gold Aurene	Jack-06/00	
0832					$145	Gold Aurene	Rago-09/00	
0832					$510	Gold Aurene	ebay-10/00	
0832					$175	Gold Aurene	Tway-10/00	
0832					$130	Gold Aurene	ebay-01/01	
0832					$160	Gold Aurene	ebay-01/01	
0832					$160	Gold Aurene	ebay-03/01	
0832					$140	Gold Aurene	ebay-05/01	
0832					$300	Gold Aurene	Cott-08/01	
0832					$165	Gold Aurene	ebay-08/01	
0832					$150	Gold Aurene	Tway-03/02	
0832					$150	Gold Aurene	ebay-08/02	
0832					$100	Gold Aurene	Tway-09/02	
0832					$75	Calcite	JDJ-05/03	
0832					$230	Gold Aurene	ebay-06/03	
0832					$210	Gold Aurene	ebay-07/03	
0832					$200	Gold Calcite (E)	ebay-08/03	
0832					$250	Gold Aurene	ebay-10/03	
0832					$155	Gold Aurene	ebay-02/04	
0832					$110	Gold Aurene	ebay-03/04	
0832					$130	Gold Aurene	ebay-03/04	
0832					$305	Gold Aurene	EAC-04/04	
0832					$225	VDS (E)	EAC-07/04	Engraved "Festoon"
0832					$170	Gold Aurene	ebay-09/04	
0832					$95	Gold Aurene	ebay-10/04	
0832					$125	Gold Aurene	ebay-10/04	
0832					$135	Gold Aurene	ebay-12/04	
0832					$190	Gold Aurene	Crft-01/05	
0832					$150	Gold Aurene	ebay-04/05	
0832					$200	Gold Aurene	ebay-07/05	

SHAPE NO.	ITEM	PAGE	COL	ROW	PRICE REALIZED	GLASS TYPE	AUCTION HOUSE	COMMENTS & PHOTO REFERENCES
0833	Shade	218	3	1	$165	VDS	JDJ-06/05	
0834	Shade	218	3	2				
0835	Shade	218	3	3				
0836	Shade	218	3	4				
0837	Shade	218	3	5	$255	Blue Pulled Feather	ebay-07/03	
0837					$240	Green Pulled Feather	ebay-09/03	
0837					$305	Green Pulled Feather	ebay-02/04	
0838	Shade	218	3	6				
0839	Shade	218	3	7	$810	Green Pulled Feather	ebay-02/05	
0840	Shade	218	3	8	$325	Blue Pulled Feather	ebay-06/04	
0841	Shade	218	3	9	$300	Decorated Aurene	ebay-04/01	
0841					$320	Green Pulled Feather	ebay-08/04	
0841					$350	Gold Pulled Feather	ebay-10/04	
0842	Bowl	141	2	6				
0843	Shade	218	3	10	$120	Gold Aurene	ebay-01/01	
0843					$165	Gold Aurene	ebay-09/03	
0843					$100	Gold Aurene	ebay-10/04	
0843					$125	Gold Aurene	ebay-10/04	
0844	Shade	218	4	1				
0845	Shade	218	4	2	$225	Pulled Feather	ebay-03/02	
0845					$210	Green Pulled Feather	ebay-02/05	
0846	Shade	218	4	3				
0847	Shade	218	4	4	$145	Gold Aurene	JDJ-05/04	
0847					$140	Gold Aurene	EAC-07/04	
0847					$165	Gold Aurene	Tway-09/04	
0847					$70	Gold Aurene	ebay-10/04	
0847					$1020	Gold Aurene	Dalla-03/05	
0847					$120	Gold Aurene	ebay-05/05	
0848	Shade	218	4	5	$150	Gold Aurene	ebay-01/01	
0849	Shade	218	4	6	$100	Gold Aurene	ebay-03/02	
0849					$120	Gold Aurene	ebay-01/04	
0850	Shade	218	4	7				
0851	Shade	218	4	8				
0852	Shade	218	4	9	$600	Green Pulled Feather	JDJ-06/05	
0853	Shade	218	4	10	$150	Decorated Calcite	ebay-02/01	
0853					$275	Decorated Calcite	ebay-05/01	
0853					$305	Gold Pulled Feather	Jack-06/02	Calcite base
0853					$290	Brown Pulled Feather	Jack-06/02	Calcite base
0853					$155	Green Pulled Feather	ebay-04/04	
0853					$415	Green Pulled Feather	EAC-10/04	
0853					$605	Gold Pulled Feather	EAC-10/04	
0853					$325	Green Pulled Feather	ebay-11/04	
0853					$270	Green Pulled Feather	ebay-11/04	
0853					$400	Green Pulled Feather	ebay-12/04	
0853					$310	Green Pulled Feather	ebay-12/04	
0853					$250	Green Pulled Feather	ebay-02/05	
0853					$480	Green Pulled Feather	Dalla-03/05	
0853					$200	Green Pulled Feather	ebay-03/05	
0853					$150	Green Pulled Feather	ebay-04/05	
0853					$230	Green Pulled Feather	ebay-05/05	
0853					$210	Green Pulled Feather	JDJ-06/05	
0853					$300	Green Pulled Feather	JDJ-06/05	
0853					$300	Green Pulled Feather	JDJ-06/05	
0854	Shade	218	4	11	$100	Gold Aurene	ebay-03/01	
0854					$1450	Green Decorated Aurene	ebay-05/04	
0854					$105	Gold Aurene	ebay-11/04	
0854					$180	Gold Aurene	ebay-05/05	
0855	Shade	218	5	1	$150	Gold Aurene	ebay-01/01	
0856	Shade	218	5	2	$125	Gold Calcite	ebay-03/03	
0857	Shade	218	5	3				
0858	Shade	218	5	4				
0859	Shade	218	5	5	$460	Pulled Feather	Jack-12/01	
0859					$260	Pulled Feather	ebay-04/02	
0859					$365	Green Pulled Feather	Jack-06/02	Gold Aurene base
0859					$260	Green Pulled Feather	Jack-06/02	Calcite base
0859					$355	Green Pulled Feather	ebay-08/03	
0859					$526	Green Pulled Feather	ebay-02/05	
0860	Shade	218	5	6				
0861	Shade	218	5	7	$180	Gold Aurene	ebay-04/02	
0861					$280	Gold Aurene	ebay-11/04	
0862	Shade	218	5	8	$170	Gold Aurene	EAC-04/04	
0863	Shade	218	5	9	$185	Gold Aurene	EAC-04/04	
0864	Shade	218	5	10				
0865	Shade	219	1	1	$175	Gold Aurene	ebay-11/03	

SHAPE NO.	ITEM	PAGE	COL	ROW	PRICE REALIZED	GLASS TYPE	AUCTION HOUSE	COMMENTS & PHOTO REFERENCES
0865					$85	Gold Aurene	ebay-07/04	
0865					$100	Gold Aurene	ebay-09/04	
0865					$125	Gold Aurene	ebay-12/04	
0865					$135	Gold Aurene	ebay-07/05	
0866	Shade	219	1	2	$150	Calcite	ebay-08/01	
0866					$165	Calcite	ebay-12/01	
0866					$100	Gold Aurene	ebay-04/02	
0866					$535	Green Aurene	ebay-07/02	
0866					$140	Gold Aurene	ebay-08/02	
0866					$115	Calcite ACB	ebay-10/02	
0866					$113	Gold Aurene	ebay-12/02	
0866					$280	Pulled Feather	Sknr-12/02	
0866					$175	Gold Aurene	Sknr-12/02	
0866					$175	Gold Aurene	ebay-02/03	
0866					$100	Calcite	ebay-03/03	
0866					$115	Gold Aurene	ebay-03/03	
0866					$135	Gold Aurene	ebay-03/03	
0866					$110	Gold Aurene	ebay-05/03	
0866					$150	Gold Aurene	ebay-05/03	
0866					$85	Gold Aurene	ebay-05/03	
0866					$110	Gold Aurene	ebay-08/03	
0866					$70	Gold Aurene	ebay-08/03	
0866					$155	Gold Aurene	ebay-08/03	
0866					$165	Gold Aurene	ebay-09/03	
0866					$165	Gold Aurene	ebay-11/03	
0866					$100	Gold Aurene	ebay-03/04	
0866					$230	Pulled Feather	ebay-07/04	
0866					$255	Pulled Feather	ebay-07/04	
0866					$75	Gold Aurene	ebay-07/04	
0866					$125	Gold Aurene	ebay-10/04	
0866					$120	Gold Aurene	ebay-11/04	
0866					$240	Gold Aurene	ebay-03/05	
0867	Shade	219	1	3				
0868	Shade	219	1	4				TPD)9.37
0869	Shade	219	1	5	$840	Green Feather/Gold Aur.	JDJ-06/05	TPT)5.49
0869					$1020	Green Feather/Gold Aur.	JDJ-06/05	
0869					$1320	Green Feather/Gold Aur.	JDJ-06/05	
0869					$1320	Green Feather/Gold Aur.	JDJ-06/05	
0870	Shade	219	1	6	$150	Gold Aurene	ebay-08/01	
0870					$185	Gold Aurene	ebay-06/02	
0870					$370	Gold Aurene	ebay-09/03	
0870					$1300	Gold Aurene	J&W-09/03	
0870					$370	Gold Aurene	ebay-10/03	
0870					$75	Gold Aurene	ebay-06/04	
0871	Shade	219	1	7				
0872	Shade	219	1	8				
0873	Shade	219	1	9				
0874	Shade	219	1	10				
0875	Shade	219	1	11				
0876	Shade	219	2	1				
0877	Shade	219	2	2				
0877½	Shade	219	2	3	$200	Gold Aurene	ebay-05/01	
0878	Shade	219	2	4				
0879	Shade	219	2	5				
0880	Shade	219	2	6	$75	Calcite ACB	ebay-07/02	
0880					$160	Gold Aurene	ebay-02/03	
0881	Shade	219	2	7	$265	Gold Aurene	Cott-02/05	
0882	Shade	219	2	8	$235	Green Pulled Feather	ebay-05/02	RFR)13,4,B
0882					$300	Blue Pulled Feather	Jack-06/02	Calcite base
0882					$215	Green Pulled Feather	ebay-09/04	
0883	Shade	219	2	9				
0884	Shade	219	2	10	$170	Gold Aurene	ebay-02/02	
0884					$225	Gold Aurene	ebay-03/02	
0884					$155	Gold Aurene	ebay-05/02	
0884					$180	Gold Aurene	ebay-12/02	
0884					$135	Gold Aurene	ebay-09/03	
0884					$150	Gold Aurene	ebay-12/03	
0884					$195	Gold Aurene	ebay-09/04	
0884					$150	Gold Aurene	ebay-07/05	
0885	Shade	219	3	1	$290	Blue Pulled Feather	ebay-01/05	
0886	Shade	219	3	2				
0887	Shade	219	3	3				
0888	Shade	219	3	4				
0889	Shade	219	3	5	$690	Green Aurene	EAC-11/03	

SHAPE NO.	ITEM	PAGE	COL	ROW	PRICE REALIZED	GLASS TYPE	AUCTION HOUSE	COMMENTS & PHOTO REFERENCES
0889					$120	Gold Aurene	ebay-03/04	
0890	Shade	219	3	6	$660	Gold Aurene	ebay-01/01	
0890					$290	Gold Aurene	EAC–04/04	
0890					$335	Gold Aurene	ebay-01/05	
0890					$50	Gold Aurene	ebay-02/05	
0891	Shade	219	3	7				
0892	Shade	219	3	8	$225	Gold Aurene	ebay-10/04	
0892					$75	Calcite	ebay-01/05	
0893	Shade	219	3	9	$285	Pulled Feather	ebay-08/01	
0893					$260	Green Pulled Feather	Jack-06/02	Gold Aurene base
0893					$350	Pulled Feather	ebay-07/02	
0893					$300	Pulled Feather	ebay-10/02	
0894	Shade	219	3	10				
0895	Shade	219	3	11				
0896	Shade	219	4	1	$195	Gold Aurene	ebay-12/00	
0896					$115	Gold Aurene	ebay-10/01	
0896					$45	VDS	ebay-02/03	
0896					$120	Gold Aurene	ebay-06/04	
0896					$110	Gold Aurene	ebay-11/04	
0896					$130	Gold Aurene	ebay-01/04	
0896					$160	Gold Calcite	ebay-02/05	
0896					$125	Calcite	ebay-06/05	
0897	Shade	219	4	2	$275	Green Feather	EAC-04/98	RFR)13,2,D
0897					$50	VDS	ebay-12/00	
0897					$490	Decorated Calcite	ebay-01/01	
0897					$430	Decorated Gold Aurene	ebay-07/02	
0897					$195	Green Pulled Feather	ebay-02/04	
0897					$340	Green Pulled Feather	ebay-09/04	
0897					$190	Green Pulled Feather	ebay-01/05	
0897					$300	Green Pulled Feather	JDJ-06/05	
0898	Shade	219	4	3	$430	Decorated Calcite	ebay-08/03	TPD)4.107
0899	Shade	219	4	4	$310	Leaves and Vines	ebay-08/03	
0900	Shade	219	4	5	$110	Gold Aurene	ebay-07/04	
0901	Shade	219	4	6	$200	Decorated Calcite	ebay-11/99	
0901					$300	Leaves and Vines	ebay-12/01	
0901					$255	Leaves and Vines	ebay-01/02	
0901					$255	Leaves and Vines	ebay-03/03	
0901					$125	Leaves and Vines	ebay-12/03	
0901					$2760	Decorated Green Aurene	JDJ-05/04	
0901					$200	Leaves and Vines	ebay-06/04	
0901					$330	Leaves and Vines	ebay-01/05	
0902	Shade	219	4	7	$425	Green Pulled Feather	ebay-09/03	
0903	Shade	219	4	8	$90	Gold Aurene	ebay-08/02	
0903					$165	Calcite	ebay-04/03	
0903					$150	Gold Aurene	ebay-12/03	
0903					$330	Gold Aurene	Cinc-11/04	
0903					$140	Gold Aurene	ebay-11/04	
0903					$165	Gold Calcite	ebay-05/05	
0904	Shade	219	4	9	$90	Gold Aurene	ebay-12/00	
0904					$150	Gold Aurene	ebay-06/03	
0904					$245	Gold Aurene	ebay-01/04	
0904					$190	Gold Aurene	ebay-06/05	
0905	Shade	219	4	10				
0907	Shade	219	4	11				
0908	Shade	219	5	1	$180	Gold Aurene	ebay-07/01	
0908					$250	Gold Aurene	ebay-02/03	
0908					$215	Gold Aurene	ebay-05/05	
0908					$140	Gold Aurene	ebay-06/05	
0909	Shade	219	5	2				
0910	Shade	219	5	3	$190	Gold Aurene	ebay-01/05	
0911	Shade	219	5	4				
0912	Shade	219	5	5				
0913	Shade	219	5	6	$85	Gold Aurene	Sknr-10/97	
0913					$210	Gold Aurene	EAC-04/98	
0913					$185	Gold Aurene	ebay-01/00	
0913					$140	Gold Aurene	Jack-06/00	
0913					$175	Gold Aurene	Rago-09/00	
0913					$350	Gold Aurene	Tway-10/00	
0913					$115	Gold Aurene	ebay-12/00	
0913					$150	Gold Aurene	ebay-01/01	
0913					$90	Gold Aurene	ebay-01/01	
0913					$35	Gold Calcite	ebay-04/01	
0913					$110	Calcite	ebay-05/01	
0913					$160	Gold Aurene	ebay-07/01	

SHAPE NO.	ITEM	PAGE	COL	ROW	PRICE REALIZED	GLASS TYPE	AUCTION HOUSE	COMMENTS & PHOTO REFERENCES
0913					$155	Gold Aurene	ebay-07/01	
0913					$180	Gold Aurene	ebay-07/01	
0913					$85	Gold Aurene	ebay-07/01	
0913					$160	Gold Aurene	ebay-07/01	
0913					$150	Gold Aurene	ebay-09/01	
0913					$210	Gold Aurene	Ogal-11/01	
0913					$155	Gold Aurene	ebay-12/01	
0913					$150	Gold Calcite	ebay-03/02	
0913					$85	Gold Aurene	ebay-03/02	
0913					$145	Gold Aurene	ebay-04/02	
0913					$170	Gold Aurene	ebay-06/02	
0913					$120	Gold Aurene	Jack-06/02	
0913					$100	Gold Calcite	ebay-07/02	
0913					$180	Gold Aurene	ebay-07/02	
0913					$115	Gold Aurene	ebay-07/02	
0913					$140	Gold Aurene	ebay-07/02	
0913					$150	Gold Aurene	ebay-08/02	
0913					$65	Gold Aurene	ebay-08/02	
0913					$110	Gold Aurene	ebay-09/02	
0913					$80	Gold Aurene	ebay-09/02	
0913					$65	Gold Calcite	Tway-09/02	
0913					$170	Gold Aurene	ebay-10/02	
0913					$115	Gold Aurene	ebay-10/02	
0913					$100	Gold Aurene	ebay-10/02	
0913					$175	Gold Aurene	ebay-11/02	
0913					$375	Gold Calcite	Jack–11/02	
0913					$110	Gold Aurene	Cinc-11/02	
0913					$80	Gold Aurene	ebay-12/02	
0913					$205	Gold Aurene	ebay-01/03	
0913					$150	Gold Aurene	ebay-01/03	
0913					$155	Gold Calcite	ebay-02/03	
0913					$200	Gold Calcite	ebay-02/03	
0913					$100	Gold Calcite	ebay-02/03	
0913					$160	Gold Aurene	ebay-03/03	
0913					$135	Gold Aurene	ebay-05/03	
0913					$50	Gold Calcite	JDJ-05/03	
0913					$110	Gold Aurene	ebay-05/03	
0913					$200	Gold Aurene	ebay-05/03	
0913					$125	Gold Aurene	ebay-06/03	
0913					$130	Gold Aurene	ebay-06/03	
0913					$105	Gold Aurene	ebay-06/03	
0913					$140	Gold Aurene	ebay-07/03	
0913					$150	Gold Calcite	ebay-07/03	
0913					$170	Gold Calcite	ebay-07/03	
0913					$75	VDS	ebay-08/03	
0913					$135	Gold Aurene	ebay-08/03	
0913					$110	Gold Aurene	ebay-10/03	
0913					$175	Gold Aurene	ebay-11/03	
0913					$125	Gold Calcite	ebay-12/03	
0913					$105	Gold Calcite	ebay-01/04	
0913					$120	Gold Aurene	ebay-02/04	
0913					$150	Gold Aurene	ebay-03/04	
0913					$200	Gold Aurene	ebay-03/04	
0913					$155	Gold Aurene	ebay-04/04	
0913					$170	Gold Aurene	ebay-05/04	
0913					$130	Gold Aurene	ebay-05/04	
0913					$100	Gold Calcite	ebay-05/04	
0913					$155	Gold Aurene	ebay-06/04	
0913					$180	Gold Aurene	ebay-06/04	
0913					$140	Gold Calcite	ebay-07/04	
0913					$135	Gold Aurene	ebay-08/04	
0913					$100	Gold Aurene	ebay-08/04	
0913					$260	Gold Aurene	ebay-09/04	
0913					$90	Gold Aurene	ebay-10/04	
0913					$170	Gold Aurene	ebay-11/04	
0913					$110	Gold Aurene	ebay-11/04	
0913					$170	Gold Aurene	ebay-11/04	
0913					$110	Gold Aurene	ebay-11/04	
0913					$130	Gold Aurene	ebay-11/04	
0913					$110	Gold Aurene	Sknr-12/04	
0913					$165	Gold Aurene	ebay-12/04	
0913					$150	Gold Aurene	ebay-01/05	
0913					$215	Gold Aurene	ebay-01/05	
0913					$145	Gold Aurene	ebay-02/05	

SHAPE NO.	ITEM	PAGE	COL	ROW	PRICE REALIZED	GLASS TYPE	AUCTION HOUSE	COMMENTS & PHOTO REFERENCES
0913					$140	Gold Aurene	ebay-02/05	
0913					$140	Gold Aurene	ebay-02/05	
0913					$150	Gold Aurene	ebay-02/05	
0913					$140	Gold Calcite	ebay-03/05	
0913					$205	Gold Aurene	ebay-04/05	
0913					$165	Gold Aurene	ebay-04/05	
0913					$135	Gold Aurene	ebay-05/05	
0913					$90	Gold Aurene	ebay-05/05	
0913					$130	Gold Aurene	ebay-05/05	
0913					$145	Gold Aurene	ebay-05/05	
0913					$95	Calcite	ebay-05/05	
0913					$160	Gold Aurene	JDJ-06/05	
0913					$125	Gold Aurene	ebay-07/05	
0913	Vase (Shade Vase)				$550	Blue Aurene	EAC-07/93	
0913					$880	Blue Aurene	JDJ-05/94	
0913					$690	Blue Aurene	Sknr-10/94	
0913					$490	Gold Aurene	Sknr-10/95	
0913					$630	Blue Aurene	Sknr-10/95	
0913					$1430	Dark Blue Jade	JDJ-06/96	
0913					$410	Gold Aurene	JDJ-06/96	
0913					$1100	Blue Aurene	EAC-10/96	
0913					$715	Blue Aurene	EAC-04/97	
0913					$575	Gold Aurene	EAC-07/97	
0913					$495	Gold Aurene	EAC-04/98	
0913					$545	Blue Aurene	Sknr-05/98	
0913					$220	Blue Aurene	GAI-02/99	
0913					$690	Blue Aurene	ebay-12/99	
0913					$300	Green Jade	ebay-03/00	
0913					$500	Blue Aurene	ebay-10/00	
0913					$366	Wisteria	ebay-12/00	
0913					$160	Ivory	ebay-12/00	
0913					$800	Blue Aurene	ebay-01/01	
0913					$60	Colorless	ebay-02/01	
0913					$345	Green Jade	Sknr-02/01	
0913					$550	Gold Aurene	Ogal-04/01	
0913					$840	Blue Aurene	EAC-04/01	
0913					$200	Gold Aurene	Midw-04/01	
0913					$175	Ivory	ebay-07/01	
0913					$155	Ivory	ebay-07/01	
0913					$300	Wisteria	ebay-07/01	
0913					$120	Ivory	ebay-11/01	
0913					$120	Ivory	ebay-11/01	
0913					$200	Ivrene	ebay-11/01	
0913					$325	Ivory	ebay-12/01	
0913					$435	Blue Aurene	ebay-02/02	
0913					$4025	Dark Blue Jade	JDJ-05/02	
0913					$590	Blue Aurene	ebay-07/02	
0913					$160	Gold Aurene	ebay-10/02	
0913					$360	Ivrene	JDJ-11/02	
0913					$540	Gold Aurene	JDJ-11/02	
0913					$540	Ivory	JDJ-11/02	
0913					$600	Blue Aurene	ebay-11/02	
0913					$660	Blue Aurene	JDJ-11/02	
0913					$385	Gold Aurene	ebay-11/02	
0913					$450	Gold Aurene	ebay-11/02	
0913					$215	Alabaster	ebay-12/02	
0913					$305	Wisteria	ebay-12/02	
0913					$455	Gold Aurene	ebay-12/02	
0913					$645	Gold Aurene	EAC-01/03	
0913					$215	Ivory	ebay-01/03	
0913					$450	Gold Aurene	ebay-03/03	
0913					$95	Ivory	ebay-07/03	
0913					$260	Pomona Green	ebay-08/03	
0913					$400	Pomona Green	ebay-09/03	
0913					$160	Ivory	ebay-11/03	
0913					$460	Green Jade	JDJ-11/03	
0913					$200	Ivory	EAC-11/03	
0913					$360	Gold Aurene	ebay-12/03	
0913					$590	Selenium Red	ebay-12/03	
0913					$690	Blue Aurene	ebay-01/04	
0913					$150	Colorless	ebay-03/04	
0913					$190	Ivory	ebay-05/04	
0913					$210	Ivrene	JDJ-05/04	
0913					$260	Ivory	JDJ-05/04	

SHAPE NO.	ITEM	PAGE	COL	ROW	PRICE REALIZED	GLASS TYPE	AUCTION HOUSE	COMMENTS & PHOTO REFERENCES
0913					$360	Ivory	JDJ-05/04	
0913					$515	Gold Aurene	JDJ-05/04	
0913					$160	Pomona Green	ebay-06/04	
0913					$350	Gold Aurene	ebay-06/04	
0913					$275	Ivory	ebay-06/04	
0913					$195	Ivory	EAC-07/04	
0913					$140	Ivrene	ebay-08/04	
0913					$510	Blue Aurene	ebay-10/04	
0913					$495	Blue Aurene	ebay-10/04	
0913					$95	Ivrene	ebay-12/04	
0913					$145	Ivrene	ebay-12/04	
0913					$160	Pomona Green	ebay-12/04	
0913					$225	Ivrene	ebay-12/04	
0913					$255	Pomona Green	ebay-01/05	
0913					$360	Blue Aurene	ebay-03/05	
0913					$120	Alabaster (FC)	ebay-04/05	
0913					$455	Gold Aurene	ebay-04/05	
0913					$420	Gold Aurene	ebay-05/05	
0913					$450	Blue Aurene	Sknr-06/05	
0913					$575	Blue Aurene	ebay-06/05	
0914	Shade	219	5	7	$125	Gold Aurene	ebay-01/04	
0914					$95	Gold Aurene	ebay-02/04	
0915	Lamp	200	1	3	$2200	Gold Aurene	JDJ-10/94	
0915					$8600	Decorated Green Aurene	ebay-07/00	
0916	Shade	219	5	8a				
0917	Shade	219	5	8b				
0918	Shade	219	5	8c				
0919	Shade	219	5	9				
0920	Shade	219	5	10				
0921	Shade	220	1	1				
0922	Shade	220	1	2	$165	Pulled Feather	ebay-08/03	
0922					$245	Pulled Feather	ebay-03/04	
0922					$410	Gold Pulled Feather	EAC-10/04	
0922					$365	Green Pulled Feather	ebay-11/04	
0923	Shade	220	1	3				
0924	Shade	220	1	4	$500	Pulled Feather	ebay-11/04	
0925	Shade	220	1	5				
0926	Shade	220	1	6	$280	Decorated Aurene	ebay-11/00	
0926					$135	Pulled Feather	ebay-09/01	
0926					$265	Pulled Feather	ebay-10/01	
0926					$205	Pulled Feather	ebay-05/02	
0926					$345	Pulled Feather	Jack-06/02	
0926					$400	Blue Pulled Feather	ebay-08/02	
0926					$300	Green Pulled Feather	ebay-07/03	
0926					$495	Blue Pulled Feather	ebay-02/04	
0926					$245	Gold Pulled Feather	ebay-11/04	
0626					$170	Green Pulled Feather	ebay-11/04	
0926					$225	Gold Pulled Feather	ebay-01/05	
0926					$1515	Pulled Feather on Green	ebay-02/05	
0926					$140	Gold Pulled Feather	ebay-07/05	
0927	Shade	220	1	7	$25	Green Pulled Feather	ebay-09/03	
0928	Lamp	200	1	4				
0929	Shade	220	1	8	$130	Gold Calcite	GAI-02/99	
0929					$75	VDS	ebay-12/00	
0929					$185	Gold Aurene	ebay-05/01	
0929					$300	Gold Aurene	ebay-08/01	
0929					$155	Gold Aurene	ebay-09/01	
0929					$130	Gold Calcite	ebay-10/01	
0929					$160	Gold Aurene	ebay-10/01	
0929					$100	Gold Calcite	ebay-02/02	
0929					$120	Gold Aurene	ebay-03/02	
0929					$50	Gold Aurene	Tway-03/02	
0929					$150	Gold Aurene	ebay-04/02	
0929					$60	Gold Calcite	JDJ-05/02	
0929					$150	Gold Aurene	Jack-06/02	
0929					$175	Gold Aurene	ebay-07/02	
0929					$125	Gold Aurene	ebay-08/02	
0929					$60	Gold Aurene	ebay-08/02	
0929					$295	Gold Aurene	ebay-02/03	
0929					$150	Gold Aurene	ebay-03/03	
0929					$135	Gold Aurene	ebay-06/03	
0929					$150	Gold Aurene	ebay-02/04	
0929					$130	Gold Aurene	ebay-03/04	
0929					$140	Gold Aurene	ebay-04/04	

SHAPE NO.	ITEM	PAGE	COL	ROW	PRICE REALIZED	GLASS TYPE	AUCTION HOUSE	COMMENTS & PHOTO REFERENCES
0929					$125	Gold Aurene	ebay-04/04	
0929					$70	VDS	EAC-07/04	
0929					$180	Gold Aurene	EAC-07/04	
0929					$130	Gold Aurene	Tway-09/04	
0929					$80	Gold Aurene	ebay-09/04	
0929					$100	Gold Aurene	ebay-11/04	
0929					$130	Gold Aurene	ebay-11/04	
0929					$40	VDS	ebay-11/04	
0929					$135	Gold Aurene	ebay-12/04	
0929					$247	Gold Aurene	ebay-12/04	
0929					$105	Gold Calcite	ebay-02/04	
0929					$135	Gold Aurene	ebay-04/05	
0929					$115	Gold Aurene	EAC-07/05	
0929	Vase (Shade Vase)				$155	Ivrene	ebay-09/01	TPD)10.48
0930	Shade	220	1	9	$180	Pulled Feather	ebay-10/02	RFR)13,1,A
0931	Shade	220	1	10				
0932	Shade	220	1	11				
0933	Shade	220	1	12				
0934	Shade	220	2	1				
0935	Shade	220	2	2				
0936	Shade	220	2	3	$215	Gold Aurene	ebay-02/03	
0936					$200	Gold Aurene	ebay-03/03	
0936					$210	Gold Aurene	JDJ-05/03	
0936					$200	Gold Aurene	ebay-06/03	
0936					$150	Gold Aurene	ebay-02/04	
0936					$80	Gold Calcite	ebay-03/04	
0936					$110	Gold Aurene	ebay-06/04	
0936					$165	Gold Calcite	ebay-09/04	
0936					$175	Gold Calcite	ebay-09/04	
0936					$225	Gold Aurene	ebay-02/05	
0936					$255	Gold Aurene	ebay-04/05	
0936					$200	Gold Calcite	ebay-06/05	
0936					$225	Gold Aurene	ebay-07/05	
0937	Shade	220	2	4	$120	Gold Aurene	ebay-02/01	
0937					$340	Gold Aurene dec. Calcite	ebay-09/02	
0937					$2000	Decorated Green Aurene	ebay-05/03	
0938	Shade	220	2	5	$185	Gold Aurene	Sknr-10/98	TPD)4.107
0938					$75	Calcite	ebay-12/00	
0938					$170	Green Pulled Feather	Sknr-02/01	
0938					$100	Calcite	ebay-06/01	
0938					$75	Calcite	ebay-10/01	
0938					$140	Gold Aurene	ebay-12/01	
0938					$175	Gold Aurene	ebay-01/02	
0938					$55	VDS	ebay-12/02	
0938					$140	Calcite ACB	ebay-01/03	
0938					$77	Calcite ACB	ebay-04/03	
0938					$120	Gold Aurene	ebay-09/03	
0938					$125	Gold Aurene	ebay-01/04	
0938					$85	Calcite	ebay-02/04	
0938					$155	Calcite ACB	ebay-02/04	
0938					$185	Gold Aurene	EAC-04/04	
0938					$150	Calcite ACB	ebay-05/04	
0938					$190	Calcite	ebay-06/04	
0938					$30	Calcite	ebay-07/04	
0938					$180	Gold Aurene	EAC-07/04	
0938					$125	Gold Aurene	ebay-10/04	
0938					$130	Calcite	ebay-10/04	
0938					$195	Calcite ACB	ebay-11/04	
0938					$90	Calcite	ebay-01/05	
0938					$235	Gold Aurene	Cott-02/05	
0938					$45	Calcite	ebay-03/05	
0938					$70	Calcite	ebay-06/05	
0938					$35	VDS	ebay-06/05	
0938	Vase (Shade Vase)	257	2	7	$440	Gold Aurene	JDJ-10/95	TPD)5.32
0938					$1090	Blue Aurene	Sknr-05/98	
0938					$1000	Blue Aurene	ebay-12/99	
0938					$795	Blue Aurene	EAC-05/00	
0938					$500	Gold Aurene	ebay-07/00	
0938					$425	Gold Aurene	Tway-10/00	
0938					$500	Blue Aurene	ebay-06/01	
0938					$155	Celeste Blue	ebay-06/01	
0938					$950	Blue Aurene	ebay-03/02	
0938					$975	Blue Aurene	JDJ-05/02	
0938					$460	Gold Aurene	Jack–11/02	

SHAPE NO.	ITEM	PAGE	COL	ROW	PRICE REALIZED	GLASS TYPE	AUCTION HOUSE	COMMENTS & PHOTO REFERENCES
0938					$700	Blue Aurene	ebay-03/03	
0938					$450	Gold Aurene	ebay-05/03	
0938					$950	Blue Aurene	ebay-06/03	
0938					$410	Alabaster	ebay-07/03	
0938					$550	Blue Aurene	ebay-09/03	
0938					$400	Gold Aurene	JDJ-11/03	
0938					$270	Green Jade	ebay-12/03	
0938					$650	Blue Aurene	ebay-12/03	
0938					$500	Gold Aurene	ebay-02/04	
0938					$280	Gold Aurene	ebay-07/04	
0938					$865	Blue Aurene	ebay-10/04	
0938					$125	Topaz	ebay-01/05	
0938					$900	Blue Aurene	ebay-04/05	
0938					$150	Ivory	JDJ-06/05	
0938					$690	Blue Aurene	Cott-06/05	
0938					$390	Gold Aurene	ebay-07/05	
0938	Vase (Footed)	257	2	8	$1870	Light Blue Jade/Flint White	EAC-04/90	PG1)312; PG2)85,D; RFR)21,3,C:21,4,B
0938					$2035	Rosaline/Alabaster ACB	EAC-07/91	Etched "Bird" RFR)25,2,B; JAS)149,BR,D
0938					$1100	Green Jade/Alabaster ACB	EAC-10/91	Etched "Bird" ACR)COLOR 2,B,D
0938					$990	Green Jade/Alabaster ACB	EAC-10/93	Etched "Bird" ACR)163,324:170,346;
0938					$330	Rosaline/Alabaster	JDJ-05/94	TPD)5.36:10.27; MDK)122
0938					$2070	Alabaster/Black ACB	Sknr-05/94	
0938					$200	Topaz/Celeste Blue	Sknr-10/95	
0938					$975	Green Jade/Alabaster ACB	Sknr-01/96	
0938					$230	Pomona Green	Sknr-01/96	
0938					$220	Amethyst Shaded	JDJ-06/96	
0938					$2255	Rosaline/Alabaster ACB	EAC-10/96	
0938					$345	Pomona Green(E)	Sknr-10/96	
0938					$285	Celeste Blue	Sknr-10/97	
0938					$60	Topaz	JDJ-10/97	
0938					$1650	Rosaline/Alabaster ACB	EAC-04/98	
0938					$145	Topaz	Sknr-05/98	
0938					$2475	Alabaster/Black ACB	EAC-07/98	
0938					$1320	Green Jade/Alabaster ACB	EAC-07/98	
0938					$190	Green Jade/Alabaster	EAC-07/98	
0938					$715	Gold Aurene	EAC-10/98	
0938					$315	Celeste Blue	Sknr-10/98	
0938					$1595	Green Jade/Alabaster ACB	EAC-07/99	
0938					$305	Bristol Yellow	ebay-12/99	
0938					$220	Rosaline/Alabaster	ebay-01/00	
0938					$660	Celeste Blue	Ogal-03/00	
0938					$400	Bristol Yellow	ebay-06/00	
0938					$385	Green Jade/Alabaster	EAC-08/00	
0938					$300	Aqua Marine	ebay-11/00	
0938					$305	Aqua Marine	ebay-12/00	
0938					$138	Aqua Marine	ebay-01/01	
0938					$200	Aqua Marine	Sknr-02/01	
0938					$2070	Green Jade/Alabaster ACB	Sknr-02/01	Etched "Bird"
0938					$178	Aqua Marine	ebay-02/01	
0938					$120	Bristol Yellow	ebay-02/01	
0938					$895	Green Jade/Alabaster (E)	EAC-04/01	
0938					$950	Light Blue Jade	JDJ-05/01	
0938					$750	Gold Aurene	ebay-05/01	
0938					$825	Light Blue Jade	ebay-05/01	
0938					$410	Aqua Marine	ebay-06/01	
0938					$1750	Green Jade/Alabaster ACB	ebay-06/01	Etched "Bird"
0938					$90	Topaz	ebay-05/01	
0938					$325	Aqua Marine	ebay-08/01	
0938					$65	Pomona Green	ebay-08/01	
0938					$230	Green Shaded	ebay-10/01	
0938					$380	Green Jade/Alabaster	ebay-10/01	Engraved "York"
0938					$50	Topaz	ebay-11/01	
0938					$715	Blue Aurene	ebay-12/01	
0938					$725	Gold Aurene	ebay-02/02	
0938					$355	Amethyst	ebay-02/02	
0938					$210	VDS	ebay-03/02	
0938					$250	Green Jade	ebay-03/02	
0938					$1525	Green Jade/Alabaster ACB	ebay-03/02	Etched "Bird"
0938					$310	Pomona Green	ebay-03/02	Engraved "10001" pattern
0938					$60	Spanish Green	ebay-03/02	
0938					$280	Bristol Yellow/threaded	ebay-03/02	Mirror Black threading
0938					$212	VDS	ebay-03/02	
0938					$670	Rosaline/Alabaster	EAC-04/02	Not ACB
0938					$1680	Rosaline/Alabaster	EAC-04/02	Etched "Fircone"

SHAPE NO.	ITEM	PAGE	COL	ROW	PRICE REALIZED	GLASS TYPE	AUCTION HOUSE	COMMENTS & PHOTO REFERENCES
0938					$720	Blue Aurene	ebay-04/02	
0938					$325	Amber/Flemish Blue rim	ebay-05/02	Flemish
0938					$500	Rosaline/Alabaster	ebay-05/02	Probably an ACB blank
0938					$525	Blue Aurene	ebay-06/02	
0938					$50	Celeste Blue	ebay-06/02	
0938					$96	Citron Yellow	ebay-06/02	
0938					$170	Aqua Marine	Jack-06/02	
0938					$230	Aqua Marine	ebay-10/02	
0938					$150	Amber/Flemish Blue rim	ebay-10/02	Flemish
0938					$355	Mirror Black	ebay-10/02	
0938					$70	VDS	ebay-10/02	
0938					$150	Amethyst	ebay-11/02	
0938					$650	Green Jade/Alabaster (E)	ebay-11/02	Engraved "10001" pattern
0938					$650	VDS	Ogal-12/02	
0938					$180	VDS	ebay-03/03	
0938					$260	Celeste Blue	ebay-03/03	
0938					$95	Celeste Blue	ebay-03/03	
0938					$895	Pomona Green (E)	ebay-03/03	Engraved "10018" pattern
0938					$200	Antique Green	ebay-04/03	
0938					$90	Topaz	ebay-04/03	
0938					$450	Gold Aurene	Free-05/03	
0938					$200	Mirror Black/Col. foot	Cinc-06/03	
0938					$805	Gold Aurene	Jack-06/03	
0938					$230	Amethyst	EAC-06/03	
0938					$305	Aqua Marine	ebay-07/03	
0938					$215	Topaz/Celeste Blue rim	ebay-08/03	
0938					$1525	Blue Aurene	ebay-09/03	
0938					$700	Blue Aurene	J&W-09/03	
0938					$750	Cyprian	ebay-10/03	
0938					$670	Gold Aurene	Ogal-10/03	
0938					$240	Topaz	ebay-11/03	
0938					$235	Topaz with Blue rim	ebay-11/03	
0938					$1400	Blue Aurene	ebay-11/03	
0938					$610	Colorless (E)	ebay-11/03	Engraved "10018"
0938					$450	Aqua Marine	Ogal-12/03	
0938					$315	Amber with Flemish rim	Rago-01/04	Flemish
0938					$315	Amber with Celeste rim	Aspr-01/04	
0938					$155	VDS	ebay-01/04	
0938					$430	Aqua Marine	ebay-01/04	
0938					$155	Pomona Green	ebay-02/04	
0938					$895	Blue Aurene	Ogal-02/04	
0938					$750	Colorless (E)	ebay-02/04	Engraved "10018"
0938					$3000	Black/Alabaster ACB	ebay-02/04	Etched "Indian"
0938					$125	Celeste Blue	ebay-02/04	
0938					$330	Aqua Marine	ebay-03/04	
0938					$310	Green Jade/Alabaster	ebay-04/04	
0938					$620	Aqua Marine	ebay-05/04	
0938					$1150	Green Jade/Alabaster ACB	JDJ-05/04	Etched "Bird"
0938					$315	Topaz/Blue rim	Aspr-05/04	
0938					$345	Celeste Blue	ebay-05/04	
0938					$1200	Green Jade/Alabaster ACB	JDJ-05/04	Etched "Bird"
0938					$90	Aqua Marine	ebay-09/04	
0938					$1200	Green Jade/Alabaster ACB	ebay-10/04	Etched "Bird"
0938					$125	VDS	ebay-12/04	
0938					$200	Ivory	ebay-12/04	
0938					$575	Rosaline/Alabaster (E)	ebay-01/05	Engraved "York"
0938					$155	Royal Purple	ebay-01/05	
0938					$175	Rosaline/Alabaster foot	ebay-02/05	
0938					$200	Rosaline/Alabaster foot	ebay-02/05	Same piece as above
0938					$55	Topaz	ebay-02/05	
0938					$250	Celeste Blue	ebay-02/05	
0938					$310	Rosaline/Alabaster foot	ebay-02/05	
0938					$245	Rosaline/Alabaster foot	ebay-03/05	
0938					$1380	Light Blue Jade/Flint White	Hrtg-03/05	Flint White foot
0938					$135	Aqua Marine	ebay-04/05	
0938					$1600	Green Jade/Alabaster ACB	ebay-04/05	Etched "Bird"
0938					$120	Flemish	ebay-05/05	
0938					$150	VDS	ebay-05/05	
0938					$115	Flemish	ebay-05/05	
0938					$155	Aqua Marine	ebay-05/05	
0938					$230	VDS	ebay-05/05	
0938					$230	VDS	ebay-05/05	
0938					$50	Topaz	ebay-07/05	
0939	Shade	220	2	6				

SHAPE NO.	ITEM	PAGE	COL	ROW	PRICE REALIZED	GLASS TYPE	AUCTION HOUSE	COMMENTS & PHOTO REFERENCES
0940	Shade	220	2	7	$325	Decorated Calcite	ebay-12/03	
0940					$590	Decorated Calcite	ebay-03/04	
0940					$225	Decorated Calcite	ebay-12/04	
0941	Shade	220	2	8	$2125	Turquoise Zipper	ebay-12/00	TPD)4.93
0942	Shade	220	2	9				
0943	Shade	220	2	10				
0944	Shade	220	2	11				
0945	Shade	220	3	1				
0946	Shade	220	3	2	$860	Leaves & Vines	Jack-06/01	TPD)10.149
0946					$715	Leaves & Vines	ebay-01/03	
0947	Shade	220	3	3				
0948	Shade	220	3	4				
0949	Shade	220	3	5	$690	Green Pulled Feather	JDJ-06/05	
0950	Shade	220	3	6				
0951	Shade	220	3	7				
0952	Shade	220	3	8				
0953	Shade	220	3	9	$75	Gold Calcite	Tway-09/02	
0953					$315	Gold Calcite (E)	Rago-01/04	
0953					$210	Gold Calcite (E)	ebay-12/04	
0953					$210	Gold Calcite (E)	ebay-12/04	
0953					$290	Gold Calcite (E)	ebay-12/04	
0953					$405	Gold Calcite (E)	ebay-12/04	
0953					$190	Gold Calcite (E)	ebay-01/05	
0953					$195	Gold Calcite (E)	ebay-01/05	
0953					$195	Gold Calcite (E)	ebay-01/05	
0953					$200	Gold Calcite (E)	ebay-01/05	
0953					$200	Gold Calcite (E)	ebay-01/05	
0953					$280	Gold Calcite (E)	ebay-02/05	
0953					$325	Gold Calcite (E)	ebay-03/05	
0953					$250	Gold Calcite (E)	ebay-06/05	
0954	Shade	220	3	10	$780	Red Pulled Feather	JDJ-11/04	
0955	Shade	220	4	1				
0956	Shade	220	4	2	$150	Gold Calcite	ebay-05/03	
0957	Shade	220	4	3				
0958	Shade	220	4	4	$430	Gold Pulled Feather	ebay-02/05	
0959	Shade	220	4	5	$200	Green Pulled Feather	Jack-06/02	Calcite base
0959					$460	Green Pulled Feather	JDJ-05/04	
0960	Shade	220	4	6				
0961	Shade	220	4	7	$650	Gold Aurene	ebay-11/03	
0962	Shade	220	4	8	$150	Gold Aurene	ebay-08/03	
0962					$295	Gold Feather on Green	ebay-11/04	
0963	Shade	227	1	3				PG1)34,62
0964	Shade	220	4	9	$150	Gold Aurene	ebay-06/02	
0965	Shade	220	4	10				
0966	Shade	220	5	1	$310	Green Pulled Feather	ebay-01/05	
0967	Shade	220	5	2				
0968	Shade	220	5	3	$250	Green Pulled Feather	ebay-07/04	
0968					$145	Gold Pulled Feather	ebay-07/05	
0969	Shade	227	1	4				
0970	Shade	220	5	4				
0971	Shade	220	5	5				
0972	Shade	220	5	6	$130	Gold Calcite	ebay-02/04	
0973	Shade	220	5	7				
0974	Shade	220	5	8				
0975	Bobeche	205	4	8				
0976	Shade	220	5	9				
0976½	Bobeche	205	4	9				
0977	Shade	220	5	10				
0978	Shade	220	5	11				
0979	Shade	221	1	1				
0980	Shade	221	1	2				
0980½	Bobeche	205	4	10				
0981	Shade	221	1	3	$100	Gold Aurene	ebay-07/01	
0981					$310	Pulled Feather	ebay-08/03	
0982	Shade	221	1	4				
0983	Shade	221	1	5				
0984	Shade	221	1	6	$125	Gold Aurene	ebay-09/02	
0985	Shade	221	1	7	$250	Green Pulled Feather	EAC-07/04	
0985					$280	Green Pulled Feather	EAC-07/04	
0985					$385	Green Pulled Feather	EAC-10/04	
0985					$135	Gold Pulled Feather	EAC-10/04	
0985					$190	Gold Pulled Feather	ebay-11/04	
0986	Shade	221	1	8	$100	Calcite ACB	ebay-04/03	
0987	Shade	221	1	9				RFR)13,1,B

SHAPE NO.	ITEM	PAGE	COL	ROW	PRICE REALIZED	GLASS TYPE	AUCTION HOUSE	COMMENTS & PHOTO REFERENCES
0988	Shade	221	1	10				TPD)9.43
0989	Shade	221	2	1				
0990	Shade	221	2	2	$995	Green Zipper	ebay-06/02	
0991	Shade	221	2	3				
0992	Shade	221	2	4				
0993	Shade	221	3	5				
0994	Shade	221	2	6				
0995	Shade	227	1	5	$220	Calcite ACB Dome	Midw-04/01	
0995					$230	Calcite ACB Dome	Wesr-09/02	
0995					$1150	Calcite ACB Dome	EAC-04/05	
0996	Shade	221	2	7				
0997	Shade	221	2	8				
0998	Shade	227	1	6				
0999	Shade	221	2	9	$105	Gold Aurene	ebay-08/02	TPD)4.93
0999					$170	Gold Aurene	ebay-05/04	
1000	Decanter	180	3	3				
1001	Decanter	180	3	4				PG1)348,I,J; TPD)7.1:7.8
1002	Decanter	180	3	5				
1003	Decanter	180	3	6				
1004	Decanter	180	4	1				
1005	Cruet	178	2	5				PG1)348,M
1006	Cologne	240	3	2				PG1)348,M
1007	Punch Cup	216	1	5				
1008	Punch Cup	216	1	6				
1009	Tea Cup	216	2	8				
1010	Punch Cup	216	1	7				
1011	Cologne	240	3	3				
1012	Pitcher	212	1	4				
1013	Pitcher	212	1	5				
1014	Pitcher	212	1	6				
1015	Pitcher	212	2	1				
1016	Pitcher	212	2	2				
1017	Vase	257	3	1				
1018	Pitcher	212	2	3				
1019	Pitcher	212	2	4				
1020	Hair Receiver	245	2	1				
1021	Vase	257	3	2				
1022	Mayonnaise Bowl	210	3	3				
1023	Sugar & Creamer	234	3	9,10				
1024	Sugar & Creamer	234	3	11,12				PG1)348,P
1025	Decanter	180	4	2				
1026	Vase	257	3	3				
1027	Vase	257	3	4				
1028	Vase	257	3	5				
1029	Basket	139	4	4				
1030	Nappie	233	1	16				
1031	Nappie	233	1	17				
1032	Vase	257	3	6				
1033	Decanter	180	4	3				
1034	Decanter	180	4	4				
1035	Pitcher	212	2	5				
1036	Centerpiece	147	1	4				
1037	Goblet	190	2	5				
1038	Cruet							See New Drawings section
1039	Cruet							See New Drawings section
1040	Decanter	180	4	5				PG1)348,J; TPD)7.1
1041	Decanter	180	4	6				
1042	Decanter	180	5	1				
1043	Goblet	197	2	4				
1044	Goblet							See New Drawings section; MDK)95
1044	Goblet				$100	VDS (E)	ebay-07/04	signed "Hawkes"
1044	Tumbler	198	4	5	$190	Gold Aurene	EAC-10/93	Shown in the 1932 Catalog. Same as 2361
1044					$110	Gold Aurene	ebay-07/01	
1044					$200	Gold Calcite	ebay-07/01	
1044					$160	VDS engraved	ebay-07/01	
1044					$40	Amethyst	ebay-08/01	
1044					$75	Col./Gold Ruby threaded	ebay-05/02	
1044					$200	Gold Aurene	ebay-10/02	signed "Haviland"
1044					$15	Pomona Green/Topaz	ebay-01/03	Topaz handle
1044					$125	Colorless/Black threaded	ebay-03/03	
1044	Vase	257	3	7				
1045	Pitcher	212	2	6				
1046	Pitcher	212	2	7				
1047	Vase	257	4	1				

SHAPE NO.	ITEM	PAGE	COL	ROW	PRICE REALIZED	GLASS TYPE	AUCTION HOUSE	COMMENTS & PHOTO REFERENCES
1048	Vase	257	4	2				
1049	Vase	257	4	3				
1050	Pitcher	212	3	1				
1051	Decanter	180	5	2				
1052	Cruet	178	2	6				PG1)348,M
1053	Decanter	180	5	3				
1054	Tea Cup	216	2	9				
1055	Decanter	180	5	4				
1056	Decanter	180	5	5				
1057	Goblet	190	2	6				
1058	Goblet	190	2	7				
1059	Decanter	181	1	1				
1060	Parfait	197	6	2	$315	Rosaline/Alabaster	ebay-01/00	
1061	Decanter	181	1	2				
1062	Decanter	181	1	3				
1063	Goblet	190	2	8				
1064	Decanter	181	1	4				
1065	Pitcher	212	3	2				
1066	Cruet	178	2	7				
1067	Pitcher	212	3	3				
1068	Decanter	181	1	5				
1069	Decanter	181	2	1				
1070	Decanter	181	2	2				
1071	Decanter	181	2	3	$1210	Gold Aurene	EAC-10/90	TPD)10.139
1072	Compote	171	2	8				PG1)347,F
1073	Centerpiece	147	1	1				
1074	Vase	257	4	4	$210	VDS	ebay-04/05	
1075	Vase	257	4	5	$1150	Yellow Silverina	Sknr-05/96	
1076	Decanter	181	2	4				
1077	Jar	209	1	5				
1078	Cruet	178	2	8				
1079	Tumbler	198	4	6				
1080	Vase	257	4	6				
1081	Vase	257	4	7				
1082	Vase	257	5	1				
1083	Vase	257	5	2				
1084	Bowl	141	2	7				
1085	Bowl	141	2	8				
1086	Bowl	141	2	9				PG1)347,C
1087	Pitcher	212	3	4				PG1)348,O
1088	Pitcher	212	3	5				
1089	Basket	139	4	5				PG1)349,W; TPD)7.2
1090	Bonbon	233	4	18				
1091	Goblet	190	3	1				
1092	Compote	171	3	1				PG1)347,E
1093	Cruet	178	2	9				
1094	Cruet	178	2	10				PG1)348,M
1095	Punch Cup	216	1	8				
1096	Basket	139	4	6				
1097	Vase	257	5	3				
1098	Vase	257	5	4				
1099	Water Bottle	199	4	4				PG1)348,N
1099	Tumbler							PG1)348,N
1100	Sugar & Creamer	234	3	13,14				
1101	Vase	257	5	5				
1102	Vase	257	5	6				
1103	Vase	258	1	1				
1104	Vase	258	1	2				
1105	Vase	258	1	3				
1106	Puff Box	244	1	8				
1107	Vase	258	1	4				
1108	Decanter	181	2	5				
1109	Puff Box	244	1	9				
1110	Compote	171	3	2				
1111	Compote	171	3	3				
1112	Compote	171	3	4				
1113	Tumbler	198	4	7				Tumbler blank #6
1114	Vase	258	1	5				
1115	Candlestick	160	2	5				
1116	Candlestick	160	2	7				PG1)347,G
1117	Tumbler	198	4	8				Tumbler blank #3
1118	Pitcher	212	3	6				
1119	Pitcher	212	4	1				PG1)348,O
1120	Bowl	141	2	10				

SHAPE NO.	ITEM	PAGE	COL	ROW	PRICE REALIZED	GLASS TYPE	AUCTION HOUSE	COMMENTS & PHOTO REFERENCES
1121	Tumbler	198	4	9				Tumbler blank #6
1122	Decanter	181	3	1				
1123	Basket	139	4	7				PG1)349,W; TPD)7.2
1124	Vase	258	2	1	$660	Gold Aurene	EAC-08/00	
1124					$660	Gold Aurene	JDJ-11/02	
1124					$600	Gold Aurene	JDJ-06/05	
1125	Tumbler	198	4	10				
1126	Tumbler	198	4	11				
1127	Tumbler	198	4	12				
1128	Tumbler	198	5	1				
1129	Tumbler	198	5	2				
1130	Tumbler	198	5	3	$65	Selenium Red	ebay-05/02	
1131	Goblet	190	3	2				
1132	Goblet	190	3	3				
1133	Bonbon	233	5	1				
1134	Bonbon	233	5	2				
1135	Bonbon	233	5	3				
1136	Bonbon	233	5	4				
1137	Bonbon	233	5	5				
1138	Bonbon	233	5	6				
1139	Bonbon	233	5	7				
1140	Bonbon	233	5	8				
1141	Bonbon	233	5	9				
1142	Bonbon	233	5	10				
1143	Vase	258	2	2				
1144	Bonbon	233	5	11				
1145	Compote	171	3	5				
1146	Compote	171	3	6				
1147	Sugar Shaker	217	5	1				
1148	Sugar Shaker	217	5	2				
1149	Sugar Shaker	217	5	3				
1150	Sugar Shaker	217	5	4				
1151	Sugar Shaker	217	5	5				
1152	Sugar Shaker	217	5	6				
1153	Salt & Pepper	217	3	7				
1154	Salt & Pepper	217	3	8				
1155	Salt & Pepper	217	3	9				
1156	Salt & Pepper	217	4	1				
1157	Salt & Pepper	217	4	2				
1158	Salt & Pepper	217	4	3				
1159	Sugar Shaker	217	5	7				
1160	Sugar Shaker	217	5	8				
1161	Sugar Shaker	217	6	1				
1162	Cruet	178	3	1				
1163	Cruet	178	3	2				
1164	Puff Box	244	1	10				
1165	Puff Box	244	1	11				
1166	Puff Box	244	1	12				
1167	Puff Box	244	1	13				
1168	Vase	258	2	3				
1169	Puff Box	244	1	14				
1170	Tray	158	2	18				
1171	Bowl	141	2	11	$440	Blue Calcite	ebay-10/02	
1171					$375	Blue Calcite	EAC-06/03	
1172	Bowl	141	2	12				
1173	Cologne	240	3	4				PG1)348,M
1174	Sugar & Creamer	234	4	1,2				
1175	Vase	258	2	4				
1176	3 Piece Dish	211	4	1				
1177	4 Piece Dish	211	4	2				
1178	3 Piece Dish	211	4	3				
1179	Dish	211	4	4				
1180	Puff Box	244	1	15				
1181	Puff Box	244	2	1				
1182	Puff Box	244	2	2				
1183	Sugar & Creamer	234	4	3,4				
1184	Decanter	181	3	2				
1185	Jar	209	1	6				
1186	Jar	209	1	7				
1187	String Box	244	2	3				PG1)348,M
1188	Tumbler	198	5	4				
1189	Bonbon	233	5	12				
1190	Bonbon	233	5	13				
1191	Limousine Vase	206	1	1				

SHAPE NO.	ITEM	PAGE	COL	ROW	PRICE REALIZED	GLASS TYPE	AUCTION HOUSE	COMMENTS & PHOTO REFERENCES
1192	Limousine Vase	206	1	2				
1193	Limousine Vase	206	1	3				
1194	Limousine Vase	206	1	4				
1195	Sardine Box	210	4	6				
1196	Limousine Vase	206	1	5				
1197	Pitcher	212	4	2				
1198	Pitcher	212	4	3				
1199	Sugar & Creamer	234	4	5,6				PG1)348,P
1200	Vase	258	2	5				J. Hoare & Co.
1201	Vase	258	2	6				J. Hoare & Co.
1202	Salt	217	1	13				
1203	Cologne	243	2	8				
1204	Limousine Vase	206	1	6				
1205	Limousine Vase	206	2	1				
1206	Cruet	178	3	3				
1207	Punch Cup	216	1	9				
1208	Basket	139	5	1				
1209	Vase	258	2	7				
1210	Vase	258	3	1				
1211	Vase	258	3	2				
1212	Vase	258	3	3				
1213	Vase	258	3	4	$975	Gold Aurene	Jack-06/02	
1213					$1100	Gold Aurene	ebay-08/02	
1213					$1540	Gold Aurene	ebay-05/04	
1214	Vase	258	3	5				
1215	Basket	139	5	2				
1216	Decanter	181	3	3				
1217	Compote	171	3	7				
1218	Watch Holder	310	1	1				
1219	Pitcher	212	4	4				
1220	Candlestick	160	2	7				
1220½	Cold Cream Jar	243	6	3	$130	Gold Ruby	ebay-09/02	PG2)97,D; JAS)148,B,D; TPD)4.62
1221	Knife Rest	237	3	7				
1222	Knife Rest	237	3	8				
1223	Pitcher	212	4	5				
1224	Goblet	197	2	5				
1225	Bowl	141	2	13				PG1)347,B,C
1226	Nappie	233	2	1				
1227	Sugar Shaker	217	6	2				
1228	Sugar Shaker	217	6	3				
1229	Tumbler	198	5	5				
1230	Salt & Pepper	217	4	4				
1231	Salt & Pepper	217	4	5				
1232	Salt & Pepper	217	4	6				
1233	Salt & Pepper	217	4	7				
1234	Salt & Pepper	217	4	8	$1065	Blue Aurene	ebay-01/05	TPD)10.140
1235	Salt & Pepper	217	4	9				
1236	Salt & Pepper	217	4	10				
1237	Salt & Pepper	217	4	11				
1238	Salt & Pepper	217	4	12				
1239	Decanter	181	3	4				
1240	Decanter	181	3	5				
1241	Cocktail Mixer							See New Drawings section
1242	Decanter	181	4	1				
1243	Misc.	211	4	7				Liner
1244	Goblet	190	3	4				
1245	Candlestick	160	3	1				PG1)347,G
1246	Candlestick	160	3	2				PG1)347,G
1247	Tea Cup	216	2	10				
1248	Decanter	181	4	2				
1249	Decanter	181	4	3				
1250	Vase	258	4	1				
1251	Vase	258	4	2				
1252	Decanter	181	4	4				
1253	Vase	258	4	3				PG1)349,R
1254	Vase	258	4	4				
1255	Vase	258	4	5				
1256	Decanter	181	4	5				
1257	Decanter	181	4	6				TPD)7.71
1258	Decanter	181	5	1				
1259	Cruet	178	3	4				
1260	Vase	258	4	6				
1261	Vase	258	5	1				
1262	Jar	209	5	3				

SHAPE NO.	ITEM	PAGE	COL	ROW	PRICE REALIZED	GLASS TYPE	AUCTION HOUSE	COMMENTS & PHOTO REFERENCES
1263	Bowl	141	2	14				
1264	Sugar & Creamer	234	4	7,8				
1265	Candlestick	160	3	3				PG1)347,G
1266	Pitcher	212	4	6				PG1)348,O
1267	Cruet	178	3	5				
1268	Water Bottle	199	4	5				PG1)348,N
1268	Tumbler							PG1)348,N; Tumbler blank #6
1269	Vase	258	5	2				
1270	Decanter	181	5	2				
1271	Tray	158	2	19				
1272	Tray	158	2	20				
1273	Nappie	233	2	2				
1274	Puff Box	244	2	4				
1275	Bowl	141	3	1	$330	Gold Aurene	EAC-10/98	
1276	Sugar & Creamer	234	4	9,10				PG1)348,P
1277	Bowl	141	3	2				
1278	Tray	158	2	21				
1279	Pitcher	212	4	7				
1280	Tumble Up	199	5	1				
1281	Cruet	178	3	6				PG1)348,M
1282	Vase	258	5	3				
1283	Vase	258	5	4				PG1)350,B
1284	Pitcher	212	5	1				PG1)91,140:350,A; TPD)7.11:7.13
1285	Vase	258	5	5				PG1)350,A; TPD)7.11
1286	Vase	258	5	6				PG1)350,A; TPD)7.11
1287	Vase	258	5	7				TPD)7.10
1288	Centerpiece	147	1	2				
1289	Vase	259	1	1				
1290	Bonbon	233	5	14				
1291	Bonbon	233	5	15				
1292	Bonbon	233	5	16				
1293	Vase	259	1	2				
1294	Vase	259	1	3				PG1)349,R
1295	Vase	259	1	4				
1296	Vase	259	1	5				
1297	Jar	210	1	4				
1298	Caviar Set	210	1	5				
1299	Loving Cup	177	2	4				
1300	Compote	171	4	1				PG1)347,F
1301	Decanter	181	5	3				PG1)348,K
1302	Vase	259	1	6				
1303	Vase	259	2	1				
1304	Vase	259	2	2	$690	Gold Aurene	EAC-04/05	Signed "Haviland"
1305	Vase	259	2	3				
1306	Lamp	200	2	1				TPD)4.66:7.5
1307	Decanter	181	5	4				PG1)348,K
1308	Vase	259	2	4				
1309	Vase	259	2	5				
1310	Vase	259	2	6				
1311	Vase	259	1	7				
1312	Vase	259	3	1				
1313	Vase	259	3	2				
1314	Cruet	178	3	7				
1315	Cruet	178	3	8				
1316	Vase	259	3	3				
1317	Vase	259	3	4				
1318	Basket	139	5	3				
1319	Vase	259	3	5				PG1)350,B
1320	Vase	259	3	6				
1321	Nut Dish	211	1	14				
1322	Nut Dish	211	1	15				
1323	Salt	217	1	14				
1323½	Salt	217	1	15				
1324	Salt	217	1	16				
1325	Caviar Set	210	1	6				
1326	Decanter	181	5	5				
1327	Decanter	182	1	1				
1328	Decanter	182	1	2				
1329	Decanter	182	1	3				
1330	Ice Tub	177	4	1				
1331	Compote	171	4	2				PG1)347,E
1332	Jar	210	1	7				
1333	Ash Tray	137	1	1				
1334	Ash Tray	137	1	2				

SHAPE NO.	ITEM	PAGE	COL	ROW	PRICE REALIZED	GLASS TYPE	AUCTION HOUSE	COMMENTS & PHOTO REFERENCES
1335	Ink Well	310	3	1				This number is an error, see #1355.
1335	Tumble Up	199	5	2				
1336	Decanter	182	1	4				
1337	Decanter	182	1	5				PG1)348,J; TPD)7.1
1338	Centerpiece	147	1	3				
1339	Decanter	182	2	1				PG1)348,I,K; TPD)7.8
1340	Vase	259	4	1				
1341	Decanter	182	2	2				PG1)348,K
1342	Candlestick	160	3	4				
1343	Vase	259	4	2				PG1)350,B
1344	Vase	259	4	3				
1345	Goblet	197	2	6				
1346	Goblet	197	2	7				
1347	Decanter	182	2	3				PG1)350,C
1348	Decanter	182	2	4				PG1)350,C
1349	Decanter	182	2	5				PG1)350,C
1350	Goblet	190	3	5				PG1)350,H
1350	Pitcher	212	5	2				
1351	Centerpiece	147	1	5				
1352	Sugar & Creamer	234	4	11,12				
1353	Jar	210	1	8				
1354	Ice Tub	177	4	2				
1355	Ink Well	310	3	1				This shape is shown as #1335 in Gardner.
1356	Goblet	190	3	6				
1357	Smoking Set	138	4	12				
1358	Vase	259	4	4				
1359	Vase	259	4	5				
1360	Vase	259	4	6				
1361	Compote	171	4	3				
1362	Compote	171	4	4				TPD)10.32
1363	Ice Tub	177	4	3				
1364	Decanter	182	2	6				
1365	Pitcher	212	5	3				
1366	Tumble Up	199	5	3				
1367	Decanter	182	2	7				
1368	Compote	171	4	5	$300	Cyprian	ebay-05/04	
1368					$100	Gold Calcite	ebay-04/05	
1369	Jar	209	1	8				
1370	Jar	209	1	9				
1371	Jar	209	1	10				
1372	Ice Tub	177	4	4				
1373	Oyster Cocktail	210	4	7				
1374	Ash Tray	137	1	3				
1375	Listerine	243	6	1				
1376	Catsup Bottle	179	3	6				
1377	Bowl	141	3	3				
1377A	Bowl	141	3	4				
1378	Decanter	182	3	1				
1379	Vase	259	4	7				
1380	Vase	259	5	1				
1381	Bowl	141	3	5				PG1)347,C&D; TPD)7.4
1382	Candlestick	160	3	5				PG1)347,H
1383	Vase	259	5	2	$150	Colorless (E)	ebay-03/05	
1384	Candlestick	160	3	6				PG1)347,H
1385	Candlestick	160	3	7				PG1)347,H
1385	Vase							PG1)350,D
1386	Centerpiece	147	2	1				PG1)349,S; TPD)7.9
1387	Centerpiece	147	2	2				
1388	Cake Plate	158	1	1				
1388½								Same as 1388 but without foot.
1389	Cake Plate	158	1	2				
1390	Compote	171	4	6				
1391	Compote	171	4	7				
1392	Salt	217	2	1				
1393	Salt	217	2	2				
1393	Vase							PG1)350,D
1394	Vase	259	5	3				PG1)350,D
1395	Decanter	182	3	2				
1396	Jar	209	1	11				
1397	Jar	209	1	12				
1397	Jar	209	4	1				
1398	Jar	209	1	13				
1399	Vase	259	5	4	$1495	Blue Calcite	Sknr-05/96	TPD)7.3
1400	Vase	259	5	5				PG1)349,V; TPD)7.3

SHAPE NO.	ITEM	PAGE	COL	ROW	PRICE REALIZED	GLASS TYPE	AUCTION HOUSE	COMMENTS & PHOTO REFERENCES
1401	Vase	259	5	6				TPD)7.3
1402	Bowl	141	3	6				PG1)347,B
1403	Nappie	233	2	3				PG1)347,A
1404	Bonbon	233	5	17				PG1)347,A
1405	Bonbon	233	5	18				PG1)347,A
1406	Cruet	178	3	9				
1407	Cruet	178	3	10				
1408	Goblet	190	3	7				
1409	Sherbet	216	4	3				
1410	Tray	158	2	22				
1411	Tray	158	3	1				
1412	Decanter	182	3	3				
1413	Decanter	182	3	4				
1414	Cologne	240	3	5	$990	Blue Aurene	EAC-10/90	RLG)136,261; RFR)21,2,A; TPD)10.145
1414					$605	Gold Aurene	EAC-10/90	
1414					$550	Rosaline/Alabaster stopper	EAC-07/92	
1414					$715	Blue Aurene	EAC-07/92	
1414					$685	Blue Aurene	EAC-07/92	
1414					$495	Gold Aurene	EAC-04/93	
1414					$715	Blue Aurene	EAC-07/93	
1414					$770	Blue Aurene	EAC-10/95	
1414					$860	Blue Aurene	Sknr-01/96	
1414					$1035	Blue Aurene	Sknr-01/96	
1414					$880	Gold Aurene	EAC-10/97	
1414					$550	Pomona Green	EAC-10/98	
1414					$330	Aqua Marine	EAC-07/99	
1414					$470	Green Jade/Alabaster	EAC-07/99	
1414					$550	Rosaline/Alabaster	EAC-07/99	
1414					$660	Green Jade/Alabaster	EAC-07/99	
1414					$525	VDS/Celeste Blue	EAC-07/99	
1414					$1380	Gold Aurene	ebay-11/99	
1414					$730	Yellow Jade	ebay-11/99	
1414					$455	Green Jade/Alabaster	ebay-12/99	
1414					$880	Blue Aurene	EAC-10/00	
1414					$660	Gold Aurene	EAC-10/00	
1414					$805	Blue Aurene	Sknr-10/00	
1414					$500	VDS/Cintra	ebay-01/01	
1414					$700	Blue Aurene	ebay-02/01	
1414					$785	Gold Aurene	EAC-04/01	
1414					$520	Rosaline/Alabaster	JDJ-05/01	
1414					$1200	Gold Aurene	ebay-05/01	
1414					$450	Rosaline/Alabaster	ebay-05/01	
1414					$410	VDS	Cott-08/01	
1414					$770	Gold Aurene	Cott-08/01	
1414					$730	Gold Aurene	EAC-11/01	
1414					$610	Rosaline/Alabaster	ebay-02/02	
1414					$460	VDS/Celeste Blue	ebay-06/02	
1414					$475	Rosaline/Alabaster	ebay-06/02	
1414					$485	Green Jade/Alabaster	ebay-06/02	
1414					$595	VDS/Green Jade stopper	ebay-07/02	
1414					$475	Alabaster over Rosaline	EAC-09/02	Alabaster foot and stopper
1414					$2080	Light Blue Jade/Flint White	ebay-10/02	
1414					$1200	Gold Aurene	JDJ-11/02	
1414					$520	Gold Aurene	ebay-11/02	
1414					$495	Alabaster over Rosaline	ebay-11/02	Alabaster foot and stopper
1414					$885	Blue Aurene	ebay-11/02	
1414					$475	Colorless/Amethyst	Cinc-11/02	Amethyst full stopper
1414					$230	Rosaline over Alabaster	ebay-12/02	
1414					$475	Rosaline over Alabaster	ebay-02/03	
1414					$760	VDS/Pomona Green	ebay-02/03	Pomona Green stopper
1414					$1300	Light Blue Jade/Flint White	Cott-06/03	Flint White foot and stopper
1414					$430	Gold Aurene	ebay-08/03	
1414					$450	Gold Aurene	ebay-10/03	
1414					$795	Blue Aurene	ebay-11/03	
1414					$460	Blue Aurene	JDJ-11/03	
1414					$515	Bristol Yellow	JDJ-11/03	
1414					$805	Rosaline/Alabaster	JDJ-11/03	
1414					$405	Blue Aurene	ebay-03/04	Stopper missing
1414					$480	Gold Aurene	ebay-03/04	
1414					$335	Blue Aurene	ebay-04/04	Stopper tip broken
1414					$70	VDS	ebay-09/04	
1414					$420	Gold Aurene	Ogal-10/04	
1414					$865	Blue Aurene	ebay-12/04	
1414					$100	Rosaline/Alabaster	ebay-06/05	Stopper missing

SHAPE NO.	ITEM	PAGE	COL	ROW	PRICE REALIZED	GLASS TYPE	AUCTION HOUSE	COMMENTS & PHOTO REFERENCES
1414					$855	Light Blue Jade/Flint White	ebay-06/05	
1414					$205	Gold Aurene	ebay-07/05	Stopper missing
1414					$495	Blue Aurene	ebay-07/05	
1414					$920	Gold Aurene	EAC-07/05	
1414					$575	Rosaline/Alabaster	EAC-07/05	Alabaster foot and stopper
1414					$1035	Pomona Green	EAC-07/05	
1414	Puff Box				$385	Blue Aurene	ebay-05/05	Cover missing
1415	Flower Pot	237	2	5				
1416	Cruet	178	4	1				
1417	Salt	217	2	3				
1418	Vase	259	5	7				
1419	Cologne	243	3	1				
1420	Salt	217	2	4				
1421	Decanter	182	3	5				
1422	Bowl	141	3	7				
1423	Tray	158	3	2				
1424	Cruet	178	4	2				
1425	Cruet	178	4	3				
1426	Tray	158	3	3	$200	VDS (E)	ebay-08/03	Hawkes signed
1427	Cruet	178	4	4				
1428	Cruet	178	4	5				
1429	Vase	260	1	1				
1430	Pitcher	212	5	4				PG1)348,I; TPD)7.8
1431	Covered Vase	305	1	1				
1432	Compote	171	4	8				
1433	Decanter	182	3	6				PG1)348,L; TPD)7.8
1433	Tumbler							PG1)348,L
1434	Cruet	178	4	6				
1435	Centerpiece	147	2	3				
1436	Salt	217	2	5				
1437	Nut Dish	211	1	16				
1438	Salt	217	2	6				
1439	Nut Dish	211	1	17				
1440	Cruet	178	4	7				
1441	Cruet	178	4	8				
1442	Nut Dish	211	2	1				
1443	Cologne	243	3	2				
1444	Sugar & Creamer	234	4	13,14				
1445	Sugar & Creamer	234	5	1,2				
1446	Compote	171	4	9	$60	VDS	ebay-02/03	
1447	Tray	158	3	4				
1448	Decanter	182	4	1				
1449	Lamp	200	2	2				
1450	Centerpiece	147	2	4				
1451	Vase	260	1	2				
1452	Vase	260	1	3	$1560	Blue Aurene	ebay-05/05	
1453	Vase	260	1	4				
1454	Basket	139	5	4	$2245	Blue Calcite	ebay-03/00	PG1)VI C,F; PG2)54,A;
1454					$970	Gold Calcite	ebay-02/01	
1455	Puff Box	244	2	5				TPD)4.57
1455	Cologne	240	3	6	$990	Blue Aurene	EAC-10/90	PG2)57,B; RFR)9,1,C;
1455					$2310	Blue Aurene/Black stopper	EAC-10/90	JAS)150,TR,B:161,BR,C;
1455					$1210	Blue Aurene	EAC-10/90	TPD)4.57:7.73:8.56:10.145:10.146
1455					$770	Gold Aurene	EAC-07/91	
1455					$440	VDS/Celeste Blue stopper	EAC-02/92	
1455					$920	Blue Aurene	Sknr-01/96	
1455					$1430	Blue Aurene	EAC-04/96	
1455					$1100	Gold Aurene	EAC-04/96	
1455					$770	Gold Aurene	EAC-07/96	
1455					$805	Gold Aurene	Sknr-10/97	
1455					$805	Gold Aurene	Sknr-10/97	
1455					$990	Green Jade	EAC-07/98	
1455					$630	Gold Aurene	Sknr-03/99	
1455					$465	VDS	EAC-04/99	
1455					$400	VDS/Celeste Blue	Sknr-06/99	
1455					$400	VDS/Gold Ruby	ebay-12/99	
1455					$400	VDS/Pomona Green	ebay-12/99	
1455					$200	VDS/Green Jade	ebay-12/99	
1455					$290	VDS/threaded	ebay-01/00	
1455					$950	Gold Aurene	ebay-04/00	
1455					$1100	Blue Aurene	ebay-04/00	
1455					$480	VDS/Gold Ruby	ebay-04/00	
1455					$305	VDS/Green Jade	ebay-04/00	
1455					$290	VDS/Celeste Blue	Rago-09/00	

SHAPE NO.	ITEM	PAGE	COL	ROW	PRICE REALIZED	GLASS TYPE	AUCTION HOUSE	COMMENTS & PHOTO REFERENCES
1455					$260	Topaz	Rago-09/00	
1455					$230	VDS/Pomona Green	ebay-10/00	
1455					$195	VDS/Celeste Blue	ebay-01/01	
1455					$175	Colorless	ebay-01/01	
1455					$975	Gold Aurene	Sknr-02/01	
1455					$450	VDS/Celeste Blue	EAC-04/01	
1455					$350	Green Jade	ebay-05/01	
1455					$475	Rosaline/Alabaster	ebay-06/01	
1455					$880	Gold Aurene	Cott-08/01	
1455					$825	Rosaline/Alabaster	Cott-08/01	
1455					$770	Green Jade	Cott-08/01	
1455					$350	VDS	ebay-08/01	
1455					$225	VDS/Amethyst	ebay-10/01	
1455					$200	Threaded VDS	ebay-11/01	Blue threads and blue stopper
1455					$225	VDS/Cintra	ebay-11/01	Gold Ruby Cintra stopper
1455					$170	VDS/Green Jade	ebay-12/01	
1455					$310	VDS/Green Jade	ebay-03/02	
1455					$630	Gold Aurene	JDJ-05/02	
1455					$265	VDS/Gold Ruby Cintra	ebay-05/02	Gold Ruby Cintra stopper
1455					$450	Colorless/Silver deposit	ebay-05/02	Marked "Alvin"
1455					$675	Rosaline/Alabaster	ebay-07/02	
1455					$200	VDS/Celeste Blue stopper	ebay-07/02	
1455					$225	VDS/Selenium Red stop.	ebay-07/02	
1455					$310	VDS/Gold Ruby Cintra	ebay-07/02	
1455					$375	Aqua Marine	ebay-08/02	
1455					$340	Light Blue Jade	ebay-10/02	Stopper missing
1455					$293	Light Blue Jade/Flint White	ebay-11/02	Flint White stopper
1455					$655	Gold Aurene	ebay-11/02	
1455					$455	Selenium Red	ebay-11/02	
1455					$355	VDS/Pomona stopper	ebay-11/02	
1455					$380	VDS/Amethyst stopper	ebay-11/02	
1455					$560	VDS/Pomona stopper	ebay-11/02	
1455					$475	VDS/Gold Ruby Cintra	Cinc-11/02	
1455					$460	Blue Aurene	ebay-12/02	
1455					$255	Pomona Green	ebay-01/03	
1455					$925	Gold Aurene	EAC-01/03	
1455					$150	VDS	ebay-02/03	
1455					$355	VDS/Green Jade	ebay-03/03	Green Jade stopper
1455					$585	VDS/Green Jade	ebay-03/03	Green Jade stopper
1455					$425	VDS/Light Blue Jade	ebay-03/03	Light Blue Jade stopper
1455					$510	VDS/Celeste Blue	ebay-05/03	Celeste Blue stopper
1455					$900	Gold Aurene	ebay-05/03	
1455					$920	Colorless/Red threaded	EAC-06/03	Gold Ruby Cintra stopper
1455					$420	Green Jade/Alabaster	ebay-06/03	
1455					$345	VDS/Black threaded	ebay-07/03	Black stopper
1455					$205	VDS/Celeste Blue stopper	ebay-08/03	
1455					$700	Gold Aurene	ebay-10/03	
1455					$515	Green Jade/Alabaster	JDJ-11/03	Alabaster stopper
1455					$2530	Blue Aurene/flower stopper	JDJ-11/03	Orange and Black flower stopper
1455					$430	VDS	EAC-11/03	
1455					$535	Rosaline/Alabaster	ebay-12/03	Alabaster stopper
1455					$355	VDS/Pomona Green	ebay-02/04	Pomona Green stopper
1455					$350	VDS/French Blue	ebay-03/04	French Blue stopper
1455					$455	VDS/Green threaded	ebay-03/04	Pomona Green stopper
1455					$480	VDS/Green threaded	ebay-03/04	Pomona Green stopper
1455					$625	Gold Aurene	ebay-05/04	
1455					$250	VDS/Pomona stopper	ebay-06/04	
1455					$760	Ivory/Black stopper	ebay-06/04	
1455					$790	Gold Aurene	ebay-06/04	
1455					$390	VDS/Gold Ruby Cintra	ebay-07/04	Gold Ruby Cintra stopper
1455					$225	VDS/Pomona Green	ebay-09/04	Pomona Green stopper
1455					$1225	Blue Aurene	Tway-09/04	
1455					$285	VDS/Pomona Green	ebay-09/04	Pomona Green stopper
1455					$415	Gold Aurene	ebay-09/04	Atomizer with bulb.
1455					$255	VDS/Gold Ruby Cintra	ebay-10/04	Gold Ruby Cintra stopper
1455					$265	VDS	ebay-10/04	
1455					$220	Gold Aurene	EAC-10/04	Stopper missing
1455					$525	Colorless/Alvin silver	ebay-11/04	
1455					$95	Colorless	ebay-02/05	
1455					$330	Colorless/Silver deposit	ebay-03/05	Marked "Alvin"
1455					$600	Gold Aurene	ebay-04/05	
1455					$170	VDS	ebay-05/05	
1455					$270	VDS/Celeste Blue stopper	ebay-05/05	
1455					$350	VDS/Gold Ruby Cintra	ebay-06/05	Gold Ruby Cintra stopper

SHAPE NO.	ITEM	PAGE	COL	ROW	PRICE REALIZED	GLASS TYPE	AUCTION HOUSE	COMMENTS & PHOTO REFERENCES
1455					$355	VDS/Gold Ruby Cintra	ebay-07/05	Gold Ruby Cintra stopper
1455					$1265	Blue Aurene	EAC-07/05	
1455					$460	VDS/Celeste Blue stopper	EAC-07/05	
1455					$920	Wisteria	EAC-07/05	
1455					$805	VDS/Gold Ruby Cintra	EAC-07/05	Gold Ruby Cintra stopper
1456	Vase	260	1	5				
1457	Goblet	190	3	8				
1458	Vase	260	1	6				
1459	Lamp	200	2	3				TPD)4.66
1460	Soap Dish	245	4	1				
1461	Cologne	240	3	7				ACR)COLOR 2,T,C; TPD)10.145
1462	Ash Tray	137	1	4				
1463	Sugar & Creamer	234	5	3,4				
1464	Sugar & Creamer	234	5	5,6				
1465	Bowl	141	3	8				
1466	Tray	158	3	5				
1467	Vase	260	1	7				
1468	Basket	139	5	5				
1469	Decanter	182	4	2				
1470	Decanter	182	4	3				
1471	Decanter	182	4	4				
1472	Decanter	182	4	5				
1473	Decanter	182	4	6				
1474	Decanter	182	4	7				
1475	Decanter	182	4	8				
1476	Decanter	182	5	1				
1477	Decanter	182	5	2				
1479	Decanter	182	5	3				
1480	Decanter	182	5	4				
1481	Decanter	182	5	5				
1482	Sugar & Creamer	234	5	7,8				
1483	Sugar & Creamer	234	5	9,10	$130	Pomona Green	ebay-12/99	
1484	Vase	260	2	1				
1485	Goblet	190	4	1				ACR)133,240
1486	Goblet	190	4	2				
1487	Goblet	190	4	3				
1489	Goblet	190	4	4				
1490	Bowl	141	3	9				
1491	Sugar & Creamer	234	5	11,12				
1492	Sugar & Creamer	234	6	1,2				PG1)350,E
1493	Spoon Holder	177	3	1				PG1)350,E
1494	Spoon Holder	177	3	2				PG1)350,F
1495	Candlestick							PG1)350,G
1495	Pitcher	212	5	5				PG1)350,F
1496	Candlestick	160	3	8				TPD)7.6
1497	Goblet	190	4	5				TPD)7.70
1498	Compote	171	4	10				
1499	Bowl	141	3	10				PG1)350,G; TPD)7.6
1500	Cologne	240	3	8				TPD)10.145
1501	Basket	139	5	6				
1502	Cruet	178	4	9				
1503	Tray	158	3	6				
1504	Goblet	190	4	6				
1505	Hair Receiver	245	2	2				
1506	Goblet	190	4	7				
1507	Goblet	190	4	8				
1508	Tray	158	3	7				
1509	Candlestick	160	4	1				TPD)7.71
1510	Compote	171	5	1				
1511	Spoon Holder	177	3	3				
1512	Mayonnaise Bowl	210	3	6				
1513	Vase	260	2	2	$225	Threaded VDS	ebay-01/00	
1514	Decanter	182	5	6				
1515	Puff Box	244	2	6	$850	Blue Aurene	EAC-10/98	TPD)7.72
1516	Cruet	178	4	10				
1517	Jar	209	2	1				
1518	Jar	209	2	2				
1519	Jar	209	2	3				
1520	Jar	209	2	4				
1521	Cruet	178	5	1				
1522	Pitcher	212	5	6				
1523	Pitcher	212	5	7	$880	Gold Aurene	EAC-10/93	
1524	Pitcher	212	5	8				
1525	Celery	158	3	8				

SHAPE NO.	ITEM	PAGE	COL	ROW	PRICE REALIZED	GLASS TYPE	AUCTION HOUSE	COMMENTS & PHOTO REFERENCES
1526	Sherbet	216	4	4				
1527	Sugar & Creamer	234	6	3,4				
1528	Ash Tray	137	1	5				
1529	Spooner	233	1	5				
1530	Champagne							MDK)71
1530					$190	Colorless Engraved	ebay-03/02	Engraved in Sinclaire's "Adams" pattern
1530	Goblet	190	4	9	$285	Colorless Engraved	ebay-03/02	Engraved in Sinclaire's "Adams" pattern
1531	Goblet	190	5	1				
1532	Compote	171	5	2				
1533	Nappie	233	2	4				
1533	Tray	158	3	9				This number is an error, see #1538.
1534	Nappie	233	2	5				
1535	Nappie	233	2	6				
1536	Cake Plate	158	1	3				
1537	Bowl	141	3	11				
1538	Tray	158	3	9				This shape shown as #1533 in Gardner.
1539	Pitcher	213	1	1				
1540	Cake Plate	158	1	4				TPD)7.74
1541	Jar	210	1	9				
1542	Jar	210	1	10				
1543	Bowl	141	3	12				
1544	Jar	209	5	4				
1545	Jar	209	5	5				
1546	Compote	171	5	3				
1547	Punch Cup	216	1	10				
1548	Punch Cup	216	1	11				
1549	Tea Cup	216	3	1				
1550	Tea Cup	216	3	2				
1551	Tea Cup	216	3	3				
1552	Bowl	141	3	13				
1553	Spoon Holder	177	3	4				
1554	Puff Box	244	2	7	$425	Gold Aurene	ebay-01/05	TPD)7.72
1554½	Spoon Holder	177	3	5				
1555	Sugar Shaker	217	6	4				
1556	Puff Box	244	2	8				
1557	Puff Box	244	2	9				
1558	Puff Box	244	2	10				
1559	Compote	171	5	4				
1560	Bowl	141	4	1				
1561	Bowl	141	4	2				
1562	Cake Plate	158	1	5				
1563	Vase	260	2	3				
1564	Jar	209	2	5				
1565	Jar	209	2	6				
1566	Pin Tray							See New Drawings section
1567	Vase	260	2	4				
1568	Decanter	183	1	1				
1569	Cruet	178	5	2				
1570	Decanter	183	1	2				
1571	Decanter	183	1	3				
1572	Decanter	183	1	4				
1573	Decanter	183	1	5				
1574	Decanter	183	2	1				
1575	Decanter	183	2	2				
1576	Decanter	183	2	3				
1577	Decanter	183	2	4				
1578	Puff Box	244	2	11				
1579	Bonbon	233	5	19				
1580	Toothpick Holder	189	3	5				
1581	Sugar & Creamer	234	6	5,6				
1582	Sugar & Creamer	234	6	7,8				
1583	Toothpick Holder	189	3	6				
1584	Decanter	183	2	5				
1585	Vase	260	2	5	$605	Gold Aurene	Cinc-12/99	
1586	Vase	260	2	6				
1587	Sugar Shaker	217	6	5				
1588	Centerpiece	147	2	5				
1589	Decanter	183	3	1				
1590	Basket	140	1	1				
1591	Sugar Shaker	217	6	6				
1592	Sugar & Creamer	234	6	9,10				
1593	Sugar & Creamer	234	6	11,12				
1594	Cruet	178	5	3				
1595	Pitcher	213	1	2				

SHAPE NO.	ITEM	PAGE	COL	ROW	PRICE REALIZED	GLASS TYPE	AUCTION HOUSE	COMMENTS & PHOTO REFERENCES
1596	Toothpick Holder	189	3	7				
1597	Vase	260	2	7				
1598	Sugar & Creamer	234	6	13,14				
1599	Bowl	141	4	3				
1600	Vase	260	2	8				
1601	Sugar & Creamer	235	1	1,2				
1602	Goblet	190	5	2				
1603	Vase	260	3	1				
1604	Jar	210	2	1				
1605	Vase	260	3	2				
1606	Cruet	178	5	4				
1607	Candlestick	160	4	2				
1608	Cruet	178	5	5				
1609	Goblet	190	5	3				
1610	Pitcher	213	1	3				
1611	Pitcher	213	1	4				
1612	Pitcher	213	1	5				
1613	Bowl	141	4	4				
1614	Bowl	141	4	5				
1615	Nut Dish	211	2	2				TPD)7.74
1616	Vase	260	3	3				
1617	Candlestick	160	4	3				
1618	Oyster Cocktail	210	4	8				
1619	Oyster Cocktail	210	4	9				
1620	Vase	260	3	4				
1621	Puff Box	244	2	12				
1622	Decanter	183	3	2				
1622	Wine	183	3	2				
1623	Sugar & Creamer	235	1	3,4				
1624								Same as 1624½ without ring on neck.
1624½	Decanter	183	3	3				
1625	Centerpiece	147	3	1				
1626	Decanter	183	3	4				
1627	Vase	260	3	5				
1628	Sherbet	216	4	5				
1629	Goblet	190	5	4				
1630	Decanter	183	3	5				
1631	Pitcher	213	1	6				
1632	Compote	171	5	5				
1633	Vase	260	3	6				
1634	Vase	260	3	7				
1635	Pitcher	213	1	7				
1636	Cruet	178	5	6				
1637	Puff Box	244	2	13				TPD)7.72
1638	Tray	158	3	10	$346	Gold Aurene	ebay-01/05	
1638					$225	Gold Calcite	ebay-01/05	
1638					$360	Blue Calcite	ebay-03/05	
1639	Jar	209	2	7				
1640	Fern Bowl	237	3	1				
1641	Fern Bowl	237	3	2				
1642	Decanter	183	3	6				
1643	Compote	171	5	6	$1850	Gold Aurene	ebay-12/02	
1644	Vase	260	4	1				
1645	Vase	260	4	2				
1646	Cologne	240	3	9				TPD)7.73
1647	Centerpiece	147	3	2				
1648	Vase	260	4	3				
1649	Lamp	200	3	1				
1650	Vase	260	4	4				
1651	Vase	260	4	5				
1652	Vase	260	4	6				
1653	Vase	260	4	7				TPD)7.12
1654	Vase	260	5	1				
1655	Cruet	178	5	7				
1656	Decanter	183	4	1				
1657	Decanter	183	4	2				
1658	Decanter	183	4	3				
1659	Decanter	183	4	4				
1660	Decanter	183	4	5				
1661	Cruet	178	5	8				
1662	Cruet	178	5	9				
1663	Decanter	183	4	6				
1664	Decanter	183	4	7				
1665	Decanter	183	4	8				

SHAPE NO.	ITEM	PAGE	COL	ROW	PRICE REALIZED	GLASS TYPE	AUCTION HOUSE	COMMENTS & PHOTO REFERENCES
1666	Vase	260	5	2				
1667	Decanter	183	5	1				
1667	Perfume				$275	VDS	Cott-08/01	
1667					$290	VDS	ebay-01/04	
1667					$220	VDS	ebay-06/04	
1667					$180	VDS	ebay-07/04	
1667					$160	VDS	ebay-10/04	
1667					$215	VDS	ebay-12/04	
1668	Bowl	141	4	6				
1669	Flower Pot	237	2	6				
1670	Cologne	240	3	10				PG2)90,B; JAS)170,B,B; TPD)7.73
1671	Puff Box	244	2	14				TPD)7.73
1672	Flower Pot Stand	237	2	7				
1673	Tray	158	3	11				
1674	Cake Plate	158	1	6				
1675	Vase	260	5	3				
1676	Tray	158	3	12				
1677	Vase	260	5	4				
1678	Vase	260	5	5				
1679	Sherbet	216	4	6	$375	Wisteria	Sknr-03/99	TPD)7.75
1680	Nut Dish	211	2	3				
1681	Nut Dish	211	2	4				
1682	Nut Dish	211	2	5				
1683	Nut Dish	211	2	6				
1684	Sugar & Creamer	235	1	5,6				
1685	Vase	260	5	6				
1686	Vase	260	5	7				
1687	Cruet	178	5	10				
1688	Cruet	178	5	11				
1689	Sugar & Creamer	235	1	7,8				
1690	Sugar & Creamer	235	1	9,10				
1691	Sugar & Creamer	235	1	11,12				
1692	Cordial				$50	VDS	ebay-09/03	
1692					$50	Celeste Blue	ebay-10/03	Colorless stem
1692					$40	VDS	ebay-11/04	
1692	Finger Bowl				$45	Celeste Blue	ebay-12/02	Bowl only, no underplate
1692					$40	Celeste Blue	ebay-01/03	Bowl only, no underplate
1692	Goblet	190	5	5	$35	Celeste Blue	Sknr-05/96	PG1)XXVIII A,C&E; ACR)COLOR 4,B,C
1692					$70	Celeste Blue	ebay-11/99	JAS)167,TL,A; MDK)38
1692					$50	Amethyst	ebay-03/00	
1692					$315	Celeste Blue	ebay-04/00	
1692					$150	VDS (engraved)	ebay-03/01	
1692					$130	Celeste Blue	ebay-04/01	
1692					$50	Pomona Green/Topaz	ebay-09/01	
1692					$60	Celeste Blue	ebay-03/02	
1692					$115	Amethyst	ebay-04/02	Colorless stem
1692					$150	Amethyst/Celeste Blue	ebay-04/02	Celeste Blue stem
1692					$105	Amethyst/Colorless stem	ebay-05/02	
1692					$125	Gold Calcite	ebay-06/02	
1692					$135	VDS	ebay-11/02	
1692					$100	Celeste Blue	ebay-12/02	
1692					$125	Celeste Blue	ebay-12/02	Colorless stem
1692					$95	VDS monogrammed	ebay-01/03	
1692					$165	Celeste Blue	ebay-01/03	Colorless stem
1692					$55	Amethyst/Colorless stem	ebay-03/03	
1692					$65	Amethyst/Colorless stem	ebay-03/03	
1692					$65	Amethyst/Colorless stem	ebay-03/03	
1692					$80	Amethyst/Colorless stem	ebay-03/03	
1692					$90	Pomona Green/Colorless	ebay-03/03	Colorless stem
1692					$100	Celeste Blue/Colorless	ebay-05/03	Colorless stem
1692					$70	Amber/Colorless stem	ebay-05/03	
1692					$35	Topaz	ebay-11/03	
1692					$170	Celeste Blue/Colorless	JDJ-11/03	Colorless stem
1692					$95	Amethyst/Colorless stem	ebay-12/03	
1692					$95	Amethyst/Colorless stem	ebay-01/04	
1692					$100	Celeste Blue/Colorless	ebay-02/04	Colorless stem
1692					$60	Celeste Blue/Colorless	ebay-04/04	Colorless stem
1692					$55	Amethyst/Colorless	ebay-04/04	Colorless stem
1692					$55	Flemish Blue	ebay-05/04	
1692					$50	Celeste Blue/Colorless	ebay-05/04	Colorless stem
1692					$40	Topaz	ebay-05/04	
1692					$200	VDS (E)	ebay-05/04	
1692					$100	Amethyst/Colorless stem	ebay-08/04	
1692					$105	VDS	ebay-09/04	

SHAPE NO.	ITEM	PAGE	COL	ROW	PRICE REALIZED	GLASS TYPE	AUCTION HOUSE	COMMENTS & PHOTO REFERENCES
1692					$30	Topaz	ebay-10/04	
1692					$45	Amethyst/Colorless stem	ebay-10/04	
1692					$50	Citron Yellow	ebay-10/04	
1692					$35	Topaz	ebay-01/05	
1692					$65	Celeste Blue/Colorless	ebay-03/05	Colorless stem
1692					$100	VDS (E)	ebay-03/05	Signed "Hawkes"
1692					$115	VDS (E)	ebay-03/05	Signed "Hawkes"
1692					$70	Celeste Blue/Colorless	ebay-06/05	
1692	Sherbet				$95	Celeste Blue	ebay-08/01	
1692					$70	VDS	ebay-05/02	
1692					$20	Olive Green	ebay-10/02	
1692					$65	Celeste Blue/Colorless	ebay-03/03	
1692					$295	Gold Calcite	ebay-05/03	
1692					$30	Topaz	ebay-05/03	
1692					$45	Amethyst/Colorless stem	ebay-06/03	
1692					$50	Celeste Blue/Colorless	ebay-12/03	Colorless stem
1692					$45	Amethyst/Colorless stem	ebay-01/04	
1692					$50	Amethyst/Colorless stem	ebay-01/04	
1692					$55	Amethyst/Colorless stem	ebay-01/04	
1692					$55	Amethyst/Colorless stem	ebay-01/04	
1692					$90	VDS	ebay-01/05	
1692					$80	VDS	ebay-04/05	
1692					$105	Blue Calcite	ebay-05/05	
1692	Wine				$75	Celeste Blue	ebay-12/01	
1692					$50	VDS	ebay-11/04	
1693	Vase	260	5	8				
1694	Decanter	183	5	2				
1695	Puff Box	244	3	1				
1696	Vase	260	5	9				
1698	Vase	261	1	1				
1699	Nut Dish	211	2	7				
1700	Vase	261	1	2				
1701	Sugar & Creamer	235	1	13,14				
1702	Compote	171	5	7				
1703	Bowl	141	4	7				
1704	Bonbon							See New Drawings section
1705	Compote	171	5	8				
1706	Nut Dish	211	2	8				
1707	Cologne	240	4	1				
1708	Toothpick Holder	189	3	8				
1709	Nut Dish	211	2	9				
1710	Nut Dish	211	2	10				
1711	Nut Dish	211	2	11				
1712	Nut Dish	211	2	12				
1713	Goblet	190	5	6				
1714	Nut Dish	211	2	13				
1715	Bowl	141	4	8				
1716	Pitcher	213	1	8				
1717	Pitcher	213	2	1				
1718	Pitcher	213	2	2				
1719	Pitcher	213	2	3				
1720	Decanter	183	5	3				
1721	Decanter	183	5	4				
1722	Decanter	183	5	5				
1723	Decanter	183	5	6				
1724	Bowl	141	4	9				
1725	Decanter	183	5	7				
1726	Decanter	184	1	1				
1727	Decanter	184	1	2				
1728	Decanter	184	1	3				
1729	Decanter	184	1	4				
1730	Decanter	184	1	5				
1731	Vase	261	1	3				
1732	Vase	261	1	4				
1733	Vase	261	1	5				
1734	Vase	261	1	6				
1735	Vase	261	1	7				
1736	Vase	261	1	8				
1737	Vase	261	2	1				
1738	Vase	261	2	2				
1739	Decanter	184	1	6				
1740	Vase	261	2	3				
1741	Sugar & Creamer	235	2	1,2				
1742	Vase	261	2	4				

SHAPE NO.	ITEM	PAGE	COL	ROW	PRICE REALIZED	GLASS TYPE	AUCTION HOUSE	COMMENTS & PHOTO REFERENCES
1743	Sugar & Creamer	235	2	3,4				
1743½	Nut Dish	211	3	1				
1744	Nut Dish	211	3	2				
1745	Sugar & Creamer	235	2	5,6				
1746	Tray	158	3	13				
1747	Limousine Vase	206	2	2				
1748	Limousine Vase	206	2	3				
1749	Limousine Vase	206	2	4				
1750	Limousine Vase	206	2	5				
1751	Vase	261	2	5				
1752	Vase	261	2	6				
1753	Bowl	141	4	11				
1754	Vase	261	3	1				
1755	Vase	261	3	2				
1756	Vase	261	3	3				
1757	Vase	261	3	4				
1758	Coffee Pot	189	3	1	$70	Colorless	ebay-04/05	"Pyrex"
1759	Sugar & Creamer	235	2	7,8				
1760	Cruet	179	1	1				
1761	Sugar & Creamer	235	2	9,10				
1762	Sugar & Creamer	235	2	11,12				
1763	Sugar & Creamer	235	3	1,2	$70	VDS (E)	ebay-03/05	Signed "Hawkes," sugar bowl only
1764	Limousine Vase	206	2	6				
1765	Limousine Vase	206	2	7				
1766	Jar	210	2	2				
1767	Vase	261	3	5				
1768	Decanter	184	2	1				
1769	Decanter	184	2	2				
1770	Vase	261	3	6				
1771	Decanter	184	2	3				
1772	Vase	261	3	7				
1773	Limousine Vase	206	3	1				
1774	Pitcher	213	2	4				
1775	Sugar & Creamer	235	3	3,4				
1776	Pitcher	213	2	5				
1777	Decanter	184	2	4				
1778	Vase	261	4	1				
1779	Jar	210	2	3				
1780	Vase	261	4	2				
1781	Goblet	190	5	7				
1782	Goblet	190	5	8				
1783	Goblet	190	5	9				
1784	Goblet	190	6	1				
1785	Vase	261	4	3				
1786	Decanter	184	2	5				
1787	Decanter	184	2	6				
1788	Cigar Jar	138	4	11				
1789	Vase	261	4	4				
1790	Limousine Vase	206	3	2				
1791	Insert	210	5	4				
1792	Bowl	141	4	10	$195	Colorless	ebay-02/05	Draped
1793	Misc.	211	4	8				
1794	Nut Dish	211	3	3				
1795	Misc.	211	4	9				
1796	Misc.	211	4	10				
1797	Misc.	211	5	1				
1798	Limousine Vase	206	3	3				
1799	Limousine Vase	206	3	4				
1800	Decanter	184	2	7				
1801	Decanter	184	3	1				
1802	Decanter	184	3	2				
1803	Decanter	184	3	3				
1804	Decanter	184	3	4				
1805	Decanter	184	3	5				
1806	Decanter	184	3	6				
1807	Jar	210	2	4				
1808	Decanter	184	4	1				
1809	Decanter	184	4	2				
1810	Limousine Vase	206	3	5				
1811	Limousine Vase	206	3	6				
1812	Limousine Vase	206	3	7				
1813	Decanter	184	4	3				
1814	Decanter	184	4	4				
1815	Decanter	184	4	5				

SHAPE NO.	ITEM	PAGE	COL	ROW	PRICE REALIZED	GLASS TYPE	AUCTION HOUSE	COMMENTS & PHOTO REFERENCES
1816	Vase	261	4	5				
1817	Ice Tub	177	4	5				
1818	Decanter	184	4	6	$1210	Gold Aurene	EAC-07/97	
1818	Perfume				$960	Blue Aurene	EAC-02/92	TPD)10.145
1818					$910	Gold Aurene	ebay-01/00	
1818					$950	Gold Aurene	ebay-12/00	
1818					$575	Gold Aurene	Jack-06/01	
1818					$450	Blue Aurene	ebay-08/01	
1818					$690	Gold Aurene	Jack-06/02	
1818					$356	Blue Aurene	ebay-06/02	
1818					$610	Gold Aurene	ebay-05/04	
1818					$305	Colorless (silver overlay)	ebay-06/04	
1818					$650	Blue Aurene	ebay-04/05	
1819	Jar	210	2	5				
1820	Finger Bowl	189	1	6				
1821	Sugar & Creamer	235	3	5,6	$50	VDS	ebay-02/02	Sugar bowl only
1821					$200	VDS	ebay-10/04	Signed "Hawkes"
1822	Sugar & Creamer	235	3	7,8				
1823	Sugar & Creamer	235	3	9,10				
1824	Sugar & Creamer	235	3	11,12				
1825	Sugar & Creamer	235	3	13,14				
1826	Sugar & Creamer	235	4	1,2				
1827	Jar	209	2	8				
1828	Jar	209	2	9				
1829	Jar	209	2	10				
1830	Jar	209	2	11	$305	VDS/Pear finial	ebay-07/02	ACR)COLOR 4,T,D
1830					$135	Citron Yellow/Fruit finial	ebay-03/04	
1830					$390	VDS/Pear finial	ebay-01/05	
1830					$220	Citron Yellow/Fruit final	ebay-02/05	
1831	Limousine Vase	206	3	8				
1832	Limousine Vase	206	4	1				
1833	Sugar & Creamer	235	4	3,4				
1834	Pitcher	213	2	6				
1835	Jar	210	2	6				
1836	Decanter	184	4	7				
1837	Sugar & Creamer	235	4	5,6				
1838	Bowl	141	4	12				
1839	Decanter	184	4	8				
1840	Compote	171	5	9				
1841	Nut Dish	211	3	4				This shape is shown as #1844 in Gardner.
1842	Decanter	184	5	1				
1843	Vase	261	4	6				
1844	Nut Dish	211	3	4				This number is an error, see #1841.
1844	Vase	261	4	7				
1845	Oyster Cocktail	210	4	10				
1846	Jar	210	2	7				
1847	Vase	261	5	1				
1848	Condiment Set	179	3	7				
1849	Vase	261	5	2				
1850	Jar	210	2	8				
1851	Jar	209	2	12				
1852	Compote	172	1	1				
1853	Vase	261	5	3				
1854	Limousine Vase	206	4	2				
1855	Insert	210	5	5				
1856	Cold Cream Jar	243	6	4				
1857	Cologne	240	4	2				
1858	Jar	209	5	6				
1859	Pitcher	213	2	7				
1860	Compote	172	1	2				
1861	Cologne	243	3	3				
1862	Compote	172	1	3				
1863	Punch Cup	216	2	1	$25	Spanish Green	ebay-01/02	
1864	Vase	261	5	4				
1865	Tea Cup	216	3	4				
1866	Punch Cup	216	2	2				
1867	Vase	261	5	5				
1868	Vase	261	5	6				
1869	Pitcher	213	3	1				
1870	Compote	172	1	4				
1872	Jar	209	3	1				
1873	Salt	217	2	7				
1874	Salt	217	2	8				
1875	Insert	210	5	6				

SHAPE NO.	ITEM	PAGE	COL	ROW	PRICE REALIZED	GLASS TYPE	AUCTION HOUSE	COMMENTS & PHOTO REFERENCES
1876	Tray	158	3	14				
1877	Limousine Vase	206	4	3				
1878	Basket	140	1	2				
1879	Limousine Vase	206	4	4				
1880	Cologne	243	5	6				
1881	Cologne	243	5	7				
1882	Bowl	141	5	1				
1883	Vase	262	1	1				
1884	Jar	209	3	2				
1885	Vase	262	1	2				
1886	Goblet	190	6	2				
1887	Jar	209	3	3				
1888	Nut Dish	211	3	5				
1889	Sugar & Creamer	235	4	7,8				
1890	Pin Tray	158	3	15				
1891	Mayonnaise Bowl	210	3	4				
1892	Decanter	184	5	2				
1893	Cologne	243	3	4				
1894	Goblet	190	6	3				
1895	Compote	172	1	5				
1896	Vase	262	1	3				
1897	Vase	262	1	4				
1898	Tray	158	3	16				
1899	Tray	158	3	17				
1900	Vase	262	1	5				
1901	Vase	262	1	6	$1540	Silverina	EAC-04/98	
1902	Vase	262	1	7				
1903	Compote	172	1	6				
1904	Vase	262	2	1				
1905	Vase	262	2	2				
1906	Puff Box	244	3	2				
1907	Vase	262	2	3				
1908	Tray	158	3	18				
1909	Tray	158	3	19				
1910	Pitcher	213	3	2	$1500	Gold Aurene	ebay-05/02	"Haviland" signature
1911	Cruet	179	1	2				
1912	Vase	262	2	4				
1913	Limousine Vase	206	4	5				
1914	Cologne	240	4	3				
1915	Puff Box	244	3	3				
1916	Jar	209	3	4				
1917	Jar	209	3	5				
1918	Vase	262	2	5				
1919	Limousine Vase	206	4	6				
1920	Nut Dish	211	3	6				
1921	Compote	172	1	7				
1922	Jar	209	3	6				
1923	Jar	209	3	7				
1924	Tray	158	3	20				
1925	Vase	262	2	6				
1926	Tray	158	3	21				
1927	Limousine Vase	206	4	7				
1928	Jar	209	3	8				
1930	Cake Plate	158	1	7				
1931	Sugar & Creamer	235	4	9,10				
1932	Decanter	184	5	3				
1933	Pitcher	213	3	3				
1934	Pitcher	213	3	4				
1935	Plate	158	1	8				
1936	Decanter	184	5	4				
1937	Decanter	184	5	5				
1938	Vase	262	2	7				
1939	Vase	262	3	1				
1940	Vase	262	3	2				
1941	Vase	262	3	3				
1942	Vase	262	3	4				
1943	Vase	262	3	5				
1944	Limousine Vase	206	4	8				
1945	Vase	262	3	6				
1946	Limousine Vase	206	5	1				
1947	Vase	262	3	7				
1948	Cologne	240	4	4				
1949	Cologne	240	4	5				
1950	Compote	172	1	8				

SHAPE NO.	ITEM	PAGE	COL	ROW	PRICE REALIZED	GLASS TYPE	AUCTION HOUSE	COMMENTS & PHOTO REFERENCES
1951	Limousine Vase	206	5	2				TPD)4.55
1952	Vase	262	3	8	$330	Gold Calcite	EAC-04/93	PG1)VI C,B; RLG)153,287
1952					$375	Gold Calcite	Sknr-10/96	
1952					$650	Gold Calcite	Ogal-09/00	
1952					$860	Blue Calcite	JDJ-11/01	
1952					$540	Gold Calcite	ebay-03/02	
1952					$300	Gold Calcite	ebay-03/03	
1952					$350	Gold Calcite	J&W-09/03	
1952					$305	Gold Calcite	ebay-12/03	
1952					$720	Gold Calcite	ebay-07/04	
1952					$225	Gold Calcite	ebay-12/04	
1952					$260	Gold Calcite	ebay-01/05	
1952					$310	Gold Calcite	ebay-06/05	
1953	Vase	262	4	1				RFR)12,3,C
1954	Tray	158	4	1				
1955	Goblet	190	6	4				
1956	Tray	158	4	2				
1957	Coffee Pot	189	3	2	$45	Colorless	ebay-05/02	"Pyrex"
1957					$60	Colorless	ebay-04/05	"Pyrex"
1958	Pitcher	213	3	5				
1959	Bowl	141	5	2	$375	Gold Calcite	EAC-07/05	
1960	Vase	262	4	2				
1961	Centerpiece	147	3	3				
1962	Decanter	184	5	6				
1963	Decanter	184	5	7				
1964	Decanter	185	1	1				
1965	Vase	262	4	3				
1966	Puff Box	244	3	4				
1967	Candlestick	160	4	4				
1968	Tray	158	4	3				
1969	Tray	158	4	4				
1970	Bell	237	3	3				
1971	Vase	262	4	4				
1972	Vase	262	4	5				
1973	Dresser Set	245	3	1				
1974	Limousine Vase	206	5	3				
1975	Limousine Vase	206	5	4				
1976	Vase	262	4	6				
1977	Vase	262	4	7				
1978	Vase	262	5	1				
1979	Vase	262	5	2				
1980	Vase	262	5	3	$385	Gold Calcite	EAC-04/90	PG1)VI C,A; RFR)14,3,A; RLG)153,287
1980					$180	Gold Calcite	ebay-11/02	
1980					$180	Gold Calcite	ebay-11/02	
1980					$225	Gold Calcite	ebay-03/03	
1980					$285	Gold Calcite	ebay-02/05	
1981	Bowl	141	5	3	$225	VDS (E)	ebay-01/04	
1982	Bowl	141	5	4				
1983	Compote	172	1	9	$385	Gold Aurene	EAC-10/91	MDK)108
1983					$285	Aqua Marine	Sknr-01/97	
1983					$160	Cyprian	Tway-10/00	
1983					$150	Cyprian	ebay-10/01	
1983					$85	Citron Yellow	ebay-10/02	
1983					$160	Gold Calcite	ebay-02/03	
1983					$325	Rosaline/Alabaster	ebay-02/03	
1983					$80	Celeste Blue/Colorless	ebay-06/03	Colorless stem
1983					$350	Gold Aurene	ebay-09/04	
1983					$215	Gold Calcite	ebay-01/05	
1983					$75	VDS	ebay-04/05	
1983					$520	Blue Calcite	ebay-05/05	
1983					$175	Gold Calcite	ebay-05/05	
1983					$205	Gold Calcite	Cinc-06/05	
1983					$150	Gold Calcite	ebay-06/05	
1984	Finger Bowl	189	1	7	$90	VDS	Cinc-06/05	
1985	Cruet	179	1	3				
1986	Cruet	179	1	4				
1987	Cologne	240	4	6				
1988	Cologne	240	4	7				
1989	Tray	158	4	5				
1990	Limousine Vase	206	5	5				
1991	Limousine Vase	206	5	6				
1992	Limousine Vase	206	5	7				
1993	Limousine Vase	206	5	8				
1994	Limousine Vase	206	5	9				

SHAPE NO.	ITEM	PAGE	COL	ROW	PRICE REALIZED	GLASS TYPE	AUCTION HOUSE	COMMENTS & PHOTO REFERENCES
1995	Limousine Vase	207	1	1				
1996	Limousine Vase	207	1	2				
1997	Limousine Vase	207	1	3				
1998	Limousine Vase	207	1	3				
1999	Limousine Vase	207	1	5				
2000	Puff Box	244	3	5				
2001	Tray	158	4	6				
2002	Tray	158	4	7				
2003	Soap Dish	245	4	2				
2004	Vase	262	5	4				
2005	Vase	262	5	5				
2006	Ash Tray	137	1	6				
2007	Ash Tray	137	1	7				
2008	Tray	158	4	8				
2009	Tray	158	4	9				
2010	Vase	262	5	6	$850	Gold Aurene	ebay-10/04	
2010					$570	Gold Aurene	JDJ-06/05	
2011	Vase	262	5	7	$150	Green Jade/Alabaster	ebay-09/02	
2011					$225	Rosaline/Alabaster foot	ebay-05/04	
2012	Vase	263	1	1				
2013	Vase	263	1	2				
2014	Puff Box	244	3	6				
2015	Puff Box	244	3	7				
2016	Sherbet	216	4	7				
2017	Bowl	141	5	5				
2018	Compote	172	1	10	$210	VDS (E)	ebay-07/05	Signed "Hawkes"
2019	Plate	158	4	10	$10	Colorless/Gold Ruby thread	ebay-08/03	TPD)9.21
2019					$20	Spanish Green	ebay-10/04	
2020	Jar	209	3	9				
2021	Jar	209	3	10				
2022	Jar	209	3	11				
2023	Limousine Vase	207	1	6				
2024	Cruet	179	1	5				
2025	Decanter Set	185	1	2	$3000	Gold Aurene	ebay-12/01	TPD)4.23
2025	Cordial	185	1	2	$550	Blue Aurene	EAC-07/96	TPD)4.23
2025					$305	Gold Aurene	ebay-05/03	
2025					$720	Gold Aurene	EAC-04/05	
2025					$360	Blue Aurene	ebay-07/05	
2025					$385	Blue Aurene	ebay-07/05	
2026	Puff Box	244	3	8				
2027	Puff Box	244	3	9				
2028	Plate (8.5" Salad)	158	4	11	$175	Oriental Poppy	EAC-07/91	TPD)4.75:9.21; MDK)113
2028					$90	Mirror Black	JDJ-10/95	
2028					$300	VDS (FC)	JDJ-06/96	
2028					$40	Pomona Green	Sknr-01/98	
2028					$45	Celeste Blue (E)	Sknr-03/99	Engraved "Kensington"
2028					$160	Green Jade (E)	ebay-11/99	
2028					$75	Amber/Threaded	ebay-11/99	
2028					$85	Bristol Yellow	ebay-11/99	
2028					$55	Green Jade	ebay-11/99	
2028					$5700	Rouge Flambé	ebay-12/99	
2028					$110	Selenium Red	ebay-12/99	
2028					$260	Colorless Cut	ebay-02/00	
2028					$260	Gold Aurene	ebay-02/00	
2028					$95	Rosa	ebay-02/00	
2028					$65	Rosaline	ebay-02/00	
2028					$75	Topaz/Celeste Blue	ebay-02/00	
2028					$35	Green Jade	ebay-02/00	
2028					$650	Red/White Cluthra	ebay-03/00	
2028					$60	Gold Ruby	ebay-03/00	
2028					$225	Colorless Cut	ebay-04/00	
2028					$115	Rosaline	JDJ-05/00	
2028					$45	VDS	JDJ-05/00	
2028					$65	Green Jade	Sknr-06/00	
2028					$130	VDS/Coral Rim	ebay-01/01	
2028					$45	Amethyst	ebay-01/01	
2028					$155	Rosaline (FC)	ebay-01/01	
2028					$30	Colorless (E)	ebay-03/01	
2028					$125	Bristol Yellow/Black	ebay-03/01	
2028					$165	Oriental Poppy	ebay-04/01	
2028					$75	Colorless/Threaded	ebay-05/01	
2028					$30	Rosaline	JDJ-05/01	
2028					$200	Opal/Cintra	ebay-06/01	
2028					$30	Pomona Green	ebay-06/01	

SHAPE NO.	ITEM	PAGE	COL	ROW	PRICE REALIZED	GLASS TYPE	AUCTION HOUSE	COMMENTS & PHOTO REFERENCES
2028					$80	Rosaline	ebay-06/01	
2028					$80	Rosaline	ebay-07/01	
2028					$190	Gold Aurene	Cott-08/01	
2028					$410	Colorless/Gold Ruby	Cott-08/01	
2028					$165	VDS (Hawkes)	ebay-08/01	
2028					$60	Colorless/Rosa (E)	ebay-10/01	
2028					$200	Gold Aurene	ebay-10/01	
2028					$45	Colorless/Gold Ruby	ebay-10/01	
2028					$285	Gold Calcite (E)	JDJ-11/01	
2028					$170	Rosaline (FC)	JDJ-11/01	
2028					$170	Green Jade (FC)	JDJ-11/01	
2028					$65	Rosaline	ebay-11/01	
2028					$35	Amethyst	ebay-11/01	
2028					$80	Bristol Yellow (E)	ebay-11/01	
2028					$160	Rosaline (E)	ebay-12/01	
2028					$75	Gold Ruby	ebay-12/01	
2028					$90	Green Jade	ebay-12/01	
2028					$30	Rosaline	ebay-12/01	
2028					$20	Spanish Green	ebay-12/01	
2028					$85	Topaz/Celeste Blue Rim	ebay-01/02	
2028					$50	Rosaline	ebay-01/02	
2028					$100	Green Jade	ebay-02/02	
2028					$30	Spanish Green	ebay-02/02	
2028					$70	Bristol/Black threaded	ebay-03/02	
2028					$440	Gold Calcite Engraved	ebay-03/02	
2028					$155	Selenium Red	ebay-03/02	
2028					$90	Green Jade	ebay-03/02	
2028					$75	Selenium Red	ebay-03/02	
2028					$20	Spanish Green threaded	ebay-03/02	
2028					$670	Gold Aurene (10" dia.)	EAC-04/02	
2028					$110	Gold Aurene	ebay-04/02	
2028					$150	VDS (Hawkes)	ebay-04/02	
2028					$900	Rosaline/Alabaster (14")	JDJ-05/02	Engraved "10012" pattern
2028					$45	Amethyst	ebay-05/02	
2028					$55	Green Jade	ebay-05/02	
2028					$70	Rosa/Rosa rim	ebay-05/02	Engraved
2028					$75	Selenium Red	ebay-05/02	
2028					$50	Green Jade	ebay-06/02	
2028					$50	Selenium Red	ebay-06/02	
2028					$40	Topaz	ebay-06/02	
2028					$40	Colorless/Black threaded	ebay-06/02	
2028					$65	VDS/Coral rim	ebay-07/02	
2028					$45	Topaz/Celeste Blue rim	ebay-08/02	
2028					$40	Pomona Green	ebay-08/02	
2028					$55	Topaz/Celeste Blue rim	ebay-08/02	
2028					$100	Green Jade	ebay-09/02	
2028					$190	VDS with Blue threading	Ogal-09/02	
2028					$60	Topaz/Celeste Blue rim	ebay-10/02	
2028					$75	Rosaline	ebay-11/02	
2028					$40	Pomona Green	Free-11/02	
2028					$1080	Rosaline/Alabaster (FC)	JDJ-11/02	Engraved and 14"
2028					$40	VDS	ebay-11/02	
2028					$85	Celeste Blue	ebay-11/02	
2028					$40	Pomona Green	ebay-11/02	
2028					$75	Rosaline	ebay-11/02	
2028					$40	Topaz/Celeste Blue rim	Cinc-11/02	
2028					$90	Green Jade	ebay-12/02	
2028					$130	Green Jade (E)	ebay-12/02	Engraved "York"
2028					$75	Colorless/Gold Ruby	ebay-12/02	Gold Ruby machine threaded on rim
2028					$160	Gold Aurene	ebay-12/02	
2028					$45	Pomona Green	ebay-12/02	
2028					$35	Celeste Blue	ebay-01/03	
2028					$90	Rosa (E)	ebay-01/03	
2028					$90	Rosaline	EAC-01/03	
2028					$25	Pomona Green	ebay-01/03	
2028					$50	Spanish Green	ebay-02/03	
2028					$40	Rosaline	ebay-02/03	
2028					$80	Rosaline	ebay-02/03	
2028					$110	Rosaline	ebay-02/03	
2028					$400	Gold Aurene	Ogal-03/03	10" dia.
2028					$100	Opal/Amethyst Cintra rim	ebay-03/03	
2028					$100	Opal/Amethyst Cintra rim	ebay-03/03	
2028					$45	Spanish Green	ebay-03/03	
2028					$85	Rosa (E)	ebay-03/03	

SHAPE NO.	ITEM	PAGE	COL	ROW	PRICE REALIZED	GLASS TYPE	AUCTION HOUSE	COMMENTS & PHOTO REFERENCES
2028					$50	Opal/Amethyst Cintra	ebay-04/03	
2028					$45	Celeste Blue (E)	ebay-04/03	
2028					$30	Celeste Blue (E)	ebay-05/03	
2028					$45	VDS	ebay-05/03	
2028					$30	Colorless (E) Renwick	ebay-05/03	"Hand Wrought" signature
2028					$135	Colorless/French Blue	ebay-05/03	French Blue threaded
2028					$50	Colorless/Pomona Green	ebay-05/03	Pomona Green threaded
2028					$30	Colorless/Rosa rim 10"	ebay-05/03	
2028					$305	Selenium Red (E)	ebay-05/03	Engraved "Grapes"
2028					$120	Green Jade	ebay-06/03	
2028					$25	Amber	ebay-06/03	
2028					$30	Rosaline (E)	ebay-06/03	Engraved "York"
2028					$45	Spanish Green	ebay-06/03	
2028					$170	Blue/White Cluthra	ebay-06/03	
2028					$85	Green Jade	Jack-06/03	
2028					$215	Rosaline/Alabaster (E)	ebay-07/03	Engraved "York," 10"
2028					$100	Bristol Yellow/White	ebay-07/03	White threaded
2028					$80	Rosaline	ebay-07/03	
2028					$210	Selenium Red	ebay-07/03	
2028					$25	Blue-gray	ebay-07/03	
2028					$90	Light Rosa (E)	ebay-08/03	
2028					$130	Selenium Red	ebay-08/03	
2028					$220	Selenium Red	ebay-08/03	
2028					$80	Rosaline	ebay-08/03	
2028					$25	Topaz	ebay-08/03	
2028					$90	Light Rosa (E)	ebay-08/03	
2028					$60	Rosaline	ebay-09/03	
2028					$85	Selenium Red	ebay-09/03	
2028					$10	Topaz	ebay-09/03	
2028					$150	Selenium Red	ebay-10/03	
2028					$290	Gold Aurene	ebay-10/03	
2028					$355	Red White Cluthra	ebay-10/03	
2028					$125	Selenium Red (E)	ebay-11/03	
2028					$315	Black over Colorless (E)	ebay-10/03	Cut and Engraved pattern
2028					$20	Colorless/Blue threaded	ebay-11/03	
2028					$30	Topaz	ebay-11/03	
2028					$30	Green Jade	JDJ-11/03	
2028					$50	Topaz	ebay-12/03	
2028					$6900	Rouge Flambé	JDJ-11/03	
2028					$100	Rosaline/Alabaster (E)	ebay-01/04	Engraved "York"
2028					$20	Topaz	ebay-01/04	
2028					$75	Selenium Red	ebay-01/04	
2028					$125	Rosaline	ebay-01/04	
2028					$5	Celeste Blue	ebay-01/04	
2028					$75	Rosaline/Alabaster (E)	ebay-01/04	Engraved "York"
2028					$40	Pomona Green	ebay-01/04	
2028					$60	Celeste Blue	ebay-01/04	
2028					$300	Colorless/Blue threaded	Ogal-01/04	
2028					$50	Bristol Yellow	ebay-02/04	
2028					$115	VDS/Coral rim	ebay-02/04	
2028					$100	Opal/Amethyst Cintra rim	ebay-02/04	
2028					$150	Pomona over Colorless (E)	ebay-02/04	Engraved "Crescent #2"
2028					$130	Rosaline/Alabaster (E)	ebay-03/04	Engraved "10008"
2028					$16	Pomona Green (E)	ebay-03/04	Engraved "10013"
2028					$25	Bristol Yellow	ebay-03/04	
2028					$30	Colorless/Gold Ruby	ebay-03/04	Gold Ruby threaded
2028					$60	Selenium Red	ebay-03/04	
2028					$150	Gold Calcite	ebay-03/04	
2028					$150	Gold Calcite	ebay-03/04	
2028					$510	Gold Aurene	ebay-03/04	10"
2028					$50	Rosaline	ebay-03/04	
2028					$50	Rosaline	ebay-03/04	
2028					$60	Bristol Yellow/Black thread	ebay-03/04	11"
2028					$60	Pomona Green (E)	ebay-03/04	Engraved "10012"
2028					$60	Jade Green	ebay-04/04	
2028					$50	Green Jade	ebay-04/04	
2028					$35	Pomona Green	ebay-04/04	
2028					$400	Gold Aurene 10"	ebay-04/04	
2028					$50	Celeste Blue with threads	ebay-04/04	
2028					$60	Pomona Green (E)	ebay-05/04	Engraved "10008"
2028					$60	Amethyst	ebay-05/04	
2028					$35	Celeste Blue (E)	ebay-05/04	Engraved "Antique"
2028					$40	Celeste Blue (E)	ebay-05/04	Engraved "Antique"
2028					$100	Rosaline/Alabaster (E)	ebay-05/04	Engraved "10008"

105

SHAPE NO.	ITEM	PAGE	COL	ROW	PRICE REALIZED	GLASS TYPE	AUCTION HOUSE	COMMENTS & PHOTO REFERENCES
2028					$15	Colorless/Green rim	JDJ-05/04	
2028					$55	Pomona Green (E)	JDJ-05/04	Engraved "10008"
2028					$60	Flemish Blue/Colorless (E)	JDJ-05/04	
2028					$50	Celeste Blue (E)	ebay-05/04	Engraved "Antique"
2028					$200	Gold Aurene 10"	Tway-05/04	
2028					$25	Pomona Green	ebay-06/04	
2028					$50	Rosaline	ebay-06/04	
2028					$60	Selenium Red	ebay-06/04	
2028					$160	Rosaline/Alabaster (E)	ebay-06/04	
2028					$80	Cyprian	ebay-06/04	
2028					$105	Rosaline/Alabaster (E)	ebay-07/04	Engraved "10008"
2028					$70	Cyprian	ebay-07/04	
2028					$60	Spanish Green w/threads	ebay-07/04	11" dia
2028					$80	Pomona Green (FC)	ebay-07/04	
2028					$80	Rosaline	ebay-07/04	
2028					$225	Selenium Red (FC)	EAC-07/04	
2028					$120	Rosaline/Alabaster (E)	ebay-08/04	Engraved "10008"
2028					$40	Colorless/Rosa rim	ebay-08/04	
2028					$10	Pomona Green	ebay-08/04	
2028					$40	Colorless/Rosa rim	ebay-08/04	10" dia.
2028					$40	Colorless/Rosa rim	ebay-08/04	10" dia.
2028					$70	Rosaline	ebay-08/04	
2028					$50	Celeste Blue	ebay-09/04	
2028					$105	Colorless/Rosa rim	ebay-09/04	
2028					$30	Celeste Blue	ebay-09/04	
2028					$50	Green Jade	ebay-09/04	
2028					$50	Rosaline	ebay-09/04	
2028					$30	Bristol Yellow	ebay-09/04	
2028					$90	Rosaline/Alabaster (FC)	ebay-10/04	Engraved "10012"
2028					$15	Colorless/Green threading	ebay-10/04	
2028					$75	Cyprian	ebay-11/04	
2028					$140	Rosaline/Alabaster (E)	ebay-11/04	Engraved "10008"
2028					$30	Green Jade	ebay-11/04	
2028					$45	Green Jade	ebay-11/04	
2028					$255	Gold Aurene	ebay-12/04	
2028					$70	Amethyst (E)	ebay-12/04	
2028					$200	Pomona Green	ebay-01/05	14"
2028					$280	Gold Aurene	ebay-01/05	
2028					$20	Bristol Yellow	ebay-01/05	
2028					$30	Bristol Yellow	ebay-01/05	
2028					$65	Cyprian	ebay-01/05	
2028					$30	Bristol Yellow/Black thread	ebay-01/05	
2028					$20	Pomona Green	ebay-02/05	
2028					$45	Green Jade	ebay-02/05	
2028					$50	Rosaline	ebay-02/05	
2028					$65	Green Jade	ebay-02/05	
2028					$50	Bristol Yellow/Black thread	ebay-02/05	
2028					$50	Opal/Amethyst Cintra rim	ebay-02/05	
2028					$175	Pomona Green	ebay-02/05	14"
2028					$40	Pomona Green	ebay-03/05	
2028					$40	Pomona Green	ebay-04/05	
2028					$140	Rosaline/Alabaster (E)	ebay-04/05	Engraved "10008"
2028					$155	Mirror Black	ebay-04/05	
2028					$15	Bristol Yellow	ebay-04/05	
2028					$45	Rosa (E)	ebay-04/05	Engraved "York"
2028					$30	Green Jade	EAC-04/05	
2028					$45	Pomona Green	EAC-04/05	
2028					$35	Grenadine	EAC-04/05	
2028					$400	Green Jade/Alabaster (E)	EAC-04/05	Engraved "York"
2028					$150	Mirror Black	ebay-05/05	
2028					$105	Mirror Black	ebay-05/05	
2028					$25	Spanish Green/threaded	ebay-05/05	
2028					$55	Jade Green	ebay-05/05	
2028					$25	French Blue	ebay-05/05	Reeded & bubbly
2028					$25	French Blue	ebay-05/05	Reeded & bubbly
2028					$125	Mirror Black	ebay-05/05	
2028					$25	French Blue	ebay-05/05	Reeded & bubbly
2028					$70	Rosaline	ebay-05/05	
2028					$50	French Blue	ebay-05/05	Reeded & bubbly
2028					$80	Rosaline/Alabaster ACB	Cinn-05/05	
2028					$780	Rouge Flambé	JDJ-06/05	
2028					$35	Green Jade	ebay-06/05	
2028					$45	Rosaline	ebay-06/05	
2028					$140	Yellow Jade	ebay-07/05	

SHAPE NO.	ITEM	PAGE	COL	ROW	PRICE REALIZED	GLASS TYPE	AUCTION HOUSE	COMMENTS & PHOTO REFERENCES
2028					$50	VDS/Coral rim	ebay-07/05	
2028					$25	Bristol Yellow	ebay-07/05	
2028					$120	Gold Ruby (E)	ebay-07/05	Engraved "Etruscan"
2028					$140	Yellow Jade	ebay-07/05	
2028					$160	Gold Ruby (E)	ebay-07/05	Engraved "Etruscan"
2028					$50	Green Jade/Alabaster (E)	EAC-07/05	Engraved "York"
2028					$20	Grenadine	EAC-07/05	
2028					$25	French Blue threaded	ebay-07/05	
2029	Vase	263	1	3				
2030	Vase	263	1	4				
2031	Vase	263	1	5				
2032	Vase	263	1	6				
2033	Vase	263	1	7				
2034	Puff Box	244	3	10				
2035	Bowl	141	5	6				
2036	Sugar & Creamer	235	4	11,12				
2037	Pitcher	213	3	6				
2038	Bowl	141	5	7				
2039	Vase	263	2	1				
2040	Vase	263	2	2				
2041	Centerpiece	147	3	4				
2042	Decanter	185	1	3				
2043	Vase	263	2	3	$405	Blue Aurene	ebay-06/01	
2044	Puff Box	244	3	11				
2045	Decanter	185	1	4				
2046	Jar	210	2	9				
2047	Puff Box	244	3	12				
2048	Vase	263	2	4				
2049	Pitcher	213	3	7				
2050	Vase	263	2	5				
2051	Vase	263	2	6				
2052	Vase	263	3	1	$975	Alabaster ACB	Sknr-10/94	
2053	Dresser Set	245	3	2				
2054	Nut Dish	211	3	7,8				
2055	Tray	158	4	12				
2056	Insert	210	5	7				
2057	Decanter	185	1	5				
2058	Decanter	185	1	6				
2059	Decanter	185	2	1				
2060	Tray	158	4	13				
2061	Cruet	179	1	6				
2062	Cruet	179	1	7				
2063	Cruet	179	1	8				
2064	Cruet	179	2	1				
2065	Shade	227	1	7				
2066	Limousine Vase	207	1	7				
2067	Bowl	141	5	8				
2068	Cologne	243	3	5				TPD)5.28
2069	Tumbler	198	5	6				
2070	Vase	263	3	2				
2071	Vase	263	3	3				
2072	Bowl	141	5	9				
2073	Vase	263	3	4				
2074	Vase	263	3	5				
2075	Vase	263	3	6				
2076	Bowl	141	5	10				
2077	Bowl	141	5	11				
2078	Goblet	190	6	5				
2079	Sugar & Creamer	235	4	13,14				
2080	Nappie	233	2	7				
2081	Vase	263	4	1				
2082	Compote	172	1	11				
2083	Compote	172	2	1	$205	VDS (E)	ebay-08/04	"Hawkes" signature
2084	Goblet	197	2	8				
2085	Goblet	197	2	9				
2086	Decanter	185	2	2				
2087	Decanter	185	2	3				
2088	Decanter	185	3	4				
2089	Vase	263	4	2				
2090	Bowl	141	5	12				
2091	Tumble Up	199	5	4				
2092	Pitcher	213	4	1				
2093	Spoon Holder	177	3	7				
2094	Jar	209	3	12				

SHAPE NO.	ITEM	PAGE	COL	ROW	PRICE REALIZED	GLASS TYPE	AUCTION HOUSE	COMMENTS & PHOTO REFERENCES
2095	Pitcher	213	4	2				
2096	Vase	263	4	3				
2097	Vase	263	4	4	$1750	Gold Aurene	Free-11/03	
2098	Vase	263	4	5				
2099	Cologne	240	4	8				
2100	Cold Cream Jar	243	6	5				
2102	Cologne	240	4	9				
2103	Vase	263	4	6	$100	VDS	ebay-02/04	
2104	Misc.	211	5	2				
2105	Vase	263	4	7				
2106	Ash Tray	137	1	8				
2107	Compote	172	2	2				
2108	Basket	140	1	3				
2109	Vase	263	5	1				
2110	Vase	263	5	2				
2111	Vase	263	5	3				
2112	Vase	263	5	4	$270	VDS (E)	ebay-03/04	"Hawkes"
2112					$610	VDS (E)	ebay-06/05	"Hawkes"
2113	Vase	263	5	5	$860	Blue Aurene	Sknr-10/97	
2114	Vase	263	5	6				
2115	Vase	263	5	7				
2116	Vase	263	5	8				
2117	Vase	264	1	1				
2118	Vase	264	1	2				
2119	Vase	264	1	3				
2120	Jar	138	4	1	$255	Topaz/Celeste finial	ebay-12/03	
2121	Puff Box	244	3	13				
2122	Puff Box	244	3	14				
2123	Cruet	179	2	2				
2124	Cruet	179	2	3				
2125	Cruet	179	2	4				
2126	Ring Stand	245	2	3				
2127	Ring Stand	245	2	4				
2128	Mayonnaise Bowl	210	3	5				
2129	Sugar & Creamer	235	5	1,2				
2130	Cologne	240	4	10				
2131	Cologne	240	5	1				
2132	Salt	217	2	9				
2133	Compote	172	2	3				
2134	Compote	172	2	4				
2135	Vase	264	1	4				
2136	Vase	264	1	5				
2137	Vase	264	1	6				
2138	Vase	264	1	7	$1000	Black/Amethyst Cintra ACB	ebay-11/03	Etched "Dover"
2139	Vase	264	2	1	$500	Gold Aurene	ebay-02/00	
2140	Vase	264	2	2				
2141	Vase	264	2	3				
2142	Vase	264	2	4	$1150	Gold Aurene	Sknr-05/94	
2142					$300	VDS	ebay-09/02	Hawkes engraved
2142					$375	VDS	ebay-02/04	Gorham collar, Hawkes engraved
2143	Vase	264	2	5				
2144	Vase	264	2	6				
2145	Vase	264	2	7	$495	Gold Aurene	JDJ-10/94	TPD)10.25
2146	Vase	264	3	1				
2147	Vase	264	3	2				
2148	Vase	264	3	3				PG1)117,189
2149	Vase	264	3	4				
2150	Tray	158	4	14				
2151	Bowl	141	5	13	$600	Blue Aurene	ebay-11/02	
2151					$510	Gold Aurene	ebay-03/04	
2152	Compote	172	2	6				
2153	Basket	140	1	4	$30	Colorless	ebay-06/03	
2154	Vase	264	3	5				
2155	Cruet							See New Drawings section
2156	Vase	264	3	6				
2157	Vase	264	3	7				
2158	Vase	264	4	1				
2159	Vase	264	4	2				
2160	Vase	264	4	3				
2161	Vase	264	4	4				
2162	Vase	264	4	5				
2163	Vase	264	4	6				
2164	Vase	264	5	1				
2165	Vase	264	5	2				

SHAPE NO.	ITEM	PAGE	COL	ROW	PRICE REALIZED	GLASS TYPE	AUCTION HOUSE	COMMENTS & PHOTO REFERENCES
2166	Compote	172	2	6				
2167	Vase	264	5	3				
2168	Compote	172	2	7	$545	Colorless	Sknr-05/96	
2169	Compote	172	2	8				
2170	Pitcher	213	4	3				
2171	Tumble Up	199	5	5				
2172	Bowl	141	5	14				
2173	Nappie	233	2	8				
2174	Jar	209	5	7				
2175	Bouillon Cup	189	2	3				
2176	Decanter	185	2	5				
2177	Cologne	243	3	6				
2178	Cologne	240	5	2				
2179	Vase	264	5	4				
2180	Cruet	179	2	5				
2181	Goblet	190	6	6				
2182	Vase	264	5	5				
2183	Cologne	240	5	3				
2184	Vase	264	5	6				PG2)70
2185	Compote	172	3	1				
2186	Compote	172	3	2				
2187	Decanter	185	2	6				
2188	Decanter	185	3	1				
2189	Mayonnaise Bowl	210	3	7				
2190	Mayonnaise Bowl	210	3	8				
2191	Mayonnaise Bowl	210	3	9				
2192	Bowl	142	1	1				
2193	Bowl	142	1	2				
2194	Bowl	142	1	3				
2195	Bowl	142	1	4				
2196	Vase	265	1	1				
2197	Vase	265	1	2				
2198	Dresser Set	245	3	3				
2200	Shade	221	2	10				
2201	Shade	221	2	11				
2202	Shade	221	3	1				
2203	Shade	221	3	2				
2204	Shade	221	3	3				
2205	Shade	221	3	4				
2206	Shade	221	3	5				
2207	Shade	221	3	6				
2208	Shade	221	3	7				
2209	Shade	221	3	8				
2210	Shade	221	3	9				
2211	Shade	221	3	10				
2217	Shade	227	1	8				
2218	Shade	221	4	1	$105	Gold Aurene	ebay-07/01	
2218					$190	Gold Aurene	ebay-09/02	
2218					$130	Gold Calcite (E)	ebay-05/03	
2218					$135	Gold Calcite	ebay-09/05	
2219	Shade	221	4	2				
2220	Shade	221	4	3				
2221	Shade	221	4	4				
2222	Shade	221	4	5	$25	Calcite ACB	ebay-09/02	
2223	Shade	221	4	6	$260	Gold Calcite (E)	ebay-11/04	
2224	Shade	221	4	7	$165	Gold Aurene	ebay-01/01	
2225	Shade	221	4	8	$230	Gold Calcite	ebay-08/03	
2226	Shade	221	4	9				
2227	Shade	221	4	10				
2228	Shade	221	4	11	$35	Calcite ACB	ebay-11/03	
2229	Shade	221	4	12				
2230	Shade	221	5	1	$150	Gold Aurene	ebay-08/03	
2230	Shade Vase				$550	Blue Aurene	JDJ-10/94	RFR)9,2,C;MDK)3
2230					$495	Gold Aurene	JDJ-10/94	
2230					$660	Blue Aurene	EAC-10/00	
2230					$500	Blue Aurene	ebay-08/01	
2230					$305	Ivory	ebay-04/02	
2230					$910	Gold Aurene	ebay-09/02	
2230					$200	Pomona Green	ebay-08/03	
2230					$1035	Blue Aurene	JDJ-05/04	
2230					$150	Alabaster	ebay-08/04	
2230					$200	Alabaster	ebay-10/04	
2230					$410	Gold Aurene	ebay-05/05	
2230					$140	Pomona Green	ebay-05/05	

SHAPE NO.	ITEM	PAGE	COL	ROW	PRICE REALIZED	GLASS TYPE	AUCTION HOUSE	COMMENTS & PHOTO REFERENCES
2230					$840	Blue Aurene	JDJ-06/05	
2231	Shade	221	5	2				
2232	Shade	221	5	3	$105	Gold Aurene	ebay-01/01	
2232					$150	Gold Aurene	ebay-04/01	
2232					$220	Gold Aurene	ebay-06/01	
2232					$180	Gold Aurene	ebay-06/01	
2232					$140	Gold Aurene	JDJ-11/01	
2232					$160	Gold Aurene	ebay-06/02	
2232					$200	Gold Aurene	ebay-02/03	
2232					$165	Gold Aurene	ebay-03/03	
2232					$180	Gold Aurene	ebay-04/03	
2232					$150	Gold Aurene	ebay-05/03	
2232					$150	Gold Aurene	ebay-05/03	
2232					$160	Gold Aurene	ebay-05/03	
2232					$75	Gold Aurene	ebay-07/04	
2232					$135	Gold Aurene	ebay-11/04	
2232					$170	Gold Aurene	ebay-01/05	
2232					$155	Gold Aurene	ebay-04/05	
2233	Shade	221	5	4	$200	Gold Aurene	ebay-03/04	
2233					$130	Gold Aurene	ebay-05/04	
2233					$150	Gold Aurene	ebay-03/05	
2233					$100	Gold Aurene	ebay-07/05	
2234	Shade	221	5	5				
2235	Shade	221	5	6				
2236	Shade	227	1	9				
2237	Shade	221	5	7				RFR)13,2,E
2238	Shade	221	5	8				
2239	Shade	221	5	9	$1025	Green/Calcite	ebay-01/01	TPD)4.105
2239					$100	Calcite ABC	ebay-10/02	
2240	Shade	221	5	10				
2241	Shade	221	5	11				
2242	Shade	222	1	1	$90	Gold Aurene over Calcite	Sknr-02/01	
2242					$185	Leaves and Vines	FtnA-08/03	
2242					$105	Calcite ACB	ebay-07/04	
2242					$120	Gold Aurene	ebay-08/04	
2242					$350	Leaves and Vines	ebay-12/04	
2242					$100	Gold Aurene	ebay-03/05	
2243	Shade	222	1	2	$50	Calcite ACB	ebay-08/02	
2244	Shade	222	1	3	$310	Gold Pulled Feather	ebay-11/04	
2245	Shade	222	1	4				
2246	Shade	222	1	5	$690	Calcite ACB	ebay-01/03	
2247	Shade	227	1	10				
2248	Shade	222	1	6	$100	Gold Calcite	ebay-07/01	
2248					$150	Calcite	ebay-01/03	
2248					$135	Gold Calcite	ebay-08/03	
2248					$200	Gold Pulled Feather	ebay-02/04	
2248					$105	Gold Calcite	ebay-03/04	
2248					$105	Gold Calcite	ebay-03/04	
2249	Shade	222	1	7				
2250	Shade	222	1	8	$255	Pulled Feather	ebay-11/03	
2250					$220	Pulled Feather	ebay-10/03	
2251	Shade	222	1	9				
2252	Shade	222	1	10	$860	Blue Pulled Feather	Jack-06/02	Calcite base
2253	Shade	222	2	1	$500	Decorated Gold Aurene	ebay-12/00	
2253					$555	Decorated Gold Aurene	ebay-11/03	
2253					$275	Decorated Gold Aurene	ebay-12/03	
2253					$305	Green Pulled Feather	ebay-04/05	
2254	Shade	222	2	2	$160	Decorated Gold Aurene	ebay-05/01	
2254					$215	Green Pulled Feather	Jack-06/02	Calcite base
2254					$185	Green Pulled Feather	Jack-06/02	Calcite base
2254					$200	Red Pulled Feather	ebay-10/02	Calcite base
2254					$235	Red Pulled Feather	ebay-10/04	
2255	Shade	222	2	3	$245	Red Pulled Feather	ebay-02/05	
2256	Shade	222	2	4				
2257	Shade	222	2	5				
2258	Shade	222	2	6				
2259	Shade	222	2	7	$275	Decorated Gold Calcite	ebay-06/03	RFR)13,4,A; TPD)4.103
2259					$420	Leaves and Vines	Rago-01/04	
2259					$500	Leaves and Vines	ebay-07/04	
2260	Shade	222	2	8	$150	Gold Aurene	ebay-03/01	
2260					$190	Gold Aurene	ebay-09/02	
2260					$200	Gold Aurene	ebay-05/04	
2261	Shade	222	2	9	$70	Gold Calcite	ebay-01/04	
2261					$70	Gold Calcite	ebay-01/04	

110

SHAPE NO.	ITEM	PAGE	COL	ROW	PRICE REALIZED	GLASS TYPE	AUCTION HOUSE	COMMENTS & PHOTO REFERENCES
2261					$70	Gold Aurene	ebay-03/04	
2261					$110	Gold Calcite	ebay-04/05	
2261					$75	Gold Calcite	ebay-04/05	
2261					$85	Gold Calcite	ebay-04/05	
2261					$345	Gold Calcite	EAC-04/05	
2262	Shade	222	2	10	$200	Gold Aurene	Midw-04/01	
2262					$180	Gold Aurene	ebay-02/02	
2262					$130	Gold Aurene	ebay-07/02	
2262					$245	Gold Aurene	ebay-11/02	
2262					$185	Gold Calcite	ebay-02/03	
2262					$150	Gold Calcite	ebay-03/03	
2262					$250	Gold Calcite	ebay-01/04	
2262					$270	Gold Aurene	ebay-01/04	
2262					$460	Gold Aurene	JDJ-05/04	
2262					$260	Gold Aurene	Crft-01/05	
2262					$215	Gold Calcite	ebay-04/05	
2262					$305	Gold Aurene	Jack-04/05	
2263	Shade	222	3	1	$230	Gold Aurene	ebay-07/01	
2263					$175	Gold Aurene	Sknr-12/03	
2263					$125	Gold Aurene	ebay-09/04	
2264	Shade	222	3	2	$130	Calcite ACB	Sknr-06/02	
2264					$94	Calcite ACB	ebay-08/02	
2264					$45	Calcite ACB	ebay-12/02	
2264					$70	Calcite ACB	ebay-12/03	
2264					$130	Calcite ACB	ebay-07/05	
2265	Shade	222	3	3	$285	Decorated Gold Aurene	ebay-11/99	
2265					$205	Pulled Feather	ebay-03/02	
2266	Shade	222	3	4				
2267	Shade	222	3	5	$230	Brown Pulled Feather	Jack-06/02	Calcite base
2268	Shade	222	3	6	$135	Gold Calcite	ebay-06/01	
2268					$115	Calcite	ebay-04/02	
2268					$125	Gold Calcite	ebay-05/02	
2268					$140	VDS	Wint-03/03	
2268					$130	Gold Calcite	ebay-01/04	
2268					$130	Gold Calcite	ebay-01/04	
2268					$130	Gold Calcite	ebay-01/04	
2268					$155	Gold Calcite	EAC-04/04	
2268					$250	Gold Calcite	ebay-07/04	
2268					$190	Gold Aurene	ebay-07/04	
2268					$85	VDS	EAC-07/04	
2268					$130	Gold Aurene	ebay-07/04	
2268					$280	Gold Aurene	ebay-09/04	
2268					$105	Gold Aurene	ebay-10/04	
2269	Shade	222	3	7	$100	Calcite	ebay-11/04	
2270	Shade	222	3	8				
2271	Shade	222	3	9				
2272	Shade	222	3	10				
2273	Shade	222	3	11				
2274	Shade	222	4	1	$430	Green Basket weave	Jack-06/02	TPD)4.90
2275	Shade	222	4	2	$125	Gold Calcite	ebay-03/02	
2275					$200	Gold Aurene	ebay-04/02	
2275					$185	Gold Aurene	Jack-06/02	
2275					$90	VDS ACB	ebay-08/04	
2276	Shade	222	4	3	$100	Gold Aurene	ebay-02/01	
2276					$125	Gold Aurene	ebay-01/04	
2277	Shade	222	4	4				
2278	Shade	222	4	5				
2279	Shade	222	4	6	$305	Decorated Aurene	JDJ-05/00	TPD)9.38
2279					$490	Decorated Aurene	ebay-11/00	
2279					$400	Green Pulled Feather	Jack-06/02	Gold Aurene base
2279					$525	Pulled Feather	ebay-09/03	
2279					$385	Pulled Feather	ebay-10/03	
2279					$900	Green Pulled Feather	JDJ-05/04	
2280	Shade	222	4	7	$910	Green Pulled Feather	ebay-05/03	
2281	Shade	222	4	8	$290	Green Decorated Calcite	Jack-06/02	
2281					$600	Decorated Gold Calcite	ebay-12/03	
2281					$560	Decorated Gold Calcite	ebay-02/04	
2281					$1150	Green Decorated	JDJ-05/04	
2282	Shade	222	4	9	$385	Pulled Feather	EAC-07/98	RFR)13,3,D; RFR)13,4,E
2282					$135	Pulled Feather	ebay-06/01	
2282					$225	Pulled Feather	ebay-08/01	
2282					$430	Blue Pulled Feather	ebay-01/02	
2282					$190	Pulled Feather	ebay-01/02	
2282					$255	Pulled Feather	ebay-04/02	

SHAPE NO.	ITEM	PAGE	COL	ROW	PRICE REALIZED	GLASS TYPE	AUCTION HOUSE	COMMENTS & PHOTO REFERENCES
2282					$145	Pulled Feather	Jack-06/02	
2282					$155	Pulled Feather	ebay-08/02	
2282					$190	Green Pulled Feather	ebay-10/02	
2282					$230	Red Pulled Feather	ebay-12/02	
2282					$305	Red Pulled Feather	ebay-05/03	
2282					$265	Pulled Feather	ebay-08/03	
2282					$275	Pulled Feather	ebay-08/03	
2282					$305	Pulled Feather	ebay-09/03	
2282					$215	Pulled Feather	ebay-02/04	
2282					$315	Gold Pulled Feather	ebay-03/04	
2282					$490	Gold Pulled Feather	ebay-03/04	
2282					$265	Green Pulled Feather	ebay-04/04	
2282					$175	Gold Pulled Feather	ebay-04/04	
2282					$180	Gold Pulled Feather	ebay-04/04	
2282					$215	Gold Pulled Feather	ebay-04/04	
2282					$230	Red Pulled Feather	JDJ-05/04	
2282					$430	Blue Pulled Feather	JDJ-05/04	
2282					$350	Gold Pulled Feather	ebay-08/04	
2282					$230	Gold Pulled Feather	ebay-08/04	
2283	Shade	222	5	1				
2284	Shade	222	5	2	$985	Green Leaves on gold curl	ebay-07/04	TPD)4.104
2284					$925	Green Leaves and Vines	ebay-11/04	
2285	Shade	222	5	3	$1380	Blue decoration on white	JDJ-05/04	
2286	Shade	222	5	4	$685	King Tut.	ebay-05/02	TPD)4.91
2286					$610	King Tut.	ebay-06/02	
2286					$685	King Tut.	ebay-07/02	
2286					$670	King Tut.	EAC-07/04	
2286					$760	King Tut.	ebay-07/04	
2287	Shade	222	5	5				TPD)4.104
2288	Shade	222	5	6				
2289	Shade	222	5	7				
2290	Shade	222	5	8	$125	VDS (E)	ebay-10/02	
2290					$75	VDS (E)	ebay-02/05	
2291	Shade	222	5	9	$300	Pulled Feather	ebay-05/01	
2291					$235	Pulled Feather	ebay-09/03	
2291					$175	Pulled Feather	ebay-12/03	
2291					$345	Gold Pulled Feather	ebay-11/04	
2292	Shade	222	5	10	$105	Calcite ACB	ebay-07/04	
2293	Shade	223	1	1				
2294	Shade	223	1	2				
2295	Shade	223	1	3				
2296	Shade	223	1	4				
2297	Shade	227	2	1				
2298	Shade	227	2	2				
2299	Shade	227	2	3				
2300	Shade	227	2	4	$320	Calcite ACB	ebay-03/04	
2301	Shade	227	2	5				
2302	Shade	223	1	5	$80	Gold Calcite	ebay-11/03	
2303	Shade	223	1	6	$260	Green Pulled Feather	ebay-05/04	
2304	Shade	223	1	7	$215	Pulled Feather	ebay-10/01	
2304					$300	Decorated Calcite	JDJ-05/04	Gold Aurene decoration
2305	Shade	223	1	8	$295	Pulled Feather	ebay-05/05	
2306	Shade	223	1	9	$420	Pulled Feather	ebay-08/01	
2306					$360	Gold Aurene	JDJ-05/03	
2306					$200	Gold Aurene	ebay-07/03	
2306					$345	Green Pulled Feather	ebay-08/03	
2306					$320	Gold Aurene	ebay-06/04	
2306					$550	Green Pulled Feather	ebay-09/04	
2306					$450	Green Pulled Feather	ebay-10/04	
2306					$170	Gold Aurene	ebay-10/04	
2306					$225	Gold Aurene	ebay-12/04	
2307	Shade	223	1	10	$450	Pulled Feather	ebay-11/02	
2307					$300	Green Pulled Feather	JDJ-05/04	
2308	Shade	223	1	11	$1125	Decorated Gold Aurene	ebay-05/02	
2308					$300	Leaves and Vines	ebay-11/04	
2309	Shade	223	2	1				
2310	Shade	223	2	2				
2311	Shade	223	2	3	$75	Calcite ACB	ebay-01/05	
2312	Shade	223	2	4				
2313	Shade	223	2	5				
2314	Shade	223	2	6				
2315	Shade	223	2	7				
2316	Shade	223	2	8				
2317	Shade	223	2	9	$135	VDS Engraved	ebay-11/01	

SHAPE NO.	ITEM	PAGE	COL	ROW	PRICE REALIZED	GLASS TYPE	AUCTION HOUSE	COMMENTS & PHOTO REFERENCES
2317					$115	VDS Engraved	ebay-10/02	
2318	Shade	223	2	10				
2319	Shade	223	3	1				
2320	Shade	223	3	2	$40	Calcite	ebay-10/02	
2320					$115	Gold Calcite	ebay-10/04	
2321	Shade	223	3	3				
2322	Shade	223	3	4				
2323	Shade	223	3	5	$235	Gold Aurene	ebay-05/05	
2324	Shade	223	3	6				
2325	Shade	223	3	7				TPD)4.109
2326	Shade	223	3	8				
2327	Shade	223	3	9	$650	Gold Aurene	Tway-10/00	RFR)13,2,C; RFR)13,3,E
2327					$330	Pulled Feather	ebay-04/01	
2327					$265	Pulled Feather	ebay-06/01	
2327					$300	Pulled Feather	ebay-07/01	
2327					$300	Pulled Feather	ebay-08/01	
2327					$350	Pulled Feather	ebay-12/01	
2327					$350	Pulled Feather	ebay-03/02	
2327					$330	Pulled Feather	ebay-04/02	
2327					$345	Pulled Feather	JDJ-05/02	
2327					$310	Pulled Feather	ebay-07/02	
2327					$405	Green Pulled Feather	ebay-02/04	
2327					$325	Green Pulled Feather	ebay-07/04	
2327					$285	Green Pulled Feather	ebay-10/04	
2327					$330	Green Pulled Feather	ebay-01/05	
2327					$205	Green Pulled Feather	ebay-05/05	
2328	Shade	223	3	10	$620	Pulled Feather	ebay-06/02	
2328					$1610	Brown Pulled Feather	JDJ-05/04	
2329	Lamp	200	3	2	$1065	Decorated Green Aurene	EAC-11/03	Lamp base only signed "Haviland"
2330	Lamp	200	3	3	$4300	Green Pulled Feather	ebay-06/04	ACR)142,266; TPD)8.50
2331	Lamp	200	3	4				
2332	Lamp	200	3	5	$360	Gold Aurene	ebay-06/03	Lamp base only
2332					$3720	Gold Aurene	ebay-05/05	Complete lamp
2333	Lamp	200	4	1				
2334	Lamp	200	4	2				
2335	Lamp	200	4	3				
2336	Lamp	200	4	4	$2310	Gold Aurene	EAC-07/90	
2337	Lamp	200	4	5	$6500	Green Decorated Calcite	Sbys-06/03	TPD)9.39
2338	Lamp	200	5	1				
2339	Lamp	200	5	2				PG2)55; JAS)162,BR; TPD)4.94
2340	Lamp	200	5	3				
2341	Shade	223	3	11	$185	Gold Aurene	ebay-02/02	
2341					$180	Gold Aurene	ebay-09/04	
2341					$230	Gold Aurene	ebay-09/04	
2342	Shade	223	4	1	$85	Light Amethyst threaded	ebay-07/02	
2344	Shade	223	4	2	$85	Calcite	ebay-05/05	
2345	Shade	223	4	3	$170	Gold Calcite (E)	ebay-09/03	
2345					$155	Gold Aurene	ebay-06/04	
2346	Shade	227	2	6	$970	Calcite ACB	ebay-09/02	Calcite dome
2347	Shade	227	2	7				
2348	Shade	223	4	4				
2349	Shade	223	4	5	$130	Calcite ACB	ebay-01/02	
2350	Shade	223	4	6	$310	Decorated Calcite	ebay-01/01	
2350					$135	Gold Aurene	ebay-07/05	
2351	Shade	223	4	7				
2352	Shade	223	4	8	$130	Calcite ACB	EAC-07/05	TPD)10.147
2353	Shade	223	4	9	$230	Blue Pulled Feather	Jack-06/02	Calcite base
2353					$60	Gold Calcite	ebay-07/02	
2353					$80	Calcite	ebay-12/02	
2353					$150	Calcite ACB	ebay-09/04	
2353					$105	Calcite ACB	ebay-01/05	
2354	Shade	223	4	10	$230	Gold Aurene	JDJ-10/97	TPD)5.49
2354					$285	Gold Aurene	JDJ-10/97	
2354					$135	Calcite	ebay-02/00	
2354					$50	Calcite	ebay-01/01	
2354					$100	Gold Aurene	ebay-01/01	
2354					$90	Calcite	ebay-02/01	
2354					$50	Calcite	ebay-04/01	
2354					$90	Calcite	ebay-04/01	
2354					$145	Calcite	ebay-04/01	
2354					$80	Calcite ACB	ebay-01/02	
2354					$120	Calcite ACB	ebay-03/02	
2354					$270	Dec. Gold Aurene	ebay-03/02	
2354					$330	Blue Pulled Feather	ebay-04/02	

SHAPE NO.	ITEM	PAGE	COL	ROW	PRICE REALIZED	GLASS TYPE	AUCTION HOUSE	COMMENTS & PHOTO REFERENCES
2354					$135	Calcite	ebay-06/02	
2354					$720	Blue Pulled Feather	Jack-06/02	Calcite base
2354					$70	Calcite ACB	ebay-08/02	
2354					$170	Pulled Feather	ebay-11/02	
2354					$50	Calcite ACB	ebay-12/02	
2354					$105	Calcite ACB	ebay-01/03	
2354					$110	Calcite ACB	ebay-02/03	
2354					$95	Calcite ACB	ebay-05/03	
2354					$70	Calcite	ebay-11/03	
2354					$95	Calcite ACB	ebay-12/03	
2354					$155	Calcite ACB	ebay-02/04	
2354					$80	Calcite ACB	EAC-07/04	Etched "Lumene"
2354					$110	Calcite ACB	ebay-01/05	
2354					$200	Calcite	ebay-03/05	
2355	Shade	223	4	11				
2356	Shade	227	2	8				
2357	Shade	227	2	9				
2358	Shade	223	5	1				
2359	Shade	223	5	2				RFR)13,2,B
2360	Dish	210	2	10	$565	Gold Aurene	ebay-04/02	Grapefruit
2360					$600	Gold Aurene	JDJ-11/02	
2360					$460	Gold Aurene	JDJ-05/04	
2360					$300	Gold Aurene	JDJ-06/05	
2361	Champagne							TPD)4.75
2361	Cordial				$110	Gold Aurene	JDJ-10/94	TPD)4.75
2361					$150	Gold Aurene	Sknr-01/97	
2361					$410	Gold Aurene	EAC-08/00	
2361					$150	Gold Aurene	ebay-12/02	
2361					$200	Gold Aurene	ebay-01/03	
2361					$270	Gold Aurene	ebay-09/03	
2361					$190	Gold Aurene	ebay-11/04	
2361					$520	Gold Aurene	EAC-04/05	
2361	Finger Bowl				$550	Gold Aurene	EAC-04/97	TPD)4.75
2361					$50	VDS	JDJ-05/00	
2361					$600	Gold Aurene	JDJ-11/02	
2361					$410	Gold Aurene	ebay-01/03	
2361					$75	Gold Aurene	ebay-05/05	Underplate only
2361	Goblet	190	6	7	$315	Gold Aurene	Sknr-10/94	RFR)9,4,B&D; TPD)4.75:6.1
2361					$360	Gold Aurene	EAC-07/96	
2361					$330	VDS	EAC-07/96	
2361					$200	Gold Aurene	Sknr-01/97	
2361					$275	Gold Aurene	EAC-04/97	
2361					$230	Gold Aurene	Sknr-01/98	
2361					$440	Gold Aurene	EAC-07/98	
2361					$425	Gold Aurene	EAC-04/99	
2361					$220	Gold Aurene	Sknr-10/99	
2361					$425	Gold Aurene	ebay-02/00	
2361					$475	Gold Aurene	Ogal-03/00	
2361					$495	Gold Aurene	ebay-04/00	
2361					$475	Gold Aurene	EAC-05/00	
2361					$430	Gold Aurene	ebay-10/00	
2361					$140	VDS	ebay-01/01	
2361					$275	Gold Aurene	Cott-08/01	
2361					$285	Gold Aurene	JDJ-11/01	
2361					$785	Gold Aurene	EAC-04/02	
2361					$785	Gold Aurene	EAC-04/02	
2361					$335	Gold Aurene	ebay-06/02	
2361					$250	Gold Aurene	ebay-07/02	
2361					$550	Gold Aurene	ebay-01/03	
2361					$250	Gold Aurene	ebay-03/03	
2361					$300	Gold Aurene	Dalla-05/03	
2361					$325	Gold Aurene	Dalla-05/03	
2361					$240	Gold Aurene	ebay-05/03	
2361					$260	Gold Aurene	ebay-06/03	
2361					$600	Gold Aurene	ebay-06/03	
2361					$690	Gold Aurene	EAC-06/03	
2361					$630	Gold Aurene	EAC-06/03	
2361					$200	Gold Aurene	ebay-07/03	
2361					$200	Gold Aurene	ebay-07/03	
2361					$300	Gold Aurene	Dalla-09/03	
2361					$290	Gold Aurene	EAC-11/03	
2361					$290	Gold Aurene	EAC-11/03	
2361					$510	Gold Aurene	ebay-02/04	
2361					$115	Colorless/Pomona stem	ebay-12/03	

SHAPE NO.	ITEM	PAGE	COL	ROW	PRICE REALIZED	GLASS TYPE	AUCTION HOUSE	COMMENTS & PHOTO REFERENCES
2361					$280	Gold Aurene	ebay-02/04	
2361					$285	Gold Aurene	ebay-03/04	
2361					$520	Gold Aurene	EAC-04/04	
2361					$350	Gold Aurene	ebay-07/04	
2361					$280	Gold Aurene	EAC-07/04	
2361					$280	Gold Aurene	EAC-07/04	
2361					$195	Gold Aurene	ebay-09/04	
2361					$525	Gold Aurene	ebay-12/04	
2361					$160	Gold Aurene	ebay-01/05	
2361					$185	Gold Aurene	ebay-01/05	
2361					$320	Gold Aurene	ebay-01/05	
2361					$325	Gold Aurene	ebay-02/05	
2361					$360	Gold Aurene	ebay-05/05	
2361					$105	Gold Aurene	ebay-07/05	
2361	Sherbet				$385	Gold Aurene	EAC-07/90	
2361					$135	Gold Aurene	EAC-07/93	
2361					$460	Gold Aurene	ebay-03/03	
2361					$310	Gold Aurene	ebay-11/03	
2361					$450	Gold Aurene	ebay-10/04	
2361					$200	Gold Aurene	ebay-11/04	
2361					$285	Gold Aurene	ebay-01/05	
2361					$160	Gold Aurene	ebay-01/05	
2361					$160	Gold Aurene	ebay-01/05	
2361	Tumbler				$440	Gold Aurene	EAC-04/98	TPD)4.75; MDK)76
2361					$685	Gold Aurene	ebay-12/99	
2361					$225	Gold Aurene	EAC-11/01	
2361					$55	Amethyst	ebay-03/02	
2361					$455	Gold Aurene	ebay-03/03	
2361					$50	Amethyst	ebay-03/03	
2361					$50	Pomona Green	ebay-03/03	
2361					$50	Amethyst	ebay-03/03	
2361					$55	Amethyst	ebay-03/03	
2361					$70	VDS	ebay-03/03	
2361					$305	Gold Aurene	ebay-03/03	signed "Haviland"
2361					$25	Topaz	ebay-03/03	
2361					$80	Celeste Blue	ebay-05/03	
2361					$215	Gold Aurene	ebay-06/03	
2361					$90	Topaz	ebay-08/03	
2361					$80	VDS (E)	ebay-09/03	
2361					$40	Topaz	ebay-10/03	
2361					$315	Gold Aurene	EAC-11/03	
2361					$45	Topaz	ebay-12/03	
2361					$50	Topaz	ebay-01/04	
2361					$50	Amethyst	ebay-01/04	
2361					$50	Amethyst	ebay-02/04	
2361					$50	Amethyst	ebay-02/04	
2361					$35	Topaz	ebay-03/04	
2361					$45	Topaz	ebay-05/04	
2361					$60	Celeste Blue	ebay-05/04	
2361					$125	Celeste Blue	ebay-08/04	
2361					$30	Topaz	ebay-02/05	
2361					$275	Gold Aurene	EAC-04/05	
2361					$245	Gold Aurene	EAC-07/05	
2362	Sherbet	216	4	8	$440	Gold Aurene	EAC-10/97	
2362					$805	Gold Aurene	ebay-10/99	
2362					$255	Gold Aurene	ebay-12/99	
2362					$200	Gold Aurene	ebay-02/01	
2362					$220	Gold Aurene	ebay-03/02	
2362					$135	Gold Aurene	ebay-04/03	Sherbet only, no underplate
2363	Vase	265	1	3				
2364	Vase	265	1	4	$330	Gold Aurene	ebay-01/02	RFR)17,2,A; TPD)10.22 Also listed as a
2364					$150	Bristol Yellow/Black thread.	ebay-10/02	Tumbler in the factory records.
2364					$100	Spanish Green w/threads	ebay-12/02	
2364					$305	Bristol Yellow, draped	ebay-01/03	
2364					$250	Colorless/Gold Ruby	ebay02/03	Gold Ruby threaded
2364					$190	Colorless/Colorless	Cinc-06/03	Colorless threaded
2364					$480	Colorless Silverina	ebay-07/03	
2364					$80	Colorless/Gold Ruby	ebay-08/03	Gold Ruby threaded
2364					$45	Bristol Yellow	ebay-12/04	
2364					$100	Colorless/Green thread.	ebay-02/05	
2364					$160	Pomona Green, draped	ebay-02/05	
2365	Vase	265	1	5				
2366	Tumbler	198	5	7				
2367	Tea Cup	216	3	5	$375	Gold Aurene	ebay-07/01	MDK)129

SHAPE NO.	ITEM	PAGE	COL	ROW	PRICE REALIZED	GLASS TYPE	AUCTION HOUSE	COMMENTS & PHOTO REFERENCES
2368	Bell	237	3	4	$1950	Gold Aurene	ebay-11/00	
2369	Nut Dish	211	3	9				
2370	Decanter	185	3	2	$1375	Gold Aurene	EAC-04/96	
2370					$2320	Gold Aurene	ebay-11/04	
2371	Shade	223	5	3	$190	VDS/Amber threaded (E)	ebay-12/03	TPD)4.104
2372	Shade	223	5	4	$275	Gold Aurene	ebay-07/01	
2372					$55	Calcite ACB	ebay-11/01	
2372					$105	Calcite ACB	ebay-04/02	
2372					$65	Calcite ACB	ebay-04/02	
2372					$65	Calcite ACB	ebay-11/03	
2372					$75	Calcite ACB	ebay-12/04	
2372					$140	Calcite ACB	ebay-07/05	
2373	Shade	223	5	5	$80	Calcite	ebay-02/01	
2373					$265	Gold Calcite (E)	ebay-11/04	
2374	Shade	223	5	6	$405	Decorated Calcite	ebay-02/01	RFR)13,3,A&B
2374					$160	Decorated Calcite	ebay-10/01	
2374					$150	Decorated Calcite	ebay-04/02	
2374					$100	Decorated Calcite	Jack-06/02	
2374					$145	Leaf & Vine on Calcite	Jack-06/02	
2374					$190	Leaf & Vine on Calcite	ebay-12/04	
2374					$275	Leaf & Vine on Calcite	ebay-02/05	
2374					$1025	Decorated Green Aurene	ebay-09/04	
2374					$400	Leaf & Vine on Calcite	EAC-04/05	
2375	Shade	223	5	7	$460	Decorated Gold Aurene	Sknr-10/94	
2375					$315	Decorated Gold Aurene	JDJ-11/00	
2375					$465	Decorated Gold Aurene	ebay-02/02	
2375					$415	Decorated Gold Aurene	ebay-05/02	
2375					$495	Gold Aurene	FtnA-08/03	
2376	Shade	223	5	8	$360	Gold Aurene	ebay-12/00	TPD)6.24
2376					$500	Gold Aurene	ebay-07/03	Intarsia border
2377	Shade	223	5	9	$90	Calcite ACB	ebay-11/00	
2377					$385	Gold Aurene	ebay-07/01	
2377					$400	Gold Aurene	ebay-07/01	
2377					$360	Gold Aurene	ebay-08/01	
2377					$390	Gold Aurene	ebay-12/01	
2377					$520	Gold Aurene	ebay-01/02	
2377					$135	Gold Aurene	ebay-11/02	
2377					$615	Decorated Gold Aurene	ebay-09/03	
2377					$105	Calcite ACB	ebay-07/04	
2377					$615	Calcite ACB	EAC-07/04	Etched "Ivy"
2377					$660	Gold Aurene	EAC-10/04	
2377					$120	Calcite ACB	ebay-11/04	
2377					$170	Gold Aurene	ebay-12/04	
2377					$100	Calcite ACB	ebay-01/05	
2377					$105	Calcite ACB	ebay-01/05	
2377					$110	Calcite ACB	ebay-01/05	
2377					$690	Gold Aurene	JDJ-06/05	
2377					$260	Gold Aurene	ebay-07/05	
2378	Shade	223	5	10				
2379	Shade	224	1	1	$300	Decorated Gold Calcite	GAI-02/99	TPD)4.107
2379					$270	"King Tut"	ebay-05/01	
2379					$200	Gold Calcite ACB	ebay-03/03	
2380	Shade	224	1	2	$415	Blue Pulled Feather	ebay-11/04	
2381	Shade	224	1	3				
2382	Lamp	200	5	4				
2383	Lamp	200	5	5				PG1)34,61
2384	Lamp	201	1	1	$2070	Calcite	Sknr-10/96	
2385	Lamp	201	1	2	$3500	Gold Aurene	Tway-03/02	
2386	Shade	224	1	4				
2387	Decanter	185	3	3	$250	VDS	ebay-05/04	
2387					$1725	Gold Aurene	EAC-07/05	
2388	Shade	224	1	5				RFR)13,1,D; TPD)4.89
2389	Shade	224	1	6	$810	Brown Aurene	ebay-02/00	TPD)6.24
2389					$800	Brown Aurene	ebay-10/00	
2389					$475	Brown Aurene	ebay-05/01	
2389					$585	Brown Aurene	ebay-12/01	
2389					$730	Brown Aurene	Jack-06/03	
2389					$600	Brown Aurene	ebay-08/03	
2389					$685	Brown Aurene	ebay-08/03	
2389					$500	Brown Aurene	ebay-11/03	
2389					$975	Brown Aurene	JDJ-05/04	
2389					$625	Brown Aurene	ebay-06/04	
2389					$735	Brown Aurene	ebay-12/04	
2389					$1320	Brown Aurene	JDJ-06/05	

SHAPE NO.	ITEM	PAGE	COL	ROW	PRICE REALIZED	GLASS TYPE	AUCTION HOUSE	COMMENTS & PHOTO REFERENCES
2390	Shade	224	1	7	$635	Brown Aurene	ebay-03/01	TPD)6.24
2390					$575	Brown Aurene	ebay-06/01	
2390					$640	Brown Aurene	ebay-12/04	
2390	Footed Shade Vase				$805	Green Silverina	Sknr-10/94	PG1)69,103; MDK)89
2390					$980	Green Silverina	ebay-04/00	
2390					$520	Colorless Silverina	ebay-01/04	
2390					$1150	Colorless Silverina	JDJ-05/04	
2390					$365	Green Silverina	EAC-07/04	
2391	Shade	224	1	8				
2392	Shade	224	1	9	$4140	Decorated Green Aurene	JDJ-06/04	
2393	Shade	224	1	10	$435	Decorated Aurene	ebay-11/00	
2394	Vase	265	1	6				
2395	Vase	265	1	7				
2396	Vase	265	1	8				
2397	Vase	265	2	1				
2398	Puff Box	244	4	1				
2399	Shade	224	1	11	$825	Green Leaves & Vines	ebay-09/04	
2400	Shade	224	2	1				
2401	Shade	224	2	2	$515	Decorated Aurene	ebay-11/00	
2402	Shade	224	2	3				
2403	Shade	227	3	1	$260	Calcite ACB	ebay-11/02	
2404	Shade	227	3	2	$80	VDS	ebay-02/03	
2405	Shade	227	3	3				
2406	Shade	224	2	4				
2407	Shade	227	3	4	$650	Calcite ACB	ebay-12/04	With hanging fixture
2408	Vase	265	2	2	$11000	Tyrian	EAC-07/91	MDK)5:107
2408					$8800	Tyrian	EAC-04/97	
2408					$880	Blue Aurene	Cott-08/01	
2408					$160	Gold Aurene	ebay-11/02	
2408					$190	Gold Aurene	ebay-08/03	
2409	Vase	265	2	3				PG1)XII A,A
2410	Vase	265	2	4				
2411	Vase	265	2	5				PG1)75,117,B; RFR)27,2,A
2412	Vase	265	2	6	$825	Gold Aurene	EAC-07/99	
2412					$760	Gold Aurene	ebay-12/99	
2412					$750	Gold Aurene	ebay-01/00	
2412					$660	VDS	EAC-10/00	
2412					$990	Gold Aurene	EAC-10/00	
2412					$390	Blue Aurene	ebay-10/03	
2413	Vase	265	2	7	$990	Blue Aurene	EAC-10/97	
2414	Vase	265	2	8				
2415	Vase	265	2	9				
2416	Vase	265	3	1				
2417	Vase	265	3	2				
2418	Vase	265	3	3				
2419	Vase	265	3	4				
2420	Vase	265	3	5				TPD)5.33
2421	Vase	265	4	1				
2422	Vase	265	4	2	$14850	Tyrian	EAC-02/92	PG1)XII A,B; JAS)154; TPD)9.26
2422					$14000	Tyrian	EAC-04/02	
2423	Vase	265	4	3				
2424	Vase	265	4	4				
2425	Vase	265	4	5				
2426	Vase	265	4	6				PG1)IX A,B; RFR)27,2,B
2427	Vase	265	5	1	$11760	Tyrian	FtnA-08/01	
2428	Vase	265	5	2				
2429	Vase	265	5	3				
2430	Vase	265	5	4				RLG)168,306;ACR)COLOR1,B,E; TPD)5.65
2431	Vase	265	5	5				
3432	Vase	266	1	1				
2433	Vase	266	1	2				PG1)XII D,A
2434	Vase	266	1	3				PG1)XII C,A
2435	Vase	266	1	4				
2436	Vase	266	1	5				
2437	Vase							See New Drawings section
2438	Vase							See New Drawings section
2439	Vase							See New Drawings section
2440	Vase	266	2	1				
2441	Vase	266	2	2				
2442	Vase	266	2	3				
2443	Vase	266	2	4				
2444	Vase	266	2	5				
2445	Vase	266	2	6				PG1)XII C,B; TPD)10.40
2446	Vase	266	3	1				

SHAPE NO.	ITEM	PAGE	COL	ROW	PRICE REALIZED	GLASS TYPE	AUCTION HOUSE	COMMENTS & PHOTO REFERENCES
2447	Vase	266	3	2	$990	Blue Aurene	EAC-07/99	
2448	Vase	266	3	3				
2449	Vase	266	3	4				
2450	Vase	266	3	5				
2451	Vase	266	3	6				
2452	Vase	266	4	1				
2453	Vase	266	4	2				
2454	Vase	266	4	3				
2455	Vase	266	4	4				
2456	Vase	266	4	5				
2457	Vase	266	4	6				
2458	Vase	266	4	7				
2459	Vase	266	5	1				
2460	Vase	266	5	2				
2461	Vase	266	5	3				PG1)IX A,C
2462	Vase	266	5	4	$25875	Decorated Blue Aurene	JDJ-11/03	
2463	Vase	266	5	5				
2464	Vase	266	5	6				
2465	Vase	267	1	1				
2466	Vase	267	1	2				PG1)IX A,A
2467	Vase	267	1	3				
2468	Vase	267	1	4	$8910	Tyrian	JDJ-05/03	ACR)COLOR 3,B,E
2469	Vase	267	1	5	$1965	Blue Aurene	Rago-01/04	
2470	Vase	267	1	6				
2471	Vase	267	2	1				TPD)5.5
2472	Lamp	201	1	3	$2600	Brown Aurene	ebay-11/02	Shade only
2473	Shade	224	2	5	$1125	Gold Pulled Feather	ebay-05/05	
2474	Shade	224	2	6	$115	Decorated Gold Aurene	Jack-06/02	RFR)13,1,C
2474					$1205	Gold Aurene zipper	EAC-04/05	
2475	Shade	224	2	7	$265	Pulled Feather	ebay-06/01	
2475					$320	Blue Pulled Feather	ebay-01/03	
2475					$440	Blue Pulled Feather	ebay-06/04	
2475					$190	Green Pulled Feather	ebay-11/04	
2476	Shade	224	2	8	$260	Pulled Feather	ebay-11/00	
2476					$450	Blue Pulled Feather	ebay-11/03	
2477	Shade	224	2	9				
2478	Shade	227	3	5				
2479	Shade	224	3	1				
2480	Shade	224	3	2	$275	VDS/G. Aurene threaded	ebay-01/02	
2481	Shade	224	3	3				
2483	Shade	224	3	4	$220	Decorated Gold Calcite	Midw-04/01	
2483					$160	Decorated Gold Calcite	ebay-08/03	
2483					$180	Decorated Gold Calcite	Cinc-11/04	
2483					$105	Decorated Gold Calcite	ebay-11/04	
2483					$150	Decorated Gold Calcite	ebay-11/04	
2483					$200	Decorated Gold Calcite	ebay-03/05	
2483					$175	Decorated Gold Calcite	ebay-04/05	
2483					$185	Decorated Gold Calcite	ebay-04/05	
2483					$250	Decorated Gold Calcite	EAC-07/05	
2484	Lamp	201	1	4				
2485	Shade	227	3	6	$505	Calcite ACB	ebay-11/02	TPD)4.102
2486	Shade	227	3	7	$690	Calcite ACB	Sknr-10/98	
2487	Shade	227	3	8	$1115	Calcite ACB	ebay-09/03	
2487					$540	Calcite ACB	ebay-11/04	
2487					$610	Calcite ACB	ebay-11/04	
2488	Shade	227	3	9				
2489	Shade	227	4	1				
2490	Shade	227	4	2				
2491	Shade	227	4	3				
2492	Shade	227	4	4				
2493	Shade	227	4	5				
2494	Shade	224	3	5				
2495	Vase	267	2	2				
2496	Vase	267	2	3				
2497	Vase	267	2	4				
2498	Vase	267	2	5				
2499	Vase	267	2	6				
2500	Lamp	201	2	1				
2501	Lamp	201	2	2				
2502	Lamp	201	2	3	$6635	Decorated Green Aurene	ebay-05/01	Shade only
2503	Shade	224	3	6				
2504	Lamp	201	3	1				
2505	Shade	224	3	7				
2506	Shade	227	4	6				

SHAPE NO.	ITEM	PAGE	COL	ROW	PRICE REALIZED	GLASS TYPE	AUCTION HOUSE	COMMENTS & PHOTO REFERENCES
2507	Shade	224	3	8				
2508	Shade	224	3	9				
2509	Shade	224	3	10				
2510	Shade	224	4	1				
2511	Shade	224	4	2				
2512	Shade	224	4	3				
2513	Shade	224	4	4				
2514	Lamp							Same as 2500 but in crackled Aurene.
2515	Lamp	201	3	2				
2516	Lamp	201	3	3				
2517	Lamp	201	3	4				TPD)4.108
2518	Lamp	201	4	1				
2519	Shade	227	4	7				
2520	Lamp	201	4	2				Tyrian base, green shade
2521	Lamp							Ivy & Green vine with Aurene border
2522	Lamp							Green cased with Aurene border
2523	Shade	224	4	5	$175	Gold Calcite ACB	ebay-09/03	TPD)10.8
2524	Shade	224	4	6	$155	Gold Aurene	ebay-01/05	
2524					$100	Gold Aurene	ebay-02/05	
2525	Vase	267	3	1				
2526	Lamp	201	4	3				
2527	Lamp	201	5	1				TPD)4.109 Three lights
2528	Lamp							Two light 2527 shade
2529	Lamp							Two light 2526 shade
2530	Lamp	201	5	2	$18720	Leaves & Vines	Cott-02/05	
2531	Shade	224	4	7				
2532	Shade	224	4	8				
2533	Shade	224	4	9	$75	Calcite ACB	ebay-11/00	
2533					$55	Calcite ACB	ebay-04/02	
2533					$35	Calcite ACB	ebay-05/02	
2533					$45	Calcite ACB	ebay-01/03	
2533					$115	Calcite ACB	ebay-09/01	
2533					$105	Calcite ACB	EAC-07/04	Etched "Warwick"
2533					$100	Calcite ACB	EAC-07/04	Etched "Oak Leaf and Acorn"
2533					$120	Gold Calcite	ebay-11/04	
2533	Vase (Shade Vase)				$1495	Dark Blue Jade	Sknr-05/94	TPD)9.29:10.3
2533					$230	Ivory	Sknr-10/96	
2533					$825	Blue Aurene	EAC-04/97	
2533					$1090	Blue Aurene	Sknr-01/98	
2533					$200	Ivrene	Sknr-05/98	
2533					$575	Blue Aurene	EAC-10/98	
2533					$460	Ivrene	JDJ-05/99	
2533					$950	Blue Aurene	ebay-12/99	
2533					$585	Blue Aurene	ebay-01/00	
2533					$370	Blue Aurene	ebay-03/00	
2533					$600	Blue Aurene	ebay-06/00	
2533					$345	Ivrene	Sknr-06/00	
2533					$695	Blue Aurene	ebay-04/01	
2533					$495	Wisteria	Cott-08/01	
2533					$165	Alabaster	Cott-08/01	
2533					$325	Blue Aurene	ebay-08/01	
2533					$450	Blue Aurene	ebay-09/01	
2533					$350	Blue Aurene	Ogal-11/01	
2533					$510	Blue Aurene	ebay-12/01	
2533					$560	Blue Aurene	ebay-12/01	
2533					$295	Gold Aurene	ebay-12/01	
2533					$230	Ivory	ebay-12/01	
2533					$230	Gold Aurene	Jack-12/01	
2533					$150	Ivory	ebay-04/02	
2533					$155	Gold Aurene	ebay-05/02	
2533					$405	Blue Aurene	ebay-09/02	
2533					$319	Green Jade	ebay-10/02	
2533					$505	Blue Aurene	JDJ-11/02	
2533					$570	Gold Aurene	JDJ-11/02	
2533					$525	Blue Aurene	ebay-03/03	
2533					$190	Ivory	ebay-07/03	
2533					$115	Alabaster	ebay-07/03	
2533					$285	Ivory	ebay-07/03	
2533					$185	Alabaster	ebay-08/03	
2533					$435	Blue Aurene	ebay-08/03	
2533					$750	Blue Aurene	EAC-11/03	
2533					$80	Calcite ACB	ebay-12/03	
2533					$690	Blue Aurene	ebay-01/04	
2533					$600	Blue Aurene	ebay-02/04	

SHAPE NO.	ITEM	PAGE	COL	ROW	PRICE REALIZED	GLASS TYPE	AUCTION HOUSE	COMMENTS & PHOTO REFERENCES
2533					$1090	Gold Aurene	EAC-04/04	
2533					$210	Ivrene	ebay-05/04	
2533					$285	Ivory	JDJ-05/04	
2533					$175	Ivrene	ebay-06/04	
2533					$610	Blue Aurene	ebay-07/04	
2533					$1010	Blue Aurene	EAC-07/04	
2533					$105	Sea Green	ebay-09/04	
2533					$610	Blue Aurene	ebay-09/04	
2533					$175	Ivrene	ebay-11/04	
2533					$85	Sea Green	ebay-11/04	
2533					$105	Sea Green	ebay-02/05	
2533					$150	Ivrene	ebay-02/05	
2533					$430	Blue Aurene	Hrtg-03/05	
2533					$125	Ivrene	ebay-03/05	
2533					$130	Alabaster	ebay-04/05	
2533					$115	Ivory	ebay-06/05	
2533					$135	Ivory	ebay-07/05	
2534	Lamp	201	5	3				
2535	Lamp	201	5	4	$2250	Brown Aurene	ebay-11/01	Shade only
2536	Lamp	202	1	1				
2537	Lamp	202	1	2				
2538	Lamp	202	1	3				
2539	Lamp	202	1	4				
2540	Lamp	202	1	5	$3000	Decorated Gold Aurene	JDJ-06/05	Complete lamp.
2541	Lamp	202	2	1				
2542	Lamp	202	2	2				
2543	Shade	227	4	8				TPD)4.111
2544	Shade	224	4	10				
2545	Shade	224	4	11	$180	Gold Aurene	ebay-09/01	
2545					$285	Gold Aurene	ebay-04/05	
2546	Shade	224	5	1				
2547	Vase	267	3	2				
2548	Vase	267	3	3				
2549	Vase	267	3	4				
2550	Vase	267	3	5				
2551	Vase	267	3	6				
2552	Decanter	185	3	4				RFR)8,3,B; ACR)135,246
2553	Nut Dish	211	3	10	$440	Gold Aurene	EAC-04/98	
2553					$1060	Blue Aurene	Ogal-02/04	
2553					$460	Blue Aurene	EAC-04/04	
2554	Vase	267	3	7				
2555	Vase	267	4	1				
2556	Vase	267	4	2	$550	Gold Aurene	EAC-04/91	
2556					$330	Blue Aurene	EAC-04/93	
2556					$430	Blue Aurene	Sknr-05/94	
2556					$285	Green Jade/Alabaster	Sknr-01/96	
2556					$290	Gold Aurene	Sknr-05/96	
2556					$525	Blue Aurene	EAC-10/96	
2556					$375	Ivory & Black	JDJ-10/96	
2556					$410	Green Jade/Alabaster	EAC-04/97	
2556					$360	Blue Aurene	EAC-10/97	
2556					$400	Blue Aurene	JDJ-10/97	
2556					$375	Blue Aurene	Sknr-01/98	
2556					$495	Gold Aurene	EAC-04/98	
2556					$220	Gold Aurene	EAC-07/98	
2556					$285	Blue Aurene	EAC-07/98	
2556					$260	Blue Aurene	Sknr-10/98	
2556					$440	Blue Aurene	EAC-04/99	
2556					$275	Rosaline/Alabaster	EAC-04/99	
2556					$550	Rosaline/Alabaster	EAC-04/99	
2556					$385	Gold Aurene	ebay-11/99	
2556					$385	Gold Aurene	ebay-11/99	
2556					$235	Gold Aurene	ebay-12/99	
2556					$385	Gold Aurene	ebay-01/00	
2556					$175	Green Jade/Alabaster	ebay-10/00	
2556					$265	Gold Aurene	ebay-11/00	
2556					$200	Green Jade/Alabaster	ebay-01/01	
2556					$660	Blue Aurene	ebay-02/01	
2556					$195	Green Jade/Alabaster	ebay-03/01	
2556					$225	Gold Aurene	EAC-04/01	
2556					$335	Gold Aurene	EAC-04/01	
2556					$185	Green Jade/Alabaster	ebay-06/01	
2556					$700	Blue Aurene 16"	ebay-07/01	
2556					$300	Gold Aurene	Cott-08/01	

SHAPE NO.	ITEM	PAGE	COL	ROW	PRICE REALIZED	GLASS TYPE	AUCTION HOUSE	COMMENTS & PHOTO REFERENCES
2556					$385	Blue Aurene	Cott-08/01	
2556					$390	Blue Aurene	EAC-09/01	
2556					$365	Blue Aurene	EAC-09/01	
2556					$500	Blue Aurene	ebay-10/01	
2556					$140	Rosaline/Alabaster	ebay-10/01	
2556					$170	Gold Aurene	Ogal-10/01	
2556					$305	Gold Aurene	ebay-11/01	
2556					$540	Blue Aurene	JDJ-11/01	
2556					$225	Green Jade/Alabaster	ebay-12/01	
2556					$355	Gold Aurene	ebay-12/01	
2556					$330	Blue Aurene	ebay-03/02	
2556					$240	Gold Aurene	ebay-03/02	
2556					$400	Gold Aurene	ebay-03/02	
2556					$150	Gold Aurene	ebay-04/02	
2556					$250	Gold Aurene	ebay-04/02	Haviland signature
2556					$230	Green Jade/Alabaster	JDJ-05/02	
2556					$400	Blue Aurene	JDJ-05/02	
2556					$120	Gold Aurene	Sknr-06/02	Haviland signature
2556					$150	Rosaline/Alabaster	ebay-08/02	
2556					$675	Blue Aurene	ebay-08/02	10" high
2556					$205	Rosaline/Alabaster	ebay-09/02	
2556					$350	Gold Aurene	ebay-09/02	
2556					$375	Gold Aurene	ebay-09/02	
2556					$350	Blue Aurene	Tway-09/02	
2556					$250	Blue Aurene	ebay-10/02	
2556					$280	Gold Aurene	ebay-11/02	
2556					$300	Green Jade/Alabaster	JDJ-11/02	
2556					$360	Gold Aurene	JDJ-11/02	
2556					$510	Blue Aurene	JDJ-11/02	
2556					$300	Blue Aurene	ebay-11/02	
2556					$390	Gold Aurene	ebay-11/02	
2556					$575	Blue Aurene	Jack–11/02	
2556					$170	Rosaline/Alabaster	Cinc-11/02	
2556					$160	VDS (E)	Cinc-11/02	
2556					$140	Blue Aurene	ebay-01/03	
2556					$170	Gold Aurene	EAC-01/03	
2556					$360	Blue Aurene	ebay-01/03	
2556					$380	Blue Aurene	ebay-01/03	
2556					$40	Gold Aurene	ebay-02/03	Price is not an error
2556					$155	Rosaline/Alabaster	ebay-02/03	
2556					$415	Gold Aurene	ebay-03/03	
2556					$300	Blue Aurene	ebay-03/03	
2556					$650	Blue Aurene	ebay-03/03	
2556					$255	Blue Aurene	ebay-05/03	
2556					$335	Blue Aurene	ebay-05/03	
2556					$390	Gold Aurene	ebay-05/03	
2556					$230	Blue Aurene	ebay-06/03	
2556					$300	Gold Aurene	ebay-06/03	
2556					$285	Gold Aurene	ebay-07/03	
2556					$130	Blue Aurene	ebay-08/03	
2556					$120	Gold Aurene	ebay-09/03	
2556					$360	Gold Aurene	ebay-10/03	
2556					$165	Gold Aurene	ebay-10/03	
2556					$280	Blue Aurene	ebay-11/03	
2556					$330	Blue Aurene	ebay-11/03	
2556					$230	Rosaline/Alabaster foot	JDJ-11/03	
2556					$400	Gold Aurene	ebay-12/03	
2556					$80	Gold Aurene	ebay-12/03	Signed "Haviland"
2556					$190	Gold Aurene	ebay-01/04	
2556					$415	Gold Aurene	ebay-01/04	
2556					$545	Blue Aurene	ebay-01/04	
2556					$155	Green Jade/Alabaster foot	ebay-02/04	
2556					$405	Blue Aurene	ebay-02/04	
2556					$295	Gold Aurene	ebay-03/04	
2556					$490	Blue Aurene	EAC-04/04	
2556					$455	Blue Aurene	ebay-04/04	
2556					$300	Gold Aurene	ebay-05/04	
2556					$100	VDS (E)	ebay-05/04	Signed "Hawkes"
2556					$265	Gold Aurene	ebay-05/04	
2556					$480	Blue Aurene	JDJ-05/04	
2556					$110	VDS	ebay-06/04	
2556					$160	Gold Aurene	ebay-06/04	
2556					$295	Gold Aurene	ebay-06/04	
2556					$340	Blue Aurene	ebay-07/04	

SHAPE NO.	ITEM	PAGE	COL	ROW	PRICE REALIZED	GLASS TYPE	AUCTION HOUSE	COMMENTS & PHOTO REFERENCES
2556					$150	Green Jade/Alabaster foot	ebay-07/04	
2556					$350	Blue Aurene	ebay-07/04	
2556					$175	Gold Aurene	ebay-08/04	
2556					$360	Blue Aurene	ebay-08/04	
2556					$200	Gold Aurene	ebay-09/04	
2556					$100	Rosaline/Alabaster	ebay-09/04	Alabaster foot
2556					$200	Gold Aurene	Crft-09/04	
2556					$280	Gold Aurene	ebay-09/04	
2556					$400	Blue Aurene	ebay-10/04	
2556					$330	Gold Aurene	EAC-10/04	
2556					$375	Gold Aurene	ebay-11/04	
2556					$300	Blue Aurene	ebay-11/04	
2556					$930	Blue Aurene	JDJ-11/04	
2556					$70	Celeste Blue	ebay-01/05	
2556					$160	Rosaline/Alabaster foot	ebay-04/05	
2556					$305	Gold Aurene	ebay-04/05	
2556					$515	Blue Aurene	ebay-04/05	
2556					$230	Gold Aurene	EAC-04/05	
2556					$345	Gold Aurene	EAC-04/05	
2556					$255	Gold Aurene	ebay-05/05	
2556					$175	Green Jade/Alabaster foot	ebay-06/05	
2556					$330	Blue Aurene	ebay-06/05	
2556					$305	Gold Aurene	ebay-07/05	
2556					$400	Blue Aurene	EAC-07/05	
2557	Shade	224	5	2				
2558	Shade	224	5	3				
2559	Shade	224	5	4				
2560	Shade	224	5	5				
2561	Shade	224	5	6				
2562	Shade	224	5	7				
2563	Shade	224	5	8				
2564	Vase	267	4	3				
2565	Shade	227	4	9				
2566	Shade	228	1	1				
2567	Shade	228	1	2	$180	Calcite ACB	ebay-03/02	
2567					$195	Calcite ACB	ebay-08/04	
2567					$260	Calcite ACB	ebay-04/05	
2567					$260	Calcite ACB	EAC-04/05	
2568	Shade	224	5	9				
2569	Shade	224	5	10				
2570	Shade	224	5	11				
2570½	Shade	225	1	1				
2571	Shade	225	1	2	$85	Calcite ACB	ebay-03/02	
2571					$130	Calcite ACB	ebay-10/02	
2571					$265	Gold Aurene	ebay-10/02	
2571					$120	Calcite ACB	ebay-12/04	
2571					$90	Calcite ACB	ebay-02/05	
2572	Shade	225	1	3				
2573	Shade	225	1	4				
2574	Shade	225	1	5	$200	Gold Calcite	ebay-03/01	
2575	Shade	225	1	6	$85	Calcite ACB	Sknr-06/00	
2575					$50	Calcite	ebay-01/01	
2575	Vase				$170	Ivrene	ebay-06/01	
2576	Shade	225	1	7	$120	Calcite	ebay-12/00	
2577	Shade	225	1	8	$175	Gold Calcite	ebay-03/02	
2577					$160	Gold Calcite	ebay-09/04	
2578	Shade	225	1	9				
2579	Shade	225	1	10	$275	Gold Aurene (E)	ebay-10/02	TPD)4.106
2580	Shade	225	2	1	$170	Gold Aurene	ebay-12/02	
2581	Shade	225	2	2	$130	Calcite ACB	ebay-06/03	
2581					$80	Calcite ACB	ebay-07/03	
2582	Shade	225	2	3	$225	Gold Calcite	ebay-02/00	
2583	Shade	225	2	4	$150	Gold Aurene	EAC-07/98	
2583					$1000	Gold Calcite ACB	ebay-06/02	
2583					$520	Gold Calcite ACB	ebay-04/05	
2584	Shade	225	2	5	$150	Gold Aurene	ebay-04/04	
2585	Bowl	142	1	5				
2586	Bowl	142	1	6	$605	Blue Aurene	EAC-07/90	RFR)27,2,C
2586					$275	Gold Aurene	EAC-02/92	
2586					$605	Blue Aurene	EAC-04/93	
2586					$990	Blue Aurene	EAC-04/93	
2586					$990	Blue Aurene	JDJ-05/94	
2586					$550	Gold Aurene	JDJ-10/94	
2586					$55	Rosaline	JDJ-10/94	

SHAPE NO.	ITEM	PAGE	COL	ROW	PRICE REALIZED	GLASS TYPE	AUCTION HOUSE	COMMENTS & PHOTO REFERENCES
2586					$385	Gold Aurene	EAC-04/96	
2586					$385	Blue Aurene	JDJ-06/96	
2586					$1265	Blue Aurene	EAC-07/96	
2586					$575	Blue Aurene	JDJ-06/97	
2586					$690	Blue Aurene	JDJ-06/97	
2586					$200	Gold Calcite	JDJ-10/97	
2586					$260	Gold Calcite	JDJ-10/97	
2586					$495	Gold Aurene	EAC-10/97	
2586					$255	Gold Aurene	Sknr-10/97	
2586					$230	VDS	Sknr-01/98	
2586					$410	Blue Aurene	EAC-04/99	
2586					$495	Yellow Jade	EAC-07/99	
2586					$440	Light Blue Jade	EAC-07/99	
2586					$260	Gold Calcite	Sknr-10/99	
2586					$510	Calcite	ebay-12/99	
2586					$450	Blue Aurene	ebay-01/00	
2586					$510	Blue Aurene	ebay-02/00	
2586					$2245	Blue Aurene (E)	JDJ-11/00	
2586					$260	Cyprian	ebay-04/00	
2586					$375	Gold Calcite	Sknr-02/01	
2586					$85	Celeste Blue	ebay-02/01	
2586					$350	Rosaline	Ogal-04/01	
2586					$1345	Blue Aurene	EAC-04/01	
2586					$150	VDS	ebay-05/01	
2586					$270	Gold Calcite	ebay-07/01	
2586					$125	VDS	ebay-09/01	
2586					$90	VDS	ebay-10/01	
2586					$225	Gold Calcite	ebay-10/01	
2586					$785	Blue Aurene	EAC-11/01	
2586					$550	Gold Aurene	ebay-12/01	
2586					$250	VDS	ebay-12/01	
2586					$345	Gold Calcite	Jack-12/01	
2586					$500	Blue Aurene	ebay-01/02	
2586					$475	Gold Calcite	ebay-03/02	
2586					$200	Blue Aurene	ebay-03/02	
2586					$435	VDS	Tway-05/02	
2586					$230	VDS	JDJ-05/02	
2586					$450	Blue Aurene	ebay-05/02	
2586					$800	Gold Aurene	ebay-05/02	
2586					$200	Gold Calcite	Jack-06/02	
2586					$345	Gold Calcite	Jack-06/02	
2586					$460	Gold Calcite	Jack-06/02	
2586					$200	Gold Calcite	ebay-09/02	
2586					$405	Gold Calcite	ebay-09/02	
2586					$250	VDS	Cinc-11/02	
2586					$585	Gold Aurene	ebay-01/03	
2586					$560	Blue Aurene	EAC-01/03	
2586					$400	Blue Aurene	ebay-01/03	
2586					$330	Gold Aurene	ebay-03/03	
2586					$170	Gold Calcite	ebay-04/03	
2586					$170	Gold Calcite	ebay-04/03	
2586					$125	Celeste Blue	ebay-05/03	
2586					$200	Gold Calcite	ebay-06/03	
2586					$300	Gold Aurene	ebay-09/03	
2586					$250	Gold Calcite	ebay-11/03	
2586					$225	Gold Calcite	ebay-11/03	
2586					$325	Gold Calcite	ebay-11/03	
2586					$690	Blue Aurene	EAC-11/03	
2586					$325	Gold Aurene	Sknr-12/03	
2586					$340	Blue Aurene	ebay-12/03	
2586					$700	Blue Aurene	ebay-01/04	
2586					$180	Rosaline	ebay-02/04	
2586					$375	Gold Aurene (FC)	ebay-02/04	
2586					$400	Blue Aurene	ebay-04/04	
2586					$405	Blue Aurene	ebay-04/04	
2586					$575	Yellow Jade	JDJ-05/04	
2586					$450	Blue Aurene	Tway-05/04	
2586					$355	Gold Calcite	ebay-05/04	
2586					$615	Blue Aurene	EAC-07/04	
2586					$430	Gold Aurene	ebay-08/04	
2586					$95	Gold Calcite	ebay-08/04	
2586					$165	Gold Aurene	ebay-08/04	
2586					$255	Gold Calcite	ebay-10/04	
2586					$275	Amethyst	EAC-10/04	

SHAPE NO.	ITEM	PAGE	COL	ROW	PRICE REALIZED	GLASS TYPE	AUCTION HOUSE	COMMENTS & PHOTO REFERENCES
2586					$190	Gold Calcite	ebay-01/05	
2586					$565	Gold Aurene	ebay-04/05	
2586					$1035	Blue Aurene	EAC-04/05	
2586					$200	Gold Calcite	ebay-05/05	
2586					$360	Gold Aurene	JDJ-06/05	
2586					$840	Blue Aurene	JDJ-06/05	
2586					$275	Gold Calcite	ebay-06/05	
2586					$400	Blue Aurene	ebay-06/05	
2586					$140	Celeste Blue	ebay-07/05	
2586					$410	Gold Aurene	ebay-07/05	With gilt metal stand
2586					$1205	Blue Aurene	EAC-07/05	
2587	Bowl	142	1	7				
2588	Vase	267	4	4	$220	Gold Aurene	JDJ-10/94	
2589	Vase	267	4	5	$8510	Tyrian	ebay-02/00	
2590	Shade	228	1	3				
2591	Shade	228	1	4				
2592	Shade	228	1	5				
2593	Shade	228	1	6	$550	Calcite	Cott-08/01	
2594	Shade	228	1	7				
2595	Shade	228	1	8				
2596	Shade	228	2	1				
2597	Shade	228	2	2,3	$430	Calcite ACB (bullet)	ebay-03/02	
2598	Vase	267	4	6	$230	Amber/Flemish Blue	ebay-01/03	TPD)10.42
2599	Vase	267	5	1				
2600	Vase	267	5	2	$1100	Gold Aurene	JDJ-05/95	
2601	Vase	267	5	3	$300	Topaz/Celeste Blue	ebay-01/01	
2602	Vase	267	5	4				
2603	Vase	267	5	5				ACR)144,273; TPD)10.85
2604	Compote	172	3	3	$1045	Gold Aurene	EAC-04/90	PG2)60,A; JAS)164,B,A; ACR)152,299;
2604					$880	Blue Aurene	EAC-10/91	TPD)10.107
2604					$770	Gold Aurene	EAC-07/92	
2604					$920	Gold Calcite	Sknr-10/97	
2604					$515	Celeste Blue	Sknr-02/01	
2604					$300	Topaz	ebay-06/01	
2604					$230	Amber/Celeste Blue dec.	ebay-07/02	
2604					$1725	Gold Aurene	ebay-10/02	
2604					$235	Celeste Blue	ebay-01/03	
2604					$1550	Blue Aurene	EAC-06/03	
2604					$1790	Gold Aurene	EAC-07/04	
2604					$215	Flemish	ebay-09/04	
2604					$1135	Blue Aurene	ebay-10/04	
2604					$275	Flemish	ebay-10/04	
2604					$90	Topaz	ebay-02/05	
2604					$2300	Gold Aurene	EAC–07/05	
2605	Nappie	233	2	9	$565	Gold Aurene	ebay-08/03	TPD)10.107
2605					$225	Flemish	ebay-12/04	
2606	Shade	225	2	6				
2607	Shade	225	2	7				
2608	Plate	158	1	15	$230	Gold Calcite	JDJ-11/03	TPD)7.50
2608					$350	Gold Aurene	ebay-02/04	
2608					$760	Gold Calcite	ebay-05/04	
2608					$300	Gold Calcite	ebay-02/05	
2609	Shade	225	2	8				
2610	Shade	225	2	9	$115	Calcite engraved	ebay-04/02	
2610					$265	Leaves and Vines	ebay-08/03	
2610					$160	Gold Aurene	ebay-10/03	
2611	Shade	225	2	10				
2612	Bowl	142	1	8				PG1)XI A; TPD)4.46
2613	Centerpiece	147	3	5				TPD)4.37
2614	Vase	267	5	6				MDK)121
2615	Vase	268	1	1				
2616	Vase	268	1	2				RFR)11,4,E
2617	Vase	268	1	3				
2618	Bowl	142	1	9	$800	Gold Aurene	Ogal-06/00	
2619	Vase	268	1	4	$1120	Blue Aurene	EAC-09/02	
2620	Vase	268	1	5				
2621	Vase	268	1	6	$860	Blue Aurene	Sknr-02/01	Haviland signature
2622	Vase	268	1	7	$265	Gold Aurene	ebay-05/05	
2622	Plate	158	1	9				This number is an error, see #2625.
2623	Vase	268	1	8				
2624	Vase	268	1	9				
2625	Plate	158	1	9				This shape shown as # 2622 in Gardner.
2626	Shade	225	2	11	$380	Gold Aurene/Green dec.	ebay-07/03	Green Pulled Feather
2627	Vase	268	2	1				

SHAPE NO.	ITEM	PAGE	COL	ROW	PRICE REALIZED	GLASS TYPE	AUCTION HOUSE	COMMENTS & PHOTO REFERENCES
2628	Vase	268	2	2				
2629	Vase	268	2	3				RFR)8,1,C
2630	Vase	268	2	4				
2631	Vase	268	2	5				
2632	Vase	268	2	6				
2633	Vase	268	2	7				
2634	Vase	268	2	8				
2635	Vase	268	2	9				
2636	Vase	268	2	10	$170	Green Jade	JDJ-11/03	
2637	Vase	268	2	11				
2638	Vase	268	3	1	$660	Blue Aurene	ebay-10/03	
2639	Vase	268	3	2	$880	Green Cintra	ebay-04/01	
2640	Vase	268	3	3	$460	Blue Aurene	JDJ-06/98	
2640					$425	Blue Aurene	ebay-02/00	
2640					$335	Blue Aurene	ebay-07/03	
2640					$520	Gold Aurene	ebay-02/04	
2640					$630	Blue Aurene	EAC-04/04	
2640					$570	Gold Aurene	Tway-03/05	
2641	Vase	268	3	4	$285	Gold Aurene	JDJ-06/98	
2641					$505	Blue Aurene	Ogal-10/04	
2641					$500	Blue Aurene	ebay-04/05	
2642	Compote	172	3	4	$660	Gold Aurene	EAC-04/90	RFR)9,3,A
2642					$440	Gold Aurene	EAC-10/91	
2642					$575	Gold Aurene	EAC-02/92	
2642					$330	Gold Aurene	JDJ-10/94	
2642					$460	Gold Aurene	Sknr-05/96	
2642					$880	Blue Calcite	EAC-04/96	
2642					$770	Gold Calcite	EAC-04/96	
2642					$990	Blue Aurene	EAC-10/96	
2642					$460	Gold Aurene	Sknr-10/97	
2642					$850	Gold Aurene	EAC-10/99	
2642					$1325	Blue Aurene	ebay-06/01	
2642					$525	Gold Aurene	ebay-06/01	
2642					$460	Gold Aurene	ebay-09/01	
2642					$1120	Blue Aurene	EAC-11/01	
2642					$350	Gold Calcite	ebay-05/02	
2642					$380	Gold Calcite	ebay-06/02	
2642					$680	Gold Aurene	ebay-08/02	
2642					$1200	Gold Aurene	JDJ-11/02	
2642					$950	Blue Aurene	Ogal-12/02	
2642					$1215	Blue Aurene	ebay-01/03	
2642					$180	Topaz/Celeste Blue rim	ebay-01/03	
2642					$1255	Blue Aurene	ebay-02/03	
2642					$575	Gold Aurene	ebay-03/03	
2642					$1175	Blue Aurene	Sknr-05/03	
2642					$790	Blue Aurene	ebay-06/03	
2642					$700	Gold Aurene	Ogal-07/03	
2642					$1120	Blue Aurene	Ogal-09/03	
2642					$475	Blue Aurene	ebay-11/03	
2642					$1065	Gold Aurene	Ogal-12/03	
2642					$65	Citron Yellow	ebay-03/04	
2642					$695	Gold Aurene	ebay-06/04	
2642					$400	Gold Aurene	ebay-09/04	
2642					$375	Gold Aurene	ebay-11/04	
2642					$700	Gold Aurene	ebay-11/04	
2642					$805	Gold Aurene	EAC-04/05	
2642					$520	Gold Aurene	EAC-04/05	
2642					$920	Blue Aurene	EAC-04/05	
2642					$685	Gold Aurene	ebay-06/05	
2643	Punch Cup	216	2	3				
2644	Shade	225	3	1	$770	Gold Aurene	EAC-07/92	
2645	Shade	225	3	2				
2646	Vase	268	3	5				
2647	Vase	268	3	6	$440	Gold Aurene	EAC-07/92	Signed "Haviland"
2647					$575	Blue Aurene	EAC-10/95	
2647					$115	Gold Aurene	JDJ-11/03	Signed "Haviland"
2648	Vase	268	3	7	$660	Blue Aurene	EAC-10/94	JAS)152,T,A; TPD)4.86
2648					$605	Blue Aurene	EAC-08/00	
2648					$410	Gold Aurene	ebay-12/00	
2648					$150	VDS	ebay-12/00	
2648					$630	Blue Aurene	ebay-02/01	
2648					$1065	Blue Aurene	EAC-04/01	
2648					$1210	Blue Aurene	Cott-08/01	
2648					$715	Gold Aurene	Cott-08/01	

SHAPE NO.	ITEM	PAGE	COL	ROW	PRICE REALIZED	GLASS TYPE	AUCTION HOUSE	COMMENTS & PHOTO REFERENCES
2648					$385	Green Jade	Cott-08/01	
2648					$330	VDS	Cott-08/01	
2648					$385	Blue Aurene	ebay-11/01	
2648					$335	Blue Aurene	EAC-11/01	
2648					$360	Gold Aurene	ebay-03/02	
2648					$435	Blue Aurene	ebay-04/02	
2648					$400	Gold Aurene	ebay-05/02	
2648					$505	Blue Aurene	ebay-05/02	
2648					$355	Blue Aurene	ebay-09/02	
2648					$360	Gold Aurene	JDJ-11/02	
2648					$615	Gold Aurene	EAC-01/03	
2648					$390	Blue Aurene	ebay-01/03	
2648					$235	Gold Aurene	ebay-04/03	
2648					$500	Blue Aurene	ebay-04/03	
2648					$445	Blue Aurene	ebay-06/03	
2648					$300	Gold Aurene	ebay-08/03	
2648					$285	Gold Aurene	ebay-09/03	
2648					$500	Blue Aurene	ebay-09/03	
2648					$250	Gold Aurene	J&W-09/03	
2648					$550	Blue Aurene	ebay-10/03	
2648					$730	Blue Aurene	EAC-07/04	
2648					$325	Gold Aurene	Sknr–12/04	
2648					$350	Gold Aurene (FC)	ebay-05/05	
2648					$460	Gold Aurene	EAC-07/05	
2649	Vase	268	3	8	$770	Gold Aurene	Cott-08/01	MDK)144
2650	Vase	268	3	9	$230	Gold Aurene	ebay-04/02	
2650					$495	Gold Aurene	ebay-02/03	
2650					$430	Gold Aurene	Jack-06/03	
2651	Vase	268	3	10	$450	Gold Aurene	EAC-11/01	
2652	Vase	268	3	11	$2650	Blue Aurene	ebay-12/99	
2652					$900	Blue Aurene	ebay-02/00	
2652					$1495	Blue Aurene	EAC-04/04	
2653	Salt	217	2	10	$405	Gold Aurene	ebay-01/00	
2654	Shade	228	2	4				
2655	Shade	228	2	5				
2656	Limousine Vase	207	1	8				
2657	Shade	228	2	6				
2658	Shade	228	2	7				
2659	Shade	225	3	3				
2660	Celery Dip	217	2	12	$220	Gold Aurene	EAC-07/96	
2660					$225	Gold Aurene	ebay-12/99	
2660					$400	Gold Aurene	ebay-03/04	
2660					$45	VDS	ebay-10/04	
2660					$25	VDS	ebay-11/04	
2660					$45	VDS	ebay-01/05	
2661	Salt	217	2	11	$440	Blue Aurene	EAC-07/96	
2661					$175	Gold Aurene	JDJ-06/98	
2661					$205	Gold Aurene	ebay-10/02	
2661					$570	Blue Aurene	ebay-12/04	
2662	Salt	217	2	13	$160	Gold Aurene	EAC-02/92	
2662					$650	Blue Aurene	ebay-01/00	
2663	Shade	225	3	4	$1100	Decorated Red Aurene	EAC-04/91	TPD)10.148
2663					$820	Decorated Red Aurene	ebay-12/00	
2663					$20	Calcite	ebay-02/02	
2663					$130	Calcite ACB	ebay-03/03	
2663					$750	Decorated Brown Aurene	ebay-05/03	
2663					$995	Decorated Red Aurene	ebay-09/03	
2663					$65	Calcite ACB	ebay-10/03	
2663					$1900	Decorated Green Aurene	ebay-12/03	
2663					$115	Calcite ACB	ebay-02/05	
2664	Shade	225	3	5	$50	Calcite ACB	ebay-09/03	
2665	Shade	225	3	6				
2666	Vase	268	3	12				
2667	Shade	228	2	8				
2668	Shade	228	3	1				
2669	Café Noir Set	216	3	10				
2670	Nappie	233	2	10	$715	Gold Aurene	EAC-04/97	MDK)98
2670					$880	Gold Aurene	Cott-08/01	
2670					$560	Gold Aurene	ebay-10/01	
2670					$1325	Gold Aurene	ebay-03/02	
2670					$690	Blue Aurene	EAC-04/05	
2671	Nappie	233	2	11				
2672	Cold Cream Jar	243	6	6				
2673	Jar	138	4	2				

SHAPE NO.	ITEM	PAGE	COL	ROW	PRICE REALIZED	GLASS TYPE	AUCTION HOUSE	COMMENTS & PHOTO REFERENCES
2674	Hair Receiver	245	3	4				
2675	Dresser Set	245	3	5				
2676	Hair Receiver	245	3	6	$660	Gold Aurene	ebay-05/04	
2677	Vase	268	4	1				
2678	Vase	268	4	2	$1540	Blue Calcite	EAC-10/97	
2678					$1295	Gold Aurene	ebay-01/03	
2679	Vase	268	4	3	$25	Topaz	ebay-10/04	
2680	Finger Bowl				$75	Amethyst	ebay-11/99	
2680					$250	Gold Aurene	ebay-06/01	
2680					$230	Gold Calcite	ebay-05/02	
2680					$50	Celeste Blue	ebay-04/04	
2680					$140	Rosaline	ebay-05/04	
2680					$265	Gold Calcite	ebay-05/04	
2680					$120	Gold Calcite	ebay-06/04	
2680					$225	Gold Calcite	ebay-06/04	
2680					$100	Celeste Blue	ebay-08/04	
2680					$180	Gold Calcite	ebay-08/04	
2680					$125	Amethyst	ebay-08/04	
2680					$100	VDS (E)	ebay-09/04	
2680					$60	Green Jade	ebay-02/05	
2680					$20	Amethyst	ebay-09/04	Fingerbowl only
2680					$185	VDS (E)	ebay-10/04	Fingerbowl only
2680					$40	Green Jade/Alabaster	ebay-10/04	
2680					$460	Gold Calcite	ebay-11/04	
2680					$180	Gold Calcite	JDJ-11/04	
2680					$150	Alabaster	ebay-11/04	
2680					$75	Green Jade	ebay-11/04	
2680					$45	Green Jade	ebay-11/04	
2680					$45	Green Jade	ebay-12/04	
2680					$80	Green Jade	ebay-01/05	
2680					$80	Green Jade	ebay-01/05	
2680					$40	Colorless (E)	ebay-05/05	Fingerbowl only, Engraved "Marguerite"
2680					$75	Gold Calcite	JDJ-06/05	Fingerbowl only
2680					$20	Amethyst	ebay-07/05	Fingerbowl only
2680	Sherbet	197	2	10	$880	Blue Calcite	EAC-07/91	PG1)XI,B,A; RFR)14,2,A;
2680					$165	Gold Calcite	EAC-10/93	MDK)52:53:69:72:120
2680					$545	Blue Calcite	Sknr-10/94	
2680					$715	Blue Calcite	EAC-04/95	
2680					$310	Light Blue Jade	EAC-04/95	
2680					$260	Gold Calcite	EAC-04/95	
2680					$230	VDS	Sknr-01/96	
2680					$495	Gold Calcite	EAC-04/96	
2680					$825	Blue Calcite	EAC-04/96	
2680					$285	Gold Calcite	Sknr-10/96	
2680					$350	Blue Calcite	EAC-10/96	
2680					$275	Gold Calcite	EAC-04/97	
2680					$250	Gold Calcite	EAC-04/97	
2680					$270	Gold Calcite	JDJ-06/97	
2680					$515	Blue Aurene	Sknr-01/98	
2680					$575	Light Blue Jade	Sknr-01/98	
2680					$520	Gold Aurene	Sknr-01/98	
2680					$135	Rosaline/Alabaster	EAC-07/98	
2680					$450	Gold Aurene	ebay-01/99	
2680					$330	Gold Calcite	ebay-11/99	
2680					$175	Green Jade/Alabaster	ebay-11/99	
2680					$715	Blue Calcite	Cinc-12/99	
2680					$825	Blue Aurene	Cinc-12/99	
2680					$325	Gold Calcite	ebay-02/00	
2680					$140	Green Jade/Alabaster	ebay-03/00	
2680					$100	Rosaline/Alabaster	ebay-03/00	
2680					$65	VDS	ebay-03/00	
2680					$350	Gold Calcite ribbed	Ogal-03/00	Sherbet only
2680					$280	Gold Aurene	ebay-04/00	
2680					$115	VDS	Sknr-06/00	
2680					$170	Green Jade	Sknr-06/00	
2680					$325	Rosaline/Alabaster	Ogal-10/00	
2680					$175	Mirror Black	Sknr-02/01	Sherbet only
2680					$200	Rosaline/Alabaster	ebay-03/01	
2680					$280	Gold Calcite	EAC-04/01	
2680					$265	Rosaline/Alabaster	ebay-05/01	
2680					$140	Gold Calcite	JDJ-05/01	
2680					$125	Gold Calcite	ebay-05/01	
2680					$245	Gold Calcite	ebay-06/01	
2680					$135	Rosaline/Alabaster	ebay-06/01	

SHAPE NO.	ITEM	PAGE	COL	ROW	PRICE REALIZED	GLASS TYPE	AUCTION HOUSE	COMMENTS & PHOTO REFERENCES
2680					$300	Rosaline/Alabaster	Ogal-07/01	
2680					$160	Green Jade/Alabaster	EAC-09/01	
2680					$285	Gold Calcite	ebay-09/01	
2680					$85	Celeste Blue	ebay-09/01	
2680					$160	Rosaline/Alabaster	ebay-11/01	
2680					$90	Rosaline/Alabaster	EAC-11/01	
2680					$175	Gold Calcite	EAC-11/01	
2680					$105	VDS	EAC-11/01	
2680					$195	Gold Calcite	EAC-11/01	
2680					$225	Gold Calcite	ebay-12/01	
2680					$250	Rosaline/Alabaster	ebay-01/02	
2680					$70	Green Jade/Alabaster	ebay-02/02	
2680					$80	Gold Calcite	ebay-02/02	Underplate only
2680					$115	Rosaline/Alabaster	ebay-02/02	
2680					$270	Gold Calcite	ebay-02/02	
2680					$60	VDS	ebay-03/02	Sherbet only
2680					$255	Gold Calcite	ebay-03/02	
2680					$325	Gold Calcite	ebay-03/02	
2680					$100	Gold Calcite	ebay-03/02	Underplate only
2680					$360	Gold Calcite	ebay-03/02	
2680					$155	Green Jade/Alabaster	ebay-03/02	
2680					$160	Rosaline/Alabaster	ebay-03/02	
2680					$420	Blue Calcite	EAC-04/02	
2680					$120	Gold Aurene	ebay-04/02	Underplate only
2680					$225	Gold Calcite	ebay-04/02	
2680					$90	Gold Calcite	ebay-04/02	Underplate only
2680					$75	VDS	JDJ-05/02	
2680					$230	Gold Calcite	ebay-05/02	
2680					$185	Gold Calcite	ebay-05/02	
2680					$100	Gold Calcite	ebay-05/02	Sherbet only
2680					$100	VDS	ebay-05/02	
2680					$155	VDS	ebay-06/02	
2680					$145	Gold Calcite	Jack-06/02	
2680					$235	Gold Aurene	ebay-06/02	
2680					$50	Amethyst/Colorless stem	ebay-06/02	
2680					$100	Gold Calcite	ebay-07/02	Sherbet only
2680					$225	Gold Calcite	ebay-07/02	
2680					$160	Gold Calcite	ebay-07/02	
2680					$300	Gold Calcite	ebay-07/02	
2680					$170	Gold Calcite	ebay-07/02	
2680					$65	VDS	ebay-08/02	
2680					$50	VDS	ebay-08/02	Sherbet only
2680					$60	VDS	ebay-08/02	
2680					$215	Gold Calcite	ebay-08/02	
2680					$50	Amethyst/Colorless stem	ebay-08/02	Sherbet only
2680					$110	VDS	ebay-09/02	
2680					$130	VDS	ebay-09/02	
2680					$200	Gold Calcite	ebay-09/02	
2680					$145	VDS	EAC–09/02	
2680					$115	Gold Calcite	ebay-10/02	
2680					$30	Gold Aurene	ebay-10/02	Underplate only
2680					$140	Green Jade/Alabaster	ebay-10/02	
2680					$150	Rosaline/Alabaster	ebay-10/02	
2680					$225	Gold Calcite	ebay-10/02	
2680					$75	VDS	ebay-10/02	
2680					$170	Gold Calcite	ebay-10/02	
2680					$35	Celeste Blue	ebay-10/02	Underplate only
2680					$85	VDS	ebay-11/02	
2680					$225	Gold Aurene	ebay-11/02	
2680					$75	Gold Calcite	ebay-11/02	Sherbet only
2680					$700	Gold Calcite	Ogal-12/02	
2680					$130	VDS	ebay-01/03	
2680					$160	Green Jade/Alabaster	ebay-01/03	
2680					$230	Gold Calcite	ebay-01/03	
2680					$230	Gold Calcite	ebay-01/03	
2680					$375	Gold Aurene	ebay-02/03	
2680					$175	Gold Calcite	ebay-02/03	
2680					$190	Alabaster/Green rim	ebay-02/03	
2680					$200	Gold Calcite	ebay-02/03	
2680					$205	Gold Calcite	ebay-02/03	
2680					$30	Topaz	ebay-02/03	Underplate only
2680					$85	Green Jade	ebay-02/03	Underplate only
2680					$130	Gold Calcite	ebay-03/03	Underplate only
2680					$160	Gold Calcite	ebay-03/03	

SHAPE NO.	ITEM	PAGE	COL	ROW	PRICE REALIZED	GLASS TYPE	AUCTION HOUSE	COMMENTS & PHOTO REFERENCES
2680					$200	Gold Calcite	Ogal-03/03	
2680					$200	Gold Calcite	Ogal-03/03	
2680					$200	Gold Calcite	Ogal-03/03	
2680					$200	Gold Calcite	Ogal-03/03	
2680					$200	Gold Calcite	ebay-03/03	
2680					$25	Amethyst/Colorless stem	ebay-03/03	Sherbet only
2680					$200	Gold Calcite	EAC-06/03	
2680					$340	Green Jade/Alabaster	ebay-03/03	
2680					$85	Gold Calcite	ebay-03/03	Underplate only
2680					$90	Gold Calcite	ebay-03/03	Underplate only
2680					$95	Gold Calcite	ebay-03/03	Sherbet only
2680					$50	VDS	ebay-05/03	Underplate only
2680					$350	Gold Aurene	Dalla-05/03	
2680					$100	Gold Calcite	ebay-06/03	Underplate only
2680					$140	Gold Aurene	ebay-06/03	Sherbet only
2680					$155	Gold Calcite	ebay-06/03	Underplate only
2680					$175	Gold Aurene	ebay-06/03	Sherbet only
2680					$50	VDS	ebay-06/03	Underplate only
2680					$65	VDS	ebay-06/03	Sherbet only
2680					$175	VDS	ebay-07/03	
2680					$55	Amethyst	ebay-07/03	
2680					$165	Gold Calcite	ebay-07/03	
2680					$60	Topaz	ebay-07/03	
2680					$250	Rosaline/Alabaster	ebay-07/03	
2680					$100	Rosaline/Alabaster	ebay-07/03	
2680					$65	Topaz	ebay-08/03	
2680					$180	Rosaline/Alabaster	ebay-08/03	
2680					$170	Rosaline/Alabaster	ebay-09/03	
2680					$150	Gold Calcite	ebay-09/03	
2680					$250	Gold Aurene	Dalla-09/03	Long Stem
2680					$170	Gold Calcite	ebay-09/03	
2680					$900	Blue Aurene	J&W-09/03	
2680					$650	Blue Calcite	J&W-09/03	
2680					$170	Rosaline/Alabaster	ebay-10/03	
2680					$225	Rosaline/Alabaster	ebay-10/03	
2680					$190	Rosaline/Alabaster	ebay-10/03	
2680					$130	Gold Calcite	ebay-11/03	Sherbet only
2680					$110	VDS	ebay-11/03	
2680					$25	Topaz	ebay-11/03	Underplate only
2680					$125	Rosaline/Alabaster	ebay-11/03	
2680					$30	Amethyst/Colorless stem	JDJ-11/03	Sherbet only
2680					$285	Gold Calcite	JDJ-11/03	
2680					$260	Gold Calcite	EAC-11/03	
2680					$185	Gold Calcite	ebay-12/03	
2680					$85	VDS	ebay-12/03	
2680					$85	VDS	ebay-12/03	Sherbet only
2680					$145	Gold Calcite	ebay-12/03	
2680					$50	Green Jade/Alabaster	ebay-12/03	Alabaster stem, Sherbet only
2680					$150	Amethyst/Colorless stem	ebay-12/03	
2680					$260	Gold Calcite	ebay-12/03	
2680					$450	Gold Calcite	Ogal-12/03	
2680					$155	Gold Calcite	ebay-01/04	
2680					$105	VDS	ebay-01/04	
2680					$15	Topaz	ebay-01/04	Sherbet only
2680					$235	Gold Calcite	Dalla-01/04	
2680					$135	Green Jade/Alabaster stem	ebay-01/04	
2680					$375	Gold Calcite	ebay-01/04	
2680					$375	Gold Calcite	ebay-01/04	
2680					$300	Gold Calcite	Ogal-02/04	
2680					$145	Rosaline/Alabaster stem	ebay-02/04	
2680					$40	Amethyst/Colorless stem	ebay-02/04	Sherbet only
2680					$130	VDS	ebay-02/04	
2680					$150	Rosaline/Alabaster stem	ebay-02/04	
2680					$225	Gold Calcite	ebay-02/04	
2680					$250	Gold Calcite	ebay-02/04	
2680					$115	Gold Aurene	ebay-03/04	Underplate only
2680					$15	VDS	ebay-03/04	Sherbet only
2680					$140	Celeste Blue/Colorless	ebay-03/04	Colorless stem
2680					$700	Blue Calcite	ebay-03/04	
2680					$160	VDS	ebay-03/04	
2680					$200	Green Jade/Alabaster	ebay-03/04	
2680					$55	Green Jade (E)	ebay-04/04	Underplate only, engraved "York"
2680					$80	Green Jade (E)	ebay-04/04	Underplate only, engraved "York"
2680					$140	Rosaline/Alabaster stem	ebay-04/04	

SHAPE NO.	ITEM	PAGE	COL	ROW	PRICE REALIZED	GLASS TYPE	AUCTION HOUSE	COMMENTS & PHOTO REFERENCES
2680					$175	Gold Calcite	ebay-04/04	
2680					$195	Gold Calcite	ebay-04/04	
2680					$230	Gold Calcite	EAC-04/04	
2680					$170	Gold Aurene	EAC-04/04	Sherbet only
2680					$170	Gold Calcite	ebay-04/04	
2680					$345	Gold Aurene	EAC-04/04	
2680					$20	Celeste Blue/Colorless foot	ebay-05/04	Sherbet only
2680					$120	Gold Calcite	ebay-05/04	Underplate only
2680					$120	Gold Calcite	JDJ-05/04	Sherbet only
2680					$35	VDS	ebay-05/04	Underplate only
2680					$75	Gold Aurene	Tway-05/04	Underplate only
2680					$95	Gold Calcite	ebay-05/04	Underplate only
2680					$100	Blue Aurene	Tway-05/04	Underplate only
2680					$10	VDS	ebay-06/04	Underplate only
2680					$30	Green Jade	ebay-06/04	Underplate only
2680					$35	VDS	ebay-06/04	Underplate only
2680					$35	VDS	ebay-06/04	Underplate only
2680					$80	VDS	ebay-06/04	Sherbet only
2680					$110	Gold Calcite	ebay-06/04	
2680					$125	Gold Calcite	ebay-06/04	Underplate only
2680					$150	Green Jade/Alabaster stem	ebay-06/04	
2680					$170	Gold Calcite	ebay-06/04	
2680					$480	Yellow Jade	ebay-06/04	
2680					$165	Gold Calcite	ebay-06/04	Sherbet only
2680					$80	Green Jade/Alabaster	ebay-07/04	Alabaster stem and foot
2680					$10	Celeste Blue	ebay-07/04	Underplate only
2680					$180	Gold Calcite	ebay-07/04	
2680					$205	Gold Calcite	ebay-07/04	
2680					$50	Gold Calcite	ebay-07/04	Underplate only
2680					$110	Green Jade/Alabaster	ebay-07/04	Alabaster stem and foot
2680					$150	Green Jade/Alabaster	ebay-07/04	Alabaster stem and foot
2680					$505	Blue Calcite	EAC-07/04	
2680					$280	Gold Aurene	EAC-07/04	
2680					$130	Green Jade/Alabaster	ebay-07/04	
2680					$135	Green Jade/Alabaster	ebay-07/04	
2680					$200	Gold Calcite	ebay-07/04	
2680					$50	Gold Calcite	ebay-08/04	Underplate only
2680					$130	Green Jade/Alabaster	ebay-08/04	Alabaster stem and foot
2680					$160	Yellow Jade	ebay-08/04	Underplate only
2680					$155	Gold Calcite	ebay-08/04	
2680					$190	Gold Calcite	ebay-08/04	
2680					$135	Gold Calcite	Tway-09/04	Sherbet only
2680					$165	Gold Aurene	ebay-09/04	Sherbet only, long stem version
2680					$180	Gold Calcite	ebay-09/04	
2680					$215	Rosaline/Alabaster	ebay-09/04	Alabaster stem and foot
2680					$180	Gold Calcite	ebay-10/04	
2680					$55	VDS	ebay-10/04	Underplate only
2680					$200	Gold Calcite	ebay-10/04	
2680					$355	Green Jade/Alabaster	EAC-10/04	
2680					$50	VDS	ebay-11/04	Sherbet only
2680					$90	VDS	ebay-11/04	
2680					$15	VDS	ebay-11/04	Underplate only
2680					$310	Yellow Jade	ebay-11/04	
2680					$420	Calcite	ebay-11/04	
2680					$85	Gold Calcite	ebay-12/04	
2680					$130	Gold Calcite	ebay-12/04	Underplate only
2680					$60	VDS	ebay-01/05	Underplate only
2680					$70	Topaz	ebay-01/05	
2680					$175	Green Jade/Alabaster	ebay-02/05	
2680					$150	Gold Calcite	ebay-02/05	
2680					$50	Green Jade/Alabaster	ebay-02/05	Sherbet only
2680					$60	Gold Aurene	Tway-03/05	Underplate only
2680					$155	Rosaline/Alabaster	ebay-03/05	Alabaster stem and foot
2680					$55	Gold Aurene	ebay-03/05	Underplate only
2680					$105	VDS	ebay-03/05	
2680					$190	VDS	ebay-03/05	
2680					$190	VDS	ebay-03/05	
2680					$220	Gold Aurene	ebay-03/05	
2680					$230	Gold Aurene	ebay-03/05	
2680					$250	Gold Aurene	ebay-03/05	
2680					$145	Gold Calcite	ebay-03/05	
2680					$165	Gold Calcite	ebay-03/05	
2680					$275	Gold Aurene	ebay-04/05	
2680					$65	VDS	ebay-04/05	

SHAPE NO.	ITEM	PAGE	COL	ROW	PRICE REALIZED	GLASS TYPE	AUCTION HOUSE	COMMENTS & PHOTO REFERENCES
2680					$75	VDS	ebay-04/05	
2680					$285	Green Jade/Alabaster	EAC-04/05	Alabaster stem and foot
2680					$230	Gold Aurene (FC)	EAC-04/05	Sherbet only
2680					$145	Gold Calcite	ebay-05/05	
2680					$95	VDS	ebay-05/05	
2680					$55	Gold Calcite	ebay-05/05	Underplate only
2680					$120	Amethyst/colorless stem	ebay-05/05	
2680					$185	Gold Calcite	ebay-05/05	
2680					$100	VDS	ebay-06/05	
2680					$140	Gold Calcite	ebay-06/05	
2680					$130	Gold Calcite	Sknr-06/05	
2680					$90	Gold Calcite	ebay-06/05	Sherbet only
2680					$120	Gold Calcite	ebay-06/05	Underplate only, Haviland sticker
2680					$150	Amethyst/Colorless stem	ebay-06/05	
2680					$115	Amethyst/Colorless stem	ebay-07/05	
2680					$95	VDS	ebay-07/05	
2681	Vase	268	4	4	$575	Gold Aurene	EAC-07/05	
2682	Vase	268	4	5	$1075	Blue Aurene	ebay-03/02	RFR)18,2,C
2682					$730	Gold Aurene	EAC-01/03	
2682					$660	Blue Aurene	JDJ-05/04	
2682					$920	Gold Aurene	JDJ-05/04	
2683	Vase	268	4	6	$1650	Blue Aurene	EAC-07/90	PG1)XXV B:XVIII A:116,186,C:312;
2683					$1045	Blue Aurene	EAC-10/90	RFR)18,1,B:20,3,B:22,1,A:22,2,A&C;
2683					$1320	Amethyst Cluthra	EAC-04/91	RFR)24,1,C:27,1,B;
2683					$1760	Ivory ACB "Stamford"	EAC-07/91	RLG)150,282; ACR)COLOR 3,T,A
2683					$1100	Blue Aurene	EAC-07/91	TPD)4.86:6.27:8.43:8.58:8.65:10.12
2683					$1265	Amethyst Cluthra	EAC-07/91	TPD)10.103:10.134
2683					$4190	Rose Cluthra	EAC-10/91	
2683					$1320	Amethyst Cluthra	EAC-10/91	
2683					$1540	Blue Cluthra	EAC-04/92	
2683					$2035	Blue Aurene	EAC-10/92	
2683					$660	Blue Cluthra	EAC-10/92	
2683					$550	Amethyst Cluthra	EAC-04/92	
2683					$660	Gold Aurene	EAC-04/92	
2683					$1100	Amethyst Cluthra	EAC-04/93	
2683					$1100	White Cluthra	EAC-04/93	
2683					$935	Green Cluthra	EAC-07/93	
2683					$685	White Cluthra	EAC-07/93	
2683					$2750	Blue Aurene	EAC-07/93	
2683					$250	Ivory	EAC-10/93	
2683					$1100	Rouge Flambé	EAC-10/93	
2683					$1705	Blue Aurene	EAC-10/93	
2683					$1925	Blue Aurene/Pomona ACB	EAC-10/93	Etched "Mansard"
2683					$715	Gold Aurene	EAC-10/93	
2683					$460	Ivory	Sknr-05/94	
2683					$605	Gold Aurene	JDJ-10/94	
2683					$1265	Blue Aurene	Sknr-10/94	
2683					$805	Ivrene	Sknr-10/94	
2683					$490	Ivrene	Sknr-10/94	
2683					$865	White Cluthra	Sknr-10/94	
2683					$880	White Cluthra	EAC-04/95	
2683					$1095	Blue Cluthra	Sknr-05/95	
2683					$990	White Cluthra	EAC-07/95	
2683					$1100	Green Cluthra	EAC-07/95	
2683					$1380	Rose Cluthra	Sknr-10/95	
2683					$2990	Black/Alabaster T-133	Sknr-10/95	
2683					$2310	Blue Aurene	EAC-10/95	
2683					$525	Ivory	EAC-10/95	
2683					$1735	Black/Alabaster T-133	Sknr-01/96	
2683					$400	White Cluthra	Sknr-01/96	
2683					$770	White Cluthra	JDJ-06/96	
2683					$385	Ivory	JDJ-06/96	
2683					$2530	Ivory ACB	JDJ-06/96	
2683					$1320	Mirror Black	JDJ-06/96	
2683					$1155	Ivory	EAC-10/96	
2683					$2200	Blue Aurene	EAC-10/96	
2683					$1130	Rose Cluthra	EAC-10/96	
2683					$2530	Rose Cluthra	EAC-10/96	
2683					$825	White Cluthra	EAC-10/96	
2683					$1430	Green Cluthra	EAC-10/96	
2683					$860	Ivory	Sknr-01/97	
2683					$1955	Blue Aurene	Sknr-01/97	
2683					$2035	Rose Cluthra	EAC-04/97	
2683					$1870	Blue Aurene (FC)	EAC-04/97	

SHAPE NO.	ITEM	PAGE	COL	ROW	PRICE REALIZED	GLASS TYPE	AUCTION HOUSE	COMMENTS & PHOTO REFERENCES
2683					$1650	Rose Cluthra	EAC-04/97	
2683					$1100	Gold Aurene	EAC-07/97	
2683					$860	Amethyst Cluthra	JDJ-10/97	
2683					$3680	Mirror Black	JDJ-10/97	
2683					$1150	Green Cluthra	JDJ-10/97	
2683					$805	White Cluthra	JDJ-10/97	
2683					$860	Mirror Black	JDJ-10/97	
2683					$1035	Gold Aurene	JDJ-10/97	
2683					$2300	Ivory ACB	Sknr-10/97	
2683					$515	Ivory	Sknr-10/97	
2683					$1380	Gold Aurene	Sknr-10/97	
2683					$6900	Black/White ACB	Sknr-01/98	
2683					$920	White Cluthra	Sknr-01/98	
2683					$805	Green Jade	Sknr-01/98	
2683					$1870	Green Cluthra	EAC-04/98	
2683					$2640	Ivory ACB	EAC-04/98	
2683					$1435	Amethyst Cluthra	JDJ-06/98	
2683					$1435	Green Cluthra	JDJ-06/98	
2683					$1815	Amethyst Cluthra	EAC-07/98	
2683					$550	Ivory	EAC-07/98	
2683					$605	Blue Cluthra	EAC-10/98	
2683					$1380	Rose Cluthra	Sknr-10/98	
2683					$1035	Blue Cluthra	Sknr-03/99	
2683					$2640	Green Cluthra	EAC-07/99	
2683					$710	Gold Aurene	ebay-11/99	
2683					$800	White Cluthra	ebay-12/99	
2683					$1000	Green Cluthra	ebay-01/00	
2683					$1125	Amethyst Cluthra	ebay-02/00	
2683					$535	Gold Aurene	ebay-02/00	
2683					$3740	Gold Aurene	Sknr-02/00	
2683					$805	Ivrene	Sknr-02/00	
2683					$2300	White Cluthra	ebay-04/00	
2683					$660	White Cluthra	ebay-04/00	
2683					$690	Green/White Cluthra	Sknr-06/00	
2683					$495	Ivrene	EAC-10/00	
2683					$1650	Blue Aurene	EAC-10/00	
2683					$800	Green Cluthra	Tway-10/00	
2683					$900	Green Cluthra	Tway-10/00	
2683					$1090	Black Cluthra	Sknr-10/00	
2683					$960	Ivrene	Sbys-10/00	
2683					$3000	Blue Aurene	Ogal-11/00	
2683					$770	Green Cluthra	Midw-11/00	
2683					$700	Green Cluthra	ebay-01/01	
2683					$750	Green Cluthra	ebay-01/01	
2683					$3105	Rose Cluthra	Sknr-02/01	
2683					$1150	Green Cluthra	Sknr-02/01	
2683					$285	Jade Green	ebay-03/01	
2683					$1455	Gold Aurene	EAC-04/01	
2683					$1090	Green Cluthra	Midw-04/01	
2683					$660	Green Cluthra	Midw-04/01	
2683					$1265	Rose Cluthra	Midw-04/01	
2683					$610	Gold Aurene	ebay-05/01	
2683					$685	Gold Aurene	ebay-05/01	
2683					$1825	Blue Cluthra	ebay-06/01	
2683					$1150	Amethyst Cluthra	ebay-06/01	
2683					$800	Gold Aurene	ebay-07/01	
2683					$1430	Rose Cluthra	Cott-08/01	
2683					$600	Blue Aurene	ebay-10/01	
2683					$700	Blue Aurene	ebay-10/01	
2683					$240	Ivory	ebay-10/01	
2683					$900	Blue Aurene	ebay-11/01	
2683					$3025	Blue Cluthra	EAC-11/01	
2683					$900	Gold Aurene	ebay-12/01	
2683					$1300	Gold Aurene	ebay-03/02	
2683					$2855	White Cluthra	EAC-04/02	
2683					$1680	Green Cluthra	EAC-04/02	
2683					$1345	Gold Aurene	EAC-04/02	
2683					$1380	Rose Cluthra	JDJ-05/02	
2683					$860	Gold Aurene	JDJ-05/02	
2683					$1600	Gold Aurene	ebay-05/02	
2683					$800	Blue Aurene	ebay-05/02	
2683					$800	Blue Cluthra	ebay-05/02	
2683					$1035	Gold Aurene	Jack-06/02	
2683	ITEM				$1265	Amethyst Cluthra	ebay-07/02	

SHAPE NO.	ITEM	PAGE	COL	ROW	PRICE REALIZED	GLASS TYPE	AUCTION HOUSE	COMMENTS & PHOTO REFERENCES
2683					$680	White Cluthra	ebay-07/02	
2683					$1000	Gold Aurene	ebay-09/02	
2683					$1125	Gold Aurene	ebay-09/02	
2683					$1510	Blue Aurene	ebay-09/02	
2683					$3360	Blue Aurene	EAC-09/02	
2683					$1345	Blue Aurene	EAC-09/02	
2683					$190	VDS	ebay-09/02	Hawkes engraved
2683					$175	VDS	ebay-10/02	Hawkes engraved
2683					$1380	Gold Aurene	ebay-10/02	
2683					$1000	Blue Aurene	ebay-11/02	
2683					$1000	Blue Aurene	Free-11/02	
2683					$950	Gold Aurene	Free-11/02	
2683					$1080	Gold Aurene	JDJ-11/02	
2683					$1105	Rose Cluthra	ebay-11/02	
2683					$1440	Blue Aurene	JDJ-11/02	
2683					$1560	Blue Aurene	JDJ-11/02	
2683					$540	Gold Aurene	ebay-11/02	
2683					$950	Gold Aurene	ebay-11/02	
2683					$455	Green Jade	ebay-11/02	
2683					$1380	Blue Cluthra	Jack–11/02	
2683					$900	Gold Aurene	Tway-12/02	
2683					$2150	Blue Aurene	ebay-12/02	
2683					$2000	Blue Aurene	ebay-12/02	
2683					$1150	Gold Aurene	ebay-02/03	
2683					$1830	White Cluthra	ebay-02/03	
2683					$1975	Rose Cluthra	ebay-02/03	
2683					$1775	Rose Cluthra	ebay-03/03	
2683					$1000	Blue Aurene	ebay-03/03	
2683					$1175	Gold Aurene	Sknr-05/03	
2683					$1225	Amethyst Cluthra	ebay-05/03	
2683					$1115	Blue Aurene	ebay-05/03	
2683					$1525	Blue Aurene	ebay-05/03	
2683					$1625	Blue Aurene	ebay-05/03	
2683					$300	Amber	ebay-05/03	
2683					$1515	Blue Aurene	ebay-05/03	
2683					$1955	Amber Cluthra	ebay-05/03	
2683					$3795	Ivory ACB	Jack-06/03	Etched "Stamford"
2683					$2415	Blue Aurene	Jack-06/03	
2683					$375	Ivory	Cinc-06/03	
2683					$910	Gold Aurene	ebay-06/03	
2683					$595	Ivrene	ebay-06/03	
2683					$880	Gold Aurene	ebay-06/03	
2683					$3737	Ivory ACB	EAC-06/03	Etched "Stamford"
2683					$2760	Green Cluthra	EAC-06/03	
2683					$1725	Blue Aurene	EAC-06/03	
2683					$1915	Rose Cluthra	ebay-07/03	
2683					$750	Gold Aurene	ebay-07/03	
2683					$2500	Alabaster/Black	ebay-07/03	Black rim and prunts
2683					$2940	Ivory ACB	ebay-09/03	Etched "Stamford"
2683					$1605	Blue Aurene	ebay-10/03	
2683					$1700	Gold Aurene	ebay-10/03	
2683					$500	Ivrene	ebay-11/03	
2683					$2700	Green Cluthra	ebay-11/03	
2683					$1725	Blue Aurene	EAC-11/03	
2683					$1265	Blue Aurene	EAC-11/03	
2683					$645	Gold Aurene	Sknr-12/03	
2683					$565	Blue Aurene	ebay-01/04	
2683					$1075	Gold Aurene	ebay-01/04	
2683					$2070	Blue Aurene	ebay-01/04	
2683					$1195	White Cluthra	ebay-02/04	
2683					$2650	Blue Aurene	ebay-02/04	
2683					$685	Gold Aurene	ebay-03/04	
2683					$725	Green Cluthra	ebay-03/04	
2683					$1300	Celeste Blue	ebay-03/04	
2683					$2650	Gold Aurene	ebay-03/04	
2683					$1450	Gold Aurene	ebay-03/04	
2683					$1760	Green Cluthra	ebay-04/04	
2683					$1300	Ivory	ebay-05/04	
2683					$1035	Green Cluthra	JDJ-05/04	
2683					$690	Gold Aurene	JDJ-05/04	
2683					$480	Green Cluthra	JDJ-05/04	
2683					$420	Blue Aurene	Crft-05/04	
2683					$880	White Cluthra	ebay-05/04	
2683					$425	Gold Aurene	ebay-06/04	

SHAPE NO.	ITEM	PAGE	COL	ROW	PRICE REALIZED	GLASS TYPE	AUCTION HOUSE	COMMENTS & PHOTO REFERENCES
2683					$300	Ivory	ebay-06/04	
2683					$425	Blue Aurene	ebay-06/04	
2683					$2320	Ivory ACB	ebay-06/04	Etched "Stamford"
2683					$650	White Cluthra	ebay-06/04	
2683					$875	Blue Aurene	ebay-06/04	
2683					$225	Ivory	ebay-07/04	
2683					$350	Blue Aurene	ebay-07/04	Poor colors
2683					$615	Green Jade	ebay-07/04	
2683					$1790	Blue Aurene	EAC-07/04	
2683					$885	Gold Aurene	EAC-07/04	
2683					$1065	Gold Aurene	EAC-07/04	Drilled for a lamp
2683					$1495	Blue Cluthra	ebay-07/04	Drilled for a lamp
2683					$650	Ivory	ebay-08/04	
2683					$1105	Amethyst Cluthra	ebay-08/04	
2683					$1175	Blue Cluthra	ebay-08/04	Drilled for a lamp
2683					$710	Blue Aurene	ebay-09/04	
2683					$1600	Blue Aurene	ebay-09/04	
2683					$1725	Blue Aurene	ebay-09/04	
2683					$200	Ivrene	Crft-09/04	
2683					$1000	White Cluthra	ebay-09/04	
2683					$1025	Blue Aurene	ebay-09/04	
2683					$1180	Gold Aurene	ebay-09/04	
2683					$915	Amethyst Cluthra	ebay-09/04	
2683					$1305	Amethyst Cluthra	ebay-10/04	
2683					$1600	Blue Aurene	ebay-10/04	
2683					$990	Pink Cluthra	EAC-10/04	Lamp
2683					$1375	Rose Quartz	EAC-10/04	
2683					$2040	Gold Aurene	Cinc-11/04	
2683					$615	Blue Aurene	ebay-11/04	Poor colors
2683					$900	Ivory	ebay-11/04	
2683					$375	White Cluthra	ebay-11/04	
2683					$510	Gold Aurene	ebay-11/04	
2683					$540	Green Cluthra	JDJ-11/04	
2683					$470	Ivrene	ebay-11/04	
2683					$750	Rose Cluthra	ebay-11/04	
2683					$780	White Cluthra	ebay-12/04	
2683					$825	White Cluthra	ebay-12/04	
2683					$395	Ivory	ebay-01/05	
2683					$1990	Blue Aurene	ebay-01/05	
2683					$815	White Cluthra	ebay-01/05	
2683					$1300	Gold Aurene	ebay-01/05	
2683					$1500	Rose Cluthra	ebay-01/05	
2683					$1790	Blue Aurene	ebay-01/05	
2683					$175	Royal Purple	ebay-02/05	
2683					$700	Ivory	ebay-02/05	
2683					$1100	Gold Aurene	ebay-02/05	
2683					$275	Ivory	ebay-03/05	
2683					$975	Blue Cluthra	Hrtg-03/05	
2683					$1200	Alabaster/Mirror Black	ebay-03/05	Black rim and prunts
2683					$1955	Blue Aurene	Hrtg-03/05	
2683					$480	Ivory	ebay-03/05	
2683					$360	Ivory	ebay-04/05	
2683					$1015	Rose Cluthra	ebay-04/05	
2683					$1150	Gold Aurene	EAC-04/05	
2683					$430	VDS	EAC-04/05	
2683					$2415	Gold Aurene	EAC-04/05	
2683					$1495	Green Cluthra	EAC-04/05	
2683					$1625	Green Cluthra	ebay-05/05	
2683					$2700	Ivory ACB	ebay-05/05	Etched "Stamford"
2683					$1920	Gold Aurene	ebay-05/05	
2683					$2280	Ivory ACB	ebay-05/05	Etched "Stamford"
2683					$500	Blue Aurene	ebay-05/05	Complete lamp
2683					$900	Blue Aurene	ebay-05/05	
2683					$1375	Blue Aurene	ebay-05/05	
2683					$1080	Blue Aurene	JDJ-06/05	
2683					$2400	Blue Aurene	JDJ-06/05	
2683					$1270	Rose Cluthra	ebay-06/05	
2683					$715	Green Cluthra	ebay-07/05	
2683					$1200	Green Cluthra	ebay-07/05	
2683					$315	Ivrene	EAC-07/05	
2683					$230	Ivory	EAC-07/05	
2683					$1495	Rose Cluthra	EAC-07/05	
2683					$630	Ivory	EAC-07/05	
2683A	Shade	228	3	2				

SHAPE NO.	ITEM	PAGE	COL	ROW	PRICE REALIZED	GLASS TYPE	AUCTION HOUSE	COMMENTS & PHOTO REFERENCES
2684	Vase	268	4	7	$1980	Blue Aurene	EAC-07/99	
2685	Decanter	185	3	5				MDK)118
2685	Tumbler	185	3	5	$150	Amber/Flemish Blue	ebay-07/03	
2686	Shade	225	3	7				
2687	Bowl	142	1	10	$2640	Plum Jade ACB "Chinese"	EAC-10/90	PG1)XXVI C:XXVII B:62,96:312; PG2)89
2687					$2860	Plum Jade ACB "Canton"	EAC-07/93	RFR)19,1,A&B; RLG)150,281;
2687					$2750	Plum Jade ACB "Chang"	EAC-10/93	ACR)162,321:162,322;
2687					$660	Blue Aurene	JDJ-10/94	JAS)152,T,C:152,B:155,T; TPD)10.115
2687					$1485	Yellow Jade	EAC-07/95	
2687					$2585	Plum Jade ACB	EAC-10/95	
2687					$1725	Light Blue Jade	Sknr-10/95	
2687					$520	Blue Aurene	Sknr-01/96	
2687					$2640	Plum Jade ACB	Sknr-05/96	
2687					$220	Gold Calcite	EAC-10/96	
2687					$410	Rosaline	JDJ-06/96	
2687					$750	Light Blue Jade	Sknr-01/97	
2687					$330	Rosaline (FC)	EAC-04/97	
2687					$2200	Plum Jade ACB	EAC-04/97	
2687					$495	Plum Jade ACB	EAC-07/97	
2687					$355	Blue Aurene	EAC-07/97	
2687					$460	Gold Aurene	Sknr-10/97	
2687					$550	Blue Aurene	EAC-07/98	
2687					$495	Light Blue Jade	EAC-07/98	
2687					$330	Gold Aurene	EAC-10/98	
2687					$745	Gold Aurene	JDJ-05/99	
2687					$3700	Plum Jade ACB	ebay-10/99	
2687					$250	Green Jade	ebay-11/99	
2687					$250	Gold Calcite	ebay-11/99	
2687					$685	Blue Aurene	ebay-04/00	
2687					$910	Blue Aurene	ebay-04/00	
2687					$700	Gold Aurene	Ogal-07/00	
2687					$400	Amethyst	Rago-09/00	
2687					$400	Green Jade	Sknr-10/00	
2687					$355	Gold Calcite	Wint-12/00	
2687					$230	VDS	ebay-12/00	
2687					$545	Rosaline	Sknr-02/01	
2687					$805	Light Blue Jade	Sknr-02/01	
2687					$200	Blue Aurene	ebay-03/01	
2687					$140	Rosaline	ebay-04/01	
2687					$200	Aqua Marine	ebay-06/01	
2687					$500	Blue Aurene	ebay-07/01	
2687					$560	Blue Aurene	ebay-07/01	
2687					$560	Light Blue Jade	EAC-09/01	
2687					$760	Gold Aurene	ebay-10/01	
2687					$1035	Blue Calcite	JDJ-11/01	
2687					$4890	Plum Jade ACB	JDJ-11/01	Etched "Canton"
2687					$975	Plum Jade not ACB	ebay-12/01	
2687					$1400	Plum Jade ACB	Wint-12/01	Etched "Canton"
2687					$200	Light Blue Jade	ebay-01/02	
2687					$120	Aqua Marine	ebay-02/02	
2687					$95	Green Jade	ebay-02/02	
2687					$245	Gold Calcite	JDJ-05/02	
2687					$5405	Plum Jade ACB	JDJ-05/02	Etched "Canton"
2687					$240	Gold Calcite	ebay-09/02	
2687					$255	Rosaline/Alabaster	ebay-09/02	
2687					$310	Gold Calcite	ebay-10/02	
2687					$1800	Rosaline/Alabaster ACB	JDJ-11/02	Etched "Murillo"
2687					$285	Gold Calcite	ebay-11/02	
2687					$3000	Plum Jade ACB	JDJ-11/02	Etched "Canton"
2687					$2880	Plum Jade ACB	ebay-11/02	Etched "Murillo"
2687					$1385	Rosaline/Alabaster ACB	ebay-12/02	Etched "Murillo"
2687					$180	Gold Calcite	ebay-01/03	
2687					$2080	Blue Aurene	Ogal-02/04	
2687					$160	Green Jade	ebay-03/03	
2687					$195	VDS	ebay-03/03	
2687					$280	Rosaline	ebay-04/03	
2687					$1150	Plum Jade ACB	JDJ-05/03	Etched "Canton"
2687					$430	Yellow Jade	ebay-06/03	
2687					$3450	Plum Jade ACB	Jack-06/03	Etched "Murillo"
2687					$330	Gold Aurene	ebay-07/03	
2687					$750	Gold Aurene	ebay-07/03	
2687					$295	Gold Aurene	ebay-08/03	
2687					$440	Gold Aurene	ebay-08/03	
2687					$860	Blue Aurene	ebay-08/03	

SHAPE NO.	ITEM	PAGE	COL	ROW	PRICE REALIZED	GLASS TYPE	AUCTION HOUSE	COMMENTS & PHOTO REFERENCES
2687					$245	Gold Aurene	ebay-09/03	
2687					$380	Blue Calcite	ebay-09/03	
2687					$1900	Blue Calcite (E)	J&W-09/03	
2687					$200	Gold Calcite	J&W-09/03	
2687					$200	Gold Aurene	ebay-10/03	
2687					$175	Green Jade	ebay-11/03	
2687					$410	Gold Aurene	ebay-11/03	
2687					$3450	Plum Jade ACB	EAC-11/03	Etched "Chang"
2687					$385	Green Jade	ebay-12/03	
2687					$350	Cyprian	ebay-12/03	
2687					$265	Rosaline	ebay-01/04	
2687					$950	Gold Aurene	ebay-01/04	
2687					$2080	Blue Aurene	Ogal-01/04	
2687					$280	Cyprian	ebay-03/04	
2687					$420	Rosaline	ebay-03/04	
2687					$375	Gold Aurene	ebay-04/04	
2687					$545	Gold Calcite (FC)	EAC-04/04	
2687					$375	Gold Aurene	ebay-06/04	
2687					$305	Rosaline	ebay-07/04	
2687					$1135	Yellow Jade	ebay-08/04	
2687					$410	Rosaline	ebay-10/04	
2687					$355	Gold Calcite	EAC-10/04	
2687					$12100	Blue Aurene/Alab. ACB	ebay-10/04	
2687					$150	Gold Calcite	ebay-11/04	
2687					$240	Celeste Blue	ebay-01/05	
2687					$135	Rosaline	ebay-02/05	
2687					$150	Rosaline/Alabaster	ebay-02/05	This was probably an ACB blank.
2687					$840	Gold Aurene	Dalla-03/05	
2687					$5750	Plum Jade ACB	Hrtg-03/05	Etched "Canton"
2687					$915	Green Jade ACB	ebay-04/05	Etched "Murillo"
2687					$270	Gold Calcite	JDJ-06/05	
2687					$1035	Gold Aurene	Cott-06/05	
2687					$3500	Plum Jade ACB	ebay-07/05	Etched "Pekin"
2687					$1895	Gold Aurene	EAC-07/05	
2688	Shade	228	3	3				
2689	Limousine Vase	207	2	1				
2690	Vase	268	5	1				
2691	Vase	268	5	2				PG2)53; JAS)159
2692	Vase	268	5	3				
2693	Vase	268	5	4				
2694	Vase	268	5	5				
2695	Vase	268	5	6				
2696	Bowl	142	1	11				PG1)VIIIB,A; RFR)12,3,B; RLG)138,266;
2696					$780	Blue Aurene	ebay-06/05	ACR)141,265
2697	Shade	225	3	8				
2698	Vase	268	5	7				
2699	Vase	268	5	8	$935	Gold Aurene	EAC-04/92	TPD)5.1
2699					$825	Gold Aurene	EAC-07/95	
2699					$805	Gold Calcite	Sknr-05/96	
2699					$1500	Gold Aurene	ebay-03/00	
2699					$1095	Gold Aurene	ebay-11/02	
2699					$1560	Gold Aurene	JDJ-11/02	
2699					$1100	Gold Aurene	Cinc-11/02	
2699					$840	Gold Aurene	ebay-02/03	
2699					$1900	Gold Aurene	ebay-05/03	
2699					$640	Gold Aurene	ebay-11/03	
2699					$1175	Gold Aurene	Sknr-12/03	
2699					$800	Gold Aurene	ebay-12/03	
2699					$1000	Gold Aurene	Tway-05/04	
2699					$1200	Gold Aurene	ebay-11/04	
2699					$745	Gold Aurene	Hrtg-03/05	
2699					$975	Gold Aurene	EAC-07/05	
2700	Bouillon Cup	189	2	4	$240	Gold Aurene	ebay-03/00	
2701	Cologne	243	3	7	$715	Gold Aurene	EAC-04/96	TPD)8.7
2701					$2640	Blue Aurene	EAC-10/97	
2701					$1810	Gold Aurene	JDJ-06/98	
2701					$500	Topaz/Amethyst	ebay-04/01	
2701					$1585	Blue Aurene	ebay-03/02	
2701					$600	Gold Aurene	JDJ-11/02	
2701					$1440	Blue Aurene	ebay-02/04	
2702	Cologne	243	3	8				
2703	Vase	269	1	1				
2704	Vase	269	1	2				
2705	Vase	269	1	3				

SHAPE NO.	ITEM	PAGE	COL	ROW	PRICE REALIZED	GLASS TYPE	AUCTION HOUSE	COMMENTS & PHOTO REFERENCES
2706	Vase	269	1	4				
2707	Vase	269	1	5	$1320	Gold Aurene	EAC-07/92	
2707					$2760	Gold Aurene	JDJ-11/02	
2707					$825	Flemish	EAC-10/04	With cover
2708	Vase	269	1	6	$3680	Blue Aurene	JDJ-11/03	
2709	Vase	269	1	7				
2711	Vase	269	2	1	$2700	Decorated Alabaster	ebay-07/05	Lamp
2712	Vase	269	2	2	$1050	Gold Aurene	ebay-05/01	
2712					$1110	Blue Aurene	Sbys-11/01	
2712					$1260	Gold Aurene	EAC-01/03	
2712					$960	Gold Aurene	ebay-07/05	
2713	Vase	269	2	3	$2250	Gold Aurene	EAC-10/90	TPD)10.23
2713					$2420	Blue Aurene	EAC-10/94	
2713					$2420	Gold Aurene	EAC-04/98	
2714	Vase	269	2	4				
2715	Vase	269	2	5				
2716	Vase	269	2	6				
2717	Compote	172	3	5				TPD)10.13
2718	Compote	172	3	6				TPD)8.4
2719	Vase	269	3	1				
2720	Cruet	179	2	6	$3850	Gold Aurene	EAC-10/90	TPD)10.121
2720					$4480	Blue Aurene	EAC-11/01	
2720					$4025	Blue Aurene	EAC-04/04	
2720					$2860	Blue Aurene	EAC-10/04	
2721	Insert	210	5	8				
2722	Oyster Cocktail	210	4	11	$260	Gold Aurene	Sknr-06/99	
2722					$110	VDS	ebay-07/04	
2722					$225	Gold Calcite	EAC-07/04	
2722					$195	VDS	EAC-07/04	
2722					$200	Gold Aurene	ebay-05/05	
2723	Oyster Cocktail	210	4	12				MDK)70
2723					$125	Gold Calcite insert	ebay-05/05	Insert in sterling holder
2723					$125	Gold Calcite insert	ebay-05/05	Insert in sterling holder
2724	Misc.	211	5	3				
2725	Ash Tray	137	1	9				
2726	Shade	225	3	9				
2727	Shade	225	3	10				
2728	Shade	225	3	11	$635	Brown Aurene	ebay-10/00	RFR)13,2,A
2728					$655	Brown Aurene	ebay-04/01	
2728					$750	Brown Aurene	Jack-06/02	
2728					$770	Brown Aurene	ebay-06/03	
2728					$710	Brown Aurene	ebay-07/03	
2728					$225	Brown Aurene	ebay-07/03	
2728					$690	Brown Aurene	FtnA-08/03	
2728					$850	Brown Aurene	ebay-04/05	
2728					$790	Brown Aurene	ebay-07/05	
2729	Shade	225	4	1	$180	Calcite	ebay-10/04	
2730	Shade	228	3	4	$675	Calcite ACB	ebay-06/04	Lamp with fittings
2731	Shade	228	3	5	$275	Calcite ACB	ebay-02/05	With ceiling fixture
2732	Shade	225	4	2				
2733	Shade	228	3	6				
2734	Shade	228	3	7				
2735	Shade	228	3	8				
2736	Pitcher	213	4	4				
2737	Vase	269	3	2				
2738	Vase	269	3	3				
2739	Vase	269	3	4				
2740	Shade	225	4	3				
2741	Vase	269	3	5	$630	Blue Aurene	EAC-04/97	PG1)88,131,A
2741					$850	Blue Aurene	EAC-04/98	
2741					$550	Gold Aurene	Cinc-12/99	
2741					$200	Amethyst	Tway-10/00	
2741					$800	Blue Aurene	Ogal-03/01	
2741					$400	Gold Aurene	ebay-05/01	
2741					$430	Gold Aurene	JDJ-05/01	
2741					$400	Blue Aurene	Ogal-11/01	
2741					$435	Blue Aurene	ebay-05/02	
2741					$430	Blue Aurene	ebay-07/02	
2741					$215	Colorless	ebay-09/02	
2741					$390	Amethyst	EAC-09/02	
2741					$500	Amethyst/Colorless foot	Cinc-11/02	
2741					$855	Blue Aurene	ebay-03/03	
2741					$775	Gold Aurene	EAC-06/03	
2741					$600	Gold Aurene	ebay-07/03	

SHAPE NO.	ITEM	PAGE	COL	ROW	PRICE REALIZED	GLASS TYPE	AUCTION HOUSE	COMMENTS & PHOTO REFERENCES
2741					$1495	Gold Aurene	EAC-07/05	
2742	Vase	269	3	6				
2743	Vase	269	3	7	$860	Gold Aurene	Rago-09/00	TPD)5.70
2743					$250	Colorless	Cinc-11/02	
2744	Vase	269	3	8	$880	Blue Aurene	EAC-07/90	PG1)88,131,B; JAS)147,B,A
2744					$770	Gold Aurene	EAC-10/90	TPD)5.70:10.17
2744					$1100	Blue Aurene	EAC-04/91	
2744					$660	Gold Aurene	EAC-04/91	
2744					$905	Blue Aurene	EAC-02/92	
2744					$1100	Green Jade/Alabaster foot	EAC-02/92	
2744					$385	Pomona Green	EAC-02/92	
2744					$990	Blue Aurene	EAC-10/92	
2744					$1210	Blue Aurene	EAC-10/93	
2744					$1045	Gold Aurene	JDJ-10/94	
2744					$745	Gold Aurene	Sknr-01/96	
2744					$200	Topaz	Sknr-01/96	
2744					$860	Blue Aurene	Sknr-05/96	
2744					$200	Pomona Green	Sknr-05/96	
2744					$220	Topaz	JDJ-06/96	
2744					$770	Green Jade	EAC-07/96	
2744					$245	Pomona Green	Sknr-01/98	
2744					$630	Gold Aurene	EAC-10/98	
2744					$230	Pomona Green	EAC-04/98	
2744					$880	Gold Aurene	EAC-07/98	
2744					$175	Topaz	EAC-10/98	
2744					$630	Gold Aurene	EAC-10/98	
2744					$990	Blue Aurene	EAC-07/99	
2744					$865	Blue Aurene	ebay-11/99	
2744					$177	Amber	ebay-11/99	
2744					$500	Amber	ebay-11/99	
2744					$1035	Blue Aurene	ebay-02/00	
2744					$450	Pomona Green	ebay-03/00	
2744					$750	Gold Aurene	ebay-03/00	
2744					$300	Topaz	ebay-03/00	
2744					$865	Mirror Black	ebay-04/00	
2744					$1315	Blue Aurene	ebay-05/00	
2744					$826	Gold Aurene	ebay-01/01	
2744					$2550	Blue Aurene	ebay-03/01	
2744					$495	Green Jade	ebay-03/01	
2744					$265	Pomona Green	ebay-04/01	
2744					$235	Pomona Green	ebay-04/01	
2744					$785	Green Jade/Alabaster	EAC-04/01	
2744					$670	VDS	EAC-04/01	
2744					$365	Topaz	EAC-04/01	
2744					$1400	Blue Aurene	EAC-04/01	
2744					$575	Blue Aurene	ebay-06/01	
2744					$500	Gold Aurene	ebay-06/01	
2744					$1595	Blue Aurene	Cott-08/01	
2744					$935	Gold Aurene	Cott-08/01	
2744					$385	VDS	Cott-08/01	
2744					$385	Pomona Green	Cott-08/01	
2744					$135	Colorless	Cott-08/01	
2744					$405	Celeste Blue	ebay-09/01	
2744					$850	Gold Aurene	ebay-10/01	
2744					$250	Topaz	ebay-10/01	
2744					$875	Blue Aurene	JDJ-11/01	
2744					$1175	Blue Aurene	EAC-11/01	
2744					$300	Topaz	ebay-12/01	
2744					$230	Topaz	ebay-12/01	
2744					$390	Pomona Green	ebay-01/02	
2744					$305	VDS	ebay-02/02	
2744					$810	Gold Aurene	ebay-03/02	
2744					$1113	Blue Aurene	ebay-03/02	
2744					$1200	Blue Aurene	ebay-03/02	
2744					$195	Topaz	EAC-04/02	
2744					$670	Gold Aurene	EAC-04/02	
2744					$895	Blue Aurene	EAC-04/02	
2744					$1120	Gold Aurene	EAC-04/02	
2744					$1120	Gold Aurene	EAC-04/02	
2744					$750	Gold Aurene	ebay-05/02	
2744					$300	Topaz	ebay-05/02	
2744					$405	Alabaster	ebay-05/02	
2744					$750	Gold Aurene	ebay-05/02	
2744					$425	Gold Aurene	Ogal-06/02	

138

SHAPE NO.	ITEM	PAGE	COL	ROW	PRICE REALIZED	GLASS TYPE	AUCTION HOUSE	COMMENTS & PHOTO REFERENCES
2744					$775	Gold Aurene	ebay-08/02	
2744					$275	Topaz	ebay-09/02	
2744					$480	Amethyst	ebay-10/02	
2744					$200	Pomona Green	ebay-10/02	
2744					$355	Topaz	ebay-10/02	
2744					$1020	Gold Aurene	JDJ-11/02	
2744					$1080	Blue Aurene	JDJ-11/02	
2744					$225	Colorless	ebay-11/02	
2744					$265	Topaz	ebay-11/02	
2744					$190	Topaz	Cinc-11/02	
2744					$985	Blue Aurene	ebay-12/02	
2744					$280	VDS	ebay-02/03	
2744					$290	Celeste Blue	ebay-02/03	
2744					$330	Celeste Blue	ebay-02/03	
2744					$355	Topaz	ebay-03/03	
2744					$600	Gold Aurene	ebay-05/03	
2744					$565	Topaz	ebay-10/03	
2744					$325	Pomona Green	ebay-10/03	
2744					$145	Colorless	JDJ-11/03	
2744					$200	Pomona Green	JDJ-11/03	
2744					$230	Topaz	JDJ-11/03	
2744					$1250	Blue Aurene	ebay-12/03	
2744					$1135	Blue Aurene	ebay-12/03	
2744					$875	Gold Aurene	ebay-01/04	
2744					$465	Topaz	ebay-01/04	
2744					$230	VDS	Cinc-05/04	
2744					$430	Rosa	ebay-04/04	
2744					$355	Topaz	ebay-06/04	
2744					$125	Pomona Green	ebay-07/04	
2744					$800	Blue Aurene	ebay-07/04	
2744					$900	Blue Aurene	ebay-08/04	
2744					$310	Pomona Green	ebay-08/04	
2744					$650	Gold Aurene	ebay-09/04	
2744					$855	Gold Aurene	Tway-09/04	
2744					$175	Topaz	ebay-09/04	
2744					$1165	Blue Aurene	ebay-09/04	
2744					$655	Gold Aurene	ebay-10/04	
2744					$470	Blue Aurene	ebay-10/04	
2744					$175	Topaz	ebay-11/04	
2744					$305	VDS	ebay-11/04	
2744					$345	VDS	ebay-11/04	
2744					$420	Pomona Green	JDJ-11/04	
2744					$610	Gold Aurene	ebay-12/04	
2744					$415	Royal Purple	ebay-12/04	
2744					$720	Gold Aurene	Crft-01/05	
2744					$390	Pomona Green	ebay-03/05	
2744					$605	Celeste Blue	EAC-04/05	
2744					$1725	Blue Aurene	EAC-04/05	
2744					$300	Topaz	ebay-05/05	
2744					$460	Celeste Blue	ebay-05/05	
2744					$200	Pomona Green	ebay-06/05	
2744					$340	Pomona Green	ebay-06/05	
2744					$255	Royal Purple	ebay-07/05	
2744					$720	Blue Aurene	ebay-07/05	
2744					$860	Blue Aurene	EAC-07/05	
2744					$745	Gold Aurene	EAC-07/05	
2744					$460	Royal Purple	EAC-07/05	
2744					$345	Topaz	EAC-07/05	
2744					$515	Pomona Green	EAC-07/05	
2744					$630	Celeste Blue	EAC-07/05	
2744					$460	VDS	EAC-07/05	
2744					$275	Pomona Green	ebay-07/05	
2744					$360	Royal Purple	ebay-07/05	
2745	Vase	269	4	1				PG2)52; TPD)8.32
2746	Vase	269	4	2				
2747	Vase	269	4	3				
2748	Vase	269	4	4				PG1)75,117,A; TPD)10.126
2749	Vase	269	4	5				
2750	Vase	269	4	6				
2751	Vase	269	4	7				
2752	Vase	269	5	1				
2753	Vase	269	5	2				
2754	Vase	269	5	3				
2755	Vase	269	5	4				TPD)10.126

SHAPE NO.	ITEM	PAGE	COL	ROW	PRICE REALIZED	GLASS TYPE	AUCTION HOUSE	COMMENTS & PHOTO REFERENCES
2756	Vase	269	5	5				
2757	Vase	269	5	6				TPD)4.12
2758	Cologne	240	5	4	$1155	Blue Aurene	EAC-10/90	TPD)10.146
2758					$715	Gold Aurene	JDJ-06/96	
2758					$880	Blue Aurene	EAC-07/98	
2758					$860	Blue Aurene	Sknr-06/99	
2758					$1725	Gold Aurene	JDJ-11/03	
2758					$1800	Blue Aurene	Dalla-11/04	
2759	Decanter	185	3	6				
2760	Compote	172	3	7	$490	Gold Calcite	Sknr-05/94	TPD)7.50; MDK)27:86
2760					$125	Celeste Blue	Sknr-10/95	
2760					$460	Yellow Jade	Sknr-01/96	
2760					$630	Light Blue Jade	Sknr-10/96	
2760					$805	Blue Aurene	Sknr-01/97	
2760					$1250	Blue Aurene	JDJ-06/97	
2760					$715	Gold Aurene	EAC-04/98	
2760					$220	Gold Calcite	EAC-04/98	
2760					$390	Green Jade/Alabaster	Sknr-10/98	
2760					$390	Gold Calcite	ebay-11/99	
2760					$400	Gold Calcite	ebay-12/99	
2760					$275	Cyprian	ebay-01/00	
2760					$505	Gold Calcite	Jack-06/00	
2760					$269	Green Jade/Alabaster	Sknr-06/00	
2760					$365	Gold Calcite	Jack-06/00	
2760					$170	Topaz	Sknr-10/00	
2760					$180	Colorless/Threaded	ebay-04/01	
2760					$1030	Blue Calcite	ebay-04/01	
2760					$240	Celeste Blue	ebay-05/01	
2760					$175	Celeste Blue	ebay-06/01	
2760					$100	Celeste Blue	ebay-07/01	
2760					$1200	Gold Aurene	ebay-07/01	
2760					$400	Blue Aurene	ebay-07/01	
2760					$300	Gold Calcite	ebay-07/01	
2760					$215	Amethyst/Colorless	EAC-09/01	
2760					$85	Topaz	ebay-09/01	
2760					$850	Gold Aurene	ebay-10/01	
2760					$805	Blue Calcite	JDJ-11/01	
2760					$175	Gold Ruby	ebay-11/01	
2760					$70	Pomona Green	ebay-11/01	
2760					$195	Rosaline/Alabaster	ebay-11/01	
2760					$405	Gold Calcite	EAC-11/01	
2760					$445	Nile Green (E)	ebay-12/01	
2760					$155	Colorless/Green threaded	ebay-01/02	
2760					$220	Celeste Blue	ebay-01/02	
2760					$200	Green Jade/Alabaster	ebay-02/02	
2760					$260	Gold Calcite	ebay-05/02	
2760					$185	VDS/Green Jade rim	ebay-06/02	
2760					$305	Gold Calcite	ebay-08/02	
2760					$85	Aqua Marine	ebay-09/02	
2760					$1680	Blue Aurene	JDJ-11/02	
2760					$2680	Gold Aurene	JDJ-11/02	
2760					$175	Gold Calcite	ebay-12/02	
2760					$195	Rosaline/Alabaster	ebay-12/02	Alabaster stem and foot
2760					$50	Celeste Bl./Colorless stem	ebay-02/03	
2760					$160	Rosaline/Alabaster	ebay-02/03	Alabaster stem and foot
2760					$400	Gold Calcite	ebay-03/03	
2760					$350	Gold Calcite	Dalla-05/03	
2760					$285	Gold Calcite	JDJ-05/03	
2760					$105	Rosaline/Alabaster	ebay-07/03	Alabaster stem and foot
2760					$460	VDS	ebay-06/03	
2760					$700	Blue Calcite	J&W-09/03	
2760					$105	Amber/Flemish Blue rim	ebay-10/03	
2760					$710	Gold Aurene	ebay-10/03	
2760					$110	Green Jade/Alabaster foot	ebay-11/03	
2760					$150	Celeste Blue/Colorless foot	ebay-11/03	
2760					$165	Celeste Blue/Colorless foot	ebay-11/03	
2760					$430	Gold Calcite	EAC-11/03	
2760					$1380	Gold Calcite (E)	EAC-11/03	
2760					$110	Green Jade/Alabaster stem	Cinc-11/03	
2760					$40	Celeste Blue/Colorless	ebay-12/03	Colorless stem
2760					$460	Blue Calcite	ebay-01/04	
2760					$100	Colorless/Green threaded	ebay-02/04	
2760					$100	Celeste Blue/Colorless	ebay-02/04	Colorless stem
2760					$2000	Gold Aurene	ebay-02/04	

SHAPE NO.	ITEM	PAGE	COL	ROW	PRICE REALIZED	GLASS TYPE	AUCTION HOUSE	COMMENTS & PHOTO REFERENCES
2760					$130	Cyprian	ebay-03/04	
2760					$210	Amethyst/Colorless stem	ebay-04/04	
2760					$105	Celeste Blue/Colorless	ebay-04/04	Colorless stem
2760					$105	Celeste Blue/Colorless	ebay-05/04	Colorless stem
2760					$180	Aqua Marine	JDJ-05/04	
2760					$240	Cyprian	JDJ-05/04	
2760					$95	Aqua Marine	ebay-06/04	
2760					$105	Aqua Marine	ebay-06/04	
2760					$125	Green Jade/Alabaster	ebay-06/04	Alabaster stem and foot
2760					$350	Gold Calcite	ebay-06/04	
2760					$175	Celeste Blue/Colorless	ebay-07/04	Colorless stem
2760					$250	Gold Calcite (FC)	ebay-08/04	
2760					$95	Topaz/Colorless stem	ebay-09/04	
2760					$115	Cyprian	ebay-10/04	
2760					$55	Green Jade/Alabaster	ebay-11/04	Alabaster stem and foot
2760					$125	VDS	ebay-11/04	
2760					$75	Rosa	ebay-12/04	
2760					$100	Sea Green	ebay-01/05	
2760					$625	Light Blue Jade/Flint White	ebay-01/05	Flint White stem and foot
2760					$630	Blue Calcite	Hrtg-03/05	
2760					$360	Gold Calcite	ebay-03/05	
2760					$155	Rosaline/Alabaster	ebay-04/05	Alabaster stem and foot
2760					$865	Blue Aurene	EAC-04/05	
2760					$330	Gold Calcite	ebay-05/05	
2760					$150	Amethyst/Colorless stem	ebay-05/05	
2760					$215	Gold Calcite	ebay-06/05	
2760					$600	Blue Calcite	Cinc-06/05	
2760					$100	Gold Calcite	ebay-07/05	
2761	Vase	269	5	7				RFR)24,3,A; TPD)5.18
2762	Vase	270	1	1	$1120	Gold Aurene	EAC-04/01	MDK)103
2762					$1120	Blue Aurene	EAC-04/01	
2762					$630	Gold Aurene	Jack–11/02	
2762					$500	Gold Aurene	Cinc-11/03	
2762					$1020	Blue Aurene	Cinc-06/04	
2762					$770	Gold Aurene	ebay-12/04	
2762					$630	Blue Aurene	Hrtg-03/05	
2762					$920	Blue Aurene	EAC-07/05	
2763	Vase	270	1	2	$1760	Blue Aurene	JDJ-06/96	
2764	Vase	270	1	3	$1650	Blue Aurene	EAC-07/98	TPD)10.119
2765	Vase	270	1	4	$3575	Blue Aurene	EAC-10/00	
2765					$75	Celeste Blue/Colorless	ebay-06/05	Colorless handles
2766	Vase	270	1	5	$800	Blue Aurene	JDJ-10/94	RFR)9,2,B
2766					$2500	Gold Aurene	ebay-02/00	
2766					$1525	Gold Aurene	Sknr-12/03	
2766					$1045	Gold Aurene	ebay-01/05	
2767	Vase	270	1	6	$700	Gold Aurene	Crft-09/04	PG1)VI A,C; JAS)161,BL,A
2767					$1700	Gold Aurene	ebay-11/04	
2768	Vase	270	1	7				
2769	Atomizer				$3120	Gold Aurene	JDJ-11/02	Not in factory records but same shape as
2769					$4310	Blue Aurene	JDJ-11/03	Decanter
2769	Decanter	185	4	1	$990	Gold Aurene	EAC-10/93	Stopper missing
2770	Bowl	142	1	12				
2771	Shade	228	4	1	$405	Calcite ACB	ebay-11/04	
2772	Punch Bowl	189	3	9				
2772	Punch Cup	189	3	9	$350	Gold Aurene	ebay-12/99	
2772					$250	Gold Aurene	ebay-10/01	
2772	Ladle Handle	189	3	9				
2773	Vase	270	1	8	$745	Gold Aurene	Sknr-05/95	
2774	Shade	228	4	2	$450	Calcite ACB	ebay-09/03	
2774					$525	Calcite ACB	ebay-01/05	Including ceiling fixture
2774					$680	Calcite ACB	ebay-04/05	
2775	Bowl	142	2	1	$495	Gold Calcite	EAC-04/95	TPD)10.46
2775					$545	Gold Aurene	Sknr-10/96	
2775					$285	VDS	Sknr-10/97	
2775					$2090	Blue Aurene	EAC-10/98	
2775					$1325	Blue Aurene	ebay-10/99	
2775					$660	Gold Aurene	ebay-03/01	
2775					$260	VDS	ebay-06/01	
2775					$1360	Blue Aurene	ebay-07/02	
2775					$1320	Blue Aurene	JDJ-11/02	
2775					$895	Gold Aurene	EAC-01/03	
2775					$480	Blue Aurene	ebay-05/04	
2775					$540	Gold Aurene	ebay-09/04	
2775					$1035	Gold Aurene	EAC-04/05	

SHAPE NO.	ITEM	PAGE	COL	ROW	PRICE REALIZED	GLASS TYPE	AUCTION HOUSE	COMMENTS & PHOTO REFERENCES
2775					$1020	Blue Aurene	JDJ-06/05	
2776	Vase	270	1	9	$470	Blue Aurene	Sknr-05/03	PG1)76,120,E; MDK)106
2776					$670	Blue Aurene	ebay-08/03	
2777	Vase	270	2	1				
2778	Vase	270	2	2	$895	Gold Aurene	Jack-06/00	
2778					$1200	Gold Aurene	Ogal-07/02	
2779	Shade	225	4	4	$260	Blue Pulled Feather	Jack-06/02	Gold Aurene base
2780	Cup & Saucer	216	3	11	$740	Blue Aurene	EAC-04/98	
2780					$785	Gold Aurene	ebay-07/02	
2780					$100	Green Jade/Alabaster	ebay-12/02	Alabaster handle
2780					$230	Green Jade/Alabaster	ebay-02/03	Alabaster handle
2780					$60	Topaz/Celeste Blue	ebay-02/03	Celeste blue handle
2781	Vase	270	2	3				
2782	Vase	270	2	4				
2783	Vase	270	2	5				
2784	Vase	270	2	6	$550	Blue Aurene	EAC-04/92	
2784					$6500	Tyrian	ebay-04/00	
2784					$325	Gold Aurene	ebay-05/03	
2784					$300	Gold Aurene	Free-05/03	
2785	Vase	270	2	7	$4830	Tyrian	EAC-06/03	PG1)76,120,A; TPD)9.26
2786	Shade	228	4	3	$4300	Decorated Red Aurene	ebay-03/03	
2786					$545	Calcite ACB	ebay-06/03	
2786					$3850	Decorated Blue Aurene	Cott-06/05	
2787	Shade	228	4	4				
2788	Shade	228	4	5				
2789	Vase	270	2	8	$840	Rouge Flambé	ebay-11/04	
2790	Sherbet	197	2	11				
2791	Vase	270	2	9	$800	Blue Aurene	ebay-05/03	
2792	Vase	270	2	10	$520	Gold Aurene	EAC-08/00	
2793	Vase	270	3	1				
2794	Vase	270	3	2				
2795	Compote	172	3	8				
2796	Compote	172	3	9				
2797	Compote	172	4	1				
2798	Vase	270	3	3				
2799	Compote	172	4	2				
2800	Plate	158	1	10				
2801	Centerpiece	147	3	6	$750	Gold Aurene	ebay-07/03	PG1)88,132,A
2802	Centerpiece	147	3	7				
2803	Bowl	142	2	2				
2804	Centerpiece	147	3	8				
2805	Covered Vase	305	1	2	$3025	Decorated Alabaster	EAC-07/93	Lamp
2805					$450	Rosaline/Alabaster	JDJ-05/01	
2806	Covered Vase	305	1	3	$490	Decorated Alabaster	Sknr-01/96	
2806					$4500	Decorated Alabaster	ebay-11/03	Lamp
2807	Covered Vase	305	1	4	$205	VDS	ebay-11/03	Cover missing PG2)56; TPD)2.25
2808	Covered Vase	305	1	5				
2809	Covered Vase	305	1	6				
2810	Covered Vase	305	2	1				
2811	Covered Vase	305	2	2				
2812	Covered Vase	305	2	3	$630	Gold Aurene	Sknr-05/98	
2812					$1250	Gold Aurene	ebay-03/00	
2812					$385	VDS	Cott-08/01	
2812					$295	Gold Aurene	ebay-09/04	
2813	Covered Vase	305	2	4				TPD)8.33
2814	Covered Vase	305	2	5	$1925	Decorated Alabaster	EAC-07/99	
2814					$3075	Decorated Alabaster	ebay-10/00	
2814					$2750	Decorated Alabaster	ebay-09/01	
2815	Covered Vase	305	2	6				
2816	Covered Vase	305	3	1				
2817	Bowl	142	2	3				
2818	Vase	270	3	4				
2819	Vase	270	3	5				
2820	Bowl	142	2	4				
2821	Vase	270	3	6				
2822	Covered Vase	305	3	2	$1330	Blue Aurene	ebay-07/01	PG1)87,129; ACR)136,247; TPD)4.60
2823	Covered Vase	305	3	3	$895	Gold Aurene	EAC-04/02	No lid
2824	Covered Vase	305	3	4	$920	Blue Aurene	Sknr-05/96	
2824					$1140	Gold Aurene	ebay-12/01	
2824					$1560	Blue Aurene	JDJ-06/05	Paper "Haviland" label
2825	Shade	228	4	6				
2826	Shade	228	4	7				
2827	Decanter	185	4	2	$700	Blue Aurene	ebay-03/04	Stopper missing
2827	Wine	185	4	2				

SHAPE NO.	ITEM	PAGE	COL	ROW	PRICE REALIZED	GLASS TYPE	AUCTION HOUSE	COMMENTS & PHOTO REFERENCES
2828	Decanter	185	4	3				
2828	Wine	185	4	3	$545	Gold Aurene	EAC-06/03	
2828					$490	Gold Aurene	Jack-06/03	
2829	Vase	270	3	7				
2830	Mayonnaise Bowl	210	3	10				
2831	Decanter	185	4	4				
2831	Tumbler	185	4	4				
2832	Cologne	240	5	5				TPD)10.141
2833	Cologne	240	5	6	$770	Gold Aurene	EAC-10/90	TPD)8.7; MDK)87
2833					$605	Gold Aurene	EAC-07/98	
2833					$315	VDS	EAC-06/03	
2833					$1150	Gold Aurene	EAC-07/05	
2834	Cologne	240	5	7	$1490	Blue Aurene (FC)	Sknr-01/96	JAS)161,BR,B; TPD)10.119
2834					$1495	Blue Aurene	Sknr-01/97	
2834					$1250	Gold Aurene	ebay-10/00	
2834					$1650	Blue Aurene	Cott-08/01	
2835	Cologne	240	5	8	$1540	Gold Calcite (E)	EAC-10/95	
2835					$745	Blue Aurene	Sknr-01/96	
2835					$715	Blue Aurene	EAC-04/99	
2835					$525	VDS/Cintra	EAC-07/99	
2835					$500	Gold Aurene	ebay-01/00	
2835					$250	VDS/Flemish Blue stopper	ebay-06/02	
2835					$690	Gold Aurene	ebay-05/05	
2836	Cologne	243	3	9				
2837	Vase	270	3	8				
2838	Vase	270	3	9				
2839	Centerpiece	147	4	1	$1045	Gold Aurene	EAC-07/97	same as 2841
2839					$1500	Gold Aurene	ebay-03/03	
2839					$260	Gold Aurene	ebay-08/03	
2839					$180	Gold Aurene	ebay-05/04	
2839					$170	Celeste Blue/Topaz foot	ebay-12/04	
2839					$155	Celeste Blue	ebay-06/05	
2839					$430	Blue Calcite	EAC-07/05	
2839	Center Vase	147	4	1	$1345	Blue Aurene	Ogal-05/04	
2840	Shade	225	4	5	$160	Gold Aurene	Midw-04/01	
2840					$320	VDS with Blue thread (E)	ebay-06/02	
2840					$170	Brown Aurene	Jack-06/02	
2840					$160	VDS with Blue thread (E)	Jack-06/02	
2840					$95	Calcite	ebay-05/05	
2841	Shade	225	4	6	$520	Gold Calcite	ebay-07/02	RFR)13,4,C
2841					$450	Calcite ACB	ebay-07/04	
2842	Shade	225	4	7				
2843	Shade	270	4	1	$105	Calcite ACB	ebay-01/05	
2843					$125	Calcite ACB	ebay-01/05	
2844	Vase	270	4	2	$770	Gold Aurene	EAC-10/92	
2845	Vase	270	4	3	$880	Blue Aurene	EAC-10/93	
2845					$3105	Gold Aurene	Sknr-10/95	
2846	Compote	172	4	3				
2847	Compote	172	4	4				
2848	Compote	172	4	5				
2849	Shade	228	4	8				
2850	Vase	270	4	4				
2851	Bowl	142	2	5	$285	Gold Calcite	Sknr-10/94	
2851					$230	Gold Calcite	Sknr-10/94	
2851	Bowl	142	2	6	$440	Light Blue Jade	EAC-10/91	Shown in 1932 Catalog. PG1)XI,B,D; MDK)36
2851					$605	Rosaline/Alabaster ACB	EAC-04/93	Etched "Fircone"
2851					$770	Calcite	Sknr-10/93	
2851					$285	Gold Calcite	JDJ-10/96	
2851					$430	Mirror Black	Sknr-10/96	
2851					$330	Gold Calcite	EAC-04/97	
2851					$115	Rosaline	JDJ-10/97	
2851					$720	Yellow Jade	ebay-11/99	
2851					$745	Light Blue Jade	ebay-11/99	
2851					$340	Amethyst	ebay-12/99	
2851					$385	Rosaline	ebay-12/99	
2851					$550	Gold Aurene	Cinc-12/99	
2851					$385	VDS	ebay-02/00	
2851					$700	Light Blue Jade	ebay-03/00	
2851					$600	Celeste Blue	Ogal-03/00	
2851					$305	Gold Aurene	ebay-03/00	
2851					$750	Blue Aurene	JDJ-05/00	
2851					$90	VDS	JDJ-05/00	
2851					$760	Blue Aurene	ebay-10/00	
2851					$105	Bristol Yellow	ebay-10/00	

SHAPE NO.	ITEM	PAGE	COL	ROW	PRICE REALIZED	GLASS TYPE	AUCTION HOUSE	COMMENTS & PHOTO REFERENCES
2851					$750	Gold Aurene	ebay-01/01	
2851					$325	Gold Aurene	ebay-02/01	
2851					$145	Rosaline/Alabaster foot	Sknr-02/01	
2851					$170	Sea Green	Sknr-02/01	
2851					$615	Blue Aurene	EAC-04/01	
2851					$670	Blue Aurene	EAC-04/01	
2851					$550	Gold Aurene	Free-05/01	
2851					$145	Aqua Marine	ebay-05/01	
2851					$660	Blue Aurene	ebay-06/01	
2851					$140	Rosaline/Alabaster	ebay-06/01	
2851					$500	Gold Aurene	ebay-06/01	
2851					$1200	Gold Aurene	ebay-06/01	
2851					$140	Sea Green	ebay-08/01	
2851					$560	Blue Aurene	ebay-09/01	
2851					$1200	Gold Aurene	ebay-10/01	
2851					$140	VDS	ebay-10/01	
2851					$270	Gold Calcite	ebay-10/01	
2851					$170	VDS	ebay-12/01	
2851					$475	Gold Aurene	Wint-12/01	
2851					$80	Celeste Blue	ebay-01/02	
2851					$185	Cyprian	ebay-02/02	
2851					$130	Rosaline	ebay-02/02	
2851					$175	Green Jade/Alabaster	ebay-03/02	
2851					$150	Green Jade	ebay-03/04	
2851					$100	Green Jade	Tway-03/02	
2851					$290	Gold Aurene	ebay-04/02	
2851					$345	Gold Calcite	Wesr-04/02	
2851					$230	VDS	JDJ-05/02	
2851					$410	Green Jade	ebay-05/02	
2851					$345	Gold Calcite	Jack-06/02	
2851					$230	Gold Calcite	Jack-06/02	
2851					$500	Light Blue Jade	ebay-10/02	
2851					$95	VDS	ebay-10/02	
2851					$2280	Gold Aurene	JDJ-11/02	
2851					$620	Rosaline/Alabaster (E)	ebay-11/02	Engraved "York"
2851					$225	Rosaline	ebay-12/02	
2851					$265	Gold Calcite	Sknr-12/02	
2851					$275	Gold Calcite	Wint-12/02	
2851					$390	Rosaline/Alabaster	EAC-01/03	
2851					$1000	Blue Aurene	ebay-01/03	
2851					$150	Green Jade/Alabaster	ebay-01/03	
2851					$200	Gold Calcite	ebay-01/03	
2851					$285	Gold Calcite	ebay-01/03	
2851					$170	Marina Blue	ebay-02/03	
2851					$100	Celeste Blue	ebay-02/03	
2851					$475	Gold Aurene	Ogal-03/03	
2851					$275	VDS	Ogal-03/03	
2851					$130	Light Blue Jade	ebay-04/03	
2851					$200	VDS	ebay-05/03	
2851					$225	Gold Calcite	Dalla-05/03	
2851					$130	Gold Calcite	ebay-06/03	
2851					$475	Gold Calcite	ebay-06/03	
2851					$455	Amethyst	ebay-06/03	
2851					$515	Gold Calcite	EAC-06/03	
2851					$405	Gold Calcite	ebay-07/03	
2851					$125	Celeste Blue	ebay-08/03	
2851					$215	Gold Calcite	ebay-09/03	
2851					$175	Rosaline/Alabaster	ebay-10/03	
2851					$365	Gold Aurene	ebay-10/03	
2851					$900	Blue Aurene	ebay-11/03	
2851					$150	Rosaline/Alabaster	ebay-11/03	
2851					$180	Gold Calcite	ebay-11/03	
2851					$200	VDS	ebay-11/03	
2851					$170	Ivory	JDJ-11/03	
2851					$805	Green Jade	EAC-11/03	
2851					$75	Celeste Blue	ebay-12/03	
2851					$125	Topaz	ebay-12/03	
2851					$250	Gold Calcite	ebay-12/03	
2851					$50	VDS	ebay-12/03	
2851					$400	Light Blue Jade	ebay-12/03	
2851					$1850	Blue Aurene	ebay-12/03	
2851					$100	Green Jade	ebay-01/04	
2851					$225	Green Jade	ebay-01/04	
2851					$270	Amethyst	ebay-01/04	

SHAPE NO.	ITEM	PAGE	COL	ROW	PRICE REALIZED	GLASS TYPE	AUCTION HOUSE	COMMENTS & PHOTO REFERENCES
2851					$160	Celeste Blue	ebay-02/04	
2851					$160	Gold Calcite	ebay-02/04	
2851					$1200	Gold Calcite	Ogal-02/04	
2851					$75	Topaz	ebay-03/04	
2851					$260	Gold Calcite	ebay-03/04	
2851					$300	Gold Calcite	ebay-03/04	
2851					$330	Gold Calcite	ebay-03/04	
2851					$355	Amber/Flemish Blue	ebay-03/04	Flemish Blue rim and prunts
2851					$320	Cyprian	ebay-03/04	
2851					$150	Gold Calcite	ebay-03/04	
2851					$355	Gold Calcite	ebay-04/04	
2851					$145	Gold Calcite	ebay-04/04	
2851					$85	Celeste Blue	ebay-04/04	
2851					$200	Amethyst	ebay-05/04	
2851					$595	Cyprian	ebay-05/04	
2851					$460	Cyprian	JDJ-05/04	
2851					$155	Celeste Blue	ebay-05/04	
2851					$255	Blue Aurene	ebay-05/04	
2851					$300	Gold Calcite	Cinc-06/04	
2851					$80	Rosaline	ebay-06/04	
2851					$850	Gold Aurene	ebay-07/04	
2851					$180	Gold Calcite	ebay-07/04	
2851					$200	Sea Green	ebay-07/04	
2851					$195	Gold Calcite	EAC-07/04	
2851					$200	Gold Calcite	ebay-08/04	
2851					$395	Flemish	ebay-08/04	
2851					$160	Green Jade	ebay-09/04	
2851					$675	Blue Aurene	Tway-09/04	
2851					$130	Green Jade	ebay-09/04	
2851					$155	Gold Calcite	ebay-11/04	
2851					$245	Gold Calcite	ebay-12/04	
2851					$125	Sea Green	ebay-01/05	
2851					$150	Royal Purple	ebay-01/05	
2851					$200	Gold Calcite	ebay-02/05	
2851					$125	Royal Purple	ebay-02/05	
2851					$245	Sea Green	ebay-02/05	
2851					$100	Celeste Blue	ebay-03/05	
2851					$150	Bristol Yellow	ebay-03/05	
2851					$115	Celeste Blue	ebay-04/05	
2851					$55	Amber	ebay-04/05	
2851					$975	Gold Aurene	EAC-04/05	
2851					$170	VDS	EAC-04/05	
2851					$220	Gold Aurene	ebay-05/05	
2851					$100	Celeste Blue	ebay-06/05	
2851					$420	Gold Calcite	JDJ-06/05	
2851					$900	Gold Aurene	JDJ-06/05	
2851					$200	Gold Calcite	ebay-06/05	
2851					$65	Amber	ebay-07/05	
2852	Bowl	142	2	7	$695	Blue Aurene	ebay-12/99	
2852					$990	Blue Aurene	EAC-05/00	
2852					$600	Blue Aurene	ebay-10/00	
2852					$265	Gold Aurene	ebay-11/00	
2852					$920	Blue Aurene	Sknr-02/01	
2852					$745	Light Blue Jade	Sknr-02/01	
2852					$385	Gold Calcite	ebay-03/01	
2852					$1100	Blue Aurene	ebay-03/01	
2852					$600	Blue Aurene	ebay-07/01	
2852					$485	Gold Aurene	ebay-11/01	
2852					$1200	Blue Aurene	ebay-12/01	
2852					$865	Gold Aurene	ebay-02/02	
2852					$565	Blue Aurene	ebay-12/03	
2852					$210	Gold Calcite	ebay-12/03	
2852					$840	Blue Aurene	Crft-05/04	
2852					$1100	Gold Aurene	Tway-09/04	
2852					$570	Gold Aurene	Tway-03/05	
2852					$300	Gold Aurene	JDJ-06/05	
2853	Shade	270	4	5				
2854	Shade	270	4	6				
2855	Cologne	240	5	9				
2856	Shade	228	4	9				
2857	Shade	229	1	1				
2858	Vase	270	4	7	$1260	Royal Purple	ebay-05/05	15" high
2859	Vase	270	4	8				
2860	Shade	226	5	2	$245	Gold Calcite	EAC-07/98	

SHAPE NO.	ITEM	PAGE	COL	ROW	PRICE REALIZED	GLASS TYPE	AUCTION HOUSE	COMMENTS & PHOTO REFERENCES
2861	Shade	226	5	3				
2862	Shade	226	5	4				
2863	Limousine Vase	207	2	2				
2864	Shade	229	1	2	$590	Calcite ACB	ebay-10/02	Calcite Dome with hanging lamp fixture.
2864					$355	Calcite ACB	Sknr-12/02	
2865	Vase	270	5	1				TPD)4.8
2866	Vase	270	5	2				
2867	Vase	270	5	3				
2868	Vase	270	5	4				
2869	Vase	270	5	5				
2870	Vase	271	1	1				
2871	Vase	271	1	2				TPD)5.14:10.46
2872	Vase	271	1	3				
2873	Vase	271	1	4				
2874	Vase	271	1	5				
2875	Vase	271	1	6				
2876	Vase	271	2	1				
2877	Shade	271	2	2				
2878	Shade	271	2	3				
2879	Bowl	142	2	8	$385	Gold Aurene	EAC-02/92	
2879					$400	Gold Aurene	Sknr-05/98	
2879					$250	Gold Calcite	ebay-01/02	
2879					$120	Green Jade	ebay-12/03	
2879					$390	Gold Aurene	ebay-07/04	
2879					$250	Gold Calcite	ebay-03/05	
2880	Bowl	142	2	9				
2881	Basket	140	1	5				
2882	Goblet	190	6	8				
2883	Mayonnaise Bowl	210	3	11				
2884	Shade	226	5	5				
2885	Shade	226	5	6				
2886	Limousine Vase	207	2	3	$690	Gold Aurene	Sknr-10/95	
2886					$565	Gold Calcite	ebay-08/01	
2887	Limousine Vase	207	2	4				
2888	Bowl	142	2	10				
2889	Finger Bowl	189	1	8	$260	Gold Calcite	Tway-10/00	
2889					$230	Gold Aurene	Rago-09/00	Bowl only; Haviland signature
2889					$80	Celeste Blue	ebay-03/02	
2889					$230	Gold Calcite	ebay-05/02	
2889					$290	Gold Aurene	Jack–11/02	
2889					$80	VDS	ebay-12/02	
2889					$75	Rosaline	ebay-02/03	
2889					$210	Gold Calcite	ebay-05/03	
2889					$95	Amethyst	ebay-05/03	
2889					$120	Gold Calcite	ebay-10/03	
2889					$105	Gold Calcite	ebay-03/04	Bowl only
2889					$200	Gold Calcite	ebay-02/05	Underplate only
2889					$65	Gold Aurene	ebay-05/05	Underplate only
2889					$185	Gold Calcite	ebay-06/05	
2889					$110	Gold Calcite	ebay-06/05	Underplate only
2889					$160	Gold Calcite	ebay-06/05	Underplate only
2890	Centerpiece	147	4	2	$850	Flemish	ebay-09/04	
2891	Vase	271	2	4				
2892	Pitcher	213	4	5				
2893	Vase	271	2	5				
2894	Vase	271	2	6				
2895	Centerpiece	147	4	3				RFR)14,1,B
2896	Bowl	142	2	11				TPD)4.58; MDK)126
2896					$650	Topaz/Celeste Blue	Cinc-11/02	Celeste Blue lattice
2897	Bowl	142	2	12				
2898	Bowl	142	2	13				
2899	Plate	158	1	11				
2900	Vase	271	2	7				
2901	Compote	172	4	6				
2902	Centerpiece	147	4	4				
2903	Compote	172	4	7				
2904	Centerpiece	147	4	5	$1090	Amber/Flemish Blue dec.	ebay-01/04	
2905	Centerpiece	147	4	6				RFR)22,1,C
2906	Plate	159	1					
2907	Vase	271	3	1	$155	Celeste Blue	ebay-01/01	
2907					$320	Celeste Blue	ebay-02/03	
2908	Vase	271	3	2	$1540	Light Blue Jade/White foot	EAC-07/93	PG1)V C,B; RFR)7,4,C:9,4,C:24,1,B
2908					$715	Blue Aurene	JDJ-10/94	RFR)25,3,B; TPD)8.30; MDK)111
2908					$660	Gold Aurene	JDJ-10/94	

SHAPE NO.	ITEM	PAGE	COL	ROW	PRICE REALIZED	GLASS TYPE	AUCTION HOUSE	COMMENTS & PHOTO REFERENCES
2908					$330	Rosaline/Alabaster	JDJ-10/94	
2908					$880	Gold Aurene	EAC-10/95	
2908					$150	Ivory	JDJ-06/96	
2908					$495	Blue Aurene	JDJ-06/96	
2908					$1645	Oriental Poppy	Sknr-10/96	
2908					$690	Rosaline/Alabaster	Sknr-01/98	
2908					$935	Gold Aurene	EAC-10/98	
2908					$920	Amethyst	JDJ-05/99	
2908					$1180	Blue Aurene	EAC-07/99	
2908					$265	Amethyst	ebay-12/00	
2908					$150	Amber	ebay-01/01	
2908					$200	Sea Green	Sknr-02/01	
2908					$200	Gold Aurene	ebay-02/01	
2908					$190	Pomona Green	ebay-03/01	
2908					$195	Topaz	ebay-03/01	
2908					$760	Gold Aurene	ebay-04/01	
2908					$840	Gold Aurene	ebay-05/01	
2908					$125	Pomona Green	ebay-08/01	
2908					$140	Pomona Green	ebay-08/01	
2908					$140	Pomona Green	ebay-08/01	
2908					$750	Blue Aurene	ebay-09/01	
2908					$330	Wisteria	ebay-02/02	
2908					$135	Bristol Yellow	ebay-05/02	
2908					$140	VDS	ebay-05/02	
2908					$80	Colorless/Green threaded	ebay-09/02	
2908					$225	Pomona Green	ebay-10/03	
2908					$360	Pomona Green (E)	ebay-11/03	
2908					$170	Celeste Blue	JDJ-11/03	
2908					$1750	Gold Aurene	ebay-01/04	
2908					$1035	Blue Aurene	ebay-01/04	
2908					$825	Gold Aurene	ebay-05/04	
2908					$180	Aqua Marine	JDJ-05/04	
2908					$175	Celeste Blue	ebay-07/04	
2908					$320	Celeste Blue	ebay-07/04	
2908					$90	VDS/Red threaded	ebay-10/04	
2908					$715	Mirror Black	EAC-10/04	
2908					$190	Green Jade/Alabaster	ebay-11/04	Alabaster foot
2908					$100	Amber	ebay-02/05	
2908					$1375	Gold Aurene	ebay-03/05	
2908					$625	Gold Aurene	ebay-04/05	
2908					$200	Colorless/Gold Ruby	EAC-04/05	Gold Ruby threading
2908					$480	Celeste Blue	Cinc-06/05	
2908					$135	Topaz (E)	ebay-06/05	Engraved "10020"
2908					$200	Colorless/Gold Ruby thread	ebay-07/05	
2909	Vase	271	3	3	$880	Blue Aurene	EAC-10/93	PG1)312;PG2)60,B;
2909					$260	Green Jade/Alabaster	Sknr-10/95	RFR)7,4,A:8,2,C:20,2,A:21,1,B;
2909					$220	Green Jade/Alabaster	EAC-04/96	RLG)152,286; ACR)COLOR 2,B,A
2909					$110	Celeste threaded	JDJ-10/97	JAS)164,B,B; TPD)4.68:8.46; MDK)43:55
2909					$375	Aqua Marine	Sknr-01/98	
2909					$275	Rosaline/Alabaster	EAC-04/98	
2909					$355	Rosaline/Alabaster	EAC-07/98	
2909					$330	Gold Aurene	EAC-10/98	
2909					$2000	Blue Aurene	ebay-12/99	
2909					$700	Amethyst	ebay-12/99	
2909					$195	Celeste Blue	ebay-01/00	
2909					$800	Selenium Red	ebay-02/00	
2909					$180	Rosaline/Alabaster	ebay-02/00	
2909					$850	Gold Aurene	Ogal-05/00	
2909					$150	Pomona Green	ebay-10/00	
2909					$260	Ruby threaded	ebay-12/00	
2909					$100	Spanish Green	ebay-12/00	
2909					$150	Aqua Marine	ebay-01/01	
2909					$740	Gold Aurene	ebay-03/01	
2909					$245	Ivrene	ebay-04/01	
2909					$395	VDS (Hawkes)	ebay-06/01	
2909					$410	Selenium Red	ebay-07/01	
2909					$1210	Blue Aurene	Cott-08/01	
2909					$160	Green Jade/Alabaster	ebay-11/01	
2909					$350	Selenium Red	ebay-12/01	
2909					$635	Blue Aurene	ebay-01/02	
2909					$200	Topaz/Celeste Blue Rim	ebay-01/02	
2909					$60	Topaz	ebay-02/02	
2909					$260	Green Jade/Alabaster	ebay-02/02	
2909					$125	Celeste Blue	ebay-04/02	

SHAPE NO.	ITEM	PAGE	COL	ROW	PRICE REALIZED	GLASS TYPE	AUCTION HOUSE	COMMENTS & PHOTO REFERENCES
2909					$1495	Blue Aurene	JDJ-05/02	
2909					$130	Bristol Yellow	ebay-05/02	
2909					$365	Gold Ruby/Colorless foot	ebay-09/02	
2909					$70	VDS	ebay-10/02	
2909					$510	Spanish Green	ebay-12/02	With colorless ring handles.
2909					$455	Gold Aurene	ebay-02/03	
2909					$225	Celeste Blue	ebay-03/03	
2909					$365	Topaz	ebay-05/03	With ring handles
2909					$100	Colorless/Green threaded	ebay-06/03	
2909					$220	Celeste Blue	ebay-07/03	
2909					$250	VDS	ebay-09/03	
2909					$225	VDS	ebay-11/03	
2909					$1090	Gold Aurene	EAC-11/03	
2909					$575	Green Jade/Alabaster	EAC-11/03	Alabaster foot and ring handles
2909					$860	Rosaline/Alabaster	EAC-11/03	Amethyst ring handles
2909					$525	Aqua Marine	ebay-12/03	
2909					$125	Spanish Green	ebay-03/04	
2909					$460	Selenium Red	EAC-04/04	
2909					$855	Gold Aurene	Sknr-06/04	
2909					$875	Gold Aurene	ebay-08/04	
2909					$160	Rosa	ebay-09/04	
2909					$1085	Gold Aurene	ebay-10/04	
2909					$1320	Blue Aurene	Cinc-11/04	
2909					$175	Green Jade/Alabaster foot	ebay-11/04	
2909					$90	Pomona Green	ebay-12/04	
2909					$145	Amethyst	ebay-02/05	
2909					$900	Gold Aurene	Tway-03/05	
2909					$210	Amethyst	ebay-03/05	
2909					$255	Green Jade/Alabaster foot	ebay-03/05	
2909					$150	Green Jade/Alabaster foot	ebay-04/05	
2909					$310	Green Jade/Alabaster foot	ebay-05/05	
2909					$150	Royal Purple	ebay-05/05	
2909					$720	Gold Aurene	JDJ-06/05	
2909					$75	Topaz	ebay-06/05	
2909					$105	Rosa	ebay-07/05	
2910	Puff Box	244	4	2				
2910½	Decanter	185	4	5				PG1)XXVIII A,D
2911	Vase	271	3	4				
2912	Vase	271	3	5				
2913	Compote	172	4	8				
2914	Bowl	142	2	14				
2915	Vase	271	3	6				
2916	Bowl	142	3	1				
2917	Vase	271	3	7				
2918	Vase	271	3	8				
2920	Shade	229	1	3				
2921	Bowl	142	3	2				
2922	Shade	225	4	8				
2923	Shade	225	4	9				
2924	Vase	271	3	9				
2925	Bowl	142	3	3				
2926	Centerpiece	147	4	7	$1035	Amethyst	Sknr-10/95	PG1)XV A,B
2926					$560	Topaz/Celeste Blue	ebay-02/02	
2926					$990	Topaz/Celeste Blue	EAC-10/04	
2927	Bowl	142	3	4				
2928	Bowl	142	3	5				
2929	Centerpiece	148	1	1				
2930	Centerpiece	148	1	2				
2931	Decanter	185	4	6				PG2)60,E; JAS)164,B,E; ACR)151,295;
2931					$3050	Blue Aurene	ebay-11/04	ACR)151,296; TPD)10.107
2931	Wine	185	4	6				
2932	Tray	158	4	15				
2933	Candlestick	160	4	5	$630	Blue Aurene	EAC-07/90	TPD)10.49:10.114; MDK)61
2933					$650	Rosaline/Alabaster	Ogal-04/01	
2933					$505	Blue Aurene	ebay-10/02	
2933					$285	Opal/Amethyst Cintra	ebay-11/02	
2933					$595	Light Blue Jade/Flint White	ebay-11/02	Flint White stem
2933					$765	Gold Aurene	ebay-06/03	
2933					$175	Topaz	ebay-07/04	
2934	Vase	271	4	1	$225	Ivrene	ebay-02/03	
2934					$160	Ivrene	ebay-10/03	
2934					$305	Ivrene	ebay-03/04	
2934					$300	Ivrene	JDJ-05/04	
2934					$475	Ivrene	EAC-07/04	

SHAPE NO.	ITEM	PAGE	COL	ROW	PRICE REALIZED	GLASS TYPE	AUCTION HOUSE	COMMENTS & PHOTO REFERENCES
2934					$425	Ivrene	ebay-01/05	
2934					$650	Ivrene	ebay-02/05	
2934					$150	Ivrene	ebay-04/05	
2935	Shade	225	4	10				
2936	Shade	225	4	11				
2937	Shade	225	5	1				
2938	Shade	229	1	4	$850	Calcite ACB	ebay-05/04	
2939	Vase	271	4	2	$1375	Green Jade/Alabaster	EAC-04/97	TPD)10.47
2939					$635	Pomona Green	ebay-04/01	
2939					$1100	Pomona Green	ebay-09/01	
2939					$2125	Green Jade/Alabaster	EAC-06/03	Alabaster handles
2940	Candlestick	160	4	6	$110	Amethyst/Topaz bowl	ebay-04/02	
2940					$190	Amber/Flemish Blue stem	ebay-10/02	
2940					$175	Amethyst	ebay-04/03	
2940					$205	Topaz/Pomona Green	ebay-05/05	Pomona Green stem and foot
2941	Centerpiece	148	1	3	$335	Amethyst	Ogal-01/04	
2941					$155	Gold Calcite	ebay-09/04	
2942	Centerpiece	148	1	4	$3300	Light Blue Jade/Flint White	EAC-10/93	PG1)XVI B,B:88,133,A; PG2)62,B;
2942					$690	Green Jade/Alabaster	Sknr-10/95	
2942					$550	Gold Calcite	EAC-10/98	RFR)20,4,B; RLG)143,274; ACR)146,278
2942					$13,200	Orange Cintra	Sbys-12/00	TPD)10.47:10.49
2942					$355	Pomona Green	ebay-03/03	No handles
2943	Bowl	142	3	6				
2944	Covered Vase	305	3	5				PG2)60,C; JAS)164,B,C
2945	Covered Vase	305	3	6				PG2)57,C; RFR)24,3,E; ACR)145,275
2945								JAS)150,TR,C; MDK)141
2946	Covered Vase	305	3	7				
2947	Vase	271	4	3				
2948	Puff Box	244	4	3				
2949	Plate	158	1	12	$400	Gold Calcite	Cinc-06/04	
2950	Shade	271	4	4	$110	Calcite ACB	EAC-07/04	
2951	Shade	225	5	2				
2952	Cologne	240	5	10				
2953	Decanter	185	5	1	$695	Gold Aurene	ebay-01/02	
2954	Puff Box	244	4	4				
2955	Nappie	233	2	12				
2956	Candlestick	160	4	7	$135	Bristol Yellow	EAC-10/91	PG1)XXVIIIA,B&F:44,79,B;PG2)62,A&C;
2956					$315	Colorless	Sknr-10/94	RFR)19,2,A&C:20,4,A&C; TPD)4.34;
2956					$250	Pomona Green	Sknr-05/95	MDK)136
2956					$230	VDS	Sknr-10/95	
2956					$805	Celeste Blue	Sknr-10/95	
2956					$175	Amethyst/Topaz	Sknr-01/96	
2956					$550	Blue Aurene	JDJ-06/96	
2956					$230	Spanish Green	Sknr-10/96	
2956					$575	Green Jade/Alabaster	Sknr-10/97	
2956					$345	Topaz	Sknr-03/99	
2956					$535	Topaz/Celeste Blue	ebay-12/99	
2956					$295	Amethyst (Royal Purple)	ebay-12/99	
2956					$565	Celeste Blue	ebay-02/00	
2956					$400	Citron Yellow	ebay-03/00	
2956					$180	Celeste Blue	ebay-04/00	
2956					$400	Rosaline/Alabaster	JDJ-05/00	
2956					$1565	Amethyst	EAC-05/00	
2956					$480	Green Jade/Alabaster	EAC-05/00	
2956					$510	Mirror Black	ebay-05/00	
2956					$145	Green Jade/Alabaster	Sknr-06/00	
2956					$215	Celeste Blue	ebay-10/00	
2956					$235	Celeste Blue	ebay-03/01	
2956					$1365	Light Blue Jade	ebay-03/01	
2956					$280	Pomona Green	EAC-04/01	
2956					$4480	Green Jade/Alabaster ACB	EAC-04/01	
2956					$770	Rosaline/Alabaster	Cott-08/01	
2956					$805	Mirror Black	ebay-10/01	
2956					$400	Rosaline/Alabaster	ebay-10/01	
2956					$315	Topaz/Amethyst	ebay-11/01	
2956					$330	Amber/Flemish Blue	ebay-01/02	
2956					$305	Alabaster	ebay-02/02	
2956					$330	Celeste Blue	ebay-04/02	
2956					$430	Topaz	JDJ-05/02	
2956					$200	Topaz/Amethyst stem	ebay-05/02	
2956					$315	Antique Green	ebay-05/02	
2956					$80	Topaz	ebay-10/02	
2956					$440	Celeste Blue	JDJ-11/02	
2956					$750	Amber/Flemish Blue	ebay-11/02	

SHAPE NO.	ITEM	PAGE	COL	ROW	PRICE REALIZED	GLASS TYPE	AUCTION HOUSE	COMMENTS & PHOTO REFERENCES
2956					$650	Amber/Flemish Blue	ebay-02/03	
2956					$285	Topaz/Amethyst stem	ebay-03/03	
2956					$360	Celeste Blue	ebay-06/03	
2956					$425	Green Jade/Alabaster stem	ebay-11/03	
2956					$225	Celeste Blue	ebay-11/03	
2956					$415	Rosaline/Alabaster stem	ebay-01/04	
2956					$225	Pomona Green	ebay-01/04	
2956					$225	Citron Yellow	ebay-02/04	
2956					$160	Topaz	EAC-04/04	
2956					$220	Celeste Blue	ebay-05/04	
2956					$200	Selenium Red	ebay-07/04	
2956					$1200	Celeste Blue/Topaz stem	ebay-07/04	14"
2956					$70	Celeste Blue	ebay-08/04	
2956					$100	Flemish	ebay-12/04	
2956					$150	Antique Green	ebay-01/05	
2956					$180	Citron Yellow	ebay-04/05	
2956					$100	Citron Yellow	ebay-04/05	
2956					$315	Flemish	ebay-07/05	
2956					$225	Topaz/Celeste Blue stem	ebay-07/05	
2957	Compote	172	4	9	$3405	Gold Aurene	Sknr-12/03	TPD)4.10
2958	Candlestick	160	5	1	$375	Topaz/Amethyst	Sknr-10/95	
2958					$1200	Topaz/Amethyst	Dalla-09/03	
2959	Candlestick	160	5	2				TPD)10.142
2960	Sherbet	216	4	9	$165	Gold Aurene	ebay-03/00	TPD)4.75
2960					$175	Gold Aurene	ebay-04/00	
2960					$150	Gold Aurene	ebay-04/00	
2960					$190	Rosaline/Alabaster	EAC-11/03	Sherbet only
2960					$140	Gold Aurene	ebay-08/04	Sherbet only
2961	Sherbet	216	4	10				
2961	Tumbler				$440	Gold Aurene	EAC-04/98	
2962	Centerpiece	148	1	5	$1200	Amber/Flemish Blue		PG1)88,133,B
2963	Centerpiece	148	1	6				
2964	Centerpiece	148	2	1				
2965	Centerpiece	148	2	2				PG1)88,133,C
2966	Centerpiece	148	2	3	$205	Aqua Marine	ebay-09/01	
2966					$345	Amber/Flemish Blue	ebay-01/02	
2967	Centerpiece	148	2	4				
2968	Covered Vase	305	4	1	$980	Aqua Marine	Sknr-10/95	
2968					$975	Aqua Marine	Sknr-10/97	
2968					$1035	Aqua Marine	Sknr-10/97	
2968					$1100	Celeste Blue	EAC-07/98	
2968					$770	Aqua Marine	ebay-11/00	
2968					$2185	Aqua Marine	EAC-01/03	
2969	Covered Vase	305	4	2	$1150	VDS with Plum finial	EAC-04/04	
2970	Covered Vase	305	4	3				
2971	Covered Vase	305	4	4	$975	Amethyst	Sknr-10/95	
2972	Centerpiece	148	2	5				
2973	Centerpiece	148	2	6				
2974	Centerpiece	148	2	7				
2975	Centerpiece	148	3	1				
2976	Jar	210	2	11				
2977	Vase	271	4	5				
2978	Vase	271	4	6				
2979	Vase	271	4	7				
2980	Vase	271	5	1				
2981	Goblet	197	3	1				
2982	Goblet	197	3	2				
2983	Bowl	142	3	7	$460	Light Blue Jade	EAC-04/04	Flint White foot
2984	Shade	225	5	3	$150	Gold Calcite	ebay-07/02	
2984					$100	Gold Calcite	ebay-09/03	
2984					$170	Gold Calcite	EAC-04/04	
2984					$125	Gold Aurene	ebay-05/04	
2984					$100	Gold Calcite	ebay-06/05	
2984					$100	Gold Aurene	ebay-04/05	
2984					$100	Gold Calcite	ebay-07/05	
2985	Vase	271	5	2				
2986	Vase	271	5	3	$300	Blue Aurene	JDJ-06/96	
2987	Vase	271	5	4	$400	Light Blue Jade	Sknr-01/98	ACR)148,287; TPD)4.50:10.45; MDK)62
2987					$250	Rosaline/Alabaster foot	ebay-11/03	
2987					$920	Gold Aurene	Jack-11/03	
2987					$300	Rosaline/Alabaster foot	ebay-01/04	Carder signed
2987					$455	Green Jade/Alabaster	ebay-07/04	Alabaster foot and ring handles
2987					$60	Topaz	ebay-01/05	
2988	Vase	271	5	5				

SHAPE NO.	ITEM	PAGE	COL	ROW	PRICE REALIZED	GLASS TYPE	AUCTION HOUSE	COMMENTS & PHOTO REFERENCES
2989	Box	138	4	3				PG1)312
2990	Covered Vase	305	4	5				
2991	Goblet	190	6	9	$130	Amber/Celeste Blue trim	ebay-09/04	
2991					$135	Amber/Celeste Blue trim	ebay-09/04	
2992	Candlestick	160	5	3				
2993	Shade	229	1	5	$215	Calcite ACB	ebay-08/03	9" dome
2994	Plate	158	1	16				
2995	Centerpiece	148	3	2				
2996	Covered Vase	305	5	1	$690	Pomona Green	Sknr-05/94	
2997	Ash Tray	137	1	10	$385	Gold Aurene	JDJ-10/94	PG2)54,Bf; TPD)10.123
2997					$380	Ivory/Mirror Black	ebay-01/01	
2997					$575	Blue Calcite	Sknr-02/01	
2997					$65	Gold Calcite	ebay-05/03	No handles, used as coasters?
2997					$460	Blue Aurene	ebay-11/03	
2998	Jar	210	3	1				
2999	Plate	158	1	17				
3000	Goblet	197	3	3				
3001	Basket	140	1	6				
3002	Ash Tray	137	1	11				
3003	Puff Box	244	4	5				
3004	Vase	271	5	6				
3005	Bowl	142	3	8				
3006	Sherbet	216	5	1				
3007	Vase	271	5	7				
3008	Vase	272	1	1				
3009	Vase	272	1	2				
3010	Vase	272	1	3				
3011	Bowl	142	3	9				
3012	Plate	158	1	18				
3013	Puff Box	244	4	6				
3014	Plate	158	1	19				
3015	Spoon Holder	177	3	6				
3016	Vase	272	1	4				
3017	Cologne	243	5	8				
3018	Covered Vase	305	5	2				
3019	Compote	172	5	1				
3020	Bowl	142	3	10				
3021	Basket	140	1	7				
3022	Basket	140	1	8				
3023	Mayonnaise Bowl	210	3	12				
3024	Marmalade Jar							See New Drawings section
3025	Vase	272	1	5				
3026	Vase	272	1	6	$155	Green Jade	ebay-02/04	
3027	Cold Cream Jar	243	6	7				
3028	Bowl	142	3	11				
3029	Bowl	142	4	1				
3030	Bowl	142	4	2				
3031	Candlestick	160	5	4				
3032	Decanter	185	5	2				
3033	Vase	272	1	7				
3034	Basket	140	2	1				
3035	Pitcher	213	4	6				
3036	Pitcher	213	4	7				
3037	Compote	172	5	2				
3038	Cologne	240	5	11				
3039	Punch Cup	216	2	4				
3040	Bowl	142	4	3				
3041	Basket	140	2	2				
3042	Pitcher	213	5	1				
3043	Cold Cream Jar	243	6	8	$1100	Gold Aurene	EAC-10/93	
3044	Vase	272	1	8	$935	Gold Aurene	EAC-04/95	
3044					$660	Blue Aurene	Tway-03/05	
3045	Vase	272	2	1				
3046	Plate	158	1	20				
3047	Cologne	240	6	1	$195	VDS/Selenium Red stopper	ebay-11/03	
3047					$205	Blue Aurene	ebay-01/05	Stopper missing
3048	Cologne	240	6	2	$1610	Opal/Cintra	Sknr-01/96	JAS)161,BR,A; TPD)10.121
3048					$1495	Gold Aurene	Sknr-01/96	
3049	Ash Tray	137	1	12				
3050	Cologne	240	6	3				
3051	Watch Holder	310	1	2				
3052	Watch Holder	310	1	3				
3053	Watch Holder	310	1	4				
3054	Watch Holder	310	1	5				

SHAPE NO.	ITEM	PAGE	COL	ROW	PRICE REALIZED	GLASS TYPE	AUCTION HOUSE	COMMENTS & PHOTO REFERENCES
3055	Watch Holder	310	1	6				
3056	Watch Holder	310	2	1				
3057	Watch Holder	310	2	2				
3058	Vase	272	2	2	$600	Blue Aurene	ebay-07/01	
3058					$495	Rosaline/Alabaster	ebay-10/01	
3058					$405	Gold Aurene	ebay-01/02	Haviland signature
3058					$495	Rosaline/Alabaster	ebay-03/02	
3058					$330	Gold Aurene	ebay-06/03	
3058					$260	Gold Aurene	ebay-10/03	
3059	Plate	158	2	1	$345	Gold Aurene	ebay-12/99	
3059					$350	Gold Aurene	Ogal-03/00	
3059					$50	Bristol Yellow	ebay-09/02	
3060	Limousine Vase	207	2	5				
3061	Cruet	179	2	7	$150	VDS (E)	ebay-05/05	
3062	Cruet	179	2	8				
3063	Cruet	179	3	1	$315	VDS (Hawkes)	Sknr-05/96	
3063					$250	VDS (E)	ebay-08/02	
3064	Tumble Up	199	5	6	$345	VDS	JDJ-06/98	PG1)XXII A,A; RFR)8,3,C:20,2,C;
3064					$460	VDS	ebay-11/99	ACR)154,304; TPD)10.144; MDK)133
3064					$635	Aqua Marine	ebay-12/00	
3064					$405	VDS	ebay-12/00	
3064					$95	VDS/Blue Handle	ebay-03/02	Pitcher only
3064					$1800	Gold Aurene	ebay-07/02	
3064					$435	Gold Aurene	ebay-06/03	Pitcher only
3064					$490	Gold Aurene	EAC-06/03	Pitcher only
3064					$610	Rosa/Pomona Green	ebay-09/03	Pomona Green handle
3064					$350	Blue Aurene	ebay-11/03	Pitcher only
3064					$635	VDS (E)	ebay-12/03	Engraved "Grape"
3064					$1025	Gold Aurene	ebay-01/04	Pitcher only
3064					$1525	Light Blue Jade	ebay-01/04	
3064					$430	Gold Aurene	ebay-05/04	Pitcher only
3064					$100	Pomona Green/Topaz	ebay-09/04	Pitcher only, Topaz handle
3064					$305	Blue Aurene	ebay-10/04	Pitcher only
3064					$1300	Blue Aurene	ebay-12/04	
3064					$350	Blue Aurene	ebay-02/05	Pitcher only
3064					$345	Flemish	EAC-04/05	
3065	Bowl	142	4	4	$285	VDS	EAC-06/03	
3066	Vase	272	2	3				
3067	Almond & Plate				$240	Gold Aurene	ebay-10/01	Probably used the 5095 saucer.
3067	Master Salt 6" dia.	272	2	14	$300	Gold Aurene	EAC-04/90	RFR)20,1,B; JAS)163,B; MDK)96
3067					$275	Gold Calcite	EAC-07/98	
3067					$650	Blue Aurene	ebay-02/01	
3067					$475	Gold Calcite	EAC-04/01	
3067					$150	VDS	ebay-08/01	
3067					$240	Gold Aurene	ebay-07/02	
3067					$340	Gold Aurene	ebay-01/03	
3067					$315	Gold Aurene	Jack-11/03	
3067					$175	Gold Calcite	ebay-03/04	
3067					$185	Gold Calcite	ebay-08/04	
3067					$355	Gold Calcite	ebay-10/04	
3067					$180	Gold Calcite	ebay-11/04	
3067					$105	Celeste Blue	ebay-12/04	
3067					$270	Gold Calcite	Cinc-06/05	
3067	Salt	217	2	14	$330	Gold Calcite	EAC-07/95	RFR)9,3,D; TPD)2.36:10.23:10.124
3067					$185	Gold Aurene	JDJ-06/96	
3067					$300	Green Jade	EAC-07/96	
3067					$385	Gold Aurene	EAC-07/96	
3067					$275	Celeste Blue	EAC-07/96	
3067					$495	Rosaline/Alabaster	EAC-04/97	
3067					$185	Gold Aurene	EAC-07/97	
3067					$130	VDS	EAC-04/98	
3067					$190	Gold Aurene	EAC-04/98	
3067					$300	Gold Aurene	EAC-04/98	
3067					$150	Gold Calcite	EAC-04/98	
3067					$315	Gold Aurene	JDJ-06/98	
3067					$550	Blue Aurene	EAC-07/98	
3067					$120	VDS	EAC-04/99	
3067					$560	Flemish Blue	ebay-11/99	
3067					$110	VDS	ebay-11/99	
3067					$460	French Blue	ebay-12/99	
3067					$115	VDS	ebay-12/99	
3067					$225	Gold Calcite	ebay-12/99	
3067					$145	Topaz	ebay-01/00	
3067					$230	Gold Calcite	ebay-01/00	

SHAPE NO.	ITEM		PAGE	COL	ROW	PRICE REALIZED	GLASS TYPE	AUCTION HOUSE	COMMENTS & PHOTO REFERENCES
3067						$230	Gold Calcite	ebay-03/00	
3067						$465	Blue Aurene	EAC-05/00	
3067						$150	VDS	ebay-10/00	
3067						$1090	Green/Threaded	ebay-11/00	
3067						$75	VDS	ebay-12/00	
3067						$75	VDS	ebay-05/01	
3067						$60	Gold Calcite	JDJ-05/01	
3067						$185	Green Jade	ebay-06/01	
3067						$105	Green Jade/Alabaster	ebay-06/01	
3067						$90	VDS	ebay-06/01	
3067						$75	VDS	ebay-06/01	
3067						$200	Green Jade	ebay-07/01	
3067						$200	Green Jade	ebay-07/01	
3067						$545	Pomona Green	ebay-09/01	
3067						$335	Blue Aurene	EAC-09/01	
3067						$230	Green Jade	ebay-10/01	
3067						$170	Gold Calcite	ebay-11/01	
3067						$155	Pomona Green	ebay-11/01	
3067						$575	Amethyst	ebay-12/01	
3067						$465	French Blue	ebay-01/02	
3067						$400	Amethyst	ebay-02/02	
3067						$1120	Light Blue Jade	EAC-04/02	Flint White foot
3067						$255	Gold Calcite	ebay-04/02	
3067						$200	Gold Aurene	ebay-05/02	
3067						$170	Rosaline/Alabaster	ebay-07/02	
3067						$175	VDS engraved	ebay-09/02	
3067						$100	VDS	ebay-10/02	
3067						$110	Celeste Blue	ebay-11/02	
3067						$375	Gold Aurene	Jack–11/02	
3067						$350	Gold Calcite	Ogal-12/02	
3067						$325	Citron Yellow	ebay-12/02	
3067						$130	Nile Green	ebay-01/03	
3067						$260	VDS	ebay-01/03	Gorham silver foot
3067						$1260	Gold Ruby/Colorless foot	ebay-02/03	Price not an error.
3067						$545	Nile Green	ebay-02/03	
3067						$435	Marina Blue	ebay-03/03	
3067						$115	VDS	ebay-03/03	
3067						$285	Spanish Green	ebay-03/03	
3067						$130	VDS	ebay-03/03	
3067						$200	Gold Aurene	ebay-03/03	
3067						$350	Green Jade	ebay-03/03	
3067						$160	VDS	ebay-05/03	
3067						$405	Gold Calcite	ebay-06/03	
3067						$860	Blue Aurene	ebay-06/03	
3067						$270	VDS (D)	ebay-07/03	
3067						$180	Green Jade/Alabaster	ebay-07/03	
3067						$230	Gold Aurene	ebay-09/03	
3067						$275	Gold Calcite	Ogal-12/03	
3067						$685	Colorless/Green threaded	ebay-01/04	
3067						$125	VDS	ebay-01/04	
3067						$150	VDS	ebay-02/04	
3067						$180	Gold Calcite	ebay-02/04	
3067						$125	VDS	ebay-03/04	
3067						$125	VDS	ebay-04/04	
3067						$185	Gold Calcite	ebay-04/04	
3067						$230	Gold Aurene	EAC-04/04	
3067						$105	VDS	ebay-05/04	
3067						$330	Colorless/Green threaded	JDJ-05/04	
3067						$125	VDS	ebay-05/04	
3067						$110	VDS	ebay-06/04	
3067						$270	Gold Aurene	ebay-06/04	
3067						$285	Gold Aurene	ebay-06/04	
3067						$635	Blue Aurene	ebay-06/04	
3067						$600	Blue Aurene	ebay-07/04	
3067						$180	Gold Calcite	ebay-07/04	
3067						$130	VDS	ebay-08/04	
3067						$125	VDS	ebay-09/04	
3067						$205	Antique Green	ebay-10/04	
3067						$440	Gold Calcite	EAC-10/04	
3067						$120	VDS	Cinc-11/04	
3067						$130	VDS	ebay-11/04	
3067						$100	VDS	ebay-12/04	
3067						$800	Blue Aurene	ebay-01/05	
3067						$240	VDS (E)	ebay-01/05	Gorham silver foot

SHAPE NO.	ITEM	PAGE	COL	ROW	PRICE REALIZED	GLASS TYPE	AUCTION HOUSE	COMMENTS & PHOTO REFERENCES
3067					$240	VDS (E)	ebay-01/05	Gorham silver foot
3067					$135	Celeste Blue	ebay-02/05	
3067					$125	Celeste Blue	ebay-02/05	
3067					$210	Gold Calcite	ebay-03/05	
3067					$200	Celeste Blue	ebay-03/05	
3067					$200	Gold Calcite	EAC-04/05	
3067					$125	VDS	ebay-05/05	
3067					$90	VDS	ebay-05/05	
3067					$150	VDS	ebay-06/05	
3067					$330	Rosaline/Alabaster	JDJ-06/05	Alabaster foot
3067					$230	Gold Aurene	EAC-07/05	
3067					$230	Gold Calcite	EAC-07/05	
3067					$345	Green Jade/Alabaster foot	EAC-07/05	
3067					$100	VDS	EAC-07/05	
3068	Jar	209	5	8				
3069	Goblet	191	1	1				
3070	Goblet	191	1	2				ACR)171,348
3071	Goblet	191	1	3				
3072	Goblet	191	1	4				
3073	Goblet	191	1	5				JSS)8-1,8-2
3074	Plate	158	2	2				TPD)9.23
3075	Plate	158	2	3				
3076	Plate	158	2	4				
3077	Jar	209	5	9				
3078	Jar	210	3	2	$1400	Blue Aurene	EAC-09/02	
3079	Vase	272	2	4	$1345	Blue Aurene	ebay-04/00	RFR)7,1,B; ACR)132,238
3079					$355	VDS	ebay-04/01	
3079					$305	Aqua Marine	ebay-01/03	
3079					$525	Aqua Marine	ebay-08/03	
3079					$575	VDS	EAC-04/04	
3079					$600	Ivrene	ebay-02/05	
3080	Bowl	142	4	5	$440	Gold Calcite	EAC-07/91	TPD)10.119
3080					$1155	Gold Aurene	EAC-07/97	
3080					$825	Gold Calcite	EAC-07/98	
3080					$210	Amethyst	ebay-12/00	
3080					$445	Topaz	ebay-02/02	
3080					$425	Amethyst	ebay-02/03	
3080					$400	VDS	EAC-06/03	
3080					$255	Pomona Green	ebay-02/04	
3080					$270	VDS	ebay-04/04	
3081	Cologne	240	6	4				
3082	Cologne	240	6	5				
3083	Vase	272	2	5				
3084	Sugar Shaker	217	6	7				
3085	Sugar Shaker	217	6	8				
3086	Goblet	191	1	6	$65	Bristol Yellow	ebay-12/99	
3086					$95	Pomona Green (E)	ebay-09/04	
3087	Nut Dish	211	3	11	$220	VDS	Cott-08/01	
3088	Candlestick	160	5	5				
3089	Vase	272	2	6				
3090	Mayonnaise Bowl	210	4	1				
3091	Vase	272	2	7				
3092	Tray	158	4	16				
3093	Cologne	240	6	6	$375	Amethyst/Colorless stopper	ebay-08/04	RFR)21,2,C; RLG)142,271;TPD)8.34
3094	Salt	217	2	15				
3095	Jar	209	5	10				
3096	Misc.	211	5	4				
3097	Puff Box	244	4	7				
3098	Jar	209	5	11				
3099	Compote	172	5	3				
3100	Candlestick	161	1	1	$185	Topaz	ebay-11/99	TPD)10.109
3100					$295	Amethyst	ebay-10/00	
3100					$200	Celeste Blue	ebay-05/02	
3100					$275	Amethyst	ebay-06/02	
3100					$175	Rosaline/Alabaster stem	ebay-12/03	
3100					$170	Topaz	EAC-04/04	
3101	Compote	172	5	4				
3102	Covered Vase	305	5	3				
3103	Bowl	142	4	6	$1955	Green Jade/Alabaster ACB	EAC-06/03	Etched "Chinese"
3104	Decanter	185	5	3				
3105	Cologne	240	6	7				
3106	Puff Box	244	4	8				
3107	Goblet	197	3	4	$140	Celeste Blue/Colorless	ebay-12/02	Colorless stem
3107					$100	Celeste Blue/Colorless	ebay-01/03	

SHAPE NO.	ITEM	PAGE	COL	ROW	PRICE REALIZED	GLASS TYPE	AUCTION HOUSE	COMMENTS & PHOTO REFERENCES
3107					$100	Celeste Blue/Colorless	ebay-03/03	
3107					$100	Celeste Blue/Colorless	ebay-05/03	
3107					$75	Rosaline/Alabaster	ebay-07/04	Alabaster stem and foot
3108	Vase	272	3	1				
3109	Covered Vase	305	5	4	$2051	Amber	ebay-01/00	TPD)8.11
3110	Vase	272	3	2				
3111	Vase	272	3	3				
3112	Plate	158	2	5				
3113	Covered Vase	305	5	5	$730	Topaz	ebay-08/01	
3114	Covered Vase	306	1	1	$825	Topaz	EAC-10/95	PG1)XV A,C; RFR)16,3,C; TPD)10.109
3115	Oyster Cocktail	210	5	1				
3116	Goblet	197	3	5	$315	Gold Calcite	EAC-06/03	Without prunts
3116					$305	Gold Calcite	ebay-10/03	Without prunts
3117	Goblet	197	3	6				
3118	Basket	140	2	3				
3119	Basket	140	2	4	$2300	Gold Aurene	JDJ-06/97	
3120	Goblet	191	1	7				PG1)88,132,B
3121	Oyster Cocktail	210	5	2				
3122	Mayonnaise Bowl	210	4	2				
3123	Mayonnaise Bowl	210	4	3				
3124	Candlestick	161	1	2				
3125	Decanter	185	5	4				
3126	Decanter	185	5	5				
3127	Ash Tray	137	1	13				
3128	Ash Tray	137	1	14				
3129	Vase	272	3	4				
3130	Covered Vase	306	1	2				
3131	Decanter	186	1	1				
3132	Vase	272	3	5				
3133	Vase	272	3	6				
3134	Covered Vase	306	1	3				
3135	Vase	272	3	7				
3136	Compote	172	5	5				
3137	Covered Vase	306	1	4				
3138	Goblet	191	1	8	$90	VDS	ebay-10/03	Signed "Hawkes"
3139	Centerpiece	148	3	3				
3140	Cordial				$150	Celeste Blue/Topaz stem	ebay-12/99	Topaz mica flecked stem
3140	Fingerbowl				$225	Selenium Red	ebay-03/00	
3140					$230	Selenium Red (E)	EAC-11/03	Engraved "Grape"
3140					$40	Selenium Red (E)	ebay-02/04	Engraved "Grape," no underplate
3140					$25	Bristol Yellow	ebay-03/04	No underplate
3140					$25	Selenium Red (E)	ebay-03/04	Engraved "Grape," no underplate
3140					$40	Selenium Red (E)	ebay-08/04	Engraved "Grape," no underplate
3140	Goblet	191	2	1	$90	Selenium Red	Sknr-05/95	PG1)XXIX,B,A; RFR)16,2,E;
3140					$75	Selenium Red	ebay-01/00	ACR)COLOR 4,T,E:150,290; RLG)162,297;
3140					$180	Selenium Red	ebay-02/00	MDK)1:6:11:59
3140					$130	Selenium Red	ebay-02/00	
3140					$95	Selenium Red	ebay-04/01	
3140					$25	Selenium Red	ebay-04/01	
3140					$70	Pomona Green	ebay-09/01	
3140					$95	Bristol Yellow	ebay-11/02	
3140					$200	Selenium Red (E)	ebay-11/03	Engraved "Grape"
3140					$75	Celeste Blue	ebay-02/04	
3140					$150	Selenium Red	ebay-12/03	
3140					$85	Bristol Yellow/Colorless	ebay-03/04	Colorless stem
3140					$115	Bristol Yellow/Colorless	ebay-03/04	Colorless stem
3140					$115	Bristol Yellow/Colorless	ebay-03/04	Colorless stem
3140					$40	Bristol Yellow/Colorless	ebay-05/04	Colorless stem
3140					$90	Citron Yellow	ebay-05/05	Cut decoration
3140	Tumbler				$225	Selenium Red (E)	ebay-06/03	Engraved "Grape"
3140	Wine				$150	Selenium Red	ebay-03/02	
3141	Vase	272	4	1				
3142	Candlestick	161	1	3				
3143	Vase	272	4	2				RFR)8,2,C:20,2,A
3144	Compote	172	5	6				
3145	Centerpiece	148	3	4				
3146	Centerpiece	148	3	5				
3147	Decanter	186	1	2				
3147	Wine	186	1	2				
3148	Nut Dish	211	3	12	$45	Nile Green	ebay-09/02	TPD)10.114
3149	Vase	272	4	3				
3150	Centerpiece	148	3	6				
3151	Decanter	186	1	3				
3152	Goblet	191	2	2				

SHAPE NO.	ITEM	PAGE	COL	ROW	PRICE REALIZED	GLASS TYPE	AUCTION HOUSE	COMMENTS & PHOTO REFERENCES
3153	Sherbet	216	5	2				
3154	Covered Vase	306	1	5	$620	Gold Aurene	ebay-05/04	TPD)5.40
3154					$1240	Gold Aurene	ebay-06/04	
3155	Covered Vase	306	1	6				
3156	Candlestick	161	1	4				
3157	Plate	158	2	6	$50	Gold Ruby, Cut	ebay-06/00	Engraved "Thistle"
3158	Shade	225	5	4				
3159	Shade	225	5	5				
3160	Shade	225	5	6				
3161	Shade	225	5	7				
3162	Vase	272	4	4				
3163	Bowl	142	4	7	$305	VDS/Blue Rim	Tway-09/04	
3164	Bowl	142	4	8				
3165	Pitcher	213	5	2				
3165	Lemonade	213	5	2	$330	VDS/Celeste Blue	EAC-10/00	
3165					$35	Pomona Green	ebay-03/01	
3165					$245	VDS/Celeste Blue	ebay-04/02	Blue foot and handle
3166	Bowl	142	4	9				
3167	Pitcher	213	5	3				
3168	Goblet	197	3	7				
3169	Goblet	197	3	8				
3170	Shade	225	5	8				
3171	Bowl	142	4	10	$300	Gold Calcite	ebay-02/04	
3171					$280	Gold Calcite	ebay-06/05	
3171					$920	Blue Calcite	EAC-07/05	
3172	Misc.	211	4	6				
3173	Bowl	142	4	11	$220	Selenium Red	ebay-12/03	
3174	Cologne	240	6	8	$1540	Blue Aurene	EAC-10/90	
3174					$1265	Blue Aurene	Sknr-01/96	
3174					$910	Rosaline	ebay-01/99	
3174					$925	Blue Aurene	ebay-02/03	
3174					$1610	Blue Aurene	Jack-06/03	
3174					$745	Green Jade/Alabaster	EAC-07/05	Alabaster foot and stopper
3175	Cologne	240	6	9	$535	Gold Aurene	ebay-08/01	TPD)10.117
3175					$920	Gold Aurene	EAC-11/03	
3175					$550	Blue Aurene	ebay-11/04	No Stopper
3176	Bowl	142	4	12				
3177	Bowl	142	4	13				
3178	Bowl							PG1)355,F
3178	Candlestick	161	1	5	$2475	Blue Cintra	EAC-07/98	PG1)355,F; RFR)23,3,A; RLG)148,279;
3178					$795	VDS/Rose duBarry	ebay-11/00	ACR)157,311; TPD)6.18
3178					$350	VDS/Rose duBarry	ebay-01/01	
3178					$375	VDS/Rose duBarry	ebay-01/03	
3178					$155	Colorless/Green disk	Ogal-05/04	Green disk is etched
3178					$170	Colorless/Green disk	EAC-07/04	Green disk is etched
3178					$500	Colorless/Gold Ruby disk	ebay-03/05	Gold Ruby disk is etched
3178					$220	Colorless/Gold Ruby disk	ebay-04/05	Gold Ruby disk is etched
3178	Compote							PG1)355,F; TPD)9.20
3179	Compote	172	5	7	$1090	Orange Cintra	Sknr-10/95	RFR)23,1,B; ACR)158,312; TPD)9.34
3179					$380	Blue Cintra/Black rim	Sknr-12/02	
3179					$195	Colorless/Green rim	EAC-07/04	Green rim is etched
3180	Candlestick	161	1	6				
3181	Bowl	143	1	1				
3181	Candlestick	161	2	1				
3182	Centerpiece	148	4	1				
3183	Centerpiece	148	4	2				
3184	Bowl							See New Drawings section
3185	Vase	272	4	5				
3186	Vase	272	5	1				
3187	Plate	159	1	2				
3188	Bowl	143	1	2				
3189	Centerpiece	148	4	3				
3190	Bowl	143	1	3				
3191	Bowl	143	1	4				
3192	Bowl	143	1	5				
3193	Candlestick	161	2	2				
3194	Compote	172	5	8				
3195	Bowl	143	1	6				
3196	Bowl	143	1	7	$400	Selenium Red.(FC)	Sknr-01/98	
3197	Vase	272	5	2				TPD)6.6
3198	Bowl	143	1	8				
3199	Bowl	143	1	9				
3200	Bowl	143	1	10				
3201	Vase	272	5	3				

SHAPE NO.	ITEM	PAGE	COL	ROW	PRICE REALIZED	GLASS TYPE	AUCTION HOUSE	COMMENTS & PHOTO REFERENCES
3202	Vase	272	5	4				
3204	Bowl	143	2	1	$220	Topaz/Celeste Blue	ebay-11/99	
3205	Vase	272	5	5				
3206	Bowl	143	2	2				
3207	Vase	272	5	6				
3208	Bowl	143	2	3				
3209	Centerpiece	148	4	4				
3210	Bowl	143	2	4				
3211	Centerpiece	148	4	5				
3212	Vase	273	1	1				
3213	Cologne	241	1	1				
3214	Vase	273	1	2				Not numbered in Gardner.
3215	Vase	273	1	3				
3216	Vase	273	1	4				
3217	Vase	273	1	5				TPD)10.100
3218	Vase	273	2	1				PG2)75,A; JAS)153,TR,A
3219	Vase	273	2	2				PG1)XVI A,B
3220	Vase	273	2	3				
3221	Centerpiece	148	4	6				PG2)75,C; JAS)153,TR,C
3221	Vase	273	2	4				This shape is shown as #3222 in Gardner.
3221								PG1)XVI A,A
3222	Vase	273	2	4				This number is an error, see #3221Vase.
3222	Cologne	241	1	2				This shape is shown as #322 in Gardner.
3223	Vase	273	2	5				PG2)75,B; RFR)23,3,B; JAS)153,TR,B
3223								TPD)10.37
3224	Vase	273	2	6				TPD)8.36
3225	Bowl	143	2	5				
3226	Vase	273	3	1				
3227	Vase	273	3	2				
3228	Vase	273	3	3				
3229	Vase	273	3	4				
3230	Centerpiece	148	4	7				
3231	Candlestick	161	2	3				PG1)77,121
3232	Compote	173	1	1				
3233	Vase	273	3	5				
3234	Compote	173	1	2				ACR)COLOR 4,B,B
3235	Bowl	143	2	6				
3236	Candlestick	161	2	4	$435	Mirror Black	ebay-07/04	PG1)XVI B,A&C; TPD)6.18
3237	Compote	173	1	3				
3238	Compote	173	1	4				
3239	Compote	173	1	5				
3240	Centerpiece	148	4	8	$1045	Gold Calcite	EAC-10/95	TPD)8.57
3240					$1650	Rosaline/Alabaster	EAC-10/95	
3240					$1875	Rosaline/Alabaster	ebay-04/04	
3241	Shade	225	5	9				
3242	Shade	225	5	10				
3243	Shade	225	5	11	$690	Gold Aurene	ebay-05/02	
3243					$150	Calcite	ebay-11/03	
3243					$160	Calcite	ebay-12/03	
3244	Shade	225	5	12				
3245	Shade	226	1	1				
3246	Shade	226	1	2				
3247	Shade	226	1	3				
3248	Shade	226	1	4				
3249	Shade	226	1	5				
3250	Shade	226	1	6				
3251	Shade	226	1	7				
3252	Shade	226	1	8				
3253	Shade	226	1	9				
3254	Shade	226	1	10				
3255	Shade	226	1	11				
3256	Shade	226	1	12				
3257	Centerpiece	148	4	9				
3258	Candlestick	161	2	5				
3259	High Ball	199	1	7				
3260	Limousine Vase	207	2	6				
3261	Centerpiece	149	1	1				
3262	Bowl	143	2	7	$410	Gold Calcite	EAC-04/96	TPD)10.43:10.123
3262					$385	Gold Calcite	EAC-07/97	
3262					$250	Blue Calcite	J&W-09/03	
3262					$180	Gold Calcite	ebay-01/04	
3262					$600	Gold Calcite	Cinc-11/04	
3263	Vase	273	3	6	$330	Gold Calcite	ebay-08/03	
3263					$550	Gold Calcite	EAC-10/04	

SHAPE NO.	ITEM	PAGE	COL	ROW	PRICE REALIZED	GLASS TYPE	AUCTION HOUSE	COMMENTS & PHOTO REFERENCES
3263					$740	Blue Calcite	ebay-05/05	
3264	Vase	273	3	7	$890	Blue Calcite	ebay-11/02	TPD)10.122
3265	Centerpiece	149	1	2	$900	Blue Calcite	ebay-03/00	
3265					$335	Gold Calcite	EAC-11/01	
3265					$575	Gold Calcite	EAC-06/03	
3266	Centerpiece	149	1	3				
3267	Cruet	179	3	2				
3268	Cruet	179	3	3	$860	VDS	EAC-07/05	
3269	Flower Block	237	1	1				
3270	Puff Box	244	4	9				
3271	Cologne	241	1	3	$455	Opal/LBJ Stopper	ebay-11/02	TPD)10.145
3272	Vase	273	4	1				
3273	Vase	273	4	2				ARC)163,327;TPD)8.24:10.131; MDK)132
3273					$2300	Black/Amethyst Cintra ACB	EAC-06/03	Lamp, complete, etched "Adams"
3274	Vase	273	4	3				
3275	Vase	273	4	4	$790	Gold Aurene	ebay-01/04	
3276	Vase	273	5	1				
3277	Vase	273	5	2				TPD)5.26:8.59
3278	Vase	273	5	3				
3279	Vase	273	5	4	$935	Green Jade/Alabaster ACB	EAC-10/93	Etched "Bird"
3279					$1095	Green Jade/Alabaster ACB	ebay-05/05	Etched "Bird"
3280	Vase	274	1	1				PG1)XXXI,C
3281	Vase	274	1	2				
3282	Vase	274	1	3	$425	Blue Aurene	EAC-10/00	
3282					$660	Gold Aurene	ebay-07/04	
3283	Vase	274	1	4	$630	Blue Aurene	Sknr-01/96	
3284	Vase	274	1	5				
3285	Vase	274	2	1	$1925	Blue Aurene	EAC-04/93	PG1)V B,B; TPD)8.46
3285					$2365	Gold Aurene	EAC-07/97	
3285					$2800	Gold Aurene	EAC-01/03	
3285					$3160	Gold Aurene	Jack-06/02	
3285					$1750	Blue Aurene	ebay-03/04	
3285					$1920	Gold Aurene	JDJ-11/04	
3286	Nut Dish	211	3	13				
3287	Nut Dish	211	3	14				
3288	Nut Dish	211	3	15				
3289	Goblet	197	4	1				
3290	Jar	209	4	2				
3291	Bouillon Cup	189	2	5				TPD)7.76
3292	Tumbler	198	5	8				
3293	Tea Cup	216	3	6				
3294	Cologne	241	1	4	$400	Amethyst	Sknr-10/96	RFR)20,1,A&C
3294					$385	Threaded VDS	EAC-07/98	
3294					$1200	Blue Aurene	ebay-11/99	
3294					$500	Green Jade	ebay-03/00	
3294					$935	Gold Aurene	Cott-08/01	
3294					$450	Rosaline/Alabaster	EAC-09/01	
3294					$975	Blue Aurene	ebay-11/02	
3294					$355	VDS (FC)	EAC-10/04	
3294					$1150	Blue Aurene	EAC-07/05	
3295	Cologne	241	1	5				
3296	Cologne	241	1	6	$685	Rosaline/Alabaster	ebay-10/04	
3297	Cologne	241	1	7				
3297½	Bobeche							See New Drawings section
3298	Coffee Pot	189	3	3	$105	Colorless (E)	ebay-07/03	Marked "Pyrex"
3298½	Bobeche							See New Drawings section
3299	Coffee Pot	189	3	4				
3299½	Bobeche							See New Drawings section
3300	Luminor	309	3	3				
3300½	Bobeche							See New Drawings section
3301	Bowl	143	2	8				
3301½	Bobeche							See New Drawings section
3302	Bowl	143	2	9	$385	Colorless/Amethyst Cintra	EAC-04/91	TPD)4.11
3302					$330	Colorless	ebay-12/99	
3302½	Bobeche							See New Drawings section
3303	Bowl	143	2	10				
3303½	Bobeche							See New Drawings section
3304	Candlestick	161	3	1	$375	Colorless/Celeste Blue	Sknr-10/95	PG1)355,G; TPD)9.1
3304					$520	Colorless/Pomona Green	Sknr-10/96	
3304					$385	Colorless/Amethyst	EAC-07/98	
3304					$250	Colorless/Celeste Blue	ebay-02/03	
3304½	Bobeche							See New Drawings section
3305	Compote	173	1	6				PG1)355,G
3305½	Bobeche							See New Drawings section

SHAPE NO.	ITEM	PAGE	COL	ROW	PRICE REALIZED	GLASS TYPE	AUCTION HOUSE	COMMENTS & PHOTO REFERENCES
3306	Jar	209	4	3				
3307	Limousine Vase	207	2	7				
3308	Limousine Vase	207	3	1				
3309	Limousine Vase	207	3	2				
3310	Limousine Vase	207	3	3				
3311	Limousine Vase	207	3	4				
3312	Limousine Vase	207	3	5				
3313	Vase	274	2	2				TPD)2.29:10.21
3314	Goblet	191	2	3				This number is an error, see #3321 Goblet.
3314	Plate	159	1	3				
3315	Candlestick	161	3	2	$875	Green Jade/Alabaster	ebay-08/03	TPD)10.114
3315					$975	Amethyst	ebay-06/04	
3316	Candlestick	161	3	3	$2285	Red and Black Cintra	EAC-04/04	
3317	Candlestick	161	3	4				
3318	Plate	159	1	4				
3319	Candlestick	161	3	5				
3320	Candlestick	161	4	1				TPD)10.26
3321	Appol. Tumbler	199	1	10				
3321	Brandy & Soda	199	1	8				
3321	Champagne				$300	Colorless/Green (E)	ebay-12/01	
3321	Finger Bowl	189	1	9				
3321	Goblet	191	2	3	$375	Colorless/Green (E)	ebay-12/01	This shape is shown as a #3314 Goblet in Gardner. MDK)48
3321	High Ball	199	1	9				
3321	Sherbet	216	5	3				
3322	Bowl	143	3	1				
3323	Candlestick	161	4	2				
3323	Compote	173	1	7				
3325	Appol. Tumbler	199	2	1	$35	Colorless/Green line	ebay-12/02	
3325					$50	Colorless/Rose line	ebay-01/05	
3325					$50	Colorless/Rose line	ebay-01/05	
3325					$50	Colorless/Rose line	ebay-04/05	
3325	Cocktail	197	4	2				
3325	High Ball	199	2	2				TPD)6.1
3325	Finger Bowl	189	1	10				
3325	Goblet	191	2	4	$145	Celeste Blue	ebay-02/00	
3325	Tumbler	199	2	3				
3325	Sherbet	216	5	4	$70	Colorless/Red decoration	ebay-03/02	Sherbet only
3325					$75	Colorless/Red decoration	ebay-07/02	Sherbet only
3325	Wine	197	4	3				
3326	Bowl	143	3	2				
3327	Candlestick	161	4	3				
3327	Compote	173	2	1				
3327	Centerpiece	149	1	4				
3327½	Bowl	143	3	3				
3328	Candlestick	161	4	4	$490	Colorless Silverina	Sknr-10/96	
3329	Pitcher	213	5	4				PG1)355,E; ACR)175,356 B
3329	Lemonade	213	5	4	$230	Colorless/Pomona Green	Sknr-05/98	
3329					$220	Colorless/Celeste Blue	ebay-04/00	
3329					$250	Amber/Celeste Blue	ebay-01/01	
3329					$150	Colorless/Lavender	ebay-02/02	
3329					$160	Colorless/Lavender	ebay-03/02	
3329					$160	Colorless/Lavender	ebay-05/02	
3329					$310	Colorless/Lavender	ebay-06/03	
3329					$190	Colorless/Lavender	ebay-07/05	
3330	Vase	274	2	3	$45	Colorless	ebay-02/00	RFR)17,1,C
3330					$650	Colorless/Rosa	Tway-10/00	
3330					$195	Colorless/Cinnamon	EAC-09/02	
3331	Vase	274	2	4				ACR)175,357
3332	Compote	173	2	2				MDK)40
3333	Sugar & Creamer	235	5	3,4				
3334	Sugar & Creamer	235	5	5,6				RFR)17,1,A&D;ACR)175,358;TPD)10.111
3335	Sugar & Creamer	235	5	7,8				
3337	Vase	274	2	5				
3338	Vase	274	2	6				
3339	Limousine Vase	207	4	1				
3340	Bowl	143	3	4				
3340	Shade	226	2	1				
3341	Bowl	143	3	5				PG1)355,C
3342	Basket	140	2	5				
3343	Jar	209	4	4	$1240	Topaz	ebay-01/00	PG1)355,C
3344	Jar	209	4	5				
3345	Shade	226	2	2				
3346	Limousine Vase	207	4	2				

SHAPE NO.	ITEM	PAGE	COL	ROW	PRICE REALIZED	GLASS TYPE	AUCTION HOUSE	COMMENTS & PHOTO REFERENCES
3347	Bowl	143	3	6				
3348	Compote	173	2	3	$740	Rosaline/Alabaster	EAC-10/90	PG1)46,83:XXVIII A,A&G
3348					$575	Amethyst	EAC-07/91	
3348					$605	Topaz	EAC-04/95	
3348					$290	Topaz/French Blue	Sknr-10/95	
3348					$575	Topaz	EAC-04/97	
3348					$410	Cyprian	ebay-02/00	
3348					$745	Celeste Blue	Sknr-02/01	Pear finial
3348					$455	Amethyst	ebay-06/01	
3348					$520	Celeste Blue	ebay-06/01	
3348					$405	Amber/Flemish Blue	ebay-01/02	
3348					$510	Amethyst	ebay-06/02	
3348					$615	Rosaline/Alabaster	EAC-01/03	
3348					$95	Topaz	ebay-02/03	
3348					$525	Amber/Fruit Finial	ebay-06/03	
3348					$650	VDS/Fruit Finial	ebay-07/04	
3348					$90	Green Jade/Alabaster	ebay-08/04	Alabaster stem and foot
3348					$360	VDS/Fruit Finial	ebay-12/04	
3348					$475	Celeste Blue/Fruit finial	ebay-01/05	
3349	Centerpiece	149	1	5				
3350	Centerpiece	149	1	6				
3351	Vase	274	3	1				PG1)355,C
3352	Vase	274	3	2				
3353	Vase	274	3	3				
3354	Candlestick	161	4	5	$800	Selenium Red/Colorless	ebay-02/02	
3354					$300	Antique Green/Colorless	ebay-12/03	
3355	Compote	173	2	4				
3356	Salt Shaker							See New Drawings section
3357	Bowl	143	3	7				
3358	Vase	274	3	4	$565	Colorless/Blue	ebay-06/03	
3359	Vase	274	3	5	$250	Colorless/Rosa	ebay-06/00	RFR)17,1,B; TPD)4.54
3360	Centerpiece	149	1	7				
3361	Bowl	143	3	8				Same as 2586
3362	Vase	274	3	6				
3363	Goblet	191	2	5				
3364	Vase	274	3	7				
3365	Centerpiece	149	1	8				
3366	Candlestick	161	5	1	$290	Green Jade/Alabaster(E)	JDJ-05/01	
3366					$890	Rosaline/Alabaster(E)	JDJ-05/01	
3366	Compote	173	2	5				
3367	Shade	229	1	6				
3368	Candlestick	161	5	2				
3369	Candlestick	161	5	3	$1265	Colorless/Mirror Black	Cott-08/01	
3369	Compote	173	2	6	$285	Colorless/Gold Ruby	ebay-10/02	Gold Ruby machine threaded
3369					$55	Colorless/Green	ebay-02/05	Green machine threaded
3369					$305	Colorless/Gold Ruby	ebay-07/05	Gold Ruby machine threaded
3369	Centerpiece	149	2	1	$530	Colorless/Gold Ruby	Ogal-01/04	Gold Ruby threaded
3369					$560	Colorless/Mirror Black	EAC-04/04	Mirror Black threaded
3370	Candlestick	161	5	4				PG1)354,B;TPD)7.20
3370					$860	Mirror Black ACB	ebay-07/04	Etched "Camillo"
3370	Compote	173	2	7				PG1)354,B;TPD)7.20
3370	Centerpiece	149	2	2				PG1)354,B;TPD)7.20
3371	Candlestick	161	5	5				
3372	Centerpiece	149	2	3				
3372	Candlestick	161	5	6				
3372	Compote	173	3	1	$500	Amber/Flemish Blue trim	ebay-06/05	TPD)4.52:10.85
3373	Candlestick	162	1	1	$250	Colorless/Black decoration	EAC-04/93	
3374	Candlestick	162	1	2	$345	Pomona Green	Sknr-05/98	
3375	Bowl	143	3	9				PG1)355,D
3375	Candlestick	162	1	3				PG1)355,D
3375	Compote	173	3	2				
3376	Bowl	143	3	10				PG1)355,B
3376					$565	Mirror Black/Green Jade	ebay-08/04	Green Jade decoration
3376	Candlestick	162	1	4	$750	Mirror Black	ebay-10/00	PG1)355,B
3376	Compote	173	3	3				PG1)355,B
3377	Shade	229	1	7				
3378	Candlestick	162	1	5	$135	Topaz/Pomona Green	EAC-07/98	RFR)16,3,A; TPD)10.89
3378					$260	Blue-gray/Amber	Sknr-06/00	
3378					$405	Blue-gray/Amber	ebay-01/02	
3378					$405	Blue-gray/Amber	ebay-02/02	
3378					$240	Blue-gray/Amber	ebay-09/04	
3378	Bowl	143	4	1				
3378	Compote	173	3	4	$560	Green/Amber (FC)	ebay-08/02	
3378					$275	Blue-gray/Amber stem	ebay-10/04	

160

SHAPE NO.	ITEM	PAGE	COL	ROW	PRICE REALIZED	GLASS TYPE	AUCTION HOUSE	COMMENTS & PHOTO REFERENCES
3379	Candlestick	162	1	6	$330	Blue-gray/Amber	ebay-07/01	
3379	Bowl	143	4	2				
3379	Compote	173	3	5				
3380	Goblet	191	2	6				
3381	Goblet	191	2	7				
3381	Mayonnaise Bowl	210	4	4				
3381	Sherbet	216	5	5				
3382	Candlestick	162	2	1				
3383	Candlestick	162	2	2				TPD)7.18
3383	Goblet	191	2	8				
3384	Goblet	191	2	9				TPD)6.1
3385	Goblet	191	3	1				
3386	Goblet	191	3	2				
3387	Goblet	191	3	3				PD)7.36:7.48:7.77
3387	½ Pt. Tumbler							See New Drawings section
3388	Centerpiece	149	2	4				
3390	Goblet	191	3	4				
3391	Shade	226	2	3	$3220	Decorated Brown Aurene	JDJ-05/04	
3392	Covered Vase	306	2	1				
3393	Candlestick	162	2	3				
3394	Vase	274	4	1				
3395	Covered Vase	306	2	3				
3396	Covered Vase	306	2	4				
3397	Candlestick	162	2	4				TPD)7.29:10.94
3398	Bowl	143	4	3				
3399	Bowl	143	4	4				PG1)96,149,B; TPD)10.94
3400	Vase	274	4	2	$4950	Amethyst/Colorless (E)	EAC-04/92	Engraved "Galleon" PG1)84,124 TPD)7.36
3401	Goblet	191	3	5				
3402	Plate	158	2	7				
3403	Cologne	241	1	8	$715	Mirror Black	EAC-10/97	PG2)90,C; JAS)170,B,C
3404	Cologne	241	1	9				
3405	Cologne	241	2	1	$200	Colorless/Gold Ruby	ebay-11/04	Gold Ruby rim and flower stopper
3406	Cologne	241	2	2				
3407	Puff Box	244	4	10				
3408	Puff Box	244	4	11				
3409	Shade	226	2	6				
3410	Oyster Cocktail	210	5	3				
3411	Shade	226	2	4				
3412	Shade	226	2	5				
3413	Vase	274	4	3				
3414	Candlestick	162	2	5				
3415	Candlestick	162	3	1				
3416	Candlestick	162	3	2				
3417	Candlestick	162	3	3				
3418	Candlestick	162	4	1				
3419	Cologne	243	4	1				
3420	Cologne	243	4	2				
3421	Peroxide Bottle	243	4	3				
3422	Cologne	241	2	3	$1760	Blue Aurene	EAC-07/91	TPD)10.146
3422					$560	Gold Aurene	ebay-02/04	
3423	Cologne	241	2	4	$1650	Blue Aurene	EAC-04/95	TPD)8.7
3423					$1650	Blue Aurene	EAC-07/95	
3423					$935	Blue Aurene	EAC-10/95	
3423					$610	Gold Aurene	ebay-10/02	
3423					$305	Gold Aurene	ebay-02/05	Stopper missing
3423					$460	Gold Aurene	EAC-04/05	Stopper missing
3424	Cologne							See New Drawings section
3425	Cologne	241	2	5	$1155	Black/Pink flower stopper	EAC-07/91	ACR)136,248; TPD)10.146
3425					$1840	Blue Aurene	Sknr-10/97	
3425					$1610	Blue Aurene	Sknr-10/97	
3425					$1100	Gold Aurene	EAC-10/00	
3425					$2415	Blue Aurene	Sknr-02/01	
3425					$515	Gold Aurene	ebay-12/01	
3425					$610	Gold Aurene	ebay-10/02	
3425					$2275	Gold Aurene	ebay-06/03	Black stopper with flower finial PG1)V A,B&C
3426	Cologne	241	2	6				No stopper
3426					$190	Gold Aurene	ebay-02/05	TPD)5.41
3427	Cologne	241	2	7				
3428	Cologne	241	2	8	$210	Colorless	ebay-07/01	
3429	Cologne	241	3	1	$190	VDS/Green Jade	EAC-07/98	
3430	Cologne	241	3	2				
3431	Ash Tray	137	2	1				
3432	Ash Tray	137	2	2				
3433	Ash Tray	137	2	3				

SHAPE NO.	ITEM	PAGE	COL	ROW	PRICE REALIZED	GLASS TYPE	AUCTION HOUSE	COMMENTS & PHOTO REFERENCES
3434	Ash Tray	137	2	4				
3435	Ash Tray	137	2	5				
3436	Ash Tray	137	2	6				
3437	Ash Tray	137	2	7				
3438	Ash Tray	137	2	8				
3439	Ash Tray	137	2	9				
3440	Ash Tray	137	2	10				
3441	Ash Tray	137	2	11				
3442	Ash Tray	137	2	12				
3443	Ash Tray	137	2	13				
3444	Ash Tray	137	2	14				
3445	Ash Tray	137	3	1				
3446	Ash Tray	137	3	2				
3447	Ash Tray	137	3	3				
3448	Ash Tray	137	3	4				
3449	Ash Tray	137	3	5				
3450	Candlestick	162	4	2				
3451	Ash Tray	137	3	6				
3452	Ash Tray	137	3	7				
3453	Ash Tray	137	3	8				
3454	Candlestick	162	4	3				PG1)96,149,A&C
3455	Cologne	241	3	3				
3456	Cologne	241	3	4	$840	Gold Aurene	EAC-11/01	
3457	Cologne	241	3	5				
3458	Cologne	241	3	6				
3459	Cologne	241	3	7				
3460	Cologne	241	3	8				
3461	Cologne	241	3	9				
3463	Cologne	243	4	4				
3548	Goblet	191	5	1				This number is an error, see #3598.
3550	Finger Bowl	189	1	11	$200	VDS/Coral trim	ebay-02/00	
3550	Goblet	191	3	6	$300	VDS/Coral trim	EAC-04/91	PG2)64,C; JAS)150,B,C
3550	Champagne	191	3	7				
3550	Claret	191	3	8				
3550	Wine	191	4	1				
3550	Cordial	191	4	2				
3550	Brandy & Soda	191	4	3				
3550	High Ball	191	4	4				
3550	Appol. Tumbler	191	4	5				
3551	Goblet	191	4	6	$285	Pomona Green/Rosa	JDJ-10/97	RFR)16,2,D;
3551					$320	Celeste Blue/Rosa	ebay-12/99	ACR)147,280:151,294:165,333
3551					$75	Pomona Green	ebay-03/00	JAS)168,B; JSS)12-23,L,C; TPD)2.41
3551					$150	Pomona Green	ebay-01/01	MDK)66
3551					$295	Colorless/Rosa (E)	ebay-02/01	Engraved "Van Dyke"
3551					$250	Rosaline/Alabaster(E)	ebay-05/01	Engraved "York"
3551					$285	Rosaline/Alabaster(E)	JDJ-05/01	
3551					$400	Colorless/Rosa (E)	ebay-02/02	Engraved "Van Dyke," polished engraving
3551					$350	Colorless/Green stem	ebay-05/02	Gold Ruby threaded
3551					$170	Colorless/Rosa stem (E)	ebay-07/02	Engraved "Van Dyke"
3551					$340	Colorless/Bristol stem	ebay-05/03	Celeste Blue threaded
3551					$100	Colorless/Pomona stem	ebay-04/04	Gold Ruby threaded
3551					$180	Celeste Blue/Topaz stem	JDJ-05/04	
3551					$130	Colorless/Rosa Stem (E)	ebay-10/04	Engraved "Van Dyke"
3551					$55	French Blue/threaded	ebay-12/04	
3551					$125	French Blue/threaded	ebay-12/04	
3551	Fruit Cocktail	216	5	8	$230	Green Jade/Alabaster (E)	EAC-04/05	Engraved "York"
3551	Oyster Cocktail				$300	Colorless/Rosa	ebay-10/01	
3551	Parfait				$270	Colorless/Rosa (E)	ebay-12/99	Engraved "Van Dyke"
3551					$85	Colorless/Gold Ruby	ebay-10/00	
3551					$45	Bristol Yellow	ebay-06/05	
3551					$50	Bristol Yellow	ebay-08/04	
3551	Sherbet	216	5	7				ACR)COLOR 2,B,E
3551					$240	Green Jade/Alabaster (E)	ebay-02/01	Engraved "York"
3551					$250	Colorless/Pomona Green	ebay-05/01	Engraved "Van Dyke"
3551					$200	Colorless/Pomona Green	ebay-07/01	
3551					$50	Celeste Blue	ebay-09/01	
3551					$420	Colorless/Rosa stem (E)	EAC-07/04	
3551	Wine				$225	Colorless/Rosa stem (E)	ebay-02/01	Engraved "Van Dyke"
3551					$205	Colorless/Pomona Green	ebay-03/01	Engraved "Van Dyke"
3551					$95	Celeste Blue/Rosa stem	ebay-01/02	
3551					$175	Green Jade/Alabaster (E)	Sknr-06/02	Engraved "York"
3551					$315	Colorless/Rosa stem (E)	ebay-02/03	Engraved "Van Dyke"
3551					$25	Topaz/Colorless stem	ebay-02/03	
3551					$175	Green Jade/Alabaster (E)	Sknr-05/03	Engraved "York"

SHAPE NO.	ITEM	PAGE	COL	ROW	PRICE REALIZED	GLASS TYPE	AUCTION HOUSE	COMMENTS & PHOTO REFERENCES
3551					$205	Bristol Yellow/Amethyst	ebay-08/03	Amethyst stem
3551					$225	Celeste Blue/Rosa	ebay-08/03	Rosa stem
3551					$190	Green Jade/Alabaster (E)	ebay-10/03	Engraved "York"
3551					$95	Pomona Green	ebay-11/03	
3551					$35	Colorless/Green threaded	ebay-03/04	
3551					$180	Celeste Blue/Topaz stem	JDJ-05/04	
3551					$160	Celeste Blue/Topaz stem	ebay-06/04	
3551					$195	Celeste Blue/Topaz stem	ebay-10/04	
3551					$115	Celeste Blue/Colorless	ebay-01/05	Colorless stem
3554	Vase	274	4	4				
3555	Vase	274	4	5				
3556	Vase	274	4	6				
3557	Vase	274	4	7				
3558	Vase	274	5	1				
3559	Lamp Spindle	207	4	3				
3560	Lamp Spindle	207	4	4				
3561	Lamp Spindle	207	4	5				
3562	Vase	274	5	2				
3563	Vase	274	5	3				
3564	Vase	274	5	4				
3565	Vase	274	5	5				
3566	Lamp Spindle	207	5	1				
3567	Candlestick	162	4	4	$250	Green Jade/Alabaster	ebay-05/01	PG2)85,B&C; JAS)149,BR,B&C
3568	Compote	173	3	6				
3569	Candlestick	162	5	1				This shape is shown as #3571 in Gardner.
3569								PG1)96,148,A&B
3569					$1925	Colorless/Flemish Blue (E)	ebay-11/02	Engraved "Rose"
3569	Compote	173	3	7				PG1)96,148,C
3569					$2025	Colorless/Flemish blue (E)	ebay-11/02	Engraved "Rose"
3569	Centerpiece	149	2	5				This shape is shown as #3570 in Gardner.
3570	Centerpiece	149	2	5				This number is an error, see #3569
3571	Candlestick	162	5	1				This number is an error, see #3569
3572	Lamp Vase	202	3	1				
3573	Lamp Vase	202	3	2				
3574	Shade	226	2	7				
3575	Shade	226	2	8				
3576	Shade	226	2	9				
3577	Compote	173	4	1	$305	Celeste Blue	ebay-01/05	TPD)10.122
3577					$1495	Gold Calcite ACB	EAC-04/05	
3578	Centerpiece	149	2	7	$775	Gold Calcite	ebay-05/01	
3579	Plate	159	1	5	$465	Blue Calcite	EAC-04/90	
3579					$715	Blue Calcite	EAC-10/92	
3579					$440	Gold Calcite	EAC-10/93	
3579					$290	Rosaline	Sknr-05/96	
3579					$690	Blue Aurene	JDJ-10/97	
3579					$690	Gold Calcite(E)	Sknr-01/98	
3579					$345	Colorless	Sknr-01/98	
3579					$200	Bristol Yellow	Sknr-03/99	
3579					$125	Pomona Green	ebay-12/99	
3579					$550	Blue Calcite	ebay-01/00	
3579					$480	Gold Calcite	ebay-03/01	
3579					$510	Blue Aurene	JDJ-05/01	
3579					$125	Pomona Green	ebay-10/01	
3579					$85	Pomona Green	ebay-11/01	
3579					$190	Bristol Yellow	ebay-11/01	
3579					$395	Gold Aurene	ebay-12/01	
3579					$90	Nile Green (E)	ebay-01/02	
3579					$125	Bristol Yellow	ebay-03/02	
3579					$115	Bristol Yellow	JDJ-05/02	
3579					$85	Bristol Yellow	ebay-07/02	
3579					$155	Pomona Green	ebay-11/02	
3579					$660	Blue Calcite	ebay-01/03	
3579					$515	Wisteria (E)	ebay-05/03	Engraved "Grapes"
3579					$410	Wisteria (E)	ebay-09/03	Engraved "Grapes"
3579					$650	Gold Calcite	ebay-12/03	
3579					$380	Gold Calcite	ebay-01/04	
3579					$345	Rosaline	EAC-04/04	
3579					$125	Pomona Green	ebay-03/05	
3579					$585	Blue Calcite	ebay-04/05	
3580	Plate	159	1	6				
3581	Candlestick	162	5	2	$770	Blue Calcite	EAC-04/90	RFR)14,1,A&C;ACR)168,340
3581					$325	Gold Calcite	EAC-10/90	
3581					$330	Gold Calcite	EAC-07/91	
3581					$880	Blue Calcite	EAC-10/92	

SHAPE NO.	ITEM	PAGE	COL	ROW	PRICE REALIZED	GLASS TYPE	AUCTION HOUSE	COMMENTS & PHOTO REFERENCES
3581					$1035	Blue Calcite	Sknr-05/95	
3581					$660	Gold Calcite	EAC-07/95	
3581					$690	Gold Calcite	EAC-04/97	
3581					$535	Gold Calcite	EAC-07/97	
3581					$550	Gold Calcite	EAC-07/98	
3581					$385	Gold Calcite	EAC-07/99	
3581					$500	Gold Calcite	ebay-11/99	
3581					$400	Gold Calcite	ebay-12/99	
3581					$450	Gold Calcite	EAC-04/01	
3581					$85	Pomona Green/Topaz	ebay-09/01	
3581					$250	Gold Calcite	Ogal-10/01	
3581					$350	Gold Aurene	Ogal-10/01	
3581					$345	Gold Calcite	JDJ-11/01	
3581					$535	Gold Calcite	JDJ-11/01	
3581					$150	Topaz/Celeste Blue	ebay-12/01	
3581					$90	Topaz/Pomona Green	ebay-12/01	
3581					$270	Gold Calcite	ebay-11/02	
3581					$550	Green Jade/Alabaster ACB	ebay-01/03	Etched "Matzu"
3581					$95	Bristol Yellow	ebay-01/03	
3581					$165	Topaz/Pomona Green	ebay-08/03	
3581					$120	Topaz/Pomona Green	ebay-10/03	
3581					$980	Green Jade/Alabaster ACB	EAC-11/03	Etched "Chinese"
3581					$280	Gold Calcite	ebay-01/04	
3581					$490	Gold Calcite	JDJ-05/04	
3581					$1305	Light Blue Jade/Flint White	ebay-09/04	Etched "Chinese"
3581					$150	Gold Calcite (E)	ebay-02/05	
3582	Vase	275	1	1	$350	Gold Calcite	Tway-10/00	
3583	Vase	275	1	2	$1380	Blue Calcite	EAC-04/04	
3583					$350	Gold Calcite	ebay-06/05	
3584	Compote	173	4	2	$715	Topaz/Celeste Blue trim	Cott-0202	
3584					$455	Bristol/Celeste Blue trim	ebay-04/02	
3584	Candlestick	162	5	3	$735	Bristol/Celeste Blue trim	ebay-04/02	
3584					$1025	Bristol/Celeste Blue trim	ebay-02/03	
3584	Centerpiece	149	2	6	$455	Bristol/Celeste Blue trim	ebay-04/02	
3585	Goblet	191	4	7				
3586	Goblet	191	4	8				JSS)12-25
3587	Whiskey	198	5	9				
3588	Vase	275	1	3				Lamp Base
3589	Vase	275	1	4				Lamp Base TPD)10.50
3589					$1090	Mirror Black/Green Jade	JDJ-05/04	Lamp with fittings, Green Jade prunts
3590	Vase	275	1	5				Lamp Base
3591	Vase	275	2	1				Lamp Base
3592	Lamp Spindle	207	5	2				
3593	Lamp Spindle	207	5	3				
3594	Vase	275	2	2				TPD)10.106
3595	Vase	275	2	3				
3596	Shade	226	2	10				
3597	Candlestick	162	5	4				
3597	Centerpiece	149	2	8				
3597	Compote	173	4	3				
3598	Goblet	191	5	1				This shape shown as 3548 in Gardner.
3598								TPD)7.37
3599	Goblet	191	5	2				
3600	Goblet	191	5	3				
3601	Goblet	191	5	4				TPD)7.38
3602	Goblet	191	5	5				
3605	Goblet							TPD)7.36
3678	Vase							TPD)8.55
4920	Vase							TPD)8.4
5000	Vase (cover opt.)	306	2	5	$2200	Rosaline/Alabaster ACB	EAC-10/90	Etched "Chinese" PG1)116,188:313;
5000					$1430	Rosaline/Alabaster ACB	EAC-10/91	Etched "Bat" PG1)XXV A,A
5000					$2860	Rosaline/Alabaster ACB	EAC-07/93	Etched "Chinese"
5000					$1870	Green Jade/Alabaster ACB	JDJ-10/95	RFR)18,1,A&C:19,2,B;
5000					$1430	Rosaline/Alabaster ACB	EAC-10/96	RFR)31,3,A; TPD)5.35:10.21:10.131
5000					$1265	Rosaline/Alabaster ACB	Sknr-10/96	
5000					$770	Rosaline/Alabaster ACB	EAC-07/98	
5000					$2695	Rosaline/Alabaster ACB	EAC-10/98	
5000					$825	Green Jade/Alabaster ACB	EAC-04/99	
5000					$1980	Green Jade/Alabaster ACB	EAC-10/00	
5000					$80	Pomona Green	EAC-10/00	
5000					$2070	Green Jade/Alabaster ACB	Sknr-02/01	Etched "Bird"
5000					$3080	Green Jade/Alabaster ACB	EAC-04/02	Etched "Dragon"
5000					$2415	Green Jade/Alabaster ACB	ebay-09/02	
5000					$340	VDS/Celeste Blue finial	ebay-08/02	

SHAPE NO.	ITEM	PAGE	COL	ROW	PRICE REALIZED	GLASS TYPE	AUCTION HOUSE	COMMENTS & PHOTO REFERENCES
5000					$5040	Grn.Jade/Yellow Jade ACB	EAC-09/02	Etched "Mockingbird"
5000					$5880	Black/Green Jade ACB	EAC-09/02	
5000					$2415	Green Jade/Alabaster ACB	ebay-10/02	
5000					$440	Rosaline/Alabaster ACB	Sknr-12/02	Etched "Bird"
5000					$1120	Rosaline/Alabaster ACB	EAC-01/03	Etched "Bird"
5000					$1955	Green Jade/Alabaster ACB	Jack-06/03	Etched "Matzu"
5000					$490	Alabaster/Black finial	ebay-10/03	
5000					$1150	Green Jade/Alabaster ACB	Jack-11/03	Etched "Bird"
5000					$1235	Rosaline/Alabaster ACB	ebay-03/04	Etched "Chinese"
5000					$1025	Green Jade/Alabaster ACB	ebay-03/04	Etched "Bird"
5000					$2660	Plum Jade ACB Lamp	ebay-04/04	Etched "Bird"
5000					$840	Green Jade/Alabaster ACB	Ogal-05/04	Etched "Bird"
5000					$1495	Green Jade/Alabaster ACB	JDJ-05/04	Lamp Etched "Bird #2"
5000					$2240	Green Jade/Alabaster ACB	EAC-07/04	Etched "Bird"
5000					$2695	Green Jade/Alabaster ACB	Tway-09/04	Etched "Galleon"
5000					$1100	Green Jade/Alabaster ACB	Crft-09/04	Etched "Bird"
5000					$1695	Green Jade/Alabaster ACB	ebay-10/04	Etched "Bird #2"
5000					$880	Green Jade/Alabaster ACB	EAC-10/04	Etched "Bird"
5000					$2090	Green Jade/Alabaster ACB	EAC-10/04	Etched "Fish"
5000					$150	Rosaline/Alabaster ACB	ebay-11/04	Single etched band around neck
5000					$760	Green Jade/Alabaster ACB	ebay-11/04	Etched "Bird"
5000					$2640	Green Jade/Alabaster ACB	ebay-11/04	Etched "Chinese" with cover
5000					$520	Green Jade/Alabaster ACB	ebay-12/04	Etched "Bird," Lamp
5000					$900	Green Jade/Alabaster ACB	ebay-01/05	Etched "Bird"
5000					$250	Green Jade/Alabaster	ebay-02/05	
5000					$500	Green Jade/Alabaster ACB	ebay-05/05	Etched "Bird," Made as a lamp.
5000					$1200	Rosaline/Alabaster ACB	JDJ-06/05	Etched "Chinese"
5000					$1150	Green Jade/Alabaster ACB	EAC-07/05	Etched "Bird"
5001	Bowl	143	4	5	$935	Rosaline/Alabaster ACB	ebay-09/03	Etched "Chinese"
5001					$1410	Rosaline/Alabaster ACB	ebay-11/03	Etched "Chinese"
5001					$1150	Rosaline/Alabaster ACB	ebay-02/04	Etched "Chinese"
5001					$805	Green Jade/Alabaster ACB	EAC-04/04	Etched "Chinese"
5001					$630	Green Jade/Alabaster ACB	EAC-07/05	Etched "Chinese"
5002	Bowl	143	4	6	$250	Gold Calcite	JDJ-05/94	PG1)116,187
5002					$1840	Black/Alabaster ACB	Sknr-10/94	
5002					$1380	Light Blue Jade ACB	Sknr-01/96	
5002					$1100	Green Jade/Alabaster ACB	EAC-04/98	
5002					$2750	Light Blue Jade ACB	EAC-07/98	
5002					$850	Gold Calcite	Ogal-07/00	
5002					$150	Gold Calcite	ebay-02/01	
5002					$240	Gold Calcite	JDJ-11/02	
5002					$300	Gold Calcite	ebay-01/04	
5002					$4830	Light Blue Jade ACB	ebay-05/04	Etched "Chinese"
5002					$175	Gold Calcite	ebay-07/04	
5002					$2425	Light Blue Jade ACB	Crft-09/04	Etched "Chinese"
5002					$360	Gold Calcite	JDJ-11/04	
5002					$225	Gold Calcite	ebay-12/04	
5002					$180	Gold Calcite	ebay-03/05	
5002					$575	Blue Aurene	EAC-04/05	
5003	Vase	275	2	4	$975	Rosaline/Alabaster handles	EAC-04/05	
5004	Vase	275	2	5	$1430	Green Jade/Alabaster ACB	EAC-04/91	Etched "Chinese"
5004					$5600	Rosaline/Alabaster ACB	EAC-04/02	Etched "Chinese"
5004					$3070	Rosaline/Alabaster ACB	ebay-05/05	Etched "Chinese"
5005	Vase	275	2	6				
5006	Vase	275	3	1	$190	Rosaline/Alabaster	ebay-03/04	ACR)147,283; TPD)10.118
5007	Vase	275	3	2	$1485	Yellow Jade	JDJ-06/96	
5007					$2070	Yellow Jade	Sknr-02/00	
5008	Vase	275	3	3				
5009	Vase	275	3	4				
5010	Vase	275	3	5	$1000	Yellow Jade	ebay-04/03	With Yellow Jade ring handles
5011	Vase	275	3	6				
5012	Vase	275	3	7	$225	Green Jade/Alabaster	ebay-06/03	
5013	Vase	275	4	1				
5014	Vase	275	4	2				
5015	Vase	275	4	3				
5016	Vase	275	4	4				
5017	Vase	275	4	5	$990	Green Jade/Alabaster ACB	EAC-10/93	
5017					$2650	Rosaline/Alabaster ACB	ebay-03/03	Etched "Carved Jade"
5018	Covered Vase	306	2	6				TPD)5.39
5019	Centerpiece	149	3	1				
5020	Covered Vase	306	2	7				PG1)113,176
5021	Covered Vase	306	2	8				
5022	Bowl	143	4	7	$145	VDS	ebay-07/04	
5023	Candelabra							No drawing in factory records.

SHAPE NO.	ITEM	PAGE	COL	ROW	PRICE REALIZED	GLASS TYPE	AUCTION HOUSE	COMMENTS & PHOTO REFERENCES
5024	Ring Stand	245	2	5				
5024	Centerpiece	149	3	2				
5025	Covered Vase	306	3	1				
5026	Ash Tray	137	3	9				
5027	Ash Tray	137	3	10				
5028	Covered Vase	306	3	2				
5029	Centerpiece	149	3	3				
5030	Vase	275	4	6				
5031	Tumble Up	199	5	7				
5032	Book End	310	2	3				
5033	Bowl	143	4	8				
5034	Bowl	143	4	9				PG1)88,134
5035	Bell	237	3	5				
5036	Compote	173	4	4				
5037	Vase	275	4	7	$315	Topaz/Celeste Blue	ebay-03/02	
5038	Compote	173	4	5				
5039	Shade	226	3	1				
5040	Vase	275	5	1				
5041	Shade	226	5	7				
5042	Shade	226	5	8				
5043	Shade	226	5	9				
5044	Shade	226	5	10				
5045	Shade	226	5	11				
5046	Shade	226	5	12				
5047	Shade	226	3	2	$410	Gold Aurene	EAC-08/00	
5048	Covered Vase	306	3	3				
5049	Covered Vase	306	3	4				
5050	Goblet	197	4	4				
5051	Covered Vase	306	3	5				TPD)10.154
5052	Covered Vase	306	4	1				
5053	Covered Vase	306	4	2				
5054	Vase	275	5	2				PG1)V C,C
5055	Vase	275	5	3				
5056	Vase	275	5	4				
5057	Cologne	241	4	1				
5058	Decanter	186	1	4				
5059	Candlestick	163	1	1				
5060	Vase	275	5	5				
5061	Centerpiece	149	3	4	$1325	Blue Calcite	ebay-11/99	
5061					$255	Gold Calcite	ebay-12/99	
5061					$825	Gold Calcite	EAC-05/00	
5061					$230	Gold Calcite	Sknr-06/00	
5061					$785	Gold Calcite	Jack-06/00	
5061					$270	Gold Calcite	ebay-02/01	
5061					$285	Gold Calcite	ebay-02/01	
5061					$920	Blue Calcite	Sknr-02/01	
5061					$295	Gold Calcite	ebay-03/01	
5061					$630	Gold Calcite	Jack-06/01	
5061					$300	Gold Calcite	ebay-07/01	
5061					$235	Gold Calcite	ebay-07/01	
5061					$275	Gold Calcite	ebay-07/01	
5061					$950	Gold Calcite	ebay-10/01	
5061					$550	Gold Calcite	ebay-10/01	
5061					$210	Gold Aurene	ebay-11/01	
5061					$510	Gold Calcite	ebay-12/01	
5061					$175	Gold Calcite	ebay-02/02	
5061					$240	Gold Calcite	ebay-03/02	
5061					$265	Gold Calcite	ebay-03/02	
5061					$250	Gold Calcite	ebay-03/02	
5061					$460	Gold Aurene	Jack-06/02	
5061					$200	Gold Calcite	ebay-07/02	
5061					$290	Gold Calcite	ebay-07/02	
5061					$240	Gold Calcite	JDJ-11/02	
5061					$240	Gold Calcite	JDJ-11/02	
5061					$210	Gold Calcite	ebay-11/02	
5061					$200	Gold Calcite	Cinc-11/02	
5061					$750	Blue Aurene	Ogal-12/02	
5061					$240	Gold Calcite	ebay-01/03	
5061					$180	Gold Calcite	ebay-01/03	
5061					$475	Gold Calcite	Ogal-03/03	
5061					$410	Gold Calcite	ebay-04/03	
5061					$900	Blue Aurene	Ogal-05/03	
5061					$200	Gold Calcite	ebay-05/03	
5061					$260	Gold Calcite	ebay-05/03	

SHAPE NO.	ITEM	PAGE	COL	ROW	PRICE REALIZED	GLASS TYPE	AUCTION HOUSE	COMMENTS & PHOTO REFERENCES
5061					$335	Gold Calcite	ebay-05/03	
5061					$150	Gold Calcite	Cinc-06/03	
5061					$430	Gold Calcite	EAC-06/03	
5061					$400	Gold Calcite	Jack-06/03	
5061					$280	Gold Calcite	ebay-07/03	
5061					$385	Blue Aurene	ebay-07/03	
5061					$205	Gold Calcite	ebay-09/03	
5061					$400	Gold Calcite	ebay-10/03	
5061					$290	Gold Calcite	ebay-10/03	
5061					$290	Gold Calcite	ebay-11/03	
5061					$180	Gold Calcite	ebay-11/03	
5061					$250	Gold Aurene	ebay-11/03	
5061					$400	Gold Calcite	ebay-11/03	
5061					$230	Gold Calcite	EAC-11/03	
5061					$180	Gold Calcite	ebay-12/03	
5061					$305	Gold Calcite	ebay-02/04	
5061					$510	Gold Calcite	ebay-03/04	
5061					$200	Gold Calcite	ebay-04/04	
5061					$90	Gold Calcite	ebay-05/04	
5061					$120	Gold Calcite	Crft-05/04	
5061					$60	Amber/Flemish Blue rim	ebay-06/04	Color is "Flemish"
5061					$175	Gold Calcite	ebay-06/04	
5061					$145	Gold Calcite	Sknr-06/04	
5061					$300	Gold Calcite	ebay-07/04	
5061					$200	Gold Calcite	ebay-08/04	
5061					$140	Gold Calcite	ebay-10/04	
5061					$270	Gold Calcite	ebay-11/04	
5061					$125	Gold Calcite	ebay-12/04	
5061					$200	Gold Calcite	ebay-12/04	
5061					$140	Gold Calcite	ebay-01/05	
5061					$200	Gold Calcite	ebay-02/05	
5061					$150	Gold Calcite	ebay-02/05	
5061					$175	Gold Calcite	Cott-02/05	
5061					$275	Gold Calcite	ebay-04/05	
5061					$275	Gold Calcite	ebay-05/05	14"
5061					$190	Gold Calcite	ebay-05/05	
5061					$175	Gold Calcite	ebay-06/05	
5061					$210	Gold Calcite	ebay-06/05	
5061					$255	Gold Calcite	ebay-06/05	14"
5061					$395	Gold Calcite	ebay-06/05	
5062	Centerpiece	149	3	5	$375	Light Blue Jade	Sknr-10/96	
5062					$230	Light Blue Jade	ebay-03/00	
5063	Vase	275	5	6				
5064	Vase	275	5	7	$355	Gold Calcite	EAC-04/95	
5064					$355	Gold Calcite	EAC-07/98	
5064					$450	Gold Calcite	Tway-10/00	
5064					$550	Gold Calcite	Cott-08/01	
5064					$285	Gold Calcite	JDJ-11/01	
5064					$450	Gold Calcite	EAC-01/03	
5064					$350	Gold Calcite	ebay-10/03	
5065	Centerpiece	149	3	6	$450	Blue Aurene	ebay-11/01	TPD)9.30
5066	Compote	173	4	6	$605	Blue Calcite	JDJ-10/94	
5066					$220	Gold Calcite	JDJ-10/94	
5066					$520	Blue Calcite	Sknr-10/95	
5066					$440	Gold Calcite	EAC-04/95	
5066					$550	Gold Aurene	EAC-04/95	
5066					$285	Gold Calcite	JDJ-06/98	
5066					$685	Blue Calcite	ebay-06/00	
5066					$715	Gold Aurene	Cott-08/01	
5066					$565	Blue Calcite	ebay-09/03	
5066					$330	Rosaline/Alabaster	ebay-01/04	Alabaster stem and foot
5066					$970	Gold Calcite	Ogal-02/04	
5066					$1080	Blue Calcite	ebay-05/04	
5066					$865	Blue Calcite	ebay-01/05	
5066					$700	Blue Calcite	ebay-02/05	
5066					$400	Gold Calcite	ebay-03/05	
5066					$1080	Blue Calcite	ebay-05/05	
5067	Finger Bowl	189	1	12				
5067	Goblet	191	5	6	$155	Topaz	ebay-04/00	PG2)64,A; RFR)9,3,E; JAS)150,B,A; MDK)32
5067					$81	Aqua Marine	ebay-11/02	
5067					$110	Aqua Marine	ebay-12/02	
5067					$155	Topaz	ebay-12/02	
5067					$90	Topaz	ebay-10/03	
5067					$690	Gold Aurene	Hrtg-03/05	

SHAPE NO.	ITEM	PAGE	COL	ROW	PRICE REALIZED	GLASS TYPE	AUCTION HOUSE	COMMENTS & PHOTO REFERENCES
5067					$170	VDS/Coral rim	ebay-03/05	
5067					$805	Gold Aurene	EAC-07/05	
5067	Pitcher	213	5	5	$550	Aqua Marine	EAC-04/91	
5067					$1000	VDS/Blue	Tway-09/02	Pitcher and 4 Tumblers
5067					$205	Topaz	ebay-01/03	
5067	Lemonade	213	5	5				
5067	Sherbet	216	5	6				
5068	Bowl	143	4	10	$75	Celeste Blue	ebay-01/03	
5068					$160	Celeste Blue	ebay-06/03	
5068					$180	Celeste Blue	JDJ-11/04	
5069	Basket	140	2	6	$2185	Gold Calcite	JDJ-10/97	PG1)VI C,E; PG2)54,D; RFR)8,1,B;
5069					$865	Blue Aurene	Sknr-10/98	RFR)14,2,B; RLG)153,288
5069					$805	VDS	Sknr-10/98	
5069					$865	Blue Aurene	Sknr-10/98	
5069					$920	VDS	Sknr-01/98	
5070	Vase	275	5	8	$385	Gold Calcite	EAC-04/95	
5070					$295	Gold Calcite	JDJ-06/97	
5070					$295	Gold Calcite	EAC-10/98	
5070					$825	Blue Calcite	ebay-12/00	
5070					$385	Gold Calcite	Cott-08/01	
5070					$375	Gold Calcite	JDJ-11/01	
5070					$950	Gold Calcite	ebay-12/01	
5070					$750	Gold Aurene	ebay-05/02	
5070					$490	Gold Aurene	ebay-03/03	
5070					$490	Gold Calcite	Jack-03/03	
5070					$595	Gold Calcite	ebay-04/03	
5070					$650	Gold Calcite	Dalla-09/03	
5070					$325	Gold Calcite	ebay-10/03	
5070					$630	Gold Calcite	EAC-11/03	
5070					$260	Gold Calcite	ebay-04/04	
5070					$230	Gold Calcite	EAC-04/04	
5070					$255	Gold Calcite	ebay-09/04	
5070					$355	Gold Calcite	EAC-10/04	
5070					$400	Gold Aurene	ebay-05/05	
5070					$345	Gold Calcite	EAC-07/05	
5071	Shade	229	1	8				
5072	Ash Tray	137	3	11				
5073	Desk Set	310	2	4				
5074	Cologne	245	2	6				TPD)10.133
5074	Puff Box	245	2	6				PG1)XXV C,D; TPD)10.123:10.133
5074					$1540	Rosaline/Alabaster ACB	EAC-10/93	Etched "Chinese"
5074	Salve	245	2	6				TPD)10.133
5075	Vase	276	1	1				
5076	Covered Vase	306	4	3				
5077	Vase	276	1	2	$850	Flemish	ebay-02/05	
5078	Shade	229	2	1				
5079	Shade	229	2	2				
5080	Shade	229	2	3				
5081	Shade	229	2	4				
5082	Shade	229	2	5				
5083	Shade	229	2	6				
5084	Covered Vase	306	4	4				
5085	Plate	158	2	8				
5086	Candlestick	163	1	2				
5087	Covered Vase	306	4	5				
5088	Champagne				$75	Selenium Red	ebay-02/04	
5088					$40	Blue-gray	ebay-06/05	
5088					$40	Blue-gray	ebay-06/05	
5088					$80	Selenium Red	ebay-06/05	
5088	Goblet	191	5	7	$145	Blue-gray/Amber	Cott-08/01	MDK)10:142
5088					$115	Selenium Red	ebay-10/03	
5088					$75	Selenium Red	ebay-03/04	
5088					$55	Selenium Red	ebay-05/04	
5088					$120	Selenium Red	ebay-08/04	
5088					$75	Selenium Red	ebay-09/04	
5088					$95	Selenium Red	ebay-10/04	
5088					$75	Selenium Red	ebay-03/05	
5088					$80	Selenium Red	ebay-03/05	
5088					$90	Selenium Red	ebay-03/05	
5088					$105	Selenium Red	ebay-03/05	
5088	Sherbet				$145	Selenium Red	ebay-01/00	
5088					$100	Blue-gray/Amber	ebay-10/01	
5088					$125	Selenium Red	ebay-10/03	
5088					$105	Selenium Red	ebay-12/03	

SHAPE NO.	ITEM	PAGE	COL	ROW	PRICE REALIZED	GLASS TYPE	AUCTION HOUSE	COMMENTS & PHOTO REFERENCES
5088					$100	Selenium Red	ebay-01/04	
5088					$75	Selenium Red	ebay-01/04	
5088					$80	Selenium Red	ebay-02/04	
5088					$65	Blue-gray	ebay-07/04	
5088					$175	Selenium Red	ebay-09/04	
5088					$25	Selenium Red	ebay-10/04	
5089	Goblet	197	4	5				
5090	Compote	173	4	7	$165	Gold Calcite	JDJ-10/94	
5090					$355	Gold Calcite	EAC-04/96	
5090					$550	Gold Calcite	EAC-10/96	
5090					$460	Gold Calcite	ebay-12/99	
5090					$345	Gold Calcite	JDJ-05/00	
5090					$525	Gold Calcite	ebay-11/00	
5090					$385	Gold Calcite	Cott-08/01	
5090					$220	Gold Calcite	ebay-10/01	
5090					$400	Gold Calcite	JDJ-05/02	
5090					$295	VDS	ebay-05/02	
5090					$175	Gold Calcite	ebay-12/02	
5090					$220	Gold Calcite	ebay-03/03	
5090					$1440	Gold Calcite	ebay-05/05	
5091	Vase	276	1	3				
5092	Candlestick	163	1	3	$465	VDS	ebay-06/03	
5093	Candlestick	163	1	4				
5094	Candlestick	163	1	5	$375	Aqua Marine	Sknr-02/01	
5094					$115	Aqua Marine	ebay-10/01	
5095	Plate	158	2	9				
5096	Plate	159	1	7				
5097	Plate	159	1	8				
5098	Centerpiece	149	3	7				
5099	Pitcher, Lemonade	213	5	6	$430	VDS/Blue	ebay-01/03	Pitcher and two tumblers
5100	Dresser Set	245	3	6				
5101	Pendant	205	3	6				
5102	Ash Tray	137	3	12				
5103	Vase	276	1	4				
5104	Vase	276	1	5				
5105	Goblet	197	5	8				
5106	Vase							See New Drawings section
5107	Cologne	241	4	2	$450	Gold Calcite (E)	ebay-06/03	
5107					$850	Gold Calcite (E)	Dalla-09/03	
5108	Compote	173	5	1				
5109	(Auto Vase)							See New Drawings section
5110	Finger Bowl	189	2	1	$230	Gold Aurene	Sknr-10/00	
5112	Candlestick	163	1	6				
5113	Candlestick	163	2	1	$380	Rosaline/Alabaster	ebay-11/02	
5113					$260	Grenadine/Flemish Blue	EAC-06/03	
5114	Candlestick	163	2	2	$190	Pomona Green/Col. stem	EAC-07/93	TPD)8.2
5114					$860	Mirror Black/Col. Spiral	Sknr-02/01	
5114					$745	Selenium Red/Col. Stem	ebay-08/02	
5114					$250	Celeste Blue/Col. Stem	ebay-11/04	
5114	Compote							See New Drawings section
5115	Plate	158	1	13	$690	Gold Aurene	Sknr-10/95	This shape shown as #5116 in Gardner.
5116	Plate	158	1	13				This number is an error, see #5115.
5116	Jar	209	4	6	$275	Celeste Blue/Fruit finial	ebay-05/05	No underplate
5117	Covered Vase	306	5	1				
5118	Covered Vase	306	5	2				
5119	Covered Vase	306	5	3				
5120	Goblet	197	4	6	$715	Green Jade/Alabaster	EAC-04/98	PG2)64,G; JAS)150,B,G; TPD)10.16
5120					$500	Rosaline	EAC-08/00	
5120					$405	Green Jade/Alabaster	ebay-05/03	Alabaster stem and foot
5120					$315	Rosaline/Alabaster	ebay-04/04	Alabaster stem and foot
5120					$535	Rosaline/Alabaster	ebay-04/04	Alabaster stem and foot
5120					$425	Rosaline/Alabaster	ebay-01/05	Alabaster stem and foot
5120					$420	Rosaline/Alabaster	ebay-04/05	Alabaster stem and foot
5120					$310	Rosaline/Alabaster	ebay-06/05	Alabaster stem and foot
5121	Plate	158	2	10				TPD)4.76
5122	Centerpiece	149	3	8				
5123	Candlestick				$290	Colorless/Celeste Blue trim	ebay-12/99	
5123	Compote	173	5	2				PG1)46,82
5124	Jar	209	4	7	$115	VDS	JDJ-05/95	
5124					$175	VDS	Sknr-05/96	
5125	Candlestick	163	2	3				
5126	Compote	173	5	3				
5127	Compote	173	5	4				
5128	Covered Vase	306	5	4	$2420	VDS with Fruit finial	EAC-10/90	PG2)57,E; RFR)24,3,B; JAS)150,TR,E

SHAPE NO.	ITEM	PAGE	COL	ROW	PRICE REALIZED	GLASS TYPE	AUCTION HOUSE	COMMENTS & PHOTO REFERENCES
5128					$770	VDS w/Blue Stem	EAC-04/96	
5128					$920	Citron Yellow	Sknr-10/96	
5128					$1100	Green/Blue	EAC-10/00	
5128					$230	Topaz/Celeste Blue	Sknr-02/01	
5129	Covered Vase	306	5	5				ACR)COLOR 1,T,C
5129					$90	VDS/Celeste handles	ebay-12/03	No cover
5130	Tumbler	199	2	4	$355	Rosaline/Alabaster	EAC-04/94	MDK)23
5130					$110	Rosaline/Alabaster	EAC-11/01	
5130					$100	Topaz/Amethyst foot	ebay-08/02	
5130					$145	Green Jade/Alabaster	Sknr-12/02	
5130					$35	Topaz	ebay-02/03	
5130					$75	Rosaline/Alabaster	ebay-09/03	
5130					$110	Rosaline/Alabaster	ebay-09/03	
5130					$180	Rosaline/Alabaster	ebay-11/03	
5131	Plate	158	2	11	$900	Blue Aurene	ebay-01/02	TPD)10.91
5132	Vase	276	1	6				
5133	Vase	276	2	1				
5134	Candlestick	163	2	4				
5135	Cruet	179	3	4				
5136	Covered Vase	306	5	6				
5137	Jar	209	4	8	$260	Amethyst/Green	JDJ-10/96	RFR)23,1,C; JAS)147,B,B; TPD)9.20
5137					$510	Opal	ebay-04/00	
5137					$1275	Orange Cintra	ebay-02/01	
5137					$230	Topaz/Green Stem	ebay-06/02	
5137					$750	Topaz/Celeste Stem (E)	ebay-08/02	
5137					$475	Pomona Green	ebay-12/04	Colorless leaf and stem
5138	Vase	276	2	2	$200	Topaz	ebay-02/00	TPD)4.24
5139	Candlestick	163	2	5				
5140	Candlestick	163	2	6				
5141	Bowl	144	1	1				
5142	Basket	140	2	7				
5143	Plate	158	1	14				
5144	Jar	209	4	9				
5145	Vase	276	2	3				
5146	Candlestick	163	3	1	$770	Gold Aurene	EAC-04/92	TPD)10.121
5146					$520	Gold Aurene	EAC-10/94	
5146					$670	Rosaline/Alabaster	EAC-09/02	Rosaline bowl, Alabaster foot and handle
5146					$75	Amber/Flemish Blue	ebay-12/02	
5146					$1175	Gold Aurene	EAC-01/03	
5146					$430	Aqua Marine	EAC-06/03	
5146					$190	Gold Ruby/Colorless foot	ebay-08/03	White bowl rim, no handle
5146					$850	Gold Aurene	ebay-01/05	
5147	Compote	173	5	5				
5148	Vase	276	2	4				
5149	Bowl	144	1	2	$450	Gold Calcite	ebay-03/00	
5149					$230	Flemish Blue	Sknr-10/00	
5149					$375	Gold Calcite	EAC-06/03	
5149					$250	Gold Calcite	ebay-12/03	
5149					$195	Gold Calcite	ebay-01/04	
5149					$590	Blue Calcite	ebay-03/04	
5149					$305	Flemish Blue	ebay-10/04	
5150	Bowl	144	1	3				
5151	Compote	173	5	6				
5152	Bowl	144	1	4				
5153	Covered Vase	306	5	7				
5154	Champagne				$440	Opal/Amethyst Cintra	EAC-07/92	ACR)150,B,D
5154					$100	Colorless	ebay-01/01	
5154					$125	Colorless/Celeste Blue	ebay-02/01	
5154					$130	Opal/Amethyst Cintra	ebay-03/01	
5154					$70	Topaz/Celeste Blue	ebay-03/01	
5154					$135	Topaz/Celeste Blue	EAC-11/01	
5154					$115	Green Jade/Alabaster	ebay-12/01	
5154					$80	Green Jade/Alabaster	ebay-06/02	
5154					$180	Grenadine/Colorless	ebay-08/02	Grenadine bowl, black rim, col. stem &
5154					$75	Topaz/Celeste Blue stem	Cinc-11/02	
5154					$90	Green Jade/Alabaster	ebay-01/03	
5154					$200	Green Jade/Alabaster	ebay-02/03	
5154					$100	Green Jade/Alabaster	ebay-02/03	
5154					$100	Opal/Amethyst Cintra	ebay-03/03	
5154					$130	Opal/Amethyst Cintra	ebay-03/03	
5154					$160	Opal/Amethyst Cintra	ebay-03/03	
5154					$95	Opal/Amethyst Cintra	ebay-03/03	
5154					$35	Opal/Amethyst Cintra	ebay-04/03	
5154					$90	Antique Green/Celeste	ebay-05/03	Celeste Blue stem

SHAPE NO.	ITEM	PAGE	COL	ROW	PRICE REALIZED	GLASS TYPE	AUCTION HOUSE	COMMENTS & PHOTO REFERENCES
5154					$115	Antique Green/Celeste	ebay-05/03	Celeste Blue stem
5154					$135	Antique Green/Celeste	ebay-05/03	Celeste Blue stem
5154					$35	Colorless/Celeste Blue	ebay-07/03	Celeste Blue stem
5154					$115	Grenadine/Colorless	ebay-09/03	Grenadine bowl, black rim, col. stem & foot
5154					$70	Green Jade/Alabaster	JDJ-11/03	Alabaster stem and foot
5154					$75	Topaz	ebay-04/04	
5154					$125	Blue-Gray/Amber stem	ebay-05/04	
5154					$125	Pomona Green/Colorless	ebay-07/04	Colorless stem
5154					$170	Rosaline/Alabaster	ebay-06/04	Alabaster stem and foot
5154					$95	Green Jade/Alabaster	ebay-09/04	Alabaster stem
5154					$130	Green Jade/Alabaster	ebay-11/04	Alabaster stem
5154					$100	Green Jade/Alabaster	ebay-11/04	Alabaster stem and foot
5154					$100	Opal/Amethyst Cintra	ebay-12/04	
5154					$55	Rosaline/Alabaster	Hrtg-03/05	Alabaster stem and foot
5154					$50	Grenadine/Colorless stem	EAC-04/05	Black rim
5154					$35	Grenadine/Colorless stem	EAC-07/05	Black rim
5154	Cordial				$70	Blue-Gray/Amber stem	EAC-07/04	
5154					$45	Pomona Green/Colorless	ebay-07/04	Colorless stem
5154					$45	Pomona Green/Colorless	ebay-07/04	Colorless stem
5154					$55	Pomona Green/Colorless	ebay-07/04	Colorless stem
5154					$50	Pomona Green/Colorless	ebay-08/04	Colorless stem
5154					$75	Rosaline/Alabaster	ebay-04/05	Alabaster stem and foot
5154					$30	Grenadine/Colorless stem	EAC-07/05	Black rim
5154	Finger Bowl				$190	Opal/Amethyst Cintra	ebay-08/02	
5154					$30	Blue-gray	ebay-05/05	Finger bowl only
5154	Goblet	191	5	8	$355	Opal/Amethyst Cintra	EAC-07/92	PG1)XVIIIC;PG2)64,D&E;
5154					$575	Opal/Amethyst Cintra	EAC-07/96	JAS)150,B,E; ACR)COLOR4,T,C;
5154					$65	Green Jade/Alabaster	EAC-07/98	ACR)159,315;TPD)6.1:10.45
5154					$410	Opal/Amethyst Cintra	EAC-07/98	
5154					$130	Colorless/Celeste Blue	ebay-12/99	Celeste Blue stem
5154					$140	Green Jade/Alabaster	ebay-02/00	
5154					$215	Green Jade/Alabaster	ebay-02/00	
5154					$200	Rosaline/Alabaster	ebay-03/00	
5154					$150	Green Jade/Alabaster	ebay-04/00	
5154					$160	Topaz	ebay-04/00	
5154					$80	Topaz/Celeste Blue	ebay-01/01	
5154					$120	Colorless	ebay-01/01	
5154					$170	Opal/Amethyst Cintra	Sknr-02/01	
5154					$70	Topaz/Celeste Blue	ebay-03/01	
5154					$355	Opal/Amethyst Cintra	ebay-05/01	
5154					$125	Topaz/Amethyst	ebay-05/01	
5154					$255	Opal/Amethyst Cintra	ebay-06/01	
5154					$150	Green Jade/Alabaster	ebay-07/01	
5154					$200	Opal/Amethyst Cintra	ebay-12/01	
5154					$85	Topaz/Celeste Blue stem	ebay-01/02	
5154					$190	Green Jade/Alabaster	ebay-07/02	
5154					$95	Topaz/Amethyst stem	ebay-11/02	
5154					$110	Topaz/Celeste Blue stem	Cinc-11/02	
5154					$150	Rosaline/Alabaster	ebay-02/03	
5154					$150	Rosaline/Alabaster	ebay-02/03	
5154					$125	Opal/Amethyst Cintra	ebay-03/03	
5154					$135	Opal/Amethyst Cintra	ebay-03/03	
5154					$130	Grenadine/Colorless	ebay-03/03	Grenadine bowl, black rim, col. stem & foot
5154					$180	Opal/Amethyst Cintra	ebay-03/03	
5154					$160	Amber/Mirror Black	ebay-03/03	Mirror Black stem
5154					$394	Flemish Blue/White rim	ebay-05/03	
5154					$85	Topaz/Amethyst stem	ebay-01/04	
5154					$95	Colorless/Celeste stem	ebay-01/04	
5154					$200	Blue-gray/Amber stem	ebay-05/04	
5154					$45	Colorless/Celeste stem	ebay-05/04	
5154					$105	Pomona Green/Colorless	ebay-07/04	
5154					$80	Pomona Green/Colorless	ebay-08/04	
5154					$150	Opal/Amethyst Cintra	ebay-09/04	
5154					$130	Amber/Amethyst stem	ebay-11/04	
5154					$70	Amber/Amethyst stem	ebay-11/04	
5154					$165	Green Jade/Alabaster	ebay-12/04	
5154					$135	Green Jade/Alabaster	ebay-12/04	
5154					$150	Green Jade/Alabaster	ebay-01/05	
5154					$200	Rosaline/Alabaster	ebay-02/05	
5154					$180	Green Jade/Alabaster	ebay-03/05	Alabaster stem and foot
5154					$110	Grenadine/Black rim	EAC-04/05	
5154					$145	Green Jade/Alabaster (E)	EAC-04/05	Engraved "York"
5154					$40	Pomona Green	ebay-05/05	
5154					$35	Grenadine/Colorless stem	EAC-07/05	Black rim

SHAPE NO.	ITEM	PAGE	COL	ROW	PRICE REALIZED	GLASS TYPE	AUCTION HOUSE	COMMENTS & PHOTO REFERENCES
5154	Sherbet							MDK)94
5154					$165	Rosaline/Alabaster foot	Cinc-12/99	Sherbet only, no Underplate
5154					$190	Rosaline/Alabaster foot	ebay-12/99	Sherbet only, no Underplate
5154					$180	Opal/Amethyst Cintra	ebay-01/00	Sherbet only, no Underplate
5154					$55	Rosaline/Alabaster	EAC-11/01	
5154					$95	Celeste Blue	ebay-03/02	
5154					$160	Green Jade/Alabaster (E)	ebay-02/02	Sherbet only, no Underplate
5154					$180	Opal/Amethyst Cintra	ebay-02/02	
5154					$45	Spanish Green	ebay-02/02	
5154					$100	Celeste Blue	ebay-03/02	
5154					$75	Opal/Amethyst Cintra	ebay-06/02	Sherbet only, no Underplate
5154					$100	Topaz/Amethyst foot	ebay-08/02	Sherbet only, no Underplate
5154					$100	Opal/Amethyst Cintra	ebay-03/03	Sherbet only, no Underplate
5154					$95	Opal/Amethyst Cintra	ebay-03/03	Sherbet only, no Underplate
5154					$95	Opal/Amethyst Cintra	ebay-03/03	Sherbet only, no Underplate
5154					$100	Opal/Amethyst Cintra	ebay-03/03	Sherbet only, no Underplate
5154					$20	Colorless/Pomona Green	ebay-03/03	Pomona junction, Sherbet only
5154					$75	Opal/Amethyst Cintra	ebay-05/03	Sherbet only, no Underplate
5154					$45	Green Jade/Alabaster foot	ebay-11/03	
5154					$35	Topaz/Amethyst foot	ebay-11/03	Sherbet only, no Underplate
5154					$35	Topaz/Celeste foot	ebay-11/03	Sherbet only, no Underplate
5154					$200	Green Jade/Alabaster (E)	ebay-05/04	Sherbet only, no Underplate
5154					$90	Blue-gray/Amber foot	ebay-09/04	
5154					$85	Blue-gray/Amber foot	ebay-11/04	
5154					$50	Celeste Blue	ebay-11/04	Sherbet only, no Underplate
5154					$110	Grenadine/Black rim	ebay-11/04	
5154					$65	Topaz/Amethyst foot	ebay-05/05	Sherbet only, no Underplate
5154					$40	Topaz/Amethyst foot	ebay-05/05	Sherbet only, no Underplate
5154					$25	Topaz	ebay-07/05	Sherbet only, no Underplate
5154					$55	Green Jade/Alabaster (E)	EAC-07/05	Engraved "York," no Underplate
5154	Wine				$75	Rosaline/Alabaster	ebay-04/05	Alabaster stem and foot
5154					$30	Grenadine/Black rim	EAC-04/05	
5155	Compote	173	5	7	$230	Topaz/Celeste Blue	Sknr-05/95	TPD)10.113; MDK)37
5156	Candlestick	163	3	2				
5156	Compote	173	5	8				
5157	Covered Vase	307	1	1	$225	Celeste Blue	ebay-11/00	
5158	Centerpiece	149	3	9				
5159	Jar	209	4	10				
5160	Goblet	191	6	1				
5160	Goblet	191	6	2				This number is an error, see #5169.
5161	Vase	276	2	5	$1320	Gold Aurene	Midw-06/02	
5162	Tumble Up	199	5	8				
5163	Puff Box	244	4	12				
5164	Cologne	243	4	5				
5165	Candlestick							See New Drawings section
5166	Compote & Plate	159	2	8	$605	Gold Calcite	ebay-09/03	
5166					$1075	Gold Calcite	ebay-11/03	
5167	Vase	276	2	6				
5168	Vase	276	3	1				
5169	Goblet	191	6	2				This shape is shown as #5160 in Gardner.
5169								PG1)XXVIII B,C
5170	Decanter	186	1	5				PG1)96,148,F
5171	Decanter	186	2	1				TPD)10.151
5172	Candlestick	163	3	3				
5173	Compote	174	1	1				
5174	Covered Vase	307	1	2	$330	Citron Yellow	EAC-04/96	
5175	Candlestick	163	3	4	$460	Green Jade/Alabaster	Sknr-01/96	
5176	Compote	174	1	2				
5177	Candlestick	163	3	5				
5178	Covered Vase	307	1	3				
5180	Covered Vase	307	1	4				
5181	Decanter	186	2	2				This is a Cologne in the factory records.
5181	Puff Box	244	4	13				
5182	Decanter	186	2	3				This is a Cologne in the factory records.
5182	Puff Box	244	5	1				
5183	Shade	229	2	7				
5184	Shade	229	2	8				
5185	Plate	158	2	12				
5186	Bowl	144	1	5	$100	Gold Calcite	Ogal-02/00	JAS)162,BL,C
5186					$370	Gold Calcite	ebay-10/02	
5186					$770	Blue Calcite	ebay-06/03	
5186					$1090	Blue Calcite	EAC-04/04	
5186					$225	Mirror Black	ebay-07/04	
5186					$255	Gold Calcite	ebay-03/05	

SHAPE NO.	ITEM	PAGE	COL	ROW	PRICE REALIZED	GLASS TYPE	AUCTION HOUSE	COMMENTS & PHOTO REFERENCES
5186					$125	Gold Calcite	ebay-04/05	
5187	Cologne	241	4	3				
5188	Sherbet	216	5	9				
5189	Covered Vase	307	1	5				
5190	Vase	276	3	2				
5191	Covered Vase	307	1	6				
5192	Ice Tea	199	2	5	$765	Cintra	ebay-03/00	PG2)60,F;JAS)164,B,F
5192					$150	Amethyst/Alabaster	Tway-10/00	
5192					$95	Rosaline/Alabaster	ebay-05/01	
5192					$105	Rosaline/Alabaster	JDJ-05/01	
5192					$35	Celeste Blue	ebay-10/01	
5192					$125	Green Jade/Alabaster	ebay-12/01	
5192					$175	Green Jade/Alabaster	ebay-08/02	
5192					$90	Rosaline/Alabaster	ebay-12/02	
5192					$145	Topaz/Celeste Blue foot	ebay-06/04	
5192					$540	Blue Aurene	Tway-03/05	
5192					$25	Pomona Green	ebay-05/05	
5192					$145	Opal/Amethyst Cintra trim	EAC-07/05	
5193	Goblet	191	6	3	$200	VDS/Blue trim	ebay-10/02	
5193	Parfait	197	6	1				
5194	Bowl	144	1	7	$265	Topaz/Celeste Blue foot	ebay-09/02	MDK)137
5194	Candlestick	163	3	6	$625	Bristol Yellow	ebay-01/00	
5194	Compote	174	1	3	$675	Green Jade/Alabaster	ebay-01/00	MDK)64:85
5194					$495	Rosaline/Alabaster	ebay-04/00	
5194					$245	Pomona Green/Topaz	ebay-04/00	
5194					$125	Pomona Green	ebay-05/02	
5194					$170	Topaz/Celeste Blue stem	Tway-05/02	
5194					$150	Topaz	ebay-07/03	
5194					$245	Topaz	ebay-07/03	
5194					$400	Rosaline/Alabaster stem	ebay-07/03	
5194					$325	Topaz	ebay-08/03	
5194					$345	Rosaline/Alabaster stem	ebay-12/03	
5194					$250	Pomona Green/Colorless	ebay-07/05	Colorless stem
5195	Bowl	144	1	6				
5195	Candlestick	163	3	7				
5196	Candlestick	163	3	8				
5197	Compote	174	1	4				
5198	Bowl	144	1	8				
5199	Goblet	191	6	4				
5200	Shade	229	2	9				
5201	Vase	276	3	3				
5202	Vase	276	3	4				
5203	Cologne	241	4	4	$160	VDS/Celeste Blue stopper	ebay-09/01	"Peggy Hoyt"
5203					$240	VDS/Celeste Blue stopper	ebay-11/01	"Peggy Hoyt"
5203					$350	VDS/Rosaline stopper	Cinc-11/02	
5203					$80	VDS/Celeste Blue stopper	ebay-01/04	
5203					$480	VDS/Celeste Blue stopper	Rago-11/04	"Peggy Hoyt"
5204	Puff Box	244	5	2	$360	Blue Aurene	ebay-07/01	TPD)9.20
5204					$900	Gold Aurene	JDJ-05/04	
5205	Puff Box	244	5	3	$630	Blue Aurene	ebay-01/03	
5205					$280	Green Jade	ebay-03/04	
5206	Puff Box	244	5	4				
5207	Goblet	191	6	5				
5208	Puff Box	244	5	5				
5209	Ash Tray	137	3	13				
5210	Ash Tray	137	3	14				
5211	Centerpiece	149	3	10				
5212	Jug & Glasses							See New Drawing section
5213	Covered Vase	307	2	1				
5214	Covered Vase	307	2	2				
5215	Covered Vase	307	2	3				
5216	Goblet	191	6	6				
5217	Goblet	191	6	7				
5218	Vase	276	3	5				
5219	Vase	276	3	6				
5220	Candlestick	163	4	1				
5221	Candlestick	163	4	2				
5222	Candlestick	163	4	3				
5223	Bowl	144	1	9				
5223	Candlestick							PG1)355,A
5223	Compote							PG1)355,A
5223	Salt							PG1)355,A
5224	Sugar & Creamer	235	5	9,10				RFR)21,1,A&C
5225	Covered Vase	307	2	4				

SHAPE NO.	ITEM	PAGE	COL	ROW	PRICE REALIZED	GLASS TYPE	AUCTION HOUSE	COMMENTS & PHOTO REFERENCES
5226	Candlestick	163	4	4				
5227	Vase	276	3	7				
5228	Vase	276	4	1				
5229	Candlestick	163	4	5	$355	Rosaline/Alabaster	EAC-07/98	
5230	Vase	276	4	2				
5231	Tea Cup	216	2	11				
5232	Covered Vase	307	2	5				
5233	Plate	158	2	13				
6000	Auto Dome Light							See New Drawings section
6001	Auto Dome Light							See New Drawings section
6002	Auto Dome Light							See New Drawings section
6003	Auto Dome Light							See New Drawings section
6004	Auto Dome Light							See New Drawings section
6005	Auto Dome Light							See New Drawings section
6001	Candlestick	163	4	6	$65	Pomona Green/Colorless	ebay-02/04	Colorless stem
6001	Centerpiece	149	4	1				
6001	Compote	174	1	5				
6002	Candlestick	163	5	1	$325	French Blue	ebay-04/04	
6002	Centerpiece	149	4	2				
6002	Compote	173	1	6	$130	Topaz	ebay-08/02	
6002					$90	Topaz	ebay-08/02	
6003	Candlestick	163	5	2				
6003	Centerpiece	149	4	3	$1100	Blue Aurene	Ogal-10/00	
6003	Compote	174	1	7				
6004	Candlestick	163	5	3				
6004	Centerpiece	149	4	4				
6004	Compote	174	2	1				
6005	Candlestick	163	5	4				
6005	Centerpiece	149	4	5				
6005	Compote	174	2	2				
6006	Pitcher	214	1	1				This number is an error, see #6007.
6007	Pitcher	214	1	1				This is shown as 6006 in Gardner.
6007	Cup	199	4	1				This cup is part of set with 6007 Pitcher.
6008	Pitcher	214	1	2				
6009	Vase	276	4	3				
6010	Vase	276	4	4				
6011	Vase	276	4	5				
6012	Vase	276	4	6				
6013	Vase	276	5	1				
6014	Vase	276	5	2				
6015	Vase	276	5	3				
6016	Vase	276	5	4				
6017	Vase	276	5	5	$1590	Celeste Blue/Amethyst	ebay-12/03	Amethyst handles and foot, PG1)XV A,A
6018	Vase	277	1	1				
6019	Vase	277	1	2	$1925	Aurene/Yellow Jade ACB	EAC-07/95	
6020	Vase	277	1	3				
6021	Vase	277	1	4				
6022	Centerpiece	149	4	6	$400	Pomona Green/Topaz	JDJ-11/03	Topaz handles
6023	Cologne	241	4	5				
6024	Cologne	241	4	6	$2100	Rosa	ebay-04/01	RLG)159,295,L
6024					$2250	Selenium Red	ebay-10/03	
6025	Pitcher	214	1	3	$300	Amethyst/Celeste Blue	ebay-01/03	Celeste Blue handle
6025	Lemonade	214	1	3				
6026	Ice Tea				$240	VDS/Coral rim & threading	ebay-02/01	PG2)64,B; JAS)147,B,C:150,B,B;
6026					$360	Amethyst/Celeste Blue	ebay-01/03	TPD)10.45; MDK)58
6026					$160	Amethyst/Celeste Blue	ebay-02/03	
6026					$155	VDS/Coral rim & threading	ebay-05/03	
6026	Pitcher	214	1	4				
6026	Lemonade	214	1	4				
6027	Pitcher	214	1	5				
6028	Pitcher	214	2	1				
6029	Vase	277	1	5				
6030	Vase	277	2	1	$385	Gold Aurene	JDJ-10/94	PG1)XXX A,C:313; RFR)26,3,A;
6030					$1840	Oriental Poppy	Sknr-10/95	JAS)165,T,A; ACR)167,336; TPD)6.16
6030					$165	Pomona Green	JDJ-06/96	MDK)50
6030					$200	Bristol Yellow	Sknr-10/96	
6030					$275	Bristol Yellow	EAC-07/97	
6030					$115	Topaz	JDJ-10/97	
6030					$345	Amethyst (10")	Sknr-05/98	
6030					$330	Oriental Poppy	EAC-10/98	
6030					$525	Gold Ruby	ebay-11/99	
6030					$495	Spanish Green	ebay-11/99	

SHAPE NO.	ITEM	PAGE	COL	ROW	PRICE REALIZED	GLASS TYPE	AUCTION HOUSE	COMMENTS & PHOTO REFERENCES
6030					$435	Selenium Red	ebay-11/99	
6030					$660	Selenium Red 10"	ebay-12/99	
6030					$340	Selenium Red	ebay-12/00	
6030					$325	Wisteria	ebay-02/00	
6030					$195	Celeste Blue	ebay-02/00	
6030					$550	Black/White Cluthra	ebay-04/00	
6030					$400	Wisteria	ebay-04/00	
6030					$1975	Oriental Poppy	ebay-04/00	
6030					$240	Amethyst	ebay-04/00	
6030					$375	Green Jade	Sknr-06/00	
6030					$170	Bristol Yellow	Sknr-06/00	
6030					$325	Green Jade 10"	Tway-10/00	
6030					$180	Gold Ruby	ebay-12/00	
6030					$235	Pomona Green	ebay-01/01	
6030					$130	Pomona Green	ebay-03/01	
6030					$375	Blue-Green 10"	ebay-04/01	
6030					$130	Colorless/Threaded	ebay-05/01	
6030					$75	Bristol Yellow	ebay-08/01	
6030					$200	Pomona Green	ebay-09/01	
6030					$110	Colorless	ebay-12/01	
6030					$225	Spanish Green	ebay-12/01	
6030					$80	Topaz	ebay-12/01	
6030					$225	Wisteria	ebay-01/02	
6030					$205	Green Jade	ebay-01/02	
6030					$105	Pomona Green	ebay-01/02	
6030					$165	Bristol Yellow	ebay-02/02	
6030					$300	Bristol Yellow	ebay-02/02	
6030					$460	Spanish Green/Black	ebay-02/02	Black threading
6030					$310	Bristol Yellow 10"	ebay-03/02	
6030					$40	Colorless	ebay-05/02	
6030					$45	Colorless	ebay-05/02	
6030					$430	Selenium Red (10")	Jack-06/02	
6030					$180	Colorless 10"	ebay-07/02	
6030					$175	Bristol Yellow	ebay-09/02	
6030					$275	Gold Ruby	ebay-10/02	
6030					$80	Pomona Green	ebay-11/02	
6030					$100	Colorless draped	ebay-12/02	
6030					$235	Ivory (10")	Sknr-12/02	
6030					$160	Ivory	ebay-01/03	
6030					$170	Amethyst	Wint-03/03	
6030					$160	Gold Ruby	ebay-06/03	
6030					$190	Green Jade (10")	ebay-08/03	
6030					$400	Selenium Red	ebay-09/03	
6030					$835	Gold Aurene (10")	ebay-11/03	
6030					$230	Topaz	JDJ-11/03	
6030					$70	Topaz	ebay-12/03	
6030					$150	Colorless	ebay-12/03	
6030					$225	Pomona Green	ebay-01/04	
6030					$460	Yellow Cintra	ebay-01/04	
6030					$230	French Blue	ebay-01/04	
6030					$65	Topaz	ebay-02/04	
6030					$125	French Blue	ebay-03/04	
6030					$360	Gold Ruby 10"	ebay-03/04	
6030					$560	Colorless/Black threaded	ebay-03/04	
6030					$285	Bristol Yellow 10"	EAC-04/04	
6030					$120	Pomona Green	JDJ-05/04	
6030					$375	Pomona Green	ebay-05/04	
6030					$180	Green Jade	ebay-05/04	
6030					$200	Pomona Green	ebay-06/04	
6030					$225	Green Jade	ebay-06/04	
6030					$280	Green Jade	ebay-06/04	
6030					$115	Bristol Yellow	ebay-07/04	
6030					$161	Jade Green	ebay-07/04	
6030					$125	Bristol Yellow	ebay-10/04	
6030					$280	Topaz 10"	ebay-10/04	
6030					$110	Topaz	EAC-10/04	
6030					$125	Topaz	ebay-11/04	
6030					$280	Celeste Blue	ebay-11/04	
6030					$980	Blue Aurene (10")	JDJ-11/04	
6030					$125	French Blue	ebay-12/04	
6030					$150	Pomona Green (10")	ebay-02/05	
6030					$180	French Blue (10")	ebay-03/05	
6030					$210	Pomona Green	ebay-04/05	
6030					$50	Pomona Green	ebay-04/05	

SHAPE NO.	ITEM	PAGE	COL	ROW	PRICE REALIZED	GLASS TYPE	AUCTION HOUSE	COMMENTS & PHOTO REFERENCES
6030					$180	Pomona Green (10")	Cinc-06/05	
6030					$360	Gold Aurene	Cinc-06/05	
6030					$85	Pomona Green	ebay-06/05	
6031	Vase	277	2	2	$1090	Yellow Cintra	Sknr-10/94	PG1)XXX A,B; PG2)90,A; RFR,23,2,A;
6031					$605	Gold Aurene	JDJ-06/96	RFR)26,3,C; JAS)170,B,A; ACR)159,316
6031					$140	Topaz (10")	JDJ-06/96	ACR)COLOR 1,T,B; TPD)4.56
6031					$200	Amethyst	JDJ-10/96	
6031					$80	Pomona Green	JDJ-10/97	
6031					$860	Red/White Cluthra	JDJ-10/97	
6031					$70	Colorless/Blue threaded	JDJ-10/97	
6031					$745	Green/White Cluthra	JDJ-10/97	
6031					$575	Green Jade	Sknr-10/99	
6031					$210	Green Jade	ebay-10/99	
6031					$165	Topaz	Cinc-12/99	
6031					$2700	Oriental Poppy	ebay-12/99	
6031					$275	Pomona Green	ebay-12/99	
6031					$70	Topaz	ebay-01/00	
6031					$220	Topaz 10"	ebay-01/00	
6031					$1440	Green Cintra	JDJ-05/00	
6031					$320	Green Jade	ebay-10/00	
6031					$155	Bristol Yellow	ebay-10/00	
6031					$300	Bristol Yellow	Tway-10/00	
6031					$100	Topaz (10")	ebay-12/00	
6031					$365	Wisteria	ebay-04/01	
6031					$65	Topaz (10")	ebay-06/01	
6031					$750	Blue Aurene	ebay-06/01	
6031					$110	Topaz	ebay-07/01	
6031					$980	Blue Aurene	ebay-07/01	
6031					$485	Green Jade 10"	ebay-08/01	
6031					$70	Bristol Yellow	ebay-01/02	
6031					$600	Blue Aurene	ebay-03/02	
6031					$155	Pomona Green	ebay-03/02	
6031					$100	Pomona Green	ebay-03/02	
6031					$175	Pomona Green	ebay-04/02	
6031					$85	Pomona Green	ebay-05/02	
6031					$450	Selenium Red	ebay-06/02	
6031					$125	Colorless/Red threaded	Jack-06/02	
6031					$350	Green Jade	ebay-08/02	
6031					$160	Celeste Blue	ebay-08/02	
6031					$195	Green Jade	EAC-09/02	
6031					$110	Amethyst	EAC-09/02	
6031					$1495	Blue Aurene	ebay-10/02	
6031					$160	Ivory	ebay-11/02	
6031					$600	Gold Aurene	JDJ-11/02	
6031					$235	Selenium Red	Sknr-12/02	
6031					$100	Colorless/Red threaded	ebay-01/03	
6031					$125	Colorless/Red threaded	ebay-01/03	
6031					$545	Selenium Red	ebay-02/03	
6031					$750	Green Jade (10")	ebay-03/03	
6031					$925	Blue Aurene	ebay-03/03	
6031					$170	Gold Ruby	EAC-06/03	
6031					$265	Nile Green	ebay-07/03	
6031					$290	Green Jade	ebay-07/03	
6031					$275	French Blue/White	ebay-07/03	White threaded
6031					$415	Pomona Green	ebay-08/03	
6031					$1035	Yellow Cintra	ebay-09/03	
6031					$385	Pomona Green (E)	ebay-10/03	
6031					$30	Amber	ebay-11/03	
6031					$130	Colorless/Green threaded	ebay-11/03	
6031					$470	Selenium Red	ebay-11/03	
6031					$75	Pomona Green	JDJ-11/03	
6031					$720	Blue Aurene	JDJ-11/03	
6031					$50	Pomona Green	ebay-11/03	
6031					$5750	Green Florentia	EAC-11/03	
6031					$210	Bristol Yellow	ebay-04/04	
6031					$225	Green Jade	ebay-04/04	
6031					$1525	Green Cintra 10"	ebay-04/04	
6031					$90	Bristol Yellow 10"	ebay-05/04	
6031					$160	Bristol Yellow	ebay-05/04	
6031					$785	Blue Aurene	ebay-05/04	
6031					$105	Topaz	ebay-07/04	
6031					$950	Yellow Cintra	EAC-07/04	
6031					$130	Topaz 10"	ebay-07/04	
6031					$80	Bristol Yellow	ebay-10/04	

SHAPE NO.	ITEM	PAGE	COL	ROW	PRICE REALIZED	GLASS TYPE	AUCTION HOUSE	COMMENTS & PHOTO REFERENCES
6031					$125	Bristol Yellow	ebay-11/04	
6031					$50	Colorless/Blue threaded	ebay-11/04	
6031					$1020	Red Cintra	Wesr-12/04	
6031					$250	Bristol Yellow	ebay-12/04	
6031					$50	Topaz	ebay-12/04	
6031					$90	Bristol Yellow	ebay-12/04	
6031					$150	Colorless/Black threaded	ebay-01/05	
6031					$230	Green Jade	ebay-03/05	
6031					$130	French Blue	ebay-03/05	
6031					$100	Bristol Yellow	ebay-04/05	
6031					$125	Amber	ebay-05/05	
6031					$90	Pomona Green	ebay-05/05	
6031					$125	Bristol Yellow 10"	ebay-05/05	
6031					$630	Rose Cintra	JDJ-06/05	
6031					$125	Pomona Green	ebay-06/05	
6031					$75	Pomona Green	ebay-06/05	
6031					$80	Topaz 10"	ebay-06/05	
6031					$145	VDS/Gold Ruby threading	EAC-07/05	
6032	Vase	277	2	3	$300	Bristol Yellow	ebay-06/04	
6033	Vase	277	2	4	$400	Topaz/Mica	Sknr-10/96	
6033					$150	Spanish Green	JDJ-11/02	
6034	Vase	277	2	5	$245	Bristol Yel./Black thread.	EAC-04/93	PG1)XXV C,B:313;RFR)18,4,A&C:27,3,B
6034					$1100	Iridescent Green Jade	EAC-10/93	RLG)136,260:146,277;ACR)147,282
6034					$1320	Rosaline/Alabaster ACB	EAC-04/96	ACR)150,289;TPD)2.44:7.40:8.49
6034					$1955	Blue Aurene	Sknr-05/96	
6034					$1380	Gold Aurene	Sknr-10/97	
6034					$920	Selenium Red	Sknr-05/97	
6034					$1650	Iridescent Green Jade	EAC-10/98	
6034					$1375	Green Jade/Alabaster	EAC-04/98	
6034					$1475	Blue Aurene	ebay-02/00	
6034					$750	Rosaline/Alabaster	ebay-03/00	
6034					$1035	Rosaline/Alabaster ACB	Sknr-06/00	Etched "Floral"
6034					$2475	Blue Aurene	EAC-08/00	
6034					$650	Selenium Red	Tway-10/00	
6034					$1200	Gold Aurene	Tway-10/00	
6034					$230	Pomona Green/Topaz	ebay-04/01	
6034					$770	Selenium Red	Cott-08/01	
6034					$300	Bristol Yellow	ebay-10/01	
6034					$750	Selenium Red (E)	ebay-01/02	Engraved "Grapes"
6034					$1900	Blue Aurene	Tway-03/02	
6034					$165	Pomona Green	ebay-05/02	
6034					$160	Pomona Green/Topaz foot	ebay-07/02	
6034					$250	Pomona Green/Topaz foot	ebay-09/02	
6034					$265	French Blue	EAC-09/02	
6034					$150	Pomona Green/Topaz foot	ebay-10/02	
6034					$315	Gold Ruby/Colorless foot	ebay-10/02	
6034					$170	Pomona Green/Topaz foot	ebay-11/02	
6034					$1200	Gold Aurene	Tway-12/02	
6034					$1200	Gold Aurene	Tway-12/02	
6034					$2065	Iridescent Green Jade	ebay-05/03	Gold Aurene threading
6034					$1725	Gold Aurene	JDJ-05/03	
6034					$1380	Green Jade/Alabaster ACB	Jack-06/03	Etched "Matzu"
6034					$8625	Amethyst/Alabaster ACB	EAC-11/03	Etched "Bird #2"
6034					$400	VDS/Green threaded	ebay-12/03	
6034					$990	Green Jade/Alabaster ACB	ebay-03/04	Etched "Fircone"
6034					$1265	Green Jade/Alabaster ACB	ebay-11/04	Etched "Fircone"
6034					$1560	Green Jade/Alabaster ACB	Wesr-12/04	Etched "Fircone"
6034					$200	Pomona Green/Topaz foot	ebay-06/05	
6034					$410	Selenium Red (E)	ebay-07/05	Engraved "Grapes"
6035	Vase	277	3	1				
6036	Vase	277	3	2				
6037	Candlestick	163	5	5				
6037	Centerpiece	149	4	7				
6037	Compote	174	2	3				
6038	Vase	277	3	3				
6039	Vase	277	3	4				
6040	Vase	277	3	5				
6041	Vase	277	4	1				
6042	Vase	277	4	2				
6043	Candlestick	164	1	1	$230	Rosa/Pomona Green stem	ebay-12/99	
6043					$240	Topaz/Pomona Green	ebay-11/00	
6043					$1435	Amethyst/Celeste Blue	EAC-07/05	Celeste Blue stem
6043	Centerpiece	149	4	8	$690	Selenium Red	Sknr-01/97	
6043					$375	Amethyst	EAC-04/05	

SHAPE NO.	ITEM	PAGE	COL	ROW	PRICE REALIZED	GLASS TYPE	AUCTION HOUSE	COMMENTS & PHOTO REFERENCES
6043	Compote	174	2	4	$355	Green Jade	EAC-07/97	MDK)15
6043					$415	Selenium Red	ebay-11/99	
6043					$300	Bristol Yellow	ebay-03/00	
6043					$80	Topaz	ebay-01/01	
6043					$440	Green Jade/Alabaster	Cott-08/01	
6043					$145	Amethyst	Jack-09/01	
6043					$300	Amethyst	ebay-10/01	
6043					$160	Bristol Yellow	ebay-03/02	
6043					$260	Amethyst	EAC-06/03	
6043					$135	Pomona Green	ebay-07/03	
6043					$130	Pomona Green	ebay-01/05	
6043					$330	Gold Ruby/Colorless stem	ebay-05/05	
6044	Candlestick	164	1	2	$225	Topaz	ebay-12/01	TPD)7.52
6044					$410	Topaz/Celeste Blue stem	ebay-08/04	
6044					$405	Pomona Green/Topaz stem	ebay-02/05	
6044					$380	Topaz/Pomona Green stem	ebay-07/05	
6044	Centerpiece	149	4	9	$285	Celeste Blue	Sknr-10/97	TPD)7.52
6044					$105	Pomona Green	ebay-11/04	
6044					$575	Celeste Blue/Amethyst foot	EAC-07/05	
6044	Compote	174	2	5	$430	Topaz/Pomona Green	Sknr-01/98	TPD)7.52
6044					$285	Topaz/Pomona Green	ebay-05/00	
6044					$390	Amethyst/Celeste	ebay-10/00	
6044					$185	Topaz/Celeste Blue	ebay-05/01	
6044					$595	Amethyst/Celeste stem	ebay-02/04	
6044					$190	Topaz/Pomona Green stem	ebay-03/05	
6045	Candlestick	164	1	3	$455	Topaz/Celeste Blue	EAC-10/93	Celeste mica flecked stem
6045					$690	Topaz/Celeste Blue	Sknr-05/96	
6045					$345	Topaz/Pomona Green	Sknr-10/95	
6045					$630	Topaz/Celeste Blue	EAC-10/98	
6045					$305	Topaz/Pomona Green	ebay-12/99	
6045					$700	Topaz/Pomona Green stem	ebay-06/02	Mica Fleck stem
6045					$200	Topaz/Pomona Green stem	ebay-11/02	
6045					$305	Pomona Green/Topaz stem	ebay-01/03	
6045					$315	Topaz/Celeste Blue stem	ebay-01/04	
6045					$620	Rosa/Mica Flecked Stem	ebay-07/04	Colorless mica flecked stem
6045	Centerpiece	150	1	1	$185	Topaz/Celeste Blue foot	ebay-01/04	
6045	Compote	174	2	6	$230	Topaz/Pomona Green	ebay-01/02	
6046	Candlestick	164	1	4	$550	Colorless/Pomona Green	EAC-07/98	TPD)10.31
6046					$400	Topaz/Celeste Blue stem	ebay-01/02	
6046					$515	Colorless/Pomona Green	ebay-05/03	Colorless mica flecked stem
6046	Centerpiece	150	1	2	$215	Pomona Green/Topaz foot	ebay-06/04	Mica flecked foot
6046	Compote	174	3	1				TPD)10.31
6047	Cologne	241	5	1				RFR)8,4,B;ACR)131,235;TPD)8.7
6048	Cologne	241	5	2	$2750	Bristol Yellow	JDJ-10/95	PG1)XV A,E; RFR)16,3,E;
6048					$2915	Opal	EAC-07/97	RLG)159,295,R; TPD)8.15
6048					$2500	Selenium Red	ebay-03/01	
6048					$1955	Bristol Yellow	JDJ-11/03	
6049	Cologne	241	5	3	$1650	Rosa	ebay-02/00	
6049					$1500	Colorless	ebay-03/01	
6050	Centerpiece	150	1	3	$225	Celeste Blue	ebay-02/02	
6050					$50	Pomona Green	ebay-01/05	
6051	Plate	159	1	9				
6052	Goblet	192	1	1				Shape discarded, replaced by 6062.
6053	Vase	277	4	3	$440	Blue Aurene	EAC-02/92	
6053					$85	Bristol Yellow	ebay-12/00	
6053					$535	Wisteria	ebay-03/01	
6053					$250	Green Jade	ebay-06/02	
6053					$405	Colorless Silverina	ebay-11/02	
6053					$95	Bristol Yellow	ebay-02/03	
6053					$25	Topaz	ebay-06/04	
6053					$205	Colorless (E)	ebay-08/04	Engraved "Marguerite"
6053					$535	Bristol Yellow Silverina	ebay-05/05	
6053					$540	Colorless Silverina	JDJ-06/05	
6054	Vase	277	4	4,5	$220	Pomona Green/Topaz	EAC-10/98	
6054					$200	Pomona Green	ebay-02/00	
6054					$150	Pomona Green/Topaz	ebay-01/01	
6055	Vase	277	5	1				
6056	Vase	277	5	2				
6057	Candlestick	164	2	1				
6057	Centerpiece	150	1	4				
6057	Compote	174	3	2				
6058	Candlestick	164	2	2	$515	Topaz/Pomona Green	Sknr-10/95	PG2)59; ACR)150,293; TPD)5.6:5.8
6058					$1495	Celeste/Topaz stem	JDJ-05/02	
6058					$3240	Gold Aurene	JDJ-11/02	

SHAPE NO.	ITEM	PAGE	COL	ROW	PRICE REALIZED	GLASS TYPE	AUCTION HOUSE	COMMENTS & PHOTO REFERENCES
6058					$5175	Gold Aurene	EAC-04/04	
6058	Centerpiece	150	1	5	$1450	Blue Aurene	ebay-05/01	
6058					$1435	Blue Aurene	JDJ-05/01	
6058					$2400	Blue Aurene	ebay-03/02	
6058					$1600	Blue Aurene	ebay-01/03	
6058	Compote	174	3	3				PG1)44,78
6059	Candlestick	164	2	3				
6059	Centerpiece	150	1	6				TPD)5.6
6059	Compote	174	3	4				
6060	Vase	277	5	3				
6061	Shade	226	3	3				
6062	Goblet	192	1	2	$550	Amethyst/Celeste Blue	ebay-10/99	MDK)41
6062					$215	Amethyst/Celeste Blue	ebay-11/99	
6063	Candlestick	164	2	4				PG1)114,182
6063	Centerpiece	150	1	7				
6063	Compote	174	3	5				PG1)43,77; TPD)8.15
6064	Candlestick	164	3	1				
6064	Centerpiece	150	1	8				
6064	Compote	174	3	6				
6065	Lamp Vase	202	3	3				
6066	Aquarium	304	3	1				
6067	Goblet	192	1	3				
6068	Ice Tub	177	4	6				
6069	Lamp Spindle	207	5	4				
6070	Vase	277	5	4				Listed as a tumbler in factory records.
6070					$205	Green cased over Colorless	ebay-07/04	Engraved "Thistle"
6071	Lamp Spindle	207	5	5				
6072	Vase	278	1	1				
6073	Goblet	192	1	4				
6074	Goblet	192	1	5				
6075	Puff Box	244	5	6	$385	Colorless	ebay-12/99	
6076	Puff Box	244	5	7				
6077	Puff Box	244	5	8	$1600	Topaz (mica-flecked)	ebay-01/00	
6078	Vase	278	1	2	$1705	Black/Alabaster ACB	EAC-04/90	Etched "Sea Holly" PG1)116,186,E:313;
6078					$2750	Plum Jade ACB	EAC-07/90	Etched "Lotus" RFR)19,3,A&C;
6078					$825	Green Jade/Alabaster ACB	EAC-10/90	Etched "Matzu" ACR)162,323; TPD)10.34
6078					$1100	Rose Quartz ACB	EAC-04/91	
6078					$660	Green Jade ACB	EAC-07/91	
6078					$1785	Rose Quartz ACB	EAC-04/92	
6078					$1100	Blue/Alabaster ACB	EAC-03/93	Etched "Sherwood"
6078					$2475	Plum Jade ACB	EAC-04/95	
6078					$605	Green Jade ACB	EAC-04/95	
6078					$1265	Black/Alabaster ACB	Sknr-10/95	
6078					$1430	Rose Quartz	EAC-10/95	
6078					$575	Green Jade/Alabaster ACB	Sknr-01/96	
6078					$975	Green Jade/Alabaster ACB	Sknr-01/96	
6078					$1375	Green Jade/Alabaster ACB	EAC-04/96	
6078					$975	LBJ/Flint White ACB	Sknr-01/97	
6078					$980	Green Jade/Alabaster ACB	Sknr-01/97	
6078					$1035	Green Jade/Alabaster ACB	Sknr-01/97	
6078					$1155	Green Jade/Alabaster ACB	EAC-04/97	
6078					$2915	Amethyst Quartz	EAC-07/97	
6078					$1595	Green Jade/Alabaster ACB	EAC-10/97	
6078					$1035	Green Jade ACB	Sknr-10/97	
6078					$1610	Rosaline/Alabaster ACB	Sknr-01/98	
6078					$1265	Green Jade ACB	Sknr-01/98	
6078					$1035	Green Jade/Alabaster ACB	Sknr-05/98	
6078					$715	Green Jade/Alabaster ACB	EAC-10/98	
6078					$990	Blue Aurene	EAC-10/98	
6078					$1715	Green Jade ACB	ebay-02/00	Etched "Sculptured"
6078					$2150	Rose Quartz	ebay-02/00	
6078					$1010	Rosaline/Alabaster ACB	ebay-04/00	Etched "Fircone"
6078					$2035	Green Jade/Alabaster ACB	EAC-08/00	
6078					$760	Rosaline/Alabaster ACB	ebay-11/00	Etched "Floral"
6078					$4310	Plum Jade ACB	Sknr-10/00	
6078					$1725	Rosaline/Alabaster ACB	Sknr-02/01	Etched "Floral"
6078					$3450	Green Jade/Alabaster ACB	Sknr-02/01	Etched "Lotus"
6078					$1000	Green Jade/Alabaster ACB	ebay-06/01	Etched "Fircone"
6078					$875	Green Jade/Alabaster ACB	ebay-07/01	Etched "Matzu"
6078					$1905	Amethyst/Alabaster ACB	ebay-10/01	Etched "Fircone"
6078					$1100	Rosaline/Alabaster ACB	ebay-10/01	Etched "Floral"
6078					$1625	Green Jade/Alabaster ACB	EAC-11/01	
6078					$1680	Green Jade/Alabaster ACB	EAC-11/01	
6078					$2750	Green Jade/Alabaster ACB	Cott-02/02	Etched "Matzu"

SHAPE NO.	ITEM	PAGE	COL	ROW	PRICE REALIZED	GLASS TYPE	AUCTION HOUSE	COMMENTS & PHOTO REFERENCES
6078					$1450	Green Jade/Alabaster ACB	ebay-03/02	Etched "Fircone"
6078					$985	Green Jade/Alabaster ACB	ebay-03/02	Etched "Fircone"
6078					$1345	Green Jade/Alabaster ACB	EAC-04/02	Etched "Matzu"
6078					$5490	Gold Aurene/Black ACB	ebay-05/02	Etched "Thistle"
6078					$1700	Rosaline/Alabaster ACB	ebay-09/02	Etched "Fircone"
6078					$1455	Green Jade/Alabaster ACB	EAC-09/02	Etched "Matzu"
6078					$1010	Green Jade/Alabaster ACB	EAC-09/02	Etched "Matzu"
6078					$1250	Green Jade/Alabaster ACB	ebay-11/02	Etched "Matzu"
6078					$1560	Rosaline/Alabaster ACB	JDJ-11/02	Etched "Floral"
6078					$1295	Green Jade/Alabaster ACB	Sknr-12/02	Etched "Matzu"
6078					$2800	Plum Jade ACB	EAC-01/03	Etched "Lotus"
6078					$2910	Rose Quartz ACB	EAC-01/03	
6078					$3135	Mirror Black/Alabaster ACB	EAC-01/03	Etched "Nedra"
6078					$1100	Green Jade/Alabaster ACB	Cinc-06/03	Etched "Matzu"
6078					$1610	Green Jade/Alabaster ACB	Jack-06/03	Etched "Matzu"
6078					$600	Green Jade/Alabaster ACB	ebay-10/03	Etched "Matzu"
6078					$1300	Rosaline/Alabaster ACB	JDJ-11/03	Etched "Floral"
6078					$1150	Green Jade ACB	EAC-11/03	Etched "Carved"
6078					$900	Green Jade/Alabaster ACB	ebay-12/03	Etched "Matzu"
6078					$960	Rosaline/Alabaster ACB	ebay-01/04	Etched "Matzu"
6078					$1775	Rosaline/Alabaster ACB	ebay-03/04	Etched "Nedra"
6078					$2285	Mirror Black/Alabaster ACB	ebay-03/04	Etched "Sea Holly"
6078					$175	Green Jade	ebay-03/04	
6078					$950	Green Jade/Alabaster ACB	ebay-03/04	Etched "Matzu"
6078					$620	Green Jade	ebay-04/04	
6078					$1200	Rosaline/Alabaster ACB	ebay-04/04	Etched "Matzu"
6078					$825	Rosaline	ebay-05/04	
6078					$995	Green Jade/Alabaster ACB	ebay-05/04	Etched "Marlene"
6078					$675	Green Jade/Alabaster ACB	ebay-07/04	Etched "Floral"
6078					$870	Green Jade/Alabaster ACB	ebay-08/04	Etched "Matzu"
6078					$800	Green Jade/Alabaster ACB	ebay-11/04	Etched "Matzu"
6078					$1680	Green Jade/Alabaster ACB	Wesr-12/04	Etched "Lotus"
6078					$1020	Rosaline/Alabaster ACB	Crft-01/05	Etched "Floral"
6078					$690	Green Jade/Alabaster ACB	Hrtg-03/05	Etched "Matzu"
6078					$660	Green Jade/Alabaster ACB	ebay-05/05	Etched "Matzu"
6078					$540	Rosaline/Alabaster ACB	Sknr-06/05	Etched "Floral"
6078					$1150	Rosaline/Alabaster ACB	EAC-07/05	Etched "Nedra"
6079	Cocktail	197	4	7				
6080	Goblet	192	1	6				
6081	Centerpiece	150	2	1	$400	Pomona Green/Topaz	ebay-03/05	PG1)108,171,B; PG2)85,A; JAS)149,BR,A
6082	Lamp Spindle	207	6	1				
6083	Lamp Spindle	207	6	2				
6084	Lamp Spindle	207	6	3				
6085	Lamp Spindle	207	6	4				
6086	Vase	278	1	3				
6087	Goblet	192	1	7				
6088	Lamp Spindle	207	6	5				TPD)4.100
6089	Lamp Spindle	207	6	6				
6090	Lamp Base	203	1	1				
6091	Lamp Base	203	1	2				
6092	Lamp Base	203	1	3				
6093	Ash Tray	137	4	1				
6094	Vase	278	1	4				PG1)115,183;RLG)150,283:151,285;
6094								ACR)COLOR 1,B,B:163,325:163,226;
6094								TPD)5.34:10.35
6094					$6325	Yellow Jade ACB	Sknr-05/96	
6094					$4070	Gold Aurene/Calcite ACB	Cinc-12/99	Etched "Ophelia" lamp with fittings
6094					$2585	Black over Yel. Jade ACB	JDJ-11/01	Etched "Dragon"
6094					$2750	Gold Aurene/Black ACB	ebay-09/02	Drilled to be a lamp.
6094					$7840	Bl. Aurene/Yel. Jade ACB	EAC-09/02	Etched "Bird #2"
6094					$2745	Gold Aurene/Alab. ACB	EAC-01/03	Lamp Etched "Ophelia"
6094					$3100	Gold Aur./Yel. Jade ACB	ebay-02/03	Etched "Dragon"
6094					$1100	Green Jade ACB	JDJ-06/05	Drilled to be a lamp.
6095	Vase	278	1	5				PG1)XXVI A,B
6096	Candlestick	164	3	2	$390	Amber	EAC-04/01	TPD)7.63
6096	Centerpiece	150	2	2	$225	Amber	EAC-04/01	TPD)7.63
6096					$675	Amber	ebay-06/03	
6096	Compote	174	4	1				
6097	Vase	278	2	1				RFR)19,4,A&C
6097					$2240	Black/Amethyst Cintra ACB	EAC-09/02	Etched "Pagoda" lamp with fittings.
6097					$2500	Black/Amethyst Cintra ACB	ebay-07/03	Etched "Pagoda" lamp with fittings.
6097					$1380	Black/Yellow Jade ACB	JDJ-11/03	Etched "Pagoda" lamp with fittings.
6097					$5400	Black/Amethyst Cintra ACB	Cinc-06/04	Etched "Pagoda" lamp with fittings.
6098	Vase	278	2	2	$2420	Blue Moss Agate Lamp	EAC-10/93	PG1)XXXI,B; RFR)25,3,C:31,4,B;

SHAPE NO.	ITEM	PAGE	COL	ROW	PRICE REALIZED	GLASS TYPE	AUCTION HOUSE	COMMENTS & PHOTO REFERENCES
6098								ACR)171,349
6099	Vase							See New Drawings section
6100	Vase	278	2	3				
6101	Vase	278	2	4				
6102	Shade	229	3	1				
6103	Ash Tray	137	4	2				
6104	Ash Tray	137	4	3				
6105	Covered Vase	307	2	6	$260	Bristol Yellow/Pomona	Sknr-06/00	
6105					$360	Topaz/Pomona trim	ebay-06/04	Pomona Green foot and finial
6106	Centerpiece	150	2	3	$385	Gold Aurene	EAC-04/93	RFR)14,3,B; MDK)54
6106					$300	Celeste Blue	ebay-12/99	
6106					$155	Pomona Green	ebay-12/00	
6106					$230	Green Jade	Sknr-02/01	
6106					$200	Sea Green	Sknr-02/01	
6106					$200	Pomona Green	ebay-04/01	
6106					$190	Topaz	ebay-06/01	
6106					$110	Bristol Yellow	ebay-07/01	
6106					$90	Bristol Yellow	ebay-11/01	
6106					$325	Pomona Green	ebay-04/02	
6106					$115	Bristol Yellow	Jack-06/02	
6106					$130	Topaz	ebay-06/02	
6106					$45	Pomona Green	ebay-06/02	
6106					$85	Bristol Yellow	ebay-06/02	
6106					$75	Celeste Blue	ebay-02/03	
6106					$100	Topaz	ebay-06/03	
6106					$80	Pomona Green	ebay-06/03	
6106					$195	Pomona Green	ebay-10/03	
6106					$200	French Blue	ebay-10/03	
6106					$105	Topaz	ebay-01/04	
6106					$75	Topaz	ebay-03/04	
6106					$140	Pomona Green	ebay-05/04	
6106					$450	Gold Aurene	ebay-05/04	
6106					$745	Gold Aurene	JDJ-05/04	
6106					$400	Green Jade	ebay-05/04	
6106					$135	Pomona Green	ebay-07/04	
6106					$65	Pomona Green	ebay-10/04	
6106					$130	Topaz	ebay-02/05	
6106					$130	French Blue	ebay-05/05	
6107	Candlestick	164	3	3	$355	Amethyst	ebay-11/01	
6107					$725	Royal Purple/Celeste Blue	ebay-01/05	Celeste Blue stem
6107	Compote	174	4	2	$350	Celeste Blue/Topaz	ebay-03/01	
6107					$765	Amethyst/Celeste stem	ebay-09/02	
6108	Centerpiece	150	2	4				
6109	Candlestick	164	3	4	$105	Pomona Green/Colorless	ebay-06/05	Colorless stem
6109	Compote	174	4	3	$805	Celeste/Rosa mica stem	Rago-09/00	RFR)16,2,C; ACR)152,300; TPD)10.33
6109					$450	Pomona/Rosa mica stem	ebay-02/03	
6110	Candlestick	164	4	1	$225	Green Jade	EAC-10/91	TPD)4.36
6110					$290	Spanish Green	Sknr-05/95	
6110					$315	Topaz	Sknr-05/95	
6110					$130	Topaz	ebay-03/00	
6110					$260	Celeste Blue	ebay-01/01	
6110					$225	Bristol Yellow	ebay-02/02	
6110					$250	Colorless/Topaz stem	ebay-09/02	
6110					$315	Topaz/Pomona stem	EAC-11/03	
6110					$1650	Gold Aurene	ebay-11/04	18"
6110	Compote	174	4	4	$355	Pomona Green/Topaz	EAC-07/98	MDK)33
6110					$560	Gold Ruby	ebay-11/99	
6110					$220	Pomona Green	ebay-10/03	
6110					$285	Green shaded/Colorless	JDJ-11/03	Colorless stem
6111	Plate	159	1	10	$540	Flemish Blue	ebay-11/99	
6112	Vase	278	2	5	$4950	Plum Jade ACB "Chang"	EAC-10/90	PG1)313
6112					$1725	Light Blue Jade	Sknr-10/95	
6112					$2950	Plum Jade ACB "Chang"	ebay-11/02	
6112					$670	Red/White Cluthra	EAC-07/04	
6112					$495	Yellow Jade	EAC-10/04	
6113	Goblet	192	2	1				
6114	Fingerbowl				$470	Gold Ruby/Colorless (E)	ebay-07/04	Engraved "Thistle"
6114	Goblet	192	2	2				PG1)XXII B,I:84,123; MDK)143
6114	Cordial				$150	Celeste/Topaz	ebay-12/99	
6114					$200	Gold Ruby/Colorless (E)	ebay-02/00	Engraved "Thistle"
6114					$285	Gold Ruby/Colorless (E)	ebay-01/01	Engraved "Thistle"
6114					$280	Gold Ruby/Colorless (E)	ebay-08/01	Engraved "Thistle"
6115	Goblet	192	2	3	$190	Bristol Yellow	ebay-05/01	
6116	Goblet	192	2	4				

SHAPE NO.	ITEM	PAGE	COL	ROW	PRICE REALIZED	GLASS TYPE	AUCTION HOUSE	COMMENTS & PHOTO REFERENCES
6117	Vase	278	3	1				
6118	Bowl	144	1	10	$170	Citron Yellow	Sknr-10/95	PG1)69,105
6118					$175	Bristol Yellow	Sknr-01/96	
6118					$230	Colorless/Blue threaded	Sknr-06/00	
6118					$175	VDS threaded	EAC-08/00	
6118					$140	French Blue	EAC-09/01	
6118					$95	Topaz	ebay-06/02	
6118					$175	Topaz	ebay-04/03	
6118					$125	Spanish Green	ebay-09/03	
6118					$1200	Gold Aurene	ebay-12/03	With Gold Aurene threading
6119	Vase	278	3	2	$275	Amethyst/Celeste Blue	Sknr-10/94	PG1)108,117,A&C; TPD)10.33; MDK)79
6119					$285	Green Jade/Alabaster	JDJ-10/96	
6119					$185	Bristol Yellow/Pomona	ebay-03/01	
6119					$200	Pomona Green	ebay-03/01	
6119					$210	Pomona Green/Topaz foot	ebay-01/02	
6119					$80	Pomona Green/Topaz foot	ebay-05/02	
6119					$215	Pomona Green/Topaz foot	ebay-10/02	
6119					$270	Pomona Green/Topaz foot	JDJ-11/02	
6119					$300	Rosaline/Alabaster	JDJ-05/03	
6119					$125	Pomona Green/Topaz foot	ebay-10/03	
6119					$130	Colorless/Topaz foot	ebay-11/03	
6119					$170	Topaz/Celeste Blue foot	ebay-12/03	
6119					$290	Colorless/Flemish Blue foot	EAC-04/04	
6119					$280	Green Jade/Alabaster foot	ebay-11/04	
6119					$170	Pomona Green/Topaz foot	ebay-04/05	
6119					$315	Pomona Green/Topaz foot	EAC-04/05	
6119					$500	Rosaline/Alabaster foot	ebay-07/05	
6120	Vase	278	3	3				
6121	Goblet	192	2	5				
6122	Shade	229	3	2				
6123	Vase	278	3	4	$100	French Blue	ebay-04/02	PG1)313
6123					$100	Bristol Yellow	ebay-12/04	
6123					$100	Topaz	ebay-01/05	
6124	Ash Tray	137	4	4				
6125	Goblet	192	2	6				
6126	Goblet	192	2	7				PG1)313
6127	Ash Tray	137	4	5				
6128	Shade	226	3	4				
6129	Ash Tray	137	4	6				
6130	Goblet	197	4	8				
6131	Goblet	192	3	1	$75	Topaz/Celeste stem & foot	ebay-04/02	
6131					$175	Topaz/Celeste stem & foot	ebay-06/02	
6132	Goblet	192	3	2	$320	Selenium Red/Colorless	ebay-10/00	
6132					$285	Selenium Red/Colorless	ebay-08/01	
6133	Goblet	197	5	1				
6134	Goblet	192	3	3				MDK)112
6135	Atomizer	239	1	1				
6136	Atomizer	239	1	2	$440	Gold Aurene	EAC-04/90	With fittings; TPD)4.2:4.3
6136					$410	Gold Aurene	EAC-10/91	With fittings
6136					$520	Blue Aurene	EAC-10/91	With fittings
6136					$410	Gold Aurene	EAC-02/92	Perfume with stopper
6136					$220	Gold Aurene	EAC-04/93	With fittings
6136					$880	Blue Aurene	EAC-04/99	
6136					$490	Gold Aurene	Sknr-10/99	With fittings
6136					$750	Gold Aurene	Ogal-01/01	With fittings
6136					$400	Gold Aurene	Jack-06/02	No fittings
6136					$510	Gold Aurene	ebay-09/02	With fittings
6136					$330	Gold Aurene	ebay-10/02	With fittings
6136					$400	Gold Aurene	ebay-10/02	With fittings
6136					$355	Gold Aurene	ebay-11/02	With fittings
6136					$360	Blue Aurene	ebay-12/02	Cap for glass only
6136					$175	Blue Aurene	ebay-01/03	Cap for glass only
6136					$705	Blue Aurene	ebay-01/03	With fittings
6136					$575	Gold Aurene	Jack-06/03	With fittings and stopper
6136					$210	Gold Aurene	ebay-08/03	Glass only
6136					$330	Gold Aurene	ebay-11/03	No bulb
6136					$250	Blue Aurene	ebay-11/03	With fittings
6136					$950	Gold Aurene	JDJ-11/03	Salt and Pepper Pair
6136					$450	Blue Aurene	ebay-01/04	With fittings
6136					$405	Gold Aurene	ebay-02/04	With fittings
6136					$480	Blue Aurene	ebay-03/04	
6136					$305	Blue Aurene	ebay-05/04	Glass only
6136					$450	Blue Aurene	ebay-06/05	With fittings
6136					$425	Blue Aurene	ebay-07/04	With fittings

SHAPE NO.	ITEM	PAGE	COL	ROW	PRICE REALIZED	GLASS TYPE	AUCTION HOUSE	COMMENTS & PHOTO REFERENCES
6136					$335	Gold Aurene	ebay-10/04	With fittings
6136					$350	Blue Aurene	ebay-11/04	With fittings
6136					$915	Gold Aurene	ebay-11/04	Perfume with stopper
6136					$615	Blue Aurene	ebay-04/05	With fittings
6136					$375	Gold Aurene	EAC-04/05	With fittings
6136					$315	Gold Aurene	EAC-04/05	No bulb
6136					$450	Gold Aurene	ebay-05/05	With fittings
6136					$405	Blue Aurene	ebay-05/05	With fittings
6136					$380	Gold Aurene	ebay-05/05	Perfume with stopper
6137	Atomizer	239	1	3				
6138	Atomizer	239	1	4				
6139	Sugar & Creamer	235	5	11,12	$410	Pomona Green/Topaz	EAC-04/95	PG1)XXII B,A&B
6140	Sugar & Creamer	235	6	1,2				
6141	Sugar & Creamer	235	6	3,4	$275	Topaz/Celeste Blue	EAC-10/04	Celeste Blue handles
6142	Sugar & Creamer	235	6	5,6				TPD)10.132
6143	Sugar & Creamer	235	6	7,8				
6144	Vase	278	3	5				
6145	Vase	278	3	6				
6146	Vase	278	3	7	$1500	Gold Aurene/Black ACB	ebay-06/03	
6147	Vase	278	4	1				PG1)113,175
6148	Vase	278	4	2	$1650	Rosaline/Alabaster ACB	EAC-04/92	Etched "Bird"
6148					$1840	Rosaline/Alabaster ACB	Sknr-01/96	PG1)114,179;RFR)18,1,A&C; RFR)31,3,A
6148					$2695	Rosaline/Alabaster ACB	EAC-10/98	
6149	Vase	278	4	3	$715	Green Jade/Alabaster ACB	EAC-04/93	Lamp Etched "Bird #2"
6150	Vase	278	4	4				
6151	Vase	278	4	5				
6152	Vase	278	5	1				PG1)XXXI A
6153	Vase	278	5	2	$350	Topaz	ebay-05/00	
6153					$265	Rosa	ebay-06/05	
6154	Bowl	144	1	11	$345	Rosa/Pomona Green	Sknr-01/96	
6154	Candlestick	164	4	2	$745	Rosa/Pomona Green	ebay-09/03	PG1)XIX B,A&C; RFR)16,3,D; TPD)10.20
6154	Centerpiece	150	2	5	$300	Topaz/Pomona Green	ebay-07/01	PG1)XIX B,B
6154	Compote	174	4	5				TPD)10.20
6155	Vase	278	5	3				
6156	Vase	278	5	4				
6157	Bowl	144	2	1				
6158	Covered Vase	307	3	1				
6159	Covered Vase	307	3	2				
6160	Centerpiece	150	2	6				
6161	Covered Vase	307	3	3	$355	Topaz/Pomona Green	ebay-03/01	
6162	Bowl	144	2	2				
6163	Puff Box	244	5	11				
6164	Cologne	241	5	4				
6165	Vase	279	1	1	$880	Blue Aurene	EAC-07/95	
6165					$790	Blue Aurene	ebay-04/04	
6165					$450	Blue Aurene	ebay-05/04	
6165					$750	Blue Aurene	ebay-08/04	
6165					$920	Blue Aurene	EAC-04/05	
6166	Parfait	197	6	3	$75	Pomona Green/Topaz foot	ebay-02/05	RFR)16,1,A; ACR)COLOR 4,B,E
6167	Parfait	197	6	4				
6168	Cologne	241	5	5				
6169	Centerpiece	150	3	1	$515	Black/White Cluthra	JDJ-05/99	
6169					$745	White Cluthra	Sknr-02/01	
6170	Bowl	144	2	3	$770	Green Jade ACB	ebay-02/00	Etched "Grape"
6170					$115	Pomona Green	ebay-11/01	
6170					$230	Gold Calcite	EAC-06/03	
6170					$225	Bristol Yellow	ebay-03/05	
6171	Vase	279	1	2	$1790	Green Jade/Alabaster ACB	EAC-02/01	
6171					$800	Rosaline/Alabaster ACB	JDJ-11/01	Etched "Floral"
6171					$1350	Gold Aurene	ebay-11/01	
6171					$950	Blue Aurene	ebay-05/03	
6171					$1000	Green Jade/Alabaster ACB	Cinc-06/03	Etched "Floral"
6171					$975	Green Jade/Alabaster ACB	ebay-07/03	Etched "Floral"
6172	Bowl	144	2	4				
6173	Centerpiece	150	3	2				
6174	Centerpiece	150	3	3	$800	Gold Calcite	ebay-08/01	
6175	Ash Tray	137	4	7	$100	Topaz/Green leaves	Cinc-11/02	ACR)168,342; TPD)10.122
6175					$130	Topaz/Green leaves	ebay-06/04	
6176	Centerpiece	150	3	4				
6177	Vase	279	1	3	$4140	Decorated Blue Aurene	ebay-03/03	RFR)15,2,B; TPD)10.120
6178	Vase	279	1	4	$2475	Decorated Gold Aurene	EAC-04/91	RFR)15,2,A&C; ARC)140,262
6178					$3105	Decorated Blue Aurene	Sknr-05/94	
6178					$3100	Decorated Gold Aurene	ebay-05/00	
6178					$2350	Decorated Gold Aurene	Sknr-06/02	

SHAPE NO.	ITEM	PAGE	COL	ROW	PRICE REALIZED	GLASS TYPE	AUCTION HOUSE	COMMENTS & PHOTO REFERENCES
6178					$1000	Blue Aurene	ebay-05/04	
6179	Candlestick	164	4	3				
6180	Candlestick	164	4	4				
6181	Cologne	241	6	1				
6182	Ash Tray	137	4	8	$300	Green Jade/Alabaster	Cott-08/01	
6183	Goblet	192	3	4	$450	Green over Colorless	ebay-06/01	Engraved "Thistle" PG1)313; JSS)12-17,L
6184	Aquarium	304	3	2				
6185	Candlestick	164	5	1	$1534	Gold Calcite	ebay-11/04	TPD)10.86
6185	Compote	174	4	6	$1840	Gold Calcite	Jack-06/02	TPD)10.86
6186	Cologne	241	6	2				
6187	Bowl	144	2	5				
6188	Bowl	144	2	6				
6189	Centerpiece	150	3	5				
6190	Candlestick	164	5	2				
6190	Centerpiece	150	3	6				
6190	Compote	174	4	7				
6190	Vase	279	1	5				
6191	Ash Tray	137	4	9				
6192	Goblet	192	3	5				JSS)12-16
6193	Centerpiece	150	3	7				
6194	Cup and Saucer	216	3	8				
6195	Cup and Saucer	216	3	9				
6196	Insert	210	5	9	$35	Jade Green	ebay-03/04	
6197	Centerpiece	151	1	1				
6198	Vase	279	1	6				
6199	Vase	279	1	7	$550	Green Jade ACB	EAC-04/90	PG1)313
6199					$285	Green Jade	Sknr-10/97	
6199					$690	Black/White Cluthra	JDJ-10/97	
6199					$1090	Green Jade ACB	Sknr-01/98	
6199					$1035	Green Jade ACB	Sknr-01/98	
6199					$805	Yellow Jade ACB	Sknr-01/98	
6199					$880	Green Jade ACB	EAC-04/98	
6199					$300	Pomona Green	Wint-09/00	
6199					$750	Green Jade ACB	ebay-12/00	Etched "Fircone"
6199					$1800	Green Jade ACB	ebay-07/02	Etched "Fircone"
6199					$160	Green Jade	ebay-07/02	
6199					$535	Green Jade ACB	ebay-08/02	Etched "Fircone"
6199					$175	Topaz	ebay-10/02	Mounted in metal holder.
6199					$290	Celeste Blue	ebay-02/03	Lamp with fixtures.
6199					$285	Bristol Yellow/Pomona	EAC-06/03	Pomona Green lion head prunts
6199					$260	Green Jade	EAC-06/03	
6199					$200	Green Jade/Alabaster	ebay-11/03	Alabaster prunts
6199					$500	Green Jade ACB	ebay-11/03	
6199					$205	Green Jade	ebay-05/04	
6199					$285	Mirror Black	ebay-09/94	Metal holder
6199					$85	Green Jade	ebay-10/04	
6199					$90	Pomona Green	ebay-10/04	
6199					$230	Yellow Jade ACB	ebay-11/04	
6199					$200	Amethyst	ebay-11/04	
6199					$200	Green Jade	ebay-11/04	
6199					$405	Green Jade ACB	ebay-01/05	Lamp with fixtures
6199					$170	Celeste Blue	ebay-03/05	
6199					$250	Green Jade	ebay-07/05	
6200	Plate	159	1	11				
6201	Bowl	144	2	7	$230	Bristol Yellow	ebay-03/04	
6202	Atomizer	239	1	5				
6203	Atomizer	239	1	6				
6204	Atomizer	239	2	1				
6205	Atomizer	239	2	2				
6206	Atomizer	239	2	3				
6207	Vase	279	2	1	$225	Green Jade	EAC-04/91	Alabaster prunts TPD)10.47
6207					$300	Green Jade	ebay-07/00	
6207					$950	Green Jade	Tway-10/00	
6207					$235	Green Jade/Alabaster	ebay-10/02	
6207					$255	Green Jade/Alabaster	ebay-11/02	
6207					$125	Bristol Yellow	ebay-02/03	
6207					$245	Green Jade	ebay-03/04	Alabaster prunts
6207					$150	Pomona Green	ebay-08/04	
6207					$160	French Blue	ebay-10/04	Built into a lamp
6207					$250	Green Jade/Alabaster	ebay-11/04	Alabaster prunts
6207					$375	Green Jade/Alabaster	ebay-11/04	Alabaster prunts
6207					$190	Green Jade/Alabaster	ebay-12/04	Alabaster prunts
6207					$380	Selenium Red/Colorless	ebay-12/04	Colorless prunts
6207					$150	Bristol Yellow	ebay-04/05	

SHAPE NO.	ITEM	PAGE	COL	ROW	PRICE REALIZED	GLASS TYPE	AUCTION HOUSE	COMMENTS & PHOTO REFERENCES
6208	Candlestick	164	5	3				
6209	Vase	279	2	2				
6210	Vase	279	2	3				
6211	Vase	279	2	4				PG1)XXVI B
6212	Vase	279	2	5	$200	Green Jade	ebay-01/02	TPD)9.19
6212					$750	Celeste Blue/Topaz foot	ebay-07/04	
6213	Vase	279	2	6				
6214	Vase	279	2	7	$410	Green Jade	EAC-07/97	TPD)4.71
6214					$375	Green Jade	Ogal-05/99	
6214					$4300	Plum Jade ACB	ebay-02/00	Etched "Chang"
6214					$185	Pomona Green	ebay-10/04	
6214					$330	Green Jade	Cinc-06/05	
6214					$145	Bristol Yellow	EAC-07/05	
6215	Vase	279	3	1	$345	Green Jade	Sknr-01/96	TPD)8.26:10.133
6215					$230	Topaz	Sknr-05/96	
6215					$385	Green Jade	EAC-04/97	
6215					$90	Topaz	Ogal-01/02	
6215					$125	Pomona Green	ebay-04/02	
6215					$175	Pomona Green	ebay-05/02	
6215					$170	Green Jade	Ogal-03/03	Lamp with fittings.
6215					$185	Rosa	ebay-09/03	
6215					$230	Green Jade	JDJ-11/03	
6215					$130	Green Jade	ebay-01/05	
6215					175	Green Jade/Alabaster	ebay-03/05	
6215					$160	Green Jade	ebay-03/05	
6215					$190	Green Jade	ebay-06/05	
6216	Vase	279	3	2				This is a Goblet in factory records.
6217	Vase	279	3	3				
6218	Vase	279	3	4				
6219	Vase	279	3	5				
6220	Goblet	192	3	6	$75	Topaz	ebay-03/01	PG1)XXII A,C; TPD)7.30
6220					$155	Bristol Yellow	ebay-11/01	
6220					$90	Green Jade/Alabaster	ebay-02/02	
6220					$75	Topaz/Celeste Blue ring	ebay-10/02	
6220					$160	Celeste Blue (E)	ebay-10/02	Engraved "Wheat"
6220					$110	Celeste Blue/Topaz ring	ebay-05/03	
6220					$125	Green Jade	ebay-03/04	
6220					$80	Green Jade/Alabaster band	ebay-02/05	
6220					$85	Selenium Red	EAC-04/05	
6221	Vase	279	4	1				
6222	Vase	279	4	2	$3300	Black/Jade ACB	EAC-04/99	
6222					$525	Green Jade ACB Lamp	ebay-08/04	
6223	Vase	279	4	3				PG2)71;JAS)155,B;TPD)9.28
6223					$3795	Plum Jade ACB	EAC-10/04	Drilled, Etched "Pekin"
6224	Vase	279	4	4				
6225	Goblet	192	3	7	$150	Colorless/Selenium Red	ebay-04/04	TPD)7.30
6226	Vase	279	5	1				
6227	Vase	279	5	2	$100	Pomona Green	ebay-11/00	ACR)COLOR 1,B,A; TPD)10.132
6227					$210	Green Jade	ebay-03/03	
6228	Vase	279	5	3	$2800	G. Aurene/Yel. Jade ACB	EAC-01/03	Lamp Etched "Lotus"
6229	Vase	279	5	4				TPD)8.31
6229					$1900	G. Aurene/Grn. Jade ACB	Tway-03/02	Etched "Fircone"
6230	Lamp Base	203	1	4				
6231	Goblet	192	3	8				TPD)6.1
6232	Cup	199	4	2	$140	Green Jade/Alabaster	ebay-01/04	Alabaster handle
6232					$160	Green Jade/Alabaster	Cinc-06/05	Alabaster handle
6232	Pitcher	214	2	2	$230	Pomona Green	Sknr-10/96	JAS)163,C,B
6232					$400	Bristol Yellow/Pomona	ebay-03/03	Pomona Green handle
6232					$230	Green Jade/Alabaster	JDJ-11/03	Alabaster handle
6232					$50	Green Jade/Alabaster	ebay-12/04	Alabaster handle
6232					$980	Green Jade/Alabaster	Cinc-06/05	Alabaster handle
6232					$500	Green Jade/Alabaster (FC)	ebay-07/05	Alabaster handle
6233	Cologne	241	6	3	$1760	Blue Aurene	EAC-04/97	
6233					$2090	Blue Aurene	EAC-04/98	
6234	Cologne	241	6	4				
6235	Cologne	241	6	5				
6236	Cologne	241	6	6	$535	Green Jade	ebay-03/00	
6236					$345	Celeste Blue	Rago-09/00	
6236					$515	Celeste Blue	ebay-01/01	
6236					$1150	Gold Aurene	ebay-07/02	
6236					$230	Celeste Blue	ebay-12/02	
6236					$1180	Green Jade	EAC-11/03	
6237	Cologne	241	6	7	$440	Bristol Yellow	EAC-07/91	PG1)XXX A,D&E; PG2)90,D; RFR)16,3,C;
6237					$935	Green Jade	EAC-10/94	JAS)170,B,D; TPD)5.29:10.145

SHAPE NO.	ITEM	PAGE	COL	ROW	PRICE REALIZED	GLASS TYPE	AUCTION HOUSE	COMMENTS & PHOTO REFERENCES
6237					$1485	Blue Aurene	JDJ-10/94	
6237					$1380	Blue Aurene	Sknr-10/95	
6237					$1220	Rosaline/Alabaster	EAC-04/98	
6237					$825	Gold Aurene	ebay-05/01	
6237					$1760	Blue Aurene	Cott-08/01	
6237					$1100	Rosaline/Alabaster	Cott-08/01	
6237					$880	Green Jade	Cott-08/01	
6237					$325	Bristol Yellow	ebay-02/02	
6237					$560	Bristol Yellow	ebay-11/02	
6237					$810	Rosaline/Alabaster	ebay-11/02	
6237					$665	Pomona Green	ebay-11/02	
6237					$300	Bristol Yellow	ebay-06/03	
6237					$650	Rosaline/Alabaster	ebay-10/03	
6237					$700	Green Jade	ebay-10/03	
6237					$975	Colorless/Light Blue Jade	JDJ-11/03	Light Blue Jade stopper
6237					$770	Blue Aurene	Rago-01/04	
6237					$1135	Gold Aurene	ebay-03/04	
6237					$745	Gold Aurene	ebay-04/05	
6237					$1075	Blue Aurene	ebay-04/05	
6237					$480	Blue Aurene	ebay-05/05	
6237					$1090	Colorless/Gold Ruby	EAC-07/05	Gold Ruby cased inside
6237	Puff Box	245	1	1	$365	Rosaline/Alabaster	EAC-09/01	TPD)10.41:10.46; MDK)25
6237					$1135	Light Blue Jade	ebay-11/02	Flint White finial
6237					$320	Rosaline/Alabaster finial	ebay-07/04	
6237					$420	Rosaline/Alabaster finial	ebay-08/04	
6238	Candlestick	164	5	4				
6239	Vase	279	5	5				
6240	Vase	280	1	1				
6241	Bowl	144	2	8,9	$275	Green Jade/Alabaster foot	EAC-02/92	RFR)7,1,A; TPD)6.5:10.114
6241					$550	Gold Aurene	EAC-07/94	
6241					$690	Blue Aurene	Sknr-10/95	
6241					$605	Gold Aurene	EAC-04/96	
6241					$165	Topaz/Pomona Green	JDJ-06/96	
6241					$230	Topaz/Pomona Green	Sknr-01/98	
6241					$245	Pomona Green	EAC-04/98	
6241					$230	Rosaline/Alabaster	ebay-12/00	
6241					$420	Green Jade/Alabaster	EAC-09/01	
6241					$275	Green Jade/Alabaster	ebay-10/01	
6241					$225	Green Jade/Alabaster	ebay-05/02	
6241					$195	Green Jade/Opal foot	ebay-10/02	
6241					$210	Pomona Green/Topaz	ebay-12/02	
6241					$115	Topaz	ebay-11/03	
6241					$400	Topaz/Celeste Blue foot	ebay-04/04	
6241					$140	Green Jade/Alabaster foot	ebay-09/04	
6241	Vase	280	1	2	$690	Gold Aurene	Sknr-05/98	TPD)10.109
6241					$130	Pomona Green	ebay-03/01	
6241					$225	Pomona Green	ebay-11/01	
6241					$160	Pomona Green	ebay-09/02	
6241					$1280	Blue Aurene	ebay-02/03	
6241					$940	Blue Aurene	ebay-02/03	
6241					$710	Blue Aurene	ebay-09/03	
6241					$1425	Blue Aurene	ebay-11/03	
6241					$280	Pomona Green	ebay-03/04	
6241					$250	Nile Green	ebay-07/04	
6241					$150	Pomona Green/Topaz foot	ebay-10/04	
6241					$230	Pomona Green/Topaz foot	ebay-10/04	
6241					$190	Green Jade/Alabaster foot	ebay-02/05	
6241					$200	Bristol Yellow	ebay-05/05	
6241					$730	Blue Aurene	ebay-05/05	
6242	Goblet	192	4	1	$75	Bristol Yellow	ebay-02/00	TPD)8.12; MDK)20
6242					$95	Bristol Yellow	ebay-04/00	
6242	Wine				$235	Bristol Yellow	ebay-04/01	
6243	Vase	280	1	3				
6244	Goblet	192	4	2				
6245	Candlestick	165	1	1	$1275	Colorless/Pomona (E)	ebay-02/03	
6245					$635	Colorless/Pomona (E)	ebay-08/04	Pomona Green foot and knob
6245	Centerpiece	151	1	2				
6246	Decanter	186	2	4				
6247	Decanter	186	2	5				
6248	Decanter	186	3	1				
6249	Decanter	186	3	2				
6250	Decanter	186	3	3				
6251	Decanter	186	3	4				
6252	Bowl	144	3	1				

SHAPE NO.	ITEM	PAGE	COL	ROW	PRICE REALIZED	GLASS TYPE	AUCTION HOUSE	COMMENTS & PHOTO REFERENCES
6253	Candlestick	165	1	2				
6253	Centerpiece	151	1	3,4				
6254	Decanter	186	4	1				
6255	Decanter	186	4	2				PG1)96,148,D
6256	Decanter	186	4	3				
6257	Candlestick	165	1	3	$465	Rosa	EAC-07/95	TPD)4.72
6257	Compote	174	5	1				
6258	Cologne	242	1	1				
6259	Puff Box	244	5	9	$590	VDS/Fruit finial	ebay-06/04	
6260	Puff Box	244	5	10				
6261	Decanter	186	4	4				
6261	Perfume							ACR)Color 4,B,D
6262	Candlestick	165	1	4				
6262	Centerpiece	151	1	5				
6262	Compote	174	5	2				
6263	Ash Tray	137	4	10				
6264	Ash Tray	138	1	1	$250	Green Jade/Alabaster	ebay-01/01	
6264					$165	Bristol Yellow (E)	ebay-09/04	
6264					$165	Pomona Green/Topaz	EAC-10/04	Topaz stem and foot
6265	Lamp Shaft	203	2	1				
6266	Saucer	203	2	2				
6267	Bobeche	203	2	3				
6268	Champagne							JSS)12-14,L
6268					$30	Colorless	ebay-02/04	Cut with leaves
6268	Cordial				$30	Colorless	ebay-02/04	Cut with leaves
6268	Fingerbowl							See New Drawings section
6268	Goblet	192	4	3				PG1)313; JSS)12-24:12-14,C; TPD)7.24
6268					$900	Alexandrite (E)	JDJ-11/02	Engraved "Old English #3"
6268					$140	Colorless	ebay-02/04	Cut with leaves
6268					$90	Colorless	ebay-02/04	Cut with leaves
6268	Wine							JSS)12-14,R
6269	Goblet	192	4	4				
6270	Candlestick	165	2	1	$595	Celeste Blue	ebay-02/00	JAS)165,T,B; TPD)10.110
6270					$355	Bristol Yellow	ebay-03/00	
6270					$385	Green Jade/Alabaster	ebay-03/01	
6270					$630	Green Jade/Alabaster	Cott-08/01	
6270					$180	Pomona Green	ebay-12/01	
6270					$545	Selenium Red	Jack-06/02	
6270					$205	Topaz	ebay-09/02	
6270					$450	Selenium Red	ebay-01/03	
6270					$690	Green Jade/Alabaster	ebay-08/03	
6270					$310	Mirror Black	ebay-11/04	
6270	Centerpiece	151	1	6	$615	Green Jade/Alabaster	ebay-10/00	
6270					$300	Topaz/Pomona Green	Tway-10/00	
6270					$150	Spanish Green	ebay-12/00	
6270					$300	Gold Calcite	ebay-03/01	
6270					$245	Green Jade/Alabaster	ebay-06/01	
6270					$100	Topaz	ebay-08/01	
6270					$105	Ivory	ebay-09/02	
6270					$160	Amethyst	ebay-05/03	
6270					$340	Rosaline/Alabaster foot	ebay-06/03	
6270					$180	Gold Calcite	ebay-07/03	
6270					$100	Pomona Green/Topaz foot	ebay-04/04	
6270					$140	Pomona Green/Topaz foot	ebay-05/04	
6270					$170	Pomona Green/Topaz foot	ebay-04/04	
6270					$250	Gold Ruby/Colorless foot	ebay-07/04	
6271	Vase	280	1	4				
6272	Vase	280	1	5				PG1)116,186,A:313; RFR)19,3,B;
6272								TPD)10.134
6272					$5990	Black/Green Jade ACB	EAC-04/02	Etched "Indian"
6272					$2530	Black/Yellow Jade ACB	EAC-06/04	
6273								
6273	Vase	280	2	1				TPD)8.27
6274	Table Decoration	236	4	4				
6275	Vase	280	2	2				
6276	Vase	280	2	3				TPD)9.14
6277	Champagne				$150	Colorless/Rosa	ebay-11/01	
6277					$225	Colorless/Rosa stem (E)	ebay-12/01	
6277					$140	Colorless/Rosa stem (E)	ebay-07/02	
6277					$180	Colorless/Rosa stem (E)	ebay-05/03	
6277					$195	Colorless/Rosa stem (E)	ebay-05/03	
6277					$182	Colorless/Rosa stem (E)	ebay-06/03	
6277					$200	Colorless/Rosa stem (E)	ebay-01/05	
6277					$260	Colorless/Rosa stem (E)	ebay-04/05	

SHAPE NO.	ITEM	PAGE	COL	ROW	PRICE REALIZED	GLASS TYPE	AUCTION HOUSE	COMMENTS & PHOTO REFERENCES
6277	Goblet	192	4	5	$340	Colorless/Rosa stem	ebay-12/99	TPD)6.1
6277					$185	Rosaline/Alabaster	Cott-08/01	
6277					$205	Colorless/Rosa	ebay-10/01	
6277					$260	Colorless/Rosa stem (E)	ebay-12/01	
6277					$265	Colorless/Rosa stem (E)	ebay-01/01	
6277					$225	Colorless/Rosa stem (E)	ebay-03/02	
6277					$225	Colorless/Rosa stem (E)	ebay-06/02	
6277					$175	Colorless/Rosa stem (E)	ebay-04/03	
6277					$135	Colorless/Rosa stem (E)	ebay-05/03	
6277					$200	Colorless/Rosa stem (E)	ebay-07/04	
6277					$200	Colorless/Rosa stem (E)	ebay-08/04	
6277					$315	Colorless/Rosa stem (E)	ebay-05/05	
6277					$105	Selenium Red/Colorless	ebay-06/05	Colorless stem
6277	Sherbet				$125	Colorless/Rosa foot	ebay-07/01	
6277					$200	Colorless/Rosa foot (E)	ebay-05/05	
6278	Goblet	192	4	6				
6279	Goblet	192	4	7				ACR)145,274; TPD)6.1
6280	Goblet	192	5	1	$690	Colorless Silverina bowl	ebay-05/05	Colorless stem, Black foot
6280					$790	Colorless Silverina bowl	ebay-05/05	Colorless stem, Black foot
6280					$1235	Colorless Silverina bowl	ebay-05/05	Colorless stem, Black foot
6280					$760	Colorless Silverina bowl	ebay-06/05	Colorless stem, Black foot
6280	Sherbet				$240	Colorless Silverina bowl	ebay-04/05	Black foot
6280					$220	Colorless Silverina bowl	ebay-05/04	Black foot
6280					$305	Colorless Silverina bowl	ebay-05/05	Black foot
6280	Wine				$195	Colorless Silverina bowl	ebay-07/03	
6280					$215	Colorless Silverina bowl	ebay-04/05	Colorless stem, Black foot, 6-5/8"
6280					$245	Colorless Silverina bowl	ebay-04/05	Colorless stem, Black foot, 7"
6280					$310	Colorless Silverina bowl	ebay-05/05	Colorless stem, Black foot, 7"
6280					$360	Colorless Silverina bowl	ebay-05/05	Colorless stem, Black foot, 7"
6280					$365	Colorless Silverina bowl	ebay-05/05	Colorless stem, Black foot, 6-5/8"
6280					$385	Colorless Silverina bowl	ebay-05/05	Colorless stem, Black foot, 6-5/8"
6280					$430	Colorless Silverina bowl	ebay-05/05	Colorless stem, Black foot, 7"
6281	Goblet	192	5	2				
6282	Goblet	192	5	3				
6283	Vase	280	2	4	$470	Gold Aurene	ebay-11/01	
6283					$1760	Dark Blue Jade	EAC-07/93	
6283					$2530	ACB	EAC-10/94	
6284	Shade	232	2	1				
6285	Goblet	192	5	4				
6286	Covered Vase	307	3	4				
6287	Vase	280	2	5	$275	Green Jade	EAC-04/90	PG1)III,B,B:XXII A,B:70,106
6287					$1320	Gold Aurene	EAC-07/91	PG1)89,137,A&E;
6287					$770	Col./Gold Ruby threaded	EAC-04/93	RFR)16,1,B:20,3,A:21,3,B;
6287					$275	Topaz (E)	EAC-07/93	ACR)COLOR 2,T,E:COLOR 4,T,A:165,331
6287					$220	Spanish Green	EAC-07/93	MDK)45:77
6287					$440	Green Jade/Alabaster	JDJ-10/94	
6287					$385	Gold Ruby	JDJ-05/95	
6287					$385	Pomona Green	JDJ-05/95	
6287					$165	Topaz/Pomona Green	Sknr-05/95	
6287					$230	Topaz/Pomona Green	Sknr-10/95	
6287					$715	Green Jade/Alabaster	EAC-10/95	
6287					$495	Flemish Blue	JDJ-06/96	
6287					$330	Pomona Green	EAC-07/96	
6287					$315	Celeste Blue	Sknr-10/96	
6287					$345	Green Jade/Alabaster	JDJ-10/96	
6287					$300	Pomona Green	EAC-04/97	
6287					$550	Rosaline/Alabaster	EAC-10/97	
6287					$330	Bristol Yellow	EAC-10/97	
6287					$550	Celeste Blue/Topaz	EAC-04/98	
6287					$300	Topaz/Pomona Green	EAC-04/98	
6287					$245	Pomona Green	EAC-07/98	
6287					$245	Pomona Green	EAC-07/98	
6287					$220	Topaz/Pomona Green	EAC-07/98	
6287					$385	Green Jade/Alabaster	EAC-07/98	
6287					$330	Green Jade/Alabaster	EAC-10/98	
6287					$330	Green Jade/Alabaster	EAC-04/99	
6287					$2275	Blue Aurene	ebay-10/99	
6287					$435	Rosa/Colorless	ebay-11/99	
6287					$395	French Blue	ebay-11/99	
6287					$175	Bristol Yellow	ebay-12/99	
6287					$605	French Blue	Cinc-12/99	
6287					$260	Topaz	ebay-01/00	
6287					$300	Bristol Yellow threaded	ebay-02/00	Mirror Black threaded
6287					$300	Topaz/Pomona Green	ebay-02/00	

SHAPE NO.	ITEM	PAGE	COL	ROW	PRICE REALIZED	GLASS TYPE	AUCTION HOUSE	COMMENTS & PHOTO REFERENCES
6287					$260	Celeste Blue/Topaz	ebay-02/00	
6287					$805	Green Jade/Alabaster	Sknr-02/00	
6287					$165	Pomona Green	EAC-10/00	
6287					$115	Topaz/Pomona Green	Sknr-10/00	
6287					$260	Topaz/Pomona Green	Tway-10/00	
6287					$210	Pomona Green	ebay-11/00	
6287					$415	Spanish Green	ebay-11/00	
6287					$455	Gold Ruby/colorless	ebay-12/00	
6287					$575	Gold Ruby/colorless	ebay-12/00	
6287					$200	Topaz	ebay-02/01	
6287					$290	Bristol Yellow	Sknr-02/01	
6287					$170	Spanish Green/Threaded	Sknr-02/01	
6287					$490	Green Jade/Alabaster foot	Sknr-02/01	
6287					$310	Green Jade/Alabaster	ebay-03/01	
6287					$180	Topaz	ebay-03/01	
6287					$140	Topaz/Pomona Green	ebay-03/01	
6287					$310	Colorless	EAC-04/01	
6287					$225	Bristol Yellow	EAC-04/01	
6287					$280	Colorless/Pomona Green	EAC-04/01	
6287					$950	Rosaline/Alabaster	EAC-04/01	
6287					$575	Topaz/Pomona Green	ebay-04/01	
6287					$350	Pomona Green	ebay-04/01	
6287					$255	Topaz	ebay-04/01	
6287					$250	Bristol Yellow	ebay-05/01	
6287					$310	Topaz	ebay-05/01	
6287					$370	Amethyst	ebay-07/01	
6287					$225	Topaz/Pomona Green	ebay-07/01	
6287					$520	Gold Ruby/Colorless	Cott-08/01	
6287					$300	Green Shaded	Cott-08/01	
6287					$190	Bristol Yellow	Cott-08/01	
6287					$145	Colorless	Cott-08/01	
6287					$410	Green Jade	Cott-08/01	
6287					$355	Topaz/Pomona Green	ebay-08/01	
6287					$920	Green Jade/Alabaster	ebay-09/01	
6287					$300	Pomona Green	ebay-09/01	
6287					$330	Topaz/Pomona Green (FC)	ebay-09/01	
6287					$230	Bristol Yellow	ebay-10/01	
6287					$150	Colorless	ebay-10/01	
6287					$1560	Gold Aurene	ebay-10/01	
6287					$340	Celeste/Topaz	ebay-11/01	
6287					$275	Topaz/Pomona Green	ebay-11/01	
6287					$530	Green Jade/Alabaster	EAC-11/01	
6287					$395	Green Jade/Alabaster	ebay-12/01	
6287					$300	French Blue	ebay-01/02	
6287					$355	Spanish Green	ebay-01/02	
6287					$380	Green Jade/Alabaster	ebay-02/02	
6287					$280	Topaz/Pomona foot	ebay-02/02	
6287					$405	Bristol Yellow	ebay-02/02	
6287					$280	Colorless/Pomona foot	ebay-02/02	Ship engraved
6287					$195	Bristol Yellow	ebay-03/02	
6287					$225	Pomona Green	ebay-03/02	
6287					$180	Topaz	ebay-03/02	
6287					$225	Topaz	ebay-04/02	
6287					$410	French Blue	ebay-04/02	
6287					$200	Pomona Green	JDJ-05/02	
6287					$130	Spanish Green	ebay-05/02	
6287					$285	Bristol Yellow	ebay-05/02	
6287					$250	Colorless/Celeste foot	ebay-06/02	
6287					$325	Pomona Green	ebay-06/02	
6287					$290	Pomona Green	ebay-07/02	
6287					$180	Colorless (E)	ebay-07/02	
6287					$230	Pomona Green	ebay-09/02	
6287					$305	Spanish Green	ebay-10/02	
6287					$385	Col./Gold Ruby threaded	ebay-10/02	Machine threaded over bottom half of bowl.
6287					$175	Pomona Green	ebay-10/02	
6287					$305	Topaz/Pomona Green foot	ebay-10/02	
6287					$175	Colorless (E)	ebay-10/02	
6287					$295	Pomona Green/Topaz foot	ebay-10/02	
6287					$305	Rosa/Pomona foot (E)	ebay-11/02	
6287					$405	Dark Amethyst	ebay-11/02	
6287					$170	Topaz/Pomona Green foot	ebay-11/02	
6287					$260	Green Jade/Alabaster foot	ebay-11/02	
6287					$260	Green Jade/Alabaster foot	ebay-11/02	
6287					$300	Green Jade/Alabaster foot	JDJ-11/02	

SHAPE NO.	ITEM	PAGE	COL	ROW	PRICE REALIZED	GLASS TYPE	AUCTION HOUSE	COMMENTS & PHOTO REFERENCES
6287					$455	Bristol Yellow (E)	ebay-11/02	
6287					$150	Topaz/Pomona Green	Cinc-11/02	
6287					$250	Green Jade/Alabaster foot	ebay-12/02	
6287					$260	Rosa/Pomona Green foot	ebay-12/02	
6287					$225	Bristol Yellow	ebay-01/03	
6287					$535	Green Jade/Alabaster	ebay-01/03	
6287					$225	Green Jade/Alabaster	ebay-02/03	
6287					$200	Topaz/Pomona Green	ebay-02/03	
6287					$270	Pomona Green/Topaz	ebay-02/03	
6287					$280	Topaz/Pomona Green	ebay-03/03	
6287					$300	Topaz/Pomona Green (E)	ebay-03/03	
6287					$165	Amber	ebay-03/03	
6287					$190	Topaz	ebay-04/03	
6287					$435	Bristol Yellow	ebay-05/03	
6287					$1850	Light Blue Jade/Flint White	Cott-06/03	Flint White foot
6287					$315	Celeste Blue/Colorless foot	EAC-06/03	
6287					$315	Pomona Green/Amethyst	EAC-06/03	Amethyst stem and foot
6287					$330	Jade Green/Alabaster	ebay-07/03	Alabaster stem and foot
6287					$235	Bristol Yellow	ebay-07/03	
6287					$200	Antique Green	ebay-07/03	
6287					$180	Celeste Blue/Colorless foot	ebay-07/03	
6287					$425	Amethyst	ebay-08/03	
6287					$410	Gold Ruby/Colorless	ebay-08/03	Colorless stem and foot
6287					$365	Pomona Green/Topaz	ebay-09/03	
6287					$405	Celeste Blue/Topaz (E)	ebay-09/03	Topaz stem and foot
6287					$280	Topaz/Pomona Green foot	ebay-10/03	
6287					$400	Green Jade/Alabaster foot	ebay-10/03	
6287					$575	Green Jade/Alabaster foot	ebay-10/03	
6287					$190	Rosa/Pomona Green foot	ebay-11/03	
6287					$250	Colorless/Pomona foot (E)	ebay-11/03	
6287					$455	Celeste Blue/Topaz foot (E)	ebay-11/03	
6287					$2300	Blue Aurene with threads	Aspr-11/03	
6287					$80	Topaz/Pomona foot	JDJ-11/02	
6287					$300	Pomona Green	ebay-11/03	
6287					$170	Light Amethyst	JDJ-11/03	
6287					$260	Topaz/Pomona Green	EAC-11/03	Pomona Green stem and foot
6287					$250	French Blue	ebay-01/04	
6287					$260	Topaz/Pomona Green	ebay-01/04	Pomona Green stem and foot
6287					$175	Topaz	ebay-02/04	
6287					$225	Green Jade/Alabaster	ebay-03/04	Alabaster stem and foot
6287					$240	Pomona Green	ebay-03/04	
6287					$170	Topaz/Pomona Green foot	ebay-04/04	
6287					$300	Pomona Green	ebay-04/04	
6287					$230	Rosa/Colorless stem & foot	EAC-04/04	
6287					$345	Pomona Green	EAC-04/04	Colorless stem and foot
6287					$230	Bristol Yellow	ebay-05/04	
6287					$250	Colorless	ebay-05/04	
6287					$210	Topaz/Pomona Green foot	ebay-05/04	Engraved
6287					$265	Celeste Blue/Topaz foot	ebay-06/04	Engraved
6287					$515	Rosa/Pomona Green foot	ebay-06/04	Engraved
6287					$380	French Blue w threading	ebay-07/04	
6287					$125	Colorless/Pomona Green	ebay-08/04	Pomona Green stem and foot
6287					$210	Spanish Green threaded	ebay-08/04	
6287					$300	Bristol Yellow/Black thread	ebay-08/04	
6287					$210	Orchid	ebay-08/04	
6287					$475	Bristol Yellow	ebay-10/04	
6287					$1600	Gold Aurene	ebay-10/04	
6287					$550	Colorless/Pomona Green	EAC-10/04	Pomona Green stem and foot
6287					$85	Colorless/Pomona Green	ebay-12/04	Pomona Green stem and foot
6287					$230	Pomona Green	ebay-12/04	
6287					$300	French Blue	ebay-01/05	
6287					$190	Topaz/Pomona Green foot	ebay-01/05	
6287					$195	Topaz/Pomona Green foot	ebay-02/05	
6287					$275	Topaz/Pomona Green foot	ebay-02/05	
6287					$135	Topaz	ebay-03/05	
6287					$200	Topaz	ebay-03/05	
6287					$140	Pomona Green	ebay-03/05	
6287					$255	Celeste Blue	ebay-03/05	
6287					$225	Pomona Green (E)	ebay-05/05	
6287					$120	Topaz/Pomona Green foot	ebay-05/05	
6287					$300	Topaz/Pomona Green foot	Cinc-06/05	
6287					$510	Topaz/Pomona Green foot	ebay-06/05	
6287					$385	Gold Ruby/Colorless foot	ebay-06/05	
6287					$410	Celeste Blue/Colorless foot	ebay-07/05	

SHAPE NO.	ITEM	PAGE	COL	ROW	PRICE REALIZED	GLASS TYPE	AUCTION HOUSE	COMMENTS & PHOTO REFERENCES
6287					$180	Topaz/Pomona Green foot	ebay-07/05	
6287					$305	Colorless/Pomona Green	ebay-07/05	Engraved "10008"
6287					$330	Green Jade/Alabaster foot	ebay-07/05	
6287					$460	Green Jade/Alabaster foot	EAC-07/05	
6288	Vase	280	2	6				
6289	Lamp Base	203	2	4				
6290	Vase	280	3	1				
6291	Vase	280	3	2				
6292	Vase	280	3	3	$1125	Gold Aurene	ebay-03/03	Lamp with fittings
6293	Vase	280	3	4				
6294	Candlestick	165	2	2				TPD)10.153
6294	Centerpiece	151	1	7				TPD)7.24
6295	Shade	232	2	2				
6296	Vase	280	3	5				
6297	Vase	280	4	1	$4125	Decorated Blue Aurene	EAC-10/90	RFR)15,1,A&B&C:15,3,A; RLG)136,259;
6297					$3025	Decorated Gold Aurene	EAC-10/90	ACR)COLOR 3,B,C; TPD)8.28:10.120
6297					$2750	Decorated Blue Aurene	EAC-07/93	
6297					$3190	Decorated Blue Aurene	EAC-10/93	
6297					$2875	Decorated Blue Aurene	Sknr-05/96	
6297					$3080	Decorated Blue Aurene	EAC-07/97	
6297					$1475	Blue Aurene	Sbys-12/97	
6297					$3400	Decorated Blue Aurene	ebay-05/00	
6297					$5225	Decorated Blue Aurene	EAC-08/00	
6297					$5225	Decorated Gold Aurene	EAC-08/00	
6297					$3465	Decorated Blue Aurene	ebay-12/00	
6297					$4950	Decorated Gold Aurene	Cott-08/01	
6297					$4480	Decorated Blue Aurene	EAC-09/02	
6297					$3405	Decorated Blue Aurene	ebay-02/03	
6297					$4025	Decorated Blue Aurene	Jack-06/03	
6297					$3600	Decorated Blue Aurene	JDJ-05/04	
6297					$2990	Decorated Blue Aurene	Hrtg-03/05	
6298	Vase	280	4	2	$5040	Decorated Blue Aurene	EAC-04/01	RFR)15,3,B; TPD)10.88:10.120
6299	Vase	280	4	3	$4675	Decorated Blue Aurene	EAC-04/97	PG1)XXIV A
6299					$2310	Decorated Gold Aurene	EAC-10/90	RFR)15,3,C:27,1,C:FRONT COVER,T;
6299					$3190	Decorated Blue Aurene	EAC-10/92	RLG)167,303;ACR)COLOR1,B,C;
6299					$3795	Decorated Gold Aurene	EAC-10/97	TPD)10.120
6299					$1700	Decorated Gold Aurene	Ogal-09/00	
6299					$6050	Decorated Blue Aurene	Cott-02/02	
6299					$2020	Decorated Gold Aurene	ebay-11/02	
6299					$2588	Decorated Gold Aurene	EAC-11/03	
6299					$3360	Decorated Blue Aurene	JDJ-11/04	
6299					$3700	Decorated Blue Aurene	Cinc-06/05	
6300	Vase	280	4	4	$3450	Decorated Blue Aurene	JDJ-11/01	
6301	Centerpiece	151	2	1	$230	Green Jade	JDJ-11/03	
6302	Basket	140	2	8	$525	Red Cluthra	EAC-07/96	TPD)10.143
6302					$315	White Cluthra	JDJ-10/97	
6302					$200	Rosaline/Alabaster	ebay-11/00	
6302					$305	Pomona Green/Bristol	ebay-02/03	Bristol Yellow handle
6302					$245	White Cluthra	ebay-10/04	
6303	Goblet	192	5	5				MDK)16
6304	Vase	280	4	5	$1400	Blue Aurene	EAC-04/01	TPD)10.135
6305	Vase	280	4	6	$255	Green Jade	ebay-04/02	
6305					$170	French Blue	JDJ-11/03	
6305					$240	Topaz	ebay-03/04	
6305					$100	Topaz	ebay-07/05	
6306	Centerpiece	151	2	2				
6307	Compote	174	5	3				
6308	Plate	159	2	9				
6309	Cologne	242	1	2				
6310	Lamp Base	203	2	5				
6311	Lamp Base	203	2	6				
6312	Lamp Base	203	3	1				
6318	Goblet	197	5	2	$75	Colorless/Black threaded	ebay-02/04	
6330	Goblet	192	5	6				
6331	Candlestick	165	2	3				
6331	Compote	174	5	4				
6332	Centerpiece-duck	151	2	3	$775	Colorless/Celeste thread.	ebay-04/02	PG1)XIII B
6333	Cocktail Glass				$190	French Blue	ebay-02/01	This is shown in the 1932 Catalog.
6333					$75	French Blue	ebay-05/01	
6333					$80	Colorless/Black threaded	ebay-02/02	
6333					$50	Spanish Green	ebay-05/02	
6333					$60	Spanish Green	ebay-05/02	
6333					$30	Colorless/Black threaded	ebay-08/02	
6333					$55	Spanish Green	ebay-11/02	

SHAPE NO.	ITEM	PAGE	COL	ROW	PRICE REALIZED	GLASS TYPE	AUCTION HOUSE	COMMENTS & PHOTO REFERENCES
6333					$35	Colorless/Pomona thread	ebay-01/03	
6333					$20	Spanish Green	ebay-01/04	
6333					$30	Spanish Green	ebay-11/04	
6333					$85	French Blue	ebay-11/04	
6333					$40	French Blue	ebay-12/04	
6333					$15	Colorless/Pomona	ebay-01/05	Pomona Green threading
6333					$30	Colorless/Pomona	ebay-05/05	Pomona Green threading
6333					$40	Spanish Green	ebay-05/05	
6333					$50	Spanish Green	ebay-05/05	
6333					$75	Colorless/Black threaded	ebay-05/05	
6333					$45	Colorless/Black threaded	ebay-07/05	
6333	Fingerbowl				$65	Spanish Green	ebay-11/04	
6333	Goblet	192	5	7				
6333	Parfait				$50	French Blue with threading	ebay-10/02	
6334	Goblet	192	6	1				
6338	Goblet	192	6	2				TPD)9.23
6339	Candlestick	165	2	4	$200	Bristol Yellow	Sknr-01/96	
6339	Vase	280	5	1	$160	Unknown Light Green	ebay-09/03	ALSO 6380; PG1)89,135,B&D
6339					$45	Unknown Light Green	ebay-12/03	
6339					$80	Bristol Yellow	ebay-12/04	
6340	Tumbler	199	2	6				
6342	Decanter	186	5	1				
6343	Decanter	186	5	2				MDK)22
6344	Decanter	186	5	3				
6352	Decanter	186	5	4				
6354	Goblet	192	6	3	$380	VDS/Coral rim (E)	ebay-05/03	Engraved "Waverly"
6355	Candlestick	165	2	5	$535	French Blue	ebay-08/01	
6355					$205	French Blue	ebay-09/03	
6355					$690	French Blue	EAC-11/03	
6355					$65	Bristol Yellow	ebay-01/05	
6355					$350	French Blue	ebay-02/05	14" high
6355	Centerpiece	151	2	4				
6355	Compote	174	5	5	$325	French Blue	Cinc-06/03	MDK)26
6356	Candlestick	165	3	1	$325	Spanish Green	Sknr-05/95	PG1)XXII B,J
6356					$270	French Blue	ebay-07/04	
6356	Centerpiece	151	2	5	$250	French Blue	ebay-07/01	TPD)10.30
6356	Compote	174	5	6	$250	Spanish Green	ebay-02/03	TPD)10.44
6356					$170	Spanish Green	Cinc-06/05	
6356	Vase	280	5	2				
6357	Candlestick	165	3	2	$665	Colorless/Gold Ruby	ebay-07/05	Gold Ruby threading
6357	Centerpiece	151	2	6	$225	Colorless/Gold Ruby	ebay-08/04	Gold Ruby threading
6357	Compote	175	1	1				MDK)65
6358	Champagne				$95	French Blue	ebay-10/01	
6358	Goblet	192	6	4	$155	French Blue	ebay-10/99	PG1)XXII A,D; TPD)10.32
6358					$180	French Blue	ebay-01/03	
6358					$170	French Blue	ebay-03/04	
6358					$120	French Blue	EAC-07/04	
6358					$95	French Blue	ebay-05/05	
6358					$70	French Blue	ebay-07/05	
6358					$90	French Blue	ebay-07/05	
6359	Champagne				$70	Spanish Green	ebay-02/00	TPD)9.21
6359					$65	Spanish Green	ebay-12/00	
6359					$80	Spanish Green	ebay-12/01	
6359					$110	Spanish Green	ebay-04/02	
6359					$95	Spanish Green	ebay-04/02	
6359					$120	Spanish Green	ebay-01/03	
6359					$90	Spanish Green	ebay-03/03	
6359					$90	Spanish Green	ebay-05/03	
6359					$80	Topaz	ebay-07/03	
6359					$70	Topaz	ebay-12/03	
6359					$45	Topaz	ebay-05/04	
6359					$125	Spanish Green	ebay-12/03	
6359					$25	Spanish Green	ebay-01/04	
6359					$90	Spanish Green	EAC-07/04	
6359					$80	Spanish Green	EAC-07/04	
6359					$80	Topaz	ebay-06/05	
6359	Finger Bowl				$50	Spanish Green	ebay-03/04	TPD)9.21
6359	Goblet	192	6	5	$65	Spanish Green	Sknr-05/95	RFR)16,2,B; TPD)9.21
6359					$70	Spanish Green	Tway-10/00	
6359					$70	Spanish Green	ebay-06/01	
6359					$35	Spanish Green	ebay-09/02	
6359					$50	Spanish Green	ebay-10/02	
6359					$105	Spanish Green	ebay-05/03	
6359					$110	Spanish Green	ebay-09/03	

SHAPE NO.	ITEM	PAGE	COL	ROW	PRICE REALIZED	GLASS TYPE	AUCTION HOUSE	COMMENTS & PHOTO REFERENCES
6359					$35	Spanish Green	ebay-01/04	
6359					$100	Spanish Green	ebay-07/04	
6359					$90	Spanish Green	EAC-07/04	
6359					$45	Spanish Green	ebay-10/04	
6359	Sherbet				$50	Spanish Green	ebay-02/00	
6359					$75	Spanish Green	ebay-11/03	
6359					$125	Spanish Green	ebay-12/03	
6359					$40	Spanish Green	EAC-07/04	No Underplate
6360	Champagne				$50	Col./Gold Ruby threading	ebay-10/03	
6360					$50	Col./Gold Ruby threading	ebay-01/05	
6360					$50	Col./Green threading	ebay-01/05	
6360	Fingerbowl				$45	Col./Gold Ruby threading	ebay-10/02	Fingerbowl only, no Underplate
6360					$25	Col./Gold Ruby threading	ebay-12/02	Fingerbowl only, no Underplate
6360					$60	Col./Gold Ruby threading	ebay-05/03	Fingerbowl only, no Underplate
6360					$65	Col./Gold Ruby threading	ebay-07/03	Fingerbowl only, no Underplate
6360					$75	Col./Gold Ruby threading	ebay-07/03	Fingerbowl only, no Underplate
6360					$45	Col./Gold Ruby threading	ebay-01/05	Fingerbowl only, no Underplate
6360	Goblet	192	6	6	$125	Col./Gold Ruby threading	ebay-11/00	
6360					$145	Col./Gold Ruby threading	ebay-01/02	
6360					$100	Col./Gold Ruby threading	ebay-12/02	
6360					$60	Col./Gold Ruby threading	ebay-09/03	
6360					$50	Col./Gold Ruby threading	ebay-10/03	
6360					$100	Col./Gold Ruby threading	ebay-01/05	
6360	Sherbet				$80	Col./Gold Ruby threading	Cinc-12/99	Sherbet only, no Underplate
6360					$95	Col./Gold Ruby threading	ebay-03/02	
6360					$95	Col./Gold Ruby threading	ebay-05/02	Sherbet only, no Underplate
6360					$95	Col./Gold Ruby threading	ebay-07/03	Sherbet only, no Underplate
6361	Goblet	192	6	7				
6362	Goblet	193	1	1				TPD)6.1
6363	Goblet	193	1	2				
6364	Finger Bowl				$30	Bristol Yellow	ebay-02/05	
6364	Goblet	193	1	3				
6365	Lamp Base	203	3	2				
6366	Lamp Base	203	3	3				
6367	Lamp Base	203	3	4				
6368	Vase	280	5	3				PG1)112,172,A&C
6368					$720	Alabaster ACB	ebay-03/05	Etched "Chippendale"
6369	Vase	280	5	4				
6370	Vase	280	5	5	$2970	Black/Amethyst Cintra ACB	EAC-10/91	Etched "Duck" RFR)19,4,B;
6370					$2310	Black/Amethyst Cintra ACB	EAC-10/93	Etched "Duck" base drilled
6370					$2750	Black/Cintra ACB	EAC-04/95	TPD)10.33
6370					$2035	Black/Cintra ACB	EAC-10/95	
6370					$3300	Black/Cintra ACB	EAC-07/98	
6370					$2830	Black/Cintra ACB	ebay-10/03	Etched "Duck" Drilled for lamp.
6371	Plate	159	1	12				
6372	Limousine Vase	203	3	5				TPD)10.18
6373	Vase	280	5	6				RLG)150,284
6374	Candlestick	165	3	3				
6375	Vase	281	1	1				
6376	Vase	281	1	2				
6377	Decanter	186	5	5				
6378	Decanter	186	5	6				
6379	Decanter	187	1	1				
6380	Bowl	144	3	2	$485	Flemish Blue	Sknr-10/96	
6380	Vase	280	5	1				ALSO 6339; PG1)89,135,C
6381	Goblet	193	1	4				
6382	Vase	281	1	3	$160	Jade Green/Alabaster	ebay-10/02	Alabaster Lion prunts.
6382					$405	Bristol Yellow/Pomona	ebay-01/05	Pomona Green Lion prunts.
6383	Candlestick	165	3	4				
6384	Candlestick	165	3	5	$265	Bristol Yellow	EAC-04/95	PG1)XXII B,E&G; TPD)4.61; MDK)35
6384					$155	Pomona Green	Sknr-05/95	
6384					$440	Gold Ruby (FC)	EAC-07/97	
6384					$190	Pomona Green	EAC-10/97	
6384					$145	Rosa	Sknr-01/98	
6384					$165	Gold Ruby	EAC-07/98	
6384					$260	French Blue	ebay-10/99	
6384					$140	Rosa	ebay-12/00	
6384					$130	French Blue	ebay-03/01	
6384					$280	Blue Aurene	EAC-04/01	
6384					$720	Gold Aurene	JDJ-11/01	
6384					$130	French Blue	ebay-09/02	
6384					$100	Celeste Blue	ebay-10/02	
6384					$165	Jade Green	ebay-10/02	
6384					$100	Spanish Green	ebay-10/02	

SHAPE NO.	ITEM	PAGE	COL	ROW	PRICE REALIZED	GLASS TYPE	AUCTION HOUSE	COMMENTS & PHOTO REFERENCES
6384					$260	Amethyst shaded to col.	ebay-04/03	
6384					$115	Topaz	ebay-09/03	
6384					$115	Pomona Green	ebay-09/03	
6384					$700	Blue Aurene	J&W-09/03	
6384					$285	Green Jade	JDJ-11/03	
6384					$150	Spanish Green	ebay-12/03	
6384					$130	Green Jade/Alabaster	ebay-02/04	Alabaster prunts
6384					$140	Bristol Yellow	ebay-04/04	
6384					$80	Amber	ebay-04/04	
6384					$85	Amber	ebay-04/04	
6384					$140	Topaz/Celeste Blue prunts	ebay-05/04	
6384					$875	Blue Aurene	ebay-05/04	
6384					$660	Gold Aurene	Cinc-06/04	
6384					$100	Bristol Yellow/Pomona	ebay-08/04	Pomona Green prunts
6384					$165	Topaz/Celeste Blue prunts	ebay-09/04	
6384					$55	Topaz	ebay-12/04	
6384					$60	Topaz	ebay-01/05	
6384					$75	Topaz	ebay-02/05	
6384					$75	Topaz	ebay-03/05	
6384					$60	Pomona Green	ebay-04/05	
6384					$115	Bristol Yellow/Pomona	ebay-06/05	Pomona Green prunts
6384					$170	Green Jade/Alabaster	EAC-07/05	Alabaster prunts
6385	Candlestick	165	3	6				
6386	Lamp	202	2	3				
6387	Lamp	202	2	4				
6388	Tumbler	199	2	7				
6389	Vase	281	1	4	$7015	Moss Agate	JDJ-11/01	PG1)314; RFR)18,2,B
6389					$2775	Rosaline/Alabaster ACB	ebay-10/02	Etched "Floral"
6390	Vase	281	1	5				TPD)5.13
6391	Vase	281	2	1	$1090	Mirror Black ACB	Sknr-05/98	PG1)113,174:314; RFR)18,2,C
6391					$1000	Green Jade ACB	ebay-10/02	
6392	Vase	281	2	2	$585	Gold Aurene	ebay-03/05	
6393	Vase	281	2	3				
6394	Goblet	193	1	5				This shape is shown as #6395 in Gardner.
6394								PG1)XXVIII C:103,157,F
6394					$1000	Colorless/Gold Ruby (E)	ebay-12/03	Engraved "Fountain"
6394	Sherbet				$210	Colorless (E)	ebay-12/01	
6394					$40	Rosaline/Alabaster foot	ebay-01/04	
6394					$35	Rosaline/Alabaster foot	ebay-01/04	
6394					$40	Rosaline/Alabaster foot	ebay-01/04	
6394					$225	Colorless/Blacked cased	ebay-06/04	Cut decoration
6395	Candlestick	165	4	1				
6395	Centerpiece	151	2	7				
6395	Compote	175	1	2				
6395	Goblet	193	1	5				This number is an error, see #6394 Goblet
6396	Covered Vase	307	3	5				TPD)7.42:9.19
6397	Goblet	193	1	6				
6398	Candlestick	165	4	2				
6398	Centerpiece	151	2	8				
6398	Compote	175	1	3				
6399	Covered Vase	307	4	1				
6400	Decanter	187	1	2				PG1)46,84,A&D
6401	Cordial				$110	Bristol Yellow	ebay-03/00	
6401	Champagne				$75	Colorless/Green threaded	ebay-07/02	
6401					$125	Colorless/Green threaded	ebay-02/04	
6401					$35	Topaz/Red threaded	ebay-08/03	
6401					$70	Colorless/Green threaded	ebay-06/05	
6401					$70	Colorless/Green threaded	ebay-06/05	
6401	Goblet	193	1	7	$150	Gold Ruby/Col. stem & foot	ebay-11/03	ACR)COLOR 4,B,A; TPD)7.54:8.12
6401					$150	Colorless/Green threaded	ebay-02/04	
6401					$90	Colorless/Green threaded	ebay-06/04	
6401					$40	Colorless	ebay-10/04	
6401					$80	Colorless/Green threaded	ebay-06/05	
6401					$80	Colorless/Green threaded	ebay-06/05	
6401	Wine				$50	Colorless	ebay-03/04	
6402	Candlestick	165	4	3				
6402	Centerpiece	151	3	1				
6402	Compote	175	1	4	$165	Pomona Green	ebay-04/02	TPD)10.112
6402					$590	Green Jade/Alabaster	ebay-02/03	Alabaster stem
6403	Candlestick	165	4	4				
6403	Centerpiece	151	3	2				
6403	Compote	175	1	5	$115	Colorless (E)	ebay-12/03	
6404	Goblet	193	2	1	$375	Smoke/Celeste Blue	ebay-02/03	PG1)355,H,I; TPD)7.54
6404					$30	Smoke/Celeste Blue	JDJ-11/03	

SHAPE NO.	ITEM	PAGE	COL	ROW	PRICE REALIZED	GLASS TYPE	AUCTION HOUSE	COMMENTS & PHOTO REFERENCES
6405	Candlestick	165	5	1				PG1)355,I
6405	Centerpiece	151	3	3				PG1)355,I
6405	Compote	175	1	6	$610	Blue Aurene	ebay-01/01	PG1)355,I; RFR)26,3,B
6405					$450	Topaz/Celeste Blue stem	ebay-09/02	
6405					$125	Colorless/Gold Ruby	ebay-04/05	Gold Ruby threaded
6406	Vase	281	2	4				PG1)314
6407	Atomizer	239	2	4	$1540	Blue Aurene (E)	EAC-10/90	With fittings; TPD)4.3
6407					$825	Blue Aurene	EAC-04/92	With fittings
6407					$385	Gold Aurene	EAC-04/99	
6407					$990	Blue Aurene Lamp	Sknr-06/02	Roycroft lamp mounts
6407					$665	Gold Aurene (E)	ebay-09/02	With fittings
6407					$1000	Blue Aurene	ebay-11/02	Roycroft lamp mounts
6407					$340	Blue Aurene	ebay-06/03	Glass only
6407					$1090	Blue Aurene	Jack-06/03	With fittings
6407					$575	Gold Aurene	Jack-06/03	With fittings
6407					$900	Blue Aurene	JDJ-11/03	With fittings
6407					$630	Gold Aurene	EAC-11/03	With fittings
6407					$400	Gold Aurene (E)	EAC-04/04	
6407					$535	Gold Aurene (E)	ebay-07/04	With fittings
6407					$920	Gold Aurene	EAC-04/04	
6407					$1100	Blue Aurene	ebay-08/04	With fittings
6407					$1320	Blue Aurene	EAC-10/04	With fittings
6407					$600	Gold Aurene (E)	ebay-01/05	With fittings
6407					$585	Gold Aurene	ebay-03/05	Missing bulb
6407					$940	Gold Aurene (E)	ebay-04/05	With fittings
6407					$1055	Blue Aurene	ebay-04/05	With fittings
6407					$690	Blue Aurene (E)	EAC-04/05	No bulb
6408	Atomizer	239	2	5				
6409	Atomizer	239	2	6				
6410	Atomizer	239	2	7				
6411	Atomizer	239	3	1				
6412	Atomizer	239	3	2				
6413	Atomizer	239	3	3				
6414	Bowl	144	3	3				
6415	Bowl	144	3	4	$1035	Colorless ACB	Sknr-05/96	PG1)XVIII A,F:314;PG2)72;ACR)155,305
6415					$440	Mirror Black	JDJ-06/96	MDK)19:131
6415					$750	Blue/White Cluthra	JDJ-10/97	
6415					$1495	Alabaster	Sknr-02/00	
6415					$235	Rosaline	ebay-11/00	
6415					$500	Jade Green	ebay-03/01	
6415					$250	Light Amethyst	ebay-06/02	
6415					$265	White Cluthra	Sknr-12/02	
6415					$500	Colorless ACB	JDJ-05/03	Etched "Dayton"
6415					$305	French Blue	ebay-06/03	
6415					$325	Bristol Yellow	ebay-07/03	
6415					$85	Colorless	ebay-01/04	
6415					$540	Amethyst Cluthra	JDJ-05/04	
6415					$1760	Amethyst Cluthra	EAC-10/04	
6415					$205	Amethyst	ebay-04/05	
6415					$200	Colorless	ebay-05/05	
6416	Vase	281	2	5	$1000	Blue Aurene	ebay-02/05	
6417	Vase	281	2	6				PG1)103,156,A
6418	Candlestick	165	5	2				TPD)4.53:7.42
6418	Centerpiece	151	3	4				
6418	Compote	175	1	7				
6419	Vase	281	3	1	$125	Bristol Yellow/Colorless	ebay-08/01	MDK)49
6420	Vase	281	3	2				
6421	Vase	281	3	3	$465	Bristol Yellow	ebay-06/02	PG1)89,135,A&E;TPD)5.45
6421					$325	Bristol Yellow	Sknr-12/02	Lamp with fittings.
6422	Vase	281	3	4				
6423	Vase	281	3	5	$80	Topaz	ebay-11/01	
6424	Vase	281	3	6	$150	Bristol Yellow	ebay-04/05	
6425	Vase	281	3	7	$120	Bristol Yellow	ebay-09/02	MDK)80
6425					$110	French Blue	ebay-03/05	
6426	Vase	281	4	1	$615	Bristol Yellow/Green	EAC-01/03	Green threading and decoration
6426					$300	Colorless/Pomona Green	ebay-04/04	Green threading and prunts
6427	Vase	281	4	2	$135	Rosa	JDJ-05/94	JAS)167,C
6427					$565	Moonlight	ebay-11/01	
6427					$410	Wisteria	ebay-02/03	
6428	Vase	281	4	3	$60	Spanish Green	JDJ-10/97	
6428					$215	Colorless/Green rings	Tway-09/04	
6428					$50	Colorless/Black rings	ebay-04/05	
6429	Covered Vase	307	4	2				PG1)103,156,B
6430	Covered Vase	307	4	3				

SHAPE NO.	ITEM	PAGE	COL	ROW	PRICE REALIZED	GLASS TYPE	AUCTION HOUSE	COMMENTS & PHOTO REFERENCES
6431	Covered Vase	307	5	1				
6432	Cologne	242	1	3				PG1)97,150; JAS)167,TR,A
6433	Vase	281	4	4	$285	Bristol Yellow	ebay-10/99	TPD)8.28
6433					$560	Green Jade/Alabaster	ebay-12/01	
6433					$355	Pomona Green	ebay-01/02	
6433					$355	Bristol Yellow	ebay-05/02	Colorless stem and foot.
6433					$512	Amethyst	ebay-08/02	
6433					$150	Topaz/Pomona Green	Cinc-11/02	
6433					$500	Green Jade/Alabaster	ebay-03/03	
6435	Pitcher	214	2	3				
6435	Lemonade	214	2	3				
6436	Atomizer	239	3	4				
6437	Atomizer	239	3	5				
6438	Atomizer	239	3	6				
6439	Atomizer	239	3	7				
6440	Atomizer	239	4	1				
6440	Cologne				$2415	Gold Aurene	EAC-11/03	TPD)8.7:10.145
6441	Vase	281	4	5	$400	Wisteria	Sknr-01/97	PG1)103,156,C
6441					$230	Pomona Green	Sknr-01/98	
6441					$285	Bristol Yellow	ebay-10/99	
6441					$130	Bristol Yellow	ebay-01/00	
6441					$345	Gold Ruby	ebay-02/00	
6441					$305	Pomona Green	ebay-04/01	
6441					$330	Pomona Green	Cott-08/01	
6441					$190	Pomona Green	ebay-09/01	
6441					$280	French Blue	ebay-11/02	
6441					$285	Gold Ruby/Colorless foot	ebay-05/04	
6441					$910	Orchid	ebay-05/04	
6441					$255	Gold Ruby/Colorless foot	ebay-11/04	
6441					$95	Rosa	ebay-01/05	
6442	Centerpiece	151	3	5				
6443	Vase	281	4	6				PG1)112,173
6444	Centerpiece	151	3	6	$575	Rosaline/Alabaster	JDJ-10/96	PG1)XXII B,C; ACR)146,279
6444					$400	Gold Ruby/Colorless foot	ebay-05/02	
6445	Champagne							JSS)12-33,L
6445	Goblet	193	2	2				TPD)7.47
6445	Sherbet				$235	Colorless/Gold Ruby	ebay-12/00	
6445					$285	Colorless/Gold Ruby (E)	ebay-02/03	Sherbet only, no underplate
6446	Candlestick	165	5	3				
6447	Bobeche	205	4	11				
6448	Table Decoration	237	1	3	$935	Gold Aurene	EAC-04/98	ACR)144,272; TPD)4.149
6448					$200	Pomona Green	ebay-10/99	
6448					$455	Gold Aurene	ebay-11/99	
6448					$130	Colorless	ebay-12/99	
6448					$190	Bristol Yellow	ebay-06/00	
6448					$200	Celeste Blue	ebay-10/00	
6448					$150	Pomona Green	ebay-09/01	
6448					$230	Bristol Yellow	ebay-05/02	
6448					$20	Colorless/Pomona leaves	ebay-11/03	
6448					$180	Topaz	ebay-11/03	
6448					$130	Pomona Green	ebay-05/05	
6449	Candlestick	165	5	4	$350	Gold Ruby/Colorless disk	ebay-02/02	
6450	Cologne	242	1	4				
6451	3 Section Dish	211	4	5				
6453	Candlestick	165	5	5				TPD)4.52
6453	Compote	175	2	1				
6454	Vase	281	5	1				
6455	Vase	281	5	2				
6456	Vase	281	5	3				
6457	Vase	281	5	4				TPD)6.28
6458	Candlestick	166	1	1				
6458	Centerpiece	151	3	7				
6458	Compote	175	2	2				
6459	Vase	282	1	1	$910	Alabaster ACB	ebay-01/04	Crest Lamp
6460	Pitcher	214	2	4	$550	Green Jade/Alabaster	EAC-07/98	
6461	Pitcher	214	2	5				
6462	Pitcher	214	3	1				
6463	Atomizer	239	4	2				
6464	Candlestick	166	1	2				
6465	Candlestick	166	1	3				ACR)166,334; TPD)10.24
6466	Candlestick	166	1	4	$100	Pomona Green	Sknr-05/94	
6466					$280	Colorless/Topaz foot	ebay-03/02	
6467	Vase	282	1	2				
6468	Vase	282	1	3	$2200	Amethyst/Alabaster ACB	EAC-10/91	PG1)XXV C,C;PG1)314; TPD)2.44

SHAPE NO.	ITEM	PAGE	COL	ROW	PRICE REALIZED	GLASS TYPE	AUCTION HOUSE	COMMENTS & PHOTO REFERENCES
6469	Centerpiece	151	3	8				
6470	Lamp Base	203	3	6				
6471	Cologne	242	1	5				
6472	Centerpiece	151	3	9				
6473	Candlestick	166	1	5				This shape is shown as #6475 in Gardner.
6474	Goblet	193	2	3	$125	Colorless/Green threaded	ebay-05/04	PG2)64,I; JAS)150,B,I
6475	Candlestick	166	1	5				This number is an error, see #6473.
6475	Wine Glass Cooler	189	2	10				
6476	Goblet	193	2	4				
6477	Centerpiece	152	1	1				
6478	Centerpiece	152	1	2				
6479	Centerpiece	152	1	3				
6480	Centerpiece	152	1	4				
6481	Plate	159	1	13				
6482	Vase	282	1	4				
6483	Table Decoration	237	1	4	$1095	Colorless	Sknr-10/00	PG1)92,142,C
6483					$635	Colorless	ebay-03/04	
6483					$365	Colorless	ebay-06/05	
6484	Candlestick	166	1	6				
6485	Vase	282	2	1				
6486	Table Decoration	236	3	6				Shoe, PG1)91,141;PG2)96,55
6487	Vase	282	2	2				
6488	Cruet	179	3	5				
6489	Centerpiece	152	1	5				
6490	Vase	282	2	3				RFR)27,1,A; TPD)8.31
6491	Vase	282	2	4				
6492	Vase	282	2	5				
6493	Vase	282	2	6				
6494	Vase	282	2	7				
6495	Flower Block	237	1	5	$365	Colorless	ebay-11/99	
6495					$495	Colorless	ebay-01/00	
6495					$335	Colorless	ebay-09/04	
6496	Covered Vase	307	5	2				
6497	Centerpiece	152	1	6	$22,500	Yellow Jade	ebay-02/00	TPD)4.149
6498	Centerpiece	152	2	1				TPD)4.150
6499	Vase	282	3	1	$3200	Yellow Jade ACB	ebay-11/99	
6500	Vase	282	3	2	$2185	Oriental Poppy	Sknr-10/94	PG1)XXX A,A; TPD)10.24
6500					$485	Green/White Cluthra	JDJ-10/97	
6500					$2200	Oriental Poppy	EAC-07/98	
6500					$245	Ivory	Cinc-12/99	
6500					$1250	Oriental Jade	ebay-09/02	
6500					$205	Ivory	ebay-07/03	
6500					$80	Colorless (E)	JDJ-11/02	
6500					$470	Blue Aurene	Sknr-12/03	
6500					$400	Gold Aurene	ebay-12/03	Signed "Haviland"
6500					$545	Ivory	JDJ-05/04	
6500					$1000	Blue Aurene	ebay-12/04	
6500					$450	Gold Aurene	ebay-01/05	
6500					$325	Ivory	ebay-03/05	
6500					$780	Gold Aurene	Dalla-03/05	
6500					$100	VDS	ebay-04/05	
6500					$145	Ivory	EAC-04/05	
6500					$230	Ivory	EAC-04/05	
6501	Vase	282	3	3	$6050	Moss Agate	EAC-04/95	PG1)314; PG2)90,E; JAS)170,B,E;
6501					$1380	Oriental Poppy	Sknr-05/97	ACR)167,335; TPD)10.19:10.88; MDK)139
6501					$690	Oriental Poppy	Sknr-10/98	
6501					$1530	Oriental Poppy	ebay-12/00	
6501					$2280	Oriental Poppy	ebay-03/01	
6501					$90	Pomona Green	ebay-07/02	
6501					$1700	Oriental Poppy	ebay-03/03	
6501					$810	Rose Quartz	ebay-10/03	
6501					$4600	Rosaline/Alabaster ACB	Jack-06/03	Etched "Chinese"
6502	Table Decoration	236	1	1	$1650	Colorless cut	Cott-08/01	Eagle, PG1)98,152
6502					$700	Colorless cut	ebay-09/03	
6503	Vase	282	3	4				
6504	Table Decoration	236	1	2	$1200	Colorless	ebay-12/00	Pheasant, JAS)170,T
6505	Bowl	144	3	5	$430	Gold Calcite (E)	ebay-02/02	PG1)314
6505	Candlestick	166	1	7				PG1)314
6505	Compote	175	2	3				PG1)314
6505	Goblet	193	2	5	$515	Green over Colorless (E)	ebay-11/00	PG1)314; JSS)12-28,R:12-35:12-53
6505					$800	Green over Colorless (E)	EAC-08/00	TPD)7.39:7.48; MDK)44
6505					$435	Amethyst over Col. (E)	ebay-01/03	
6505					$370	Amethyst over Col. (E)	ebay-02/03	
6505					$560	Gold Ruby over Col. (E)	ebay-04/03	

SHAPE NO.	ITEM	PAGE	COL	ROW	PRICE REALIZED	GLASS TYPE	AUCTION HOUSE	COMMENTS & PHOTO REFERENCES
6505					$145	Colorless (E)	ebay-08/04	
6505					$150	Colorless (E)	ebay-08/04	
6505					$155	Colorless (E)	ebay-08/04	
6505					$95	Colorless (E)	ebay-08/04	
6505					$130	Colorless (E)	ebay-09/04	
6505					$160	Green over Col. (E)	EAC-04/05	Engraved "Harvard"
6505	Parfait				$375	Amethyst over Col. (E)	EAC-11/03	Engraved "Harvard"
6506	Centerpiece	152	2	2				
6506	Candlestick	166	2	1	$280	Colorless/Threaded	EAC-11/01	Gold Ruby threaded 6" high
6506	Compote	175	2	4	$340	Colorless/Pomona Green	ebay-09/01	
6507	Candlestick	166	2	2				
6507	Centerpiece	152	2	3				
6507	Compote	175	2	5				PG1)76,120,D
6508	Vase	282	3	5				
6509	Bowl	144	3	6				
6510	Goblet	193	2	6				
6511	Goblet	193	3	1				
6512	Vase	282	3	6				MDK)148
6513	Centerpiece	152	2	4				
6514	Centerpiece	152	2	5				TPD)7.35
6515	Centerpiece	152	2	6				PG1)47,85:314; TPD)4.150
6516	Decanter	187	1	3				
6517	Goblet	193	3	2				
6518	Parfait	199	2	8	$375	Oriental Jade	Sknr-05/94	
6518					$385	Oriental Poppy	JDJ-06/96	
6518					$600	Oriental Poppy	ebay-05/01	
6518					$100	Gold Calcite	ebay-11/01	
6518					$425	Oriental Poppy	ebay-11/01	
6518					$560	Oriental Poppy	EAC-09/02	Pomona Green foot
6518					$60	Colorless/Black threaded	ebay-08/03	
6518					$150	Bristol Yellow (E)	ebay-03/04	
6518					$125	Bristol Yellow (E)	Cinn-05/05	
6519	Vase	282	3	7				
6520	Goblet	193	3	3				
6521	Goblet	193	3	4				
6522	Goblet	193	3	5	$935	Oriental Poppy	EAC-07/96	PG2)64,H; JAS)150,B,H; TPD)6.1;MDK)14
6522					$660	Oriental Poppy/Pomona	EAC-11/03	Pomona Green stem and foot
6522					$225	Selenium Red/Colorless	ebay-07/04	Colorless stem
6523	Goblet	193	3	6	$200	Green Jade/Alabaster	ebay-04/00	PG2)64,F; JAS)150,B,F
6523					$200	Gold Ruby/Colorless	ebay-11/01	
6523	Parfait				$115	Rosaline/Alabaster foot	ebay-03/04	
6524	Goblet	193	3	7				
6525	Vase	282	4	1	$330	White Cluthra	JDJ-06/96	
6526	Vase	282	4	2				
6527	Vase	282	4	3				
6528	Vase	282	4	4				
6529	Vase	282	4	5				
6530	Vase	282	4	6				
6531	Goblet	193	4	1				
6532	Goblet	193	4	2	$130	Flemish Blue	Cinc-06/05	
6532					$175	Gold Calcite	ebay-06/05	
6533	Candlestick	166	2	3				
6534	Vase	282	5	1				
6535	Vase	282	5	2				PG1)113,177; TPD)10.132
6536	Covered Vase	307	5	3				
6537	Centerpiece	152	3	1				
6538	Vase	282	5	3				
6539	Centerpiece	152	3	2				PG1)46,84,B; TPD)7.62
6540	Vase	283	1	1	$1495	ACB	Sknr-05/97	PG1)XXIV B,B; PG2)97,C; RLG)146,276;
6540					$1265	ACB	Sknr-05/97	JAS)148,B,C
6541	Lamp	202	5	1				
6542	Lamp	202	4	2				TPD)4.181
6543	Lamp	202	4	3				TPD)4.116
6544	Lamp	202	4	1				
6545	Vase	283	1	2				TPD)4.50
6546	Vase	283	1	3				
6547	Vase	283	1	4	$345	Green Jade	EAC-04/95	
6547					$125	VDS/Blue threaded	Sknr-06/00	
6547					$305	Flemish Blue	ebay-02/03	
6547					$135	Green Jade	ebay-03/03	
6547					$295	VDS/Yellow threaded	ebay-08/03	
6547					$70	Celeste Blue	ebay-06/04	
6547					$150	Topaz	ebay-09/04	
6547					$180	Bristol Yellow/White thread.	ebay-02/05	

SHAPE NO.	ITEM	PAGE	COL	ROW	PRICE REALIZED	GLASS TYPE	AUCTION HOUSE	COMMENTS & PHOTO REFERENCES
6548	Vase	283	1	5				
6549	Lamp Base	203	4	1				
6550	Lamp Base	203	4	2				
6551	Lamp Base	203	4	3				
6552	Vase	283	1	6				
6553	Compote	175	2	6				
6554	Vase	283	1	7				
6555	Decanter	187	1	4				
6556	Centerpiece	152	3	3				
6557	Candlestick	166	2	4				
6557	Centerpiece	152	3	4				TPD)4.72
6558	Candlestick	166	2	5				
6558	Centerpiece	152	3	5				
6559	Covered Vase	308	1	1				PG1)314
6560	Vase	283	2	1				
6561	Vase	283	2	2				PG1)XXVIII B,B; PG1)76,120,C
6562	Goblet	193	4	3				
6563	Champagne				$170	Green Jade/Alabaster	ebay-07/01	
6563					$60	Green Jade/Alabaster	ebay-01/02	
6563	Goblet	193	4	4				JSS)12-36,C
6563	Fingerbowl				$235	Rosaline/Alabaster foot	ebay-07/04	No underplate
6564	Goblet	193	4	5				
6565	Champagne				$60	Marina Blue (E)	ebay-02/05	Engraved in Lenox "Fountain"
6565	Goblet	193	4	6	$180	Bristol Yellow	ebay-02/00	PG1)49,86,A; TPD)7.45:7.69
6565					$60	Marina Blue (E)	ebay-02/05	Engraved in Lenox "Fountain"
6565	Parfait				$50	Marina Blue (E)	EAC-01/03	Engraved in Lenox "Fountain"
6565	Sherbet				$70	Marina Blue (E)	EAC-01/03	Engraved in Lenox "Fountain"
6566	Covered Vase	308	1	2				PG1)94,147; PG2)80; TPD)7.31:9.18
6567	Goblet	193	5	1				
6568	Water Bottle	199	4	6				
6569	Covered Vase	308	1	3				
6570	Shade	229	3	3				
6571	Shade	229	3	4	$1320	Gold Aurene	JDJ-06/05	
6571					$1440	Gold Aurene	JDJ-06/05	
6572	Shade	229	3	5				
6573	Bowl	144	3	7				
6574	Goblet	193	5	2				
6575	Vase	283	2	3				
6576	Vase	283	2	4				
6577	Vase	283	3	1				PG1)76,120,B
6578	Bowl	144	3	8				
6579	Covered Vase	308	1	4				
6580	Shade	229	3	6				
6581	Shade	229	3	7				
6582	Goblet	193	5	3	$195	Green Jade/Alabaster	ebay-08/04	Alabaster stem and foot
6582					$195	Green Jade/Alabaster	ebay-09/04	Alabaster stem and foot
6582	Champagne				$190	Rosaline/Alabaster	ebay-11/00	
6582	Parfait				$100	Rosaline/Alabaster	ebay-06/04	
6583	Goblet	193	5	4				TPD)7.69
6583	Wine				$90	Spanish Green	ebay-05/04	
6584	Vase	283	3	2				
6585	Vase	283	3	3				PG1)46,81
6586	Jar	209	5	1				
6587	Listerine	243	6	2				
6588	Vase	283	3	4	$2875	Rose Quartz ACB	JDJ-11/03	Etched "Sculptured"
6589	Vase	283	4	1				
6590	Toilet Bottle	243	4	6	$355	French Blue	ebay-11/99	JAS)167,B,A&C;TPD)5.47; MDK)146
6590					$300	Amethyst	ebay-12/99	
6590					$265	Gold Ruby	ebay-12/99	
6590					$2750	Oriental Orchid	ebay-05/00	
6590					$230	Colorless/Black threaded	ebay-01/01	
6590					$100	Colorless/Green threaded	ebay-08/01	
6590					$600	Bristol/Black threaded	ebay-03/02	
6590					$270	Bristol Yellow/Black thread.	ebay-12/03	
6590					$255	French Blue	ebay-02/04	
6590					$200	French Blue	ebay-10/04	
6590					$300	Gold Ruby	EAC-10/04	
6590					$275	Amethyst/Flower stopper	ebay-11/04	
6590					$180	Amethyst	ebay-12/04	
6590					$145	Colorless/Black threaded	ebay-02/05	
6590					$170	Amethyst	ebay-02/05	
6590					$180	Amethyst	ebay-02/05	
6590					$255	Amethyst	ebay-02/05	
6590					$155	Colorless/Green threaded	ebay-03/05	

SHAPE NO.	ITEM	PAGE	COL	ROW	PRICE REALIZED	GLASS TYPE	AUCTION HOUSE	COMMENTS & PHOTO REFERENCES
6590					$205	Colorless/Black threaded	ebay-03/05	
6590					$205	Green Jade/Alabaster	ebay-05/05	Alabaster stopper, set of 5 @ $1020
6590					$130	Colorless/Black threaded	ebay-05/05	Black stopper
6590					$205	French Blue	ebay-05/05	
6590					$90	Flemish Blue	ebay-06/05	
6590					$80	Amethyst	ebay-06/05	
6591	Lamp Base	205	3	5				Art Light Special
6592	Centerpiece	152	3	6	$220	Bristol/Black threaded	Cinc-12/99	
6593	Candlestick	166	3	1	$315	Threaded VDS	Sknr-05/95	MDK)51
6593					$400	Threaded VDS	JDJ-06/97	
6593					$50	Green Jade	ebay-03/00	
6593					$160	Threaded VDS	ebay-04/00	
6593					$175	Bristol Yellow	EAC-10/00	
6593					$180	Gold Ruby	ebay-01/01	
6593					$220	Colorless/Threaded	ebay-03/01	
6593					$450	Blue Aurene	EAC-04/01	
6593					$60	Topaz	ebay-03/02	
6593					$125	Green shaded	ebay-01/03	
6593					$125	Spanish Green	ebay-02/03	
6593					$225	Bristol Yellow	ebay-06/03	
6593					$85	Colorless/Red threaded	ebay-12/03	
6593					$100	Colorless/Red threaded	ebay-12/03	
6593					$75	Pomona Green	ebay-08/04	
6593					$50	Pomona Green	ebay-12/04	
6593					$100	Bristol Yellow	ebay-05/05	
6593					$120	Gold Ruby	Cinc-06/05	
6593					$120	Bristol Yellow	Cinc-06/05	
6594	Candlestick	166	3	2				PG1)49,86,B
6594	Centerpiece	152	3	7				
6594	Compote	175	2	7				
6595	Vase	283	4	2				
6596	Champagne				$350	Colorless/Gold Ruby (E)	ebay-04/03	
6596	Goblet	193	5	5	$1155	Colorless/Gold Ruby	EAC-07/94	PG1)314; PG2)87,B; TPD)7.41
6596					$750	Colorless/Gold Ruby	ebay-06/02	
6596	Sherbet				$650	Colorless/Gold Ruby (E)	ebay-04/03	MDK)46
6597	Candlestick	166	3	3				PG1)XXX A,F
6597	Centerpiece	152	3	8				
6597	Compote	175	3	1				
6598	Champagne							
6598					$380	Oriental Jade/Opaline	ebay-08/02	Opaline stem and foot
6598					$390	Oriental Jade/Opaline	ebay-08/02	Opaline stem and foot
6598					$775	Oriental Jade/Opaline	ebay-07/03	Opaline stem and foot
6598					$240	Oriental Jade/Opaline	ebay-01/04	Opaline stem and foot
6598					$310	Oriental Jade/Opaline	ebay-09/04	Opaline stem and foot
6598					$250	Oriental Jade/Opaline	ebay-10/04	Opaline stem and foot
6598					$335	Oriental Jade/Opaline	ebay-12/04	Opaline stem and foot
6598	Goblet	193	5	6	$395	Oriental Jade	ebay-04/00	
6598	Sherbet				$200	Oriental Jade/Opaline foot	ebay-10/04	
6598					$250	Oriental Jade/Opaline foot	ebay-12/04	
6599	Goblet	193	6	1				PG1)314
6600	Cologne							See New Drawings section. MDK)56
6600					$450	VDS threaded	ebay-12/01	This shape shown in 1932 catalog.
6600					$250	VDS/Pomona threaded	ebay-11/02	
6600					$255	VDS/Red stopper	ebay-11/02	
6600					$150	VDS/Red threaded	ebay-04/04	
6600	Puff Box	245	1	2	$200	VDS threaded	ebay-11/00	MDK)13
6600					$450	Alabaster and Black	J&W-09/03	Black cover
6601	Vase							See New Drawings section
6602	Candlestick							See New Drawings section
6602					$125	Colorless	ebay-08/04	"Low" version, threaded and bubbly
6602	Comport							See New Drawings section
6602	Bowl							See New Drawings section
6603	Goblet	193	6	2	$250	Colorless/Black threading	ebay-07/04	MDK)115
6603					$230	Colorless/Black threading	ebay-07/05	
6603	Wine				$175	French Blue	ebay-07/04	
6603	Sherbet				$15	Colorless/Blue threaded	ebay-11/04	
6604	Cologne	242	1	6				PG1)105,161
6605	Cologne	242	1	7	$170	Green/Threaded	Sknr-10/96	
6605					$355	Bristol/Black threaded	ebay-06/02	
6605					$200	Colorless/Black threaded	ebay-07/02	
6605					$455	Bristol/Black threaded	ebay-02/03	
6606	Cologne	242	2	1				
6607	Basket	140	3	1				This Line Drawing is Missing in the
6607								Original Printing

SHAPE NO.	ITEM	PAGE	COL	ROW	PRICE REALIZED	GLASS TYPE	AUCTION HOUSE	COMMENTS & PHOTO REFERENCES
6608	Vase	283	4	3	$2700	Amethyst /Alabaster ACB	EAC-06/03	Etched "Honesty"
6609	Table Decoration	236	4	1				
6610	Lamp	208	1	1				PG2)99
6611	Covered Vase	308	1	5				PG1)105,163; TPD)7.55
6612	Decanter	187	2	1				TPD)7.55
6613	Vase	283	4	4				
6614	Candlestick	166	3	4				PG1)XXX A
6614	Centerpiece	152	3	9				
6614	Compote	175	3	2				PG2)91,Br; JAS)153,B,Br
6615	Champagne				$880	Oriental Poppy	EAC-07/91	
6615					$715	Oriental Poppy	EAC-02/92	Pomona stem and foot
6615					$715	Oriental Poppy	EAC-07/92	Pomona stem and foot
6615					$250	Oriental Poppy	EAC-10/98	
6615					$285	Oriental Poppy	Sknr-10/98	
6615					$275	Oriental Poppy	EAC-04/99	
6615					$575	Oriental Poppy	Jack-06/03	
6615					$575	Oriental Poppy	JDJ-11/03	
6615					$630	Oriental Poppy	JDJ-11/03	
6615					$400	Oriental Poppy	Jack-11/03	
6615					$480	Oriental Poppy	ebay-06/04	
6615					$610	Oriental Poppy	ebay-06/04	
6615					$365	Oriental Poppy	EAC-07/04	
6615					$400	Oriental Poppy	ebay-09/04	
6615					$485	Oriental Poppy	ebay-10/04	
6615					$200	Oriental Poppy	ebay-11/04	
6615					$390	Oriental Poppy	JDJ-06/05	
6615	Goblet	193	6	3	$605	Oriental Poppy	EAC-04/91	PG1)XXX B,C; ACR)COLOR1,T,D
6615					$1095	Oriental Poppy	Sknr-10/95	
6615					$825	Oriental Poppy	EAC-04/97	
6615					$490	Oriental Poppy	Sknr-01/98	
6615					$440	Oriental Poppy	EAC-07/98	
6615					$825	Oriental Poppy	EAC-08/00	
6615					$700	Oriental Poppy	ebay-12/00	
6615					$500	Oriental Poppy	ebay-10/01	
6615					$1570	Oriental Poppy	EAC-04/02	
6615					$400	Oriental Poppy	Jack-11/03	
6615					$860	Oriental Poppy	JDJ-05/04	Green stem and foot
6615					$585	Oriental Poppy	ebay-05/04	Green stem and foot
6615					$550	Oriental Poppy	ebay-11/04	Green stem and foot
6615					$295	Oriental Poppy	ebay-01/05	
6615					$840	Oriental Poppy	Cinc-06/05	Green stem and foot
6615	Sherbet				$200	Oriental Poppy	EAC-10/98	
6615					$145	Oriental Poppy	Sknr-10/98	
6615					$105	Oriental Jade	ebay-05/02	Sherbet only, no Underplate
6615					$375	Oriental Poppy	ebay-05/02	Sherbet only, no Underplate
6615					$660	Oriental Poppy	ebay-01/03	Sherbet only, no Underplate
6615					$575	Oriental Poppy	Jack-06/03	Sherbet only, no Underplate
6616	Bowl	144	3	9	$130	Bristol Yellow	ebay-05/05	
6617	Pitcher	214	3	2				
6617	Lemonade	214	3	2				
6618	Cigarette Holder	138	3	3				
6619	Cologne	242	2	2	$385	VDS/Threaded	EAC-10/97	MDK)13
6619					$300	VDS/Green threaded	ebay-04/02	
6619					$665	Ivory/Black stopper	ebay-06/03	
6619	Puff Box	245	1	3				
6620	Bowl	144	3	10				
6621	Goblet	193	6	4				
6622	Cologne	242	2	3				
6623	Cologne	242	2	4				
6624	Cologne	242	2	5				
6625	Cologne	242	2	6				
6626	Candlestick	166	3	5	$460	Selenium Red/Colorless	Sknr-05/94	PG1)314; TPD)10.95; MDK)28
6626					$390	Selenium Red/Colorless	EAC-04/01	
6626	Centerpiece	153	1	1				PG1)314
6626	Compote	175	3	3				
6627	Vase	283	4	5	$905	Gold Aurene	EAC-04/95	RFR)9,3,C; ACR)135,244; TPD)8.30
6627					$2230	Blue Aurene	ebay-01/02	
6627					$1775	Gold Aurene	ebay-03/02	
6627					$410	Blue Aurene	Sknr-12/02	
6627					$2800	Blue Aurene	ebay-07/03	
6627					$1540	Gold Aurene	ebay-02/04	
6627					$2160	Gold Aurene	Crft-05/04	
6627					$2400	Blue Aurene	ebay-06/04	
6627					$2800	Blue Aurene	ebay-07/04	

SHAPE NO.	ITEM	PAGE	COL	ROW	PRICE REALIZED	GLASS TYPE	AUCTION HOUSE	COMMENTS & PHOTO REFERENCES
6627					$2280	Gold Aurene	ebay-10/04	
6627					$3050	Blue Aurene	ebay-06/05	
6628	Vase	283	5	1				
6629	Vase	283	5	2				
6630	Vase	283	5	3	$990	Blue Aurene	JDJ-06/96	
6630					$3000	Gold Aurene	ebay-01/00	
6630					$3850	Blue Aurene	Cott-08/01	
6630					$3220	Gold Aurene	JDJ-11/01	
6630					$1790	Gold Aurene	EAC-01/03	
6630					$2100	Gold Aurene	Aspr-05/04	
6630					$1250	Blue Aurene	ebay-10/04	
6630					$5265	Blue Aurene	Cott-02/05	
6630					$3495	Blue Aurene	ebay-02/05	
6630					$960	Blue Aurene	ebay-05/05	Drilled for a lamp
6631	Tumbler	199	2	9				
6632	Aquarium	304	3	3				
6633	Vase	283	5	4				
6634	Vase	283	5	5	$195	Green Jade	ebay-07/04	
6635	Vase	283	5	6				
6636	Covered Vase	308	2	1				PG1)315; TPD)7.32
6637	Bowl	144	4	1	$1000	Oriental Poppy	ebay-01/03	
6637	Candlestick	166	3	6	$260	Green Jade	Sknr-01/97	RFR)26,1,A&C; TPD)9.27
6637					$430	Silverina	Sknr-01/98	
6637					$750	Gold Aurene	JDJ-11/01	
6637					$1315	Gold Aurene	ebay-01/03	
6637					$100	French Blue/White thread.	ebay-05/05	
6637					$450	Gold Aurene	ebay-05/05	
6637					$140	French Blue/White thread.	ebay-05/05	
6637					$100	French Blue/White thread.	ebay-06/05	
6637					$85	French Blue/White thread.	ebay-07/05	
6637	Compote	175	3	4	$865	Silverina	Sknr-01/98	RFR)26,1,B; TPD)4.26:9.27
6637					$805	Amethyst Silverina	Sknr-06/00	
6637					$200	Green Jade	ebay-10/01	
6637					$580	Colorless Silverina	ebay-07/02	
6637					$1680	Oriental Poppy/Pomona	ebay-10/02	Pomona Green stem and foot.
6637					$355	Green Jade	ebay-08/03	
6637					$380	Green Jade	ebay-08/03	
6638	Vase	283	5	7	$860	Oriental Poppy	ebay-10/00	
6639	Vase	284	1	1	$230	French Blue	EAC-04/04	
6639					$540	Gold Aurene	Crft-01/05	
6640	Bowl	144	4	2	$1850	Cintra	ebay-02/00	
6640					$105	Colorless/Threaded	ebay-05/01	
6641	Bowl	144	4	3				TPD)10.91
6642	Goblet	197	5	3				
6643	Vase	284	1	2				
6644	Pitcher	214	3	3				
6644	Lemonade	214	3	3				
6645	Vase	284	1	3				
6646	Vase	284	1	4				
6647	Vase	284	1	5				
6648	Vase	284	1	6				
6649	Vase	284	2	1				
6650	Vase	284	2	2				PG1)XXVII A,A; JAS)156
6650					$2070	White Cluthra ACB	Sknr-03/99	Lamp with fittings
6651	Pitcher	214	3	4				
6651	Lemonade	214	3	4				
6652	Pitcher	214	3	5				
6653	Pitcher	214	3	6				
6654	Pitcher	214	4	1				
6655	Decanter	187	2	2				TPD)10.19
6656	Decanter	187	2	3	$3450	Oriental Jade	ebay-11/03	
6657	Decanter	187	2	4				
6658	Vase	284	2	3				
6659	Bowl	144	4	4				
6660	Vase	284	2	4				
6661	Shade	229	3	8				
6662	Table Decoration	237	1	6	$100	Alabaster	ebay-06/01	
6662					$150	Alabaster	ebay-03/02	
6662					$100	Alabaster	ebay-06/02	
6662					$80	Colorless/Pomona rim	ebay-03/04	
6662					$40	Colorless/Pomona rim	ebay-10/04	
6662					$100	Colorless/Black rim	ebay-11/04	
6662					$175	Colorless	ebay-03/05	
6662					$50	Colorless	ebay-04/05	

SHAPE NO.	ITEM	PAGE	COL	ROW	PRICE REALIZED	GLASS TYPE	AUCTION HOUSE	COMMENTS & PHOTO REFERENCES
6663	Cigarette Holder	138	3	4	$410	Green Jade	Cott-08/01	
6664	Candlestick	166	3	7				
6664	Centerpiece	153	1	2				
6664	Compote	175	3	5				
6665	Pitcher	214	4	2	$460	Spanish Green	Sknr-03/99	
6665					$330	Spanish Green (E)	ebay-12/02	
6666	Centerpiece	153	1	3				
6667	Covered Vase	308	2	2				TPD)7.58
6668	Candlestick	166	3	8				
6668	Centerpiece	153	1	4				
6668	Compote	175	3	6				TPD)10.15
6669	Candlestick	166	4	1				
6669	Centerpiece	153	1	5				
6669	Compote	175	3	7	$490	Gold Ruby (E)	ebay-11/00	
6670	Candlestick	166	4	2				
6671	Cologne	242	2	7				TPD)7.78
6672	Cologne	242	2	8				
6673	Cologne	242	2	9				
6674	Cologne	242	3	1				
6675	Cologne	242	3	2				PG1)108,170
6676	Flower Pot	237	2	8	$365	Green Jade/Alabaster rings	EAC-04/02	ACR)148,285; TPD)10.50; MDK)90
6676					$195	French Blue	ebay-07/04	
6677	Cologne '	242	3	3				
6677	Puff Box	245	1	4				
6678	Vase	284	2	5				
6679	Vase	284	3	1	$1870	Oriental Poppy	EAC-04/95	TPD)8.29; MDK)21
6679					$2135	Gold Calcite (E)	ebay-05/04	
6680	Vase	284	3	2				PG1)315
6681	Bowl	144	4	5				PG1)114,180; TPD)10.137
6682	Finger Bowl	189	2	2				
6683	Aquarium	304	3	4				
6684	Ash Tray	138	1	2				RFR)9,1,A; ACR)132,236; TPD)10.121
6685	Ash Tray	138	1	3				
6686	Cologne	242	3	4				
6687	Cologne	242	3	5	$3740	Black/White Cintra	EAC-07/93	PG1)315
6688	Puff Box	245	1	5				PG1)71,109; PG1)315
6689	Candlestick	166	4	3				
6689	Centerpiece	153	1	6				
6689	Compote	175	3	8				
6690	Candlestick	166	4	4				
6690	Centerpiece	153	1	7				
6690	Compote	175	4	1				
6691	Goblet	193	6	5				
6692	Goblet	193	6	6	$65	Nile Green	ebay-02/02	TPD)7.49; MDK)42
6693	Goblet	193	6	7				TPD)7.49
6694	Centerpiece	153	1	8				
6694	Vase	284	3	3				
6695	Candlestick	166	4	5	$90	French Blue/White thread.	ebay-12/01	
6695	Centerpiece	153	1	9				
6695	Compote	175	4	2				
6696	Bowl	144	4	6				
6697	Ash Tray	138	1	4	$140	Pomona Green	ebay-02/03	
6698	Centerpiece	153	1	10				
6699	Vase	284	3	4	$1875	Iridescent Green Jade	ebay-12/00	
6699					$785	Rosaline/Alabaster ACB	ebay-11/03	Etched "Chinese"
6700	Vase	284	3	5				TPD)4.39
6701	Compote	175	4	3				
6702	Vase	284	4	1				
6703	Vase	284	4	2				
6704	Goblet	194	1	1				TPD)7.49
6705	Goblet	194	1	2				TPD)7.49
6706	Covered Vase	308	2	3				This shape is shown as #6760 in Gardner.
6706								TPD)7.56
6707	Cologne	242	3	6				PG2)76,B; RFR)25,1,B; JAS)168,T,B;
6707								TPD)10.92
6708	Cologne	242	4	1				PG2)76,C; RFR)25,1,C; RLG)168,304;
6708								JAS)168,T,C;ACR)COLOR 3,T,B;TPD)6.37
6709	Candlestick	166	4	6				
6709	Centerpiece	153	2	1				
6709	Compote	175	4	4				
6710	Candlestick	166	5	1				
6710	Centerpiece	153	2	2				
6710	Compote	175	4	5				
6711	Table Decoration	236	4	2				

SHAPE NO.	ITEM	PAGE	COL	ROW	PRICE REALIZED	GLASS TYPE	AUCTION HOUSE	COMMENTS & PHOTO REFERENCES
6712	Cologne	242	4	2				
6713	Vase	284	4	3				PG1)XVII B; ACR)158,313; TPD)6.7
6714	Goblet	194	1	3	$80	Colorless	ebay-01/01	JSS)12-27,R; TPD)7.69
6714					$185	Gold Ruby/Colorless	ebay-12/03	Colorless stem and foot
6714					$185	Gold Ruby/Colorless	ebay-12/03	Colorless stem and foot
6715	Goblet	194	1	4				
6716	Goblet	194	1	5				
6717	Goblet	194	1	6	$230	Colorless	ebay-02/00	
6718	Covered Vase	308	3	1				
6719	Vase	284	4	4				
6720	Covered Vase	308	3	2				
6721	Table Decoration	237	1	7				PG1)46,84,B
6722	Table Top	238	1	1	$7500	Aurene Table	Tway-12/00	TPD)10.134
6722					$4250	Aurene Table	ebay-04/05	
6723	Table Top	238	1	2	$7295	Aurene Table	ebay-01/03	
6723					$8150	Aurene Table	ebay-04/04	
6724	Candlestick	166	5	2				
6724	Centerpiece	153	2	3				
6725	Candlestick	166	5	3				
6725	Centerpiece	153	2	4				
6726	Ash Tray	138	1	5				
6727	Goblet	194	1	7				PG1)103,158,TOP; PG1)315; JSS)12-34,L
6728	Goblet	194	2	1				PG1)85,125; PG2)87,C; PG1)103,157,A
6728								JSS)12-29,C:12-33,C:12-34,C
6728	Wine							JSS)12-33,R
6729	Vase	284	4	5				
6730	Jar	209	5	2	$440	Pomona Green	EAC-04/98	
6730					$295	Topaz	ebay-01/02	
6730					$70	VDS with Fruit finial	Jack-06/02	
6731	Vase	284	5	1				TPD)5.63:10.102; MDK)60
6731					$6050	Yellow Florentia	EAC-02/92	drilled for lamp
6731					$3500	Yellow Florentia Lamp	ebay-11/02	Crest fittings
6732	Soap Dish	245	4	3				
6733	Cold Cream Jar	243	6	9	$770	Black/Green Jade stopper	EAC-07/91	PG2)97,E; RFR)17,2,B&D; RLG)159,293;
6733					$300	Threaded	ebay-05/99	JAS)148,B,D:167,B,B; ACR)165,332;
6733					$350	Amethyst	ebay-11/99	TPD)10.111
6733					$80	French Blue	ebay-03/01	
6733					$350	Colorless/Threaded	ebay-05/01	
6733					$550	Gold Ruby	Cott-08/01	
6733					$300	Colorless/Blue threaded	ebay-10/02	
6733					$2640	Oriental Jade	ebay-01/04	
6733					$100	French Blue	ebay-10/04	Missing cover
6733					$150	Colorless/Green threaded	ebay-05/05	Pomona Green cover
6733					$260	VDS/Green Jade cover	ebay-07/05	
6734	Candlestick	166	5	4				
6734	Centerpiece	153	2	5				
6734	Compote	175	4	6	$440	Celeste Blue	ebay-02/03	
6735	Goblet	194	2	2				JSS)12-36,R
6735	Wine							JSS)12-36,L
6736	Loving Cup	177	2	5				
6737	Bouillon Cup	189	2	6				
6738	Bouillon Cup	189	2	7				
6739	Bouillon Cup	189	2	8				
6740	Bouillon Cup	189	2	9				
6741	Vase	284	5	2				
6742	Vase	284	5	3				
6743	Vase	284	5	4				
6744	Vase	285	1	1				
6745	Bowl	144	4	7				
6746	Bowl	144	4	8				
6747	Candlestick	167	1	1				
6747	Centerpiece	153	2	6				
6747	Compote	175	4	7				
6748	Lamp Base	203	4	4				
6749	Lamp Base	203	4	5				
6750	Lamp Base	203	4	6				
6751	Vase	285	1	2				
6752	Vase	285	1	3				
6753	Vase	285	1	4				
6754	Vase	285	2	1				
6755	Shade	230	1	1				
6756	Vase	285	2	2	$1590	Grn. Jade/Yel. Jade ACB	EAC-07/91	Etched "Acanthus"
6756					$2300	Opal/Green Cintra ACB	EAC-04/04	
6757	Centerpiece	153	2	7				

SHAPE NO.	ITEM	PAGE	COL	ROW	PRICE REALIZED	GLASS TYPE	AUCTION HOUSE	COMMENTS & PHOTO REFERENCES
6758	Candlestick	167	1	2				
6759	Candlestick	167	1	3	$120	Amber	ebay-10/01	
6759	Centerpiece	153	2	8				
6759	Compote	175	4	8				
6760	Bowl	144	4	9	$1300	Red Cintra	ebay-05/01	
6760					$1435	Red Cintra	JDJ-05/01	
6760					$615	Green/White Cluthra	ebay-01/02	
6760	Covered Vase	308	2	3				This number is an error, see #6706.
6761	Vase	285	2	3	$690	ACB	Sknr-05/97	TPD)4.51
6761					$770	Colorless ACB	EAC-10/98	
6762	Vase	285	2	4	$420	Green/White Cluthra	ebay-05/02	
6762					$1090	Yellow Cintra	JDJ-05/04	
6763	Vase	285	2	5	$2000	Red Cintra	ebay-01/00	PG1)315; RFR)23,3,C; ACR)160,317;
6763					$495	Colorless ACB "Mansard"	EAC-04/91	TPD)4.51
6763					$330	Colorless ACB "Mansard"	ebay-11/04	
6764	Bowl	144	4	10				TPD)4.51
6765	Champagne				$70	Colorless/Green threading	ebay-11/03	
6765					$575	Oriental Jade/Opaline	EAC-11/03	Opaline stem and foot
6765					$145	Colorless/Green threading	ebay-07/05	
6765	Goblet	194	2	3	$180	French Blue	ebay-11/99	PG1)105,162,B; JSS)12-30,L
6766	Vase	285	3	1	$3335	Rose Quartz	Sknr-01/97	PG1)XVIII B,B; PG2)78; JAS)153,TL;
6766					$2970	Rose Quartz	EAC-07/98	ACR)159,314; TPD)4.20
6767	T'brush Holder	245	4	5	$100	Colorless/Black threaded	ebay-03/00	MDK)2:117
6767					$30	Pomona Green	ebay-08/02	
6768	Candlestick	167	1	4				PG1)315
6768	Centerpiece	153	2	9				PG1)315
6768	Compote	175	5	1				PG1)315
6769	Bowl	144	4	11	$235	Persian Blue/Bristol thread.	ebay-05/02	TPD)10.22
6769					$200	Persian Blue/Bristol thread.	EAC-04/05	No handles
6770	Vase	285	3	2	$150	Colorless/Green threaded	ebay-08/03	
6770					$90	Colorless/Green threaded	ebay-05/05	No handles, minor thread damage
6771	Sugar & Creamer	235	6	9,10				PG1)86,127
6772	Vase	285	3	3	$135	Celeste Blue	JDJ-05/94	RFR)27,3,C:31,4,D; TPD)10.88
6772					$300	Colorless/Red threaded	ebay-02/00	
6772					$155	Colorless/Black threaded	ebay-06/02	
6772					$125	Colorless/Green threaded	ebay-10/04	
6772					$250	Colorless/Black threaded	ebay-10/04	
6772					$400	Pomona Green/White	ebay-10/04	White threaded
6772					$300	Pomona Green/White	ebay-02/05	White threaded
6773	Centerpiece	153	3	1	$280	Colorless/Green threaded	ebay-12/99	
6774	Centerpiece	153	3	2	$860	Iridescent Green Jade	Sknr-10/96	
6774					$220	Bristol Yellow/threaded	ebay-11/01	
6774					$80	Colorless/threaded	ebay-11/01	
6774					$495	Pink threaded VDS	ebay-11/01	
6774					$325	Bristol Yellow/Black	ebay-01/03	Mirror Black threaded
6774					$155	Pink threaded VDS	ebay-03/03	
6774					$125	Colorless/Black threaded	ebay-03/03	
6774					$90	Bristol Yellow/White thread	ebay-05/03	
6774					$175	Colorless/Blue threaded	ebay-11/03	
6774					$90	Green threaded VDS	JDJ-05/04	
6774					$110	Green threaded VDS	ebay-02/05	
6774					$100	Colorless/Green threaded	ebay-06/05	
6775	Vase	285	3	4				
6776	Vase	285	3	5	$200	Blue/Yellow threaded	JDJ-10/97	
6776					$505	Amethyst Silverina	EAC-04/01	
6776					$760	Colorless Silverina	ebay-10/01	
6776					$4025	Opal/Green Cintra ACB	JDJ-11/03	
6777	Vase	285	3	6	$2300	Iridescent Green Jade	Sknr-05/96	TPD)6.25
6777					$250	Colorless/Blue threaded	ebay-10/01	
6777					$1500	Green Jade/Alabaster ACB	ebay-11/02	
6777					$125	Colorless/Blue threaded	ebay-09/03	
6777					$9085	Blue Aur./Alabaster ACB	EAC-11/03	Etched "Corintha"
6777					$75	VDS/Amber threaded	ebay-10/04	
6777					$120	VDS/Blue threaded	Cinc-06/05	
6778	Centerpiece	153	3	3	$345	VDS/Blue threaded	Sknr-02/01	ACR)144,272
6778					$205	Colorless/Green threaded	ebay-01/04	
6778					$110	Colorless/Green threaded	ebay-03/04	
6778					$160	Colorless/Red threaded	ebay-05/04	
6778					$90	Colorless/Green threaded	ebay-10/04	
6779	Centerpiece	153	3	4				
6780	Vase	285	4	1				PG1)XXX B,A; RFR)26,2,A; RLG)168,307;
6780								ACR)COLOR1,T,E
6781	Vase	285	4	2	$1430	Cinnamon Florentia	EAC-07/92	TPD)5.67
6781					$3735	Cinnamon Florentia	Sknr-05/94	

SHAPE NO.	ITEM	PAGE	COL	ROW	PRICE REALIZED	GLASS TYPE	AUCTION HOUSE	COMMENTS & PHOTO REFERENCES
6781					$1160	Cinnamon Florentia	Sknr-05/95	
6781					$3850	Florentia	JDJ-06/96	
6781					$3135	Cinnamon Florentia	EAC-07/98	
6782	Centerpiece	153	3	5	$2200	Cinnamon Florentia	EAC-07/93	RFR)26,2,B
6782					$1840	Florentia	Sknr-01/96	
6782					$5000	Cinnamon Florentia	ebay-11/04	
6783	Centerpiece	153	3	6				
6784	Centerpiece	153	3	7	$2200	Green Florentia	EAC-04/98	PG2)91,Bf; JAS)153,B,Bf; TPD)5.30
6784					$2500	Cinnamon Florentia	ebay-04/00	
6784					$4715	Green Florentia	Sknr-02/01	
6785	Centerpiece	153	3	8				TPD)5.67
6786	Puff Box	245	1	6	$825	Rosa	EAC-04/98	MDK)18:82:83
6786					$85	Colorless/Black threaded	ebay-05/04	
6786					$265	Amethyst	ebay-03/05	
6786					$150	Amethyst	ebay-05/05	
6787	Vase	285	4	3				
6788	Vase	285	4	4	$550	Green Jade ACB	ebay-09/02	Lamp with fittings.
6789	Covered Vase	308	3	3				
6790	Goblet	194	2	4				
6791	Goblet	194	2	5				
6792	Goblet	194	2	6				
6793	Goblet	194	2	7				
6794	Goblet	194	3	1	$45	Colorless	ebay-04/05	
6795	Vase	285	4	5	$770	Green Jade	JDJ-10/94	
6795					$540	Green Jade	ebay-03/00	
6795					$1750	Green Jade/Alabaster	ebay-07/01	
6795					$525	Colorless/Blue handles	ebay-01/03	
6795					$1440	Green Jade/Alabaster	Wesr-12/04	Alabaster handles
6795					$325	Pomona Green/Colorless	ebay-03/05	Colorless handles
6795					$865	Colorless/Amber handles	EAC-04/05	
6796	Vase	285	4	6	$1760	Iridescent Green Jade	EAC-07/93	
6796					$140	Colorless/Green threaded	JDJ-05/95	
6796					$545	Threaded Black	Sknr-05/96	
6796					$575	Bristol/Threaded	JDJ-05/00	
6796					$110	Colorless/Green threaded	Cinc-06/05	
6796					$180	Bristol Yellow/Green	Cinc-06/05	Green threaded
6797	Pitcher	214	4	3				
6798	Pitcher	214	4	4				
6799	Candlestick	167	1	5				
6800	Candlestick	167	2	1	$962	VDS/Pink threaded	ebay-06/00	
6801	Candlestick	167	2	2	$255	VDS/Threaded	Sknr-10/95	
6802	Candlestick	167	2	3				
6803	Candlestick	167	2	4				
6804	Bowl	145	1	1				MDK)81
6805	Vase	285	5	1				
6806	Vase	285	5	2	$2760	Opal ACB	Sknr-05/94	
6806					$410	Colorless ACB	ebay-10/01	
6807	Bowl	145	1	2				
6808	Bowl	145	1	3				
6809	Shade	230	1	2				
6810	Shade	230	1	3				
6811	Shade	230	1	4				
6812	Vase	285	5	3	$200	VDS/Red threaded	ebay-03/00	
6812					$125	Colorless/Blue threaded	ebay-03/00	
6812					$805	Colorless/Green threaded	Sknr-02/01	
6812					$230	Colorless/Red threaded	ebay-10/01	
6812					$225	Colorless/Green threaded	EAC-11/01	
6812					$250	Colorless/Green threaded	ebay-01/02	
6812					$2125	Green Cintra	ebay-04/02	
6812					$170	VDS/Gold Ruby threaded	JDJ-05/03	
6812					$25	Colorless/Blue threaded	ebay-09/03	
6812					$50	Colorless/Green threaded	ebay-10/03	
6813	Vase	285	5	4	$550	Ivory	EAC-05/97	RFR)23,2,C; MDK)140
6813					$935	Blue Aurene	EAC-07/98	
6813					$550	Bristol Thread	EAC-10/98	
6813					$65	Colorless/Green threaded	EAC-10/00	
6813					$105	Colorless/Blue threaded	ebay-05/01	
6813					$385	Bristol/Threaded	Cott-08/01	
6813					$180	Colorless/Red threaded	ebay-04/02	
6813					$360	VDS/Blue threaded	ebay-05/02	
6813					$75	Colorless/Red threaded	ebay-07/02	
6813					$95	Colorless	ebay-08/02	
6813					$125	Colorless/Green threaded	ebay-12/02	
6813					$150	Colorless/Green threaded	Aspr-01/03	

SHAPE NO.	ITEM	PAGE	COL	ROW	PRICE REALIZED	GLASS TYPE	AUCTION HOUSE	COMMENTS & PHOTO REFERENCES
6813					$75	VDS/Yellow threaded	ebay-04/03	
6813					$250	VDS/Red threaded	J&W-09/03	
6813					$150	Green Jade	ebay-11/03	
6813					$140	Colorless/Green threaded	ebay-12/03	
6813					$105	VDS/Black threaded	ebay-12/03	
6813					$65	Colorless/Green threaded	ebay-03/04	
6813					$30	Colorless/Yellow threaded	ebay-07/04	
6813					$200	VDS/Red threaded	ebay-11/04	
6813					$390	VDS/Yellow threaded	Cinc-11/04	
6813					$150	Colorless/Red threaded	ebay-01/05	
6813					$95	Colorless/Green threaded	ebay-03/05	
6813					$60	Colorless/Red threaded	ebay-04/05	
6813					$205	Colorless/Black threaded	ebay-04/05	
6813					$230	Persian Blue/Bristol thread.	EAC-04/05	
6813					$130	VDS/Blue threaded	ebay-05/05	
6813					$50	VDS/Amber threaded	ebay-06/05	
6814	Vase	285	5	5	$115	Celeste Blue	ebay-04/00	
6814					$1690	Iridescent Green Jade	ebay-06/00	
6814					$200	French Blue	ebay-03/01	
6814					$895	Yellow Cintra	EAC-04/01	
6815	Vase	285	5	6	$355	Colorless/Green threaded	ebay-07/00	Green threaded ACR)144,271; TPD)10.97
6815					$185	Bristol/Threaded	ebay-03/01	Mirror Black threaded
6815					$125	Colorless/Threaded	ebay-03/01	Gold Ruby threaded
6815					$110	Pomona Green	Wint-04/01	
6815					$140	Colorless/Threaded	Wint-04/01	Blue threaded
6815					$65	Colorless/Threaded	ebay-06/01	Blue threaded
6815					$150	Colorless/Threaded	EAC-09/02	Black threaded
6815					$80	Bristol Yellow/White	JDJ-11/03	White threaded
6815					$170	Bristol Yellow/Black	ebay-05/04	Black threaded
6815					$735	VDS/Blue threaded	Tway-09/04	
6815					$155	Bristol Yellow/White	ebay-04/05	White threaded
6816	Vase	286	1	1				
6817	Vase	286	1	2	$1210	Iridescent Green Jade	EAC-10/93	RFR)16,2,A:27,3,A; TPD)10.85
6817					$60	VDS threaded	JDJ-06/98	
6817					$105	VDS/Red threaded	Sknr-02/01	
6817					$170	VDS/Green threaded	JDJ-11/02	
6817					$225	Colorless/Red threaded	ebay-06/02	
6817					$50	Colorless/Red threaded	ebay-07/02	
6817					$285	VDS/Green threaded	ebay-02/04	
6817					$165	Persian Blue/Yellow thread	ebay-07/04	
6817					$265	VDS/Blue threaded	ebay-09/04	
6817					$125	Persian Blue/Yellow thread	ebay-11/04	
6818	Vase	286	1	3	$5500	Green Florentia	EAC-07/91	PG2)91,A; JAS)153,B,A; TPD)5.67
6819	Vase	286	1	4				
6820	Goblet	194	3	2				
6821	Luminor	208	1	2	$640	Ball with Black base	ebay-10/02	PG1)69,104,B
6821					$350	Ball with Black base	Sknr-12/02	
6821					$865	Ball with Black base	ebay-01/03	
6821					$1000	Ball with Black base	ebay-12/03	
6821					$105	Colorless ball	ebay-11/04	No base
6821					$150	Colorless ball	ebay-01/05	No base
6821					$495	Colorless ball	ebay-06/05	No base
6822	Table Decoration	236	1	3	$1275	Colorless	ebay-10/03	Pigeon
6823	Lamp	208	1	3				
6824	Table Decoration	236	1	4	$1265	Colorless	EAC-04/04	Pigeon TPD)4.45
6825	Shade	226	3	5				
6826	Shade	226	3	6				
6827	Vase	286	1	5				
6828	Candlestick	167	2	5				PG1)315
6828	Centerpiece	153	3	9				PG1)315
6829	Pitcher	214	4	5				
6829	Lemonade	214	4	5				
6830	Pitcher	214	4	6				
6830	Lemonade	214	4	6				
6831	Ice Tub	177	4	7	$710	Wisteria	ebay-01/04	
6831					$900	Wisteria	ebay-01/05	
6832	Candlestick	167	3	1				TPD)7.62
6832	Centerpiece	153	3	10				
6832	Compote	175	5	2				TPD)7.62
6833	Candlestick	167	3	2				
6833	Centerpiece	153	3	11				
6833	Compote	175	5	3				
6834	Pitcher	215	1	1				
6834	Lemonade	215	1	1				

SHAPE NO.	ITEM	PAGE	COL	ROW	PRICE REALIZED	GLASS TYPE	AUCTION HOUSE	COMMENTS & PHOTO REFERENCES
6835	Pitcher, Lemonade	215	1	2	$275	Colorless/Green threaded	ebay-06/05	
6836	Vase	286	2	1				
6837	Vase	286	2	2				
6838	Vase	286	2	3	$270	Bristol Yellow	ebay-04/00	Mirror Black threaded
6838					$190	Colorless/Gold Ruby	ebay-01/03	Gold Ruby threaded
6838					$125	Colorless/Blue threaded	ebay-08/03	
6838					$280	Colorless/Gold Ruby	ebay-11/03	Gold Ruby threaded
6839	Vase	286	2	4				
6840	Vase	286	3	1				
6841	Goblet	194	3	3				
6842	Box	138	4	4				
6843	Candlestick	167	3	3				
6844	Champagne				$480	Black over Colorless (E)	ebay-02/05	Engraved "Poussin"
6844	Goblet	194	3	4				PG1)315; ACR)151,297
6844	Plate				$720	Black over Colorless (E)	ebay-12/04	Engraved "Poussin," 11"
6844					$1135	Black over Colorless (E)	ebay-04/05	Engraved "Poussin," 11"
6844					$805	Black over Colorless (E)	EAC-07/05	Engraved "Poussin," 11"
6844	Sherbet				$360	Black over Colorless (E)	ebay-08/02	Engraved "Poussin"
6844					$390	Black over Colorless (E)	ebay-02/05	Engraved "Poussin"
6845	Bowl	145	1	4	$900	Opal ACB	ebay-12/00	
6846	Centerpiece	154	1	1				
6847	Covered Vase	308	4	1				PG1)XV A,D
6847					$330	Light Amethyst (E)	ebay-08/04	No cover, Engraved "Marina"
6848	Shade	226	3	7				
6849	Vase	286	3	2				RFR)25,3,A
6850	Shade	230	1	5	$1350	Brown Aurene	ebay-04/01	
6851	Lamp Base	203	5	1				Special for Art Lighting
6852	Lamp Base	203	5	2				Special for Art Lighting
6853	Table Top	238	1	3				
6854	Vase	286	3	3	$3850	ACB	EAC-10/94	
6855	Vase	286	3	4				
6856	Bowl	145	1	5	$1495	Rose Quartz	Sknr-05/97	PG1)XVIII B,A:80,122:315; TPD)4.20
6856					$1150	Amethyst Quartz	Sknr-10/98	
6856					$3360	Amethyst Quartz	EAC-01/03	
6857	Vase	286	3	5				
6858	Candlestick	167	3	4	$745	Yellow Silverina	Sknr-01/96	RFR)25,2,A&C; TPD)10.1
6858	Bowl	145	1	6				
6858	Compote	175	5	4	$160	Colorless/Gold Ruby	ebay-04/02	
6859	Goblet	194	3	5				
6860	Goblet	194	3	6				
6861	Goblet	194	4	1				PG1)106,164:315:103,157,C;
6861								JSS)12-26,R; MDK)39
6862	Vase	286	4	1	$1320	Red/White Cluthra	EAC-04/96	PG1)XVIII A,E ; TPD)6.3:8.28
6862					$1800	Red/White Cluthra	ebay-03/03	
6862					$1435	Red/White Cluthra	EAC-06/03	
6862					$700	Green/White Cluthra	ebay-11/04	
6862					$400	Green Jade	ebay-01/04	
6863	Candlestick	167	3	5	$415	Amethyst over Colorless (E)	ebay-07/02	MDK)123
6863					$265	Amethyst over Colorless (E)	ebay-09/04	Engraved "Harvard"
6863	Centerpiece	154	1	2				
6863	Compote	175	5	5				
6864	Vase	286	4	2				
6865	Bowl	145	1	7				
6866	Goblet	194	4	2	$105	Amethyst	ebay-01/04	TPD)4.76:6.1:7.51
6866	Sherbet							TPD)4.76
6866	Wine							TPD)4.76
6867	Candlestick	167	3	6				TPD)7.65
6867	Centerpiece	154	1	3				TPD)7.65
6867	Footed Dish							TPD)7.64
6868	Candlestick	167	4	1				TPD)7.68
6868	Centerpiece	154	1	4				TPD)7.68
6868	Compote	175	5	6				TPD)7.68
6869	Champagne				$170	Flemish Blue/Colorless	ebay-12/03	Colorless stem
6869	Goblet	194	4	3				PG1)XXII A,E:315; JSS)12-20
6870	Vase	286	4	3				Superceded by 6862.
6871	Vase	286	4	4				
6872	Centerpiece	154	1	5				
6873	Vase	286	4	5	$1375	Black/White Cluthra	EAC-10/92	TPD)4.7
6873					$880	Ivory	EAC-04/93	
6873					$880	Mirror Black	EAC-04/95	
6873					$1210	Green/White Cluthra	EAC-10/95	
6873					$385	Pomona Green	JDJ-06/96	
6873					$990	Wisteria	JDJ-06/96	
6873					$520	Mirror Black	JDJ-10/96	

SHAPE NO.	ITEM	PAGE	COL	ROW	PRICE REALIZED	GLASS TYPE	AUCTION HOUSE	COMMENTS & PHOTO REFERENCES
6873					$460	Mirror Black	Sknr-10/96	
6873					$860	Green Jade/Alabaster	Sknr-10/97	
6873					$925	Green/White Cluthra	ebay-02/00	
6873					$800	Mirror Black	ebay-06/00	
6873					$410	Sea Green	ebay-12/00	
6873					$315	Spanish Green	Sknr-02/01	
6873					$575	Ivory	ebay-03/01	
6873					$1840	Green Jade/Alabaster	JDJ-05/02	
6873					$1700	Green/White Cluthra	J&W-09/03	
6873					$2945	Flemish Blue	ebay-05/04	
6873					$305	Spanish Green	ebay-08/04	
6873					$1200	Red/White Cluthra	ebay-10/04	
6873					$1115	Mirror Black	ebay-11/04	
6873					$300	Colorless	ebay-01/05	
6873					$240	Colorless	ebay-02/05	
6873					$300	Colorless	ebay-04/05	
6874	Vase	286	4	6	$880	Green/White Cluthra	EAC-10/90	
6874					$1430	Green/White Cluthra	EAC-10/97	
6874					$275	French Blue	ebay-02/00	
6874					$185	Pomona Green	ebay-08/02	
6874					$180	Bristol Yellow	ebay-08/03	
6874					$340	Bristol Yellow	ebay-03/05	
6875	Vase	286	5	1	$605	Ivory with Black base	EAC-04/91	
6875					$825	Black/White Cluthra	EAC-10/93	Colorless foot
6875					$1045	Red/White Cluthra	EAC-10/95	
6875					$1325	Red/White Cluthra	JDJ-10/97	
6875					$155	Colorless	ebay-02/00	
6875					$430	Ivory	Sknr-02/01	
6875					$1595	Black/White Cluthra	Sknr-02/01	
6875					$1000	Green Jade/Alabaster	ebay-03/01	
6875					$135	Colorless	ebay-08/01	
6875					$225	Mirror Black	Ogal-10/01	
6875					$450	Mirror Black	ebay-01/02	
6875					$325	Green Jade/Alabaster	ebay-01/02	
6875					$415	Mirror Black	ebay-10/02	
6875					$675	Black/White Cluthra	ebay-01/03	
6875					$375	Mirror Black	ebay-02/03	
6875					$205	Green Jade/Alabaster	ebay-07/03	
6875					$275	Ivory	ebay-07/04	
6875					$285	Green Jade/Alabaster foot	EAC-07/05	
6875					$745	Mirror Black	EAC-07/05	
6876	Vase	286	5	2	$230	Flemish Blue	ebay-06/00	PG1)90,139
6876					$150	Pomona Green	ebay-11/00	
6876					$40	Colorless	Midw-01/01	
6876					$255	Mirror Black	ebay-02/01	
6876					$300	Wisteria	ebay-07/01	
6876					$90	Gold Ruby	ebay-10/02	
6876					$50	Colorless	ebay-10/02	
6876					$180	Green Jade	ebay-12/02	
6876					$40	Colorless	ebay-05/04	
6876					$90	Colorless	ebay-04/05	
6876					$50	Colorless	ebay-05/05	
6878	Bowl	145	1	8				
6879	Shade	230	1	6				PG1)315
6880	Ash Tray	138	1	6				
6881	Cologne	242	4	3	$1100	Cluthra	EAC-07/95	ACR)156,307C
6881					$1650	Green Cluthra	Cott-08/01	
6881					$250	Blue/White Cluthra	ebay-08/03	Stopper missing
6881					$1025	Red/White Cluthra	ebay-11/03	
6881					$150	Red/White Cluthra	ebay-08/04	Stopper missing
6881	Puff Box	245	1	7	$770	White/Rose Cluthra	EAC-10/90	PG1)XVIII A,C
6881					$1150	Green/White Cluthra	Sknr-02/01	
6881					$5175	Blue Aurene/Pomona ACB	EAC-11/03	
6882	Vase	286	5	3	$575	Red/White Cluthra	Sknr-10/96	PG1)72,111; TPD)6.16
6882					$900	Blue/White Cluthra	ebay-12/00	
6882					$500	Black/White Cluthra	ebay-06/03	
6882					$1035	Red/White Cluthra	EAC-11/03	
6882					$660	Red/White Cluthra	JDJ-05/04	
6882					$410	Red/White Cluthra	ebay-12/04	
6882					$515	Red/White Cluthra	ebay-01/05	
6883	Vase	286	5	4	$1210	Black/White Cluthra	EAC-10/90	TPD)6.16
6883					$685	Green/White Cluthra	EAC-04/91	
6883					$660	Amethyst Silverina	JDJ-11/01	
6883					$820	Blue Silverina	Sknr-06/02	

SHAPE NO.	ITEM	PAGE	COL	ROW	PRICE REALIZED	GLASS TYPE	AUCTION HOUSE	COMMENTS & PHOTO REFERENCES
6883					$700	Black/White Cluthra	ebay-07/02	
6883					$950	Amethyst Silverina	ebay-12/02	
6884	Vase	286	5	5				TPD)10.52
6885	Bowl	145	1	9	$860	Red/White Cluthra	Sknr-05/96	
6885					$1035	Red/White Cluthra	JDJ-10/97	
6885					$575	Blue/White Cluthra	JDJ-06/98	
6885					$510	Red/White Cluthra	ebay-03/02	
6885					$335	White Cluthra	ebay-11/03	
6885					$890	Red/White Cluthra	ebay-08/04	
6885	Candlestick	167	4	2				PG2)79,B&C; JAS)164,T,B&C
6885	Compote	175	5	7	$700	Red/White Cluthra	ebay-08/03	RFR)22,3,C
6886	Compote	175	5	8	$315	Colorless/Red threaded	Sknr-03/99	MDK)110
6886					$165	Colorless/Red threaded	Cinc-12/99	
6886					$200	Parisian Blue/Y. threaded	Sknr-06/00	
6887	Cologne	243	4	7	$230	Flemish Blue	Sknr-10/96	
6887					$130	Mirror Black	ebay-02/00	
6887					$195	Bristol Yellow	ebay-11/00	
6887					$285	Amethyst	Sknr-02/01	
6887					$190	French Blue	Midw-04/01	
6887					$225	French Blue	ebay-06/01	
6887					$225	French Blue	ebay-01/02	
6887					$100	Colorless/Black threaded	ebay-02/02	
6887					$250	Colorless/Green threaded	ebay-07/02	
6887					$200	Colorless/Gold Ruby Thrd.	ebay-07/02	Gold Ruby Cintra flower stopper
6887					$60	Gold Ruby	ebay-10/02	
6887					$280	Pomona Green	ebay-11/02	
6887					$295	Bristol/Black threaded	ebay-02/03	
6887					$405	Gold Ruby	ebay-07/03	
6887					$320	Bristol/Black threaded	ebay-07/04	
6887					$250	French Blue	ebay-09/04	
6888	Shade	226	3	8				
6889	Cocktail Shaker	215	3	1				RLG)158,292
6890	Centerpiece	154	1	6	$530	Ivory	ebay-12/99	
6890					$160	Mirror Black	ebay-03/02	
6890					$185	Amber	ebay-03/03	
6890					$260	Green Jade	JDJ-05/04	
6890					$150	Pomona Green	ebay-07/04	
6890					$105	Colorless	ebay-01/05	Cut in "Punty" pattern
6891	Centerpiece	154	1	7				
6892	Vase	286	5	6				
6893	Vase	287	1	1				PG1)316
6894	Cold Cream Jar	243	6	10	$325	Green Jade	ebay-09/03	
6895	Candlestick	167	4	3				
6896	Soap Dish	245	4	4				
6897	Covered Vase	308	4	2				
6898	Vase	287	1	2	$1840	Green/White Cluthra	JDJ-10/97	PG1)XVIII A,D; PG2)77; JAS)157,TR
6899	Covered Vase	308	4	3				ACR)153,302,C
6900	Vase	287	1	3				ACR)153,302,B
6900					$480	Colorless (E)	ebay-04/05	
6901	Vase	287	1	4				ACR)153,302,A; TPD)6.13
6902	Candlestick				$205	Nile Green	ebay-02/02	TPD)6.30
6902					$175	Amethyst	ebay-05/02	
6902	Centerpiece	154	1	8				PG2)79,A;JAS)164,T,A
6903	Centerpiece	154	1	9	$125	Bristol Yellow	ebay-09/04	
6904	Vase	287	2	1	$5750	Blue Aurene/Pomona ACB	Sknr-05/95	
6904					$1790	Red/White Cluthra	ebay-09/00	
6905	Bowl	145	2	1	$495	Green/White Cluthra	EAC-07/92	
6905					$495	Red/White Cluthra	EAC-04/95	
6905					$770	Red/White Cluthra	EAC-07/95	
6905					$630	Black/White Cluthra	JDJ-10/97	
6905					$690	Green/White Cluthra	Sknr-06/00	
6905					$330	White Cluthra	ebay-02/03	
6905					$545	Red/White Cluthra	ebay-07/03	
6905					$660	Green/White Cluthra	Aspr-11/03	
6905					$400	Green/White Cluthra	JDJ-05/04	
6906	Bowl	145	2	2	$660	Black/White Cluthra	EAC-10/95	MDK)67
6906					$545	Cluthra	JDJ-06/98	
6906					$810	Blue/White Cluthra	ebay-01/02	
6906					$650	Black/White Cluthra	ebay-02/03	
6907	Vase	287	2	2				
6908	Vase	287	2	3	$1155	Green/White Cluthra	EAC-10/92	TPD)6.19
6908					$1035	Red/White Cluthra	JDJ-10/97	
6908					$600	Green/White Cluthra	ebay-03/03	
6909	Finger Bowl				$805	Blue Cluthra	Sknr-05/94	

SHAPE NO.	ITEM	PAGE	COL	ROW	PRICE REALIZED	GLASS TYPE	AUCTION HOUSE	COMMENTS & PHOTO REFERENCES
6909					$935	Red/White Cluthra	EAC-07/96	
6909					$880	Red/White Cluthra	Cinc-12/99	
6909					$250	Red/White Cluthra	ebay-05/01	
6909					$190	Green/White Cluthra	ebay-12/03	Fingerbowl only
6909					$230	Red/White Cluthra	JDJ-05/04	
6909	Goblet	194	4	4	$660	Red/White Cluthra	EAC-04/91	RFR)22,1,B
6909					$605	Black/White Cluthra	EAC-10/97	
6909					$375	Yellow Silverina	ebay-12/99	
6909					$800	Blue/White Cluthra	ebay-10/01	
6909					$900	Green/White Cluthra	JDJ-11/02	
6909					$1090	Red/White Cluthra	EAC-04/04	
6909					$285	Red/White Cluthra	EAC-04/05	
6910	Vase	287	2	4	$4125	Amethyst Quartz	EAC-07/98	TPD)5.27
6911	Vase	287	2	5				
6912	Vase	287	3	1	$1205	Red/White Cluthra	JDJ-10/97	
6912					$1265	Black/White Cluthra	JDJ-10/97	
6912					$1035	Green/White Cluthra	JDJ-05/99	
6913	Vase	287	3	2	$1650	Black/White Cluthra	JDJ-06/96	
6913					$1725	Black/White Cluthra	JDJ-10/97	
6914	Vase	287	3	3	$490	Green Silverina	Sknr-10/96	
6915	Puff Box	245	1	8				
6916	Cologne	242	4	4				PG2)76,A; RFR)25,1,B; JAS)168,T,A;
6917	Cologne	242	4	5				TPD)6.34
6917								
6917					$4600	Green Cintra	Sknr-06/00	
6917					$4310	Black/White Cluthra	Sknr-06/00	
6918	Centerpiece	154	2	1				
6919	Vase	287	3	4				
6920	Goblet	194	4	5				
6921	Vase	287	4	1				
6922	Vase	287	4	2				TPD)6.31
6923	Vase	287	4	3				
6924	Vase	287	4	4				
6925	Vase	287	4	5				
6926	Vase	287	5	1				
6927	Table Decoration	236	2	1	$310	Rosa	ebay-05/99	PG1)90,138; TPD)5.46
6928	Goblet	194	4	6				PG1)316; JSS)12-27,L
6929	Goblet	194	5	1				
6930	Candlestick	167	4	4				
6930	Centerpiece	154	2	2				
6930	Compote	175	5	9				
6931	Candlestick	167	4	5				
6931	Centerpiece	154	2	3				
6932	Goblet	194	5	2				
6933	Vase	287	5	2				
6934	Goblet	194	5	3	$35	Orchid	ebay-05/04	
6935	Goblet	194	5	4	$65	Threaded	Sknr-10/95	
6935					$70	Colorless/Green threaded	ebay-04/03	
6936	Fingerbowl							MDK)68
6936	Goblet	194	5	5				PG1)316; TPD)7.26; MDK)75
6937	Table Decoration	237	2	1				
6938	Bowl	145	2	3				
6939	Vase	287	5	3				
6940	Cologne	242	5	1				
6941	Cologne	242	5	2				TPD)6.34
6942	Cologne	242	5	3	$3850	Cintra	EAC-07/98	ACR)178,364
6943	Cologne	242	5	4				
6944	Cologne	242	5	5	$4760	Black/White Cluthra	ebay-02/02	TPD)6.11
6944					$8155	Black/White Cintra (FC)	ebay-11/04	
6945	Cologne	242	6	1				
6946	Goblet	194	5	6				
6947	Goblet	194	5	7				PG1)107,167,A; JSS)12-29,L
6948	Goblet	194	6	1				
6949	Goblet	194	6	2				
6950	Cologne	242	6	2				
6951	Cologne	242	6	3				
6952	Cologne	242	6	4				
6953	Cologne	242	6	5				
6954	Bowl	145	2	4				
6954	Bowl	145	2	9				Error, see #6984 Bowl
6955	Goblet	194	6	3				TPD)7.53
6956	Tumbler	198	5	10				
6957	Shade	226	3	9				
6958	Shade	226	4	1				

SHAPE NO.	ITEM	PAGE	COL	ROW	PRICE REALIZED	GLASS TYPE	AUCTION HOUSE	COMMENTS & PHOTO REFERENCES
6959	Goblet	194	6	4				PG1)96,148,E&G; PG1)107,167,B;
6959								JSS)12-22; MDK)74
6960	Goblet	194	6	5				PG1)107,167,C
6961	Bowl	145	2	5				
6962	Bowl	145	2	6				
6963	Goblet	194	6	6				
6963	Wine				$140	Selenium Red	Cinc-06/03	
6964	Vase	287	5	4	$330	Gold Aurene	ebay-10/03	
6965	Goblet	194	6	7				
6966	Goblet	195	1	1				
6967	Candlestick	167	4	6				
6967	Centerpiece	154	2	4				
6967	Compote	176	1	1				
6968	Vase	288	1	1	$905	Green Jade/Alabaster foot	EAC-04/92	MDK)127
6969	Goblet	195	1	2				MDK)149
6970	Vase	288	1	2				
6971	Luminor	208	1	4	$315	Colorless/Black base	ebay-03/03	PG1)69,104,A; TPD)4.115
6972	Goblet	195	1	3				TPD)7.53
6973	Table Decoration	236	4	3				
6974	Goblet	195	1	4				
6975	Cologne	242	6	6				
6976	Goblet	195	1	5				TPD)2.42
6977	Goblet	195	1	6				PG2)86
6978	Vase	288	1	3	$115	Colorless/Green threaded	ebay-08/04	
6979	Vase	288	1	4				
6980	Vase	288	1	5	$295	French Blue	ebay-12/99	
6980					$145	Colorless/Black threaded	Sknr-06/00	
6980					$220	Colorless/Black threaded	ebay-08/01	
6980					$200	Bristol Yellow/White	Wint-12/01	White threaded
6980					$100	Bristol/White threaded	ebay-08/02	
6980					$180	VDS/Bristol threaded	ebay-11/02	
6980					$90	Colorless/Black threaded	ebay-12/03	
6980					$100	Colorless/Black threaded	ebay-04/04	
6980					$365	Colorless/Green threaded	EAC-07/04	
6980					$130	Colorless/Black threaded	ebay-11/04	
6980					$150	Colorless/Green threaded	ebay-12/04	
6980					$65	Colorless/Colorless thread	ebay-03/05	
6981	Bowl	145	2	7	$30	Colorless threaded	JDJ-11/03	
6982	Goblet	195	1	7				
6983	Bowl	145	2	8				PG1)XXVIII B,A; ACR)164,329;
6983								TPD)8.30:10.136
6984	Bowl	145	2	9	$160	Flemish Blue	ebay-11/03	This is a 6954 Bowl in Gardner
6985	Candlestick	167	4	7				
6985	Centerpiece	154	2	5	$420	Colorless Engraved	Wint-07/03	
6985	Compote	176	1	2	$160	Colorless Engraved	ebay-11/01	
6985					$225	Colorless Engraved	Wint-07/03	
6986	Centerpiece	154	2	6				
6987	Bowl	145	2	10	$1035	Cluthra	JDJ-10/97	TPD)7.57
6987	Candlestick	167	5	1				TPD)9.32
6987	Compote	176	1	3				TPD)6.3:7.57
6988	Vase	288	1	6	$860	Silverina	ebay-05/00	
6989	Vase	288	2	1				This is a duplicate shape of #7008.
6990	Vase	288	2	2	$840	Blue Aurene	JDJ-05/04	
6990					$1650	Blue Aurene	ebay-05/04	
6991	Vase	288	2	3	$690	Black/White Cluthra	JDJ-10/97	
6991					$75	Colorless/Blue threaded	ebay-05/05	
6992	Vase	288	2	4	$825	Gold Aurene	EAC-04/97	
6993	Vase	288	2	5	$975	Gold Aurene	Sknr-02/01	
6993					$2035	Blue Aurene	Cott-08/01	
6993					$1175	Bristol Yellow Silverina	ebay-07/03	
6993					$935	Gold Aurene	ebay-07/03	
6993					$750	Gold Aurene	ebay-11/04	
6994	Vase	288	3	1				
6995	Centerpiece	154	2	7	$650	Green Jade/Alabaster (E)	ebay-04/05	Engraved "Grapes"
6996	Centerpiece	154	2	8	$495	Yellow Silverina Air Trap	EAC-04/93	TPD)4.26
6996					$250	Ivrene	ebay-11/03	
6997	Centerpiece	154	2	9				MDK)128
6998	Candlestick	167	5	2	$575	Amethyst Silverina Air Trap	EAC-07/91	
6998					$230	Amethyst	ebay-05/04	
6999	Candlestick	167	5	3				TPD)4.26
7000	Vase	288	3	2	$7700	Green/Red Cluthra	EAC-04/96	PG1)114,178; RFR)18,4,B; TPD)10.129
7000					$2125	Rose Cluthra	JDJ-05/04	
7000					$3500	Green/Rose Cintra ACB	ebay-07/04	Etched "Cliffwood"
7001	Vase	288	3	3	$3450	Green Cintra ACB	Sknr-01/98	

SHAPE NO.	ITEM	PAGE	COL	ROW	PRICE REALIZED	GLASS TYPE	AUCTION HOUSE	COMMENTS & PHOTO REFERENCES
7001					$1800	Green Jade/Alabaster ACB	EAC-10/00	
7001					$1230	Blue Aurene	ebay-06/01	
7001					$810	Blue Aurene	ebay-02/02	
7001					$1915	Blue Aurene	ebay-04/02	
7001					$4440	Gold Ruby/White Cluthra	JDJ-11/02	Etched "Heaton"
7002	Vase	288	3	4				TPD)6.10:6.26
7003	Centerpiece	154	3	1				
7004	Centerpiece	154	3	2				
7005	Centerpiece	154	3	3				
7006	Table Top	238	1	4				
7007	Vase	288	4	1	$5060	Cintra/Pomona Green ACB	EAC-07/98	PG1)316
7007					$6500	Opal/Green/Rosa ACB	ebay-12/03	Etched "Boothbay"
7008	Vase	288	4	2	$1095	Mirror Black	Sknr-10/95	MDK)125
7008					$575	Mirror Black	Sknr-01/96	
7008					$630	Mirror Black	Sknr-10/96	
7008					$345	Mirror Black	Sknr-01/97	
7008					$920	Green Jade ACB	Sknr-06/00	Lamp and fittings etched "Sculptured"
7008					$255	Cyprian	ebay-11/01	
7008					$325	Pomona Green	ebay-02/02	
7008					$200	VDS	ebay-03/02	
7008					$840	Pomona Green	ebay-03/02	
7008					$780	Mirror Black ACB	ebay-01/03	Etched "Bird"
7008					$500	Cyprian	ebay-01/05	
7008					$250	Cyprian	ebay-02/05	
7009	Vase	288	4	3				
7010	Table Decoration	236	1	5				Pegasus TPD)4.45
7011	Bowl	145	3	1				
7012	Vase	288	4	4				
7013	Cologne	243	5	4,5				
7014	Vase	288	4	5	$9775	Blue Aurene/Yellow Jade	Sknr-10/98	
7015	Pitcher	215	1	3				
7016	Pitcher	215	1	4				
7017	Pitcher	215	1	5				
7018	Pitcher	215	2	1				
7019	Goblet	195	2	1				
7020	Centerpiece	154	3	4				
7021	Vase	288	5	1				
7022	Vase	288	5	2				
7023	Bowl	145	3	3	$605	Light Blue Jade	EAC-10/95	
7024	Tray	159	2	1	$190	Topaz/Celeste Blue rim	Cinc-11/02	16" diameter
7025	Ash Tray	138	1	7	$545	Gold Aurene	Sknr-10/94	ACR)136,249; TPD)10.22
7025					$275	Green Jade	Cott-08/01	
7025					$520	Gold Aurene	Cott-08/01	
7025					$355	Amethyst (FC)	Cott-08/01	
7025					$530	Blue Aurene	ebay-06/03	
7026	Ash Tray	138	1	8				MDK)88
7027	Ash Tray	138	1	9	$260	Green Jade	Sknr-05/94	
7028	Goblet	195	2	2				
7029	Ash Tray	138	1	10	$155	Green Jade	ebay-04/02	
7029					$225	Green Jade	ebay-05/02	
7029					$215	Green Jade	ebay-09/02	
7030	Ash Tray	138	1	11				
7031	Bowl	145	3	2				
7032	Candlestick	167	5	4	$110	Colorless (E)	ebay-06/05	
7032	Compote	176	1	4	$175	Colorless	ebay-07/01	
7032					$230	Colorless/Green rim	ebay-08/04	Green rim has acid etched pattern
7032					$250	Colorless (E)	ebay-12/04	Engraved "Glendale"
7032					$325	Colorless (E)	ebay-12/04	Engraved "Glendale"
7032					$300	Colorless (E)	ebay-01/05	Engraved "Glendale"
7033	Tray	159	2	2				TPD)7.50
7034	Vase	288	5	3				RFR)18,3,B; TPD)8.24
7034					$785	White Cluthra ACB	ebay-09/02	
7034					$5060	Black/Alabaster ACB	Jack-03/03	Etched "Nimrod"
7035	Vase	288	5	4				PG1)316
7036	Vase	288	5	5	$880	White Cluthra	EAC-10/98	PG1)316
7036					$805	Red/White Cluthra	JDJ-05/99	
7037	Vase	289	1	1				
7038	Cocktail Shaker	215	3	2				
7039	Flower Block	237	2	2	$480	Colorless	ebay-10/99	PG1)92,142,B; PG1)92,143
7039					$925	Bristol Yellow	ebay-01/00	
7039					$760	Colorless	ebay-05/01	
7040	Goblet	195	2	3	$260	Ivory with Black foot	Sknr-02/01	
7040					$41	Nile Green	ebay-11/02	
7040	Sherbet				$140	Mirror Black	ebay-07/05	

SHAPE NO.	ITEM	PAGE	COL	ROW	PRICE REALIZED	GLASS TYPE	AUCTION HOUSE	COMMENTS & PHOTO REFERENCES
7041	Vase	289	1	2				RFR)28,3,B; ACR)COLOR 3,T,E; TPD)8.47
7042	Bowl	145	3	4				
7043	Vase	289	1	3				
7044	Bowl	145	3	5				
7045	Vase	289	1	4				
7046	Goblet	195	2	4				PG1)316
7047	Goblet	195	2	5				
7048	Vase	289	1	5				
7049	Centerpiece	154	3	5	$165	Gold Calcite	ebay-07/04	MDK)17
7050	Vase	289	1	6				PG1)73,113,A&C:316
7051	Bowl	145	3	7				PG1)73,114,A&C:316; RFR)28,2,C;
7051								JAS)165,B,Cf; TPD)5.51
7052	Vase	289	2	1				RLG)163,298
7053	Vase	289	2	2				PG1)316
7054	Covered Vase	308	5	1				
7055	Goblet	195	1	6				
7056	Cocktail Shaker	215	3	3	$180	Colorless/Black threaded	ebay-01/03	PG1)87,128; RFR)17,2,C:24,3,D;
7056					$280	VDS/Jade Green stopper	ebay-04/04	TPD)9.22
7056					$150	Colorless/Green threaded	JDJ-05/04	
7056					$440	Colorless/Black threaded	EAC-10/04	Black faceted stopper
7056					$150	Colorless/Black threaded	ebay-05/05	Black faceted stopper
7057	Centerpiece	154	3	6				
7057	Cordial				$40	Selenium Red	ebay-12/04	
7057					$125	Selenium Red	ebay-12/04	
7057	Champagne				$155	Flemish Blue	ebay-01/03	MDK)114
7057					$90	Flemish Blue	ebay-02/03	
7057	Goblet	195	2	7	$255	Flemish Blue	ebay-01/03	
7057					$190	Flemish Blue	ebay-08/04	
7058	Goblet	195	3	1				
7059	Bowl	145	3	6				PG1)73,114,B
7060	Vase	289	2	3				PG1)73,113,B; PG2)102; ACR)171,350;
7060								TPD)4.80:8.22
7061	Vase	289	2	4				
7062	Vase	289	2	5				
7063	Vase	289	3	1	$990	Green Jade/Alabaster	EAC-07/97	RFR)22,3,B; ACR)156,308; TPD)6.12
7064	Flower Block	237	2	3	$105	Celeste Blue	ebay-08/01	PG1)92,142,A; TPD)10.30
7065	Vase	289	3	2				
7066	Bowl	145	3	8				
7067	Bowl	145	3	9				
7068	Bowl	145	3	10	$400	Green Jade	Tway-10/00	
7069	Bowl	145	3	11				
7070	Bowl	145	4	1				
7071	Bowl	145	4	2				
7072	Bowl	145	4	3				
7073	Table Top	238	2	1				
7074	Table Top	238	2	2				
7075	Table Top	238						Not numbered. Third row second item.
7076	Bowl	145	4	4	$90	Mirror Black	ebay-06/02	
7077	Bowl	145	4	5				
7078	Covered Vase	308	5	2				PG1)106,165; PG1)316
7079	Goblet	195	3	2				PG1)106,166,A
7080	Goblet	195	3	3				PG1)106,166,B
7081	Goblet	195	3	4				PG1)106,166,C
7081	Wine							JSS)12-19
7082	Vase	289	3	3	$3920	Blue Aurene	EAC-11/01	RFR)8,4,A
7083	Vase	289	3	4				PG1)72,110; ACR)157,309
7084	Ash Tray	138	1	12				
7085	Ash Tray	138	1	13				
7086	Candlestick	167	5	5				
7086	Centerpiece	154	3	7				
7086	Compote	176	1	5				
7087	Vase	289	3	5				
7088	Vase	289	4	1				
7089	Vase	289	4	2	$470	Amethyst Shaded	EAC-10/95	PG2)67,D; JAS)169,D; RFR)31,4,A
7089					$1150	Amethyst Shaded	JDJ-06/97	
7089					$285	Green Shaded	JDJ-10/97	
7089					$605	Amethyst Shaded	EAC-10/99	
7089					$665	Red Shaded	ebay-05/01	
7089					$320	Green Shaded	ebay-06/01	
7089					$270	Green Shaded	Cinc-06/05	
7090	Vase	289	4	3	$490	Blue Shaded	Sknr-01/96	PG1)XIX A,A&B&C&G; PG2)67,A&E;
7090					$635	Ivory	EAC-10/96	
7090					$440	Red Shaded	EAC-07/97	RFR)17,3,A&B&C:24,1,D; JAS)169,A&E;
7090					$200	Ivory	JDJ-10/97	ACR)176,359; TPD)5.55

SHAPE NO.	ITEM	PAGE	COL	ROW	PRICE REALIZED	GLASS TYPE	AUCTION HOUSE	COMMENTS & PHOTO REFERENCES
7090					$410	Ivory	EAC-07/98	
7090					$275	Ivory	EAC-10/98	
7090					$300	Green Shaded	EAC-10/98	
7090					$520	Amethyst Shaded	Sknr-06/99	
7090					$415	Red Shaded	ebay-04/00	
7090					$385	Red Shaded	EAC-10/00	
7090					$500	Green Shaded	ebay-11/00	
7090					$500	Green Shaded	ebay-02/00	
7090					$260	Amethyst Shaded	Sknr-02/01	
7090					$405	Amethyst Shaded	ebay-03/01	
7090					$180	Colorless	ebay-03/01	
7090					$785	Red Shaded	EAC-04/01	
7090					$530	Ivory	EAC-04/01	
7090					$550	Red Shaded	Midw-04/01	
7090					$230	Ivory	JDJ-05/01	
7090					$200	Ivory	ebay-05/01	
7090					$395	Red Shaded	ebay-06/01	
7090					$550	Red Shaded	ebay-11/01	
7090					$350	Green Shaded	ebay-12/01	
7090					$265	Green Shaded	ebay-01/02	
7090					$520	Amethyst Shaded	Cott-08/01	
7090					$330	Amethyst Shaded	ebay-04/02	
7090					$515	Amethyst Shaded	JDJ-05/02	
7090					$155	Colorless	ebay-05/02	
7090					$280	Green Shaded	ebay-10/02	
7090					$305	Amethyst Shaded	ebay-11/02	
7090					$305	Green Shaded	ebay-01/03	
7090					$115	Green Shaded	ebay-01/03	
7090					$495	Amethyst Shaded	ebay-02/03	
7090					$350	Green Shaded	ebay-03/03	
7090					$580	Red Shaded	ebay-06/03	
7090					$650	Blue Shaded	Cinc-06/03	
7090					$370	Red Shaded	ebay-06/03	
7090					$310	Green Shaded	ebay-09/03	
7090					$400	Ivory	JDJ-11/03	
7090					$325	Amethyst Shaded	ebay-11/03	
7090					$460	Ivory	EAC-11/03	
7090					$410	Amethyst Shaded	ebay-12/03	
7090					$255	Green Shaded	ebay-02/04	
7090					$270	Amethyst Shaded	ebay-05/04	
7090					$315	Amethyst Shaded	JDJ-05/04	
7090					$400	Green Shaded	JDJ-05/04	
7090					$165	Green Shaded	ebay-05/04	
7090					$525	Green Shaded	ebay-08/04	
7090					$335	Amethyst Shaded	ebay-09/04	
7090					$750	Colorless	ebay-09/04	Price seems much too high
7090					$280	Green Shaded	ebay-01/05	
7090					$275	Green Shaded	ebay-02/05	
7090					$400	Red Shaded	ebay-02/05	
7090					$330	Green Shaded	ebay-05/05	
7090					$345	Blue Shaded	Cinn-05/05	
7091	Bowl	145	4	6	$110	Ivory	JDJ-10/94	PG1)XIX A,D; ACR)176,360;
7091					$400	Red Shaded	Sknr-05/96	TPD)5.54:5.55
7091					$330	Red Shaded	JDJ-06/96	
7091					$195	Ivory	JDJ-06/96	
7091					$285	Ivrene	JDJ-10/97	
7091					$345	Ivory	Sknr-01/98	
7091					$355	Ivory	EAC-04/98	
7091					$220	Ivory	EAC-10/98	
7091					$650	Red Shaded	ebay-12/99	
7091					$300	Red Shaded	ebay-12/99	
7091					$330	Red Shaded	ebay-12/99	
7091					$275	Red Shaded	ebay-01/00	
7091					$180	Ivory	ebay-02/01	
7091					$200	Blue Shaded	Sknr-02/01	
7091					$140	Ivory	ebay-03/01	
7091					$225	Amber Shaded	ebay-04/01	
7091					$330	Amethyst Shaded	ebay-06/01	
7091					$440	Amber Shaded	Cott-08/01	
7091					$405	Red Shaded	ebay-11/01	
7091					$900	Wisteria	ebay-12/01	
7091					$245	Green Shaded	ebay-03/02	
7091					$300	Red Shaded	ebay-04/02	
7091					$190	Colorless	ebay-04/02	

SHAPE NO.	ITEM	PAGE	COL	ROW	PRICE REALIZED	GLASS TYPE	AUCTION HOUSE	COMMENTS & PHOTO REFERENCES
7091					$100	Amethyst Shaded	ebay-06/02	
7091					$95	Colorless	ebay-07/02	
7091					$210	Ivory	ebay-10/02	
7091					$285	Red Shaded	ebay-11/02	
7091					$215	Green Shaded	ebay-01/03	
7091					$55	Colorless	ebay-03/03	
7091					$1240	Wisteria	ebay-05/03	
7091					$495	Red Shaded	ebay-05/03	
7091					$360	Amethyst Shaded	JDJ-05/03	
7091					$375	Ivory	Cinc-06/03	
7091					$460	Blue Shaded	EAC-06/03	
7091					$260	Ivory	ebay-08/03	
7091					$405	Amethyst Shaded	ebay-09/03	
7091					$655	Red Shaded	ebay-10/03	
7091					$230	Ivory	JDJ-11/03	
7091					$400	Amethyst Shaded	EAC-11/03	
7091					$945	Wisteria	ebay-12/03	
7091					$560	Blue Shaded	ebay-02/04	
7091					$510	Red Shaded	ebay-03/04	
7091					$335	Red Shaded	ebay-03/04	
7091					$145	Green Shaded	EAC-04/04	
7091					$400	Green Shaded	EAC-04/04	
7091					$230	Red Shaded	ebay-06/04	
7091					$145	Ivory	Cinc-06/04	
7091					$180	Amethyst Shaded	ebay-06/04	
7091					$380	Amethyst Shaded	ebay-09/04	
7091					$275	Green Shaded	ebay-10/04	
7091					$80	Colorless	ebay-10/04	
7091					$245	Amethyst Shaded	ebay-10/04	
7091					$275	Ivory	ebay-11/04	
7091					$255	Red Shaded	ebay-11/04	
7091					$130	Blue Shaded	ebay-01/05	
7091					$400	Ivory	ebay-01/05	
7091					$200	Red Shaded	ebay-03/05	
7091					$240	Red Shaded	ebay-05/05	
7091					$300	Ivory	Cinc-06/05	
7091					$270	Red Shaded	ebay-06/05	
7091					$405	Green Shaded	ebay-07/05	
7092	Vase	289	4	4				
7093	Candlestick	168	1	1	$520	Wisteria	Sknr-03/99	
7093	Centerpiece	154	3	8				
7093	Compote	176	1	6				
7094	Candlestick	168	1	2				
7094	Centerpiece	154	3	9				
7094	Compote	176	1	7				
7095	Vase	289	4	5				
7096	Bowl	145	4	7				RFR)7,3,A
7097	Vase	289	5	1	$1700	Gold Aurene	ebay-11/03	PG1)VI B,A; TPD)8.24
7097					$10925	Black/Green Jade ACB	EAC-11/03	Etched "Tropic"
7098	Vase	289	5	2				
7099	Bowl	145	4	8				TPD)10.131
7100	Vase	289	5	3	$3360	Blue Aurene	EAC-11/01	PG1)V B,A
7100					$3000	Blue Aurene	ebay-10/04	
7101	Bowl	145	4	9				RFR)7,3,C
7102	Vase	289	5	4				JAS)162,BL,B
7103	Vase	289	5	5				RLG)139,269; TPD)10.38
7104	Vase	290	1	1				PG1)VI B,B
7105	Vase	290	1	2				TPD)8.4
7106	Vase	290	1	3				TPD)10.130
7107	Vase	290	1	4	$1870	Gold Aurene	Cott-08/01	
7108	Ash Tray	138	1	14				
7109	Ash Tray	138	1	15				
7110	Ash Tray	138	2	1				
7111	Decanter	187	2	5				
7112	Decanter	187	3	1				
7113	Decanter	187	3	2				
7114	Decanter	187	3	3				
7115	Decanter	187	3	5,6				
7116	Decanter	187	4	1				
7117	Decanter	187	4	2				
7118	Decanter	187	4	3				
7119	Cigarette Holder	138	3	5				
7120	Cigarette Holder	138	3	6				
7121	Lighter	138	4	8				

SHAPE NO.	ITEM	PAGE	COL	ROW	PRICE REALIZED	GLASS TYPE	AUCTION HOUSE	COMMENTS & PHOTO REFERENCES
7122	Goblet	195	3	5				
7123	Goblet	195	3	6				
7124	Goblet	195	3	7				
7125	Cologne	243	4	8	$255	Colorless/Green threaded	ebay-08/03	
7125					$380	Colorless/Green threaded	ebay-10/03	
7126	Cologne	243	4	9				
7127	Cologne	243	5	1				
7128	Vase	290	1	5	$840	Ivory	Cinc-06/05	
7128					$610	Mirror Black	ebay-06/05	
7129	Vase	290	2	1	$1380	Spanish Green	Sknr-01/96	PG2)100; RLG)143,275; TPD)6.20
7129					$920	Colorless	Sknr-01/98	
7130	Vase	290	2	2				
7131	Vase	290	2	3				
7132	Vase	290	2	4				
7133	Table Decoration	236	2	2	$920	Colorless	Sknr-01/97	PG1)92,142,D; TPD)10.33
7133					$490	Alabaster	Sknr-05/98	
7133					$400	Amethyst	Sknr-01/98	
7133					$590	Spanish Green	ebay-01/00	
7133					$400	Colorless	ebay-01/00	
7133					$440	Alabaster	ebay-02/00	
7133					$150	Colorless	ebay-02/00	
7133					$410	Pomona Green	ebay-07/00	
7133					$535	Amethyst	ebay-01/01	
7133					$515	Light Amethyst	Sknr-02/01	
7133					$250	Colorless	ebay-07/02	
7133					$130	Colorless	ebay-10/02	
7133					$125	Colorless	ebay-08/03	
7133					$950	Alabaster	EAC-11/03	
7133					$405	Alabaster	ebay-04/04	
7133					$230	Bristol Yellow	ebay-06/04	
7133					$310	Green Jade	ebay-01/05	
7134	Ash Tray	138	2	2				
7135	Atomizer	239	4	3				
7136	Atomizer	239	4	4				
7137	Atomizer	239	4	5	$90	Celeste Blue	ebay-02/04	With fittings
7138	Atomizer	239	4	6				
7139	Atomizer	239	4	7				
7140	Atomizer	239	4	8				
7141	Atomizer	239	4	9				
7142	Atomizer	239	5	1				
7143	Atomizer	239	5	2				
7144	Atomizer	239	5	3				
7145	Atomizer	239	5	4				
7146	Atomizer	239	5	5				
7147	Atomizer	239	5	6				
7148	Atomizer	239	5	7				
7149	Atomizer	239	5	8				
7150	Lamp Base	205	1	1				
7151	Lamp Base	205	1	2				
7152	Ash Tray	138	2	3				
7153	Vase	290	3	1				
7154	Vase	290	3	2				
7155	Candlestick	168	1	3				
7156	Vase	290	3	3				
7157	Lighter	138	4	9				ACR)136,250
7158	Lighter	138	4	10				
7159	Candlestick	168	1	4				
7159	Centerpiece	155	1	1				
7159	Compote	176	1	8				TPD)4.70
7160	Goblet	195	4	1				
7161	Goblet	195	4	2				
7161	Sherbet							MDK)130
7162	Candlestick	168	2	1				
7162	Bowl	146	1	1				
7162	Centerpiece	155	1	2				
7163	Covered Vase	308	5	3				
7164	Centerpiece	155	1	3				
7165	Vase	290	3	4	$595	Green/White Cluthra	ebay-12/04	RFR)22,3,A
7166	Vase	290	4	1				
7167	Vase	290	4	2				
7168	Vase	290	4	3				TPD)4.70
7169	Vase	290	4	4				TPD)4.70
7170	Vase	290	4	5				
7171	Candlestick	168	2	2	$490	Green	Sknr-10/96	

SHAPE NO.	ITEM	PAGE	COL	ROW	PRICE REALIZED	GLASS TYPE	AUCTION HOUSE	COMMENTS & PHOTO REFERENCES
7171					$180	Colorless/Amber	ebay-01/01	
7171	Centerpiece	155	1	4				
7171	Compote	176	2	1				
7172	Cologne	243	5	2				
7173	Candlestick	168	2	3				
7173	Centerpiece	155	1	5				TPD)7.67
7173	Compote	176	2	2				
7174	Goblet	195	4	3				
7175	Cologne	243	5	3				
7176	Vase	290	5	1				
7177	Vase	290	5	2				
7178	Bowl							See New Drawings section
7179	Vase	290	5	3				
7180	Vase	290	5	4				
7181	Goblet	195	4	4				PG1)99,155
7182	Goblet	195	4	5	$290	Wisteria	Sknr-03/99	MDK)24
7182					$530	Wisteria	ebay-01/00	
7183	Candlestick	168	2	4	$690	Celeste Blue(E)	Sknr-10/95	
7183					$975	Colorless/Celeste Blue	ebay-03/01	
7183	Centerpiece	155	1	6				
7183	Compote	176	2	3				MDK)30
7184	Vase	290	5	5				
7185	Vase	291	1	1				
7186	Vase	291	1	2				
7187	Vase	291	1	3				
7188	Vase	291	1	4	$1350	Gold Aurene	ebay-03/00	
7188					$630	Gold Aurene	JDJ-11/03	
7188					$215	Topaz/Green foot	ebay-11/04	
7189	Vase	291	1	5				
7190	Vase	291	2	1				
7191	Vase	291	2	2				
7192	Vase	291	2	3				
7193	Shade	226	4	2	$55	Marbelite	EAC-07/04	
7194	Tray	159	2	3				
7195	Vase	291	2	4				
7196	Vase	291	3	1	$1800	Gold Aurene	JDJ-06/05	
7197	Vase	291	3	2	$4885	Lace Cintra	Sknr-05/96	TPD)8.35
7198	Covered Vase	308	5	4				
7199	Pitcher	215	2	2				
7200	Vase	291	3	3				
7201	Vase	291	3	4				
7202	Vase	291	3	5				
7203	Vase	291	4	1	$2800	Blue Cintra	ebay-12/99	
7203					$400	Wisteria	ebay-06/01	
7204	Centerpiece	155	1	7	$1100	Iridescent Green Jade	EAC-10/93	
7204					$495	Green/Colorless (E)	JDJ-06/96	
7204					$250	Green/White threaded	ebay-05/02	
7205	Vase	291	4	2				
7206	Vase	291	4	3				
7207	Vase	291	4	4				
7208	Vase	291	4	5	$805	Wisteria	Sknr-01/98	TPD)10.116
7208					$715	Alabaster/Black	ebay-08/00	
7209	Vase	291	4	6				
7210	Vase	291	5	1				
7211	Candlestick	168	3	1				
7211	Centerpiece	155	2	1				
7211	Compote	176	2	4				
7212	Vase	291	5	2				
7213	Cigarette Holder	138	3	7				
7214	Lamp	208	2	1				
7215	Lamp	208	2	2				
7216	Lamp	208	2	3				
7217	Lamp	208	2	4				
7218	Pitcher	215	2	3	$985	Green Jade/Alabaster	ebay-11/99	
7218					$785	Green Jade/Alabaster	ebay-02/03	Pitcher and 4 Glasses
7218	Lemonade Glass	215	2	3	$130	Green Jade/Alabaster	ebay-03/00	
7218					$85	Green Jade/Alabaster	ebay-07/01	
7218					$100	Green Jade/Alabaster	ebay-08/01	
7218					$200	Green Jade/Alabaster	ebay-12/01	
7218					$150	Green Jade/Alabaster	ebay-01/02	
7218					$230	Green Jade/Alabaster	ebay-12/02	
7218					$80	Pomona Green/Topaz	ebay-01/03	
7218					$130	Green Jade/Alabaster	ebay-01/03	
7218					$180	Alabaster/Black handle	ebay-02/03	

SHAPE NO.	ITEM	PAGE	COL	ROW	PRICE REALIZED	GLASS TYPE	AUCTION HOUSE	COMMENTS & PHOTO REFERENCES
7218					$80	Green Jade/Alabaster	ebay-02/03	
7218					$85	Green Jade/Alabaster	ebay-02/03	
7218					$40	Bristol/Pomona handle	ebay-05/03	
7218					$80	Green Jade/Alabaster	ebay-08/03	
7218					$155	Green Jade/Alabaster	ebay-08/03	
7218					$20	Celeste Blue/Topaz	ebay-09/03	Topaz handle
7218					$55	Colorless/Blue handle	JDJ-11/03	
7218					$100	Green Jade/Alabaster	ebay-04/04	Alabaster handle
7219	Vase	291	5	3				
7220	Bowl	146	1	2				
7221	Centerpiece	155	2	2				
7222	Vase	291	5	4				
7223	Luminor	208	3	1				PG1)93,144
7224	Luminor	208	3	2				PG1)93,145
7225	Lamp	208	3	3				
7226	Lamp	208	3	4				
7227	Vase	291	5	5				
7228	Vase	292	1	1	$880	Wisteria	EAC-04/93	
7229	Panel	208	4	1				
7230	Bowl	146	1	3				
7231	Table Decoration	237	2	4				PG1)92,142,E; RFR)24,1,E; TPD)4.152
7231					$1495	Mirror Black	EAC-07/05	
7232	Bowl	146	1	4	$400	Green/White Cluthra	JDJ-10/97	
7232					$50	Pomona Green	ebay-11/00	
7232					$190	Pomona Green	ebay-03/02	
7233	Bowl	146	1	5				PG1)316
7234	Goblet	195	4	6	$920	Black/Colorless (E)	Sknr-05/94	PG1)316; MDK)124
7235	Goblet	195	5	1				
7236	Goblet	195	5	2				PG1)316
7237	Goblet	195	5	3				PG1)316
7238	Cordial				$150	Colorless (E)	ebay-11/00	Engraved "Strawberry Mansion"
7238	Goblet	195	5	4				PG1)316; PG2)87,E-H; TPD)9.17
7238					$200	Colorless (E)	ebay-11/00	Engraved "Strawberry Mansion"
7238					$175	Colorless (E)	ebay-11/00	Engraved "Strawberry Mansion"
7238	Vase							TPD)9.17
7239	Covered Vase	309	1	1				
7240	Covered Vase	309	1	2				
7241	Tray	159	2	4				
7242	Candelabra	170	1	1				TPD)7.34
7243	Candelabra	170	1	2				
7244	Ash Tray	138	2	4	$335	Selenium Red	ebay-11/01	
7244					$410	Selenium Red/Colorless	EAC-10/04	Colorless handle
7245	Candelabra	170	1	3				
7245	Candlestick	168	3	2				PG1)316
7245	Centerpiece	155	2	3				PG1)316
7245	Compote	176	2	5	$770	Colorless	EAC-10/04	PG1)316
7246	Vase	292	1	2	$650	Green/White Cluthra	ebay-05/02	
7247	Vase	292	1	3	$1485	Gold Aurene	JDJ-06/96	
7248	Vase	292	1	4				
7249	Candlestick	168	3	3				
7249	Centerpiece	155	2	4				
7249	Compote	176	2	6				
7250	Candlestick	168	3	4				PG1)317
7250	Centerpiece	155	2	5				PG1)317
7250	Compote	176	3	1				PG1)317
7251	Cologne	242	6	7	$265	Colorless (E)	ebay-12/01	
7252	Cologne	242	6	8				
7253	Candlestick	168	4	1				
7253	Centerpiece	155	2	6				
7253	Compote	176	3	2				
7254	Compote	176	3	3	$200	Green Jade/Alabaster	ebay-09/01	TPD)10.36
7255	Candlestick	168	4	2				
7255	Centerpiece	155	2	7				
7255	Compote	176	3	4				
7256	Candelabra	170	2	1				
7256	Candlestick	168	4	3				
7256	Compote	176	3	5				
7257	Door Stop	236	4	5	$290	Colorless	Sknr-05/98	PG1)116,186,B&D
7257					$305	Colorless	ebay-03/00	
7258	Cologne	243	1	1				
7259	Cologne	243	1	2				
7260	Vase	292	2	1				
7261	Vase	292	2	2				
7262	Vase	292	2	3				

SHAPE NO.	ITEM	PAGE	COL	ROW	PRICE REALIZED	GLASS TYPE	AUCTION HOUSE	COMMENTS & PHOTO REFERENCES
7263	Vase	292	2	4				
7264	Vase	292	2	5				
7265	Vase	292	3	1				
7266	Vase	292	3	2				
7267	Shade	230	1	7				
7268	Goblet	195	5	5				
7269	Candlestick	168	4	4				
7269	Centerpiece	155	2	8	$105	Ivrene	ebay-04/04	
7269					$150	Gold Calcite	ebay-06/04	
7270	Dessert							MDK)135
7270	Goblet	195	5	6				TPD)7.25; MDK)134
7270	Plate							TPD)7.25
7270	Sherbet							TPD)7.25
7270	Tumbler							TPD)7.25
7271	Vase	292	3	3	$1265	Cluthra	JDJ-06/98	
7272	Vase	292	3	4	$660	White Cluthra	EAC-07/92	TPD)10.52
7272					$1375	Cluthra	JDJ-06/96	
7272					$1380	Amethyst Cluthra	JDJ-10/97	
7273	Vase	292	4	1	$2090	Rose Cluthra	EAC-10/90	
7273					$745	White Cluthra	Sknr-10/97	
7273					$1380	Green Cluthra	JDJ-10/97	
7274	Vase	292	4	2				
7275	Vase	292	4	3	$250	Red Shaded	ebay-01/05	PG2)69
7276	Vase	292	4	4	$940	Gold Aurene	ebay-09/04	
7277	Vase	292	4	5				PG1)XIX A,F
7278	Vase	292	5	1				
7279	Vase	292	5	2				
7280	Vase	292	5	3	$450	Red Shaded	ebay-10/99	
7281	Vase	292	5	4	$1200	Blue Aurene	ebay-03/00	
7281					$1035	Blue Aurene	Jack–11/02	
7282	Vase	292	5	5	$1920	Blue Aurene	ebay-01/05	
7282					$110	Blue Aurene	ebay-06/05	
7283	Goblet	195	6	1				JSS)12-32,C
7284	Goblet	197	5	4				PG1)107,168
7285	Goblet	197	5	5				
7286	Cocktail Glass							TPD)7.66
7286	Cocktail Shaker	215	3	4				RLG)159,296; TPD)7.66
7287	Cocktail Shaker	215	3	5				
7288	Vase	293	1	1				
7289	Vase	293	1	2	$400	Green Jade	Tway-10/00	PG1)317
7289					$865	Wisteria	ebay-10/02	
7289					$350	Colorless	ebay-11/03	Cut decoration
7289					$590	Colorless ACB	ebay-11/04	
7290	Candlestick	168	4	5				
7290	Centerpiece	155	3	1				
7290	Compote	176	3	6				
7291	Shade	226	4	3				
7292	Centerpiece	155	3	2				TPD)7.27
7293	Vase	293	1	3				
7294	Vase	293	1	4				
7295	Vase	293	2	1				
7296	Goblet	195	6	2				
7297	Goblet	195	6	3				
7298	Goblet	195	6	4				
7299	Goblet	195	6	5	$350	Gold Ruby/Colorless (E)	ebay-11/04	TPD)7.46
7300	Tumbler	199	3	1				
7301	Champagne							JSS)12-15,L
7301	Goblet	195	6	6				
7302	Candlestick	168	5	1				
7302	Centerpiece	155	3	3				
7302	Compote	176	4	1	$1500	Wisteria	ebay-06/00	
7303	Goblet	195	6	7				
7304	Vase	293	2	2				
7305	Vase	293	2	3				PG1)XXVIII C,D
7306	Vase	293	2	4				
7307	Centerpiece	155	3	4	$1210	Blue Aurene	EAC-10/90	PG1)317; RFR)20,2,B; TPD)4.63;MDK)7
7307					$605	Ivory & Black	EAC-02/92	
7307					$550	Ivory & Black	JDJ-10/95	
7307					$345	Ivory & Black	JDJ-10/96	
7307					$460	Ivory & Black	Sknr-10/96	
7307					$385	Ivory	EAC-10/97	
7307					$385	Ivory & Black	EAC-10/98	
7307					$550	Ivory & Black	EAC-10/98	
7307					$170	Black	Sknr-01/98	

SHAPE NO.	ITEM	PAGE	COL	ROW	PRICE REALIZED	GLASS TYPE	AUCTION HOUSE	COMMENTS & PHOTO REFERENCES
7307					$190	Sea Green	ebay-06/99	
7307					$430	Ivory	Sknr-06/99	
7307					$630	Wisteria	Sknr-06/00	
7307					$385	Green Jade/Alabaster	ebay-11/00	
7307					$860	Ivory	Sknr-02/01	
7307					$745	Ivory & Black	Sknr-02/01	
7307					$1500	Gold Aurene	ebay-05/01	
7307					$475	Ivory & Black	ebay-07/01	
7307					$245	Ivory	ebay-11/01	
7307					$500	Ivory	ebay-12/01	
7307					$280	Ivory	ebay-02/02	
7307					$250	Ivory	ebay-03/02	
7307					$335	Ivory	EAC-04/02	
7307					$1905	Blue Aurene	EAC-04/02	
7307					$480	Ivory & Black	JDJ-11/02	
7307					$175	Colorless	ebay-01/03	
7307					$1050	Wisteria	ebay-04/03	
7307					$230	Ivory	EAC-11/03	
7307					$355	Ivory	ebay-12/03	
7307					$60	Colorless	ebay-02/04	
7307					$255	Ivory	ebay-04/04	
7307					$575	Celeste Blue	ebay-04/04	
7307					$1495	Blue Aurene	JDJ-05/04	
7307					$665	Ivory/Black foot	ebay-05/04	
7307					$215	Ivory	ebay-11/04	
7307					$240	Ivory	ebay-12/04	
7307					$275	Ivory	ebay-02/05	
7307					$300	Ivory	ebay-04/05	
7307					$315	Ivory	EAC-04/05	
7308	Lamp	208	1	5				
7309	Centerpiece	155	3	5				
7310	Vase	293	2	5				
7311	Vase	293	3	1	$400	Green Jade	Sknr-10/96	
7311					$60	Colorless	ebay-05/01	
7311					$200	Ivory	ebay-07/01	
7311					$175	Colorless	ebay-08/02	
7311					$300	Ivory	ebay-02/03	
7311					$80	Colorless	ebay-06/04	
7311					$250	Green Jade	ebay-06/04	9"
7311					$85	Ivory	ebay-09/04	
7311					$200	Colorless	ebay-07/05	
7312	Vase	293	3	2				
7313	Brandy Snifter	197	6	5				
7314	Goblet	197	5	6				
7315	Candlestick	168	5	2				
7315	Centerpiece	155	3	6				
7315	Compote	176	4	2				PG2)92,B; JAS)148,T,B
7316	Vase	293	3	3	$230	Ivory	Sknr-05/98	
7316					$440	Green Jade/Alabaster	EAC-07/98	
7316					$575	Ivory	Sknr-02/01	
7316					$630	Wisteria	Sknr-02/01	
7316					$305	Green Jade/Alabaster	ebay-07/01	
7316					$275	Green Jade/Alabaster	ebay-08/01	
7316					$380	Ivory/Black foot	Sknr-12/02	
7316					$150	Topaz	ebay-04/03	
7316					$160	Ivory	ebay-08/04	
7317	Candelabra	170	2	2	$960	Ivory & Black	EAC-10/91	PG2)92,A&C; JAS)148,T,A&C; TPD)5.68
7317					$860	Ivory & Black	Sknr-10/95	
7317					$545	Ivory	Sknr-01/98	
7317					$1650	Green Jade/Alabaster	EAC-05/00	
7317					$1285	Ivory & Black foot	ebay-09/04	3 Arm version
7318	Vase	293	3	4				
7319	Vase	293	3	5				TPD)6.32
7320	Vase	293	4	1	$805	Ivory	Sknr-10/95	
7321	Vase	293	4	2				TPD)8.38
7322	Vase	293	4	3				
7323	Candlestick	168	5	3				TPD)6.9
7324	Goblet	197	5	7				
7325	Cologne	243	1	3	$375	Amethyst	ebay-08/01	MDK)47
7325					$375	Amethyst	ebay-12/01	
7325					$275	Colorless/Red threaded	ebay-04/05	
7326	Cologne	243	1	4				TPD)4.57
7327	Cologne	243	1	5	$485	Green/White Cluthra	ebay-01/04	ACR)156,307,A&B; TPD)6.21
7328	Cologne	243	1	6				

SHAPE NO.	ITEM	PAGE	COL	ROW	PRICE REALIZED	GLASS TYPE	AUCTION HOUSE	COMMENTS & PHOTO REFERENCES
7329	Cologne	243	1	7				
7330	Cologne	243	1	8				
7331	Vase	293	4	4	$260	Ivory & Black	Sknr-05/94	ACR)147,281
7331					$550	Ivory	ebay-10/99	
7331					$300	Ivory	ebay-03/00	
7331					$170	Ivory	Rago-09/00	
7331					$200	Pomona Green	Rago-09/00	
7331					$325	Ivory	Tway-10/00	
7331					$200	Ivory	ebay-02/02	
7331					$80	Ivory	ebay-05/02	
7331					$310	Green Jade/Alabaster foot	EAC-01/03	
7331					$575	Ivory & Black	JDJ-05/02	
7331					$200	Amethyst	ebay-04/04	
7331					$660	Ivory	EAC-10/04	
7331					$310	Green Jade/Alabaster foot	ebay-02/05	
7331					$180	Ivory	Cinc-06/05	
7332	Goblet	196	1	1			JDJ-05/04	
7333	Vase	293	4	5	$145	Colorless (E)	ebay-02/02	Engraved "Renwick"
7334	Cologne	243	1	9				
7335	Cologne	243	1	10				
7336	Goblet	196	1	2				JSS)12-32,L
7337	Bowl	146	1	6	$430	Ivory	Sknr-03/99	
7337					$200	Ivory	JDJ-05/04	
7338	Goblet	196	1	3				
7339	Goblet	196	1	4				
7340	Vase	293	5	1				
7341	Goblet	196	1	5				JSS)12-28,L
7342	Centerpiece	155	3	7				
7343	Goblet	196	1	6				
7344	Goblet	196	2	1				PG2)87,D
7345	Goblet	196	2	2				
7346	Goblet	196	2	3				
7347	Cologne	243	2	1	$180	VDS/Blue stopper	JDJ-05/04	JAS)167,TR,B
7348	Decanter	187	4	4				
7349	Decanter	187	4	5				PG1)317
7350	Decanter	188	1	1				
7351	Decanter	188	1	2				
7352	Vase	293	5	2				
7353	Goblet	196	2	4	$50	Colorless cut	ebay-11/01	JSS)12-21:12-32,R
7354	Shade	232	3	1				
7355	Shade	232	3	2				
7356	Shade	226	4	4				
7357	Shade	226	4	5	$145	Gold Aurene	ebay-05/02	
7358	Shade	226	4	6	$95	Gold Aurene	ebay-05/05	
7358					$175	Gold Aurene	ebay-06/05	
7359	Shade	226	4	7	$230	Gold Aurene	ebay-09/04	
7360	Shade	226	4	8				
7361	Shade	232	4	3				
7362	Shade	232	3	4				TPD)5.13
7363	Vase	293	5	3				
7364	Vase	293	5	4				
7365	Bowl	146	1	7				
7366	Bowl	146	1	8				
7367	Vase	293	5	5				
7368	Vase	293	5	6				
7369	Vase	293	5	7				
7370	Vase	294	1	1				
7371	Vase	294	1	2				
7372	Vase	294	1	3				PG1)317; RFR)18,4,C
7373	Vase	294	1	4				PG1)317
7374	Vase	294	1	5				PG1)317
7375	Vase	294	1	6				PG1)317
7376	Compote	176	4	3				PG1)317
7376					$150	Colorless (E)	ebay-02/04	Engraved "Marguerite"
7376					$560	Colorless (E)	ebay-12/04	Engraved "Marguerite"
7377	Vase	294	2	1				PG1)317
7378	Centerpiece	156	1	1				PG1)317
7379	Vase	294	2	2	$220	Ivory	EAC-04/98	PG1)317
7379					$935	Blue Aurene	EAC-07/98	
7380	Candlestick	168	5	4				PG1)317
7381	Centerpiece	156	1	2	$520	Green Jade	Sknr-06/00	PG1)317
7381					$660	Gold Ruby	ebay-05/02	
7382	Goblet	196	2	5				JSS)12-31,L,C
7383	Goblet	196	2	6				JSS)12-31,R

SHAPE NO.	ITEM	PAGE	COL	ROW	PRICE REALIZED	GLASS TYPE	AUCTION HOUSE	COMMENTS & PHOTO REFERENCES
7384	Goblet	196	3	1				PG1)XXVIII C,C
7385	Goblet	196	3	2	$375	"Special Green"	ebay-03/03	ACR)148,286; TPD)10.29;MDK)8
7385					$400	"Special Green"	ebay-04/03	
7386	Ash Tray	138	2	5				
7387	Vase	294	2	3	$190	Colorless	JDJ-10/97	PG1)318
7388	Vase	294	2	4				PG1)318; TPD)10.42:10.89
7389	Vase	294	2	5	$1035	Colorless (not engraved)	Sknr-03/99	PG1)318
7389					$89	Colorless (not engraved)	ebay-01/04	
7390	Champagne							JSS)12-18,R
7390	Goblet	196	3	3	$275	Ivory & Black (FC)	ebay-09/01	JSS)12-18,L
7391	Vase	294	3	1	$1650	Green Jade/Alabaster ACB	ebay-12/99	Etched "Valeria" PG1)318
7391					$4200	Green Jade/Alabaster ACB	EAC-04/02	
7391					$1500	Green Jade/Alabaster ACB	ebay-08/02	Etched "Peony"
7391					$3640	Green Jade/Alabaster ACB	EAC-07/04	Etched "Peony"
7391					$1440	Green Jade/Alabaster ACB	EAC-04/05	Etched "Peony"
7392	Candelabra	170	2	3				
7393	Shade	230	1	8				PG1)115,185
7394	Vase	294	3	2				
7395	Ash Tray	138	2	6				
7396	Cigarette Holder	138	3	8				
7397	Cigarette Holder	138	3	9				
7398	Table Decoration	236	1	6				Peacock, PG2)82; TPD)2.40
7399	Table Decoration	236	1	7	$860	Colorless	Sknr-01/98	Gazelle, TPD)4.130; MDK)93
7399					$575	Colorless	Sknr-05/99	
7399					$300	Colorless	ebay-10/00	
7399					$290	Colorless	ebay-03/01	
7399					$385	Colorless	ebay-10/01	
7399					$350	Colorless	ebay-11/01	
7399					$225	Colorless	EAC-11/01	
7399					$350	Colorless	ebay-01/02	
7399					$405	Colorless	ebay-06/02	
7399					$250	Colorless	ebay-10/02	
7399					$200	Colorless	ebay-11/02	
7399					$330	Colorless	ebay-03/03	
7399					$285	Colorless	ebay-05/03	
7399					$200	Colorless	ebay-10/03	
7399					$245	Colorless	JDJ-11/02	
7399					$230	Colorless	JDJ-11/02	
7399					$510	Colorless	ebay-12/03	
7399					$400	Colorless	ebay-02/04	
7399					$235	Colorless	ebay-05/04	
7399					$355	Colorless	ebay-05/04	
7399					$345	Colorless	ebay-11/04	
7399					$305	Colorless	ebay-01/05	
7399					$385	Colorless	ebay-03/05	
7399					$375	Colorless	ebay-04/05	
7399					$245	Colorless	ebay-07/05	
7400	Table Decoration	236	1	8				Duck
7401	Candlestick	168	5	5				PG1)318
7401	Centerpiece	156	1	3				PG1)318
7401	Compote	176	4	4				PG1)318
7401	Goblet	196	3	4				
7402	Champagne				$30	Colorless Eng. "Renwick"	ebay-05/03	"Hand Wrought" signature
7402	Goblet	196	3	5				PG1)318; RFR)28,3,A; TPD)4.74
7402	Wine				$40	Colorless Eng. "Renwick"	ebay-05/03	"Hand Wrought" signature
7403	Candlestick	169	1	1				PG1)318
7403	Centerpiece	156	1	4				PG1)318
7403	Champagne				$55	Colorless (E)	ebay-01/02	Engraved "Renwick"
7403	Compote	176	4	.5				PG1)318
7403					$395	VDS (E)	ebay-09/03	Signed "Hawkes"
7403	Goblet	196	3	6				PG1)318
7404	Vase	294	3	3				
7405	Vase	294	3	4				
7406	Vase	294	4	1	$40	Colorless	ebay-02/00	Teague #T-132 pattern MDK)138
7407	Vase	294	4	2	$400	Colorless (Cut #2)	ebay-10/04	PG1)319
7408	Vase	294	4	3				
7409	Vase	294	4	4	$1150	White Cluthra	Sknr-01/96	PG1)III B,D
7410	Vase	294	4	5	$2820	Green Cluthra	JDJ-06/97	
7410					$1090	Green Cluthra	JDJ-05/01	
7410					$1200	Green Cluthra	ebay-05/01	
7410					$400	White Cluthra/Colorless	ebay-11/02	Colorless handles
7411	Vase	295	1	1				
7412	Vase	295	1	2				
7413	Vase	295	1	3				

SHAPE NO.	ITEM	PAGE	COL	ROW	PRICE REALIZED	GLASS TYPE	AUCTION HOUSE	COMMENTS & PHOTO REFERENCES
7414	Vase	295	1	4				
7415	Vase	295	2	1	$550	Gold Aurene	EAC-10/93	
7415					$405	Green Jade	ebay-02/04	
7415					$650	Blue Aurene	ebay-07/04	
7415					$995	Blue Aurene	ebay-09/04	
7416	Vase	295	2	2	$510	Blue Aurene	ebay-03/01	
7416					$1610	Blue Aurene	ebay-10/02	
7417	Vase	295	2	3	$1525	Blue Aurene	ebay-02/01	
7418	Vase	295	2	4				
7419	Vase	295	2	5				TPD)8.4
7420	Vase	295	3	1	$2280	Blue Aurene	ebay-11/00	
7420					$3200	Blue Aurene	ebay-06/05	
7420					$2415	Gold Aurene	Cott-06/05	
7421	Vase	295	3	2	$1200	Gold Aurene	Cinc-06/05	TPD)8.46
7422	Centerpiece	156	1	5				
7423	Centerpiece	156	1	6	$2300	Blue Aurene	Sknr-10/97	
7423					$835	Gold Aurene	JDJ-11/01	
7423					$1825	Gold Aurene	Rago-01/04	
7424	Vase	295	3	3				PG1)319; RFR)18,3,A&C; TPD)10.96
7425	Vase	295	3	4				PG1)319; TPD)10.96
7426	Vase	295	3	5				PG1)319
7427	Vase	295	3	6				
7428	Vase	295	4	1				
7429	Vase	295	4	2	$410	Selenium Red	ebay-02/01	
7429					$2700	Dark Blue Jade	ebay-03/04	
7429					$335	Selenium Red	ebay-12/04	
7430	Vase	295	4	3				
7431	Vase	295	4	4	$300	Selenium Red	ebay-07/01	
7432	Vase	295	4	5				RFR)21,2,B; ACR)COLOR 2,T,D;TPD)10.48
7433	Vase	295	4	6	$1915	Dark Blue Jade	ebay-05/04	MDK)12
7434	Vase	295	4	7	$550	Wisteria	JDJ-06/96	PG1)XXIV B,C; TPD)10.48
7434					$520	Wisteria	ebay-01/00	
7434					$300	Sea Green	Cott-08/01	
7435	Vase	295	4	8	$360	Selenium Red	ebay-12/01	TPD)10.110
7435					$435	Selenium Red	ebay-11/04	
7436	Vase	296	1	1	$2530	Dark Blue Jade	Rago-09/00	
7437	Vase	296	1	2	$385	Ivrene	EAC-10/92	
7437					$715	Green Jade	Cinc-12/99	
7438	Vase	296	1	3				
7439	Vase	296	1	4	$1705	Flemish Blue over Col.	ebay-02/03	PG1)319; PG2)83
7440	Vase	296	1	5	$1815	Rosaline/Alabaster ACB	EAC-04/98	PG1)319
7441	Vase	296	1	6				PG1)XXV C,A:319; TPD)6.8
7442	Vase	296	2	1	$2090	Rosaline/Alabaster ACB	EAC-10/97	PG1)319
7442					$1375	Rosaline/Alabaster ACB	EAC-04/98	
7443	Vase	296	2	2	$385	Green Jade/Alabaster ACB	EAC-07/93	Etched "Alicia" PG1)319
7444	Vase	296	2	3				PG1)319
7445	Vase	396	2	4	$1725	Gold Calcite ACB	Sknr-05/96	PG1)319
7446	Vase	296	2	5				
7447	Vase	296	2	6	$245	Ivory	EAC-02/92	RFR)9,2,A; ACR)134,243; TPD)10.42
7447					$690	Blue Aurene	Sknr-01/96	
7447					$1210	Blue Aurene	EAC-04/96	
7447					$630	Gold Aurene	EAC-10/97	
7447					$220	Ivory	EAC-10/98	
7447					$985	Blue Aurene	EAC-07/99	
7447					$315	Ivory	ebay-01/00	
7447					$430	Gold Aurene	ebay-01/01	
7447					$610	Gold Aurene	ebay-04/01	
7447					$1010	Blue Aurene	EAC-04/01	
7447					$1010	Blue Aurene	EAC-04/01	
7447					$980	Blue Aurene	EAC-04/01	
7447					$535	Blue Aurene	ebay-07/01	
7447					$445	Gold Aurene	ebay-07/01	
7447					$630	Gold Aurene	Sknr-10/01	
7447					$415	Gold Aurene	ebay-11/01	
7447					$395	Green Jade	ebay-12/01	
7447					$715	Blue Aurene	ebay-01/02	
7447					$1010	Blue Aurene	EAC-04/02	
7447					$400	Gold Aurene	ebay-04/02	
7447					$720	Gold Aurene	JDJ-11/02	
7447					$150	Colorless	ebay-02/03	
7447					$265	Ivory	ebay-02/03	
7447					$1175	Blue Aurene	Sknr-05/03	
7447					$785	Wisteria	ebay-05/03	
7447					$250	Ivory	ebay-07/03	

SHAPE NO.	ITEM	PAGE	COL	ROW	PRICE REALIZED	GLASS TYPE	AUCTION HOUSE	COMMENTS & PHOTO REFERENCES
7447					$330	Green Jade	ebay-09/03	
7447					$860	Blue Aurene	EAC-11/03	
7447					$465	Green Jade	ebay-12/03	
7447					$225	Ivory	ebay-02/04	
7447					$645	Blue Aurene	ebay-07/04	
7447					$835	Wisteria	ebay-10/04	
7447					$160	Ivory	Hrtg-03/05	
7448	Table Decoration	236	3	1,2				
7449	Bowl	146	1	9	$520	Amethyst Shad.	ebay-11/99	
7449					$175	Colorless	ebay-11/99	
7449					$200	Green Shaded	ebay-03/01	
7449					$180	Colorless	ebay-09/01	
7449					$130	Colorless	ebay-10/01	
7449					$205	Green Shaded	ebay-02/03	
7449					$100	Colorless	ebay-03/03	
7449					$135	Colorless	ebay-05/03	
7449					$180	Colorless	ebay-05/03	
7449					$260	Green Shaded	ebay-05/03	
7449					$145	Colorless	ebay-06/03	
7449					$140	Colorless	ebay-06/03	
7450	Table Decoration	236	3	3				Hollow Ball
7451	Vase	296	2	7				
7452	Panel	208	4	2				
7453	Candlestick	169	1	2				
7453	Centerpiece	156	1	7				
7453	Compote	176	4	6				
7454	Candlestick	169	1	3				
7454	Centerpiece	156	1	8				
7454	Compote	176	4	7				
7455	Centerpiece	156	1	9				
7456	Vase	296	3	1	$825	Alabaster and Black	ebay-09/03	
7457	Vase	296	3	2	$560	Alabaster and Black	ebay-05/02	
7457					$650	Alabaster and Black	ebay-05/02	
7458	Vase	296	3	3	$545	Alabaster and Black	ebay-08/03	
7459	Vase	296	3	4				MDK)29
7460	Centerpiece	156	2	1				
7461	Centerpiece	156	2	2				
7462	Goblet	196	3	7				
7463	Cocktail Shaker	215	4	1,2				PG2)98,C; JAS)149,BL,C; ACR)148,284;
7464	Vase	296	3	5				PG2)98,B;JAS)149,BL,B; TPD)4.40:4.54
7465	Vase	296	3	6	$2990	Alabaster/Mirror Black	Sknr-10/95	
7466	Candelabra	170	3	1				PG2)98,A; JAS)149,BL,A
7467	Vase	296	4	1				PG1)66,99; RFR)24,2,C; TPD)4.9:8.30
7468	Vase	296	4	2	$605	Ivrene	EAC-04/95	
7468					$1035	Ivrene	Sknr-01/98	
7468					$160	Colorless	ebay-04/03	
7468					$255	Colorless	ebay-05/03	
7468					$355	Colorless	ebay-09/03	
7468					$200	Ivrene	J&W-09/03	
7468					$160	Colorless	ebay-11/03	
7468					$500	Colorless	ebay-02/04	
7468					$150	Colorless	ebay-05/04	
7468					$60	Colorless	ebay-02/05	
7468					$180	Colorless	ebay-02/05	
7469	Ash Tray	138	2	7				
7470	Centerpiece	156	2	3				
7471	Vase	296	4	3	$610	Colorless (E)	ebay-11/00	Teague #T-7 pattern PG1)319
7471					$265	Colorless (E)	ebay-03/05	Teague #T-100 pattern
7472	Centerpiece	156	2	4				PG1)319
7472	Compote	176	5	1	$405	Colorless	ebay-03/00	
7472	Sherbet							MDK)116
7472	Tumbler	199	3	2	$205	Colorless/Color Bands	ebay-05/01	MDK)116
7472	Vase	296	4	4,5				PG1)320
7473	Tumbler	199	3	3,4				PG1)320
7474	Table Decoration	236	3	7	$355	Ivory Pear	EAC-04/98	RFR)24,1,A; ACR)169,344; TPD)8.6
7474					$405	Ivory Pear	ebay-04/02	
7474					$405	Ivory Apple	ebay-04/02	
7474					$400	Ivory Pear	JDJ-11/03	
7475	Vase	296	4	6				PG1)320
7476	Centerpiece	156	2	5				PG1)320
7477	Pitcher	215	2	4				
7477	Lemonade	215	2	4				
7478	Place Setting	237	3	9	$180	Colorless	ebay-10/04	TPD)5.11; MDK)57
7479	Vase	296	5	1				ACR)173,354

SHAPE NO.	ITEM	PAGE	COL	ROW	PRICE REALIZED	GLASS TYPE	AUCTION HOUSE	COMMENTS & PHOTO REFERENCES
7480	Centerpiece	156	2	6				ACR)174,355
7481	Candlestick	169	1	4				PG1)320
7481	Centerpiece	156	2	7				PG1)320
7481	Compote	176	5	2				PG1)320
7481	Goblet	196	4	1	$45	Colorless	ebay-12/00	Teague #T-111 pattern PG1)320
7481					$45	Colorless	ebay-05/03	Teague #T-24 pattern
7481					$100	Colorless	ebay-11/03	Teague #T-24 pattern
7481					$145	Colorless	ebay-11/04	Teague #T-24 pattern
7482	Vase	296	5	2	$1725	Teague Pattern	Sknr-05/95	PG1)320; TPD)4.47
7482					$775	Colorless	ebay-05/00	Teague #T-107 pattern
7482					$30	Teague Pattern	Tway-10/00	
7482					$305	Colorless/Teague pattern	ebay-03/04	Teague #T-35 pattern
7483	Vase	296	5	3				PG1)320
7484	Vase	296	5	4				This shape not numbered, PG1)321
7485	Candlestick	169	1	5				
7485	Centerpiece	156	2	8				PG1)321
7485	Compote	176	5	3				PG1)321
7485	Goblet	196	4	2				PG1)321
7486	Candlestick	169	2	1	$300	Blue Aurene	EAC-10/04	PG1)321
7486	Centerpiece	156	2	9				PG1)321
7486	Compote	176	5	4				PG1)321
7486	Goblet	196	4	3				PG1)321
7487	Plate	158	2	14				PG1)321
7488	Old Fashion	197	6	6	$70	Colorless/Cut punties	ebay-06/04	PG1)321
7488					$20	Colorless/Cut punties	ebay-10/04	
7489	Vase	296	5	5	$130	Colorless/Black threaded	ebay-06/02	PG1)321
7490	Vase	297	1	1	$330	Amethyst Shaded	JDJ-10/94	
7490					$400	Amethyst Shaded	Sknr-05/96	
7490					$405	Red Shaded	ebay-04/00	
7490					$495	Red Shaded	ebay-05/02	
7490					$515	Red Shaded	JDJ-05/02	
7490					$500	Amethyst Shaded	ebay-07/02	
7490					$255	Green Shaded	ebay-05/03	
7490					$575	Amethyst Shaded	EAC-04/04	
7490					$325	Red Shaded	ebay-04/05	
7491	Panel	208	4	3				
7492	Candlestick	169	2	2	$150	Ivory	ebay-01/00	PG1)321; PG1)322
7492					$390	Colorless/Teague Pattern	ebay-03/04	Teague #T-114 pattern
7493	Tumbler	199	3	5				
7494	Vase	297	1	2				PG1)322
7495	Vase	297	1	3				PG1)322
7496	Cocktail Shaker	215	4	3				
7497	Vase	297	1	4				PG1)322
7498	Vase	297	1	5				PG1)322
7499	Vase	297	2	1				PG1)322
7500	Vase	297	2	2	$200	Colorless	Sknr-03/99	PG1)322
7501	Candlestick	169	2	3				PG1)322
7501	Centerpiece	156	3	1				PG1)322
7501	Champagne							TPD)7.33
7501	Compote	176	5	5				PG1)322
7501	Goblet	196	4	4	$230	Flemish Blue/Colorless	ebay-10/04	PG1)322; TPD)7.33
7501	Plate							TPD)7.33
7501	Sherbet							TPD)7.33
7501	Wine							TPD)7.33
7502	Covered Vase	309	1	3				
7503	Candlestick	169	2	4				
7503	Centerpiece	156	3	2	$400	Colorless (E)	ebay-05/05	T-114 decoration
7503	Compote	176	5	6				
7504	Candlestick	169	2	5				
7505	Candlestick	169	2	6	$270	Selenium Red	ebay-03/00	
7506	Candlestick	169	2	7	$520	Ivrene	JDJ-06/98	RFR)24,2,B&D; ACR)COLOR 2,B,B
7506					$90	Colorless	ebay-12/99	
7506					$65	Colorless	ebay-03/00	
7506					$180	Colorless	ebay-03/05	
7507	Vase	297	2	3				
7508	Tumbler	199	3	6				
7509	Cologne	243	2	2				
7510	Candlestick	169	3	1				
7511	Candlestick	169	3	2				
7512	Candlestick	169	3	3				
7513	Vase	297	2	4	$225	Amethyst	ebay-03/05	
7514	Ash Tray	138	2	8				
7515	Bowl	146	2	1				
7516	Candlestick	169	3	4,5	$115	Colorless	Sknr-05/94	PG1)87,130

SHAPE NO.	ITEM	PAGE	COL	ROW	PRICE REALIZED	GLASS TYPE	AUCTION HOUSE	COMMENTS & PHOTO REFERENCES
7516					$335	Colorless	ebay-07/00	
7517	Vase	297	2	5				TPD)6.2
7517					$3820	Green Jade/Alabaster ACB	Sknr-12/04	Etched T-130
7518	Vase	297	3	1				
7519	Aquarium	304	3	5				
7520	Bowl	146	2	2	$200	Blue Shaded	JDJ-10/97	MDK)31
7520					$185	Green Shaded	ebay-10/03	
7520					$315	Blue Shaded	ebay-11/04	
7520					$250	Amethyst Shaded	ebay-05/05	
7521	Vase	297	3	2	$230	Green Shaded	JDJ-11/03	PG1)XIX A,E
7522	Goblet	196	4	5				TPD)7.79
7523	Panel Holder	208	3	5				
7524	Cocktail Shaker	215	4	4				
7524	Cocktail	215	4	4				
7525	Cologne	243	2	3				
7526	Cologne	243	2	4				
7527	Goblet	196	4	6	$160	Colorless	ebay-11/99	
7527					$160	Colorless	ebay-12/00	
7528	Ash Tray	138	2	9				
7529	Ash Tray	138	2	10				MDK)9
7530	Cigarette Holder	138	3	10				
7531	Cigarette Holder	138	3	11				
7532	Ash Tray	138	3	1				
7533	Centerpiece	156	3	3				
7534	Centerpiece	156	3	4	$345	Colorless	Sknr-10/96	
7534					$125	Colorless	ebay-12/99	
7534					$200	Green Shaded	Wesr-09/02	
7534					$305	Green Shaded	ebay-12/02	
7534					$310	Green Shaded	ebay-02/03	
7534					$265	Green Shaded	ebay-08/04	
7535	Centerpiece	156	3	5	$250	Ivory	EAC-07/93	PG2)68,67,B; JAS)169,B;
7535					$375	Green Shaded	Sknr-05/94	TPD)5.55:8.3:10.99
7535					$4255	Dark Blue Jade	Sknr-05/96	
7535					$430	Ivrene	Sknr-05/96	
7535					$275	Ivory	JDJ-06/96	
7535					$400	Topaz	Sknr-10/96	
7535					$690	Ivrene	Sknr-01/97	
7535					$285	Ivrene	JDJ-10/97	
7535					$285	Ivory	JDJ-10/97	
7535					$345	Ivrene	Sknr-05/98	
7535					$230	Colorless	Sknr-10/98	
7535					$3335	Dark Blue Jade	Sknr-10/98	
7535					$220	Colorless	Cinc-12/99	
7535					$165	Colorless	ebay-12/99	
7535					$300	Ivrene	ebay-01/00	
7535					$465	Blue Shaded	ebay-10/00	
7535					$200	Amethyst Shaded	Sknr-02/01	
7535					$200	Amber	Sknr-02/01	
7535					$235	Colorless	ebay-04/01	
7535					$305	Ivrene	ebay-04/01	
7535					$230	Ivory	JDJ-05/01	
7535					$450	Red Shaded	ebay-06/01	
7535					$105	Colorless	ebay-06/01	
7535					$350	Ivrene	ebay-08/01	
7535					$200	Amber	ebay-09/01	
7535					$200	Colorless	ebay-09/01	
7535					$340	Blue Shaded	ebay-10/01	
7535					$250	Colorless	ebay-10/01	
7535					$150	Colorless	ebay-11/01	
7535					$230	Sea Green	ebay-11/01	
7535					$160	Sea Green	Ogal-11/01	
7535					$430	Amethyst Shaded	ebay-12/01	
7535					$360	Amethyst Shaded	ebay-12/01	
7535					$310	Colorless	ebay-12/01	
7535					$270	Colorless	ebay-12/01	
7535					$270	Green Shaded	ebay-01/02	
7535					$180	Colorless	ebay-02/02	
7535					$315	Green Shaded	ebay-03/02	
7535					$305	Sea Green	ebay-03/02	
7535					$450	Ivrene	EAC-04/02	
7535					$105	Colorless	ebay-06/02	
7535					$20	Colorless	ebay-06/02	
7535					$220	Colorless	ebay-06/02	
7535					$350	Ivrene	Wint-09/02	

SHAPE NO.	ITEM	PAGE	COL	ROW	PRICE REALIZED	GLASS TYPE	AUCTION HOUSE	COMMENTS & PHOTO REFERENCES
7535					$269	Ivrene	ebay-10/02	
7535					$370	Ivory	ebay-10/02	
7535					$450	Blue Shaded	ebay-11/02	
7535					$100	Colorless	ebay-11/02	
7535					$165	Colorless	ebay-11/02	
7535					$275	Ivrene	ebay-11/02	
7535					$405	Red Shaded	ebay-11/02	
7535					$390	Green Shaded	EAC-01/03	
7535					$300	Ivrene	ebay-01/03	
7535					$280	Ivory	ebay-02/03	
7535					$405	Ivory	ebay-04/03	
7535					$130	Amber	ebay-06/03	
7535					$400	Green Shaded	ebay-06/03	
7535					$75	Colorless	ebay-06/03	
7535					$170	Colorless	ebay-06/03	
7535					$155	Colorless	ebay-06/03	
7535					$180	Colorless	ebay-06/03	
7535					$6035	Dark Blue Jade	EAC-06/03	
7535					$205	Colorless	ebay-07/03	
7535					$100	Colorless	ebay-08/03	
7535					$125	Colorless	ebay-08/03	
7535					$250	Colorless	ebay-09/03	
7535					$175	Colorless	ebay-09/03	
7535					$35	Colorless	ebay-10/03	
7535					$100	Colorless	ebay-10/03	
7535					$110	Colorless	ebay-11/03	
7535					$135	Colorless	ebay-11/03	
7535					$200	Colorless	ebay-11/03	
7535					$375	Colorless	ebay-11/03	
7535					$375	Colorless	Free-11/03	
7535					$170	Colorless	ebay-01/04	
7535					$200	Colorless	ebay-02/04	
7535					$190	Colorless	ebay-02/04	
7535					$130	Colorless	ebay-03/04	
7535					$400	Ivrene	EAC-04/04	
7535					$360	Ivory	JDJ-05/04	
7535					$210	Ivrene	ebay-05/04	
7535					$160	Colorless	ebay-06/04	
7535					$255	Ivory	ebay-06/04	
7535					$175	Colorless	ebay-06/04	
7535					$90	Colorless	ebay-09/04	
7535					$130	Colorless	ebay-09/04	
7535					$425	Colorless	ebay-09/04	
7535					$125	Colorless	ebay-10/04	
7535					$125	Colorless	ebay-10/04	
7535					$140	Colorless	ebay-10/04	
7535					$235	Colorless	ebay-10/04	
7535					$375	Sea Green	ebay-10/04	
7535					$130	Colorless	ebay-11/04	
7535					$295	Colorless	ebay-11/04	
7535					$150	Colorless	ebay-11/04	
7535					$220	Green Shaded	ebay-11/04	
7535					$205	Green Shaded	ebay-11/04	
7535					$160	Colorless	ebay-12/04	
7535					$335	Ivory	ebay-12/04	
7535					$450	Ivrene	ebay-01/05	
7535					$360	Blue Shaded	ebay-02/05	
7535					$280	Colorless	ebay-03/05	
7535					$535	Colorless	ebay-03/05	
7535					$180	Colorless	ebay-03/05	
7535					$195	Colorless	ebay-03/05	
7535					$100	Colorless	ebay-04/05	
7535					$125	Green Shaded	ebay-04/05	
7535					$125	Colorless	ebay-04/05	
7535					$200	Colorless	ebay-05/05	
7535					$150	Colorless	ebay-05/05	
7535					$145	Colorless	ebay-05/05	
7535					$180	Colorless	ebay-06/05	
7535					$180	Ivory	Cinc-06/05	
7535					$270	Ivrene	Cinc-06/05	
7535					$185	Colorless	ebay-06/05	
7535					$140	Colorless	ebay-07/05	
7535					$130	Colorless	ebay-07/05	
7536	Vase	297	3	3				

SHAPE NO.	ITEM	PAGE	COL	ROW	PRICE REALIZED	GLASS TYPE	AUCTION HOUSE	COMMENTS & PHOTO REFERENCES
7537	Centerpiece	156	3	6	$225	Blue Shaded	ebay-12/99	MDK)84
7537					$250	Ivrene	ebay-12/04	
7538	Vase	297	3	4				
7539	Vase	297	3	5	$1020	Flemish Blue over Colorless	JDJ-11/02	TPD)4.48:4.84
7540	Puff Box	245	1	9	$495	Celeste Blue/Pink finial	EAC-10/90	
7540					$1035	Oriental Poppy	Sknr-05/97	
7540					$175	Celeste Blue	Sknr-01/98	
7540					$200	Colorless/Green threaded	ebay-06/02	
7541	Vase	297	4	1	$850	Green Jade/Alabaster foot	ebay-02/05	
7542	Vase	297	4	2				
7543	Candlestick	169	3	6				
7544	Tile							See New Drawings section
7545	Tumbler	199	3	7	$230	Colorless	Sknr-10/96	
7546	Vase	297	4	3				
7547	Tumbler	199	3	8	$900	Colorless T-152	ebay-04/01	TPD)4.49
7547					$355	Colorless T-152	ebay-09/01	
7547					$550	Colorless T-152	ebay-10/02	
7547					$55	Colorless T-152	ebay-09/03	
7547					$420	Colorless T-152	ebay-05/05	
7548	Salt	217	3	1				
7549	Salt	217	3	2				
7550	Salt	217	3	3				
7551	Bowl	146	2	3				
7552	Vase	297	4	4				
7553	Vase	297	4	5				
7554	Candlestick	169	3	7				
7555	Goblet	196	4	7				
7556	Table Decoration	236	2	3				
7557	Vase	297	5	1				
7558	Tray	159	2	5				
7559	Vase	297	5	2				
7560	Vase	297	5	3	$495	Ivrene	EAC-10/98	TPD)5.1
7560					$495	Ivrene	EAC-10/98	
7560					$675	Ivrene	ebay-02/00	
7560					$1075	Gold Aurene	ebay-03/00	
7560					$460	Ivrene	JDJ-11/01	
7560					$385	Ivrene	ebay-03/02	
7560					$1000	Gold Aurene	ebay-04/02	
7560					$870	Gold Aurene	ebay-03/03	
7560					$355	Ivrene	ebay-06/03	
7560					$345	Ivrene	ebay-08/03	
7560					$200	Ivrene	ebay-09/03	
7560					$220	Ivrene	ebay-09/03	
7560					$400	Ivrene	JDJ-05/04	
7560					$200	Ivrene	ebay-03/05	
7561	Tray	159	2	6	$350	Ivrene	ebay-01/05	
7563	Candelabra	170	3	2	$465	Ivrene	EAC-07/93	PG1)XXV A,B&C; TPD)4.81:5.71
7563					$225	Ivrene	ebay-05/01	
7563					$145	Ivrene	JDJ-05/01	
7563	Centerpiece	156	3	7	$430	Ivrene	Sknr-01/96	PG2)94; TPD)5.71
7563					$460	Ivrene	JDJ-06/98	
7563					$415	Ivrene	ebay-06/01	
7563					$335	Ivrene	EAC-09/02	
7563					$135	Colorless	ebay-03/04	
7563					$460	Ivrene	JDJ-05/04	
7563					$1155	Ivrene	EAC-10/04	
7563	Compote	176	5	7	$455	Ivrene	ebay-08/01	TPD)5.71
7564	Candlestick	169	3	8	$215	Ivrene	Sknr-10/96	TPD)5.12:9.16
7564					$215	Ivrene	Sknr-05/98	
7564					$170	Ivrene	ebay-05/01	
7564					$175	Ivrene	ebay-06/01	
7564					$275	Ivrene	ebay-08/01	
7564					$210	Ivrene	ebay-10/01	
7564					$55	Colorless	ebay-10/02	Post 1932 diamond point signature.
7564					$80	Colorless	ebay-12/04	Post 1932 diamond point signature.
7564					$50	Colorless	ebay-12/04	
7564					$130	Colorless	ebay-02/05	
7564					$85	Colorless	ebay-06/05	
7564	Vase	297	5	4,5	$825	Ivrene	EAC-10/90	TPD)5.12:9.16
7564					$550	Ivrene	ebay-12/99	
7564					$670	Ivrene	EAC-04/01	
7564					$335	Ivrene	ebay-04/02	
7564					$335	Ivrene	EAC-09/02	
7564					$315	Ivrene	ebay-07/03	

SHAPE NO.	ITEM	PAGE	COL	ROW	PRICE REALIZED	GLASS TYPE	AUCTION HOUSE	COMMENTS & PHOTO REFERENCES
7564					$610	Ivrene	ebay-01/04	
7564					$170	Ivrene	ebay-12/04	
7564					$180	Ivrene	Cinc-06/05	
7564					$205	Ivrene	Cinc-06/05	
7565	Vase	297	5	6	$550	Ivrene	Sknr-10/93	TPD)4.82
7565					$1625	Ivrene	ebay-01/00	
7566	Vase	298	1	1	$990	Ivrene	EAC-04/93	TPD)5.69
7566					$865	Ivrene	Sknr-10/95	
7566					$960	Ivrene	EAC-10/98	
7566					$850	Ivrene	EAC-10/98	
7566					$1100	Ivrene	EAC-07/99	
7566					$1955	Ivrene	Rago-09/00	
7566					$890	Ivrene	ebay-09/01	
7566					$1405	Ivrene	Rago-01/04	
7566					$1360	Ivrene	ebay-01/04	
7566					$1090	Ivrene	JDJ-05/04	
7566					$1080	Ivrene	Cinc-06/05	
7566					$1320	Ivrene	Cinc-06/05	
7568	Vase	298	1	2	$1380	Ivrene	Sknr-10/98	TPD)4.82
7568					$1495	Ivrene	JDJ-05/02	
7568					$415	Ivrene	ebay-04/05	
7570	Vase	298	1	3	$630	Ivrene	EAC-10/96	RFR)24,2,E
7570					$920	Ivrene	Sknr-02/01	
7575	Vase	298	1	4	$190	Ivrene	ebay-09/03	
7575					$300	Ivrene	ebay-06/04	
7575					$375	Ivrene	ebay-09/04	
7575					$330	Ivrene	EAC-10/04	
7576	Plate	158	2	15				
7577	Centerpiece	156	3	8				
7578	Bowl	146	2	4				
7579	Vase	298	1	5	$465	Ivrene	EAC-04/91	ACR)167,337
7579					$550	Ivrene	EAC-10/91	
7579					$230	Ivrene	JDJ-06/98	
7579					$605	Ivrene	EAC-07/98	
7579					$330	Ivrene	Cott-08/01	
7579					$250	Ivrene	ebay-11/01	
7579					$280	Ivrene	ebay-02/03	
7579					$260	Ivrene	ebay-03/03	
7579					$25	Colorless	ebay-07/04	
7579					$100	Ivrene	ebay-09/04	
7579					$90	Colorless	ebay-10/04	
7579					$75	Colorless	ebay-04/05	
7579					$145	Ivrene	Cinc-06/05	
7579					$300	Ivrene	ebay-06/05	
7580	Vase	298	2	1				
7581	Vase	298	2	2	$160	Colorless	ebay-01/04	
7581					$155	Colorless	ebay-01/04	
7582	Centerpiece	157	1	1				
7583	Vase	298	2	3				
7584	Pilsner	197	6	7				
7585	Goblet	196	5	1				
7586	Champagne	198	1	1				
7587	Martini	198	1	2				
7588	Sherry	198	1	3				
7589	Wine	198	1	4				
7590	Claret	198	1	5				
7591	Burgundy	198	1	6				
7592	Wine	198	1	7				
7593	Liqueur	198	2	1				
7594	Vermouth	199	1	1				
7594	High Ball	199	1	2	$125	VDS	ebay-05/02	
7595	Vase	298	2	4	$1650	Ivrene	EAC-07/91	PG2)93; RFR)24,2,A; RLG)149,280;
7595					$1265	Ivrene	JDJ-10/94	
7595					$1035	Ivrene	Sknr-10/95	ACR)167,338; JAS)149,T
7595					$1705	Ivrene	EAC-04/98	
7595					$2090	Ivrene	Cott-08/01	
7595					$1275	Ivrene	ebay-06/05	
7596	Vase	298	3	1				
7597	Bowl	146	2	5				TPD)10.138
7598	Bowl	146	2	6				
7599	Bowl	146	2	7				
7600	Champagne	198	2	2				
7601	Vase	298	3	2				
7602	Decanter	188	1	3				

SHAPE NO.	ITEM	PAGE	COL	ROW	PRICE REALIZED	GLASS TYPE	AUCTION HOUSE	COMMENTS & PHOTO REFERENCES
7602	Goblet	196	5	2				
7602	Water	198	2	3				
7603	Hock	198	2	4				
7604	Sherry	198	2	5				
7605	Centerpiece	157	1	2				
7606	Cologne	243	2	5				
7607	Vase	298	3	3				PG1)XXVIII C,B
7608	Covered Vase	309	1	4				
7609	Liqueur	198	2	6				
7610	Whiskey	198	2	7				
7611	Goblet	196	5	3				
7612	High Ball	198	5	11				
7613	Candlestick	169	4	1	$3620	Gold Aurene	JDJ-11/01	PG1)63,98; RFR)9,4,A&E; TPD)5.6
7613					$2640	Gold Aurene	JDJ-11/02	
7613					$3450	Gold Aurene	Cinc-06/04	
7613	Centerpiece	157	1	3	$1500	Gold Aurene	JDJ-06/05	
7613	Compote	176	5	8				
7614	Vase	298	3	4				
7615	Toddy	199	1	3				
7616	Candelabra	170	3	3				
7623	Goblet	196	5	4				
7624	Decanter	188	1	4				
7625	Decanter	188	2	1				
7626	Decanter	188	2	2				
7627	Decanter	188	2	3				
7627	Wine	188	2	3				
7628	Box	138	4	5				
7629	Goblet	196	5	5				
7630	Martini	198	3	1				
7631	Claret	198	3	2				
7632	Chablis	198	3	3				
7633	Liqueur	198	3	4				
7634	Goblet	196	5	6				
7635	Claret	198	3	5				
7636	Box	138	4	6				
7637	Candlestick	169	4	2				
7638	Table Decoration	236	2	4				
7639	Tray	158	4	17				
7640	Vase	298	4	1				
7641	Table Decoration	236	3	4				
7643	Large Vase	140	3	3				
7644	Goblet	196	5	7				
7645	Ink Well	310	3	2				
7646	Vase	298	4	2				
7647	Vase	298	4	3				
7648	Vase	298	4	4				
7649	Vase	298	5	1				
7650	Bowl	146	2	8	$200	Gold Calcite	ebay-12/03	
7651	Box	138	4	7				
7652	Candlestick	169	4	3				
7654	Decanter	188	2	4				
7655	Decanter	188	3	1				
7656	Covered Vase	309	1	5				
7657	Decanter	188	3	2				
7658	Cologne	243	2	6				
7658	Cologne	243	2	7				
7659	Decanter	188	3	3				
7660	Decanter	188	3	4				
7661	Centerpiece	157	1	4				
7662	Centerpiece	157	1	5				
7663	Cocktail	198	3	6				
7664	Cocktail	198	3	7				
7665	Decanter	188	4	1				
7666	Goblet	196	6	1				
7667	Goblet	196	6	2				
7668	Cocktail Shaker	215	4	5				
7668	Whiskey	215	4	5				
7669	Vase	298	5	2				
7670	Covered Vase	309	1	6				
7671	Vase	298	5	3	$300	Ivrene	Sknr-10/93	MDK)34
7671					$150	Ivrene	ebay-02/02	
7671					$85	Ivrene	JDJ-05/04	
7671					$160	Ivrene	ebay-01/05	
7672	Centerpiece	157	1	6				

SHAPE NO.	ITEM	PAGE	COL	ROW	PRICE REALIZED	GLASS TYPE	AUCTION HOUSE	COMMENTS & PHOTO REFERENCES
7673	Bowl	146	3	1				
7674	Champagne Cooler	177	4	8				
7675	Tumbler	199	1	4				
7676	Whiskey	199	1	5				
7677	Centerpiece	157	1	7				
7678	Vase	298	5	4				
7679	Vase	298	5	5				
7680	Bowl	146	3	2				
7681	Centerpiece	157	2	1				
7684	Vase	299	1	1				
7685	Bowl	146	3	3				
7687	Centerpiece	157	2	2				
7688	Goblet	198	3	8	$60	Amethyst	ebay-01/02	
7689	Vase	299	1	2				
7690	Vase	299	1	3				
7691	Vase	299	1	4				
7692	Vase	299	1	5				
7693	Vase	299	1	6				
7694	Vase	299	1	7				
7695	Vase	299	2	1				
7696	Bowl	146	3	4				
7697	Vase	299	2	2				
7698	Table Decoration	236	2	5	$630	Colorless	Sknr-01/97	Fish,TPD)4.85
7698					$750	Colorless	Sknr-10/98	
7698					$600	Colorless	ebay-12/99	
7698					$600	Colorless	ebay-12/99	
7698					$505	Colorless	ebay-07/01	
7698					$360	Colorless	ebay-04/02	
7698					$405	Colorless	ebay-02/04	
7698					$505	Colorless	ebay-04/04	
7698					$350	Colorless	ebay-06/04	
7698					$495	Colorless	ebay-12/04	
7698					$465	Colorless	ebay-01/05	
7698					$215	Colorless	ebay-04/05	
7699	Centerpiece	157	2	3	$165	Alabaster	ebay-12/99	
7699					$600	Amethyst	ebay-10/00	
7699					$750	Green Jade	Ogal-04/01	
7699					$270	Mirror Black	ebay-08/01	
7699					$355	Green Jade	ebay-05/02	
7700	Centerpiece	157	2	4				
7702	Bowl	146	3	5				
7703	Covered Vase	309	2	1				
7704	Bowl	146	3	6				
7705	Vase	299	2	3				
7706	Vase	299	2	4	$55	Colorless	Jack-06/00	ACR)154,303
7706					$170	Colorless	ebay-04/01	
7706					$90	Colorless	ebay-08/01	
7706					$140	Colorless	ebay-10/02	
7706					$110	Colorless	ebay-01/03	
7706					$45	Colorless	ebay-08/03	
7706					$260	Colorless	ebay-10/03	
7706					$125	Colorless	ebay-11/03	
7706					$320	Colorless	ebay-04/04	
7706					$200	Colorless	ebay-01/05	
7706					$100	Colorless	ebay-04/05	
7706					$100	Colorless	ebay-07/05	
7707	Vase	299	2	5				
7708	Basket	140	3	2				
7709	Vase	299	2	6				
7710	Candlestick	169	4	4				
7711	Tumbler	199	1	6	$130	Gold Aurene	EAC-11/01	
7712	Decanter	188	4	2	$105	Colorless	ebay-04/04	
7713	Ash Tray	138	3	2				
7714	Vase	299	3	1				
7715	Centerpiece	157	2	5				
7715	Punch Cup	157	2	6				
7716	Wine Glass Cooler	189	2	11				
7717	Bowl	146	3	7				
7718	Salt	217	3	4				
7719	Salt	217	3	5				
7720	Lamp	208	1	6	$500	Colorless with Black Stand	ebay-05/02	
7721	Covered Vase	309	2	2				
7722	Tankard	199	4	3				
7723	Misc. Item	189	3	10				

SHAPE NO.	ITEM	PAGE	COL	ROW	PRICE REALIZED	GLASS TYPE	AUCTION HOUSE	COMMENTS & PHOTO REFERENCES
7724	Sugar & Creamer	235	6	11,12				
7725	Sherry				$100	Colorless	ebay-04/05	
7730	Vase				$35	Colorless	ebay-02/05	MDK)119
7730					$60	Colorless	ebay-02/05	
7730					$140	Colorless	ebay-02/05	
7730					$55	Colorless	ebay-04/05	
7730					$90	Colorless	ebay-05/05	
7730					$65	Colorless	ebay-05/05	
7730					$80	Colorless	ebay-06/05	
7730					$45	Colorless	ebay-07/05	
7730					$65	Colorless	ebay-07/05	
7736	Decanter							See New Drawings section
7736	Liqueur							See New Drawings section
7737	Goblet							See New Drawings section
7738	Beer Glass							See New Drawings section
7739	Umbrella Stand							See New Drawings section
7740	Ash Tray							See New Drawings section
7741	Cigarette Holder							See New Drawings section
7742	Vase	299	3	2				
7743	Cocktail	198	4	1				
7744	Vase	299	3	3				This shape not numbered in Gardner.
7745	Covered Vase	309	2	3				
7746	Candlestick	169	4	5	$250	Colorless	ebay-03/04	TPD)4.35
7746					$525	Colorless	ebay-08/04	
7746					$200	Colorless	ebay-09/04	
7746					$310	Colorless	ebay-10/04	
7746					$500	Colorless	ebay-04/05	
7746					$360	Colorless	ebay-07/05	
7747	Sherry	198	4	2				
7748	Tumbler	198	4	3				
7749	Roll-edge Pan	159	2	7				
8001	Lamp Base	203	5	3				
8002	Lamp Base	203	5	4	$460	Green Jade	Sknr-01/98	
8002					$635	Green Jade/Black	ebay-03/03	Black decoration, complete lamp
8002					$405	Green Jade/Black	ebay-03/04	Black decoration, complete lamp
8004	Vase	299	3	4				
8005	Vase	299	3	5				
8006	Vase	299	3	6	$1150	Alabaster ACB	Sknr-03/99	Lamp
8006					$1035	Yellow Cintra ACB	JDJ-05/03	Lamp base
8006					$1495	Ivory ACB	EAC-04/04	Lamp
8006					$595	Alabaster ACB	ebay-08/04	Drilled for a lamp
8006					$685	Yellow Cintra ACB	ebay-06/05	Lamp
8007	Covered Vase	309	2	4				PG1)112,172,B
8021	Lamp Base	203	5	5				
8022	Lamp Base	203	6	1				
8023	Lamp Base	203	6	2	$2645	Moss Agate	Sknr-10/98	
8023					$2415	Purple Moss Agate	Sknr-03/99	Lamp with fittings
8023					$3680	Purple Moss Agate	EAC-06/03	Lamp with fittings
8023					$5750	Blue Moss Agate Lamp	JDJ-05/04	Lamp with fittings
8024	Lamp Base	203	6	3				
8025	Lamp Base	203	6	4				
8026	Lamp Base	203	6	5	$850	Green Jade Lamp	ebay-04/04	Lamp with fittings
8026					$550	Green Jade Lamp	ebay-09/04	Lamp with fittings
8026					$1305	Black/Green Cintra ACB	ebay-10/04	Lamp with fittings
8027	Shade	232	2	3				
8028	Shade	230	2	1				
8029	Shade	230	2	2				
8030	Lamp Base	202	2	5				
8031	Lamp Base	204	1	1				
8032	Lamp Base	204	2	3				This is shown as 8302 in Gardner.
8033	Lamp Base	204	2	4				This is shown as 8303 in Gardner.
8034	Lamp Base	204	1	2				
8035	Lamp Base	204	1	3				
8036	Lamp Base	204	1	4				
8037	Lamp Base	204	2	1				
8038	Lamp Base	204	2	2				
8302	Lamp Base	204	2	3				This number is an error, see #8032.
8303	Lamp Base	204	2	4				This number is an error, see #8033.
8315	Candlestick	169	5	1				
8315	Champagne				$120	French Blue/White thread.	ebay-05/03	
8315	Compote	177	1	1				
8315	Goblet	196	6	3				
8315	Vase	299	4	1				
8316	Candlestick	169	5	2				

SHAPE NO.	ITEM	PAGE	COL	ROW	PRICE REALIZED	GLASS TYPE	AUCTION HOUSE	COMMENTS & PHOTO REFERENCES
8316	Compote	177	1	2				
8316	Centerpiece	157	2	7				
8316	Goblet	196	6	4				
8316	Champagne				$140	Spanish Green	Sknr-10/96	
8316 .					$155	Spanish Green	ebay-10/01	
8317	Candlestick	169	5	3				
8317	Compote	177	1	3				
8317	Centerpiece	157	2	8				
8317	Decanter	188	4	3				
8317	Champagne				$90	Colorless/Red threaded	ebay-10/04	
8317	Goblet	188	4	3	$170	Colorless/Red threaded	ebay-01/02	TPD)10.111
8317					$165	Colorless/Red threaded	ebay-02/02	
8317					$100	Colorless/Red threaded	ebay-02/02	
8317					$100	Colorless/Red threaded	ebay-03/02	
8317					$90	Colorless/Red threaded	ebay-04/02	
8317					$100	Colorless/Red threaded	ebay-12/02	
8317					$75	Colorless/Red threaded	ebay-07/03	
8317					$80	Colorless/Red threaded	ebay-02/04	
8317	Parfait				$100	Colorless/Red threaded	ebay-07/01	
8317	Sherbet				$45	Colorless/Red threaded	Sknr-02/01	Sherbet only
8317					$25	Colorless/Red threaded	ebay-03/05	Underplate only
8317	Short Parfait (3" tall)				$65	Colorless/Red threaded	ebay-06/05	
8320	Vase	299	4	2				
8321	Vase	299	4	3				
8322	Vase	299	4	4				
8323	Vase	299	4	5				
8324	Bowl	146	4	1				
8325	Vase	299	4	6				
8326	Vase	299	5	1	$290	Spanish Green	ebay-04/05	
8327	Vase	299	5	2				
8328	Vase	299	5	3				
8336	Decanter	188	4	4				
8336	Goblet	196	6	5				
8336	Tumbler				$85	Bristol Yellow	ebay-05/00	
8337	Decanter	188	4	5				
8339	Bowl	146	4	2				
8339	Vase	299	5	4				
8341	Decanter	188	5	1				
8345	Bowl	146	4	3				
8346	Bowl	146	4	4				
8347	Bowl	146	4	5				
8348	Bowl	146	4	6				
8349	Decanter	188	5	2				Special for "M. F. Co."
8350	Decanter	188	5	3				Special for "M. F. Co."
8351	Goblet	196	6	6				PG1)XIII A:103,158,BOT:105,162,A;
8351								PG1)103,157,B&D; PG2)87,A; JAS)166;
8351								JSS)12-26,L; TPD)7.48:10.9
8351								Special for "M. F. Co."
8351	Wine				$105	Bristol Yellow/Black thread	ebay-05/05	
8352	Goblet	197	1	1				Special for "M. F. Co."
8353	Goblet	197	1	2				
8354	Goblet	197	1	3				
8355	Centerpiece	157	2	9				
8356	Shade	230	2	3				
8357	Lamp Base	204	2	5				
8358	Lamp Base	204	3	1				
8359	Lamp Base	204	3	2				
8360	Lamp Base	204	3	3				
8361	Lamp Base	204	3	4				
8362	Lamp Base	204	3	5				
8363	Shade	230	2	4				
8364	Candlestick	169	5	4				
8365	Vase	299	5	5				
8366	Vase	299	5	6				
8367	Vase	300	1	1				
8368	Vase	300	1	2	$125	Bristol Yellow	ebay-04/04	ACR)COLOR 4,B,F; MDK)78
8368					$125	Bristol Yellow	ebay-04/04	
8369	Centerpiece	157	3	1				
8370	Lemon Dish	177	2	3				
8371	Lamp Base	204	3	6				
8372	Lamp Base	204	4	1				Special for "Art Light"
8373	Lamp Base	204	4	2				Special for "Art Light"
8374	Lamp Base	204	4	3				Special for "Art Light"
8375	Lamp Base	204	4	4				

SHAPE NO.	ITEM	PAGE	COL	ROW	PRICE REALIZED	GLASS TYPE	AUCTION HOUSE	COMMENTS & PHOTO REFERENCES
8376	Centerpiece	157	3	2	$475	Gold Ruby	Ogal-10/99	
8377	Goblet	197	1	4				
8378	Goblet	197	1	5				
8381	Goblet	197	1	6	$160	Bristol Yellow/Black Thrd.	ebay-08/02	
8381					$125	Bristol Yellow/Black Thrd.	ebay-05/04	
8381	Wine				$130	Bristol Yellow/Black Thrd.	ebay-05/04	
8381	Parfait				$110	Bristol Yellow/Black Thrd.	ebay-05/03	
8381	Wine				$200	Bristol Yellow/Black Thrd.	ebay-08/03	
8382	Candlestick	169	6	1				
8382	Compote	177	1	4	$145	Bristol Yellow/Black Thrd.	Sknr-12/02	
8382	Centerpiece	157	3	3				
8383	Lamp Base	204	4	5				
8384	Vase	300	1	3				
8385	Vase	300	1	4	$305	Bristol Yellow	ebay-05/05	PG1)XXIX A,C
8386	Lamp Base	204	5	1				
8387	Vase	300	1	5				TPD)7.59:7.60
8388	Vase	300	2	1				
8389	Vase	300	2	2	$665	Alabaster ACB	ebay-08/04	Lamp
8389					$480	Alabaster ACB	JDJ-06/05	Lamp
8390	Lamp Base	204	5	2				
8391	Centerpiece	157	3	4				
8392	Vase	300	2	3				PG1)IV B; PG1)XXVI A,C; RFR)18,2,A
8392					$2240	Blue Aur./Yellow Jade ACB	EAC-07/04	Lamp, See Gardner XXVI A,C
8393	Compote	177	1	5				
8394	Candlestick	169	6	2				
8395	Lamp Base	204	5	3				
8396	Lamp Base	204	5	4				
8397	Lamp Base	204	5	5				
8398	Lamp Base	204	6	1				
8399	Lamp Base	204	6	2				
8400	Vase	300	3	3				
8401	Vase	300	3	4				
8402	Vase	300	3	5				PG1)44,80,A
8403	Vase	300	2	4				
8404	Vase	300	2	5				
8405	Vase	300	3	1				PG1)44,80,B
8406	Vase	300	3	2				
8407	Candelabra	170	3	4				
8407	Compote	177	2	2				
8407	Bowl	146	4	7				
8408	Candlestick	169	6	3				
8408	Centerpiece	157	3	5				
8408	Compote	177	2	1				
8409	Candlestick	169	6	4				
8409	Compote	177	1	6				
8409	Centerpiece	157	3	6				
8410	Decanter	188	5	4				
8411	Vase	300	4	1	$1700	Green Jade/Alabaster ACB	ebay-07/04	Lamp Etched "Pagoda"
8411					$1000	Green Jade/Alabaster ACB	ebay-09/04	Lamp Etched "Pagoda"
8411					$2520	Yellow Cintra ACB	Cinc-11/04	
8411					$880	Green Jade/Alabaster ACB	ebay-03/05	Crest Lamp Etched "Pagoda"
8412	Lamp Base	204	6	3	$1700	Oriental Poppy	EAC-07/92	Tiffany lamp base
8412					$860	Oriental Jade	Sknr-10/98	
8413	Vase	300	4	2				PG1)XXVII A,B; PG1)320; ACR)161,320
8414	Vase	300	4	3	$1550	Gold Aur/Grn. Jade ACB	ebay-06/03	Lamp with fittings
8414					$2520	Blue Aur/Grn. Jade ACB	JDJ-06/05	Lamp with fittings
8415	Vase	300	4	4	$1540	Cintra ACB	EAC-04/99	
8416	Centerpiece	157	3	7				
8417	Vase	300	5	1				TPD)10.104
8417					$1750	Oriental Poppy lamp	Tway-12/02	Tall lamp with metal shaft, one of a pair
8417					$2500	Oriental Poppy lamp	Dalla-05/03	Tall lamp with metal shaft, one of a pair
8417					$1610	Oriental Poppy	EAC-04/04	Green threaded
8418	Shade	226	5	1				
8419	Vase	300	5	2	$5320	Bl. Aurene/Grn. Jade ACB	EAC-09/02	Etched "Bird #2" Lamp with fittings.
8419					$5320	Bl. Aurene/Yel. Jade ACB	EAC-09/02	Etched "Bird #2" Lamp with fittings.
8419					$1275	Rose Quartz ACB	ebay-07/04	Lamp with fittings
8420	Vase	300	5	3				RLG)142,273
8421	Shade	230	2	5				
8422	Vase	300	5	4				PG2)74; RLG)165,300;ACR)COLOR 3,T,C;
8422								TPD)5.13
8423	Finial	205	4	1				
8424	Finial	205	4	2				
8425	Finial	205	4	3				
8426	Finial	205	4	4				

SHAPE NO.	ITEM	PAGE	COL	ROW	PRICE REALIZED	GLASS TYPE	AUCTION HOUSE	COMMENTS & PHOTO REFERENCES
8427	Finial	205	4	5				
8428	Finial	205	4	6				
8429	Finial	205	4	7				
8430	Vase	300	5	5				PG1)71,108
8431	Covered Vase	309	3	1				
8432	Vase	301	1	1				
8433	Vase	301	1	2				
8434	Vase	301	1	3				TPD)5.37
8435	Vase	301	1	4				
8436	Vase	301	2	1	$1045	Cinnamon Florentia	EAC-10/93	drilled PG1)XXX B,B
8436					$550	Cinnamon Florentia	EAC-04/95	
8437	Shade	230	2	6				
8438	Shade	230	3	1				
8439	Shade	230	3	2				
8440	Shade	230	3	3				
8441	Vase	301	2	2				
8442	Vase	301	2	3				
8443	Vase	301	2	4				
8444	Vase	301	2	5	$475	Alabaster ACB	ebay-05/05	Complete lamp
8445	Vase	301	2	6				ACR)COLOR 2,T,B
8446	Vase	301	3	1				
8447	Vase	301	3	2				
8448	Vase	301	3	3				
8449	Vase	301	3	4				ACR)152,298
8450	Vase	301	3	5				
8451	Vase	301	3	6				
8452	Vase	301	4	1				
8453	Vase	301	4	2				
8454	Lamp Base	204	6	4				
8455	Table Top	238	2	3				
8456	Shade	230	3	4				
8457	Vase	301	4	3				
8458	Vase	301	4	4				
8459	Shade	230	3	5				
8460	Panel	208	4	4				TPD)4.117
8461	Panel	208	4	5	$4800	Colorless	ebay-01/04	Complete lamp
8462	Table Decoration	236	3	5				Solid Ball, ACR)178,363
8463	Vase	301	4	5				
8464	Vase	301	4	6	$1250	Peach Quartz	ebay-06/03	Complete lamp
8465	Vase	301	4	7				
8466	Lamp Base	205	1	3				
8467	Table Top	238						Fourth row, second item.
8468	Table Top	238						Fourth row, third item
8469	Vase	301	5	1				
8470	Lamp Base	205	1	4				
8471	Vase	301	5	2				RLG)142,272; JAS)163,TL; TPD)10.104
8471					$1100	Citron Yellow	EAC-10/93	Light Blue Jade decoration
8471					$470	Peach Sculptured Quartz	ebay-12/02	Lamp with fittings
8471					$920	Amber Cintra/Turquoise	JDJ-05/04	Turquoise leaves and vines
8472	Centerpiece	157	3	8				
8473	Shade	230	3	6				
8474	Shade	231	1	1,2,3				
8475	Shade	231	1	4				
8476	Shade	231	1	5				
8477	Vase	301	5	3				
8478	Shade	231	1	6				
8479	Vase	301	5	4				PG1)VI B,C
8480	Vase	301	5	5				
8481	Vase	302	1	1				
8482	Vase	302	1	2				
8483	Vase	302	1	3				
8484	Vase	302	1	4				
8485	Vase	302	1	5				
8486	Vase	302	2	1				
8490	Lamp Base	205	1	5	$575	Oriental Poppy	Sknr-01/98	
8490					$2000	Oriental Poppy	ebay-09/03	Table lamp
8491	Vase	302	2	2				PG1)XXVI A,A; ACR)161,319; TPD)2.43
8491					$1925	Blue Aurene/Yellow Jade	EAC-07/90	Lamp
8492	Vase	302	2	3	$3450	ACB	Sknr-01/98	TPD)4.25
8493	Vase	302	2	4	$4800	Blue Moss Agate	JDJ-06/05	
8494	Vase	302	2	5	$3735	Cluthra ACB	Sknr-10/96	PG1)XXVII A,C
8494					$6000	Rose over Green Cluthra	ebay-01/04	Etched "Cliffwood"
8495	Vase	302	3	1				
8496	Vase	302	3	2				ACR)161,318

SHAPE NO.	ITEM	PAGE	COL	ROW	PRICE REALIZED	GLASS TYPE	AUCTION HOUSE	COMMENTS & PHOTO REFERENCES
8496					$4025	Dec. Black/Yellow Jade	Sknr-02/00	Pegasus lamp
8496					$12075	Dec. Black/Yellow Jade	JDJ-05/04	Pegasus lamp
8497	Vase	302	3	3				
8498	Shade	231	1	7				
8499	Vase	302	3	4				
8500	Vase	302	3	5				
8501	Vase	302	3	6				
8502	Lamp Base	205	1	6				
8503	Vase	302	4	1				
8504	Vase	302	4	2				
8505	Vase	302	4	3				
8506	Vase	302	4	4				
8507	Vase	302	4	5				RFR)8,2,B; JAS)161,BL,C; TPD)4.6
8507					$2285	Yellow Jade/Red threaded	ebay-05/05	Lamp, Alabaster handles
8508	Vase	302	4	6	$1100	Blue Cluthra/Opal handles	EAC-04/93	PG1)XVIII A,B; RFR)8,4,C;
8508					$1100	Green Jade	JDJ-10/94	
8508					$2900	Amethyst Cluthra	EAC-04/95	JAS)161,BL,B; RLG)147,278;
8508					$805	Green Jade	Sknr-10/95	
8508					$805	Green Jade/Alabaster	Sknr-01/96	
8508					$2970	Rose Cluthra	EAC-04/96	ACR)155,306; TPD)4.79:10.52
8508					$990	Green Jade	EAC-04/96	
8508					$1705	Rose Cluthra	EAC-07/97	
8508					$745	Green Jade/Alabaster	Sknr-10/97	
8508					$1265	Ivrene	Sbys-12/97	
8508					$1090	Green Jade/Alabaster	Sknr-06/99	
8508					$1635	Green Cluthra/Opal	ebay-12/99	Opal handles
8508					$3440	Rose Cluthra	ebay-02/00	
8508					$675	Green Jade/Alabaster	ebay-03/00	
8508					$1265	White Cluthra	Sknr-10/00	
8508					$690	Ivory	Sknr-10/00	
8508					$1485	Green Jade/Alabaster	Cott-08/01	
8505					$1760	Ivory/Black	Cott-08/01	
8508					$885	Green Jade/Alabaster	ebay-08/01	
8508					$1655	Ivrene	ebay-03/02	
8508					$2300	Green Jade/Alabaster	JDJ-05/02	
8508					$930	Green Jade/Alabaster	ebay-06/02	
8508					$4400	Blue Aurene	EAC-09/02	
8508					$1500	Rose Cluthra/Opaline	ebay-10/02	
8508					$100	Colorless	ebay-12/02	
8508					$1890	Mirror Black	ebay-12/02	
8508					$1625	Green Jade/Alabaster	EAC-01/03	
8508					$1625	Green Jade/Alabaster	EAC-01/03	
8508					$925	Ivory	ebay-02/03	
8508					$1200	Ivrene	ebay-06/03	
8508					$1050	Green Jade/Alabaster	ebay-08/03	
8508					$910	Ivrene	ebay-11/03	
8508					$1430	Green Jade/Alabaster	ebay-08/04	Alabaster handles
8508					$920	Ivrene	Tway-09/04	
8508					$1500	Green Jade/Alabaster	ebay-09/04	Alabaster handles
8508					$1210	Ivory/Black handles	EAC-10/04	
8508					$480	Ivrene	ebay-11/04	Lamp
8508					$1440	Green Jade/Alabaster	Wesr-12/04	Alabaster handles
8508					$1345	Ivrene	ebay-01/05	
8508					$1130	Ivrene	ebay-04/05	
8508					$1250	Ivrene	ebay-04/05	
8508					$1800	Green Jade/Opal	JDJ-06/05	Opal handles
8508					$360	Ivrene	ebay-07/05	Lamp
8508					$2300	Amethyst Cluthra/Opal	EAC-07/05	Opal handles
8509	Vase	302	5	1				
8510	Vase	302	5	2				
8511	Vase	302	5	3				
8512	Vase	302	5	4				
8513	Vase	303	1	1				
8514	Vase	303	1	2				ACR)157,310; TPD)4.101
8515	Vase	303	1	3	$1155	Red/White Cluthra	EAC-10/95	TPD)6.3
8515					$1250	Green/White Cluthra	ebay-04/00	
8515					$2530	Green/White Cluthra	Cott-08/01	
8516	Lamp Base	205	2	1				
8517	Vase	303	1	4				
8518	Vase	303	1	5	$1675	Flemish Blue/Colorless	ebay-05/04	Acid etched and engraved
8519	Table Top	238	2	4				
8520	Insert	210	5	10				
8521	Insert	210	5	11				
8522	Vase	303	2	1				TPD)7.61

SHAPE NO.	ITEM	PAGE	COL	ROW	PRICE REALIZED	GLASS TYPE	AUCTION HOUSE	COMMENTS & PHOTO REFERENCES
8522					$6400	G. Ruby/Green Cintra ACB	ebay-08/03	Etched "Daphne"
8522					$1200	Blue Aurene	ebay-11/04	
8523	Vase	303	2	2				
8523½	Shade	231	1	8				
8524	Shade	231	1	9				
8525	Shade	231	2	1				
8526	Shade	231	2	2				
8527	Shade	231	2	3				
8528	Shade	231	2	4				
8529	Vase	303	2	3				
8530	Vase	303	2	4				
8531	Vase	303	3	1				
8532	Lamp Base	205	2	2	$860	Green Jade/Alabaster ACB	Jack-11/03	Etched "Floral"
8533	Shade	231	2	5				
8534	Shade	231	2	6				
8535	Shade	231	3	1				
8536	Vase	303	3	2				
8537	Vase	303	3	3				
8538	Vase	303	3	4				
8539	Vase	303	4	1				
8540	Vase	303	4	2				
8541	Vase	303	4	3				
8542	Shade	231	3	2				
8543	Shade	231	3	3				
8544	Vase	303	4	4				
8545	Vase	303	5	1	$825	Rose Quartz	ebay-05/04	Lamp with fittings
8545					$750	Rose Quartz	ebay-03/05	Lamp with fittings
8546	Vase	303	5	2				
8547	Shade	231	3	4				
8548	Lamp Base	205	2	3				
8549	Bowl	146	4	8				Special for "Miss Clay"
8550	Shade	231	3	5				Special for "Kaplin"
8551	Vase	303	5	3				Special for "Crest"
8551					$1840	Rose Quartz Lamp	ebay-02/04	Lamp with fittings
8552	Shade	231	3	6				Special for "Crest"
8553	Vase	303	5	4				This shape is shown as #8554 in Gardner.
8553					$1815	Plum Jade ACB	EAC-04/93	Lamp with fittings etched "Chinese"
8553					$1840	Plum Jade ACB	Sknr-06/99	Lamp with fittings etched "Chinese"
8553					$2550	Plum Jade ACB	ebay-10/03	Lamp with fittings etched "Chinese"
8554	Vase	303	5	4				This number is an error, see #8553.
8554	Shade	231	3	7				Special for "Crest"
8555	Vase	303	5	5				
8556	Shade	232	1	1				
8557	Shade	232	1	2				
8558	Vase	304	1	1				Special for "Art Lamp"
8558					$3450	Black/Green Cintra ACB	JDJ-05/04	Lamp
8559	Vase	304	1	2				Special for "Art Lamp"
8560	Vase	304	1	3				Special for "Art Lamp"
8561	Goblet	197	1	7				Special for "Doolittle"
8562	Shade	232	1	3				Special for "Crest Co. #300"
8563	Shade	232	1	4				Special for "Crest Co. #301"
8564	Shade	232	1	5				Special for "Crest Co. #302"
8565	Vase	304	1	4				Special for "Crest Co."
8565					$3360	"Pink" Dec. Aurene Lamp	EAC-07/04	Crest
8566	Vase	304	2	1				Special for "Crest Co."
8567	Torchere	304	2	2	$2750	Decorated Selenium Red	EAC-04/97	TPD)4.92 Special for "Crest Co."
8568	Shade	232	1	6				Special for "Crest Co."
8569	Lamp Base	205	2	4				Special for "Crest Co."
8570	Vase	304	2	3				PG1)85,126;ACR)COLOR 1,B,D;TPD)10.87
8571	Vase	304	2	4				Special for "Crest Co."
8572	Vase	304	2	5				Special for "Windsor Lamp Studios"
8573	Lamp Base	205	2	5				Special for "Windsor Lamp Studios"
8574	Lamp Base	205	2	6				Special for "Windsor Lamp Studios"
8575	Lamp Base	205	3	1				Special for "Windsor Lamp Studios"
8576	Lamp Base	205	3	2				Special for "Windsor Lamp Studios"
8577	Lamp Base	205	3	3				Special for "Windsor Lamp Studios"
8578	Lamp Base	205	3	4				Special for "Windsor Lamp Studios"
Architectural Pieces								
A2008		336			$1345	Colorless	ebay-07/04	With Bronze Frame
A2012		336			$580	Colorless	ebay-03/01	
Edison panel					$540	Colorless	ebay-05/05	
Edison panel					$580	Colorless	ebay-06/05	

Steuben Drawing Numbers

When Frederick Carder began designing for Steuben in 1903 he started with number one and continued numerically from there. The first number found in the existing factory records is for a cruet number 97. There are gaps in the records either because the records are currently lost or because some numbers were skipped and were never used. There are major gaps between 3678 and 5000 and between 5233 and 6000. It is felt by some that when Steuben was acquired by Corning Glass in 1918 the numbers were in the 3600 range and when design resumed under Corning the numbers started at 5000. There is only one piece known that falls within that gap and that is a Blue Aurene vase with the number 4920. It is felt that that number is probably legitimate because it was collected before the numbers and shapes had been published. The last number known in the regular series is 7749. There is a whole series of numbers beginning with 8001 and ending at 8578 that were special orders and given a number in this series. There are also a number of gaps in this series, which may be due to incomplete data or numbers that were not assigned.

Each Steuben shape does not necessarily have a unique number. There are a few shapes known that have two numbers, for reasons that are now lost, and there are also a larger number of designs that use an earlier number as a blank. It is presumed that the "blank" would have been used for months or years and at some point the same shape was used in some special way and was given a new number. The existing records include both the new number and the number of the piece that it was derived from. The list below is an attempt to show which shapes had multiple numbers and which were used as blanks for others. All references are to *The Glass of Fredrick Carder*.

Number	on page	is the same as	Number	on page
2941	148		2839	147
3361	143		2586	142
5195	144		2851 (1st version)	142
6395 (actually 6394*)	193		6445	193
6989	288		7008	288
*See Appendix 3.				

Number	on page	has as its blank	Number	on page
7159 bowl	155		2851(2nd version)	142
7160	195		5154	191
7164	155		6995	154
7165	290		6884	286
7166	290		8326	299
7167	290		6879	230
7170	290		6991	288
7174 decanter	not shown		6612 decanter	187, 7174 Decanter engraved "Garfield"
7167	290		6994	288
7177	290		7083	289
7178	not shown		8327	299, for 7178 see New Drawings section
7179	290		6817	286
7180	290		6884	286
7181	195		6844	194
7183 compote	176		6668 compote	175
7184	290		6919	287
7185	291		6991	288
7186	291		6854	286
7187	291		6813	285
7188	291		6241	280
7189	291		6575	283
7190	291		6577	283
7193	226		843	218
7194	159		7033	159
7195	291		6795	285

Number	on page	has as its blank	Number	on page
7197	291		7130	290
7202	291		6814	285
7203	291		6815	285
7204	155		6778	153
7205	291		6030	277
7227	291		7168	290
7228	292		7169	290
7249 stick	168		6709 stick	166
7249 compote	176		6709 compote	175
7249 bowl	155		6709 bowl	153
7250 stick	168		6710 stick	166
7250 compote	176		6710 compote	175
7250 bowl	155		6710 bowl	153
7253 stick	168		6506 stick	166
7253 compote	176		6506 compote	175
7253 bowl	155		6506 bowl	152
7284	197		3107	197
7285	197		3551	190
7290 stick	168		6668 stick	166
7290 compote	176		6664 compote	175
7290 bowl	155		7183 bowl	155
7335	243		6952	242
7372	294		6034	277
7373	294		6030	277
7374	294		6123	178
7375	294		6500	282
7377	294		2909	271
7378	156		2839	147
7379	294		6813	285
7381	156		6616	144
7387	294		6031	277
7388	294		7316	293

Abbreviations Used For Colors and Techniques

ACB	Acid Cut Back (Etched)
Alab.	Alabaster
Aur.	Aurene
Bl.	Blue
Blue Calcite	Blue Aurene over Calcite
Col.	Colorless
Dec.	Decorated
(E)	Engraved
(FC)	Frederick Carder postproduction signature
G.	Gold
Grn.	Green
Gold Calcite	Gold Aurene over Calcite
(Hawkes)	Carder Steuben VDS engraved and signed by Hawkes
LBJ	Light Blue Jade
Pomona	Pomona Green
Stop.	Stopper
T + number	Teague pattern number
Thread.	Threaded
VDS	Verre de Soie
Y	Yellow
Yel.	Yellow

Auction Companies

Aspr   Aspire Auction, 12730 Larchmere Blvd, Cleveland, OH 44120, (216) 231-5515

Cinc   Cincinnati Art Galleries, 225 E. Sixth Street., Cincinnati, OH 45202, (513) 381-2128

Cott   Cottone Auctions and Appraisals, 15 Genesee St., Mt. Morris, NY 14510, (617) 658-3119

Crft   Craftsman Auctions, 333 N. Main Street, Lambertville, NJ 08530, (609) 397-9374

Dalla   Dallas Auction Gallery, 1518 Slocum Street, Dallas, TX 75207, (214) 653-3900

EAC   Early Auction Company, 123 Main St. Milford, OH 45160, (513) 831-4833

ebay   eBay Internet Auction Site, www.ebay.com

FtnA   Fountain's Auction Gallery, 1485 W. Housatonic, Pittsfield, MA 01201, (413) 448-8922

Free   Freeman's, 1808 Chestnut St., Philadelphia, PA 19103, (215) 563-9275

GAI   Garth's Auctions Inc., 2690 Stratford Rd., P.O. Box 369, Delaware, OH 43015

Hrtg   Heritage Galleries and Auctioneers, 3500 Maple Ave., 17th Floor, Dallas, TX 75219-3941, (214) 528-3500

Jack   Jackson's International Auctioneers and Appraisers, 2229 Lincoln St., Cedar Falls, IA, (319) 277-2256

J&W   Jackson & Wickliff, 12232 Hancock St., Carmel, IN 46032, (317) 844-7353

JDJ   James D. Julia, Inc., Rt. 201, Slowhegan Rd., P.O. Box 830, Fairfield, ME 04937, (207) 453-7125

Midw   Midwest Auction Galleries, 13015 Larchmere Blvd, Shaker Heights, OH 44120 (216) 421-9742

Ogal   O'Gallerie, 228 Northeast Seventh Ave., Portland, OR 97232, (503) 238-0202

Sknr   Skinner, Inc., 63 Park Plaza, Boston, MA 02116, (617) 350-5400

Sbys   Sotheby's, 215 W. Ohio St., Chicago, IL 60610

Rago   David Rago Auctions Inc., 333 N. Main Street, Lambertville, NJ 08530, (609) 397-9374

Tway   Treadway Galleries Inc., 2029 Madison Road, Cincinnati, OH 45208, (513) 321-6742

Wesr   Weschler's, 909 E. Street N.W., Washington, D.C. 20004, (202) 628-1281

Wint   Winter Associates, Inc., 21 Cooke Street, Box 323, Plainville, CT, (860) 793-0288

Appendix 3
Anomalous Features of *The Glass of Frederick Carder*

The Glass of Frederick Carder was originally printed in 1971 by Crown Publishers, Inc. It was reprinted in about 1979 but there was no change in the text and no recognition of the second printing in the book. The book underwent a third printing in 2001, when it was reprinted by Schiffer Publishing Ltd. Basically all of these printings are the same, but there are some differences. Using the original 1971 printing as a reference, the 1979 reprint has a few line drawings missing. On page 137 of the 1979 reprint, all of the ash trays numbered 3431 through 3449 consecutively and numbers 3451, 3452, and 3453 are missing. This is a total of 22 items. The 1979 reprint also has Plate XXIII as a mirror image of the original and the Rouge Flambé bowl 2687 is shown as the second from the left in the reprint while it is second from the right in the original version. In the 2001 Schiffer reprint, the line drawings on page 137 re-appear but Plate XXIII is still a mirror image.

All of the printings have a short list of items that might be considered errors. Some of these are well known and some may not be so well known. Most are listed below. In addition, I have added information that may help in identifying Steuben where the line drawings may not be particularly clear.

1.	Shapes 2843, 2853, 2854, 2877, 2878, and 2950 are shown in the line drawing as vases but they are actually lamp shades. Shape 8567 is shown as a vase but is also a lamp shade.

2.	Shape 913 is a lamp shade that was inverted and used as a vase in about 1932. This shape should be included with 929, 938, 2230, 2390, and 2533.

3.	Bowl shape 2586 is shown in the drawings having three feet. This bowl was also made without the feet.

4.	Pedestal salt 3067 is usually seen as an individual salt with a diameter of about 2.25". It was also made as a master salt with a diameter of about 6".

5.	Vase shapes 2908, 2909, and 2987 are shown in the drawings with ring handles. All of these shapes were also produced without the handles.

6.	Compote 3348 was available both with and without a cover, as was vase 2707.

7.	Compote 2760 is shown in the line drawings with a scalloped bowl and it was also made with a bowl that didn't have scallops.

8.	Vase shape 5000 is shown in the drawings as a covered vase. It was also available without the cover.

9.	Vase shape 2812 is shown in the drawings as a covered vase. It was also available without the cover.

10.	It is not unusual for several different objects to carry the same drawing number. Dinnerware sets often had matching pieces such as bowls, candlesticks, and compotes that had the same number. Examples are numbers 3375, 3376, and 7472.

When the line drawings in *The Glass of Frederick Carder* are compared with the archival line drawing information at the Rakow Library and the Gardner Glass Center at Alfred University, one discovers that there are some omissions and errors in the Gardner book. The following list has been generated to allow the corrections necessary in the Gardner book. Note that where necessary the location of a line drawing is given in parenthesis, such as (145,2,4) to mean page 145, column 2, and line 4.

1.	On page 140 of the original printing, the drawing associated with number 6607 is missing. The drawing appears in both of the reprints.

2.	On page 145, there are two bowls of considerably different shape that seem to carry the same number of 6954 (145,2,4 and 145,2,9). The first bowl is 6954 while the second is 6984.

3.	On page 149, the bowl numbered 3570 is actually 3569.

4.	On page 158, the item numbered 2622 is actually 2625.

5.	On page 158, the tray numbered 44 is actually 411.

6.	On page 158, the item numbered 1533 is actually 1538.

7.	On page 162, the candlestick numbered 3571 is actually 3569.

8.	On page 155, the candlestick numbered 6475 is actually 6473.

9.	On page 172, the compote numbered 20 is actually 2083.

10.	On page 172, the compote numbered 2017 is actually 2107.

11.	On page 173, there is a compote that is not numbered (173,4,1). This compote is number 3577.

12.	On page 178, the cruet numbered 200 is actually 206.

13.	On page 191, the goblet numbered 3314 is actually 3321.

14.	Again on page 191, the goblet numbered 3548 is actually 3598.

15.	On page 191, there are two goblets that are numbered 5160. The upper goblet is number 5160 and the second one is 5169.

16.	On page 192, the goblet numbered 6395 is actually 6394.

17.	On page 204, the lamp shaft numbered 8302 is actually 8032 and the one numbered 8303 is actually 8033.

18.	On page 206, the item numbered 1813 is actually 1831.

19.	On page 211, the dish numbered 1844 is actually 1841.

20.	On page 214, the pitcher numbered 6006 is actually 6007.

21. On page 217, the salt numbered 1324 is actually 1323½ and the one numbered 1325 is number 1324.

22. On page 226, the shade numbered 3340 is actually 3348.

23. On page 226, there is a shade that appears to be numbered 5041 (226,3,2). This is actually shape 5047. There is another shade on this page with the number 5041.

24. On page 227, there is a shade that is numbered 2501. This shade is number 2506.

25. On page 238, there is a table top in the center of the page that is not numbered. This top is number 7075.

26. On page 241, there is a perfume numbered 322 (241,1,2). This is actually 3222.

27. On page 249, the vase numbered 341 is actually 344.

28. On page 260, there is a drawing (260,5,6) with the last digit indistinct. This is shape number 1685.

29. On page 273, there is a vase (373,1,2) that is un-numbered. This vase is number 3214.

30. On page 273, the vase numbered 3222 is actually 3221.

31. On page 296, there is a vase with no number (296,5,4). This vase is number 7484.

32. On page 299, there is a vase with no number (299,3,3). This vase is number 7744.

33. On page 303, the vase numbered 8554 is actually 8553.

34. On page 308, the vase numbered 6760 is actually 6706.

35. On page 310, the ink well numbered 1335 is actually 1355.

There are three errors associated with the captions for color plate XXVIII. In the caption for XXVIII A, the drawing number for the covered compote is 3348 and not 3384. In the same caption, the number for the candlesticks is 2956 and not 2596. In the caption for XXVIII B, the number for the goblet is 5169 and not 5160.

There is also an error in the caption for XXVII B, where the drawing number should be 2687 and not 2928. The caption for color plate VI B should read "Right to left" rather than "Left to right." The shape number for the compote shown in Ill. 83 on page 46 is incorrect. The shape of this compote is 3348.

The factory records indicate that a "shade vase" was made from shape 2390 in 1929. It is almost certain that the vase shown in Ill. 103 on page 69 is a 2390 vase.

Cross Reference of Colors and Finishing Techniques

This lists many of the Carder Steuben colors and finishing techniques and references them to color photographs in the same nine reference books that were used to reference the line drawing numbers. It is not a complete listing, but covers perhaps 90 to 95% of the colors and finishing techniques that one is likely to see.

Alabaster	TPD)9.29:10.42
Alabaster and Mirror Black	PG2)98; JAS)149,BL; TPD)4.9:4.32:5.68:10.42; MDK29
Alabaster with Aurene decoration	PG1)XXV A; PG2)56; TPD)2.25
Alexandrite	PG2)84; JAS)163,TR; JSS)12-24; TPD)7.24:10.153
Amber	TPD)8.15
Amber and Flemish Blue (Flemish)	TPD)10.107; MDK)118:121
Amber and French Blue	TPD)8.11
Amethyst	PG1)XXVIII A; RFR)16,3,C; ACR)COLOR 4,B,D; JAS)167,TL; JSS)12-25; TPD)2.36:4.76:7.33:7.39:9.31:10.109; MDK)47
Amethyst and Celeste Blue	MDK)41
Amethyst and Topaz	PG1)XXVIII A
Amethyst over Alabaster ACB	TPD)2.44
Amethyst over Colorless	PG2)81; TPD)7.30:9.23:10.94; MDK)17:44:123
Amethyst Quartz	PG1)XVIII B; TPD)4.20:5.27
Antique Green	MDK)11:59
Aqua Marine	PG1)XI B; MDK)141
Black over Alabaster ACB	RFR)18:19; RLG)150,282 ; TPD)6.2:6.25:6.27:8.24
Black over Amethyst Cintra ACB	TPD)5.34
Black over Celeste Blue ACB	PG2)70; TPD)8.31
Black over Green Jade ACB	TPD)4.86:8.24
Black over Light Blue Jade ACB	TPD)10.131
Black over Pomona Green ACB	RFR)19
Black over Turquoise ACB	TPD)8.24
Black over white Cintra ACB	PG2)72
Blue Aurene	PG1)IV A:V; PG2)48:69; RFR)7:9; RLG)139,269; JAS)162,BL; TPD)2.36:4.23:4.36:4.60:4.86:5.18:8.4; MDK)21:69:97
Blue Aurene, decorated	RFR)15; RLG)136,259; ACR)COLOR 3,B,C; TPD)8.28:10.120
Blue Aurene over Alabaster ACB	PG1)XXVI C; RLG)150,281; TPD)10.134
Blue Aurene over Pomona Green	PG1)XXVII C
Blue Aurene over Yellow Jade	PG1)IV B:XXVI A; ACR)COLOR 1,B,B; TPD)2.43
Blue Calcite	PG1)VI,C; PG2)54; RFR)14; RLG)153,287; TPD)2.36:9.30
Blue-gray	MDK)58:94:111
Bristol Yellow	PG1)XXIX A; ACR)COLOR 4,B,A; JAS)167,TR; TPD)2.36:4.61:8.12:10.108; MDK)20:49
Bristol Yellow, threaded	RFR)16,2,A; JAS)167,B; TPD)10.22
Brown Aurene	PG1)IX A; PG2)52:6.24
Brown Aurene, decorated	PG2)50:51; RLG)137,264; ACR)COLOR 3,B,D; JAS)162,T,C; TPD)5.10
Burmese, decorated	TPD)5.57
Calcite	TPD)4.109:4.111; MDK)4:36
Calcite, decorated	TPD)4.31:5.7
Celeste Blue	PG1)XXII A; RLG)159,295; ACR)COLOR 4,B,C; TPD)2.36:7.30:8.15; MDK)18:32:82
Cintra	PG1)XVI:XVII B; PG2)75; RFR)23; RLG)148,179; ACR)COLOR 1,T,A; JAS)153,TR:168,T; TPD)4.39:4.51:4.71:6.6:6.18; MDK)140
Cintra paperweight	PG1)XVII A; PG2)76; RFR)25,1; RLG)168,304; ACR)COLOR 3,T,B; PD)6.11:6.37
Cire Perdue	PG2)104-111; RFR)29; RLG)154,289; JAS)158,T&BL; TPD)3.24:4.27:4.157-4.164:5.44:8.42:8.48
Citron Yellow	MDK)6
Colorless with Black threading	RLG)159,293; MDK)2

Cluthra	PG1)XVIII A; PG2)77; RFR)22; RLG)147,278; ACR)COLOR 3,T,A; JAS)157,TR; TPD)4.79:6.3:6.12:6.13:10.52; MDK)67:81
Cyprian	PG1)XI B; RFR)24,3,C; TPD)10.85:10.154; MDK)112
Dark Blue Jade	PG1)XXIV B; PG2)68; RFR)21; RLG)146,276; ACR)COLOR 2,T,D; TPD)10.36:10.48:10.116; MDK)3
Decorated Blue Aurene	TPD)10.148
Decorated Green Aurene	PG1)VIII; PG2)50:51:55; RFR)10:11:12; RLG)138,266; ACR)COLOR 3,B,E; JAS)161:162,T,B:162,BR; TPD)5.5:5.14:5.16
Decorated Red Aurene	PG1)VII; PG2)50; RFR)10:11:12; RLG)137,263; ACR)COLOR 3,B,A&B; JAS)162,T,A; TPD)4.56:5.15
Diatreta	PG1)XXXII A,B; PG2)112-114; RFR)30; RLG)155; JAS)151,T&B; TPD)2.38:4.174-4.176
Flemish Blue	PG1)XXII A; TPD)4.7; MDK)10:114:149
Flemish Blue over colorless	TPD)7.33:7.79
Florentia	PG1)XXX B; PG2)91; RFR)26,1:26,2; RLG)168,307; ACR)COLOR 1,T,E; JAS)153,B; TPD)5.30:5.63:5.67:9.27; MDK)51:60
French Blue	PG1)XXII A; PG2)61; TPD)10.32; MDK)9:26
Gold Aurene	PG1)III:VI A,B; PG2)47:58:59; RFR)8:9; RLG)139,270; JAS)161; TPD)2.36:4.6:4.10:4.13:4.75:4.79:5.6:5.17:8.7; MDK)35:98:99:100
Gold Aurene, decorated	PG2)49; RFR)15; RLG)166,301; JAS)160; TPD)9.336:10.93:10.120
Gold Aurene decorated Turquoise	PG1)IX B; RLG)138,265; TPD)10.127
Gold Aurene over Alabaster ACB	RFR)18:8.43
Gold Aurene over Black ACB	PG1)XXVI B; TPD)10.134
Gold Aurene over Green Jade ACB	TPD)4.25:10.134
Gold Calcite	PG1)VI C; PG2)54; RFR)14; RLG)153,288; TPD)2.36:4.37:4.106:5.1:10.43
Gold Ruby	RFR)16,1,B; RLG)159,294; ACR)COLOR 4,T,A&B; TPD)10.17; MDK)25:54
Gold Ruby over Colorless	PG1)XIII A:XIII C; JSS)12-33,A; TPD)7.39:7.42:10.91:10.111
Green Jade	TPD)2.36:4.79:4.86:4.149:4.152:8.28; MDK)77:90
Green Jade and Alabaster	PG2)65:100; RFR)20:21; RLG)143,275; JAS)150,B,E; JAS)163,C; TPD)4.54:4.68:4.79:6.5:6.20:10.26:10.27
Green Jade, Iridescent	RFR)27; RLG)136,260; TPD)6.31:10.88
Green No. 5	TPD)2.36
Green Jade over Alabaster ACB	RFR)18:19; RLG)150,284; TPD)4.84:5.36:7.40
Green Jade over Flint White ACB	TPD)10.131
Green Jade over Yellow Jade ACB	RLG)150,283
Grenadine	ACR)COLOR 4,T,C; MDK)23
Grotesques	PG1)XIX A; PG2)67; RFR)17,3; JAS)169; TPD)5.55:10.99
Heliotrope over Alabaster ACB	TPD)8.27
Intarsia	PG1)XX:XXI; PG2)101:102; RFR)28; RLG)163,298; ACR)COLOR 3,T,E; JAS)165,B; TPD)4.74:4.80:5.31:5.51:8.22
Ivory	PG1)XXV B; RFR)24,1; ACR)COLOR 2, B,A; TPD)4.86:4.152:5.54:8.6:10.129; MDK)50
Ivory and Mirror Black	PG2)92; RLG)152,286; JAS)148,T; TPD)4.57:4.79:10.41
Ivrene	PG1)XXV A; PG2)93:94; RFR)24,2; RLG)149,280; ACR)COLOR 2,B,B; JAS)149,T; TPD)4.81:4.82:5.12:5.69
Lace Glass	TPD)4.70:8.35
Light Blue Jade (w/Flint White)	PG1)XXIV B; PG2)62; RFR)20:21; RLG)143,274; ACR)COLOR 2,T,E; JAS)163,B; TPD)2.36:4.34:4.68:10.39:10.49; MDK)55
Mandarin Yellow	PG1)XXIII B:XXIX,A; PG2)88; ACR)COLOR 2,T,B; JAS)152,T; TPD)2.29:10.21:10.106
Marbelite	TPD)4.109
Marina Blue	PG1)XXVIII B; RFR)16,1,A; TPD)7.45; MDK)28
Mat-su-noke	RFR)17,1; TPD)4.11:4.54
Millefiori	PG1)XIV; PG2)63; RFR)28; RLG)168,305; JAS)157,B; TPD)8.23:9.15
Mirror Black	PG2)97; JAS)148,B; JAS)167,TR; TPD)2.36:4.58:6.29:8.6; MDK)52
Moonlight	PG2)80; TPD)4.52:7.47:8.29
Moresque	TPD)4.40:10.96
Moss Agate	PG1)XXXI; PG2)74; RFR)25,3; RLG)165,300; ACR)COLOR 3,T,C; TPD)5.13:5.26:10.103
New Intarsia	TPD)10.90
Nile Green (unconfirmed)	MDK)42
Olive Green	MDK)38
Opal with Cintra decoration	PG1)XVIII C; MDK)61:62
Opaline, decorated	TPD)4.8

Orchid	MDK)22:73
Oriental Jade	PG1)XXX A; PG2)65:90; RFR)26,3; ACR)COLOR 1,T,B; JAS)150,B,I:170; TPD)5.28:10.24
Oriental Orchid	TPD)5.47
Oriental Poppy	PG1)XXX A; PG2)65:90; RFR)26,3; JAS)150,B,H:170,B; TPD)5.29:10.19; MDK)117
Pate de Verre	PG2)103; ACR)COLOR 2,B,C; JAS)158,BR
Peachblow	ACR)COLOR 1,B,D; TPD)10.87
Peach Quartz	TPD)10.104
Persian Blue	MDK)110
Plum Jade	PG1)XXVII B; PG2)71; RFR)19:21; JAS)155,B; TPD)9.28:10.115
Pomona Green	PG1)XXII B; RFR)16,2,D; ACR)COLOR 4,T,D; TPD)4.121; MDK)43:78
Pomona Green over Colorless	JSS)12-33,C
Rosa	PG1)XIX B; RFR)16,1,C; TPD)2.41; TPD)4.53:4.63:4.72
Rosa and Celeste Blue	TPD)2.36
Rosa and Pomona Green	TPD)10.20
Rosaline and Alabaster	PG2)65; PG2)85; RFR)20:21; ACR)COLOR 2,B,D&E; JAS)149,BR; JAS)150,B,D&F&G; TPD)2.36:5.35:5.40:8.26; MDK)19:64
Rosaline over Alabaster ACB	PG1)XXV C; RFR)18; RLG)146,277
Rose duBarry	TPD)4.62
Rose Quartz	PG1)XVIII B:XXVII A; PG2)78; JAS)153,TL:156; TPD)4.20; MDK)139
Rouge Flambé	PG1)XXIII A:XXIV A; PG2)89; RFR)27; RLG)167; ACR)COLOR 1,B,C; JAS)152,B; TPD)8.31:8.58:8.65
Russian Amber	MDK)34
Sea Green	MDK)7
Selenium Red	PG1)XIII B; RFR)16,2,E; RLG)162,297; ACR)COLOR 4,T,E; JAS)165,T; TPD)2.36:8.49:10.15:10.110:10.152; MDK)14:15:76
Selenium Red, decorated	TPD)4.92
Silverina Air Trap	PG2)79; RFR)25,2; JAS)164,T; TPD)4.26:6.23:6.30:9.32:10.1:10.25; MDK)89:128
Spanish Green	PG1)XXII B; RFR)16,2,B; TPD)4.150:9.21:9.22:10.30; MDK)45:57
Special Green	TPD)10.29; MDK)8
Straw Opal	PG1)XV B
Topaz	PG2)60; ACR)COLOR 4,B,B; JAS)164,B; TPD)2.36; MDK)1:80
Tyrian	PG1)XII; PG2)66; RFR)27; RLG)168,306; ACR)COLOR 1,B,E; JAS)154; TPD)2.36:4.108:5.33:5.65:9.26; MDK)5
Verre de Soie (VDS)	PG1)XI B; PG2)57; RLG)158,292; ACR)COLOR 1,T,C; JAS)147,B,A&B; TPD)4.50:5.39:10.46
VDS, threaded	TPD)2.36:10.85:10.97; MDK)13
VDS with Celeste Blue	TPD)4.24
VDS with Coral decoration	PG2)64; JAS)147,B,C:150,B,A&B&C; MDK)37
VDS with Green Jade decoration	MDK)86
VDS with Turquoise prunts	PG1)XI A
Wisteria	PG1)XXVIII,C; PG2)95; ACR)COLOR 4,B,F; JSS)12-31; TPD)5.32:7.75; MDK)12:24:30
Yellow Jade	PG1)XXIX A; RFR)20:21; RLG)142,271; ACR)COLOR 2,T,C; JAS)163,TL; TPD)8.34:10.23:10.118; MDK)27
Yellow Verre de Soie	MDK)122:136